Mourning Philology

Mourning Philology

Art and Religion at the Margins of the Ottoman Empire

MARC NICHANIAN

TRANSLATED BY G. M. GOSHGARIAN AND JEFF FORT

FORDHAM UNIVERSITY PRESS *New York* 2014

Library of Congress Cataloging-in-Publication Data

Nichanian, Marc, 1946–
    Mourning philology : art and religion at the margins of the
Ottoman Empire / Marc Nichanian ; translated by G. M. Goshgarian
and Jeff Fort. — First edition.
        pages cm.
    Includes bibliographical references and index.
    ISBN 978-0-8232-5524-5 (cloth : alk. paper)
    1. Armenian literature—20th century—History and criticism.
2. Art and literature—Armenia.   3. Religion and literature—Armenia.
4. Varuzhan, Daniel, 1884–1915—Criticism and interpretation.
I. Goshgarian, G. M., translator.   II. Fort, Jeff, 1966– translator.
III. Title.
    PK8516.N47 2014
    891'.99209—dc23

                                        2013016259

Printed in the United States of America

16 15 14   5 4 3 2 1

First edition

CONTENTS

A NOTE ON THE TRANSLITERATION

Armenian words have been transliterated as follows:

ա	a	կ	k	ս	s
բ	b	հ	h	վ	v
գ	g	ձ	dz	տ	t
դ	d	ղ	gh	ր	r
ե	ye, e	ճ	j	ց	ts'
զ	z	մ	m	ւ	v
է	ê	յ	h, y, –	փ	p'
ը	ë	ն	n	ք	k'
թ	t'	շ	sh	o	o
ժ	zh	ո	vo, o	ֆ	f
ի	i	չ	ch'	ու	u
լ	l	պ	p	իւ	iu
խ	kh	ջ	j	ոյ	uy
ծ	ts	ռ	r'		

This system avoids most diacritical marks. It takes into account the fact that pronunciation of the letters ե, յ, and ո depends on their position within the word, and it provides for diphtongs.

ACKNOWLEDGMENTS

This book was originally written and published in French (MétisPresse, 2007). Part II was translated into English by Jeff Fort. Introduction, Part I, and Epilogue were translated by G.M. Goshgarian. The latter is also responsible for most of the literary translations from Armenian (and, in one case, German) into English that are offered in the appendices. In appendix 3, I included some poetic translations from Armenian done by Lena Takvorian and Nanor Kebranian. I owe a word of gratitude to each of them.

I must also acknowledge a debt. I owe my belated courage to two people, Gil Anidjar and Catherine Coquio. It goes without saying that I have learned a great deal from them. As importantly, they convinced me that it was possible to expose the history of the ethnographic nation at the margins of the Ottoman empire as the unfolding of something contained in germ in the matrix that governs the relations between art and religion. This thumbnail history is, in reality, a history of mourning, a mourning that remains hidden to the end. Coquio and Anidjar made it possible for me to say that the mourning that was at stake here was the mourning of philology.

Finally, I am especially thankful to Ann Miller for the fabulous work she has done as the editor of this volume.

Mourning Philology

Art, Religion, and Philology

In winter semester 1802–03, F. W. J. von Schelling gave one of the last courses he was to give at the University of Jena. It was entitled Philosophie der Kunst (Philosophy of Art). There is no mistaking the significance of this choice. For the first time ever, someone holding a chair of philosophy was giving a course on art, thus conferring upon art the dignity of being something more than an object of reflection: namely, a form of philosophy. Schelling uses a somewhat different term: he calls art, simply, a "power," that is, a presentation of the Absolute as a whole raised to a certain power. To give his course, he mobilized all the philological knowledge he had amassed in the few years that he had just spent in Jena; most of it stemmed from exchanges with the Schlegel brothers and their wives or mistresses. Not only did Schelling steal all their philological knowledge; the elder Schlegel also continued to provide him, in letter after letter, with all the information he needed to meet the philological requirements of his philosophical program, and he did so most graciously, although Schelling had diverted rather more than just Schlegel's philological expertise to his own ends. In his course, then, Schelling writes: "The basic law of every figuration of the gods is the law of beauty."[1] Even if this passage does not spell it out and even if Schelling seems to be very explicit when he says "*every* figuration of the gods," what is in question here is plainly figuration, that is to say, mythological production. At the same time, of course, religion is in question as well: not just any religion, but the kind the nineteenth century would somewhat later label "mythological religion" in order to distinguish it from "prophetic" or "monotheistic" religion. It was already Aryans versus Semites, and none of the subsequent scholarly precautions would alter that in the least. Of course, a philology of the Semites would also eventually come into existence. But, plainly, philology began as Aryan philology. The philology of the Semites sprang up only in counterpoint to it and in reaction against it; moreover, as a general rule, it borrowed its instruments and concepts from its predecessor. It was also careful to point out, at all times, that the Aryans' "mythopoetic" capacity had philological precedence—meaning their capacity (good or bad) for fabricating myths and figuring gods. In any case, there we have it: art is at the origins of religion.

But that is not all. A bit further on, Schelling writes, invoking a new proposition that links art to mythology, historically this time: "Mythology is the necessary condition and raw material for all art."[2] Thus we have a circular relationship between mythological religion and what might be termed the "aesthetic principle." For, at the origins of religion, we find art in the form of a law of beauty. It is by means of art, by means of an operation of a manifestly artistic kind, that the "figuration" of the gods is realized. Conversely, however, art itself, in its historical reality, presupposes religion, at least in its mythological form (whatever Schelling means by that here). It presupposes a mythological religion that has withdrawn and ceded its place, while continuing to have effects even in its absence. It is by coming to an end that mythology becomes something eternal. It becomes something eternal in mourning. Art is mourning for mythology. Thus we have to do with a complex, twofold relationship between art and mythology or between art and religion. Art presents itself once as origin and a second time as mourning. And it is the origin or mourning of the same thing each time: of mythology and the gods.

A philosophical interest in myths and mythology is a constant in Schelling's work throughout, from the essays of his youth to the posthumous *Philosophy of Mythology*. Yet it seems to me that the circular relation between mythology and the aesthetic principle, between art and religion, is altogether characteristic of the early Romantic period in general, of the small group of people who, from Jena to Berlin, during the fabulous ten years that ran from 1795 to 1805, invented philology out of whole cloth, and with it, of course, literature as well. This circular relation is already the object of Friedrich Schlegel's pastiche or paraphrase in his 1800 *Dialogue on Poetry* (pastiche is largely synonymous with adherence here). The same relation, again, presides over the (utopian?) project for a "new mythology" that was common to the two men, and, in fact, to the entire group of early Romantics who came together for a time in Jena. A short quotation to this effect will suffice for the moment. It is drawn from the *Dialogue* just mentioned; more exactly, from the "Speech on Mythology" held by one of the participants in the conversation—most probably, Schelling: "Our poetry, I maintain, lacks a focal point, such as mythology was for the ancients; and one could summarize all the essentials in which modern poetry is inferior to the ancient in these words: We have no mythology. But, I add, we are close to obtaining one or, rather, it is time that we earnestly work together to create one."[3]

One century later, under altogether different circumstances, an Armenian poet rediscovered mythology as the past of art and put art at the origins of religion: Daniel Varuzhan (1884–1915), the founder of what he called "poetic paganism." The term appears for the first time in his writings in a letter written in 1908, when Varuzhan was a student in Ghent: "Pagan life fascinates me a little more every day. If it were still possible now, I would change religions, happily accepting poetic paganism. Judaism is lifeless, even if the prophets embellished it somewhat."[4] It may be said without reserve that, with these lines, Varuzhan inaugurated a neo-paganism, a kind of "return to the Greeks" that was to constitute the essence of his poetry in the seven years he had left to live. (He was deported in April 1915 and killed in August of that year in atrocious fashion, at the age of thirty-one.) His first poem in a neo-pagan vein dates from the year he wrote the letter just mentioned, 1908. The poem is dedicated to the god Vahagn, who corresponds to Verethragna of the Indo-Iranian pantheon, as had been established by the nineteenth-century tradition of German comparative mythology. Of course, there remains nothing, or almost nothing, of these pagan gods. At most, their names and memory survive. Perhaps their force also survives, or—who knows?—their power! Moreover, is Vahagn not the god of power? The god of power intervenes, then, in order to evoke the power of the gods, now all but lost. It might also be said, if we put matters the other way around, that, even if we find ourselves on the far side of the Christian parenthesis, we no longer speak the language of the pagan gods. Indeed, the ancient Greeks themselves, perhaps, no longer spoke it. They had perhaps already lost the gods' language, together with the memory of their power. In any case, like it or not, these pagan gods are already philological gods, a circumstance that, it will be agreed, immensely complicates the question whether the Greeks themselves still spoke this language, that of the gods. Indeed, it is only today (in the present of philology) that we can conceive of the loss of the gods. And since in foreign lands, as Hölderlin would say, we have almost lost our tongue—lost the language of the gods—we need philologists, obviously, in order to restore it to us. The philologists will give language back to us. No doubt about it: the mythological gods are philological gods. But to restore a language philologically is, for us, who have arrived late, to establish and confirm the loss of it. The native element of philology is plainly mourning.

We have lost the gods' language. Yet something of the gods is still active, since, in Varuzhan's 1908 poem, the first written in the neo-pagan vein, the poet declares that he is the last Vahuni, that is (as I shall explain at length at the appropriate moment), the last of the race of priests employed in the service of the god Vahagn. He is the end of the line. As the god's last priest, he necessarily voices mourning for the god and the gods. In that, he differs from the real Vahunis, the historical Vahunis, those who served the god in his temples and acted as the agents and officiants of his cult. But what do we know about that, after all? It may be that, two thousand years ago, the real Vahunis did the same thing the poet does. It may be that they, too, were already agents of mourning. At any event, art is, once again, mourning, mourning for the gods and mythology. One year later Varuzhan wrote "The Light," a poem that was inspired by his reading of the Rig Veda (a collection of religious poems in Sanskrit that was, according to the philologists who had reconstructed and published it, the oldest surviving trace of religious humanity and therefore, obviously, of humanity *tout court*, of civilized humanity, of Aryan humanity) and was meant to be included in his 1912 collection *Het'anos yerger* (Pagan Songs). In "The Light" the poet writes: "The light is the marble quarried in heaven / From which Art, with its deathless dream, / Carves gods with bodies of snow." Thus, quite independently of Schelling, Varuzhan redefines the function that Schelling called "the figuration of the gods." He describes an activity of erection that is also, necessarily, the Apollonian activity known as art. Art as figuration, as a sculpting of the gods, art as erection, is clearly at the origins of mythological religion. Here Varuzhan simply repeats "after Schelling"—incredibly, word for word—what is dictated to him by the "aesthetic principle" and its idealist matrix. To do so, as the reader will have guessed, he did not need to read Schelling, whose name he had quite possibly never heard. The same 1912 collection contains a poem called "To the Dead Gods," in which we find the following lines, which I cite for the moment without comment: "Under the bloody-glorious cross / Whose stretched arms flow in sadness / On the whole world, / I, vanquished, from the bitter heart of my art / I mourn your death, O pagan gods." This time (again, in the form of an astounding repetition of Schelling), art is essentially the space in which the mourning of (mythological) religion can find expression. The intervention of the Christian parenthesis somewhat complicates the schema of this mourning reception, since, in one form or another, it must already have intervened in ancient Greece, if it is true that there too art was the reception of the dead gods of mythology. In fact, this schema is quite as complicated in Schelling as it was in Friedrich Schlegel before him. It calls for treatment in its own right, a treatment that I have to defer for the moment. The gods, in any case, belong to the past. Only mourning allows us to maintain a relationship to them.

Thus Daniel Varuzhan invented neither the structure of this relationship between art and religion, which is identical in his work and in Schelling's, nor the idealist matrix by means of which art and religion form a system and can be thought. But they did not come to him as a result of the direct influence of German Idealism and its representatives, either; nor by way of acquaintance, direct or indirect, with the early Romantics, whom he had certainly not read. One might suppose that this relationship and its idealist matrix reached him, in part, by way of Nietzsche, the Romantics' obligatory relay. I shall not neglect this hypothesis. What I wish to show in this book, however, and shall doubtless too often repeat, is that they came to him, in the main, through the sharply distorting lens of the philological century, the nineteenth century, and through the orientalism that was constructed generation after generation, beginning with the pioneering works of comparative linguistics: this orientalism had elaborated a philological memory of the Eastern religions. Let me spell out that, by *orientalism*, I mean the phenomenon described by Edward Said in his celebrated 1978 book of that title. Let me state the matter (which is rather troubling, after all) still more simply. We could endlessly repeat (as people have been repeating for two centuries, with interruptions, intermezzos, and spectacular rediscoveries) Schelling's philosophy of art in Schelling's terms, which are also idealism's terms. We shall not have taken a single step forward, however, if we fail to see that that philosophy is like a closed shell regulated secretly from within; better, it is like a clock regulated by the invention of philology, an invention that, historically, occurred at exactly the same time and, what is more, in the same place. Yet as soon as we grasp that the same matrix governs the relations between art and religion in a poet who, a century later, activates or reactivates the end of mythological religion in his verse, matters appear in a different light. For the space of a century lies between the German philosopher and the Armenian poet (and also between the orientalist West and the East of the ethnographic nations), and this is the space in which philology unfolded in all its glory and splendor. Was it not Renan who declared, sometime in the latter half of the nineteenth century (in a work of his youth, *L'Avenir de la Science*), that philology was the science of the sciences? It was the science that would at last reveal the secrets of both primitive and civilized humanity, hence of humanity at its origins as well as in the course of its historical development; indeed, it had already begun to reveal those secrets. Be that as it may, philology had to develop for a century and travel from Germany to the ethnographic nations before art could afford to repeat Schelling's formula—"I am the point of departure as well as the mourning (for religion, for mythology)"—in the belief that it was repeating it in opposition to philology (for that is what Varuzhan very explicitly believed). In fact, it was philology which, from the outset, made art say what it did.

I am getting ahead of myself. Let me sum up: 1) Philology knows nothing about the loss of the gods as such, except (and this it knows from the very first) that the gods are dead, and no mistake; as dead as they were during the Christian parenthesis and, perhaps, because of it. In this respect, philology coincides with Christianity. There can be no philology without Christianity. 2) Philology institutes the loss by instituting the mythological gods. In every sense of the phrase, philology is *an institution of mourning*. I shall expatiate upon this at length in what follows. Let us say, provisionally, that the myth thus "discovered" in the late eighteenth century (in fact, we should rather say *invented*, in the sense in which one speaks of the "invention of the Cross") has always already been lost. We do not live in this myth. It is discovered (invented) *as* lost. Hölderlin was alluding to that loss, consubstantial with the discovery of the myth, when in his poem "Mnemosyne" he said that "we have almost lost our tongue in foreign lands," and went on to ask whether it was at all possible to mourn that loss. 3) But, inversely, philology discovers the loss; or, at any rate, it is philology which makes discovery of it possible. Once again, Hölderlin would never have been able to utter his sentence about the loss of language in foreign lands if, from the outset, he had not found himself confronting the philological present, that is, the mourning of philology. 4) But then it is not quite true that mourning is philology's native element. At least, one would have to say, conversely, that we know nothing about mourning today (I mean mourning for the Catastrophe, catastrophic mourning), absolutely nothing, other than what philology tells us about it. This is serious. What is more, it heavily compromises the understanding that we thought we had of art as mourning, and aggravates even further our indecisiveness about the question of what it is, precisely, that art mourns. For already, from the very beginning, philology has decided everything about mourning (as I shall argue later, it has also decided everything about the disaster that it mourns). Art accordingly is, in its function and tenor, wholly dependent on this decision of philology's. This is precisely what Foucault said (albeit in other terms) about the invention of literature in the nineteenth century, literature as philology's twin sister. It is perhaps time to try to understand what he meant.

I now need to say a few words about the structure of the present book. Part II is wholly given over to a patient, detailed interpretation of the poetry of Daniel Varuzhan; it constitutes an essay in its own right and can be read independently of the rest. By means of this interpretation, it reinvents, with Varuzhan, the concepts that make it possible to understand the history in which this poetry takes its place. For there can be no doubt about the fact that Varuzhan's poetry seeks to awaken the history of a period of which it, too, is a part. This period is that of orientalist philology and its two great inventions, the "native" and "mythological religion." We must therefore follow Varuzhan step by step in order to see how he radically reinterprets, precisely in terms of the aesthetic principle, the nineteenth-century emergence of the nation, the advent of the figure of the native, philological nationalism, and auto-ethnography. Varuzhan's poetry is thoroughly contextual and, as such, demands to be read contextually. This does not simply mean that we have to read it in its historical context. It means, essentially, that we have to observe how the national context surges up in it, interpreted through the grid of art, mourning, and the inadequacy of mourning, or, again, through the idea of disaster and the aesthetic logic of the emergence of the nation. Only a patient reading of this kind can show that orientalist philology is the central phenomenon of the century to which Varuzhan was heir. If he is in competition with this philology, if he forces it to cough up what it has inside, the fact remains that he is also wholly dependent on it. That is what makes it hard to decide what "the context" is.

Vauzhan wrote his major poetry (or, at least, the great poems that I shall be patiently glossing in Part II of the present book) between 1907 and 1912. Scarcely two years later, in 1914, the review *Mehyan* made its appearance in Constantinople. The major representatives of Varuzhan's generation (a generation whose surviving members went on to become the most eminent writers of the diaspora) had soon gathered around it. The "aesthetic principle" manifested itself most fully in this review, with all its *collective force* and terrible *ambiguities*, and in its many different variants. That is why I shall begin by closely examining the theses advanced in *Mehyan*, mainly under the signatures of Hagop Oshagan and Constant Zarian, or under their supervision. I shall also, of course, detail the careers of these two personalities, explain their roles, and discuss their *a posteriori* interpretations of the collective movement represented by *Mehyan*. This review is an extraordinary phenomenon in the literature of the Western Armenians. It represents the moment on the very eve of the Catastrophe when these associated writers decided to create a showcase for the aesthetic principle. For that reason, before we read Varuzhan's poetry and reinvent, with his help, a set of concepts reflecting his poetic reaction to philological nationalism and the ethnographic nation, we have to read the texts published in *Mehyan* and consider the image of the aesthetic principle forged in them. That is the subject of chapter 1. On the other hand, thought based on the aesthetic principle, which is on a continuum with philological orientalism—its vehement opposition to this orientalism notwithstanding—constantly runs the risk of becoming racialist thought, and sometimes is quite openly just that. This emerges with blinding clarity in the texts published in the review in which Zarian and Oshagan tried to explain, for the first time, the goals they had set themselves and the movement that their review intended to herald. An attempt has been made to translate these texts as faithfully as possible (the reader will find translations in appendix B), in a way that respects their phraseology and rhetoric and resists the temptation to tone down their racialist character. Since Zarian was the editor-in-chief of *Mehyan*, it was his texts which, issue after issue, presented the thinking, often in all its naïveté, that derived from the aesthetic principle. I have therefore included in appendix B nearly all the articles and essays he wrote for the review. This was a ticklish business, inasmuch as Zarian represents only one facet of the aesthetic principle, the moment when, setting out from the racialist positions into which it inevitably risks lapsing as a result of its unconditional belief in a "mythopoetic" power, it turns into an overtly racist ideology. There could be no ignoring this. It had to be put on display. It was necessary to try to understand what, in the thinking based on the aesthetic principle, motivated the shift toward this extreme. That is the subject of the epilogue, which opens with a review of the reception of Nietzsche in Armenian literature, and then focuses exclusively on Zarian, who bears the main responsibility for the racist turn of a body of thought that is always potentially racialist, judged by the criteria of nineteenth-century philology as a whole. Thus I have parceled out the reading and interpretation of the collective phenomenon represented by the Armenians' implementation of the "aesthetic principle" between the two chapters that frame the present volume, the first and the last. I should point out that chapter 1, a general chapter about *Mehyan* in which Oshagan's later interpretation of it holds pride of place, takes up analyses of the review already presented in my book *Ages et usages de la langue arménienne*. These analyses make no sense outside the context of a history of the "aesthetic principle." Varuzhan's poetic reception and reframing of all the questions bearing on the end of religion and the mourning of philology have afforded me an opportunity to repeat and revise what I said on the subject in *Ages et usages*. The revision is extensive. It is responsible, in any event, for a circularity that the reader will not fail to notice. Understanding Varuzhan's work calls for explication of its philological context. But this philological context, in its turn, takes on meaning (and is of interest) only as it is shaped by the transformation that it underwent at the hands of poetic "paganism," and, therefore, the aesthetic principle in its entirety.

Thus the first part of the present volume proposes to describe the appearance and evolution of philology in the nineteenth century and the concomitant emergence of the national "form," or, if one prefers, of the "nation" as a form (obviously "imaginary") of collective perception. What is presented here is, then, a history of the ethnographic nation, its formation, and its gradual solidification, which extended over a century, from the attempts to found an "archeological geography" in the second decade of the century down to the work of the ethnomusicologist Komitas in the 1890s. Indeed, Komitas's work already represented a conscious, accomplished implementation of the aesthetic principle and was accordingly to become a powerful inspiration for the *Mehyan* generation. The first part of the book has a sharply polemical tenor, at two levels. First, it proposes to trace the course that the "imaginary" self-invention of the nation followed as the century wore on, from the archeology with which national philology began through the articulation of the properly ethnographic project and its realization, to, finally, the implementation of the aesthetic principle carried out by Komitas and the group around *Mehyan*. Let us attach dates to these different stages: 1815 for archeological geography, 1841 for the auto-ethnographic project, 1874 for its realization, 1890 for the project of aestheticization that Komitas pursued in the field, 1914 for the formulation of this project in *Mehyan*. This formulation has it, quite simply, that the process of becoming a nation is, in reality, an "aesthetic" process. I can put that differently, in a sentence or proposition that sums up the thinking of the *Mehyan* group as a whole (it has taken me a lifetime to understand this sentence, which I can now serenely repeat after the *Mehyan* writers). The sentence alters the usual sense of the word *nationalization* to make it signify the process of becoming a nation or, if one likes, the self-invention of the nation. The proposition reads: *Nationalization is an aestheticization.* For the members of the *Mehyan* group, this was self-evident. They did not have to convince themselves or their readers of it. They embodied it. Self-evident, this proposition constituted, at the same time, an imperative. At stake here was the aesthetic principle as affirmation and imperative. It manifested itself as both in 1914, on the eve of the Catastrophe, which is, after all, food for thought. Why on the eve of the Catastrophe? Why so late? It took Oshagan three more decades to reformulate this proposition and reinterpret it in another context, that of his *Panorama* (ten volumes containing five thousand pages) reviewing the literature of the Western Armenians (roughly speaking, a mere sixty years of literature). Here he does no more than repeat, volume after volume, over thousands of pages, the idea that nationalization is an aestheticization. He repeats it not only so that people will learn it. He repeats it, obviously, in order to accomplish both "nationalization" and "aestheticization," that is, to bring these processes to completion. His aim is to create a war machine. I discuss this in greater detail in a subsequent volume on the "writers of disaster," wholly devoted to Oshagan.

But if this is how matters stand, then how am I to describe the stages of the imaginary self-invention of the nation? I had to bring out the historical necessity of this central statement of the aesthetic principle—nationalization is an aestheticization—before beginning to criticize it. This proposition is blinding. Its incredible power blinded me for years. Is it *that* history which I wanted to write? Had Oshagan, in his *Panorama*, not done so before me? What had he fought, with such constancy, his whole life long? Philology, of course! If credit for the principle of "nationalization" goes to art, then it will, at the very least, not go to philology. My demonstration bears on that very point, which is likewise the object of my doubts. What if, in fact, just the opposite were the case? What if the truth of the matter were that art and philology go hand in hand? What if art, the aesthetic-religious matrix (whose institution in Schelling and repetition in Varuzhan a century later I have just rapidly sketched), were in fact just another name for the unfolding of philology? What if this matrix, initially established by the philological project, could only develop and produce effects by way of this project and its history? Let us, moreover, not forget that the history of the philological project can only be understood with reference to the gradual institution of the ethnographic nation. There we have the kernel of the schema that will guide us here.

I have, however, so far ignored that which appears at the heart of philology when it invites itself onto the public stage at the dawn of the nineteenth century with the archeological geography of the nascent nation, and again at mid-century with the ethnographic moment of the self-invention of the nation. What we find at the heart of philology is orientalism and its corollary, the invention of the native. Thus we must ultimately observe European orientalism at work as it is internalized in the form of autoscopy and that central figure of orientalist philology (or philological orientalism) known as *the native*. This is, finally, the only way to account for the development of philology, to show that it is thoroughly bound up with the auto-emergence of the imaginary national form, and to describe the secret connivance between art (which is both the source of religion, and mourning for it) and philology. It so happens, however, that neither of these two aspects, neither aesthetic nationalization nor the emergence of the nation as an *effect* of philological orientalism, find their place in run-of-the-mill theories of nationalism. That is why the first part of the present book is not merely descriptive. It is also a fierce (albeit implicit) polemic directed at the theories of nationalism put forward by the sociologists, who totally ignore "aestheticization" and, incidentally, autoscopic orientalism as well (even when these theoreticians have the best intentions in the world, as is sometimes the case). Thus I must also be in a position to explain what distinguishes an approach like mine from all the approaches to the nineteenth-century nationalist phenomenon that are currently in fashion. I attempt to provide this explanation throughout Part I. Nationalization is an *event*, an irreversible event. It is an *Ereignis*. That is how Varuzhan and Oshagan understood it, and that is how I understand it after them. The sole problem is that, beholden as they were to the aesthetic principle, they considered the event in question to be "artistic." In any case, we are entirely dependent on this event, artistic or not, that is now, like modern philology, two centuries old. It has made us what we are and we have no means of escaping it. We do not live in a vacuum in which we might simply have an opinion (good or bad) of nationalism that we could back up with theories. We have therefore to return to the appropriating event, the one that has made us what we are, "properly" are, and has, additionally (but is it merely an addition?), given us our literary language. We must explore the reasons for it and the forms of its historical advent. We must prove capable of changing direction and working our way back through all the historically sedimented layers between us and the initial event, if it is possible to envisage such a thing. In sum, we have to prove capable of "replaying" the event of nationalization. Foucault called that an "archeology." But, whatever one calls it, and whether or not one appeals to Foucault's archeology of the human sciences in pursuing it (as I, for my part, am ready to do), the means of analysis at our disposal are those which the inaugural event has put at our disposal. It is this which, I believe, distinguishes my work on the advent of the nation from all other critical theories of nationalism. The other characteristic is that the event in question cannot be immediately, straightforwardly classified. It is obviously not a "political" event. But neither is it "cultural." Distinctions of this kind (which are to be found everywhere in the literature on nationalism, especially at those moments when it becomes absolutely indispensable to explain the primacy of the cultural model in terms of a failure to realize "political aspirations") ignore everything having to do with nationalization as an appropriating event (one that creates a supposedly political "us" at the very moment it expresses what is supposed to be culturally specific to this "us"). Such distinctions also ignore everything about the other facet of the event, to which the whole second part of the present volume is basically devoted: the discovery of (mythological) religion as religion in the past tense. In the case of both these aspects ("nationalization" as appropriating event as well as the invention of religion), we have to do with the same aesthetical-philological event. We have to give a name to this unclassifiable event, this event with multiple contents, informing both works of comparative mythology and nineteenth-century national movements. That name is orientalism, of course; but, thanks to this two-sided orientalism,[5] it is also, and above all, *the mourning of philology*. But then why is it unclassifiable? It is unclassifiable because it is a vortex-event. Philology bears mourning within itself, a mourning that is also its own mourning. It is, obviously, incapable of recognizing its own mourning. It is this incredible incapacity that philology projects onto the "nationalizing" project. There can be no self-invention of the nation, no nationalism, and no formation and "planning" of literary languages (which are both nationalized and, in the same measure, nationalizing) without the mind-boggling operation by which philology occults its mourning for itself. Among the Armenians before Varuzhan, once and once only, mourning declared itself (only immediately to negate itself) to be in accord with philology. This happened in 1841; it took the form of the preface that Abovean wrote for his novel *Wounds of Armenia*. The year 1841 also saw the birth of the native in the "national" consciousness, and, secondarily, the birth of modern literature and the auto-ethnographic project (all this at one and the same time, in the same burst of enthusiasm and by the same necessity). That is why I devote a separate chapter to Abovean—in order to pay homage to his multivalence.

Let me sum up once again. My opening chapter recapitulates the questions raised by the aesthetic principle in the form in which I was able to state them before engaging in a close reading of Varuzhan's poetry, that is, as I formulated them in chapter 9 of my 1989 book *Ages et usages de la langue arménienne*, at a time when I did not have the foggiest notion that the only possible answer to these questions turned on philology's twofold invention (that of mythological religion and the parallel invention of the figure of the native). This chapter accordingly sketches the three facets of the aesthetic principle: the "end of religion" (Varuzhan), "nationalization" (Oshagan), and "racialist thought" (Zarian); it should be understood that none of these three facets is independent of the others, but also that it is not possible clearly to bring out the reasons for their interdependence in my initial approach to them. Chapter 1 nevertheless constitutes an introduction to the period as well as to aestheticization's "literary personnel." There follows the chapter on Abovean, written on the same principles; the sole objective here is to establish historical benchmarks and describe an "experience," precisely the experience of disaster that presents itself under the name of "mutism." Together, chapters 1 and 2 illustrate what the Armenians experienced, between 1840 and 1915, under a "seal of silence." In chapter 3, I take up the problem of orientalism in the framework of a discussion of the very first moment of the national imagination, that of "neo-archeology," which made its appearance in the 1810s. Chapters 4 to 8 form the heart of the book, and can be read, as I have said, independently of the rest; for this reason, they go back over some of the names and passages cited and analyzed earlier in the context of our thumbnail history of the ethnographic nation (whence, as well, a dense web of cross-references). The title of this second part is "Daniel Varuzhan: The End of Religion." Finally, the epilogue devotes a few pages to Constant Zarian in particular, in the broader framework of a discussion of the racist culmination of the philological-aesthetic project.

I should also remind my readers that, at the end of this volume, they will find appendices containing previously unpublished translations. My enterprise would have made no sense without them, for the simple reason that the history of the ethnographic nation, from its imaginary formation to its irremediable collapse, is not part of the basic philosophical and literary stock of my presumed audience (Armenian or not, be it said in passing). Virtually nothing of this history and literature has been translated to date. This is an unsettling symptom, after all. Nothing of what has gone on within these confines has reached Western ears (or, consequently, Armenian ears). That is why the appendices and my analyses form a whole. The first of the appendices presents translations of different extracts from authors and texts decisive, in my estimation, in the history of national philology and the philological-ethnographic-aesthetic nation (which I have been calling and will continue to call the *ethnographic nation*, keeping only the middle term for the sake of brevity), a history that, on my understanding of it, represents the coming of the nation to itself while simultaneously constituting a "self-invention" and an "appropriation." Assembling the texts in appendix A, often drawn from the prefaces to philological works, was for me a way of scanning the trajectory of the ethnographic nation that had its point of departure in them. All these texts are briefly glossed in the first three chapters of the book, and glossed again from a different angle (because of the inevitable circularity of my project) in Part II. Of course, the appendices also contain the poems by Varuzhan (appendix C) that we analyze below, as well as most of the texts by Constant Zarian published in the review *Mehyan* (appendix B).

—*Translated by G. M. Goshgarian*

"The Seal of Silence"

CHAPTER I

Variants and Facets of the Literary Erection

THE CONSTELLATION OF THE TEMPLE

In January 1914, in Constantinople, a monthly review called *Mehyan* began to appear. The name is printed in Latin letters on the masthead of the review, followed by the words "Revue arménienne de littérature et d'art." The exact meaning of the Armenian word *mehyan* is "pagan temple." The review appeared for only seven months in all. Its publication was suspended in July 1914 because of the declaration of war and the departure of its main promoter, Constant Zarian. All together, the seven issues form a slim volume of about one hundred pages.[1] In the first of these seven issues, a "Manifesto" announced the conceptions and objectives of the group responsible for the review. This Manifesto—a translation of which may be found in appendix B (text 9)—contains the fabulous phrase that will serve as our springboard in this chapter: "We want to found an aesthetics of the language." The Manifesto bears five signatures: Daniel Varuzhan, Hagop Kufejian (who was to become Hagop Oshagan a few years later[2]), Constant Zarian, Aharon, and Kegham Parseghian. Three of these authors, Oshagan, Zarian, and Aharon, survived the storm that was to break over the heads of the Armenians of the Ottoman Empire one year later. The three writers met very different fates in the diaspora. As for Varuzhan and Parseghian, they were deported and killed in summer 1915, Varuzhan in Changere, Parseghian in Ayash. Let us recall that all the intellectuals arrested in April 1915 in Constantinople were deported to Changere and Ayash. Among the hundreds of intellectuals, writers, and activists on the black list, very few survived. The ones who did owed their survival to chance and circumstance; some, such as Zabel Esayan, Hagop Oshagan, and Hagop Sirouni, went underground, where they were able to call on their skills at eluding police dragnets. Changere is the best-known place of deportation, because it was there (or in the immediate environs, since the killing did not always occur on the spot) that virtually all the writers and intellectuals that Armenian Constantinople boasted were murdered in short succession in summer 1915. Those deemed "political cases" were exceptions; they were deported to Ayash. Fifteen people in all returned from Changere. Some testified to what they had seen. Almost no one came back from Ayash, and we have only two eye-witness accounts containing information about it. It was in Ayash that Kegham Parseghian was killed. The exact circumstances of his death are unknown. I shall not have much to say about him or about Aharon in the following pages. "Aharon" was the pseudonym of the poet Aharon Dadurian (who was born in 1886 in Ovajek, near Izmit, and died in 1965 in Paris, where he had been living since 1928). Apparently, his name was not on the police's wanted lists in April 1915. Until 1922, overwhelmed, it seems, by the personality and force of Daniel Varuzhan, Aharon faithfully served the "poetic paganism" that Varuzhan had invented. It later took him years to find his own path and forge his own style, which, however, remained well within the boundaries of the "aesthetic principle." It was in Paris that Aharon published, very late, his two most important books: *Magaghat'ner* (Parchments) in 1937 and *Bohemakank'* (Bohemian Poems) in 1939. For a long time, he was hardly known, if not altogether unknown, to the reading public, in part because he was the "ill-timed" or even "untimely" poet par excellence.[3] As for Kegham Parseghian, his essays and articles have been collected in a volume, *Amboghjakan gortsë* (Complete Works).[4] His short, tragic life did not leave him enough time to produce work of importance.

I open the present chapter with a consideration of these writers as they appeared in the very limited space of a journal and in the exceedingly brief period immediately preceding the Catastrophe. To the five names already cited should be added that of Hagop Sirouni (1890–1972); Sirouni, as I said a moment ago, was among those who eluded death by successfully hiding underground to the end.[5] He was a close friend of Varuzhan, with whom he published the first and only issue of the review *Navasard,* in 1913. He would most probably have signed the *Mehyan* Manifesto and taken part in the adventure of the review if he had not been in prison from 1913 on,[6] in the few months in which that adventure ran its course. *Mehyan* and *Navasard* accordingly comprise the essence of the encounter that brought these writers together, and we trace the pattern of a constellation in them. That encounter and that constellation constitute one of the most important moments in the short history of Western Armenian literature, the first major collective movement to occur in it. Other such movements would follow, notably that which crystallized in the early 1930s around the Paris review *Menk'.* Proper attending to such encounters is not a matter of reconstituting an anecdotal history of them, but rather, I believe, of reconstructing the common space that made them possible.

In the period during which the encounter that spawned *Mehyan* took place, around 1913, Varuzhan (born in 1884) was already a famous poet. In 1909, he had published *Tseghin sirtë* (The Heart of the Race), and, in 1912, *Het'anos yerger* (Pagan Songs). These two books had immediately revealed him as the greatest poet of his day, the early twentieth century, for reasons we shall discuss in Part II, the essay on Varuzhan. The other *Mehyan* authors, Zarian, Oshagan, and, of course, Aharon, would produce their works only much later. In the encounter of all these writers, a generation discovered itself and announced that it *was* a generation. It is true that dissensions and divergences were not long in coming, notably a conflict between Zarian and Varuzhan that led Varuzhan to distance himself from the group as early as February 1914 and provoked a volley of ripostes from Zarian, on which we shall comment in the epilogue. Yet the fact remains that the autoproclamation of a generation perfectly conscious of its role and novelty constituted an event, and remains one even today, for us. The conflicts in the group did not stem from the opposition of irreducibly different worlds, as did many of the other critiques leveled at Varuzhan in the same period (critiques aimed at his undue "attachment to the past," his immoderate use of classical Armenian, and his sensuality, described as pornographic). Quite the opposite: they were the sign of a strange proximity.

The event constituted by this encounter, let us repeat, has endured down to our own day and has lost nothing of its mystery. The titles of the two reviews, *Mehyan* and *Navasard*, seem to indicate that "paganism" constituted the heart of that event. ("Navasart" was the name of a month in the pre-Christian Armenian calendar, corresponding to our month of July.) The moving spirit behind "paganism" was, above all, Varuzhan. And if Aharon was still, to some extent, one of Varuzhan's epigones in this period, the three other writers were by 1914 already far from subscribing to Varuzhan's paganism in articulating their literary project. Moreover, the divergence between Varuzhan and Zarian nearly became a matter of public concern when, in the fifth issue of *Mehyan*, Zarian published an essay entitled "Paganism?"[7] in which he contrasted his conception of a "Futurism" nominally inherited from Marinetti to what he believed he was justified in interpreting as a longing to return to the past in Varuzhan's poetic paganism. In any case, this paganism was no more than the operationalization of, and a particular name for, an event that the emergence of *Mehyan* marks but by no means exhausts. The authors grouped around the review endowed this event with its social and literary form and attempted to define it in their theoretical writings.

FACETS OF THE ERECTION

At the same time, nothing can justify forgetting that all this occurred on the eve of the Catastrophe. The watchmen of the Catastrophe were the strange heralds of an upwelling of the sacred (that was how they saw things) whose destructiveness they did not fully anticipate. In this respect, they were heirs to an event that took the form of a destiny, which means that, for them, the event had no name. Literature was only its depositary. The deposit itself had been made long before the generation of Varuzhan, Zarian, and Oshagan arrived on the scene. It had begun to be made even before literature, in the modern sense of the word, came into being among the Armenians, around 1840 or perhaps even earlier, but these writers themselves had no idea of that. Of what, then, was the event the destiny? Only literature has a voice capable of answering the question. We should not be surprised that the answer it gave has, since the *Mehyan* generation, taken perfectly circular form: the event was the destiny of literature itself. This circular response characterizes the literary erection in its two-sidedness. Indeed, the *Mehyan* Manifesto proclaims: "It was necessary to erect a temple. We want to help erect it."[8] The "we" here is that of "artists." Here are the opening lines of the Manifesto: "Toward what veiled goal is the Armenian artist staggering, amid the turbulent scenes that uncertain Destiny has cruelly forged with the sweeping blows of affliction? . . . What statue's form will his body assume? What kind of dance will his feet trace, weighed down with their leaden burden? And what magic will his tongue utter?" (*Mehyan*, no. 1, p. 1) The artist sees, he makes his body into a statue, he dances, he utters magic formulas. Moreover, the whole Manifesto hammers home the verb "create," casting it in the imperative. At the entrance to the temple, above the door, the initiate will see, in bas relief, the inscription "Let us create." This imperative is clearly associated with a finality: "A race that wants to live is under an obligation to create" (ibid., p. 3). To erect a temple, a statue, or one's body as a statue: these are the forms of the imperative, and there is nothing surprising about this twofold formulation. The artist is, as we shall again have occasion to emphasize, a man who erects and who erects himself. The Manifesto says that art is a "temple." And when, beginning in this period, Zarian makes a racist theme of the artist's auto-erection, he is, after all, faithfully extending an idea that here finds expression on every page, that of art as erection and of the erection of art. This kind of thinking runs all the way through the nineteenth century in Europe and, as is well known, crystallizes in Nietzsche's work, with which this generation of Armenian writers was perfectly familiar.

There is, however, another side to the erection. The penultimate stanza of Varuzhan's poem "Luysë" (The Light) begins: "The light is the marble quarried in heaven, / From which Art, with its deathless dream, / Carves gods with bodies of snow."[9] In these lines, we find, of course, the first side as well, that of art as erection. Art carves out figures and makes them into bodies of light; it casts the gods in a marble made of light. The lines that follow show, however, that, as always in the constellation of *Mehyan*, the "erectors" are those who work upon language, the "brooding Dantes and titanic Homers," themselves self-erected upon this breast of light. Thus the fundamental and founding activity of figuration has devolved upon literature. Figuration does not take the form of a mere representation of the gods—of a secondary, mimetic activity. The "creation" of the gods consists in their erection by art within the luminous "breast" that precedes them, as if art were at the origin of religion. As art, literature is erected in this way as a founding activity that establishes the figure of the gods for men. Which gods are in question here? To what system of thought does that kind of affirmation about the erection of the gods belong? We will have ample occasion to return to these questions. But we already have here the second aspect of what I shall call, in this chapter, the literary or aestheticizing erection. This second aspect finds expression, in its diverse variants, throughout the *Mehyan* period. I shall be gradually elucidating the essential forms of this double erection— erection of art and erection through art—in order to show that, for the whole *Mehyan* generation, art is the response to mutism, alienation, and fragmentation. It is likewise art that provides a relay for the "legendary sources" and "popular treasures."

That which constitutes a twofold self-evidence for the *Mehyan* generation and period offers us, from the outset, occasion for a twofold interrogation. Why is art, at this precise historical moment, apprehended, understood, and defined as an "erection"? Why is every figuration, beginning with the creation of the figures of the gods, conceived as something that takes place within the horizon of art, in what Varuzhan describes as a breast and an orb of light? It has first to be shown that these two questions are essential. In other words, they have to be confirmed and reformulated. That is the first objective of the present attempt to reconstruct what presents itself as the system of the "erection," which is already the system of the "aesthetic principle." This examination presupposes, and demands, a project: that of reconstructing these declarations about, and conceptions of, art, the activity of "figuration," and the relationship between art and the popular production of myths, or between art and the gods. These declarations and conceptions are not simply "theoretical." They are advanced by writers, not philosophers. They are put to work and, consequently, diffused throughout these writers' works. Conversely, reconstructing the system of the "literary erection" also means decomposing or undoing it. Where does one stand when one adopts this position and project: in the history and theory of literature? Not really, because both are determined, from one end to the other, by the system of the "aestheticizing erection" itself. I do not mean to say that this holds for the Armenian context alone; every informed reader can see that this system, as presented in *Mehyan*, owes much to Nietzsche (either directly or through the deforming lens of the readings of him that prevailed at the time); it transposes, under conditions that are surprising and, in any case, rather unfamiliar to contemporary readers, a Nietzschean aesthetics, that is, a metaphysics understood as an aesthetics. I shall have occasion to return (much later) to everything that this Nietzschean aspect of aestheticization implies. It must be understood historically, to begin with—simply as a result of the fact that these authors, three of whom had received part or all of their university education in Europe, lived in a period in which Nietzsche's influence was pervasive. They read and understood Nietzsche the way everyone read and understood him in Europe around 1910. Obviously, here, too, this recourse to Nietzsche has an internal dimension that I shall have to elucidate. The history of literature will be of no help to us, because it comprehends its object only through the prism of the "aesthetic erection," while literature is merely the depositary of an experience (or a history) that engenders the *Mehyan* period: in a word, aestheticization.

But what was this experience? If it is the experience of a disaster, as everything would seem to indicate (whatever other names one gives it: mutism, alienation, fragmentation, disintegration, all terms we shall be encountering, one after the other), we must nevertheless ask, insistently: just what kind of a disaster is involved? And, above all: does this disaster have anything at all to do with the subsequent Catastrophe? It is true that the experience of the *Mehyan* generation is the experience of this pre-Catastrophic disaster, an experience of the prelude-to-death. And it is also true that, for a very long time, I believed that the Catastrophe was already inscribed in this experience. That is why, throughout all the years in which the present book had already been conceived but could not yet materialize, I thought (I wrote and also declared to everyone who was willing to listen, and have done so even here, echoing those dated formulations) that the *Mehyan* generation had claimed to be the watchman of the Catastrophe on the eve of it.

VERSIONS AND CIRCUMSTANCES

It seems that it is hard to say why these writers came together around *Mehyan*, and hard to account for the significance of their encounter, without making a detour through the affirmations later put forward by one of the movement's leading figures, Hagop Oshagan, in *Hamapatker arevmtahay grakanut'ean* (Panorama of Western Armenian Literature). Oshagan's declarations and reminiscences, which date from the 1940s, remained unpublished for many years, for reasons having nothing to do with literature.[10] It must, however, also be admitted that the point of view expressed in the *Panorama* is already an interpretation of the adventure inaugurated in 1914. To reconstruct the phenomenon as a whole, we have to take both of the aspects we have already mentioned into account, and, as well, different people's versions of it. This explains the constant toing-and-froing, in what follows (and in the pages of the epilogue, on Zarian and Nietzsche), between interpretations on the one hand and the texts assembled in the review on the other.[11]

We must, however, begin by saying a few words about the circumstances and historical world that presided over the birth of *Mehyan*. In 1914, the Armenians of the Ottoman Empire had already enjoyed six years of relative freedom, after twelve years (1896–1908) of terror, persecution, and censorship. Exiled writers and intellectuals had returned to Constantinople after the Young Turks' constitutional revolution; some, such as Arshag Chobanian (1872–1954) and Vahan Tekeyan (1878–1945),[12] remaining only briefly, others, such as Rupen Zartarian (1874–1915)[13] and Zabel Esayan (1879–1943), settling there permanently. Political organs, such as, from 1909 on, the newspaper *Azatamart*, had assumed a prominent public role. Literary reviews were published without interruption, notably *Hay grakanut'iun* (Armenian Literature) in Smyrna and *Shant'* in Constantinople. This climate of relative, and illusory, freedom was punctuated in 1913 by a public celebration, in Constantinople, of the 1500th anniversary of the Armenian alphabet, during which Constant Zarian read the famous poem by Siamanto (1878–1915) dedicated to Mesrop Mashtots, the creator of the Armenian alphabet according to both legend and history. In spring of the same year, the entire Armenian intellectual class in Constantinople was mobilized around the "Literary Lectures" organized by Hagop Sirouni; they successively examined *Hin astvatsner* (Ancient Gods), a play by Levon Shant that had just been produced in Constantinople; collections of short stories by Krikor Zohrab (1861–1915), the most prominent writer of the realist school; Varuzhan's *Pagan Songs*; Zartarian's *Ts'aygaluys* (Night Light); the poetic work of Hovhannes Setian (1853–1930); and Siamanto's complete poetical works.[14] There is something tragic about this liberation of creative powers, when one is aware of the fate that lay in store for them just a few months ahead. Nearly all the writers we have just mentioned were brutally murdered after being deported in summer 1915.

In the literary field, after the dizzying emergence of two great writers of the Armenian poetry of the dawn of the twentieth century, Indra (1875–1921) and Medzarents (1886–1908),[15] the reading public was overcome by an almost demented passion for the works of Varuzhan and Siamanto, at the junction where poetry, nationalistic rhetoric, the breath of freedom, and the gathering tragedy met. The newspaper *Azatamart* launched the slogan of a "return to the old country," in which a segment of the younger generation sincerely believed. The "paganizing" current took shape under the influence of the poems published by Varuzhan between 1908 and 1912. Aharon and Sirouni belonged to this current, writing verse directly inspired by Varuzhan's paganism, even if they took up its neo-Romantic aspects alone. Komitas (1869–1935) himself was in Constantinople. The first confluence of these various currents came late in 1913 with the review *Navasard*, named after the great annual festival in honor of the three main gods in the Armenian pantheon.[16] Incontestably, a feeling of "rebirth" was in the air, a general, generous appeal to the long-suppressed "vital forces" of the "nation" or "race," in the expression of the day. This is what Varuzhan writes in his August 1913 poem "*Navasardian*" (For the Feast of Navasard), in the guise of a preface to the review that he and Sirouni would publish together.

> O Hayg, you genius, may you be reborn from the ruins
> In your sunlike glory during these Navasardean festivals,
> And take your lyre with you
> That your cry of glory may be heard. . . .

We will often be encountering the elements of the "solar" rhetoric typical of Varuzhan in the second part of the present volume. In any case, everything about this atmosphere was such as to appeal to the younger generation. Oshagan had moved to Constantinople in 1909, Varuzhan in 1912, Zarian in 1910 and again in 1912.[17] It was in this atmosphere that the *Mehyan* group was born.

In *Mayrineru shuk'in tak* (In the Shade of the Cedars), Oshagan says: "When we founded the review, our literature was showing signs, I won't say of exhaustion, but of going stale. Six years of freedom of the press had given free rein to our rhetorical powers, and our writers, long since drained of their creative energies and youthfulness, had not had the time to try new things, carried away as they were by slogans and politics."[18] This is one of Oshagan's favorite themes: the younger generation, he repeatedly says, reacted against the literary aridity provoked by the undue place given to political rhetoric. Thus we see that the climate of freedom that we just described had not had exclusively positive effects. Freedom reigned, be it added, only in a very relative sense. Abandoning their democratic and constitutional promises, the Young Turks gradually slid toward authoritarianism, a movement that culminated, in 1913, in the party's total control over government and state, followed by the Ottoman Empire's entry into the war and the decision to carry out the extermination. What is more, the Armenians did not, after all, simply go down the garden path. The April 1909 massacres in Adana and Cilicia, in which 30,000 people died, twelve years after the vast wave of pogroms carried out in 1895–96 across the Armenian plateau at the sultan's instigation, had considerably dampened the Armenians' enthusiasm and their hope for the creation of an Ottoman society in which the notion of citizenship would prevail. Zabel Esayan's book *Averaknerun mej* (Among the Ruins), which appeared two years after the 1909 events, was the report of a great woman of letters on the massacres in Cilicia, where she had gone as an official representative of the Patriarchate in July 1909 and remained for three months. It is a terrible, very finely written testimony.[19] As we shall see, Varuzhan wrote the poem "*Kilikioy averaknerun*" (To the Ashes of Cilicia) in 1909; in it, addressing the "Stranger," the foreign traveler to whom he has shown the ruins of the region, he advises, "Leave this bitter country for your peaceful shores," and "When . . . / You reach the laps of your golden brothers—don't forget / To tell them how Cilicia was slaughtered / To the treacherous rhythms of freedom's melody"(*YLZ* 1:150).[20] In a word, Varuzhan appealed to the foreigner to offer his own testimony, without believing that such testimony would ever reach the ears of those to whom it was addressed.[21] Meanwhile, the poet himself must go down to the plain, for "I too now descend / From this height, and wrapped in my morose cape . . . / I must dig countless graves tonight, / And weave resplendent shrouds until dawn. / I must construct tombs, raise monuments, / And on the marble, my epitaph I must engrave" (*YLZ* 1:151). Light may well serve as the marble out of which art sculpts the gods, but it can also, as we see here, serve as a shroud for the tombless dead. Similarly, the erection may be that of a "temple," but it may also, described at the same time and in the same terms, be that of the mausoleums and the memorials.

According to Oshagan, *Mehyan*'s aim was, in any case, to shake apathetic contemporaries awake, initiate a renewal, and introduce a little reflection, a little "madness," and a good deal of "the West" into "our literature." Here is his description of the primary driving forces behind the movement: it sought "to negate, overthrow, praise newcomers to the skies, adopt an attitude of rebellion against the prevailing aesthetic, and utter words that would impress people (necessary in any manifesto)."[22] The reserve that informs these lines has to do with the collective nature of the enterprise and, in particular, the role played in it by Zarian, who, returning from Europe, probably brought back with him the idea of the Manifesto, its imposing language, its scathing attacks on the Philistines, and, secondarily, its "Futurism." *Mehyan* is characterized, then, by this explosive dimension above all, this spirit of revolt and "madness." It should be added that Oshagan himself had by no means showed restraint when it came to rebellion against the older generation, sweeping negations, and the determination to turn things upside down, as his still celebrated series *Hart'enk'* shows.[23] This was even one of the postures that made for *Mehyan*'s vitriolic glory. The basic significance of the enterprise, however, lies elsewhere. In the first volume of *Panorama*, Oshagan says about *Mehyan* that "this group . . . entered the public arena and raised a number of questions that shook literary thinking to its foundations" (1:41). Of these questions, we shall, for the moment, focus on those raised in the Manifesto as well as those which appear in the third issue of the review. Our first approach to them will be descriptive, (almost) indistinguishable from the usual approach of literary history and the history of aesthetic conceptions.

THE EXPRESSION OF A SOUL

The Manifesto puts forward four imperatives, which it goes on to elaborate one by one. Let us simply state them in all their apparent naïveté:

1. worship and express the Armenian Soul;
2. pursue originality and individuality in matters of form;
3. cultivate the Armenian language with the help of revitalizing grafts;
4. keep pure literature at a far remove from politics and journalism.

(Mehyan, no. 1, p. 1)

The expression of these imperatives is marked by the weakness inherent in any Manifesto. In the fourth point, we will recognize Oshagan's distrust of political rhetoric and the misdeeds of political journalism. The third point is developed later in the Manifesto in connection with Armenian dialects and classical Armenian, both of which are supposed to enrich the literary language. The Manifesto speaks of the "inadequacy" of the elements used in the literary Armenian of the day. Varuzhan had made a similar argument in 1911.[24] The inadequacy that all the writers of this generation perceived had to do with the literarization of the language as it had been carried out among the Western Armenians; it seemed to suggest that the result of this literarization had now to be rectified. "Literarization" had, indeed, occurred in the absence of all contact with "popular sources." It was now up to art, the aesthetic principle, to correct the defect. Whence a formula to which we shall often return: "We want to found an aesthetics of the language" (ibid., p. 2).

That said, the fact remains that, of the four imperatives in the Manifesto, the first, the will to "express the Armenian soul," is the one that remained engraved in the collective memory and was later identified by teachers of literature as the defining characteristic of the *Mehyan* group. Today, this imperative strikes us as outdated or ideological, insofar as it depends on the assumption of a pre-existent "essence," and also, it has to be said, for a much more disturbing reason: the Manifesto speaks of this "Soul" being "embodied" in the "*Aryan* race to which we belong." (*Mehyan*, no. 1, p. 2).[25] This is a rhetoric typical of the entire period; its resurgence in *Mehyan* seems to be due, once again, to Zarian, the only member of the group to develop this theme explicitly in his articles, and, later, in his essays and novels.[26] The group as a whole, however, necessarily accepted such rhetoric, if to different degrees. We can certainly not ignore this aspect of matters, even if everyone is familiar with the European context in which such declarations were quite common; they came essentially (and unfortunately) by way of Nietzsche. The gravity of this subject requires that we come back to it. Later on, simplifying outrageously, Oshagan would declare in *Panorama* that *Mehyan*'s great merit resided in its "discovery of the Armenian soul" (9:185). He meant, of course, the rediscovery of popular sources and their distillation in written texts or art, since he had no other "soul" in mind. Yet the fact remains that his phrase—torn out of context and, certainly, considered in isolation from the aesthetic principle, of which it is, albeit secretly, the spokesman— has, despite or perhaps because of its naïveté, enjoyed great success with the Armenians. That is why a reconstruction of the system of the aestheticizing erection must be very explicitly associated with a destruction of the very same principle. Those who bandy Oshagan's naïve formula about have obviously never realized that "soul" is precisely what is lacking or absent from one end of Armenian literature to the other, on the witness of Oshagan himself, who frequently bewails the "absence of [the Armenian] people" from Armenian literature (*Panorama* 1:110; 6:21). "Soul" is even characterized precisely by this absence, by the fact that it is not manifest. Thus the Manifesto affirms, in its pretentious, bloated style, that "[t]he Armenian Soul is an element in the intellectual universe [*imats'akan tiezerk'*] which, once It has been *made manifest*, will amaze all thinking mankind"(*Mehyan*, no. 1, p. 2; emphasis added). It must be said that thinking mankind had other things on its mind. Is the one and only reason that art constitutes a luminous space for the reception of concealed sources the fact that it universalizes the particular, thus making the particular audible for the "foreigner" before making it audible for "us"?

TOTALITY AND RELIGION

The second question raised by *Mehyan* is the one that the third issue of the review calls the question of *Hayastaneats' grakanut'iun*, a phrase that might be translated "the literature of all Armenians." Oshagan would later say that "when the people associated with *Mehyan* . . . brought this formula before the public, they were aware of the seriousness of what they were about" (*Panorama* 1:41). We must therefore ask, if only in passing, just what this "seriousness" was. The phrase *Hayastaneats' Yekeghets'i* means "the Church of all the Armenians," the semi-official name for the Armenian Church. Oshagan's formula, strangely, presents the task of literature as a substitute for the task that had, for centuries, been incumbent on the Church. Indeed, he says this in so many words in volume 9 of *Panorama* (9:23).[27] Manifesting an essence down to the moment of its disappearance and standing in for an institution with a totalizing mission: such are the two functions that have now devolved upon literature. But this account of the two functions in terms of the group's project as the group consciously conceived it sheds very little light on things. It does not, in any case, reveal anything about the group's "experience" or the literary and aesthetic "erection." Nonetheless, for better than eighty years, nothing else in the *Mehyan* group's project held the attention of any of those who, among the Armenians, claimed to be intellectuals. This means, at the very least, that the project was open to interpretations of the most naively nationalistic sort.[28]

A third obvious characteristic, finally, is the omnipresent reference to religion. It appears, to begin with, in the title of the review, *Mehyan*, "(Pagan) Temple" a direct allusion to pagan religion. The Manifesto affirms, moreover, that "[i]tself a species of religious zealotry, [Art] stands above every religion" (*Mehyan*, no. 1, p. 3). The reference to religion is made even by Oshagan, for whom literature becomes the ark (*tapanak*) of the Torah (*Mehyan*, no. 3, p. 40);[29] it is above all present in Zarian, who writes: "The absence among us of quests inspired by religious crises is striking" (*Mehyan*, no. 2, p. 19). Zarian links this, once again, to the absence of "Aryan consciousness," but also, still more strangely, to the fact that "this people . . . has never experienced an inner . . . Golgotha" (ibid.). This desideratum was soon made good. At all events, the sum total of Zarian's contradictory or scandalous formulations remains incomprehensible unless we relate them to the system of the aestheticizing erection in which they find their place, if not their justification. We shall attempt to do so here.

We have brought out three characteristics of art and literature as understood by *Mehyan* and described in explicit statements enshrined in the review: art manifests essence, art accomplishes the totality, art measures itself against religion. In each case, art plays a role in the emergence and development of a collectivity. With these three characteristics, however, we have, so far, only repeated what lies on the surface. We shall now proceed to chart the underlying system of this aesthetic erection, concentrating on its Oshaganesque variant.

THE LAST EVENING SPENT TOGETHER: THE NATIONAL

The most fully developed passage that Oshagan devotes to the *Mehyan* group occurs in the ninth volume of *Panorama*, at the beginning of his monograph on the poet Rupen Sevag (1885–1915).[30] Here Oshagan recounts the last evening, as he remembered it thirty years later, that the members of the group spent together, a week before the fateful date of April 11/24, 1915.[31] He focuses on their discussion of what, in his view, constituted *Mehyan*'s "message." The gathering, at which Varuzhan and many others were also present, is recounted at length, in a style dear to Oshagan's heart, one that turns on seizing, at a particular moment, the whole spirit of a mini-epoch by representing the various tendencies that informed it, while, in the present case, keeping the reader constantly aware of the tension and terror engendered by the deterioration of the political climate. Oshagan tells us that the least little details of this evening remained forever engraved in his memory. It was the group's last meeting: one week later, the unimaginable was to begin and would soon run its course. The heart of the gathering is, in Oshagan's account of it, his conversation with Sevag, as he recalled it very many years later. He recounts other aspects of this encounter in at least two other texts, a 1924 essay and the monograph in *Panorama* on Varuzhan.[32] The conversation developed around the question of what *Mehyan* had been a year earlier and what I have just called its "message": literature as the manifestation of a collective essence and as a stand-in for the totalizing mission of the Church, now no longer capable of carrying out this mission. Oshagan's interlocutor Sevag (who was also hosting the soirée) took a humanist position, which had it that both the suffering and "collective essence" of this people, his people, were transcended by, or enveloped within, a more general form of suffering. Oshagan, needless to say, was not bent on single-minded pursuit of the particular. Simply, it seemed to him that the specific question of the collective essence of the people—in a word, its founding or coalescence as a people torn apart by an uncontrollable, nameless form of violence—disappeared in Sevag's approach it. The collective essence and internal divisions of the collectivity and the specific kinds of violence visited upon it did not really become themes of the conversation. What did, in contrast, was the need for a literature without universalizing pretensions, one that would confine its attention to the people's characteristic culture, the cultural forms of its existence. Oshagan's constant theme is that these "cultural forms" had never really been brought to light and enshrined in writing, which for him means, of course, literary writing. Thus we once again encounter a formulation and preoccupation with which we are already quite familiar: they revolve around the idea that the sources of the culture have been abandoned to themselves and left in the dark, that they have had no contact with writing and have not been sublated by art.

Just before recounting this evening, Oshagan introduces one of the long footnotes typical of his work. I shall cite it at length. It is, in its entirety, about the *Mehyan* movement, which Oshagan calls the movement of the "Leftists" (in Armenian, *Tsakherë*):

> This label is appropriate for a movement that materialized in 1914 under the name *mehenakan* ("pertaining to the *Mehyan* group"), with, as its mainsprings, renewal and nationalization [*azgaynats'um*]. . . . The renewal pursued by the Leftists was a vast project, a sort of reaction to the exaggerated pursuit of fashion prevailing in 1900. . . . Furthermore, the nationalization pursued by the Leftists was a profound negation of the rhetorical utilitarianism of the 1860 generation, of their historicism and liberalism, which were sociopolitical movements much more than they were literary tendencies. (*Panorama* 9:13)[33]

Patently, Oshagan is hard put, in this, the first part of his note, to provide a precise definition of the movement. That is why he falls back on historical contrasts, affirms that the movement was innovative, and, above all, recites the pivotal formula of "nationalization." Finally, he insists on what *Panorama* sometimes calls "the emancipation of the concept of literature," as if the concept of pure literature (mentioned explicitly in the *Mehyan* manifesto) had until then been the captive of a language foreign to it. In the middle of the note, Oshagan cites the names of the leading "provincial" writers of the diaspora (Ohan Garo, Hamasdegh)[34] as a sort of counterargument, as if these writers had announced or pursued *Mehyan*'s project without drawing all the consequences. Given what we have seen so far, the best description of the project in its Oshaganesque variant is encapsulated in the word *azgaynats'um*, which I have translated as "nationalization." The goal was to "nationalize" literature, to endow it with a "national" character. Is the desire or the thesis involved here nationalistic? We have to do, in any case, with one of the most powerful formulations of the "aesthetic principle," one I have sometimes interpreted as plainly antinationalistic. On what grounds? Simply because this formulation has to be read against the grain, in the awareness that nothing "national" exists prior to art or before the intervention of art. There is, in particular, nothing "national" about the productions "of the people." Once this is understood, Oshagan's formulation takes on a very precise meaning: if it is true that literature has to be "nationalized," the "national" itself comes into being only by way of art, particularly literature. It comes into being only as a result of the sublation or aestheticization of its popular sources. It so happens that nationalism, in the political sense of the word, was not problematic for Oshagan. In contrast, it did become problematic a little later—in an altogether different universe—for Charents. Yet Charents would affirm exactly the same thing: the national comes into being only by way of art.[35] I do not mean to say that this formulation is not inherently ambiguous. The ambiguity in question is, however, genuinely abyssal; it subsists throughout the nineteenth century in Europe and presides over the birth of the ethnographic nations. At any rate, the fact is that all the nationalistic readings of Charents and Oshagan (and, to date, there exists no reading of the one or the other that is not effectively nationalistic) presuppose, for their part, that the national pre-exists art, thereby rendering all the critical work that these writers accomplished pointless, if not, indeed, ridiculous. If the reader puts these nationalistic interpretations aside for a moment, she can no doubt already grasp what we mean when we say that, for Oshagan and Varuzhan, nationalization was an appropriating event, an *Ereignis* in the Heideggerian sense. The principle that presides over this event is the aesthetic principle. It is a question of a coming to one's self, a coming of the self to the self, which is thought under the name of "art" and carried out by means of art. Hence it presupposes, at the origin, a radical alienation of the "self."

THE LAST EVENING SPENT TOGETHER: AESTHETICIZATION
AS DISCLOSURE

Oshagan's note continues:

> This nationalization [*azgaynats'um*] was directed above all against the Mkhitarists. . . . It consisted in leading our literature back toward its authenticity, content, and true color, those of the people, while following a path different from that taken by the work that came forward under the label "provincial literature."[36]

The Leftists believed in the emotion and beauty inherent in the hitherto unsuspected reserves of their race. *To dig down to these depths and bring the treasures buried there to light*: this meant accepting the fact that Western Armenian literature was defective and fragmentary, and it meant extending the boundaries of this literature well beyond Constantinople, Smyrna, and Venice toward the East, our country's heartland. (*Panorama* 9:14; emphasis in the original)

So reconstructed, the *Mehyan* project appears to be identical to the one pursued by Komitas, who, in the same period, was systematically collecting folk songs in order to restore them to, and reclaim them for, the sphere of art. I have already coined a formula for this effort, which consisted, I said, in reclaiming previously concealed popular sources for an artistic medium. Indeed, in his essay published in the March 1914 issue of *Mehyan*, Oshagan invokes Komitas, whose work he identifies as paradigmatic of what he himself was championing: "A Priest of Labor has transformed our songs into music as marvelous as a revelation for us, for whom they had become something foreign"(*Mehyan*, no. 3, p. 40).[37] Here we can also readily see how the opposition between the manifest and the nonmanifest works. The "popular sources" and "cultural forms" of existence of the people are invisible, hidden, buried in the land's depths. They must be brought into the light. Into what light? That of Art. Art (which clearly deserves to be capitalized from now on) ensures this passage from the nonmanifest to the manifest. Art functions as a means of reflection. It is this passage to the manifest in the form of self-reflection which is described and formulated as an imperative. We must erect a temple, we must "create," we must bring Art into being. It is a question of survival! But then how are we to account for the fact that the demand to forge a link of this sort (between "art" and the "popular sources") is formulated at a particular point in time, around 1908, somewhat earlier by Komitas, somewhat later by Varuzhan, Oshagan, and their associates in the *Mehyan* group? Why the need for art here, when, previously, the popular sources were sufficient unto themselves? They have to be "brought into the broad light of day," exhibited in what is deemed the "light" and "day" of art, but that is "light" and "day" thanks only to a persistent sense that the "popular sources" are buried or under wraps. As we shall see in chapter 2, the same experience was explored seventy years earlier among the Eastern Armenians, in Khachatur Abovean's work: an experience of radical mutism, of a "people's" voice that has become inaudible for the people itself and must be saved in a certain way, so that it may be heard by the people whose voice it is. Thus *Mehyan* called for a "disclosure" of the popular sources that were under wraps, which is to say, in effect, for an "appropriation" or a coming to the self of what was already most intimately the self's. This appeal took a number of different forms. Yet, always, one and the same phenomenon was to be found at the source of the call, that of a diffuse threat, an underlying disaster, a chronic insufficiency in literature, which is to say, as well, in the way the literarization of the language and thus, ultimately, "nationalization" had taken place. Hence we find an incredible drive toward aestheticization in the whole of this generation, in reaction to what seems to be a hidden tragedy that has overcome the collective voice and condemned it to silence. Art has to take over where the popular sources have left off. Art is the "broad light of day" in which the popular sources can become manifest only because popular forms are now threatened with the suffocation and extinction that have abruptly become realities in this place.

How, then, are we to conceive of the necessity of an event of this kind, thanks to which "art" suddenly becomes indispensable where there was previously no mention of it? The question will sound odd, of course, because, from a contemporary standpoint, the answer seems self-evident. What could be more manifestly necessary than the art of someone like Komitas, to whom the whole subsequent Armenian musical tradition appeals—without whom it seems impossible even to conceive of Armenian popular music? Nevertheless, when the *Mehyan* period encountered this self-evident necessity in the first decade of the twentieth century, it perceived it as something altogether new. Thereafter, it could not conceive of the popular sources as, precisely, anything other than "sources" to be put on exhibit, sources calling, from their profoundest depths, for their own reception and aestheticization.

We have spoken of a depth that was "buried," left under wraps, hidden away underground, and of treasures awaiting their manifestation and "aestheticization." The next section of Oshagan's note in volume 9 of *Panorama* sets up an opposition between this "depth" and the transfer of its treasures into the light of art, on the one hand, and the pedestrian activity of the "collection" of ethnographic material on the other: "The Leftists were not afraid to encounter another pedestrian reality on this path, the utilitarian, sociojournalistic attitude that was winning converts in Tblisi." The sacred, subterranean depth of that which had never before been made manifest comes to the fore in the "telluric" significance with which the project of the aestheticizing erection was endowed:

> We were very different people, advocating theses about aesthetics that were very nearly at loggerheads. But we were of a single mind as far as the fierce desire to nationalize [*azgaynats'nel*] literature went, and we invested the term with telluric significance. (*Panorama* 9:14)[38]

What is more, it is precisely this point which, in Oshagan's view, ensured the unity of the group and motivated those making it up to join forces: "Whence a spiritual unity whose other face was the pugnacious attitude informing our effort to put an end, once and for all, to the onerous legacy of the artistic tastes typical of the two generations preceding ours." Once again, we have translated literally: "to nationalize literature." It should be clear by now that "national," in this context, can only be understood if the project of "aestheticization" is presupposed.

OCCULTED MISFORTUNE AND THE LUMINOUS RESPONSE

I have reproduced long sections of this note because of its value as testimony, to begin with. The note presents itself as a balance sheet, one of the central formulations of which bears on the "telluric" significance of *Mehyan*'s project, the desire to "dig down to [the] depths" in order to "bring . . . to light" "unsuspected reserves" and buried "treasures." It is this desire which defines *nationalization*, a term that must, accordingly, be employed in a transitive sense. Nevertheless, this balance sheet, drawn up in Oshaganesque terms, is fundamentally ambiguous. The ambiguity is due, first of all, to the questions thrown up by the term *nationalization*. Secondly, the balance sheet seems to require that the *Mehyan* project and movement engage in an act of self-representation of the kind that Abovean, several decades earlier, had described as a necessity, as if it were a question, in sum, of ethnography. Quite the contrary is true: the first characteristic singled out here is that of aestheticization, manifestation in the light. This balance sheet also obscures the acuteness of the other question that quite naturally comes to the fore: what kind of experience is responsible for the fact that the "popular sources" cease to suffice unto themselves at a particular moment in time and thus require "aestheticization"? That it is an experience of a hidden and then suddenly unveiled "tragedy" changes nothing here. It does not tell us why it should be art which provides the response to this tragedy. What is more, Oshagan and his generation would have been hard put to formulate the question in this way. They took it for granted that the response should come from art. They were capable only of noting the demand for aestheticization and acting upon it. They were certainly not capable of interrogating it. They operated within the confines of the system of the aestheticizing erection, and were consequently unable to question the core of this demand and system. For them, there was, perforce, a blind spot there. It is our task as readers and heirs to inquire into the nature of this blind spot, and explore it.

Folk songs offer the best illustration of these "sources" waiting to be revealed. Folk songs were not only buried and inaudible, but also had no "name" and no identity thanks to which we might recognize and appropriate them. Someone had to come along to "reveal" them, to endow them with the luminosity of art. For Oshagan, that someone was Komitas. Art is that which has the power of revelation and manifestation. Komitas is the paradigm of the aestheticizing erection. Moreover, these popular "sources" include not only the people's "tragic songs," but also its narratives, tales, and myths, which resemble an "undreamed dream" (*antes yeraz*). Constant Zarian, in "The Heart of the Fatherland," an essay in the third issue of *Mehyan*, puts this more naively: it is necessary, he says, to return to the "heart" of things, to the place where the "myths" and "songs" were produced.[39] But the heart must "manifest itself." How can we ensure that it will? By means of style. "For the Style will have been discovered" (*Mehyan*, no. 3, p. 37), which is to say, to put it plainly, that we will discover Art, which is, for the moment, "hidden" (*t'ak'nëvats*). "The Heart of the Fatherland shall live by Art and in Art." In each case, the allusion is plainly to popular sources and treasures, songs, narratives, and myths. Zarian adds, "then the choral song of the new *ashough*s shall rise joyous and clear, declaiming the new Mythology" (ibid.).[40] When he wrote the essay "The Heart of the Fatherland," he was certainly unaware that the first generation of German Romantics had called for a "new mythology," nor did he know anything about the doctoral dissertation that Manuk Abeghean (1865–1944) had published in 1899, a dissertation that likewise concerned itself with these songs, narratives, and myths, which it grouped under the rubric "lower (or secondary) mythology."[41] Along with the major work by Ghevond Alishan (1820–1901) on the Armenians' ancient religion,[42] Abeghean's thesis offers something like a prehistory of the literary erection and the *Mehyan* project; I shall examine both in that light in the following chapters. To be sure, neither Alishan nor Abeghean issued a call, on the eve of the annihilation, for "aestheticization" as a luminous manifestation of inaudible, nameless, hidden sources. Yet these are the characteristics that Abeghean attributes to his object, "secondary mythology," when he affirms that "many aspects of the ancient pagan faith, although they are, to be sure, on the way to extinction, have been preserved [to the present day] . . . especially among the lower classes of the people." It is much too early to appreciate this passage at its full value. After all, it makes very simple affirmations about things with which we are all familiar, such as the crisis of oral literature (real or supposed), the preservation of ancient beliefs in the form of folklore, and the continuity between ancient paganism and modern beliefs. However, as we shall see, the passage constitutes a magnificent culmination of the development of philology. It draws a connection between the two great philological inventions: the native, and mythological religion. These matters will become clearer in the following two chapters. The novelty of these questions (especially the thematization of philology as the protagonist of literary aestheticization) explains why we have to take one hesitant step at a time in this exploration of the national imagination.

The songs, narratives, and myths were nameless and voiceless, buried, and doomed to silence. Thus the Manifesto speaks of a "seal of silence" (*lr'utean dataknik'ë*) that must be broken (*Mehyan*, no. 1, p. 3). It is of course art and aestheticization that are summoned to break this seal. Aestheticization will restore the voice of those who have so far been mute. This power that aestheticization possesses bears not only on "popular productions," but also on what the Manifesto calls "language," when it declares: "We want to found an aesthetics of language." This is an extraordinary formulation that does not at all mean "we want to embellish our language" or develop an aesthetic theory of language. It follows on the heels of the paragraph about the need to exploit the dialects and the classical language, assimilating them to the literary language while raising them to its level. Varuzhan, in one of the pair of remarkable essays he wrote in 1911 and 1913, had already said the same thing in much the same terms. We shall have occasion to return, later, to the idea that it is no longer possible to write in the dialects, since they comprise natural languages that are, as such, incomprehensible and inaudible. Yet one cannot *not* refer to them, precisely because they are perceived as being nameless and mute. They have to be brought out of their "darkness" into the bright light of day and of aestheticized language. This is a process exactly identical to the one just described. Natural languages, like popular productions, are "sources" that have to be made manifest by way of an "aestheticization," by being carried over into the so-called literary language. This language will "bring into the light" the buried treasures of the language.[43] The notion of bringing into the light or aestheticizing is expressed in Varuzhan in yet another way: he calls it "giv[ing] the language its integral form" (*amboghjakan dzevë*). That which is thus brought into the light is something drawn from a "mine," and, as well, something that awaits "adoption": namely, the styles, expressions, and individual words of the natural languages. The earlier literarization of the language failed to take the form of an aestheticization.

INTEGRITY AND FRAGMENTATION

After the opposition of the manifest and nonmanifest and the concomitant need for aestheticization—as that which gives a voice to that which has no voice, a substitute paternity for that which no longer has a father as such, a luminous space for that which is buried underground—we shall now consider, more briefly, the second opposition: that between what is whole and what is disintegrating.

"It would be absurd," writes Varuzhan, "to think that this integral form of the language will come about when the grammarians and philologists . . . impose it. This is rather the task of the writer-aesthetes" (*YLZ* 3:163). This affirmation will eventually constitute one of the nodal points in our explication of the aesthetic principle. It explains, in part, why it is necessary to examine the project of aestheticization and the emergence of philology side by side. It is the continuation of what was said a moment ago about Varuzhan's 1913 essay. To found an aesthetic of the language is to endow the language with a wholeness that it no longer has or, rather, never had. In question is not only the dispersion of the dialects, but also their naturalness. In the same vein, in his essay in the third issue of *Mehyan*, Oshagan began by saying, in the form of a wish rather than a statement, "our literature is one"(*Mehyan*, no. 3, p. 38).[44] We should understand him to mean not only unity here, but also wholeness. The counterexample or counterreality appears immediately thereafter, in the guise of "the diversity of our dialects"(ibid.). Literature is "one" over against that diversity. Obviously, the aim of Oshagan's plea is not to suppress the dialects. He presupposes the integrity of the body of the community, an integrity that is not only in jeopardy, but already crumbling. The goal is "to transform our fragmented existence into a whole" (ibid., p. 40). In question here is not, obviously, geographical fragmentation, the divisions between "dialects." What is at stake is, rather, an essential internal fragmentation, a sort of disassembling of the core. The wholeness of this core has to be restored; this body has to be given back its integrity. Integrity, wholeness: the Armenian word for both is *amboghjut'yun*, the word we saw Varuzhan using, a moment ago, to describe the "integral form of the language." Later in Oshagan's essay, this "fragmentation" of our existence is described in still starker terms:

> Fragmented, aged, driven from its center, land, and religion, vagabond, humiliated by its aimless wanderings, without a name or body, a tottering multitude stands before us. (ibid.)

Here again, the center and the land from which the people have been driven are not geographical concepts. Oshagan is quite clearly describing a mortal fragmentation that scatters the fragments of the integral core and center, people, land, and religion. He is plainly describing a process of *disintegration*. It is because this is what is at stake that the term *amboghjut'iun* must be translated as "integrity" in the sense of "wholeness." What is needed to restore integrity to our disintegrated existence, to ward off the catastrophic end threatening the body of our community? Let us not forget that Oshagan is writing in 1914. The Catastrophe has not happened yet. What is in question is nonetheless the catastrophic disintegration of a community. For a long time, I believed that the term *amboghjut'iun* had to be translated as "integrity" because the Catastrophe was already on the horizon. We shall see that matters are somewhat more complicated when we discuss the "disaster" of the "native." In reality, the disaster at issue here is the one that philology has always considered to be the disaster of the native. Hence we shall be observing a gradual but total reversal of perspective. That is why we had to begin our survey of the situation without considering any of the elements that will, one by one, subsequently emerge into the light: "philology," the "native," the loss of the gods, the "disaster" constitutive of the native. In a word, we had to begin without considering the process of *mourning* that is characteristic of orientalist philology, the process that it is precisely the function of orientalist philology to hide. On the other hand, this means that we shall have to reread the same pages and passages in the second part of the present book, with full awareness, the second time around, of the profoundly *philological* content of the experience of disaster (and, of course, all the questions and doubts that go hand-in-hand with it).

For as long as philology and its "native" do not enter into our analysis, we may suppose that the *Mehyan* writers were already talking about the Catastrophe here. We may say, with them, that the Catastrophe is a form of total violence. We may add that it affects the whole precisely because it takes aim at wholeness or integrity. We may conclude that the *Mehyan* writers succeeded, on the verge of the Catastrophe, in writing this blow directed against the whole and, consequently, that they were the night watchmen of the Catastrophe, the watchmen of the last night. And this is indeed what I told myself again and again for years. It is not altogether wrong, of course, as long as one simultaneously bears in mind that such formulations are utterly oblivious to the mourning of philology, which, however, cannot simply be neglected. It will therefore be necessary to return to all these interpretations with new premises in mind: the incontestable fact of the mourning of philology.

In the meantime, we can always ask, with the *Mehyan* writers: What is needed to restore the integrity of that which has already disintegrated? Here is their answer, a crazy answer that is nevertheless stated in black and white: "To forge the unity of our fragmented existence, we await our Dante. The Dantes did not come from India." The Dantes, that is, will not come to us from the outside, from just anywhere. They will be born in our midst, they will rise to their feet, they will erect themselves on their own power. Here we see the system of the aesthetic erection at work. The erection of the artist and that of the work will gather around themselves the dispersed vestiges of the process of disintegration. They will reproduce, in the unity of an aesthetic illumination, that is, of the aestheticized language, the originary assembly, the paradigmatic instance of integrity. A crazy answer! Yet all these writers say the same thing, with an utterly fascinating consistency. Thus Varuzhan declares, in an April 2, 1909 letter to the editor Theotig:[45] "We have to gather up the vestiges of our heart, dispersed among three million people; we have to bring them together in a single breast and then apprehend the Life that is its own, even if only briefly, for the love of Art and the love of the Song of Life" (*YLZ* 3:408). The artist's auto-erection will spark this regrouping, leading back to the originary assembly of that which is assembled, that which we call a "people."[46] Art—aestheticization as auto-erection—is thus the other side of disintegration. At the same time, the system of the aestheticizing erection leads to the "cult" of the self-erected individual, the artist. That is why, in Zarian, Christ is the first self-erected individual, and therefore also, Zarian says, the "proto-artist," a formula that occurs in his article "The Jesus of the Armenians." It remains to ask what delirious historical logic could transform this first auto-erected individual, the proto-artist and, as well, the proto-Aryan, into the man who proved capable of "overcoming Semitism." No "internal" logic can explain this. What is needed is a historical logic, the logic of the invention of mythological religion by nineteenth-century philology.[47] Thus Oshagan, again, can say: "The individual focuses the countless rays diffused by the furnace of the race, in all their colors, burning bright or on the point of dying out"(*Mehyan* no. 3, p. 38).[48] And Zarian, more naively, as usual: "Admirable are those who, slinging sacks over their shoulders, set out on rocky roads to find the scattered fragments of the Heart of the Fatherland. . . . it is necessary to gather up its fragments and seek the new form of its emergence and manifestation" (ibid., p. 37).[49] Here we find, once again, the imperative of "manifestation," bound up with the imperative to re-establish the "fullness" or integrity of that which has disintegrated. The "sack slung over the shoulder" is hardly just a metaphor. Since the 1830s, indigenous travelers had been setting out for "the fatherland"—attracted by what mirage, what figure? Driven by what force? We shall see. But the image corresponds closely to that of the "discoverers" who, like Servantsdeants (1840–1892) between 1870 and 1890, or Komitas somewhat later, wandered through "the heart of the fatherland" in order to bring back scraps of the oral tradition or ethnographic observations. It remains for us to discover these "discoverers" whom Zarian named in March 1914:

> Reverend Father Khrimian, a true Father,
> Abovean, the man of tough Ideals,
> Servantsdiants, the intelligent Traveler,
> Alishan, whose Eyes were trained on the fatherland, and others, many others . . .

and to understand the cultural history of their "discovery."

CHAPTER 2

Abovean and the Birth of the Native

Khachatur Abovean (1809–1848) is the favorite author of those who produce national-istic discourse among Armenians. He enjoys extraordinary favor in such discourse, since he is considered to be not only the father of modern literature—meaning, I sup-pose, literature written in the modern language—but also the herald and architect of this modern language itself. I showed at length in my 1989 book *Ages et usages de la langue arménienne* that nationalistic discourse has been deliberately deceiving itself on both points. Abovean was neither the herald nor the architect of the modern lan-guage, which, under the name "civil language," existed in fully developed form long before his day, and in its two variants, Eastern and Western, at that. Moreover, while he did indeed produce, in the nineteenth century, the first *novel* written in Armenian, he wrote it in a language inaccessible to most ordinary mortals: to all intents and purposes, the dialect of his own village. Nationalistic discourse thus needed to "make a hero" of Abovean, and, profiting from the occasion, to forget, for reasons we shall learn in the following pages, all those whose efforts had, before him, contributed to bringing the modern language into being (and, *ipso facto*, the modern nation as well). In particular, nationalistic discourse has erased from Armenians' memory, almost without a trace, the Mkhitarist monks Pzhshgean (1777–1851) and Injijean (1758–1833), the first great architects of the modern language, whom I discuss at length below. This is, all things considered, an extraordinary lapse, a virtually immediate suppression of all that had been produced prior to 1840. There exists, to be sure, a myth about "mod-ernization" among the Armenians, a myth about a "renaissance" (roughly correspond-ing to the process of nationalization). This myth has it that modernization and the renaissance began with Abovean; it takes no account at all of what was underway among Western Armenians in the first half of the nineteenth century. The Western Armenians, too, have done their part to consign Abovean's predecessors to oblivion, forgetting their great writers of the modern language active in the 1810s and 1820s even before the earth was cold on their graves.[1] I shall disinter these writers later, with-out the least intention of rehabilitating them (from the nationalistic viewpoint). I shall do so simply in order to see how nationalistic discourse works, and also how, before any such discourse existed, the self-invention of the nation came about. Let us assume that it was with Abovean that modern literature did in fact come into existence among the Armenians. The fact remains that what was established at the moment of this birth, in literature and before literature, was the *auto-ethnographic project*, which was to absorb the bulk of the Armenians' intellectual energies throughout the last quarter of the century. What was established at that time, to be more exact, was the auto-ethnographic moment of the process of becoming a nation, or of the nation-inventing process. It is thus incumbent upon us to understand why this moment immediately took a central place in the nationalistic imagination, to the point of eclipsing everything else. To do so, we need to reread Abovean's preface to his novel *Verk' Hayastani* (Wounds of Armenia), which he wrote in 1841.

The present chapter contains two sections. The first offers a fairly detailed commentary on Abovean's preface, following the analysis of it that I proposed in 1989 in *Ages et usages de la langue arménienne*. Thus the present commentary takes up and supersedes what I had to say about Abovean twenty years ago.[2] I have deliberately engaged in this sort of repetition as a way of zeroing in (so that I can grasp it myself) on the point where the divergence from what I wrote then begins, especially as concerns both the "paternal reference" and myth as a vehicle for a foundational paternity. My analyses of Yeghishe Charents and Gurgen Mahari in *Writers of Disaster: The National Revolution* (and my insistence on comprehending disaster as a "disaster of the father," that is, on following or even anticipating those two authors' own interpretation of the Catastrophe) already tended, it seems to me, in the direction I take here. They were designed to set the framework for the strange theme of "foundational paternity," the object of the disaster and thus, as these authors saw it, the key to understanding what the Catastrophe was and what had actually occurred at the heart of it, in its black box or blind spot. Ultimately, as goes without saying, we will have to reinterpret this theme, too, as *an effect* (no doubt, one of the most powerful effects) of *philological mourning*. In sum, I propose to describe the experience of the disaster as it appears in Abovean, and to bring out, for the first time, behind the birth of literature and the auto-ethnographic project, the figure of the "native," surreptitiously or in all its glory, while simultaneously trying to understand why the disaster had to be experienced and articulated as a disaster "of the father." The first section of the present chapter is consequently devoted to the "mutism" of "the son." The second section seeks to give the reader, succinctly, an idea of the extensive historical posterity of the auto-ethnographic project drawn up by Abovean.

I. THE STORY OF THE MUTE SON AND ITS ALLEGORICAL INTERPRETATION

In his *History* (book 1, chapter 85), Herodotus says that King Croesus of Lydia (who died in 546 B.C.) had a mute son. The king did all he could to cure him, but in vain. He even sent messengers to Delphi to ask the Pythia what to do. The Pythia replied,

"Do not desire to hear the voice of your son under your roof. Hope rather that his lips may never open. For he shall first speak on the day on which it is decided whether you shall live or die." The kingdom of Lydia was later invaded by the Persians under Cyrus the Great. During the final battle, which put an end to Croesus' kingdom and led to the destruction of his last stronghold, a soldier spotted the king and raised his sword in order to kill him. Croesus made no attempt to defend himself. All was lost; the end was at hand. His mute son, mute since his birth, was terrified by the scene. Opening his lips, he uttered human language for the first time in his life, crying out: "Do not kill him! It is Croesus!" Herodotus adds that the mute son continued to speak to the end of his days.

This story of the mute son obsessed the nineteenth-century Eastern Armenians. In 1829, Nerses Ashtaraketsi, then Patriarch of the Armenians, recalled this story in a still-unpublished letter in which he slightly alters Croesus' son's words to "Do not kill him; it is my father!" Nerses uses the story as an allegory to express his own helplessness as a "son" confronting the disastrous state of his people. He writes, "I can neither keep silent nor cry out."[3] In his wake, Abovean twice utilized the story of Croesus' mute son. He first did so while a student at the University of Dorpat in Estonia, between 1830 and 1836, as he was translating, from the German, a book of ancient history that related the downfall of the Kingdom of Lydia—in particular, the passage inspired by Herodotus.[4] He used it again in the extraordinary passage that opens his preface to his novel *Wounds of Armenia*, written in 1841 but published only in 1858, ten years after its author's death. At the threshold of the novel, at the inaugural moment of modern Armenian literature (in fact, as was just noted, at a moment reconstructed as such by the nationalistic tradition inaugurated, precisely, by Abovean), we find this striking story about a mute son, devastation, and a slain father.

Abovean immediately interprets the story that he has inherited from Herodotus and Patriarch Nerses. He interprets it as an allegory. For he says, to begin with, that the "father" is his people or "nation" ("my dear father and my beloved nation";[5] the Armenian word he uses is *azg*) and, thereafter, that the "father" is the language ("the Armenian language was running away from me like Croesus").[6] This allegorical interpretation may be reconstructed to mean "I was unable to speak before this because I lacked an adequate language. I had not yet understood that I should make use of my people's language in order to make myself heard. My nation was in a state of disaster, on the verge of collapse. I am crying out in order to prevent it from perishing." This reconstruction, however close it may be to what Abovean actually intended, is nevertheless not entirely convincing. It suggests that he merely wanted to make this story over into an allegory, as Patriarch Nerses had before him. Of course, he had a perfect right to make it whatever he wished; in particular, he had the right to transform it into an allegory for his purposes. We, in our turn, have the right to assume that this story of mutism at the very beginning of modern Armenian literature says more than Abovean was capable of making it say. At the end of the preface, he again confirms the allegoric interpretation by translating the words of the once mute son as follows:

"Who is that you are raising your sword to strike? Do you not recognize the great Armenian nation?" (*Verk' Hayastani*, 1981, 48). Who raises his arm here to strike down the "great Armenian nation"? The answer is not clear. It seems, at any event—this is what I would like to show—that the obsession of the mute son is, in Abovean's mind, inherently more powerful than his allegorical interpretation of it.

A Novel of the Son and the Birth of Literature

What is beyond doubt is that Abovean identified with the son. He himself was the mute son. He had the impression that he was opening his mouth for the first time. He was thirty-two years old at the time. He was to commit suicide seven years later. He had already produced volumes of poetry, fables, historical works, and reflections on child education, mainly in classical Armenian. Yet this was not the first time that he was writing or preparing to write in modern Armenian. Where, then, did the difference lie? Why did it now seem to him as if he had never before opened his mouth? This is not an easy question to answer. We have to read the preface closely if we hope to find a convincing response to it. In the meantime, we must bear in mind that this story about the mute son appears in what is only the preface to a novel. No novel had been previously written in (or even translated into) Eastern Armenian. Abovean "opened his mouth" for the first time by way of literature, in the process of inaugurating what we call "literature" and creating a character inspired by the oral chronicles of his village, Kanaker, located just outside Yerevan. A legend had already been built up around this character, Aghasi. This legend recounted, in Oriental style, a feat of valor performed to defend a woman whom the Persian khan's henchmen were trying to abduct; it tells of resistance to the oppressor, struggle side-by-side with the liberators, and heroic death in battle. These are also the themes of the novel, which narrates, in sum, by way of a literary reprise of this oral tradition, the first thirty years of the nineteenth century, down to the Russians' 1829 capture of the citadel of Yerevan. It relates the suffering of a people and that people's subsequent liberation. Of his main character, Abovean very explicitly says, in the preface in question: "Aghasi opened my lips, which had been sealed for thirty years" (*Verk' Hayastani*, 1981, 46).

Thus when Abovean had the impression that he was opening his lips for the first time, he was getting ready not only to write a novel in modern Armenian (or rather, as we shall see, in dialectal, colloquial Armenian), but also to make a transcription: he was about to take a narrative from the oral tradition and transpose it into writing, into a medium other than that of the spoken word. Let us read a bit more of this preface in order to analyze the reasons and conditions for this "first time," this tragic, stunning linguistic inauguration. At stake here are the inauguration of literature in the modern sense of the word and its conditions of possibility. It is thus this literature's destiny which is at stake. Under what conditions did a literature in the modern sense become possible and, therefore, necessary? What was its destiny? I had long read Abovean's preface with these questions in mind. Beneath them, however, what is at stake is the

birth of the "native." This cannot be immediately understood. The present book is being written to give form and substance to this secret figure, that of the native, which
animated all the philological practices of the nineteenth century and presided over the
emergence of the "national," hence also, in particular, over the emergence of the so-
called "national literatures." Because the figure of the native was covered up for so long,
because it remained for so long in the background of the national project, we, too, have
to ignore it a little longer (the space of a chapter) in order to describe the experience of
mutism in its own terms. We need to focus on the experience of tragedy, the nameless
tragedy that obsesses Abovean, which he casts, in altogether overdetermined fashion,
in the form of a disaster that happens to the father.

The Two Subdivisions and Their Languages

The birth of modern literature occurred in the two subdivisions of the Armenian
people at approximately the same time: around 1840 in Tblisi, somewhat after 1850 in
Constantinople. (It should be pointed out that these were not Armenian cities.) The
differences between these two subdivisions were both linguistic and geopolitical. The
bulk of the Armenians who spoke the Eastern dialect found themselves concentrated
or scattered, until 1828, in the Persian Empire, the Khanate of Yerevan, and Karabagh,
but also in the Teheran area and what today comprises Iranian Azerbaijan. Southern
Georgia and the city of Tblisi had large Armenian populations. There were also big
communities in Crimea and further to the north, on the banks of the Don, in Moscow and in St. Petersburg. The Transcaucasus did not come under Russian control
until 1828, a date that marked the beginnings of a slow migration of Armenians toward what is today known as "Armenia." As for the Western Armenians, a majority
lived on their ancestral lands, as they are called, in Eastern Anatolia: the regions of
Erzerum, Van, Mush and Bitlis, Sevas, Diarbekir, Urfa, and northern Mesopotamia.
Very old communities existed throughout the territory of the Ottoman Empire, especially in areas that had once constituted the outlying districts and eastern border regions of the Byzantine Empire, west of the Euphrates, around Caeserea and Malatya,
and in the Pontus region. Moreover, a sizable fraction of the population had emigrated
in the seventeenth century, moving to the western districts of Turkey: Izmir, the Bursa
region, and, above all, Constantinople.[7] The division between Eastern and Western
Armenians thus went back a long way. Hand-in-hand with this geopolitical division
went a linguistic division that was simultaneously powerful and subtle. The natural
languages spoken by Armenians, that is, their local dialects, were in an advanced state
of "decomposition" by the nineteenth century, because they had for centuries had no
contact with writing or, needless to add, with one another. A centralizing principle,
whether literary or political, was lacking. Mkhitar, the founder of the Mkhitarist
Congregation, had already noted this in the preface to his *Bar'girk' Haykazean lezvi*
(Dictionary of the Armenian Language), published in 1749 in Vienna:

From all this, it plainly follows that, until the Lord gives us a well-made dictionary, our language runs the risk of rapid deterioration. For a dictionary is the guide
to writing well for those who have business with texts, and motivates the multitudes to use the language in a uniform manner when they speak or write. In the
absence of a dictionary, everything is subject to confusion or disintegration, as is
shown by our vulgar language [*ashkharhabar*], which, because it is irregular and
has no guide, has broken down into as many fragments as there are regions, or
even towns and villages. It has sometimes disintegrated to the point that people do
not even seem to be speaking Armenian. They speak a barbarous dialect.[8]

In addition to the natural languages that the Armenians spoke, however, there existed a "civil" language. Such, at any rate, was the name that the Armenians of the day
gave to this language from the late seventeenth century on. Morphologically and syn-
tactically, it was essentially the modern Armenian spoken today, the vehicular language known as *ashkharhabar*. It was also the "civilized" language, the one spoken by
the elites, by merchants and the clergy, and in the schools and tribunals. From the
early eighteenth century on, this civil language was already divided, in its turn, into
two varieties. They would yield, in the nineteenth century, literary Eastern and Western Armenian. The civil language existed; no one had invented it. The Western civil
language took written form very early. The Mkhitarist fathers, particularly those
based in Venice, wrote hundreds of books and tens of thousands of pages in this language, at a time when it was still a civil, not a literary, language. They wrote books on
contemporary history, the natural sciences, and geography, and they published alma-
nacs and monthly reviews. In exceptional cases, they even translated literature into
this language.[9] The Western civil language was the language of the Enlightenment.
Until 1850, on the other hand, Eastern civil Armenian rarely took written form. Short
books on religion published in limited runs by the Protestants in the 1830s and an 1843
translation of the Psalms were (as far as I know) virtually all that saw the light. In the
same period, the first half of the nineteenth century, the language of literature, the
noble language, was still classical Armenian, or *grabar*, in a restored state, and yet
identical to itself since the fifth century of our era. Between 1800 and 1850, the Venetian Mkhitarists systematically translated all the great works of the Western literary
tradition into, not the modern or civil language, but into, precisely, this classical language, which they hoped would rise from its ashes. They translated Homer, Virgil,
Horace, Milton, Racine, Byron, and Tasso, clearly putting the accent on epic works.
In so doing, they paved the way for the composition of a national epic which they very
much wished to see come into being. This epic would have to be written in the classical language, they firmly believed, if it was to exist at all! Similarly, among the Eastern
Armenians, when Abovean began writing poems and turning out translations in 1828
in Echmiadzin, he of course wrote in *grabar*, like all young people of his generation.

The civil language, while it existed, was not yet a literary language. This is not just to say that it was not yet the language of literature. The phenomenon that materialized in both subdivisions of the Armenian population around 1840 involved a literarization of the civil language. This means, first of all, that a very rapid diffusion of the civil language could be observed after 1840, thanks to schools, newspapers, translations, and the theater. The stake was, above all, a unification of the language, the immediate effect of which was to check the fragmentation of the dialects and the dispersion or decomposition of the natural languages.

Tragedy and the Literarization of the Language

To explain the transition, within modern Armenian, from civil language to literary language, it is not enough to take account of the two features of homogenization and unification. It must also be borne in mind that modern Armenian rapidly replaced classical Armenian, basically in the space of a decade (1845–55), in every field in which classical Armenian had been utilized until then: most notably, in literature and scholarship. At the same time, there took place a secularization of the intelligentsia, now composed of young people who, almost always after returning from a stay in Europe, announced their intention to take the destiny and education of the nation in hand. In question here was, in fact, a twofold secularization: that of the personnel charged with producing writing, if I may be forgiven the expression, and that of writing's general functions. Among the Western Armenians, this secularization had been firmly underway for quite some time, thanks to the dissemination of works written in Western civil Armenian and published in Venice. Among the Eastern Armenians, in contrast, there sprang up an emotionally charged rhetoric of secularization, incarnated principally by Abovean. He was, among the Armenians of the East, one of the first (perhaps the very first) to have received a higher education in Europe at, precisely, the German University of Dorpat, beginning in 1830, that is, immediately following Czarist Russia's annexation of Armenia. He was the only one to have made the transition, after a terrible inner crisis, from the ecclesiastical to the secular state (his higher education was to have prepared him for the priesthood). Thus he embodies, in exacerbated form, the crisis of the transition, a crisis that finds its most powerful expression in the preface to *Wounds of Armenia*. Before returning to that preface, we should note that Abovean found himself (like, be it added, all his contemporaries) in a strange linguistic situation. He had three languages at his disposal, three "states" or varieties of Armenian (in addition to all the foreign languages he had mastered, including Russian, German, French, Latin, Persian, and Turkish, and probably also Georgian). These three states of Armenian, these three perfectly distinct languages, were his natural language (the dialect of his native region), the civil language, and the classical language. We have already seen that he wrote in *grabar* in his youth. Upon returning to the Caucasus, he was obsessed by the fact that the children whom he had brought together and come to know as a teacher and educator found themselves, as it were, cut off from themselves because they did not have texts to read in their own language. Yet he hesitated over what to do to remedy the situation. He wrote a short work, *Parap vakhti khaghalik'* (A Toy for One's Free Time, 1838–40), a strangely composed work that begins in dialect, continues in civil Armenian, and concludes in *grabar*. He wrote a short book in civil Armenian, *An Introduction to Pedagogy for Beginners* (1838). He then wrote, in 1841, the novel that was to win him fame, *Wounds of Armenia*, in his native dialect this time. Thus he made, as it were, the "bad choice," opting for a natural over the civil language. That is why his novel is very hard to read and in places incomprehensible for readers accustomed to the civil/literary language. Abovean must have had his reasons for preferring to write in dialect. It would be another fifteen years before Eastern civil Armenian imposed itself as a literary language, under very different circumstances and mainly in Moscow, thanks to the efforts of Stepanos Nazareants (1812–1879) and Mikael Nalbandean (1829–1866). Yet it was in Abovean that the necessity of this transition made itself felt with the greatest force, taking the form of a violent break that resembled a fit of madness or mystical crisis. It was a question, with Abovean, of a *revelation* that heralded a new mode of being. We can, if we set out from this point, attempt to come to terms with what is involved in this transition or birth: it allows us to discern what the "literarization" of the language really amounted to.

We find, in Abovean, the expression of a very profound crisis, about which I have just said a word. It goes hand-in-hand with the desire, which seems so natural to us today, to write in the language of the people, a language that everyone could understand, one that belonged to each and every one of its speakers. It was truly a question, for Abovean, of putting an end to the "mutism" afflicting the popular language, the language of a human community, the language in which and by means of which this community should have been able to communicate with itself, to hear itself speak. The fact that this language was condemned to "mutism" thus means that it had undergone a kind of tragedy or disaster. It could no longer hear itself speak. Abovean's experience, an experience incarnated in a body, has to do with this disaster, which affected what might be called *the community's relationship with itself in its language*. This relationship was mutilated because the language of the people was condemned to mutism, had dried up, had been attacked at its source. The experience of the disaster appears in this author in the form of a mystic crisis that manifestly brings him to the brink of madness. In the preface that we are here analyzing, Abovean writes: "Not a day but I saw my grave before me, not an hour but death's fiery sword danced over my head" (*Verk' Hayastani*, 1981, 42). If, departing from custom, we take this passage seriously, the term "tragedy," which I have just used, will not seem excessive. Here is another passage from the preface:

> I wasted whole days of my life brooding over all this. I was very often tempted to stick my head in a noose. . . . Believe it or not, as you like, but this tragedy weighed so heavy on my soul that I often went roaming like a madman over

hill and dale, walking and thinking, and came back home with an overflowing heart. (ibid., 44)[10]

I said a moment ago that Abovean wanted to plunge back into tragedy, the tragedy of this community which was incapable of hearing itself speak and thus could no longer relate to itself. But whence came his conviction that it could no longer hear itself speak? I have been asking myself that since commenting on the passage above and, with it, the whole of the preface to *Wounds of Armenia* in *Ages et usages de la langue arménienne*. I shall therefore begin to answer it by returning to the commentary I made then, considering it, this time, in the context of all the circumstances that spawned it.

Self-Representation and the Popular Sources

Abovean speaks of a double crisis: he is afflicted by the sufferings of his people, but also by seeing that the children who have been entrusted to his care gladly read Western literary works (no doubt in Russian translation, but that is not important here) and only Western literary works. The desire that this breeds is articulated as a desire to create for the Armenians, in their and their children's language, works that they will just as eagerly read, while finding in them a reflection of their own experience. This amounts to a demand that the collectivity be able to enter into relation with itself. The demand passes by way of language, the language, precisely, that is spoken by the people. "Our books were in *grabar* and our modern language didn't count, so that I could not express my heart's wish in words. . . . If I prayed or even begged, no one would understand my language" (*Verk' Hayastani*, 1981, 42).

In his anguish over the fact that children can read nothing comparable to Western books in Armenian, Abovean writes:

> In those days, God also sent me several children I was supposed to educate. My heart wanted to break when I saw that they didn't understand any of the books by Armenians that I put in their hands, although whatever they read in the language of the Russians, Germans, or French delighted their innocent souls. I often wanted to tear out my hair because they loved those foreign languages better than ours. Yet there was a very natural reason for this. In those languages, they read about the exploits of famous people, what they said and what they did; they read about things that captivate the heart because they are things of the heart. Who hasn't delighted in reading such things? Who hasn't delighted in learning what love, friendship, patriotism, parents, children, death, and battle are . . . ? In Europe, [people say] that the Armenian nation must be heartless, since, despite all the storms that have broken over its head, not a single Armenian has come along to write about these things of the heart[.] What exists is about the Church, or God and his saints. But the books children tuck under their pillows are the pagan works of Homer, Horace, Virgil, and Sophocles. (ibid., 43)

Here, then, is what these children read: Homer, Horace, Virgil, and Sophocles. Those are the works that Abovean has in mind and the authors with whom he has to compete to win these children's attention. Logic would seem to dictate that he notice that the authors he names are not Germans or Russians who offer the children a view or representation of themselves: they are the authors on whom the Western tradition was founded. Indeed, they are the authors Abovean himself read and loved. Yet he was never tempted to translate them into Armenian or to teach his pupils this Western tradition. Thus the break that he advocates does not consist solely in writing in the modern language, in bringing translation and tradition into the realm of the modern language. Abovean does not simply wish to compete with the foreign languages that the children and he himself loved. He wants to struggle against himself and his own appreciation of the major works in the Western tradition. He wants to compete with the very idea of the tradition. This is a demand for self-representation. We might also call it a demand for self-consciousness. Afflicted with mutism, the Armenians can no longer hear themselves speak. Hence we can readily understand why Abovean deems it essential to write in the language of the people. He has to put writing in a position of mediation. It is, for him, the object of a revelation and a liberation:

> Parents, home, childhood, things once heard or said, had all come alive in such a way that I forgot the world around me. All the nameless, stray, lost thoughts inside me blossomed and returned. Only now did I begin to see that *grabar* and the other languages I had learned had closed my mind and held it prisoner until that moment. (ibid., 47)

This demand for self-representation has, however, another component, one quite as essential as the literarization of the language of the people: the collection of popular customs and nonliterary narratives. It was at this point that Abovean began to write and that his tongue was loosened:

> On that morning, and for the whole of the next week, the next month, I had only one desire, and still have only one: to go throw myself at the feet of a prince, beg him to give me a crust of bread, and then wander from village to village, day and night, in order to collect and write down the exploits of our nation. (ibid., 47–48)

How could he collect and record "exploits" if not by listening to the narratives that the people would recite for him, or already had? It is thus a question, this time, of the popular sources in a general sense: narratives, songs, and customs. It is essentially a question of popular, oral narrative, not necessarily elaborated on a grand scale, but, importantly, collected at the source. Abovean here expresses a desire that would seem to qualify as ethnographic, at least on first sight. It is a question of collecting the popular sources, to be sure. But for whom? Obviously, for the "people" itself, so as to give back to the "people" what the "people" itself has produced. We have to do, once again, with the demand for self-representation. This demand is at the source of the ethnographic project. In Abovean, at the moment when this demand is articulated in this way for the first time, the literarization of the language and the desire to return to the popular sources join forces. They are articulated at one and the same time. It is often said, absurdly enough, that Abovean decided to write in the language of the people so that he might be heard by a majority of the people (this was also what is suggested by my attempt, at the beginning of the present chapter, to reconstruct Abovean's logic, that is, the logic commonly attributed to him). The statement is absurd because Abovean's aim was not to make *himself* heard. It was, rather, to make it possible for the people to hear *themselves* and enter into a relation with themselves. That is something quite different. His aim was to give a voice to those who had so far been deprived of a voice, to restore the spoken word to those whose utterance had been cut off at the root, because what they said did not reach their own ears. That is what mutism is. Mutism is characteristic of "the native." The task was to put the native's own utterance back in his mouth and his ears.

Hence it was not only a question of forging the kind of "communal transparency" in which everyone could communicate with everyone else. To accomplish that, it would have been more than enough to diffuse the civil language in consistent fashion. (This was, moreover, the model proposed by Mikael Nalbandian a few years later.) Abovean's aim clearly was the very different one of enabling the "people" to hear its own voice at its epic or mythological source. Apparently, the mythological source is the capacity to recount, to produce epic narratives and, thereby, to create a past of one's own, a temporality. This capacity, presumed to be lost, had accordingly to be restored. But this is a strange demand, after all. The native cannot hear his own narratives and does not live according to his own customs: why, then, is there a need for a reduplication, a supplementary organ, one more mouth or ear, so that people can finally hear themselves? Why does it devolve upon writing to play this role? Whatever the answer to these questions may be, the project is clear enough: it is to go from village to village in order to collect customs, feats and exploits, actions and narratives, and ensure their mediation through a representation (written or not). Without this supplementary organ of writing, the native will continue to be cut off from himself. The project consists in confronting him with himself by way of a mediation (a corpus of knowledge, a common language, a written culture, an informed memory) so that he may once again hear his own voice resonating from its mythological source. This is the defining project of philology, here presented in the form of an ethnographic demand. The ethnographic collection will in fact make its appearance later, and will do no more or less than meet the demand first stated by Abovean, which means, as well, that it will take its place in a program elaborated in direct relation with the literarization of the language. At the root of this project, we find the violent threat of irremediable silence vis-à-vis oneself, and thus the strange need for a mediation allowing the native to hear his own voice again at its epical-mythological source. We here encounter, for the first time, the "native," that crucial philological personage, that central figure suddenly invented in the nineteenth century. Who is this native? We will have ample occasion to give a precise answer in many different contexts. But we can already affirm the following: the native is like the figure I have just described, cut off from himself, his past, and his own memory. He is a personage lacking the capacity to represent himself. It is therefore necessary that an external agency intervene in order to serve as a crutch in the process of auto-representation. That is the philologist's role; that is the role of the various branches of philology. Is the purpose to come as close as possible to the native again? If so, then one must go back to his "natural" language. This leaves its trace, quite simply, in the fact that the novel *Wounds of Armenia* is written in the dialectal language that was Abovean's own language from this moment on: in the fact that the novel is not written in the civil language, although it was as easily available to Abovean as the dialect and would become, a little later, the literary language of the Eastern Armenians.

Abovean was reacting to a vague threat (real or supposed, as always). He had been the first to register its existence; self-representation was his way of trying to overcome it. He thought it would allow him to ward the threat off or eliminate it. But he did no more than register it. The mediation of the written word (philological, ethnographic, or literary) was obviously incapable of re-establishing the mythic circulation of "popular" discourse. Abovean would have liked to see self-representation rectify the increasing aridity of the spoken word and recreate an audience for the nation's feats and exploits. He reacted to mutism with a self-representation inspired by the philological project and the invention of the native. In reality, it was the inadequacy of self-representation (an inadequacy inherent in the very figure of the native invented by philology) which compelled him—compelled him personally—to write his fable about mutism. Thus there is an absolute reciprocity between mutism on the one hand and the project of finding a remedy for it, a reciprocity that is sometimes called "nationalism." This is, at any event, why Abovean was not able to *think mutism*. As a "son," he could not but incarnate the disaster of mutism and mutism as disaster. He could not but make himself into a native (*natif*), and thus be "born" (*naître*) to the spoken word, by remaining faithful to the father, which means, very precisely, faithful to the father's disaster. Involved here is a fidelity to disaster that goes very much further than the nascent nationalistic discourse of the time could itself say (because it is its hidden source) and, obviously, much further than any of the theories of nationalism have succeeded in seeing.

What I have just described as a "fidelity to disaster" requires that we return for a moment to Herodotus' story. Like Partriarch Nerses before him, Abovean interpreted it badly; he needed to interpret it badly. He needed to believe that the son cried out to save his father. When the son opens his mouth, however, he is no longer capable of saving anything. The end has already arrived. He opens his mouth to speak because his father is dying before his very eyes. Herodotus suggests, moreover, that his father allows himself to be killed because he is despondent. The devastation of the kingdom plainly bears a relation to the son's mutism. If it did not, the story would be meaning-less. The son opens his mouth to cry out at the moment of his father's death. He opens it to say that his father is dying, that it is the father who is dying. Abovean does not want to know anything about that, even if he repeats the whole story point by point. It is in this sense that the story transcends him and, what is more, ceases to be an allegory of the fate of the "fatherland." The radical consciousness of a disaster that has to be remedied at any price is doubtless nowhere more powerfully expressed than in this preface. We do not understand very well what comprises this disaster, why it has come about, or why the son is mute. Yet the history that so fascinates Abovean had already provided a response to this question even before we formulated it. Of course, Herodotus' history does not declare that it is the disaster of the philological creature known as the "native," that it is the mutism of the native. The history says that it is the disaster of the father. The mutism of the son is the as-yet-unrevealed disaster of the father. The Pythia says this in her way, magnificently: this mutism will come to an end after the disaster has become palpable, after it has been brought into the broad light of day. It would be hard to put it more plainly. It is because the story says this as plainly as it does that it so fascinates Abovean, and me as well, every time I tell myself the story, every time I have the son say, "it is my father." Abovean has to do with a collectivity that lives on its myths, an oral collectivity. The disaster that comes over it, that has already come over it from (apparently) time immemorial, is that of the paternal reference. It is the disaster of *mythic* paternity. There is a father. Plainly enough, there has to be a father. The father holds the keys of the kingdom in his hands. He is the keystone of the collectivity. It is this keystone which is in the process of crumbling, of falling apart before the son's eyes. The problem, obviously, is that it has never ceased crumbling and falling apart! The nationalistic version of the story (which is also, almost immediately, Abovean's as well) has it that *the son saves the father from the disaster*. That is quite possible. But if literature is the strange activity which, since Abovean (in fact, since the emergence of philology and the institution of its mourning), has accompanied the downfall of the father, what the whole story says, what Abovean's obsession says, is, rather, that the son *saves the father's disaster*. And, if this is true, Herodotus' little fable says exactly the opposite of what Abovean the nationalist makes it say. Yet Abovean relates this inverted version of the story as well, with blinding clarity. He relates the institution of mourning, of an impossible mourning.

This inversion and transformation of the embryonic nationalistic interpretation into the institution of mourning is, to be sure, the most radical possible interpretation of it. We need to back up for a moment, because it seems to me that, in advancing as we have, we have forgotten one of the questions that arise naturally in this context. Why, if there is indeed a disaster, is it the disaster of a father, of the father?

Beyond a doubt, a rhetoric of the father and the disaster is at work here, even if this rhetoric presents itself in the form of an experience. This rhetoric will be repeated time and again. The first repetition, as will appear, is that of the philologists busy justifying the ethnographic collection of "folklore." Later, in the twentieth century, it will be repeated by Charents and Mahari, and, more or less simultaneously, by Hagop Oshagan and Zareh Vorpuni. Every time, we have to do with the discovery of a disaster and, every time, this disaster is interpreted as the "father's." Every time, then, the son discovers mythical paternity. Let us say, for the sake of clarity, that he discovers (in altogether implicit fashion) the myth as the vehicle of a foundational paternity. Or, even more simply, that *he discovers the myth as foundational.* This holds much more clearly for Abovean than for the others. Abovean, it is true, does not make a philosophy of this implicit discovery; he does not triumphantly announce it; he does not himself translate it into ethnographic work; he does not transform it into a science of religion. Ethnography was to be the task of the next generation. The science of religion and mythology in the modern sense would hover in the background of a series of works stretching from Moscow (Mkrtich Emin and his 1850 book on the Armenians' ancient epic or mythological narratives) to Venice (Ghevond Alishan and his 1895 book on the Armenians' ancient religion) and, somewhat later still, would become the object of an immense rediscovery due to Daniel Varuzhan. I am, of course, also in the process of sketching a genealogy of Varuzhan's poetic work. Abovean, at any rate, does not do all this: he does not talk about myth or ethnography or the science of religion. But he had read Herder, like his contemporary and classmate Stepanos Nazareants, who translated Herder into Russian, discussing the translation with him.[11] Abovean was perfectly well aware of Herder's popularity with his German contemporaries. By way of Herodotus' story and a figure like that of the father, then, he discovered this foundational paternity. In sum, he understood the myth and its function the way everybody else had begun to in the nineteenth century. It is not surprising that he should simultaneously have discovered "mythical paternity" as something that has crumbled or disintegrated. There simply is no myth or mythical paternity that is still "upright" or "whole," that is, no living myth—neither for us nor for Abovean. The essential thing about the birth of modern literature is, without a doubt, that this disintegration (which Varuzhan will later call an "interruption," *ëndhatum*) "at last" makes itself felt. Moreover, literature is the only place in which it ever makes itself felt. Neither nationalistic discourse nor the theories of nationalism would ever say anything about it. We might say that modern literature has been living on this interruption of the myth since the nineteenth century. Let me be very clear: I do not mean to say that there was first a myth, with its foundational function, and that it was then interrupted. That would be the nostalgic version of the myth and foundational mythic paternity. What I mean to say is, rather, that toward the end of the eighteenth century, with Herder, Schelling, or the Schlegel brothers, all of them taken together, or, again, with nascent philology, myth was discovered (or invented) *as* interrupted. It was discovered or invented at the same time as the mourning of it. I shall be repeating this in a dozen different ways in the following chapters. But I must also now say that I would never have understood this if I had not read the chapter on "interrupted myth" in Jean-Luc Nancy's *La Communauté désoeuvrée* (1986), which I shall be discussing at some length later.[12]

I said a moment ago that the son saved the disaster; I wanted to show, in this way, that the nationalistic interpretation demands that we discern its inversion in the text. For a long time, indeed, I believed that it was enough to bring out this inversion of the formula of nationalism in order to expose the historical truth (or, rather, the lie) of nationalism.[13] But this was doubtless to remain within the terminology and logic of philology and the complicity between nationalism and philology. The problem is that, even if the difference is patent (saving the father/saving the disaster), reversing the formula of nationalism does not make it possible to liberate oneself from the structural and historical complicity between nationalism and philology (a complicity that maintained itself throughout the nineteenth century in order to culminate in the formulations of the *Mehyan* group at the beginning of the twentieth, and in the whole body of literature that the members of the group produced). Above all, it does not make it possible to reveal this complicity. The turbulent logic of nationalism is working at full capacity here. The reader can easily imagine that I needed time to understand and then explain all this in satisfactory fashion. The perplexity in which I found myself resurfaces in my claim (which I will be putting forward again) that the central formula of the aesthetic principle ("nationalization is an aestheticization") is not nationalistic in its essence because it declares the "truth" of nationalism. It is true that this formula is incomprehensible for nationalism itself. But we might just as well say that this is the *nec plus ultra* of the hidden complicity between nationalism and philology. We shall find ourselves confronting the same problems when we read Varuzhan's poetry in the next section of this book. Since Abovean, the idea of the paternal disaster has accompanied the institution of national philology from one end to the other. From one end to the other, therefore, it is the mourning of philology which is at work, that is to say, philology as an institution of mourning. The more effectively mourning was concealed, the more effectively it worked below the surface. Adopting another tone, now, literature takes its place within the interruption of the myth; it is itself this interruption. Thereby, perhaps, it escapes the national. Does the "national" not come into existence by denying that the newly discovered myth is discovered as interrupted, that the revealed father is never revealed except in his dereliction, that the foundational paternity necessarily sustained by this myth has already, in advance, disintegrated?

Thus, by way of this discussion of the native and his disaster, we have, altogether unexpectedly, entered upon a discussion of the invention of myth (and, with it, the philological discovery of mythological religion).

2. ETHNOGRAPHIC RECEPTION AND POPULAR EPIC

I now turn back to auto-ethnography. Abovean himself did not carry his project through to the end. The auto-ethnographic model which he articulated for the first time in his preface to *Wounds of Armenia* was gradually put in place in the second half of the century. When he speaks of "beg[ging] for a crust of bread so that [he] could wander from village to village, day and night, in order to collect and write down the feats and exploits of our nation," what is at stake is quite clearly this auto-ethnographic model of reception. When, even today, we envisage the reception of oral narratives in line with the ethnographic model (exemplified by, among other things, the immense, vain enterprise of collecting oral testimony from the survivors of the Catastrophe), we do nothing more nor less, in this sense, than obey the nineteenth century's injunctions, in accordance with the old program sketched by Abovean. We do nothing else, in sum, than react to the timeless "disaster of the father." Is it truly "timeless"? Our studies of Charents and Mahari have amply demonstrated that it is, in any case, an old story that continued to be told to the mid-twentieth century, in relation, this time, to the historical Catastrophe. That is why we must now rapidly review the properly ethnographic elaboration of the program introduced by Abovean, and, especially, the fate of the popular epic from the moment that philology took hold of it to the fatal date of 1939.

In 1874, there appeared, in Constantinople, a short book entitled, in Armenian, *Grots' u Brots'*, which might be translated as "Written in a Rush,"[14] a very unassuming title for one of the essential books of the day. Its author was a clergyman by the name of Karekin Servantsdeants.[15] This book is essential because it constitutes the first step, among the Armenians, in the immense auto-ethnographic enterprise which, for some forty years, preoccupied intellectuals, sometimes to the exclusion of everything else, claiming a good deal of their energies and time. It is essential, again, because it includes fragments of the popular epic *Sasna Tsr'er* (The Daredevils of Sasun), better known to the public today under the generic name *David of Sasun*. This popular epic, a heroic-mythical narrative, had until then never merited the honor of a written transcription and had therefore never appeared in book form. It had never been collected on the basis of recitations by "bards." Servantsdeants recounts, with religious devotion, the efforts it cost him to secure the co-operation of one of these bards, among the last of those who had committed the epic to memory, and then convince him to chant or recite, over a three-day period, one of its central episodes, which he called "Mher's Gate." The reaction to Servantsdeants's book among general readers and even among men of letters, when it was published in Constantinople, was one of stupefaction. Urban Armenians had been quite simply unaware of the existence of a major oral tradition among their people. This people, which doubtless represented, in their eyes, the empire of the uncultured, was now recognized as possessing another culture, and thus also a memory other than the one based on the written word. At that, the fragments collected by Servantsdeants offered only a very partial idea of the vast scope of the popular epic cycle, revealing the tip of the iceberg at best. This was just the beginning of the ethnographic movement among the Armenians, an endeavor that was to stretch over several decades: it consisted of finding informers and asking them to recount narratives that had been handed down from generation to generation. These narratives had become a sort of local property that varied with dialect and place, although they formed a unified cycle diffused throughout the Armenian collectivity. Ethnographers recorded not only the myths, but also the circumstances under which they were recited, local customs, and the various communities' ways of life. They collected narratives that had never before been written down. The activity inaugurated at this time can plainly be described as the entry of the popular sources into the literary language, where they were taken up without further elaboration: this was, that is, a purely ethnographic reception, which, from now on, subjected the narratives that were collected and transcribed to a form of "utilization" altogether different from the original one. In a word, the oral tradition now became the nation's "testament." From the moment it was collected in line with philological practice, which reinvented it as part of "national" culture, it no longer had anything to do with what it had been before philology stepped in. It had now to be read and understood as an integral part of the nation's philological discourse. That is, moreover, as the reader will readily understand, why the content of this tradition, the details of the legendary narratives and popular customs, and the "natural" reality of these narratives and customs, will not concern us here. I have never, for my part, been particularly interested in them. What is fascinating, in contrast, is the philological operation thanks to which a supposedly natural oral tradition became "testamentary," that is, was bequeathed in writing, under the rubric of culture, to the people who were presumed to have produced it, and this at the very moment when it was disappearing; by the same token, this operation made the nation heir to the legacy that it was thus bestowing upon itself. In this testamentary legacy, philology obviously brought off the feat of making the naturalness of the object credible, along with the continuity and authenticity of its reception. But it did something else as well, something still more essential: it succeeded in masking the testamentary aspect of the operation—which means, as well, the nature of the supposed disaster—inherent to a culture collected and transmitted in this way. I shall return to the testamentary aspect of this phenomenon, which seems to me to hold a pivotal place in the operation of philology read as the driving force behind the auto-invention of the ethnographic nation. We are clearly not there yet.[16] But we can already make out the testamentary operation, which I here mention in passing, as that which is characteristic of philology, the invisible institution of its mourning.

There can be no doubt that Servantsdeants was not acting under Abovean's influence when he conceived the idea of collecting myths, legends, and customs, lending his ear to the "people" living on their land, and reproducing their utterances and oral productions in a work exclusively devoted to this forgotten "culture" that had never before been paid any attention. *Wounds of Armenia* was first published in 1858, in Tblisi, so that Servantsdeants cannot have found his inspiration in that work. He was from Van, had been the pupil and closest disciple of Father Mkrtich Khrimian (1820–1907), had followed and would continue to follow him on the troubled path that led him from Van to Mush and then to Constantinople, and had been, de facto, the editor of the newspaper *Artsvi Vaspurakani* (The Eagle of Vaspurakan), which Khrimian published in the monastery of Varak. Although Servantsdeants was a clergyman who held posts of the first rank, he spoke no foreign languages and was in no sense a professional ethnologist or ethnographer. He had certainly never read Herder, as had the young Eastern Armenian intellectuals studying at the Germanophone universities of the Baltic countries thirty years earlier. Yet he had received the message of national philology. He had heard its slogans about rediscovering a "popular culture" utterly ignored until then, about the authenticity and the supposedly ancient character of the legends and customs that were part and parcel of the lives of ordinary people in the provinces. In his works, he revived the probably unadulterated "taste" for these authentic traditions. Yet, when he had occasion to define the nature of his research project, he did not yet make a distinction between the geographical archeology of the previous generation and that other kind of archeology that he was the first to pursue in a systematic, exclusive manner: an *ethnographic archeology*. I believe that that is the term which is called for here, and I will explain why (I am obviously already broaching what is to be the explicit subject of the next chapter: the neo-archeological project as constitutive of the nation). In paragraph 39 of his first book, just before entering into a discussion of the circumstances in which he transcribed an episode of the popular epic, Servantsdeants names his predecessors, priests who spent their time doing work similar to his; he does so, he says, "to satisfy philologists' [*banasirats'*] curiosity." The priests he mentions have had no posterity, and their discoveries, as far as I know, never saw the light. I therefore need not concern myself with their names and texts here. Let us look rather at what Servantsdeants says about their work:

> For several years . . . [they] have been pursuing a worthwhile task: wherever they have gone, they have jotted down archeological descriptions [*storagrut'iun*] of antiquities, transcribed the colophons of old manuscripts and the inscriptions on stone crosses found in the ruins . . . and also written down popular tales as well as curses, legends [*ar'aspel*], and many dialectal words, in the intention, of course, of one day publishing all this material. Reverend Poghos Tomayan of Trebizond, a scholar doing similar work, has, for his part, been producing archeological descriptions of the Trabizond and Taron regions on the Holy Father's recommendation,[17] and has also turned out important commentaries on the ancient traditions and toponyms of those two regions. He has, further, made a description [*nkaragrut'iun*] of the customs and language of Taron's inhabitants. (*Yerker* 1:182)[18]

This passage seems to me to be important precisely because it mentions the two types of archeology, without really distinguishing them. This is our first encounter with geographical archeology. We must, then, say a few words on the subject. Geographical archeology constitutes the first moment of national philology and, consequently, of the self-invention of the nation. It was inaugurated very early among the Armenians, in the 1810s, by the Mkhitarist Fathers, especially Lucas Injijean and

Minas Pzhshgean. We will provide, somewhat later, a more detailed commentary on the beginnings of modern philology around 1810. For the time being, we can gather, from Servantsdeants's evocation of it sixty years later, a sense of what was involved. The philologists (amateurs or not) of the latter half of the century were very fond of antiquities. Everywhere they went, they deemed it their duty to note down descriptions of them, copy the inscriptions on the stone crosses that they found serving as tombstones in various ruins, and look for the colophons of old manuscripts. As we shall see, Father Pzhshgean had already done such work on his many voyages to Transylvania, the Pontus region, and Poland between 1810 and 1820, in quest of the Armenian communities that had been scattered far and wide centuries earlier. The sole difference is that Father Pzhshgean did not, at the time, have access to the native, in both the literal and figurative senses of the term. In the literal sense: the provinces, in which no organized Catholic communities were to be found, were inaccessible to the Mkhitarist Fathers. In the figurative sense: the native had yet to be born and, in 1815, it would never have occurred to Pzhshgean to transcribe "popular tales," dialectal forms, or the legends the native told himself. Yet it was the Mkhitarist fathers who generalized the use of the word *storagrut'iun* to designate their activity: making archeological descriptions of the places they either visited or didn't (precisely because one need not visit an archeological site to describe what it had looked like in antiquity). Thus it was that Injijean published, in 1822, a book that was to inaugurate the entire Armenian philological tradition, *Storagrut'iun hin Hayastaneayts*, or Description (in the sense the word has in geographical archeology) of Ancient Armenia. Injijean had of course never set foot in "Armenia." This did not deter him from describing the country archeologically, even if the project presented certain paradoxes, which we shall have occasion to describe more fully. It is because the word *storagrut'iun* holds a strategic place in the inauguration of the national and philological project that I would like to discuss it in greater detail later. This discussion has to come at the end of our examination of these matters, precisely because what is structurally "lacking" in archeological geography is the figure of the native. This figure, which appears for the first time (awash in the pathos of mourning) in Abovean's 1840 or 1841 preface, does not begin to produce concrete effects until several decades later, with the triumphant unfolding of ethnographic archeology.

Let us return to Servantsdeants. It is easy to see that the two archeologies are not entirely distinct in his mind. He evokes, in the same breath and with equal enthusiasm, the description of the antiquities in the field or the manuscripts, on the one hand, and, on the other, the culling of popular tales, curses, and dialectal forms directly from the lips of the natives. Again, in the last example he cites, we find, ranged side-by-side, both "archeological descriptions" and "commentaries" on old traditions, customs, and the language. This juxtaposition itself, this unified project, is a hallmark of the period. The archeological endeavors mentioned were carried out with the official encouragement of Khrimian Hayrik, who is here called the "Holy Father"; he assumed the role of "mentor" for Servantsdeants and all his fellow scholars. In 1878, Servantsdeants was dispatched on a mission to the provinces, doubtless at his own request: his task was to "travel throughout the native regions [*bnagavar's mayreni*] and make a topographical description [*teghagrel*] of everything to be found there."[19] His mission required him to carry out a general census of the whole of the provincial Armenian world in its then existing form, that is, in the form of natives living on their native soil; it likewise required him to complete and refine the archeological work of previous generations, in systematic fashion this time. Servantsdeants successfully carried out his ethnographic task. He did so not only by publishing, after *Grots' u Brots'*, other books that combined field observations, descriptions of customs and traditions, and transcriptions of tales and legends—*Manana* (Manna) in 1876 and *Hamov Hotov* (The Way It Tastes and Smells) in 1884—but also by publishing his account and statistical census of the provincial Armenian world in his two-volume *T'oros Yeghbayr, Hayastani champord* (Brother Thoros, a Traveler in Armenia; 1879–84). The encounter of the "traveler" and the "native" thus took an official turn, ceasing to be the adventure of a single man.

The juxtaposition, in the passage cited above, of these two archeologies, geographical and ethnographic, like the whole of the philological project underlying this juxtaposition, can be understood only on two conditions. What, after all, did these scholars, envoys, and travelers do? What did they do in the ruins, churches, cemeteries, and villages? They amassed archives. This means that, behind their activity, in total silence, a first revolution had taken place. Their business was with a historical object. But the ruins, churches, manuscripts, and villages were not historical in and of themselves. They were part of the landscape, played a role in worship, transmitted knowledge, and provided a common resting-place for the dead. They became historical only at the moment in which someone began making his way through them with the aim of constituting archives. The silent revolution to which all these people—clergymen, travelers, amateur or professional scholars—were heir was thus that of a "historicization" of the subject. Of course, the indigenous traveler set out to encounter "himself" when he visited the provinces: he was already a twofold personage, was already divided into the traveler he was and the native he also necessarily was. We shall see, later, why this remark has its importance. For the time being, let us note that this "self" is a historicized subject. That is the general condition subtending the philological intervention of the whole nineteenth century. However, against the background formed by historicization, a second revolution occurred, and it is this revolution that interests me at the moment. It was a question, for these philologists and voyagers, of collecting archives not only in the ruins and graveyards, where "antiquities" were to be found, but also among the living, by collecting and writing down their utterances and constituting files, by gathering up elements of an oral discourse that went back to the dawn of time. To what end? To found a future science? That was never Servantsdeants's intention. It is true that he sometimes entertained the question. The only reasonable answer to it that ever crossed his mind lay in the notion that these elements of an ancient, oral discourse would one day serve as material for writers. This is plainly not the right answer and, in any case, it is not a consistent answer. It will be granted that the archives of the ancient spoken word were constituted by a purely internal necessity, the fact, precisely, that the native's utterance was assumed to come from times long past. That the two kinds of archeology co-existed in so natural a fashion is patent proof that the oral discourse of the living was itself apprehended as an "antiquity." The native's oral discourse was an antiquity in quite the same sense as the inscriptions found on gravestones or the colophons of forgotten manuscripts.

The antiquity of the native's utterance is self-evident for philologists because it enters into the very structure of this figure constituted by nineteenth-century philology. The native is an individual whose utterance comes down to us through the centuries, somewhat faintly, to be sure, and partly effaced, but no more faintly or more effaced than the inscriptions on ancient monuments in ruins. This self-evidence, I said, was the sign of a revolution; I shall continue to use the word. Among the Armenians, Servantsdeants was the vector of this revolution, discussed in a single line by Michel Foucault in *The Order of Things*, where it is treated as one consequence of the philological revolution.[20] We must rather, I think, assign it a place apart and a significance all its own. The fact that the historical antiquity of the native's utterance, *qua* principle, produced its effects very late in the ethnographic nation that the Armenians gradually became in the course of the nineteenth century clearly shows that we have to do with a special phenomenon here. Moreover, what I just called self-evident was in reality so far from being self-evident that Servantsdeants and the philologists who came after him all felt the need to repeat that what comes from the native's lips comes from times long past. Servantsdeants was the first to say so in so many words, at the beginning of his second book, *Manna*, published in 1876:

> Those of my readers possessed of even a modicum of learning will have realized that, both in my observations [*tesut'eants'*] and in the popular utterances I cite, there occur passages that have been preserved orally by the inhabitants of Armenia exactly as they were preserved in writing by the best writers of our national fifth century. This allows us to appreciate how old and ancient [*hin yev vaghemi*] they are. (*Yerker* 1:124)

Servantsdeants then proceeds to list, one after the next, all the passages of manifestly mythological origin (or drawn directly from the oral tradition) in Moses of Khoren, as well as in Eznik of Kolb and other writers. Manuk Abeghean would, twenty years later, say the very same thing in the introduction to his doctoral dissertation (here, too, the first work of its kind) on "Armenian popular beliefs." But if that is so, the reader will reply, there must have been some truth to what they said. There is, of course; yet my own readers, if they are possessed of even a modicum of perspicacity, will surely have realized that what matters here is not whether what they said was true or false. Everything that the scientific community (and, with it, ordinary public opinion) considers true at a given moment is, obviously, true. What matters is the antiquity of the native's utterance as such, *as* the utterance of the native (that inevitable philological personage), together with the fact that this kind of antiquity could not be articulated or enounced before 1874. Abovean had made no mention of it thirty years earlier, although this is not to say that his work did not make the native available and ready for utilization (ready to meet the needs of nationalism in particular). In any case, later in his 1876 book, Servantsdeants again names all the epic or mythical writings found in Khorenatsi, with a view to establishing that the "legends" (*vep u zruyts'*) available for collection in his own time are in no wise inferior to the ancient legends, which, after all, were themselves nothing but legends: "It is by way of myths of this kind that all ancient nations came into being and have maintained themselves as they were primordially" (ibid., 1:180).[21] This sentence is, however, ambiguous. It can also mean that it was by way of those myths that the primordial character (*nakhnakanut'iun*), that is, the antiquity of these nations was maintained. Thus, by way of a sentence whose grammar is unclear, Servantsdeants succeeds in saying that the "ancient nations" first emerged as such thanks to the creation and recitation of myth, a statement that is quite similar to certain theses of the German Romantics that we will be examining in Part II. Or, more simply, he affirms that the ancient nations have always spoken of their origins through the mediation of myths, like that of Romulus and Remus. In any case, what is involved is the reiterated, continuous antiquity of the native's utterance.

Servantsdeants's first two books, we said, enjoyed great success with both philologists and the ordinary reading public. Included in his books of 1876 (*Manna*) and 1884 (*The Way It Tastes and Smells*) are a number of the letters he received from Venice (Alishan), Moscow (Mkrtich Emin and Grigor Khalateants), Constantinople (Patriarch Nerses), and Saint Petersburg (Kerovbé Patkanean), as well as from Vienna and Tblisi. Everyone, it seems, had been waiting to hear the oral discourse of the native, because of both its antiquity and its authenticity; Servantsdeants offered it up for the first time, with all the passion and in all the detail they wished. Thus Alishan writes: "For many years, I have felt the desire, from time to time, to hear with my own ears, and faithfully transcribe, the local traditions of the different regions of the Armenian world; and now you yourself and a few other patriotic priests whom you mention have done just that. I am impatiently waiting for you to publish more collections of the sort. The promise to publish this kind of texts was made in the Armenian newspapers years ago" (*Yerker* 1:621–22). Oddly, here too Alishan conflates the archeology of monuments and colophons with that of the native, for he adds that, among these eagerly awaited publications was, precisely, a collection of the colophons of Armenian manuscripts. Thus, for him as well, the spoken word of the native was an "antiquity" comparable to ancient ruins and monuments. Besides Alishan's, one of the most astonishing of the letters Servantsdeants received was sent him by Grigor Khalateants, who was teaching, at the time, at Moscow's Lazarian Academy (which would later, following its natural penchant, become an orientalist institute). Khalateants had been a pupil of Mkrtich Emin, the scholar who, with his 1850 *Vepk' hnuyn Hayastani* (Epic Narratives of Ancient Armenia), had been the first to echo, among the Armenians, the modern discovery (or invention) of mythology. Khalateants's letter is most instructive. He wants to know everything. He has already made a Russian translation of the part of the popular epic published by Servantsdeants, but he wants a great deal more. In fact, he expresses his desire to have an overall idea of Servantsdeants's ethnographic collection in order to publish it in its entirety using money available to him in Moscow; that is to say he expresses, quite simply, his desire to appropriate it, so that he can at last have the archives of ethnographic philology at his disposal.[22] I like this letter (if one may say so) and I like this philological personality, Khalateants, because he is also the man who, fifteen years later, would write a book of a rare poverty on "mythemes" in the work of Moses of Khoren, for the sole purpose of demonstrating that the episodes that this author claims to have taken from the oral tradition were all, without exception, fabrications of his own devising. With that thesis Khalateants annulled (or thought he had annulled) the fundamental contribution of his intellectual father, Mkrtich Emin, whose 1850 *Vebk' hnuyn Hayastani* [Epic Narratives of Ancient Armenia] had explored the traces of a national historical epic preserved in Moses's *History*. This strange patricide thus went hand-in-hand with a total failure to grasp the modern meaning of mythology. For someone who had boundless admiration for Servantsdeants, this was a very sad end.

Servantsdeants, in one of his replies to the long letters he received from all over the world (a reply to one of his benefactors), spoke in tones that Abovean would not have disowned: "To save the Armenians from the exactions to which they are subject [*harstaharut'ene*], one has to make them acquainted with themselves. To bring the Armenians back from the confines of the cemetery of indifference, one has to speak to them in their native dialect [*hayrenakan parpar'ov*]. The flute of Masis has to be made to sound in their ears. It is time to wipe the dust from our lyres . . . set the printing presses turning in order to diffuse national songs, the narratives of the popular tradition [*veperë*], critical, archeological texts and oral discourses, and individual popular biographies and local customs, in the same way in which we distribute food and clothing" (*Yerker* 1:626).[23] It may well be that we already find ourselves, here, at the level of the conscious, elaborated nationalistic project, not that of the self-invention of the nation. Against indifference or the self-inflicted disappearance and loss of the self, we must, according to Servantsdeants, marshal native dialects, as well as national songs, antiquity, and local customs and legends in the form in which they are still ringing out, somewhere—back where the natives have not lost their authenticity or customs. The reader will have understood that I continue to repeat their argument, an argument about the authenticity of the native that circulates from Abovean to Servantsdeants and beyond, because I am fascinated by the obstinacy with which it returns, and also (if I may be forgiven the term) by its incongruity. I am not disputing the authenticity that the argument implicitly (and sometimes quite explicitly) assumes. What fascinates me is the absurdity of the argument and, at the same time, its extraordinary force, the power it exercised, its extremely natural, self-evident character, and the fact that, as a result of all this, it had a shaping effect on the whole of the national phenomenon from the moment it was articulated and even before, since it shaped, in advance, the work of several generations of very learned, influential people. Yet I did indeed write "the absurdity of the argument." Why should one have to assemble and circulate something that exists in and of itself? Why should the circulation of philological material save the "nation" from disaster, ruin, and indifference? Moreover, what disaster is involved? Is it not clear that it is the intervention of philology which reduces the "oral tradition" and "local customs" to their status as witnesses and vestiges, which is to say, in both cases, to traces and ruins? Yet, notwithstanding this absurdity, the "national" constituted itself before our eyes by means of this argument. From the moment that "the national" is constituted and the ethnographic nation imposes itself on people's minds, effacing the past of collective forms without a trace, the argument is nothing more than that of nationalism. This, furthermore, is what explains the fact that Armenian nationalism later took up Hagop Oshagan's formulations about authenticity without understanding anything at all about the equivalence that he and his generation had established between "nationalization" and "aestheticization" and, consequently, without understanding anything about the imperative of aestheticization itself: of the becoming-oneself, the appropriation of the self by art. It further explains why the philologists (and the ethnographic institutes, the very definition of which is based on Servantsdeants's inauguration of national ethnography) have never read what Oshagan wrote about the founder of their discipline. And, Oshagan aside, they will never admit that their discipline, in its close complicity with nationalism, is orientalist through and through. But that is practically redundant. It is the explanation of this redundancy (the orientalism inherent in philology and its foundational role for nationalistic discourse) which we have decided to put off until the next chapter.

The Fate of the Oral Tradition

The philological effervescence around Servantsdeants's work continued unabated for several decades. In particular, it took a number of generations of ethnographers to digest the heroic-mythical manna represented by the popular epic. It may be said without fear of exaggeration that the work to receive, compile, and publish went on for nearly seventy years. The problem resided in the fact that this epic narrative with its four "branches," which came into being in the Sasun region in, roughly, the ninth century, gradually spread to virtually all the regions inhabited by Armenians, taking on diverse aspects in the course of the centuries. In 1936, when the Armenian Academy of Sciences or, rather, what stood in for it at the time,[24] deemed that the moment had come to begin publication (this was a decision with a "political" dimension, the authorization to publish having come directly from Moscow), some fifty variants had been collected; they were similar in content, yet differed in their treatment of the various episodes. These variants were published in three volumes in 1936, 1944, and 1951.[25] But the work of publication did not stop there, because a "standard," homogenized, integral version was also published in 1939; it is this version that I especially wish to discuss. This volume was apparently published for a practical reason: the many different transcriptions put the whole out of reach of nonspecialist readers; moreover, these variants reflected all the dialects of the Armenian world. The standard, integral version published by the Academy in 1939, under the general editorship of Manuk Abeghean, aspired to linguistic uniformity. Abeghean's complete works include a defense of the work he now undertook, which involved replacing some of the words that smacked too heavily of the dialectal with their equivalents in the (Eastern) literary language, and also harmonizing the narrative structure.[26] This version was very widely distributed, and Frédéric Feydit published a well-known French translation of it; an English version by Artin Shalian was published in 1964.[27] It so happens, however, that the project for a "national epic" was drawn up and realized between 1936 and 1939, when the Stalinist persecutions peaked. This was in no sense fortuitous. The same officials who were killing intellectuals by the dozens in the NKVD's prisons also found the time to publish books and ponder the "national" dimension of their enterprise. Valorizing the epic corpus and transforming it into a national epic were purely political acts, strictly contemporaneous with the persecution of Charents and the writers in his entourage. The same sanguinary nationalism that imprisoned Charents and drove him to his death also homogenized the Armenians' oral epic, transforming it into a pseudo-national epic. This was one of the last twentieth-century avatars—one of the worst—of the ideological interpretation to which the desire and need to establish a written record of popular sources were subjected. Here, there is no longer any crisis, no "paternal" disaster, no testamentary legacy, no mourning or institutionalization of mourning. Instead, we have a national epic! But the need to turn out an integral, linguistically homogenized version of the text must be understood as the product of another desire as well, one that did not date from 1939 and the efforts of the Academy or the Armenian government. In question here is, in a word, the desire to have an epic in the national sense of the word, not just a popular, oral narrative with a thousand and one variants. In their desire to create a literary epic where there had existed only an oral tradition of heroic-mythological narrative and an ethnographic record of this tradition, the leaders of the Republic of Armenia were simply complying with what had been suggested to them by the Armenians' desire to possess a "national" epic of their own, with all the distortions that this necessarily implied (obviously, more variants had been collected in Western than in Eastern dialects, whereas the national imperative to create a literary epic apparently made it necessary to homogenize the whole in literary Eastern Armenian).[28]

Oshagan and Servantsdeants

To close the second section of the present chapter, about Karekin Servantsdeants's place in the history of the ethnographic nation, we shall now examine Hagop Oshagan's discussion of Servantsdeants in his *Panorama of Western Armenian Literature*. We have already mentioned Oshagan's *Panorama* in the previous chapter. We must nevertheless begin here with a brief account of the nature of this work, the last large-scale enterprise Oshagan undertook.

Oshagan's *Panorama* is a philological work, for its author sets out to write a gargantuan history of the literature of the Western Armenians in the form of a series of monographs devoted to the producers of this literature and its literary language, Western Armenian. At the beginning of his career, before 1915, Oshagan's philological models were doubtless Charles Augustin Sainte-Beuve, Hippolyte Taine, and Ferdinand Brunetière, French critics of the latter half of the nineteenth century. However, when he began to write *Panorama* in 1939 (the work was effectively composed between 1939 and 1943, even if some of the monographs it contains had already been written and were simply incorporated into the new project), Oshagan had had the time to change his philological models completely. His references now were the great German philologists, of whom he had already said in 1931 that

> rather than judging, they subjected ideas to a labor resembling a metaphysics of a new kind. Having acquired vast learning and a vast experience of life, and after pursuing the loftiest intellectual activities for a long time, these people succeeded in grasping the fundamental structure of their period in their work. . . . Considered at this level, criticism is the supreme form of creation.[29]

One of the philologists Oshagan so admired was Ernst Curtius. He could obviously not have been familiar with Curtius's great, comprehensive study of medieval Latin literature, interpreted as the bedrock of the European literature that came after it. But Curtius was, from the 1920s on, well known in France thanks to his friendships with a number of French writers and the fine studies he had made of them. It is also possible that Oshagan's great interest in him went back to the essay Curtius had written on the Abbé Brémond.[30] For Henri Brémond was Oshagan's other great model in philology, from the 1930s on. Let us recall that Brémond (1865–1933) was the author of an eleven-volume *Histoire littéraire du sentiment religieux en France*.[31] This is certainly not the place to explain why Oshagan was fascinated by Brémond's critical and philological work, but it is clear that he saw in him a sort of anticipation of his own desire to recreate an entire epoch, both comprehensively and in detail, by way of a discussion of its literary writers. The unstated underlying assumption was that each of these authors "condensed," in his work, the totality of his period. In this sense, the work becomes a "witness" to the period in which it is written, and is, at the same time, a product of that period; it presents its author's "lived" experience. (In Brémond's case, the authors were leading clergymen, mystical authors, and spiritual advisers of a kind to be found in few historical periods). What is more, Brémond opens his work with the following notice: "I am writing a literary history, not a history tout court, of religious sentiment in France." Hence he concerns himself with written "documents" and "testimony" in which religious sentiment had already been shaped by the experience of an individual and found literary expression. I shall leave the discussion of Brémond there in order to note that this was precisely Oshagan's project in *Panorama*. His subject, obviously, was not religious experience. Yet it was plainly, in its turn, an experience. It was the Armenians' pre-Catastrophic experience as such.

Let us now add two things, again very briefly, on the "comprehensive" project of *Panorama*, simply in order to make Oshagan's treatment of Servantsdeants intelligible. The goal of Oshagan's grand critical work was to bring out what he calls the "literary idea." Thus he does not content himself with describing the pre-Catastrophic world on the basis of testimony provided by its writers. He also assesses the contribution each of them made to what we have called, in the previous chapter, the "aestheticizing erection," which is simultaneously an erection of art and an erection of popular sources through the "medium" of art. At the same time, Oshagan assesses his writers' contribution to the discovery of these sources, the discovery of a hidden "essence" awaiting its manifestation; ostensibly, the life of the people. Yet there are precious few modern Western Armenian writers who fulfill this last criterion. Not all of them wrote, fortunately, in conformity with the stipulations of an "aesthetic principle" that they could not, in any case, have anticipated. Only Oshagan's own literary work was capable of fully meeting his requirements. That is the real reason that his vast critical oeuvre is crowned by a tenth volume in which he presents himself as the culmination of this literary history: in his work, the literary idea (leaving the question of what that might mean aside for the moment) is said to have been fully emancipated; at the same time, the popular sources supposedly attain their complete artistic (and therefore also national) metamorphosis in it.

The trouble with Servantsdeants is that he is, on the one hand, the "discoverer" par excellence and even, most likely, the *only* "discoverer" of popular sources in the whole Armenian literary field of his time; on the other hand, it is impossible to consider him as belonging in any sense at all to the Armenian literary field. He was quite simply not a writer, in the sense that he made no contribution whatsoever to the liberation of the "literary idea." Indeed, he had not the foggiest notion about what the "literary idea" might be. This is, after all, a serious paradox. It was, in any event, a problem for Oshagan, as is indicated by the fact that he devotes one of the most generous monographs in *Panorama* to Servantsdeants (*Panorama*, as a rule, does not treat the writers it discusses kindly, whether as writers or as "witnesses" to their period), yet also one of the shortest. (It is short when measured by the criteria and standards that Oshagan apparently set himself: it is only seventeen pages long.) Here is what Oshagan says of "this priest" in the opening pages of this study, which I cite at some length:

> Some things are priceless; there is no haggling over their worth. Such is the most uncertain but also precious spiritual system of the Armenian fatherland—to put it differently, the Armenian soul's warp and woof, its inner expanses and the ultimate arrangement of its elements—that was saved [*p'rkvats*] by Servantsdeants. . . . Servantsdeants collected everything that spilled from the lips of those who lived on

that soil, all the images that had sprung from the land over the centuries, all the opulence of all the libraries that had for centuries been honored guests in monk's cells or in chapels or huts, in the guise of manuscripts, miniatures, paintings, books. He felt, for the very last time (after him, we never had, from anyone's pen, a depiction of the experience of the Armenian fatherland or the feelings called forth by its soil; for more than twenty years, the censors outlawed descriptions of local conditions in the fatherland), the nameless, profound, indecipherable plastic manifestations [*patkerakerpum*] of that fatherland, salvaged for all time by his writings. . . . And yet Servantsdeants's work hardly even approaches the concept of literature as I present it in the introduction to the present volume. This man, who rescued elements of such inestimable value for the ethnographic history of Armenian civilization, hardly considers the possibility (let alone the actual existence) of something called literature. Fate has decreed that, with his perfect indifference to art [*gegharvesd*] . . . and thanks to the vivid results that this eyewitness [*akanates*] and collector took straight from the land, Karekin Servantsdeants is more than just an Armenologist and ethnographer; he enters the field of Western Armenian literature, head held high.[32]

We must, first, provide a few words of explanation. We already know that, in 1878, the Armenian Patriarchate charged Servantsdeants with organizing a census of the Armenians in the six *vilayets* where the majority of them lived, and also with drawing up an inventory of their cultural riches (manuscripts, monuments, and artifacts). Oshagan alludes to this when, after evoking the oral tradition that this priest-scholar and ethnographer recorded in the field, he talks about "images," the pictures in illustrated manuscripts, which had been waiting in the monasteries for their improbable visitor; or again, when he mentions the vestiges of the past that took the form of monuments or ruins. For Oshagan as well, then, the old equation was still in force, that between geographical archeology, which collects objects presumed to stem from High Antiquity, and ethnographic archeology, which collects whatever "spilled" from the lips of the native. The next sentence is an important link, of course, in his implicit chain of reasoning: "[Servantsdeants] felt, for the very last time . . . the nameless, profound, indecipherable plastic manifestations [*patkerakerpum*] of [the] fatherland." I am not entirely certain that *patkerakerpum* is the word Oshagan actually wrote. The "fatherland" must take graphic material form and be crystallized in concrete, pictorial manifestations, in the guise of architectural or intellectual constructs. But the word Oshagan wrote may have been *patkerakertum*, which, albeit similar in meaning, puts the accent on the creation of such forms, rather than on their physical manifestation or graphic nature. Why should it have been "for the very last time"? This has to do with the subaltern conditions in which the Armenians of the Ottoman Empire lived. After 1885—indeed, even as early as 1880—no sign of the "fatherland" (I use Oshagan's terminology) could appear directly, as such, in Constantinople newspapers or in books. The increasing rigidity of Abdül Hamid's regime, followed by the terror, pure and simple, that it visited on the provinces, ruled out all ethnographic work calling itself a "science of the fatherland." We must never lose sight of this dimension, the consequence of a generalized censorship. It explains, in part, why it was among the Eastern Armenians that ethnographic work was developed further. But only in part! Eastern Armenian scholars, as we have seen, were eminently familiar with the science of folklore as it had been developed in German universities. Western Armenians, in contrast, had no contact with these philological circles. This, too, is part of the explanation. Further, Oshagan's "for the last time" is an overly dramatic way of putting matters. The ethnographic spirit continued to hold a central place in Western Armenians' consciousness after 1880. Have I already said that, between 1880 and 1915, there was not a single schoolteacher in the provinces who did not, in one way or another, make a contribution to the ethnography of his village or native region? Ethnography as such was not deemed dangerous by the sultan's Censors and it was not outlawed. It was, however, impossible to make an inventory of cultural riches, since that would have created the impression that there existed a nation that had an identity of its own and formed a separate whole within the Empire's borders. On this point, Oshagan was obviously right. The Censors had not yet fully grasped that the ethnography of the native was engaged in producing nothing more or less than an inventory of cultural riches! The Censors read (and censured) writers, not ethnographers. Can one not, however, put the matter the other way around, and argue that the sultan's Censors knew more here than the ethnographers—that they had perfectly well understood the importance of the role of art, and thus of aestheticization, in the nationalization of the nation? If so, we can begin to see why, for Oshagan, censorship was another name for the radical subjection of the subject people (the process of depriving them of selfhood). The subaltern condition, the condition of being a "subject people," and the extent of this subjection of the Armenians will be explored later, following Hagop Oshagan, who seems to me to have said crucially important things on this score; he was, in any case, the only one to suggest the significance of total subjection in an imperial system of domination. He was the only one to suggest that this subjection of a subjugated people could comprise the core of a necessarily irremediable disaster. With that idea as one's starting point, one can begin to pose certain questions: did Khachatur Abovean have this disaster in mind when he described the calamitous state of the community, conceiving it, from the outset, in the form of a disaster of the father and the mutism of the son? Was it this disaster that Karekin Servantsdeants was evoking when he pointed to the "cemetery of indifference" from which it was imperative to save the Armenians by "acquainting them with themselves"? Again, was it this disaster that was at issue when even Oshagan, in 1914, mentioned this people alienated from itself, this multitude "driven from its center, land, and religion"?

These questions are so troubling that I shall be repeatedly coming back to them in Part II of the present volume, in essentially the same terms. I shall be asking myself what precisely is in question when it is a question of "disaster," a question that recurs in such regular, uniform fashion in Abovean, Servantsdeants, Oshagan and, of course, Varuzhan. In the passage on Servantsdeants just quoted (a passage which, let us recall, was written thirty years after *Mehyan*), Oshagan seems to say clearly (this, at any rate, is the plain inference) that censorship, an expression of the total subjection of the people on which it is imposed, in fact forbids, whether the Censors know it or not, the transfer of popular sources to the sphere of art, when this transfer alone was capable of "nationalizing" the nation. This explains why the liberation of the "literary idea" was a genuine emancipation, from censorship and from subjection, and thus constituted an eminently political act. *Panorama* is the history and inauguration of an emancipation. This, finally, is the reason that Servantsdeants holds a special place in Oshagan's voluminous literary history, even if his "work hardly even approaches the concept of literature," even if he "barely considers the possibility . . . of something called literature," even if he was perfectly indifferent to art. If so, Servantsdeants may be said to have saved "the inexhaustible storehouse of popular creation" "for literature," and only secondarily for ethnography (*Panorama* 4:323). What, indeed, is a writer, if not "someone who saves a moment, a world, a spirit [*pah më, ashkharh më, vogi më*]" (ibid., 324)?

CHAPTER 3

Orientalism and Neo-Archeology

Going from chapter 1 to chapter 2, we have proceeded backwards in time. The school of the review *Mehyan*, associated with the names Daniel Varuzhan, Hagop Oshagan, and Constant Zarian—the school of the aesthetic principle that dominated the world of Armenian letters in the first half of the twentieth century—made explicit reference to the ethnographic movement of the middle of the previous century in order to define its own position and demand recognition of its distinctiveness. It engaged in a polemic with philology, although it was not exactly clear how much it depended on philology. The *Mehyan* school competed with philology in the struggle to accomplish what it called (speaking through the mouth of Oshagan) the "nationalization" of the nation. At the same time, it was clear that it wanted this competition with philology to be amplified, and understood, in yet another way. If art (according to the *Mehyan* Manifesto) was "above" religion, or if criticism (according to Oshagan's later declarations) could be fully practiced and understood only as a modern avatar of the experience of the "sacred" in the religions of antiquity, then the affirmation of art against philology called religion itself into question. The problem is that we do not know exactly what the religions of antiquity were; this holds in particular for the religions of the "pagan" societies, which, as the nineteenth century endlessly repeated, were the only ones to have had a mythological dimension. We know nothing about these religions other than what philology tells us about them. For all these reasons, we have had to make our way back to the mid-nineteenth century in order to examine the modalities of the ethnographic discovery of the Armenians by themselves. This first step backwards has not yet allowed us, however, to see that, between ethnographic practice and the aesthetic demand, the fate of the "nation" was at stake, and, consequently, that it was the national imagination that was at work here. Furthermore, when the writers of the *Mehyan* group spoke of mythology and mythological religion, they were utterly unaware of the fact that the very idea of mythology was altogether new—that, thanks to philology, it had surreptitiously insinuated itself into the national consciousness only a few decades earlier. Thus their debate with philology was at all events skewed. Moreover, nationalistic discourse, as soon as it was put in place, effaced everything that had preceded it. This discourse had it that the Armenians' national modernity commenced with what has ever since been called the *Zart'onk'*, the "Renaissance" of mid-century, and that this Renaissance was characterized by rhetorical jousting around the literary language, although this jousting was in fact a rear-guard action, since there could no longer be any doubt as to the outcome of the fight. Here, too, the *Mehyan* writers had no notion of these origins of the ethnographic nation or the part philology played before it was harnessed to the ethnographic cart. Thus we must turn around again and take another step into the past, this time toward the moment that inaugurated the national imagination and the beginnings of philology. It is situated, to be precise, in the 1810s, that is, twenty years before Abovean wrote the preface to his novel *Wounds of Armenia*, thirty years before Mkrtich Emin's discovery of the mythological idea in *The Epic Narratives of Ancient Armenia*, and fifty years before Servantsdeants's *Written in a Rush*.

This second step backwards is in fact two steps. It is clearly a matter, first, of returning to a moment that, chronologically speaking, precedes auto-ethnography. Yet it is, second, also a question of accounting for the autoscopic phenomenon constituted by the ethnography of the self by the self, in which the subject's vision and knowledge (*le voir et le savoir*) are turned on himself as object. The aim of this chapter is thus, first of all, to show that the national imagination made its debut under the mantle of archeology, by forcibly establishing the necessity for a voyage toward the self. At the outset, all that was involved was a necessity the more fascinating in that nothing of the sort yet existed in actual fact. The fashion of the real voyage back to the "fatherland" (echoed and sustained, as we shall see, even by Daniel Varuzhan as late as 1908) did not set in before 1820, when the archeological decade was drawing to a close. The present chapter also aims, however, to describe the beginnings of the national imagination in the context of orientalism, which makes its triumphant entry onto the terrain of the future ethnographic nations in precisely the same period. In our humble opinion, this orientalism remains unintelligible if we do not take its realization in the midst of the ethnographic nations into account. Now, it so happens that the phenomenon of European orientalism was elucidated in an extraordinary conjuncture by an individual, Edward Said. Overnight, Said compelled philology as a whole to acknowledge the existence of orientalism. The discipline had a rather hard time of it recovering from the experience (according to the most recent reports, however, it has bucked up and is again doing just marvelously). Said, a respected, honored American academic, accomplished this feat with a single book, *Orientalism*, published in 1978. His work is not, however, of a piece; quite the contrary, in fact. That is why it seems to me worthwhile to begin the present chapter with a general (and, necessarily, very brief) overview of the paradoxes of the activity and historical concept of "orientalism," as I interpret it in reading Said in conjunction with philology (in a way different from the one in which he would have presented it himself). *Orientalism* is the finest illustration of the resolutely anti-humanist approach taken by Michel Foucault, whom Said, moreover, explicitly identifies as one of the inspirations for his own work. The fact remains, however, that "humanism" dominates Said's thinking both before and after the appearance of his masterpiece—humanism or, in other words, a defense and illustration of philology that grew more tenacious as the years went by. Furthermore, as the American reception of the book has never explicitly highlighted the book's treatment of philology and never read it as a critique of philology, all this will require that we engage, to a certain extent, in a rewriting of it. The work this requires has been undertaken before me by Stathis Gourgouris, although he never presents it in this light. There was no reason that I should not avail myself of the results of Gourgouris's work.

THE UNFOLDING OF PHILOLOGY

It was in 1786 that William Jones, then working as a judge, a translator, and a scholar in India, first advanced the thesis that different languages were probably related—more precisely, related historically—although he was unable to explain why they should be or to forge a method capable of revealing either the filiation between languages or the derivation of some languages from others. The news of the discovery of Sanskrit, however, had already, in the space of four or five years, made its way from one end of the intellectual world to the other. In 1803, the year that Hölderlin wrote "Mnemosyne" and Schelling gave his course on the philosophy of art, Friedrich Schlegel, who had just published a book on Lessing and produced a play, and apparently had nothing more to do in Germany, went to Paris to study Sanskrit with Hamilton.[1] The result was Schlegel's 1808 *Über die Sprache und Weisheit der Indier* (*On the Language and Wisdom of the Hindus*).[2] This book was the first to formulate the whole set of hypotheses about the affiliation and derivation of the Germano-Indo-European languages; these hypotheses are fully worked out, in a way that makes no concessions to and exhibits no traces of the eighteenth-century conception of language. Schlegel's hypotheses nevertheless continue to be marked by the notion, which he would subsequently rectify to a certain extent, that Sanskrit was at the root of European humanity—in other words, of that segment of humanity endowed with the capacity to mythologize. Things developed quickly in this regard. In 1815, Wilhelm Humboldt was already planning to create chairs of Sanskrit in Germany; they would become the first chairs of the comparative philology of the Indo-European languages. Involved here was, so to speak, the political institutionalization of mythological religion. In 1818, August-Wilhelm Schlegel, who had, in the meantime, himself learned Sanskrit, started teaching in Bonn. In 1821, Franz Bopp began teaching in Berlin. Max Müller, who may be called, with Ernest Renan, the most renowned philologist of the nineteenth century, had studied in Bonn with August-Wilhelm Schlegel's first assistant (he would also, somewhat later, attend Schelling's courses on mythology).[3] Thus there is, unsurprisingly, a direct relationship between this central philological current and the Jena Romantics.

From the outset, Bopp and August-Wilhelm Schlegel equitably divided up their task. Bopp concentrated on grammatical elucidation of the relations between languages, while Schlegel focused mainly on the philologist's task in a different sense of the term, leaving aside strictly linguistic work: he spent most of his energy on editing and translating texts and writing historical commentaries. None of this offers a full response to the question of what philology is, but one thing is already clear: there will never be any question here of philology as an institution of mourning. Nor is that all. It must further be recalled that Friedrich Schlegel, after publishing his book on India in 1808, more or less definitively abandoned his study of Sanskrit in order to devote part of his talent and energy to the Catholic unification of Europe. This did not prevent him from giving lectures in Vienna that were very well attended. Thus he delivered, in 1812, a series of lectures on the history of world literature that he published in book form three years later. A general history of literature, the reader will say (for that is what Schlegel sought to produce), is a pedestrian sort of project. The same would doubtless hold for Schlegel's enterprise, too, if it were not for the fact that, just as his 1808 book was the first to discuss the Indo-European languages in detail, so its 1815 successor was the first history of literature ever written, which is to say, very precisely, the first real literary history in which the interpretation of the texts treated depends on their context, while their context is reconstituted on the basis of the texts. Before Schlegel, literary history was inconceivable.[4] Only in his day, because literature now existed as such, as philology's twin, did it become possible to envisage writing a history of it. There, indeed, is the point at which philology initiates its method and project. The first defining feature of this project is its universality: Schlegel considers all the national literatures. The second aspect is the idea that the national context is the one in which it is possible to write a history of literatures. The third aspect has already been mentioned: to understand texts, one has to understand their context; conversely, however, there is no way of understanding the context other than that offered by the texts themselves! This is not a vicious circle. The redoubling and interdependence of text and context within the framework of a project that aims at a purely historical understanding is the very definition of philology, which can only exist as a circular, comprehensive enterprise. One hundred fifty years later, Auerbach would reproduce this philological program term for term, in extremely naïve fashion. Whence, after all, a fourth aspect: because the comprehensive enterprise that philology necessarily comprises concerns itself, in the nineteenth century (at least), with national cultures and the spirit of the peoples considered as hermeneutical contexts, there was no reason that literature should have a special role to play in this project of historical elucidation. Yet it did: literature, the definition of which was of course broadened to include written and nonwritten, religious and poetic traditions, that is, the whole field of "aestheticized" language, as we shall see as soon as we come to the next aspect—literature, I say, was taken to form the heart of national cultures. Whence the fifth and last aspect, which is quite as crucial as all the others: it is not possible to bring the relationship text / context into play unless one has, from the outset, transformed everything into literature ("everything": for example, the Rig Veda, Hebrew poetry, and the ancient hymns to the Armenian god Vahagn, as well as, say, religion, the oral tradition, epics, and popular legends—for everything is literature, whatever its aesthetic value; in other words, everything counts as a possible object of philology). Summing up all these aspects, we can say that philology is an ideological-conceptual apparatus that has two operational phases: it transforms what is usually defined as literature into a witness; but, historically, what is defined as literature is so defined only in reaction to philology's inauguration of its own comprehensive, contextual, and secularized project, which is present from the beginning. The implication is that literature, in its twofold dependence on philology, must itself be constantly practiced in the form of an attempt to break free of philology. This is the operation by which documents are transformed into monuments. (This is also, in a strange reversal, how Giorgio Agamben defines testimony: as that which emancipates itself from the rule of the archive and, shedding its status as document, becomes a monument.)

If we cast a glance at chapter 8 of Foucault's *The Order of Things*, we will see that he retraces the birth of philology and its object, language in its historical depth and density, in essentially the same terms. The difference is that he systematically employs the word *philology* to mean the grammatical study of the Indo-European languages, as if the diverse other aspects of philology regarded as a comprehensive, historical enterprise (see our list) were secondary. Thus Foucault privileges one dimension of philology, the one that, at the outset, encounters the object language; he takes basically very little interest in the other dimension, namely, philology as historical criticism of texts and comprehensive recreation of a context. However, from this one aspect, he deduces the others that I have mentioned, treating them as its consequences. He deduces everything, with the exception of philology's orientalism. But it is not possible to understand what philology is without orientalism as Said conceptualizes, defines, and situates it in *Orientalism*. Here, everything changes, requiring that we enter on a new discussion.

Before we broach philology as orientalism, however, let us make sure that we have a firm grasp on what has been said so far. We have seen how the speculative matrix that governs the relations between art and religion and defines art as both the informing principle and the mourning of mythological religion was put in place. We have understood that philology unfolded between 1803 and 1908, between the two defining moments ("philosophical" and "poetic," "Western" and "Eastern") of the emergence of the formula "art is mourning," and that it gradually asserted its supremacy while remaining wholly oblivious to its own "humanist" project and inventions, that is, wholly ignorant of itself as the institution of mourning. Nothing in all this, at any event, is grounds for the suspicion that philology would reflexively (or even speculatively) revisit its own project as the central project of European humanism (that is, in fact, a formulation of the project in which philology itself would at last take its place at the heart of humanism, even if this had already been done in great part by Renan).[5] More-over, we do not yet know how and why the philological project played so influential a role outside the field in which it first emerged, that of the invention of the (national) self in nineteenth-century Europe. We do not yet know why it was at the center of the crucial phenomenon of the formation of the ethnographic nations. And, above all, we do not yet know the forms that the relationship between these two disparate realities can assume: on the one hand, the accomplishment of philology in its own right, as pure speculation; on the other, the revelation of the orientalist genealogy of the na-tional. Not to speak of the fact that, in all this, we see nothing that has to do with mourning, which was nevertheless at the center of the philological workshop, with the discovery of mythological religion as the mournful discovery of the lost gods and as the prelude to the only way of conceiving of disaster that the ethnographic nations have at their disposal to the present day.

Must we, then, demolish philology? Or must we rather announce its end and work incessantly to hasten it, as Foucault so effectively and powerfully did with the Man of the human sciences? In either case, we will perhaps ultimately be able to liberate mourn-ing from philology and take the full measure of the disaster. As to those who have not fully grasped the nature of the "anthropological thinking" denounced by Foucault, it is time to announce that it is, eminently, philological thought. I do not mean that philol-ogy is an example of such thinking but, rather, that it is its core, its matrix, its driving force. True, philosophers have not understood this any better than anyone else.

When Said published *Orientalism* in 1978, he struck a blow that rocked the Ameri-can academy to its foundations, in all its departments and in every discipline. It was, obviously, a blow struck at the orientalists first of all: broadly, all those who had made the literatures and traditions of the (Middle) East their stock-in-trade, had recounted the history of the world's civilizations and the benefits of colonialism in the same breath, and had never lost a moment's thought on the historical inscription of their discipline—in a word, academics in departments of Middle Eastern or Indian civiliza-tion. Abruptly, the whole philological approach was called into question. But Said's book also sent shock waves rippling through anthropology departments. It so happens that it was well received in departments of English (and thus of humanism), which obviously did not deem it dangerous to read or put on syllabuses. These departments had long since incorporated the study of colonialism or imperialism into their pro-grams. (To be sure, this is not the only reason for the tremendous success the book had with philologists, as will appear in a moment.) *Orientalism* was, however, also re-ceived with open arms by fundamentalists of all stripes. A Western work that targeted the Western stranglehold on the tradition of the Eastern countries, especially the Is-lamic countries, what a godsend! And, surprisingly, this criticism commanded atten-tion and circulated pretty much everywhere. There was no need to take the book's subtleties into account. Was orientalism an ideology, a false, erroneous, warped repre-sentation, or was it a discourse? No matter! It was intimately bound up with the exercise of colonial power. Here were themes aplenty on which one could serenely hold forth. Fundamentalist circles did not hold forth on them any less enthusiastically than the Anglo-Saxon intellectual world; and in Anglophone academe, *Orientalism* was no doubt one of the bestsellers of all time.

We just asked whether orientalism was an ideology, a representation, or a discourse. Do these three things differ? Said's strength resides in the fact that he, too—he above all—never asked himself these questions. He blazed a path by making use of all of the theoretical weapons he encountered on his way. The most extraordinary of these theoretical weapons at the time was Michel Foucault, as represented not only by *The Order of Things* but also by the imposing works of his next period, in which he conjugated knowledge with power. My conviction is that *Orientalism* is the best illustration of all that Foucault says about epistemological breaks; it is the best practical application of his ideas about how history is written and of his way of showing how an object, here the (Middle) East, emerges in step with the knowledge of it, and is never independent of the simultaneously epistemic and political conditions for the production of knowledge. The object is brought within the compass of knowledge there only to be the more effectively negated. The problem is that orientalism did not really have a precise theoretical status for Said. Even if it is true that his analyses as a whole would have been strictly impossible without Foucault, the fact remains that Said hesitates, when it comes to determining the status of orientalism, between ideology, representation (of a reality), institution, political project, and style.

The most terrible thing is that Said was his own book's worst reader. After *Orientalism*, he not only lost all interest in the Foucaldian historical problematic but, worse, waged an ongoing war against Foucault, covertly at first and, before long, in the open. In defense of what? Quite simply, in defense of humanism. Thus his covert war against Foucault was a war against antihumanism. The enormous success of *Orientalism*, even and especially with American philologists, obviously had to do with the fact that the book enabled them, simply by referring to its author, to wash their hands of, precisely, the orientalist aspect of philology. This is, it will readily be agreed, sheer paradox. Thus people read everything in *Orientalism* except for the critique (or autocritique) of philology. But it so happens that the book also presented itself as the accomplishment of the philological enterprise. How could one book be these two things at once? This question calls for a separate study that I cannot undertake here. Let us say simply that *Orientalism* is a book of such importance that there must be something that explains its power apart from the theme that everyone in the Anglo-Saxon world reads in the book: the anticolonialist critique that dovetails as a critique of European culture from within. This something is the Foucaldian aspect of the book, which Said later wholly abjured and repudiated; it is its antihumanism, the critique of philology. I just spoke of "the accomplishment of the philological enterprise." Is it so utterly surprising that philology should be at the heart of the critique *Orientalism* offers? The book clearly sets out a description of the Western world, its determinations, and its main project over the course of two centuries; it sets out, therefore, one more philological history, centered, this time, on philology itself, which is, un-mistakably, at the heart of the action here. Cast in a critical light (rather than in a self-celebratory light, as in Renan) for what is doubtless the first time, philology here appears for what it is: the pivotal discourse of the West for the past two hundred years, the discourse of its power. Hence we have to read *Orientalism* as the last of the great Western philological *summas*; but we also have to understand why this last *summa* had to put philology (and thus criticism as well) on prominent display (or, if one prefers, *en abyme*) at the heart of its own text. This further implies that Said's book obeys two imperatives at once: on the one hand, an antihumanist imperative that leads to a historical deconstruction of the philological project and its imple-mentation; on the other, an essentially humanist imperative that leads to philology's triumphant accomplishment. Thus, in one and the same book, philology makes a radical self-critique while also gloriously fulfilling its own two-hundred-year-old proj-ect, which came into the world with the Schlegel brothers and a few others associated with them around 1800.

ORIENTALISM'S NATIVE

At the very beginning of *Orientalism*, Said quotes a remark made in Beirut in 1976 by a French journalist who aired the nostalgic or learned view that, until the war, Beirut had still been part of Chateaubriand's and Gérard de Nerval's East. Said then has an easy time of it mocking the Frenchman. He immediately reminds us that the East was, in any case, an invention of the West, teeming with exquisitely exotic (and erotic) creatures as well as haunting landscapes and memories; he adds that, happily, that East is doubtless on the verge of disappearing, if it ever existed anywhere other than in the imagination of Western travelers, esthetes, or flâneurs. Whatever the truth of the matter, the journalist in question did not consider it particularly important to know whether there were Easterners living in this East, people who might themselves, after all, have lost something: these Easterners who were already there in the age of Chateaubriand and de Nerval—in short, the natives. In his book, Said repeatedly comes back to a twofold question about natives and travelers. At bottom, what have these travelers to the East, these flâneurs, come to see? Why does the native interest them as much as he does, the thrills of exoticism aside? Furthermore—or, perhaps, conversely—if orientalism is a fantasy representation (and one that serves certain interests) or a form of knowledge the object of which has been defined within an inevitable knowledge-power relationship, that is to say, as well, if it is something that has been created as an object of knowledge in order to be subjected in one and the same move, an object subjected by the knowledge of it, then (once this relationship has been laid bare), how is it possible to enter into a "true" relationship with the reality of the East, one that is neither rooted in fantasy nor determined in advance by the elaboration of this empirical object-subject known as the native? Of course, as can readily be imagined, there is no answering the second question, because it is poorly formulated. There can be no encounter with reality here, because there is no reality behind the native to encounter or know. We have to do with exactly the same structure of the Other as object found in ethnology. That is why the first penetrating—both sympathetic and critical—reader of *Orientalism* was a cultural anthropologist, James Clifford.[6]

There is no "realer" reality behind the native that the Western gaze (say, the gaze of the voyager and flâneur in Eastern climes) can encounter and recognize. The native is a figure: he is, when all is said and done, philology's most remarkable invention, the one that turned the history of the last two centuries upside down. The real problem is that this advent of the native thanks to his becoming-an-object was also, necessarily, a becoming-subject, as with Foucault's madman or criminal as well. The native had to become a subjected subject, as is obvious, but he was in reality (this is the crux of the matter) a self-subjected subject. The significance of this phenomenon is unimaginable. It bears a name, coined by Stathis Gourgouris, the only writer to have taken its full measure, in the extraordinary fourth chapter of his *Dream Nation*. In his wake, we have called this phenomenon of self-subjection "autoscopic mimicry." Chapter 4 of Gourgouris's book, on the "punishment of Philhellenism,"[7] begins by developing the idea of autoscopic mimicry not with regard to the ethnographic nation but, first and foremost, in the European context—more precisely, in that of early-nineteenth-century Germany. It does so in order to explain the emergence of Philhellenism and, in opposition to it, the emergence of Western (and, of course, German) "identity," the kernel of which was formed by what Gourgouris calls a "colonization of the ideal." This is his way of formalizing the remarkable equation (which is not a pure and simple equivalence) between orientalism and philology that we have already described. The formation of the modern nation proceeds, Gourgouris says, philologically, not politically (as we had reason to suspect), in the movement that discovers and re-enacts Greece. But, still more essentially, it proceeds by way of colonization. The desire to repeat the Greek experience peaked, as is well known, in late-eighteenth-century Germany. It was this desire that motivated Hölderlin, both as a translator and a poet. It was what motivated Humboldt to write, in 1807: "Our study of Greek history is a matter quite different from our other historical studies. . . . For us, the Greeks step out of the circle of history. . . . Knowledge of the Greeks is not merely pleasant, useful, or necessary of us—no, in the Greeks alone we find the ideal of that which we ourselves should like to be and to produce."[8] This mad logic of imitation is well known; it has been examined at length by Philippe Lacoue-Labarthe in his essays on Hölderlin.[9] The aim is to be "like them" so as to become wholly ourselves. We have to "imitate" in order to be "independent." What is incredible here is that Humboldt says these things altogether explicitly. It is of course the idealization of the Greek past which allows us Germans to establish our historical identity. What is described in this way, by Humboldt as cited by Gourgouris, is an "appropriation" of the type described at length in my preceding two chapters under the rubric of the aesthetic principle. It is an appropriation of the self, a paradoxical appropriation of what is absolutely specific to ourselves, hence already an "autoscopy," a gaze turned on the self by the self, an inaugural division effected by the gaze. What is more, this multiple "appropriation" (of the self by the self, of the Greeks by the self, of the self by the Greeks) is realized only by means of imitation of the ideal, by a sublimation of the Greek past. This sublimation is what Gourgouris calls, rather surprisingly, after all, the "colonization of the ideal":

> In so far as this sublimation partakes of the ambivalent exercise of mimicry—here, an autoscopic mimicry grounded in the ideal—the classical Bildung is no less than an explicit and programmatic *colonization of the ideal*. (*Dream Nation*, 124; emphasis in original)

Would the theme of appropriation not have sufficed? Why must Gourgouris here introduce the idea of "colonization"? The reason, obviously, is that he is himself motivated by the desire to assimilate the achievements of "postcolonialism" (Edward Said, Partha Chatterjee, Robert Young, Subaltern Studies) in its twofold theorization of the Western and then the ethnographic nation as imaginative form. We should not be unduly troubled by the fact that the first autoscopy, the Western one, is here conceived with regard to the German example, which is then extended—logically speaking, in a second phase, but in fact almost immediately—to the nascent ethnographic nations.[10] As Derrida says, setting out from other categories, the nation is in any case a "philosopheme"; he adds that "nationalistic affirmation is thoroughly philosophical" (formulations that Derrida explains by way of a commentary on Fichte's *To the German Nation*).[11] It was necessary to describe the constitution of the "nation" as a colonization in order to be able to grasp, in a second step, the constitution of the "ethnographic nation" as a repetition, and thus, once again, an imitation modeled after the previous one: that is to say, ultimately, a self-colonization. This is how Gourgouris proceeds. Undeniably, it was the Germans who, in this period, cultivated "Philhellenism" most intensively. Yet this was clearly a European, not just a German, phenomenon. The reader perhaps knows about the extraordinary vogue that the Abbé Barthélémy's *Voyage du jeune Anacharsis en Grèce* enjoyed.[12] The book was published in Paris in 1788, reissued in 1789, saw five further editions between 1792 and 1796 and another twelve by 1821, and was translated into all the European languages, including, in 1819, modern Greek. The Armenians were perfectly well aware of its importance, and they, too, were swept up by the Philhellenist vogue. Father Injijean, in the final volume of his *Darapatum* (History of the Century), a work in eight volumes that saw the light between 1823 and 1828, voices his admiration for Barthélémy's *Voyage* and his desire to see it translated into Armenian. I shall discuss *Darapatum* somewhat later: it is a superb book in modern Armenian, unknown to the philological fraternity down to the present day. As for *Le Voyage du jeune Anacharsis*, it was in fact translated into (classical) Armenian a little later by Father Edward Hurmuz, one of the Mkhitarist Congregation's great translators, and published in Venice in 1843.

Let us now turn back to the "internalization" of the orientalist gaze. I am not certain that this term is altogether adequate, given its psychological overtones; I shall explain what I mean gradually. To begin with, it will already have become clear that orientalism was not restricted to the emergence of the European gaze on the object then constituted as the native of the East, together with a body of knowledge about this object. In reality, orientalism was the process by which the Easterner was compelled to adopt this gaze. From the moment the phenomenon was put in place, orientalism was invincible, since it was adopted, without restrictions, by the native himself. It was adopted both as a way of seeing and as a body of knowledge. What imposed itself was thus twofold. There was, on the one hand, the need to be the object of a gaze. But this gaze could obviously only be the Westerner's. The native of the East was condemned to turn the gaze of the Westerner upon himself once and for all. This is sometimes called philology, "national" or not. And, national or not, it is a pathology that nothing can escape. Philology's all-encompassing ambition was powerful.[13] Every historical object became philological by its nature. However, limiting ourselves for the time being to the most strictly orientalist aspect of philology, we discover that the phenomenon of "internalization" took hold almost immediately, from one end of the Europe of the "nationalities" and "minorities" to the other, spreading, immediately thereafter, to the confines of the Ottoman Empire. What I have repeatedly called the "ethnographic nation" is simply the result of this orientalist autoscopy, which is a philological autoscopy (that is why all psychological explanations fall short of the mark). The phenomenon took root with the Greeks and the Balkan nations (first and foremost, the Serbs) between 1810 and 1815, spearheaded by the grand figures of Adamantios Korais (1748–1833) and Vuk Karadžić (1787–1864).[14] In 1814, Karadžić (a fervent partisan of the vernacular, which was, in his opinion, the only possible candidate for the "literarization" of the language and "nationalization" of the nation) published his *Grammar of Modern Serbian*, which was translated into German by Jakob Grimm in 1824. In 1818, Karadžić's *Serbian Dictionary* (a trilingual dictionary, Serbian-German-Latin) appeared. Three years earlier, he had also issued two series of popular Serbian songs, never before transcribed, that he had collected from his informers. In 1823–24, he succeeded in publishing an initial version of epic narratives in the oral tradition. Thus we can see that Karadžić, very early in the century, played the role that devolved upon several different individuals among the Armenians: Abovean, as far as the plea in favor of the modern language is concerned; Servantsdeants and even Abeghean or Komitas when it came to collecting the oral tradition and popular songs and carrying out the philological work required to publish them. We should also note the immediate interest that Goethe and the brothers Grimm took in the elements of the oral tradition exhumed by Karadžić. The personality and activities of Adamantios Korais are harder to sum up in a few words. Born in Izmir, Korais lived in Paris from 1787 on. It was from Paris that he called on his contemporaries to rise up against the Ottomans. It was likewise in Paris that he laid the groundwork for "Neo-Hellenism" by way of an ongoing defense of the idea of a restored, purified Greek language, editions of ancient Greek authors, and philological and philosophical prefaces: in a word, through his neo-archeological works. It would appear that Korais remained a partisan of the Enlightenment to the end of his days, after being educated in the spirit of its leading thinkers. His immense book series, the Hellenic Library, dates from the period 1807–27, while his most famous "Impromptu Reflections" (cast in the form of prefaces to his editions of ancient authors) date, precisely, from the 1810s. Of course, what is most representative of this author, the most famous of all those associated with the Neo-Hellenistic movement, is not, properly speaking, his editorial work, that is, his philological activity in the sense that the classical age would have recognized as its own. Rather, it is the combination of this editorial activity with his role as a reformer of the language and his calls for the creation of a modern culture, for the "education" of the nation. The commentators (especially Gourgouris) exhibit a certain hesitation when it comes to Korais's place between Enlightenment thinkers (Étienne Bonnot de Condillac, language as a form of knowledge) and nineteenth-century neo-archeology. This hesitation reappears with the grand Armenian figures (all of them Mkhitarist monks) who inaugurated modern philology and the discourse on the nation, while also, incidentally, beginning to write in vernacular Armenian, unsystematically to be sure (that is, with no will to bring about reforms and initiate a politics of language), but also without feeling any particular anguish or dramatic sense of disaster.

EXCHANGING GLANCES

The Armenians, at any event, did not lag behind when it came to philological mimicry and autoscopy, for national philology begins, in their case, too, at exactly the same moment. Geographically, of course, they found themselves a bit further to the east than the Greeks and the Balkan peoples, but they had, let us not forget, a European bridgehead in Venice. The Congregation of Mkhitarist Fathers threw itself wholeheartedly into the movement of philological autoscopy, with which, moreover, it ultimately identified without reserve. A "Neo-Armenism" accordingly came into being on the model of the Greek "Neo-Hellenism" of the day. (In contrast, there was, to the best of my knowledge, no direct relationship between Armenians and Serbs.) If this was already a form of nationalism, it was, like that of the Greeks and Serbs, a "diasporan nationalism."

The relations Lord Byron cultivated with members of the Congregation during his 1816–17 stay in Venice offer an especially telling illustration of the link between Neo-Armenism and Neo-Hellenism. Neo-Armenism, to repeat, emerged in the second decade of the nineteenth century in a climate of European Philhellenism, which had, of course, a determining influence on nascent Greek "nationalism," but just as powerfully shaped the philological auto-invention of the nation among the Armenians. As for

Byron, he had become acquainted with the writings of Adamantios Korais during his first, 1810–11, stay in Greece. While his feelings toward his Greek contemporaries were not particularly warm, he was nevertheless one of the foremost supporters of their internal struggle to free themselves (psychologically, to begin with) from the Ottoman yoke. The tremendous success of his 1812 *Childe Harold's Pilgrimage* is a sign, not to say a symptom, of the dimensions that Philhellenism had taken on in Europe. Four years later, in 1816, Byron left England, never to return. It was during his fall 1816 stay in Venice that he met the members of the Mkhitarist Congregation and took it into his head to learn Armenian. It should be pointed out that this odd resolution differed somewhat from his long-standing propensity to learn the languages of the natives. In Venice in 1816, the language of the natives was the Venetian dialect of Italian; it was certainly not Armenian. Moreover, the Armenian that Byron was taught by his main contact among the Mkhitarist monks, Father Harutiun Avkerian (whose Europeanized name was Pascal Aucher), was not the vernacular Armenian that the monks spoke among themselves, but, of course, the classical language, the only form of Armenian which, in their view, was worthy of being taught and learned. Byron did not get very far in his study of Armenian. At the time, he was preoccupied by his marital problems, his divorce, the terrible campaign of denigration of him orchestrated by his wife and, finally, by his Venetian mistress. He did, however, learn the language well enough to make a few translations (or to pretend that he had), and he agreed to co-edit an Armenian grammar in English, even after Father Aucher turned down the preface that Byron had written for it. All these matters are well known, even if they hold, all in all, a very small place in the English poet's correspondence. The most interesting thing, however, is the place Byron implicitly assigned the Armenians and, conversely, the role they made him play. Let us put it simply: the Armenians were surrogates for the Greeks. Like the Greeks, they lived under the Ottoman yoke. Like the Greeks, they needed to be psychologically emancipated from the domination of their masters, or to emancipate themselves from it. And Byron reacted very harshly when Father Aucher rejected his preface, probably because of an allusion it contained to the pashas who had "devastated the region in which God created man in his image."[15]

However, a great deal more than this was involved, because the Armenians themselves came forward as surrogates for the Greeks—in a word, as ersatz Greeks. It is certain that there was no "Philarmenism" comparable to Philhellenism in the Europe of the day. The Mkhitarist fathers consequently attempted to pull themselves up by the bootstraps and achieve visibility in Europe (and, consequently, in their own eyes as well) within the framework of the Philhellenist movement. Their aim was to make the Armenians an object of the European gaze and then to bask in it. But the European gaze was Philhellenic. The Armenians therefore had to sow confusion so that, profiting from an ambiguity, they could occupy the Greeks' place in the European field of vision and thus engender the Philarmenism that the Mkhitarist fathers so badly wanted. How was that possible?

Before answering, I have to say something about the Byron cult that the Mkhitarists had been building up from the 1817 episode on. The monastery on the Venetian island of San Lazzaro possesses a small library that is also known as "Byron's Room." The museum has piously preserved several paintings bearing on the poet's visit. A part of the garden in which olive trees have been planted has been named after one of these paintings (unless it is the other way around): it is known as "Lord Byron's Olive Grove."[16] The olive trees here are those to whose shade Father Harutiun and Byron were in the habit of retiring. This short description shows how deep an impression Byron left on the little island and, accordingly, how desperately nascent Neo-Armenism, that is, the national imagination in its infancy, needed Philarmenism. The only problem is that the national imagination has, in the case of the Mkhitarist fathers, remained at exactly the same infantile stage in which it was then, in the 1810s.

How could the Mkhitarists, then, pull the wool over their own eyes and divert the Philhellenic gaze in order to induce it to become "Philarmenic"? This was entirely within the realm of possibility, for the simple reason that the works of the Christian High Middle Ages had long since been translated from Greek into Armenian (for the most part, between 450 and 750 A.D.) and were, in some cases, extant only in their Armenian translations. This held for a number of texts by Philo of Alexandria as well as Eusebius' *Chronicle*. In 1804, a Mkhitarist father named Zohrabian, who had only just graduated from the seminary, aired his unhappiness over European scholars' ignorance of "Armenian literature" in a letter. "To arouse their curiosity," he went on, "I tell them about Eusebius' *Chronicle* and also about Philo, so that they will respect Armenian literature and take an interest in studying it; the number of those who wish to become acquainted with it is growing daily."[17] European "respect" for "Armenian literature" and Armenian solicitation of the Western gaze would thus come by way of Eusebius of Caeserea and Philo. In 1807, Father Agonts, then the Abbot of the Congregation, again spoke (in a letter to the historian Father Mikaël Chamchean, who was in Constantinople at the time) about European philologists' enthusiasm and pending plans to turn out a Latin translation of the *Chronicle*. This dependence on the European gaze (audible in the lyrical, perfectly childish tone in which these very learned monks report on the Europeans' interest in letter after letter) is, for us, the distinguishing feature of the period.

The translation announced by Father Agonts was indeed to see the light, but in wildly improbable circumstances worth pausing over for a moment, simply for the pleasure of the anecdote and in order to savor the ridiculousness of the situation. The task of translating Eusebius was entrusted to the Congregation's best philologist of the day, Father Mkrtich (Baptist) Aucher, the brother of Pascal Aucher, who, be it recalled, was to teach Byron Armenian in 1816–17. The story goes that this unhappy decision aroused the anger (or jealousy) of Father Zohrabian, who considered himself to be the discoverer and promoter of the Greek treasures in the Congregation's possession; he is therefore supposed to have purloined a copy of the original manuscript and run off with it to Milan, where, at all events, he diligently translated Eusebius' *Chronicle* into

Latin with the help of a Milanese scholar, Angelo Mai, and then published it with considerable fanfare. This was in 1818.[18] Zohrabian, needless to say, paid for these shenanigans with his exclusion from the Congregation. Be it added that the date of the book's appearance is uncertain, because (as we shall now see) this translation had a competitor in Father Aucher's. Angelo Mai, then in charge of Milan's Biblioteca Ambrosiana, was a Jesuit priest who had disinterred a great many previously unpublished and even unknown ancient Greek and Latin texts. While collaborating with Zohrabian, he wrote *De Philonis Iudaei et Eusebii Pamphili scriptis ineditis aliorumque libris ex armeniaca lingua convertendis*, an eighty-page essay on the thirteenth-century manuscript that contained, among other texts, Philo's works in Armenian translation. Mai's essay dates from 1816. We should also mention the friendship that sprang up, a little later, between Mai and the poet Giacomo Leopardi, a friendship to which we owe Leopardi's short book on the product of Mai's 1818 collaboration with Father Zohrabian: *Annotazioni sopra la Cronica d'Eusebio*.[19] Meanwhile, back in Venice, Father Aucher had prepared his own translation of Eusebius' *Chronicle*, but was unable to publish it, for reasons that are not directly related to our story, but interesting in their own right: from 1815 to 1817, the printing-house at Saint Lazarus was closed on the Pope's orders, which were motivated by the investigation, underway since 1815, of Father Chamchean, who was strongly suspected of having taken his distance from Catholic orthodoxy in his unpublished *Vahan Havadoy* (The Shield of Faith), a work stolen from his apartments in Constantinople by a zealous servitor of Rome and submitted to the critical regard of the guardians of the purity of the dogma. Mkrtich Aucher's translation was not issued until January 1819, in Venice, yet includes the words "first translation" in its title (as does the other translation, incidentally).[20] All this brouhaha as well as the display of scholarship, erudition, and contained or uncontained rage date from the period in which Lord Byron was making his matinal trips to the Island of Saint Lazarus to take his Armenian lessons and then stroll under the cypresses and olive trees with Father Pascal (the learned translator's brother), who of course told the English poet about the importance of the Greek books of which there existed only one copy on earth, in Armenian translation. Byron faithfully relayed what he was told in his letters to his publisher, John Murray: "I can assure you that they have some very curious books and MS., chiefly translations from Greek originals now lost."[21] I suspect that Giacomo Leopardi was carried away by the same sort of philological, neo-archeological fever a few years later, when Angelo Mai acquainted him with the Armenian-Greek *Chronicle*. The Mkhitarist fathers, although they were fine connoisseurs of Italian poetry, never said a word about the subject.

I do not know if the reader can fully savor the piquancy of the situation. Admittedly, Byron's 1817 visit to Venice and the double publication of Eusebius of Caesarea in 1818 and 1819 are only the stuff of anecdote. Yet they are extraordinarily revelatory nonetheless. Byron was, at the time, European Philhellenism's most renowned representative. His 1812 *Childe Harold* describes a pilgrimage to a present in ruins and to an archeological Greece, even if Byron himself was entirely committed to "Neo-Hellenic modernity," a conception of Greek culture as a modern culture, which makes him altogether "exceptional in the discourse of Philhellenism." Here I am, once again, following Gourgouris, who writes: "His is a Philhellenism of modernity, a Philhellenism of the Orient one might say, and thus a perfect illustration as well of the astonishing relation between exoticism, orientalism, and *flânerie*"(*Dream Nation*, 139).[22] In fact, there is no contradiction or even ambiguity here. It is indeed within this twofold relationship, to an archeological past on the one hand and the present of the native who was its heir on the other, that European orientalism was constituted, together with, in reaction to it, the orientalism of the modern Greeks (and Armenians). There is nothing surprising about this. In the moment in which the orientalist himself is coming into being, he gathers up the elements of a past that is not his own, introduces historicity into scattered elements that had remained outside history of any sort, transforms all the texts and other vestiges of the past into so many "documents," and thereby creates the nation's testament in the guise of its "culture" (something that sustains the existence of the nation in its testamentary reality: the nation receives from its own past the message it has itself invented under the name of culture, a message that, in its evanescence, makes the nation what it is). But the same orientalist has to do, after all, with the present and those who live in it. He must therefore establish a relationship or, at least, find a modus vivendi with the present. He can decide to neglect it, above all when this present seems to him to be nationalistic—even if nationalistic thought is merely the inversion of orientalism, inasmuch as it subjects the historical facts to exactly the same operations. Alternatively, he can decide to take an interest in the present and hence to approach the native, this newly visible product of philology and its historicization of history.[23] All the orientalist travelers of the nineteenth century—Byron was one of the first—did no more than approach this mysterious native, Eastern, Greek, and, sometimes, Armenian. What Gourgouris says of Hellenism thus holds, in fact, for all orientalism and, as well, for the "Philarmenism" that the Mkhitarist fathers wished to bring into existence (and whose emergence they witnessed as if witnessing a miracle) with the help of Byron's visit and the sudden interest taken by European philologists (and poets) in Eusebius: "First, we can speak of a Philhellenism of ancient traces. . . ." I here interrupt the quotation in order to replace the word *Philhellenism* with the word *Philarmenism* in Gourgouris's sentence (my alterations are in italic):

> First we can speak of a *Philarmenism* of ancient traces, which seeks and enjoys its intoxication amidst ruins and legends—this constitutes *Philarmenism's* explicit utterance. Second, we can speak of a *Philarmenism* of a contemporary resurrection of ancient traces, if you will. Byron exemplifies this second site, which is inextricably interwoven with the Oriental. (*Dream Nation*, 139)

Why do I take the liberty of thus changing *Philhellenism* to *Philarmenism* in a statement that seems very obviously to center on the attitude of European travelers and philologists in Greece and the East? Because, as I must now remind my reader, the philologist's and the orientalist traveler's seeing and knowing (*voir-savoir*) is not an external seeing and knowing that leaves the native it takes as its object in a passive position. It is the seeing and knowing of the native himself, and has the native himself as its object; it is the imposition of the gaze on the native. The native springs into existence when he ardently solicits the philologist's gaze, in accordance with a necessity inherent in the configuration of the native. Once all this has been pointed out, it can readily be seen that the term *internalization* of the orientalist gaze is of no use or, at any rate, rather misleading. For it is now clear that the native has no "inside" in which to internalize the orientalist gaze, since he is invented at the very instant that this solicitation of the gaze occurs. I shall nevertheless continue to employ the term from time to time for the sake of convenience. At all events, orientalism is precipitated in the historical moment when these figures are ranged face-to-face in their reciprocal unity: the philologist-traveler on the one hand and the native on the other. The philologist-traveler does not have to come from Europe. The Mkhitarist monks were quite capable of playing all the roles in question. They could be the objects of their own philology; they could travel toward themselves. As the occasion demanded, they could also, as Armenians, be the natives and the archeological remains toward which the philologist's gaze was turned and the traveler's footsteps were directed. This and this alone comprises orientalism's distinguishing feature. Ultimately, Byron's stay with the Mkhitarist fathers in Venice and his odd interest in the Armenians, which waned after a few months, are in no sense catalysts and, for that reason, remain anecdotal. Yet they are revelatory in the sense that they clearly bring out the nature of autoscopic imitation and identification, of the circulation of the gaze, and of the inaugural relationship with the self that constitutes the national imagination in the archeological stage. Philology's gaze is, here, Byron's; it is the orientalist gaze. This is how the "transposition of European traveling flâneurs onto indigenous, native philologists" comes about. (Gourgouris, *Dream Nation*, 151). What is more, the orientalist gaze, once internalized as the indigenous philological gaze, endows the self with a historical depth that puts it in relation with a history and calls on an elaborate archeology of texts and inscriptions (and, soon enough, legends) to bolster its identity. It is also, of course, a gaze situated in the present, a present resurrection of ancient traces.

The irony of the Armenian case (here too, Byron's presence in Venice, at the very moment when the Armenian-Greek Eusebius was being translated into Latin so that he might exist in the civilized world's eyes, clearly exposes this irony for what it is) resides in the fact that Armenian autoscopic mimicry is a threefold mimicry. The early-nineteenth-century Greek intellectuals invented Neo-Hellenism by internalizing the Philhellenic gaze of the Germans and, secondarily, the French. They invented the nation by way of this reduplication, thanks to which they saw themselves philologically as orientalists by reiterating the initial act of mimicry or the first imitation, the Germans' (who obviously could become what they were only by imitating the

Greeks: as we know today, everyone couched the matter in these terms, from Hölder-lin through Humboldt to, thereafter, Nietzsche and beyond). But the unfortunate Armenians were not lucky enough to be Hellenes, descendants of the ancient Greeks. On the other hand, it was their good fortune to be able to present themselves to the Western world (and thus, autoscopically, to their own gaze) as surrogate Hellenes, Hellenes by proxy, since no other nation possessed Eusebius' and Philo's unpublished writings, which had for fourteen centuries been waiting in their archives to be trium-phantly presented to the Europeans 1,400 years after they were composed. This is how the Armenians became a nation, with or without Lord Byron—thanks to this substi-tutive triumph. (Have I given the reader a sense of how ridiculous I find this triumph, because of both the puerile excitation that informed it and the Armenians' enthusias-tic delight in existing only in the gaze of the Other?) Of course, this process of becom-ing a nation had a prehistory in its turn, since the Mkhitarists had first to have encountered Europe, to establish themselves there, to collect mountains of manuscripts by buying them from Armenian monasteries wherever they were to be found, using funds provided by the Vatican or the Most Christian states of Europe, and this throughout the eighteenth century; they had to learn Greek and Latin over a period of several generations, so that they could ultimately boast of having scholars of the caliber of a Mikaël Chamchean by the end of the eighteenth century and a Zohrabian or the Aucher brothers early in the nineteenth, and could take pride not only in the fact that they had the *Chronicle* of Eusebius of Caesarea in archives that were more than a thousand years old, but, above all, in their ability to turn out a critical edition of the *Chronicle* for the scholarly community of the day. This is a long list of precondi-tions. These preconditions and this prehistory merit examination in their own right. Obviously, I cannot undertake such an examination here. To conclude this section of the present chapter, let us say that Neo-Armenism, like the Neo-Hellenism that Gour-gouris has studied, was "an immanently antiquarian discourse, which is why during the nineteenth century its most elaborate proponents were, besides history, the most refined of philological disciplines: folklore and archeology" (*Dream Nation*, 142). But let us also recall that, in Philarmenism's first period, the one in which it was manufac-tured and internalized while the national imagination was in its archeological stage, it took its greatest pleasures in ruins and monuments rather than "legends." As we have already seen, the interest in "legends" and, along with it, the invention of "folklore" as a philological discipline, did not crystallize in the form of a project until around 1840; and it was not until around 1874 that it took the form of concrete work in the field.

TRAVELERS AND ARCHEOLOGISTS

We have not yet seen all the surprises that this inaugural moment of the establishment of the national imagination holds in store. We now turn to two Mkhitarist monks who were, by themselves, the grand artisans of modern Armenian: Father Minas

Pzhshgean (1777–1851) and Father Lucas Injijean (1758–1833), both of whom I have already mentioned. Pzhshgean came from Trebizond, a fact that has its importance for our understanding of his literary career. Injijean, like many other Mkhitarist fathers, was born in Constantinople. He was a nephew of the illustrious Mikaël Chamchean, the first great critical, if not modern, historian among the Armenians, and his ambition was to follow in the footsteps of his uncle. Everything of importance published in vernacular Armenian between 1790 and 1820 was the work of these two men, Pzhshgean and Injijean, or of others working under their lead. In 1791, Injijean published a geography manual for the use of the students of the Congregation.[24] It is, to my knowledge, the first book published in the vernacular in Venice since the appearance of Mkhitar's catechism in 1727. These two Mkhitarist fathers wrote comedies in the vernacular (laced with Turkish and Greek) that were performed by their students, in accordance with Mkhitarist tradition, which they contented themselves with simply continuing, at least on this point. None of these plays was ever published. It was, again, Injijean who in 1798 launched the publication of a *Taregirk'* (Almanac), the first Armenian periodical in the modern language. This Almanac was published in Venice and distributed mainly in Constantinople. It was also in his native Constantinople that Injijean later began to issue, again in the vernacular, the periodical *Yeghanak Biuzantean* (Seasons of Byzantium), followed, from 1812 on, by *Ditak Biuzantean* (The Observer of Byzantium); both appeared in more or less regular fashion from 1803 to 1820.[25] The second of these periodicals was the organ of the Literary Society that Injijean helped found, *Arsharuneayts Ënkerut'iun*. This Society presented itself as a sort of club; there were several other examples of such clubs in the latter half of the nineteenth century. Its avowed aim was to promote the Armenians' education and modernization (the word used at the time was "enlightenment"); the review offered its readers political and scientific news from the civilized world. In 1815, Injijean published a short book, again in the vernacular, entitled *Azgaser* (The Patriot), in which he explained that one had to "love" one's nation. These were the major steps toward a self-conscious nationalism, cast in the form of a doctrine addressed to "the people," that is, to readers without much literary education. Later, between 1824 and 1828, Injijean released, in the vernacular, his eight-volume *Darapatum* (History of the Century), which I mentioned in passing earlier. This was a truly extraordinary work, by virtue of both its ambition and scope. Injijean set himself the goal of retracing all of European political history from 1750 to 1800, and of presenting, in the last two of its eight volumes, all the European artists and scholars who had been active in the eighteenth century. At the same time, *Darapatum* is, of course, a work of popularization, composed partly with the help of Italian encyclopedias and written in the Western Armenian that the Mkhitarist fathers favored at the time, a language that they made no effort to correct, that was close to spoken Armenian and teemed with Turkish words. This by no means diminishes its value, even if Injijean was frequently held up to scorn later, once vernacular Armenian had been transformed into a literary language.

For his part, Father Pzhshgean composed in 1812, in the vernacular, the first Armenian musicological book.[26] He also produced the first modern Armenian translation of a literary work, *Robinson Crusoe*, which saw the light in 1817. The intentions informing this enterprise, too, were didactic: the translation was intended for use in the schools. Nonetheless, it was a literary translation into Western Armenian, the first of its kind, produced well before there existed anything resembling a literature in this language. Finally, in 1819, Pzhshgean published what must be considered the first real book in the modern language written without a didactic or scholastic purpose: a text, published in Venice, called *Patmut'iun Pontosi* (History of Pontus). I shall say a few words about it, because this book that inaugurated "literature" in Western Armenian has a certain importance for the questions of interest to us here, the beginnings of the national imagination as a reaction to European orientalism and the archeological expression of that imagination in the 1810s. We must, to begin with, take note of an important fact: this book (and, massively, its author) was crossed off the maps or charts that the national memory drew up in producing its own history. In fact, as I have already indicated, the whole neo-archeological moment of the process of becoming a nation was effaced from the nation's nationalistic memory. The result is that Pzhshgean and Injijean are utterly absent from the national and nationalistic tradition, not only as writers, educators, and philologists, but in yet another of their capacities: as architects of the modern language and thus, already, of the nation. The Armenian nationalistic tradition stubbornly repeats that Abovean introduced the use of the modern language—a pure and simple falsehood consequent upon the heroization of the native. Of course, Pzhshgean and Injijean had, emphatically, nothing to say about the native. The native did not exist for them. He had not yet manifested himself as such. Furthermore, while their aim was to "translate," they never proposed to translate themselves. Self-translation would have called for a manifestation of the native and an aesthetic project. Among the Western Armenians, as we now know, the aesthetic project of "self-translation" emerged a century later, with the *Mehyan* group. In the second decade of the nineteenth century, the encounter with the present passed by way of the translation of the foreign(er), not the self. We are here in the period of the initial internalization of Europe's archeological, idealizing gaze—in a word, the orientalizing gaze.

In another sense, the encounter with the present could only involve the ruins and monuments of the past, and the native as ruin and monument. This is the reason that, in this first phase of the process of becoming a nation, the Mkhitarist fathers never considered traveling toward the native who was the bearer of legends, the one who lived on his "native" soil. They always traveled toward the exterior, those in exile, those who represented the vestiges of an ancient civilization. But this is also the explanation for the fact that, after Pzhshgean, the Mkhitarist fathers, inspired by their dream of possessing a national epic in classical Armenian, would not again produce vernacular translations until late in the century. For the orientalism shaped by archeology, the native was incapable of speaking. The Mhkitarists would have been astounded to see him producing literature. Among the Western Armenians, the native did not speak until 1874, if not 1914. I say this in a polemical spirit. Literary criticism and the "science of literature" in Soviet Armenia never understood the relationship that the Mkhitarists established with the vernacular. To assess the Congregation's literary production, they made use of ostensibly Marxist, anticlerical, or, simply, nationalistic categories, obviously without so much as suspecting that there lurked, behind the Mkhitarists' classical dream, orientalist archaeology and the tragic belatedness of the emergence of the native.

THE TRAVELS OF FATHER PZHSHGEAN

What, then, is this *Patmut'iun Pontosi*, or History of Pontus? Pzhshgean was a traveler. True, the Mkhitarist monks traveled a great deal in order to pay visits to their communities, which were scattered throughout Europe and the Ottoman Empire. But Pzhshgean was the first to conceive the idea of becoming a literary traveler and publishing a record of the results of his travels.[27] He went on his maiden journey in 1808, visiting the communities of Hungary, Bulgaria, Rumania, and Moldavia. Why this predilection for Eastern Europe? The practical reason was that Pzhshgean could visit the communities converted to Catholicism that were settled there. But behind this obvious reason lay another, a wish characteristic of this writer and the project that fueled it: Pzhshgean was searching for the traces of an old wave of emigration, one that, from the eleventh to the fourteenth centuries, had led the Armenians of Ani to the cities of Pontus, thence to the Crimea, and on to Transylvania and even Poland. After his 1808 voyage, Pzhshgean settled for a time in Constantinople, founded a Mkhitarist secondary school in Pera, and served as its principal until 1817, when he returned to the town of his birth, Trebizond, and tried, unsuccessfully, to found a new school there. It is not known why he failed. It was, in any case, during this 1817–19 period that he traveled, on his own witness, throughout the Pontus region (on mission as an "apostolic vicar")[28] and wrote his book on its history, a book of the sort that we would today call either a "tourist guide," modeled on Pausanias, or a travel narrative, on the model that had been provided by Arrian in antiquity and by Joseph Pitton de Tournefort in the seventeenth century. Moreover, Pzhshgean had works of the two last-named writers to hand as he wrote, Arrian's *Periplus Ponti Euxini* and Tournefort's *Relation d'un voyage du Levant,* both of which he cites and even occasionally corrects. When all is said and done, we cannot even be sure whether Pzhshgean really traveled to all the places and "archeological" sites he mentions. On a number of occasions, he takes the information he gives straight from Tournefort. In other instances (the northern Black Sea coast), it is all but certain that he simply follows an ancient source or repeats information he has learned by hearsay. We should also mention Pzhshgean's third important voyage, an 1820 journey that took him first to Germany and Poland and then to the Crimea (where he was later to settle, remaining there practically to the end of his days). He conflated his two voyages to Eastern Europe, undertaken in 1808 and 1820, to produce a single, continuous travel narrative (this time, in classical Armenian) that he published in 1830 under the title *Chanaparhordut'iun i Lehastan yev hayl koghmans bnakeals i Haykazants' sereloy i nakhneats' Ani k'aghak'in* (Journey to Poland and Other Places Inhabited by Armenians from Ancient Ani). This book is today used and cited by historians of Armenian emigration and those specializing in the history of Ani. But to limit it to such uses is not to do it full justice. We need to account for the fact that it is still (or already) a work of geographical archeology whose author traces the trajectory of a voyage realized on the model of the voyages undertaken by early-nineteenth-century orientalist travelers: in other words, that it is a philologist's voyage in the natives' present, although that present never appears as such. In particular, Pzhshgean (as author) never takes an interest in the current situation of the communities through which he travels; he does not record what the living members of these communities have to say about their more or less recent history. He regards these communities as nothing more than vestiges, traces, monuments, ruins. He describes churches, copies colophons, records the inscriptions he finds on monuments; he never concerns himself with the "culture" characteristic of what remained of these Armenians, who had been living in exile for centuries. The living interest him only as monuments; that is to say, very precisely, as traces of, and witnesses to, their own past. For Pzhshgean, that past was summed up in the fact that their ancestors hailed from Ani. That is why the title of the book is careful to point out that the author has traveled to places inhabited by the Armenians from that city.

In short, working in the archeological mode of the national imagination, Pzhshgean, as writer and traveler, is not interested in the living. His interest is in "survivors"; living people interest him only insofar as they are "from" somewhere. He seeks, everywhere, traces of their origins. It is, plainly, an archeological desire that is at work here, an intoxication with the trace, and a transformation of the present into testimony, all things that we can grasp here virtually in the pure state, because it is here that they are expressed for the first time and because they appear in embryonic form, prior to their transformation into history and philological science. At the same time, because it is a question of a real (if stylized) voyage, we can here see with the naked eye the inaugural movement that gave rise to the philologist-traveler, the scholar who approaches the native even before the native has been manifest as a figure capable of talking about himself. This movement toward the native *infans* is simultaneously a movement that "genealogizes" or historicizes the present, because it always reads it as a palimpsest in which one can discern its historical origins. Pzhshgean goes so far as to hear, in the language spoken by some of these Armenians, a relationship with the intonations and locutions of the Armenians of Trebizond, who were themselves, in fact or in the author's imagination, descendants of inhabitants of Ani.[29] This discovery of a linguistic filiation, a "family resemblance," is quite striking: it would have been quite simply unthinkable twenty years earlier. Visible between the lines here is the historicity of language, that is, the characteristic feature of the nascent philology of the early nineteenth century. A language can be perceived as a residue of its own past; it can have an internal history that allows it to be transformed in accordance with its own laws, even while preserving within itself, in fossil form, the stages of its development. A language speaks in the present, yet one can hear Ani's past in it. The historicized structure of the native is already fully present here. The native is never just someone whom one hears and sees now. If he speaks, one hears, through him, the centuries of which he is the remnant or fossilized vestige—what Gourgouris calls the "trace." A brief citation will suffice to show how Pzhshgean very precisely defines his intentions as an archeological traveler and his stubborn quest for the ancient in the modern, that is, his way of historicizing the present and giving the national imagination form:

> To round out the history of our journey, we have had to furnish indispensable information about Ani and its inhabitants. It is now time to move on to a description [*storagrut'iun*] of the cities through which I traveled. The special aim of my history is to describe the cities inhabited by our compatriots from Ani who are, today, scattered throughout the world and whom it seemed to us appropriate to visit in 1820, after our first visit of 1808. We shall present the narrative of these two voyages together. . . . We deal rapidly with places in which none of our compatriots are living. Where we encounter Armenians whom we consider to be children of Ani, in contrast, we pause in order to examine their history and old buildings. Moreover, since the old inhabitants of Ani fled not only to Poland, but also to the new Russia and the Crimea, where they built many buildings, we have decided to visit all the sites of the peninsula one by one, in order to describe them as well, supplying such geographical information as is indispensable. (*Voyage to Poland*, 91)

In what does the orientalism of such a project reside? Quite simply in the circumstance that this is the self-conscious description of a voyage toward the self and, consequently, of an orientalist voyage, the first of its kind cast in philological form, a voyage toward a historical and historicized self—the description, in fact, of a double voyage, in 1808 and 1820, at the beginning and end of the astonishing decade in which we have seen philological orientalism come into being, provoking an immediate reaction on the part of the natives in the guise of the emergence of a national imagination. The native who is exiled from himself because he is exiled from his fatherland must first come to know the history of "his" past in order to know himself. Who if not the philologist can provide him with the memory of this past? Moreover, Pzhshgean clearly says in his prologue that Ani here serves as a paradigm. "It is preferable to leave all that to one side [the successive disasters and the history of this people's tragedies] so that, in the narrative [*vep*] of this trek northwards, we may consider only the events that took place in Ani, the capital, since a majority of the Armenians living along this route [the one the author followed as he traveled toward the north] are descendants of Ani; it is therefore desirable that they know what happened to the city and learn its history, the history of their former fatherland" (*Voyage to Poland*, 4). The author accordingly proceeds to preface his travel narrative with a history in the proper sense, that is, a history of the grandeur and downfall of Ani. There can be no identifiable present without history and, therefore, without philology. By means of a voyage (and by that means alone), the new world, the world of the native, is opened up to time. Conversely, it is the opening up to time, the location of the native in time, and the decrypting of the signs of the past in the native's present, which invest the voyage with significance. Thus we plainly have the whole genealogical program of nascent archeology here—the nascent archeology for which, as the reader may recall, the Mkhitarist fathers were to utilize the general term *storagrut'iun* (description), which they used so often in the special sense they gave to the word that, in the nineteenth century, it came to mean nothing but the operation of "reading" ruins as traces, and thus the operation of opening something up to time through the intervention of an archeological traveler. We shall see this again in a moment with Injijean.

The most astounding thing, perhaps, is that between Pzhshgean's two journeys to Transylvania and Poland, we find that other voyage (the subject of the first book written in modern Armenian), the ostensible voyage to Pontus, the region that, of course, served as the Ani Armenians' first refuge, a region that the author knew perfectly well but, above all, one set apart by the fact that it was much more heavily populated by Greeks than by Armenians. Thus we already have, with *History of Pontus*, a geographical archeology doubled by a travel narrative; here, however, the monuments that the author describes, the sites through which he passes, the ruins the inventory of which he serenely draws from Arrian and Tournefort, and the churches whose inscriptions he records are all, without exception, of Greek origin, vestiges of antiquity or the Byzantine Middle Ages (prolonged for a few more decades, in the Pontus region, as the Greek kingdom of Trebizond). Only occasionally does Pzhshgean describe Armenian churches, which, more often than not, are converted Greek churches in which the oldest inscriptions are in Greek or else commemorate the moment when the church was handed over to the Armenians. Thus we find exactly the same structure that we earlier saw at work in the emergence of Neo-Armenism, an emergence patterned after that of Neo-Hellenism: it was based on both a diabolical and yet comic trading of glances involving the solicitation of the European's promptly internalized gaze, and the confusion maintained (consciously or not) with the help of ancient translations, a confusion between what was Greek and what was Armenian. It is easy to understand, at the same time, why the nationalist tradition has completely ignored Pzhshgean, although he was the representative par excellence of the national imagination in its archeological phase. Pzhshgean turns to the exile, not the native. He remains wholly within the bounds of geographical archeology. He never so much as entertains the notion that it is the native's utterance that has to be heard and retransmitted to the native (retransmitted to him as if the utterance that the native hears, thanks to this restitution, is the one he himself made). In brief, even if the whole archeological project is present here and even if this project is already wholly informed by orientalist autoscopy, the native is here only surmised. What is more, all this is too Greek. The superimposition of things Armenian on things Greek and the substitution of the former for the latter are not well done; they do not go unnoticed. The mimicry is too obvious. Neo-Armenism, here, is too patently born in exile, rather than on its native, ancestral soil. Were things to continue along these lines, there could be no fatherland. It is all too plain, in this birth of the idea and image of the nation, that the translation that presides over the formation of a national identity in the orientalist exchange of glances (the translation of Greek into Armenian, for example) is the experience of a limit or frontier. But frontiers are always ambiguous. They unite as much as they separate. Hence the translation, the mimicry, had to be effaced as well. It is like the Hamshentsi of the Trebizond region, known as the *kes-kes*, the half-this-half-that, about whom Pzhshgean writes repeatedly in his book: no one knows to which side they belong. Are they Armenians or Turks? Christians or Muslims? They themselves do not know. This is intolerable. Once the national imagination reaches the auto-ethnographic stage, it moves rapidly to forget all this; it sweeps its uncertain beginnings aside. At the same stroke, it effaces the Hamshentsi from the national map for two centuries and, with them, Pzhshgean as well, who was not national enough because he was not nativist enough. For us, however, coming two centuries later, it is apparent how these uncertain, hesitant beginnings and these all-too-revelatory "first times" were the bearers of a different kind of thought, and that the nationalism of the rectified national imagination, the one that rewrites history to its own ends, was not inevitable, even if it was, in the form it took, a historical necessity.

ARCHEOLOGY'S "DESCRIPTION"

It remains to describe Lucas Injijean's archeological project. Before I do, I would like to observe once again that my objective is not to provide a general account of Armenian philology in its early stages. The aim is rather to show how philology functions when it belatedly invents the figure of the native and how, with that as its starting point, the very special form we have called the ethnographic nation is put in place by means of autoscopic mimicry. Secondly, I would like to show that it is indispensable to take the nineteenth-century emergence of the ethnographic nations into consideration if we are to account for the appearance of philology as a discursive form at the turn of the nineteenth century. However—and this is what makes studies of the present kind difficult—it must not be supposed that the description of embryonic Armenian philology is simply an illustration of phenomena that occurred independently of it. It is true that scholarship has, to date, managed quite well without this description. But it is also true that it has never told us anything about either the native in his twofold anthropological structure or nationalizing autoscopy and, therefore, it has told us nothing about philology's part in the process of "nationalization." One has to pause over the history of the national imagination in order to bring these matters into the light. They are invisible to the naked eye. In the final analysis, we are plainly still dealing with philology here.

The first works of philology, then, were archeological and geographical. They were descriptions of places. They did not depict them as they were in modern times, in the philologists' day. To do the kind of archeology involved, the nascent philologist did not have to go somewhere and carry out an archeological dig. Places were described as they had been in ancient times; these descriptions were constructed, purely and simply, on the basis of texts. It was a question of past places that were patiently recreated, one by one, in writing. But how does one create the places of the past, if not by putting them in the context of a geography of the present? In that sense, philology does not escape the present, even if the project presents itself as being strictly archeological. The oddest thing, in the Armenians' case, is that there were, at all events, no sites to go visit. The subject people of the Ottoman Empire could not create archeological sites and organize digs, even if they wanted to, as they almost never did. There was only one exception, at the very end of the century, in, precisely, Ani, the Bagratunis' ancient capital. The archeological team that planned the dig, mapped the area, and returned from its work in the field with a significant quantity of photographic documents was headed by a Russian, the renowned Nikolai Marr. This took place in what was already a different period, one that no longer had much to do with the general project, a geographical project, of philological "description" pursued by the Mkhitarists in the grand decade, the second decade of the nineteenth century. What did such description entail? We now turn to that question.

The task of archeological and geographical "description" was successfully carried out for the first time by Lucas Injijean. This is the same Mkhitarist monk who, in 1791, wrote, in modern Armenian, a general geography for beginners; who published, in 1798, his *Almanac*, the first Armenian periodical in the vernacular; who wrote an educational defense of patriotism entitled *Azgaser* in 1815; and who later, in 1824, began issuing his voluminous encyclopedic history of the eighteenth century. Injijean made two or perhaps even three new attempts to complete his archeological project. We have a book of his published in 1822, called *Storagrut'iun hin Hayastani* (Description of Ancient Armenia), as well as a posthumous 1835 work in three magnificent volumes entitled *Hnakhosut'iun ashkharhakragan Hayastaneayts' ashkharhi* (Geographical Archeology of the Armenian World). The editor of this posthumous work (the Congregation's head abbot) explains in his preface that Injijean finished the first version of *Geographical Archeology* before 1815, but that the text was destroyed in a fire in Istanbul. We can only presume, then (because we know nothing about the contents of the 1815 text), that this was part of the same project that Injijean realized only partially in 1822, and then in more complete fashion in the last years of his life. The 1835 work offers a general description of the ancient Armenian world as it is presented in the fifth-century historians, with its political and administrative system, crafts and arts, trading routes, roads and means of navigation, and, as well, its laws, sciences, and military organization. I have produced this little list on the basis of what the author says in the introductory passages of his work. In a word, we have, ideally, a description of what we would call a "civilization." Let us note that Nina Garsoïan has successfully carried out a similar project in a relatively recent work, her translation of *Buzandaran* and the vast textual apparatus she has appended to it,[30] which thus presents itself as the fulfillment of Injijean's program of archeological description. Conversely, it must also be said that Injijean approaches his descriptive project as if the civilization in question had engendered itself, for there is nothing comparative in a project of this sort. But in what sense is such a project "geographical" in any case? In this respect, it is, rather, Injijean's book of 1822 that answers to the more narrowly focused project of geographical archeology. That is why we shall now proceed to read the first paragraphs of his preface to this book and then try to describe its author's philological project:

> Motivated by a sublime passion, we have undertaken to examine the archeology [*hnagrut'iun*] of the world of the Armenians at greater length than that of other nations, as is the duty of a patriot, by culling information about our own geography from a large number of detailed works by ancient writers, classing it systematically according to province and locality, and adding a description [*storagrut'iun*] of each locality. For proper archeology not only describes the past [*hnakhosel*], but also identifies its auctorial sources.
>
> We approached this task too lightly on our first attempt and encountered two major problems as a result. Initially, we decided to select, not everything that the archeological geographers had cited . . . but only that which seemed necessary for a modern geographer seeking to provide archeological place descriptions [*hnagrel*]. Thus contenting ourselves with what seemed essential, we often omitted to note what ancient authors said. Secondly, with the aim of simplifying our task, we began to mix descriptions [*sdoragrel*] of the old and the new. However, on due reflection, we understood that we would not be able successfully to complete the task of establishing the relationship between modern and ancient sites and then placing them side by side so as to facilitate comparison and correlation, and that it would be even more difficult to make a satisfactory comparison of the divisions, regions, and borders of the old provinces with those of the new ones.[31]

I break the quotation off here. The two-page preface is followed by eight hundred pages of text proper, in which the main divisions of Greater Armenia are considered one by one. The ancient authors are indeed mobilized. There are discussions of sites and toponyms. In addition to geographical descriptions, the book offers precise historical information about names, regions, villages, and towns. It is, then, similar to what we would today call a historical geography. Yet the prevailing criteria for such a geography are not met here. Injijean offers no comparison with modern geographical divisions. Conversely, however, it can also be said that his project goes beyond the prevailing standards for a historical geography. To begin with, no project of this kind had ever before been pursued among the Armenians. We are truly in the very first phase of native philology and the national imagination. The world described by the author (*world* is the term he uses for the country and its inhabitants, in line with ancient usage) is a human world, and therefore one traversed by history. Injijean never describes a site without also recounting the legends associated with it and the events that took place in it, the whole on the basis of testimony offered by ancient authors (mainly Greek and Roman). Without a doubt, a world opens up before our eyes. Yet it is never presented for its own sake, but, rather, always in relation to written accounts of it. Nevertheless, this description of ours says nothing about the difficulties the author encountered, that is, at least one of the "major problems" he evokes at the very beginning of his preface. The first of these difficulties is that he had not anticipated the magnitude of his task and therefore repeatedly had to abandon it and take it up again. He had failed to note everything that the ancient authors say about this or that site, and it sometimes happened that he ignored matters that later turned out to be indispensable. In the following paragraphs of the preface, Injijean comes back to this first difficulty, as a result of which, he says, he had to make exhausting rereadings. Thus he discovered, thanks to his own practice, a twofold law of philology: the need to compare sources and the need to reconstruct a context. In both cases, very obviously, every new rereading opened up, and mandated, new perspectives.

It is, however, the second of the two difficulties mentioned by Injijean which is of special interest to us here. It resides in his discovery that he could not "mix descriptions . . . of the old and the new." This is an extremely simple formulation of a situation that was in reality utterly novel—a formulation that conceals the very essence of the philological project as expressed in Injijean's text. What, indeed, is a "historical geography" if not a description that mixes the old and the new? To produce such a description, one has to situate all the places that appear in the ancient authors, each province and each border, whether it is explicitly named or not; and one has to find the corresponding place in the "new" geography. Conversely, one has to be able to "reread" every site in the new geography in terms of its historical significance, the events for which it served as a stage, and its place in the world of antiquity. In this sense, if historical geography is an archeology, a discourse on the past assigned a location in space, there can be no archeology worthy of the name without "neology," that is, without a discourse on a present that is likewise situated in space.

Thus Injijean needed a "neology" to make archeology possible. Let us note that the word *archeology* itself is invented here and endowed with a meaning it could not have had before—exactly as with the word *storagrut'iun*. In the classical language, the noun *hnakhosut'iun* is used to designate any discourse about the past. The corresponding verb is *hnakhosel*. Until Injijean, however, "discourse about the past" by no means implied the necessity of a simultaneous "discourse about the present." The emergence of the new meaning of the word *hnakhosel* marks the invention of modern philology. Injijean also uses the neologism *hnagrel* in the paragraphs quoted above. It is a question of writing about the past. The fact that our author has to employ a neologism, however, indicates that he is clearly aware of the novelty of his project. But then why is it impossible to realize this project? Why does Injijean have to fall back on a description of the past in and of itself, by way of the authors available to him, and why does he have to postpone the very essence of his project, which was to write past and present together, to describe the sites of present-day geography as the same ones mentioned in these authors of the past? Why is he unable to match up the two toponymies, past and present? He seems to say that that would have required too much work and that the task could not have been accomplished in a single lifetime. That is no doubt true. But the real reason is that he did not have the description of the "new" human geography at his disposal, so that he could establish the necessary correspondences with the old—the geography of the towns and villages, narratives and legends, temples and palaces, battles and councils—such as he found it in the ancient authors. The veritable archeological project is therefore present here, and its formulation is fully worked out, but it is, at the same time, altogether unrealizable. What would have been required to make at least the beginnings of a realization of it possible? Obviously, *travelers*, or something even better: European travelers. The problem is not that no Europeans traveled through historical Armenia in the seventeenth and eighteenth centuries. Tournefort did, for example. Yet philological orientalism had not yet appeared on the horizon, and the European travelers (who, moreover, visited the Caucasus and Persia more often than the Ottoman part of former Armenia) were not yet concerned to produce descriptions of use to a future historical geography and a philology of traces and monuments. Only after the vogue of orientalist voyages began (that is, voyages already motivated by a project identical to Injijean's, but in its modern dimension), and several generations of travelers had crossed the Armenian regions of the Ottoman Empire and northern Persia, could correspondences be fully established between modern toponymy, or the modern description of the sites, on the one hand, and ancient toponymy on the other. By the end of the century, Ghevond Alishan had all the necessary documentation at his disposal, and had read all the travel narratives and descriptions of the Armenian provinces: he had even made that his specialty and obsession. Without ever having set foot in Armenia—Persian, Russian, or Ottoman—he knew every nook and cranny, every little hill, every ruin, and every rock of the country that once bore the name, the political name, of Greater Armenia (and, also, Cilicia). Thus he was in a position to go back over the whole of Injijean's geographical archeology, taking its modern dimension, this time, as his point of departure, and to carry the project through to a successful conclusion by providing a full description of the historical background of the sites that he had visited with his imaginary everyday companions, the voyagers. He did so in vast, magnificent works. Needless to say, no one reads them today.[32] Were they, however, written to be read? Was the enterprise in question not already anachronistic, even before Alishan envisaged it? It was, in fact, the project of the philological decade, the neo-archeological project, the one on which Injijean had set out around 1815 and which was successfully completed eighty years later. Conceiving it plainly mattered more than realizing it.

The difficulty evoked by Injijean and the fact that the *Description* published in 1822 accomplished only half the work required by the project of "description" show, to begin with, something that we have already noticed: the interdependence of the philologist and the orientalist traveler. In reality, these are two faces of one and the same personage. Moreover, the orientalist voyage itself (let us say, the voyage to the interior of the territory, the voyage to the "fatherland") could not be conceived before the neo-archeological project had been formulated, the essence of which consisted in describing the historical contents of the present, or the past as inhabiting (or haunting) the sites of present-day geography. In the Armenians' case, as I have said, the voyage to the fatherland began only in the 1820s. It was thus effected after the archeological decade. It is, after all, paradoxical that Injijean's contemporary and, doubtless, his pupil, Father Pzhshgean, the first great "philologist-traveler," never once considered undertaking a voyage to the fatherland, which emphatically took its time constituting itself as such in the minds of these scholars and pioneers of Neo-Armenism. Thus it was not the fatherland that came first, or even the fashion and vogue of the voyage. The throw of the dice that inaugurated this astonishing adventure was, beyond a doubt, the project of "description." I shall therefore come back to it briefly, for one more point remains to be elucidated.

Description, ideally, was to be a reading of the past in the empirical present. Thus it involved the opening up of a temporal dimension behind all that appeared, or ought to have appeared, before the traveler's eyes (a traveler who, to be sure, had not yet heard the call to travel when Injijean wrote his preface in 1822). It is an inscription of the empirical in time or, rather, a reading of the temporal dimension off the surface of the seen and known object, an object now recognized as a vestige, a temporal palimpsest, an archival document, or a witness. As I have said several times, a "reading" of this sort, the establishment of communication between the "old" and the "new," between the information provided by ancient geographers and real descriptions by modern travelers, would have been unthinkable a scant decade earlier. We can say about the objects of spatial geography what Foucault says about the fate of all empiricity in exactly the same period: it "is henceforth traversed by History, through the whole density of its being. The order of time is beginning." And because Foucault's analyses bear, in part, on the science of language as it appeared in the 1810s in Franz Bopp or the brothers Grimm, we can say that the neo-archeological "description" promoted by Father Injijean was, in its turn, an *etymology* (in the sense given the word by comparative linguistics, not in that of the eighteenth-century grammarians). *"Description" is an etymology of spatial geography.* It regards every object in this space as permeated by its own history. Foucault, again, says, in a seemingly redundant formulation: "The historicity of language . . . reveals its history immediately, and without intermediary. . . . Philology was to untie the relations that the grammarians had established between language and external history in order to define an internal history."[33] Exactly the same thing may be said of the historicity of geographical space and philology's intervention in the relationship between this space and outer history. This space that, from now on, carries its history within itself, in its very body, and is traversed by history in all the density of its being, is the space of the nation. It can thus be readily seen why I have been constantly using the expression "national imagination" to designate the collective mental operation, itself historical, that gives rise to it. "Reading" temporal depth in the very objects of geographical space, opening these objects up to their historical temporality, is clearly a labor of the imagination.[34]

But then how are we to integrate the two phenomena that, it seems, preside over the archeological project—that is, the appeal of the voyage and the genesis of the "national"? On the one hand, we have the historicization of a space that has now become national. This historicization is an epistemic phenomenon that shook the whole scholarly community to its foundations (and, as we can see, all cultural and political reality as well) at the turn of the nineteenth century. On the other hand, we have orientalism, after all, the internalization of the European gaze, speculary and speculative imitation, and the construction of Neo-Armenism as a pure effect of this orientalism, one that would find a concrete translation in philological works and travel narratives and, later, auto-ethnography. How are we to account for the historicization of the object and, simultaneously, the orientalism of the gaze? How are we to describe, in a single logical movement, the opening up to time of which "description" is at once the project and model, on the one hand, and, on the other, autoscopy, which mandates this enthusiastic turn toward "the self"? Why do they emerge at the same moment? Do we have to do with one and the same phenomenon, described in two different ways according to our perception of the neo-archeological project?

It seems to me that the central moment here is, once again, the emergence of the native. In Injijean's project of archeological description as well as in Pzhshgean's travel narratives, the native is present only between the lines. He has not yet been discovered as such. His place is there, but he himself is not yet in his place. Yet he produces concrete effects even in his absence. He is a breath, a sudden flux. It is the native who, in the distance, calls out to the traveler and incites him to travel. It is the native who determines the basic features of the archeological program: gathering up everything that the ancients have said about a region so as to be able to read the whole past behind each place in the present, even if one does not yet possess an overall or detailed description of the world of the present. It is the native, finally, who will carry in his very flesh and his voice all the historical density that characterizes him, although he himself, of course, knows nothing about it.

Let us not, however, lose sight of the fact that there is a structure of subjugation in all this. The "destruction" of memory and the tradition, which lies in the background of the figure of the native as vestige, also coincides perfectly with one form of subjection of the subjected peoples. Does this make the destruction of memory and the tradition something objective, a historical reality, rather than a philological invention? This objection calls for a special study, which I will carry out in detail in Part II of the present book. From the outset, however, we know that the native is the one who carries the disaster within himself. He is the figure of the disaster of the tradition. The native is a residue. *The invention of the native, that shadow of the philologist, as residue is orientalism's way of carrying out the historicization of the object.* For philological thought, the disaster came about historically. The native no longer remembers. He no longer re-members either his history or, needless to add, his historicity. It is philology that would have things this way. Conversely, however, philology has to remain wholly unaware of the fact that it is itself on a continuum with the residual, vestigial figure of the native as the bearer of disaster. Thus it is philology that invented the historical disaster. We might just as well say that the historical disaster invented itself with philology. I would, furthermore, ask the reader to recall what I said at the beginning of the chapter about Abovean and auto-ethnography (and what I have suggested again, here and there, in the present chapter). Everything that I have just explained about national philology's first steps, which correspond to the archeological moment of autoscopy and the open-ing up of the ethnographic nation to itself, stand outside the national tradition, the one that the nation, in the process of its constitution, accorded itself and presented to the world as its own history. The names of the monks Pzhshgean and Injijiean are utterly unknown, appearing nowhere in the "official" history of the Armenian entry into mo-dernity and the community of nations, the history that the Armenians teach them-selves, the history of what is called "national consciousness." That history begins later, with, among the Eastern Armenians, Abovean, not the Mkhitarist Fathers. It begins with Eastern, not Western Armenian. Pzhshgean and Injijiean have been definitively blotted out of national history. This censorship goes back a long way: their names had been forgotten by the mid-nineteenth century. They were the first real and imaginary travelers, the first archeologists, the first geographers, the first to write all or some of their works in modern Armenian and, therefore, the first to respond fully to the im-perative call for an autoscopic mimicry made necessary by the unfolding of philology. The national tradition has expunged their names from the archives, without a trace. This strict censorship and rigorous ignorance, this oblivion and historical silence are also part of history. They are part of the ethnographic nation's history, of autoscopy, of the nation's orientalist and philological history. The nation had clearly to forget the mimicry and autoscopy, that is, precisely, the orientalism that presided over its consti-tution. But it also had to forget its aleatory birth, the experience of limits induced by translation, and the crossing of the frontier.

A NEO-ARCHEOLOGY

In the face of this silence imposed by the nationalist tradition, I must now put all that has been said about the auto-ethnographic movement (Abovean, Servantsdeants, the frenzied activity of the last quarter of the nineteenth century, Edouard Lalayan's *Ethno-graphic Journal*,[35] Abeghean's dissertation) back in the context of the ongoing creation of Neo-Armenism. Hence I have to repeat about Neo-Armenism what Gourgouris has said of Neo-Hellenism: it is clear that it bears within itself, immanently, the "anti-quarian" nature of its own discourse. To that end, it was plainly necessary that it be taken in hand by the philological disciplines par excellence: archeology, to begin with, and then folklore. What I have called a "neo-archeology" in the present chapter must accordingly be understood in a twofold sense. First, of course, it must be understood as a new archeology, different from the one that had prevailed until then. In what precedes, I have not mentioned Injijean's sources. The scholars to whose authority he appeals are philologists and archeologists of the Leiden school, active from the end of the seventeenth to the early eighteenth century.[36] One might suppose that this fact by itself invalidates everything I have said, in the wake of Foucault and Said, about the early nineteenth-century "philological revolution." But that is not the case. The seventeenth-century philologists and archeologists also studied languages, to be sure, and wrote learned treatises about ancient authors. Some also concerned themselves with the history of the Holy Land, which they treated "descriptively," in the sense in which the Mkhitarists employed the term. They did not, however, transform literature into a witness to its age and an eminent representative of a nation's culture. They had not yet invented the figure of the native, nor, for that matter, the "place" in which the native might be present or absent. They knew nothing of the foundational function of mythology and, therefore, nothing of the function of mythological religion or the birth of the nations unto themselves. The "colonization of the ideal" and the structural incitement to autoscopy are yet to be found in these writers; there was no anthropological doublet, no internalization of the European gaze, no voyage toward the "fatherland." Geographical space was not saturated by its own history (this held only for the space of the Holy Land: there have to be, after all, continuities and ruptures from one period to another). To bring the difference into sharper relief, let us look at what Tournefort writes in the preface to his posthumous *Relation d'un voyage du Levant*: "My Lord the Count of Pontchartrain, *Secrétaire d'Etat*, charged with overseeing the Academies, and always attentive to all that can contribute to the perfection of the Sciences, suggested to His Majesty, toward the close of the year 1699, that he dispatch competent observers to foreign countries to make observations not only of their Natural History and ancient and modern Geography, but also of everything touching on the Commerce, Religion, and Customs of the different peoples living in them."[37] Let us note the expression "ancient and modern Geography," which seems to correspond to the collective project of the first generation of modern philologists among the Armenians, that of the archeology that called for a description of modern geography; let us also recall that Father Pzhshgean had Tournefort's book to hand when he wrote his *History of Pontus* in 1819. What, then, so radically distinguishes, despite all, the voyages of the modern period from Tournefort's *Voyage*? The answer, obviously, is the modern project's orientalism, that is, the fact that the voyage is, always (whether it is undertaken by foreigners or by indigenous travelers), a voyage toward the native, even if the native is conspicuous thanks to his absence from the scene. The voyage through the Pontus region undertaken by Pzhshgean is in some sort a turning point, because it participates in both programs, that of the classical age and that of (modern) neo-archeology. The same holds for Injijean's classic references, in the middle of the neo-archeological decade, which was also the decade in which the incitement to autoscopy was already in full swing. Thus there can be no neo-archeology in the absence of orientalism; Injijean was no more exempt from this than anyone else. The only specifically Armenian trait (over against the Greeks or Serbs, for example) was that the actual deployment of auto-ethnography occurred, in the Armenian case, very late in the century, almost fifty years after the purely archeological moment. It is not hard to guess why the Armenians were so incredibly late here. I will later discuss the reasons at greater length than I have so far, especially in my discussion of Oshagan. So much for the first way of coming to grips with neo-archeology.

There is, however, another way of approaching it. I have used the term *neo-archeology* to highlight the fact that *archeology* is also a *neology*. It studies traces of the past in the present. In everything "new," it sees only the vestige of something "old." Only in this sense is the "new" of interest to it; it is in this sense that, by an essential, structural necessity, it needs voyagers, who will soon be crisscrossing the whole country, constantly undertaking all manner of pilgrimages to the fatherland, and describing the slightest antiquity and the least nook and cranny in which antiquity has something to say. It is also as a "neo-archeology" that we have to read everything that the folklorists (whom I am coming to now), the amateur scholars and, soon, the specialists of the oral tradition, the mythology of the grand era and "secondary mythology" (the reader will recall this fascinating term of Abeghean's, which I cited earlier and to which I shall return), everything that Abovean's distant disciples and Servantsdeants's admirers would say about modern customs and legends and, as well, about the significance they attached to their endless labor of collecting, recording, and systematizing data. They say, first of all: we must allow the people to hear their own voice. Why? Could they no longer hear it? Why did philologists have to come along and suddenly perceive that the people's spoken utterance was no longer reaching the people's own ears? The anthropological doublet, of course (and already, therefore, orientalism, in the full sense), is responsible for this. The figure of the native, even when it is absent, summons the philologist like a black hole, like an absence of matter that sucks in matter. It summons the traveler as well: there is no difference here. The neo-archeological traveler is no longer dispatched by His Royal Highness as, in the seventeenth century, Tournefort was when he was charged with the mission of collecting observations on the "Religion and Customs" of the peoples living in the regions through which he traveled. He is no longer summoned by the Holy Land, which never counted as anything other than archeological terrain capable of satisfying the needs of the Christians' biblical tourism. He is summoned by the native. On the other hand, however, and simultaneously, this movement toward the people's living (and, already, dead) utterance goes hand-in-hand with another archeological movement, that of the discovery of the oral tradition, mythology, and (somewhat later) mythological religion. The finest example of the pure, folkloric neo-archeology among the Armenians before Abeghean is provided by Mkrtich Emin, mentioned once or perhaps twice in the preceding pages. I shall expand a bit here on what has already been said about him, adding what new information we now need.

Mkrtich Emin (1815–1890) received his secondary education at the Lazarian Academy in Moscow. After earning a doctorate as an orientalist philologist at the University of Moscow, he taught Armenian and Armenian literature at the Academy for the rest of his life. He published his first original book in 1850; entitled *Epic Narratives of Ancient Armenia*, it was a veritable revelation, because it contained an unprecedented interpretation, couched in terms of oral tradition and mythology, of the narratives recounted by the historian Moses of Khoren. It so happens that Emin, although he was familiar with the newly established German tradition of comparative mythology, did not take the full measure of his own discovery: he did not distinguish among the various levels of the oral tradition in the narratives related by Moses and, in particular, did not trace them back to the mythemes at their origin in order to interpret them in accordance with methods already coming into use in the Germany of his day. That task would be accomplished by Abeghean fifty years later.[38]

This, however, is not what matters here. The fact is that Emin's work on the oral tradition was in every respect analogous to Injijean's work on "Ancient Geography." The analogy lies in the fact that Emin had the archeological elements at his disposal, yet knew absolutely nothing about the "neological" elements or, in other words, modern oral traditions. These were simply presupposed. It is essential that we understand that archeological work itself would never have commenced had it not been for this presupposition—had it not been for the *implicit* project of a voyage toward the native. In 1850, Emin could not have read Abovean's preface to *Wounds of Armenia*, in which we find this project set out in black and white, since the preface (along with the full version of the novel) was not published until 1858. This explains the enthusiasm with which Emin's whole entourage and, of course, Emin himself, greeted the very first example of "field work," that carried out by Servantsdeants in 1874, which completed and valorized the neo-archeological work that he himself had begun much earlier. In question now, of course, is no longer a geographical, but a folkloric, religious archeology. The structure of both, however, is strictly the same. The summons to the voyage is there; it is to be found between the lines of Emin's text just as it is in Injijean's. In both cases, the summons comes from the native whose existence is the premise for the neo-archeological project. That, ultimately, is why the grand decade that culminated in the "Geographical Description" of ancient Armenia is clearly the first moment of a grand history of the national imagination, which is, from one end to the other, an orientalist imagination.

Let us recall, by way of illustration, what Servantsdeants wrote in 1876 about the age or antiquity of the oral traditions. We cited these passages in the previous chapter. Servantsdeants had surely read Emin's 1850 book; but, in any event, the discovery of mythology, mythological religion, and the oral tradition in ancient Armenia had, between 1850 and 1874, more than enough time to become the common property of all intellectuals. Servantsdeants's argument, when he quotes the narratives taken from the oral tradition by the historian Moses of Khoren and other supposedly fifth-century authors, is the argument that typically underpins the neo-archeological project from the outset. I now complete, therefore, what I have said so far about the first way of understanding neo-archeology. Neo-archeology is an operation with two faces. One is orientalist: it involves autoscopic internalization of the gaze and imitation of the European model, itself an autoscopic imitation that created a self by way of imitation of an ideal past. The other involves historicization of the object, in other words, the self. These two faces are absolutely inseparable. The birth of the "human sciences" (and, therefore, of philology) is impossible without orientalism, and, conversely, there can be no orientalism without philology. It is these two faces that I bring together when I speak of the neo-archeological program. That program does not consist solely in giving a people its forgotten past again or allowing a people to hear its own voice, suddenly become inaudible for some unknown reason. It is because neo-archeology is there from the start, because, in neo-archeology, historicization is inseparable from the imitative autoscopy of orientalism, that Servantsdeants could elaborate his argument about the antiquity of the oral tradition as well as the link between old and new folklore; we should perhaps say, however, between the old and the new mythology—the old one considered as a religion and the new one as belief.

It is here, in the articulation and implementation of the neo-archeological program, that the provisional formulation we offered in chapter 2 about the testamentary structure of the "oral culture" discovered by philology and promoted to the rank of folklore—and therefore also to the rank of the nation's will and testament—can be made fully explicit. Here is what Gourgouris says on this subject. Earlier I contented myself with alluding to him; here I shall quote him at some length, for the simple pleasure of pointing to the convergence that I underscore by replacing the word *Greek* with the word *Armenian*:

> As an academic practice, folklore is constitutively philological. It is, as Renan points out, the practical consequence of the intimate link between comparative linguistics and comparative mythology, its inquiry specifically directed at the self-perpetuation of a people's "primitive laws." Folklore's object of study is the implicit and anonymous coherence of customary culture, conceived as a kind of naturally preserved, but contemporary, expression of myth. The specifically mythifying character of so-called "oral tradition," embodied best in the customary practices of peasant populations, becomes in this sense the privileged cultural object. Folklore often builds its discourse on the extraction of certain practices from their integral place in the everyday life of certain communities and their subsequent nomination as *cultural* practices—indeed as marks of cultural inheritance. . . . Folk songs, in other

words, may reflect the spirit of, say, the [Armenian] people in themselves, but they are actually studied for (and as) *inscriptions* of the development of this spirit through the ages. . . . In the discourse of the nation, oral culture is interesting (or indeed, *is*) only as testament—Scripture—of the nation's legacy.[39] (*Dream Nation*, 148)

The discourse of the nation is neo-archeological in its essence, and it has an essential need for the cultural practices reinvented by philology. I need not comment further on this extract from Gourgouris, which I have transposed to the Armenian case by altering just one word: my previous two chapters are already a long commentary on it. I would simply like to conclude my discussion here by once again quoting at length, for purposes of illustration, the passage of Abeghean's 1899 doctoral dissertation in which he speaks of *niedere Mythologie*, counterposing to this "secondary mythology" (altogether explicitly, this time) a high mythology that is, quite simply, a religion, an established body of beliefs, with the corresponding institutions. Here is the passage in question:

> Popular Armenian beliefs are certainly Christian, in the first instance. But a people clings to its old traditions when it is deprived of writing and formal education (as most Armenians are) and lives in close proximity to nomadic peoples who do not possess writing. Consequently, many aspects of the ancient pagan faith, although they are, to be sure, on the way to dying out [*allerdings schon im Verschwinden begriffen*], have been preserved in the form of vestiges [*Überbleibsel*] of the past in contemporary popular belief, especially among the lower classes of the people, such as old peasant women. . . . Thus [contemporary Armenian popular belief has] two main components: Christianity and paganism.
>
> The pagan component, the subject of the present examination, represents a secondary mythology [*eine niedere Mythologie*] like that possessed by almost all the world's peoples. It comes to the fore in the belief in souls and the cult of the dead, in the veneration and mythical conceptions of physical phenomena and natural objects, in the belief in demons, and in magical practices.
>
> The imaginary representations of Armenian popular faith, as well as most of its sagas and legends, are also found, of course, among other Indo-European and non-Indo-European peoples. Many of its notions, like those of every popular faith, may well constitute elementary ideas common to all humankind, and yet be authentically Armenian. However, most such aspects of Armenian popular faith are doubtless owing to borrowings or transfers. The neighboring peoples as well as those who have lived together with the Armenians in their historical homeland [*Heimatland*] were always present in large numbers, and still are today. They have all certainly had some kind of influence on Armenian mores, customs, and popular beliefs. It is thus difficult to determine what has been borrowed from one or another foreign people in ancient or modern times.[40]

This passage merits a long commentary that would bring out, on the one hand, the fact that Abeghean here applies a program of folkloric studies that he learned from his German teachers of comparative mythology, and, on the other, the fact that he lays bare the logic of the native (which is of course by no means evidence of originality). I have always wondered whether these old peasant women, presumed to hand down the fantastic narratives comprising the remains of an ancient tradition, were ever young. The standard answer has it that the tradition was disappearing, that the world was in the process of being modernized. I have always wondered, consequently, whether ethnographers consistently arranged to arrive on the scene at the moment when the inevitability of the disappearance of tradition was being confirmed, at precisely the moment when the tradition was in such a state of decomposition that only old women, not a single young person, still knew something about it. Furthermore, I have included in brackets in this passage a few German words that seem to me to be of capital importance. These words are *Überbleibsel*, meaning the vestiges or remnants of a tradition to which we have access only in the form of ruins, which have, to be sure, been preserved, but after a colossal collapse, a boundless forgetting; *Heimatland*, meaning the fatherland, big or small, that is, one's native country (*terre natale* in my original French translation), the territory or land of the native; finally, *niedere Mythologie*, meaning the lower, derived mythology that now exists only in fossilized form, but that has nevertheless existed through the centuries as a memory that is not conscious of itself, the memory of an ancient mythology that was, for its part, authentic or authentically pagan, and thus superior because still alive and still in circulation, forming a system and corresponding to an effectively practiced religion. I shall not engage in the pointless exercise that consists in speculating about what is truly native and what has been borrowed from the surrounding peoples. I must, however, add that what fascinates me most is the phrase *allerdings schon im Verschwinden begriffen*: the process of disappearing (in my French translation, *évanouissement*, literally, fainting), the state in which the ethnographer-philologist works. No tradition is worthy of being recorded by ethnography unless it is on the verge of disappearing, unless it has already begun to disappear.

To all this, it must be added that, in the case to hand, the ethnographer, in reflecting on questions of method, never once considers the fact that the people (the lower classes) from whom he takes his sub-mythological knowledge is a long-subjugated people, a people crushed under the weight of a domination so massive that no tradition whatever could survive it intact. The philologists are in quest of a tradition that has managed to survive intact despite centuries of domination and the supposed disaster of the native. This domination, according to them, could therefore only have been political; it could not have been cultural. They think, in other words, in the very terms of nationalistic thought. For if there is one thing characteristic of that thought, it is plainly the idea that something has survived intact, has been preserved at the cultural level. As to the presumption of the disaster of the native, an essential premise of orientalist philology that defines it as philology and constitutes the philologist's raison d'être (in other words, the raison d'être of the scholar who is now the native's memory, interpreter, and analyst), it was there between the lines, but only between the lines, of everything that we began by saying about the aesthetic principle defended by the *Mehyan* group, and then about the auto-ethnographic principle of the "fatherland's" would-be discoverers. This "disaster" of the native will stand at the center of our concerns in everything that follows. We have to bring out what is between the lines and state it in black and white. Let us anticipate the result in a sentence: if it is true that the memory of the native is inherently defective and must be supplemented by the philologist who restores the native's past and living voice to him, thus saving him, in some sense, from his strange mutism, it is equally true that this defect itself has no memory. And because it is a defect with no memory of itself, it is a loss without mourning.

That is why, in 1803, that is, at the moment when philology began to establish itself as a discourse, phenomenon, discipline, and science, the moment when its object emerged from the limbo of the absence of knowledge, Hölderlin could speak, in his poem "Mnemosyne," of a loss without pain, in other words, without mourning, without the pain of mourning:

> Ein Zeichen sind wir, deutungslos,
> Schmerzlos sind wir und haben fast
> Die Sprache in der Fremde verloren.[41]

> A sign we are, undeciphered,
> Painless we are, and have almost
> Lost our tongue in foreign lands.[42]

The native is a sign (*ein Zeichen*) that it has become absolutely impossible to decipher, since the key to his original language has been lost and the world in which he signified no longer exists. This sign is no more than a vestige, a monument, a Rosetta Stone that will never find its Champollion. It is a relic, a silent witness to the past, a monument standing defiantly erect in the midst of nature, an expression of the myth that is at once memorable and immemorial; it has been naturally conserved, thanks to God-knows-what miracle, but will remain mute for as long as the key to deciphering it is not found. Hölderlin did not anticipate the philologists, of course, but did he really need to concern himself with philology? This sign that "we" are, as natives, is *deutungslos*. It is true that the hieroglyphic inscription has been preserved intact, or very nearly so; yet its meaning has been lost, perhaps forever (we cannot be sure: that is why we say that the native's original language, the language of the original myth and of mytho-poetic power, which is also a capacity for mourning, has been "almost" lost). Along with this meaning, the means of recovering it has also been lost. Most important, the loss has been lost as well. What native could ever have been aware that he was by nature a linguistic vestige, a relic, a silent monument preserved by nature, an archeological object, a mysterious palimpsest, had it not been for the philologists? Which native could ever have discovered and recorded his own disaster in himself, the disaster constitutive of his being (that is, his being as a native)? The loss in question is thus plainly a loss without mourning. That is why we are painless, *schmerzlos*, petrified in our turn. Hölderlin reverses the whole structure that binds the native to the philologist, the structure responsible for the fact that they function in tandem from the outset. He reverses it and responds to it even before this structure has had the time to crystallize and produce historical effects. He even succeeds in bringing this structure into the light, in stripping it bare, in revealing the disaster of the native for what it is. He can do all this for a very simple reason that I need not elaborate and explain: he does not identify with the philologist. He identifies with the native in the nascent structure that no one had ever perceived before him (and that it was given to no one to perceive in the two centuries after him). Finally, if we may say that the native is someone who has lost mourning, there can be no question of restoring his own history to him without first restoring his capacity to mourn. Was philology designed for that purpose? Such was the conviction of some who sought to compete with philology in nationalizing the nation and taking charge of mourning; they failed to realize that the mourning they wished to take in hand was nothing other than the mourning of philology. Who are those I have in mind here? Naturally, all those who tried to imagine the disaster (and "put it to rights") on the basis of the "aesthetic principle." I can now repeat: it is through the ethnographic nation's destiny (from the initial impulse provided by orientalism and Philhellenism down to the "aesthetic" repetition or culmination of the process) that one is able to understand what was at stake in the idealist matrix established by Schelling, the one that governs the relationship between art and religion.

—Part One translated by G. M. Goshgarian

Daniel Varuzhan: The End of Religion

CHAPTER 4

The Disaster of the Native

On February 2, 1908, in a letter from Ghent, Belgium, where he was attending university, Daniel Varuzhan used the phrase *poetic paganism* for the first time, a phrase that clearly indicates the religious turn in his writing. In the years that followed, "paganism" would take on more and more importance in his work; indeed, because of this work and its immediate effects—virtually unparalleled within the history of cultural production—this notion would take on more and more importance in every part of Armenian intellectual life during the period from 1908 to 1915, and beyond, in the diaspora as well as in Armenia. The letter of February 1908 was addressed to Arshag Chobanian, the editor of the journal *Anahit*, published in Paris, in which Varuzhan had already published many of his poems. Here is an excerpt:

> It will be a pleasure to read the books you recommended to me, although
> I already know quite a few of them, particularly Leconte de Lisle. His poems
> are well done, with some fine effects. It may well be that he is a master worth
> following in matters of art, and I know that that is why you mention him. But,
> unfortunately, his writings are soulless, and that is why I don't much like him.
> His poems are like those deserted marble palaces, seen through white columns
> through which only a cold and chilling wind passes. With every stroke of his
> pen, the poet's heart must let out a drop of blood, until he stands before his work
> like Jesus and consumes himself to the very end, until no one can hear his last
> words drift from his pale lips. But in fact that is not the ultimate condition for
> becoming a great poet. How I envy these Unreachable Ones, who have formed
> and molded all the elements into one great unity!
>
> Recently I have written nothing new or important, except a prayer addressed to
> Vahagn. Perhaps I will give it to *Bazmavep* to publish. Pagan life seduces me a little
> more with each passing day. If it were possible today, I would change my religion
> and would joyfully embrace poetic paganism. Judaism is dull, though the prophets
> were able to beautify it somewhat. I am surrounded by ancient works. If only I
> could free myself from this mediocre condition and become a Pindar or an Isaiah.
> Of course it makes you smile to read such silly remarks, but you should know that

my soul has grown sad in the monkish solitude that is mine, and that all my attempts to smile are forced, are almost impossible.[1]

This first mention of "poetic paganism" is made in association with the poem "Vahagn," which was published one year later, first in the Constantinople periodical *Azdak* (and not in *Bazmavep*, as Varuzhan expects here); it was then republished in the first large collection of the poet's work, the 1909 book *Tseghin sirtë* (The Heart of the Race), which had been preceded in 1905 by *Sarsur'ner* (Shivers). But the book in which this "paganism" was given its full expression did not appear until four years later, with *Het'anos Yerger* (Pagan Songs) in 1912. *The Heart of the Race* and *Pagan Songs* are two of the most important works of Armenian poetry from the beginning of the twentieth century, a period when "paganism" became culturally fashionable for Western Armenians, largely (but not only) because of Varuzhan's influence. The question here, then, will be to understand these two conjoined terms: "paganism" and "poetry." Is it really a religious project, requiring a kind of conversion? Is it a purely literary or artistic project? What is the context in which such a project could emerge? If it is an artistic project, why does art have to be defined here in relation to religion? Or must we speak here of a "religion of art," as certain declarations from the journal *Mehyan*, written in the same context in 1914, might suggest? These are questions that will be addressed in some detail in the subsequent chapters of this essay on Daniel Varuzhan.

Judging by the 1908 letter quoted above, it appears that Varuzhan began to write the first segment of his "pagan" series of poems partly in reaction to his reading of Leconte de Lisle. This clearly indicates the importance for him (a negative importance, at least) of the Parnassian poets, who were attempting to reconstruct, in France, a certain architectural and sculptural antiquity. We must acknowledge Chobanian's astonishing intuition in recommending to Varuzhan a Parnassian poet steeped in Greek antiquity, without at all suspecting his young correspondent's state of mind or the direction that his poetry was taking. It is striking also to note Varuzhan's "Romantic" and generally anti-Parnassian profession of faith, his doctrine of poetry as sacrifice, and of the poet as an object of self-sacrifice. There is of course no originality in this doctrine, which was prevalent throughout Europe during the nineteenth century. But, as we will see, a reading of "Vahagn" shows that this initial poem of poetic paganism is not only a prayer addressed to a pagan god, as Varuzhan designates it here, but also, and simultaneously, a detailed description of a pagan sacrifice. With the announcement of the project of "converting" to the religion of poetic paganism, it is clear that Varuzhan insists on a relation between art and religion and thus initiates a creative reflection on the theme of sacrifice. Finally, it is especially important not to overlook the presence of Pindar and Isaiah in this letter, that is, two religious poets whom Varuzhan thus considered his models—one of whom represents a "mythological" religion, while the other represents a "theological" religion, as the poet wrote in a text from the same period.[2] All these themes merit careful reflection. It is clear that they are all inscribed within a systematic conception of art and religion—and of their reciprocal relations—which Varuzhan and his contemporaries would gradually develop, and which they would bring to a provisional culmination in their collaborative work on the "Journal of Literature and Art" called *Mehyan*. This journal would be created a little later, at the end of the brief period that we will examine here (1908–14)—and on the eve of the Catastrophe.

A PRECOCIOUS GLORY

When Daniel Varuzhan wrote the lines cited at the beginning of this chapter, he had been in Ghent for three years. Of course, his personal trajectory, in and of itself, cannot explain the emergence of this desire to "convert" to a new religion, however we might understand this conversion or this religion for now. But it will be useful if we know something about Daniel Varuzhan's life up to this point. Born in 1884 into a Catholic Armenian family in Prknig, a village in the Sebastea (Sivas) region, he followed his father into exile in Constantinople after the massacres in 1896. He attended the Mkhitarist school of Chalcedon between 1898 and 1902, and was sent to the school of the Congregation of the Mkhitarist Fathers in Venice, where he stayed until 1905. He received his entire education from the teachers of this Congregation, which played such an essential role in Armenian intellectual life from the beginning of the eighteenth century. We will return to the question of Varuzhan's involvement with the Mkhitarist school later, not only because it gave him a rigorous literary education, but also and especially because Varuzhan became (without exactly meaning to) the heir and continuation of a national project that had been formulated and stubbornly pursued to its logical conclusion (or its absurd breakdown) by several generations of writer-translators (the fathers in the Congregation) throughout the nineteenth century. But of course, in order to realize the national-literary project of the Congregation, it was first necessary for Varuzhan to separate himself from it abruptly and spectacularly, and he did precisely that just after his first book of poems, *Shivers*. This book gained immediate recognition by his peers, the intellectuals and critics of his time, such as Rupen Zartarian, Theotig, and Vahan Tekeyan.[3] Barely twenty years old, Varuzhan had already become the poet of suffering and exile, the poet of death, the one who opens the anonymous tombs and sees nothing but bottomless darkness and silence, the poet of sacrifice who says that life is a "sacrificial altar,"[4] the poet of corpses and ashes, the poet of aborted destinies and human misery—all in a language that, already at this stage, is the most exquisite ever found in modern Armenian, a language inherited from the ancients and inflected by classical Armenian, but also armed with a powerful rhetoric that the poet had learned from nineteenth-century poetry.

For four years after that, while pursuing his studies in political sciences and sociology at the University of Ghent, Varuzhan worked on his first major book of poetry, *The Heart of the Race*, which appeared in 1910 in Constantinople, a few months after Varuzhan had left Belgium to return to his country. It was this book that brought renown to Varuzhan, for it spread his name far beyond the literary circles. A number of accounts have come down to us describing public recitations and declamations of poems from this work. This is particularly true for the long poem "Djardë" (The Massacre), which had been previously published as a separate volume; it deals with the mass pogroms of 1895–96. Contemporaries report that this poem was recited several times in public, at events commemorating the victims of 1896.[5] It must be recalled that the Young Turk revolution of April 1908 had changed the political situation of the Ottoman Empire and had given hope for a better future to minorities in the region, in a burst of fraternal spirit that appears to us today as simply unbelievable. *The Heart of the Race* has three parts: "On the Altar," "In the Arena," and "Epic Poems." According to Arakel Badrig, who was Varuzhan's student in 1910, the poet commented on these titles: In the first part he tried to "render the tragic episodes of the sacrifices of our people"; in the second part he included "poems devoted to their heroic struggles"; the third part's title speaks for itself.[6] On the whole, then, these are "patriotic" poems written partly under the pressure of recent events, and partly under the influence of the national liberation movement, which was still awaiting its poetic voice. On the one hand, collective death, desolation, ruins; on the other, the announcement of a renaissance, the glorification of armed struggle, a call to the "slumbering forces"[7] hidden deep within the children of the fatherland. An attentive reading, however, reveals another very different set of concerns behind this altogether conventional scheme. These concerns bear on the function, both central and contradictory, of art (that is, in fact, of poetry) in the becoming of the nation, or—to put it another way—in the production of the cultural forms and mentalities that accompanied the invention of the "nation." A brief analysis of the book's introductory poem, entitled "Nemesis," will allow us to provisionally situate these elements, in a first attempt to understand their scope.

THE ABILITY TO MOURN

The poem "Nemesis" was written in November 1908, just after the Young Turk revolution in Istanbul and the reestablishment of the Ottoman constitution—and therefore in a period of exaggerated revolutionary optimism. This optimism was felt at every level of the population after the fall of the sultan and the institution of a constitutional government;[8] it was accompanied by an enthusiasm—no doubt unfounded—on the part of the minorities, particularly among Armenians, for a possible or even an already established reconciliation between the "nationalities" that made up the Empire. It was in this atmosphere that Varuzhan wrote this long poem to the Greek goddess of justice and revenge. The poem is divided into two parts. In the first part, the "poet" sculpts the statue of Nemesis; after completing his work, he falls into an exhausted sleep. In the second part, the people march forth; they pour out of the factories and the prisons, break their chains and liberate themselves from secular oppression, find their heroes again, assemble around the statue of Nemesis, cry out for revenge, and venerate the poet who gave birth to the work of art. It is time to avenge the weak and oppressed, and time for the final uprising of the proletariat, the fall of the powerful, and the liberation of the people held in bondage. During this time, the poet-sculptor sleeps, and indeed, all this may only be his dream, his vision of the future, but this future is ineluctable. The political intention of the poem is clear. Varuzhan presents his socialist vision of a world to come, a world in which the tyrants have been overthrown and man's exploitation of man has been eliminated. Throughout his entire work, Varuzhan will never swerve from this socialist orientation, which is found also in the second part of his next book (which we will discuss in a moment), published in 1912. However, it is not a matter here of a poetry engaged in the service of a political and social *ideal*. In its self-reflexivity and its metaphorization of poetry, the poem presents itself, in effect, as creating a pure form, and therefore an idea, the only one capable of mobilizing the masses. Art is not in the service of an ideal that could be defined independently of it as political or social. It is the very element in which the idea comes to be, in which "the eagle's wing of the idea" shows up on the pure faces of the disaggregated masses, and teaches them freedom (*YLZ* 1:78). Art is the production of the idea, and thus the element of freedom.

In conformity with the assumptions of his age, Varuzhan is uncertain about the precise meaning of the oppression and freedom in question. What is clear is that the fatherland will be restored to its inhabitants by the overthrow of the tyrant. But which fatherland? During the same period, Zabel Esayan understood this "fatherland" as that of the multiethnic state, as a state that would make possible a democratic coexistence among peoples, in which ethnicity would finally have a merely private status, and in which the principle of interethnic submission or subjection would be eliminated.[9] That is how Esayan interpreted the Young Turk revolution. This was of course only a pious wish, another illusion, conforming to the ideal or the ideology of the Young Turk revolution itself, to which the revolutionary Armenian parties had contributed through aid and collaboration. This illusion was necessary after the pogroms of 1909 in Cilicia, barely nine months after the Young Turks had taken power, establishing a regime that claimed to be democratic. That was the last homicidal rehearsal before the impending apocalypse, and Esayan wanted to understand this bloody orgy (which repeated the one in 1895–96) as the last ethnic sacrifice that would bring the end of ethnicities—that is, in reality, the end of the Empire as a system of domination between the ethnicities. And this sacrifice would thus bring freedom to the state in which, she thought, minorities could survive and cohabitate, without domination and without subjection, as "reconciled" ethnicities.[10] In Varuzhan's poem, there is of course no explicit reference to the Ottoman Empire or to the revolution that had just taken place a few months before. But the placement of this poem (at the beginning of a collection of "patriotic" poems) and even the date of its composition (halfway between the revolution of July 1908 and the prelude to the Catastrophe in April 1909) strongly suggest that this is the political and historical context in which it has to be read. In a famous letter dated October 4, 1908, just before the composition of "Nemesis," Varuzhan wrote the following to Chobanian (who had returned to Constantinople after hearing about the revolution and the overthrow of the sultan, hoping to get a sense of the situation and to see whether he would be able to continue publishing his journal *Anahit* in the Ottoman capital):

> You are probably in Constantinople as I write this letter. . . . You are not far from the land of our fathers and already you must feel, in the depths of that red earth, the trembling of a joy covered with laurels. When you are there, drinking wine from Van in a celebration of victory, at least at the moment when you take the last drop from your glass, remember your friend who is wandering under strange skies, and in you this drop will form into a sacrament of love.
>
> I hope that the circumstances may provide you with the possibility of living and working there. The projects of *Anahit* are necessary for our intellectual evolution, especially now that the journal will have a direct influence on the population. We must take up in our own hands the thread of this magnificent civilization that has been interrupted [*ëndhatvats*] for centuries. This thread, woven with such a pure hand, was cut-interrupted [*khzvats-ëndhatvats*] since the time of the Bagratids, for it was entangled in the ruins of Ani. At the university, I am surrounded by currents of socialist thought, but—think of it what you will—every time I awaken our ancient glory within myself by the force of imagination, I am transported completely out of myself. I have a "nostalgia" not only for our own heroic centuries, but also for the heroic centuries of all humanity. When will paganism return, and with it the ancient triumphs, for which heroism was necessary, rather than mere diplomacy?
>
> These sentiments will be more comprehensible to you when you read the poem I have included with my letter. "Native Mountains" was written a few days before the Constitution. It took shape in my mind as I was passing through Switzerland on my way to Italy. I have no doubt that you will be glad to publish it. After the Constitution, it may appear rather badly timed and out of place to strike this *tone*. In that light, and in order to correct this impression to some extent, I wondered if you might add a brief note describing the particular circumstances and influences that led to its composition. (*YLZ* 3:385–86)

This letter is an essential element in the context that concerns us, and it will require a certain amount of commentary, which I will provide at relevant points throughout this essay. We will therefore return to it several times, particularly since this is the second time that Varuzhan mentions "paganism" in his published correspondence. What captures our attention first of all is Varuzhan's remark about "Native Mountains" at the end of the letter. The fact is that Chobanian declined to publish this poem. He even warned Varuzhan that it was important to be careful at this delicate "turn" of historical events, that is, the shift in Armeno-Turkish relations. He advised him to delay publishing *Heart of the Race* for the same reasons.[11] Varuzhan therefore had good reason to anticipate misunderstandings or even hostile reactions to the "patriotic" tone of this poem, at a moment when the political situation had not settled, and when it was still very unclear what the new status of subject peoples and "minorities" would be. The poet did not follow Chobanian's advice to show moderation; instead, he published the poem in his book the next year.[12] And yet it is clear that Varuzhan was unable to harmonize or to reconcile the call to heroism in his patriotic poems with the Ottoman patriotism that was also being called for in that period. The mountains of the fatherland are the dwelling place of the epic figures of national history (Armenian, of course), and it is in their "solar marble" that the "genius of the ancestors" was incised into "titanic forms." They put forth the call to "struggle," and out of this same marble, the statues of future heroes will be carved. Thus we find in Varuzhan's poetic thought the constant presence of the heroic figure, erected in the original marble of the fatherland, a figure that requires an act of creation and an engagement of art's "formative" function, its function as a producer of forms. It will be necessary to reflect in greater detail on this function of the hero within the *explicitly aesthetic* process of becoming a nation.

If we can trust Varuzhan's letter to Chobanian (which of course we are not obliged to do), "Native Mountains" was written before the reestablishment of the constitution. However, Varuzhan wrote another "patriotic" poem immediately after receiving news of the Young Turk revolution. This was the poem entitled "The Lady of the Ruins," with the subtitle "On the Occasion of the Ottoman Constitution"; it was published in a literary journal in Bulgaria in August 1908.[13] In this poem, Varuzhan celebrates in his own way the Young Turk revolution and the removal of the sultan, Abdül-Hamid. He does this by comparing it to the French Revolution. He addresses the Tyrant, proclaiming that Phrygian caps are now being carried on the end of bayonets, and that the nations are gathered for the Festival of Fraternity on the banks of the Bosphorus. But he also says that the Lady of the Ruins, the Widow, the Lady in Tears, has been invited to the celebration by the reveling crowds, and that she believes in Liberty. So she is dressed as a queen, as she was long ago, and comes to sit at the table of the feast. All around her, the crowd sings praises for the heroes whom the Lady has nourished at her breast. She gathers around her the Turks and the Circassians, the Jews and the Greeks, she removes her mourning veil, she dances with them, as at the festivals of Dionysus. And the participants in the celebration, all the races joined together, call for the engagement ring to be brought from the depths of the Bosphorus for the Lady's marriage to "the great Ottoman nation." During the night, she buried her heroes; the next morning, she was a young bride, bound together with all these reconciled peoples. But at the end of this long poem to the glory of the Ottoman constitution, there are twelve more lines:

Hurrah! they said, but in the distance
Awakened by the clamor of this feast
Vahan the Wolf, David Beg the Leopard, and all the others,

The ancient heroes of the Old Idea
Saw very well that she was drunk
Their mother who danced before all these strangers.
Horrified, drunk with anger, they tore
Their shrouds with vengeance
And triumphantly carrying the stones of their tombs
They wept with rage, for the first time,
And in the darkness they called to their mother:
"Oliaba, Salomé . . ."[14]   (*YLZ* 1:202–03)

According to contemporary sources, the poem was translated into Turkish in 1909 by some ecclesiastical admirers of Varuzhan (among them the Armenian Primate of Sebastea, the bishop Torkom Kushagean, who later became the Patriarch of Jerusalem), in order to present it to Mehmet Emin, the literate governor of the villayet of Sebastea. At the time (after his return home), the poet held a post as a teacher in a secondary school in Sebastea, the capital of his native region; a meeting was arranged between him and this erudite governor, who was known to court the muses in his spare time,[15] and who wanted to meet this man who was constantly being praised in the highest terms. However, the zealous translators omitted the last part of the poem, the twelve lines quoted above, and Varuzhan complained of this in private: "They castrated my poem, that's how they were able to sneak it into the harem."[16] But how are we to understand the noncastrated poem? Do the last twelve lines render the rest of the poem somehow obsolete? Is Varuzhan giving a warning to his compatriots, intoxicated by the climate of Ottoman fraternization, and to his revolutionary friends, subjugated by the success of their struggle against the bloody Tyranny, marching hand in hand with the Young Turks? Had this struggle been in vain? Was the enthusiasm of the masses after the revolution premature? Was the alliance between the Armenian revolutionaries (the Dashnaktsakan party, in fact, to which Varuzhan felt very close) and the Young Turks a terrible error of judgment?[17] Or was it that, as one might think, Varuzhan was attempting to distinguish for himself between the anti-Hamidian Ottoman revolution and the national revolution? It must be said that the end of the poem remains rather mysterious. Varuzhan seems to say that the Lady of the Ruins, she who produced the heroes of liberty, the queen in mourning for so long, is at the origin of the national revolution. Does she then become the whore of the Ottoman revolution, forgetful of her sons, suddenly betraying their cause out of drunkenness? This is the ambiguity and uncertainty that was mentioned at the beginning of this section, and it is the same uncertainty that will later bring Zabel Esayan to assign a meaning to the pre-Catastrophic sacrifice by making every possible effort to understand it in the context of the "Ottoman fatherland," the fraternization between the peoples of the Empire and therefore, in fact, in the context of the end of the Empire as a system of domination. This ambiguity and this uncertainty overlap with another supposed contradiction,

clearly expressed by Varuzhan in the letter of October 4, 1908, which opposes the socialist revolution to any nostalgia for the heroic ages. The ancient triumphs required
heroes, not diplomacy, says Varuzhan. But at the same time, it is very clear that Varuzhan does not exclude the socialist revolution in favor of heroes past or to come, or
in favor of the ages of glory and heroic times. On the contrary, he sets up a confrontation between them in his work, and will do so even more clearly in the years that follow. But this is not a matter of contradiction or of a political type of confrontation, at
least not entirely. In any case, a purely political interpretation of this debate that takes
place within Varuzhan's work would itself be confronted by the same contradiction.
Should one let oneself be carried along by the current of fraternization, seeing the Ottoman revolution as an avatar of the French Revolution, but refusing the logic of national revolution, while also distrusting the new Turkish leaders? Or should one, on
the contrary, push this logic to its extremes, seeing the Lady of the Ruins dancing
with the reconciled nations and ethnicities as a new Salomé? These are naïve questions, to be sure. They are naïve because, in reality, these twelve lines of the poem say
something much more terrible than a poet's hesitation between two types of revolution.
The "heroes of the old Idea" suddenly realize that their "mother" has given up her
mourning. As long as she remained prostrate in her pose as Widow and Lady in Tears,
and as long as she wore her mourning garments, they were not forgotten as heroes.
Regardless of whether it was an illusion, they could still believe that the language of
mourning was also a memory and that the ability to mourn was still intact. But when
their mother is adorned in her finery as an Ottoman bride, when she prostitutes herself to all the nations, suddenly the truth is bared. They awaken from their deathly
sleep and abruptly realize that what was being taken away and extracted from them
during all those years of servitude was the ability to mourn, and that now nothing else
remains. The poem thus makes a complete turnaround, saying, at the end, the opposite of what it seemed to say in the beginning about the glory of the Ottoman revolution. And this is not because the poet prefers the national revolution to the Young Turk
revolution. Rather it is because there is nothing left to prefer. The cry let out by the
heroes of the Idea is a definitive and powerless cry of rage. The sacrificial Empire did
not periodically extract wealth and blood, it did not extract milk and wine, it did not
extract the gold and marble of the mountains; it extracted the symbolic power to articulate the loss of wealth, blood, milk, wine, gold, and marble, the loss of the heroes
and the fathers, the loss of the Father. It extracted the ability to mourn. That was what
it accomplished. It extracted the power to articulate loss. That is where catastrophic
mourning begins, the impossible mourning of mourning. But this last remark is
somewhat extraneous here, since Varuzhan never says these things explicitly.

After the Young Turk revolution, the patriotic *tone* of Varuzhan's poem will seem
somewhat out of place, as he wrote in the letter of October 4. He did not know yet
where he stood. He had to choose between two different possibilities; he had to choose
whether to emphasize the patriotic tone or that of fraternization. But at the same time

he dreamed of heroic ages. "We must take up in our own hands the thread of this magnificent civilization that has been interrupted for centuries. This thread, woven with such a pure hand, was cut-interrupted since the time of the Bagratids, for it was entangled in the ruins of Ani." Here too, in the double characterization of the destiny of this "thread" of the nation, an uncertainty is expressed. It is the uncertainty of aesthetic nationalism. If the continuity of the national destiny was merely interrupted, it can be taken up today and restored to its ancient glory, in other forms, without denying anything of the past. If it was cut, however, it seems that there is indeed nothing left but "nostalgia." And yet this is not entirely true. Nostalgia remains, certainly, but mourning also remains. It is true that Varuzhan says nothing about mourning in this letter from October 4, 1908; and in general, he never says anything about mourning in his dialogues with his correspondents. He speaks of it only in his poetry, in the space that for him was the element of the true dialogue with the present and the past. This is what we will have to read in what follows. But already we see that the fundamental uncertainty of the aesthetic nationalism specific to Varuzhan—an uncertainty that hesitates between the "interruption" (*ëndhatum*) and the "cut" (*khzum*), between a possible "renaissance" and a vague "nostalgia" for the historical, mythic, or heroic past (or, we must add, on a completely different level: between revolt and mourning)—will remain unresolved as long as we do not understand what is at stake in the ability to mourn that we just mentioned. For Varuzhan himself, it remained unresolved outside of his poetry. Only poetry is capable of speaking of mourning. *At least now we have the ability to mourn*: that is what Varuzhan's poetry will say again and again, despite everything; and it is what Varuzhan's commentators have never been able to read in his poetry, since they too are caught in the trap of renaissance and nostalgia, that is, the trap of nationalism, in the most banal sense of the term.[18] But this trap leads directly to the denial of the Catastrophe. When we read these lines in which aesthetic nationalism is explicitly formulated for the first time, we must never forget that they were written at a moment when the Catastrophe was approaching. Seven years later, this entire people—which was supposedly undergoing a renaissance, a rebirth to itself (through the reveries of Varuzhan and the festivals of fraternization)—would disappear without a trace in the genocidal torment. We can thus rightly interrogate the interruption of the national destiny and the "renaissance" of which, among other things, Varuzhan became a kind of herald. Only the memory of the Catastrophe allows one to ask (but it also *obliges* one to ask) how Varuzhan could imagine for a single moment that in his day (in 1908, let's say), finally, Armenians had regained the ability to mourn; and this is the only question worth asking, because it is a question that we are compelled to ask. To the very end, Varuzhan will never renounce the patriotic tone, the aesthetic project of a renascent "race," betrothed to the "red soil" (this is the subject of the last book he was able to complete during his lifetime, *The Song of Bread*, but it is also the title of a poem in the book of Varuzhan's poems that was published in 1909).[19] But the fatherland is the land of mourning. Consequently, it is necessary to understand what this "ability to mourn" is, how it could have been lost over the centuries, and how one can imagine having re-gained it. We might recall here that around the same time, in 1911, with her book *Aver-aknerun mej* (Among the Ruins), Zabel Esayan raised a monument of mourning in memory of the victims and those stricken by the massacres of April 1909 in Cilicia. We might also recall that in doing this, she claimed a certain "ability to mourn," against those who decided on and "perpetrated" these massacres, whose ultimate aim was ap-parently the definitive interdiction of mourning. With this definitive interdiction (which of course was not decreed by the government; we are not in ancient Greece or the The-bes of Creon; these things happen in secret and hidden ways, in a zone of the human psyche to which only the victim, at times, has access, and even then it is only a fleeting and anaphoric access), the perpetrators wanted definitively to seal the failure, the falter-ing, or the default of mourning, a default that bore directly on the collectivity under the system of imperial domination. In the end, it is this default of mourning (or per-haps we should say, the default *in* mourning) that must be considered. It is this default that is spoken of in Varuzhan's work, and it was this same default that Hölderlin spoke of a century before him, when he wrote: "dem / gleich fehlet die Trauer"—"Mourning is in default." Once again, what is this mysterious ability to mourn? How does it come to be? Does it coincide with what is called political freedom?

THE TOMB AND THE IDEA

The Bagratids mentioned in Varuzhan's letter of October 4, 1908 were the royal dynasty ruling in Ani until the eleventh century. The thread of national destiny is entangled or interwoven in the ruins of Ani, Varuzhan writes, and it remains tied to these ruins, it cannot be extricated from them. It is there that one must begin to take up this interrupted thread of heroic history. It is necessary, then, to return to the ruins of Ani, the ruins of that phantom city, which changed hands so often beginning in the eleventh century, which was struck by several upheavals, and was finally entirely deserted by its inhabitants in the fourteenth century. It remains today as it was in Varuzhan's time, in a deserted landscape, with its churches ruined but still magnifi-cent after almost a millennium, and its truncated walls, like a strange witness to past glory. It is located at the far edge of present-day Turkey, on the steep banks of the Akhourian River, which separates this (formerly Soviet) part of Armenia from Turkey. It was not until the nineteenth century that archaeologists began to show interest in Ani, when the expeditions of Nicolai Marr made it possible to reconstruct a descrip-tion of the city, which now shows us the state in which the ruins were found a little more than a hundred years ago. This archaeological description (accompanied with photographs) was for a long time the only document available on the ruined city. After 1914, there was no access at all to Ani for a very long period. It was quite simply forbid-den for travelers and archaeologists to visit the ruins of Ani. It should also be noted that we possess very few descriptions of Ani and its ruins by Armenian travelers in the nineteenth century. The city remained a purely mythical object for the national imagination.[20] It is thus to this mythic city that Varuzhan refers in his letter of October 4. But this reference, as is often the case in the poet's correspondence, is itself an echo of a poem written one year earlier, in 1907. This poem is called "Anii averaknerun mej," "Among the Ruins of Ani" (which of course sounds to us like a first version of Zabel Esayan's title, *Among the Ruins*), and was included at the very beginning of *The Heart of the Race* (*YLZ* 1:86–92).[21] Varuzhan guides his reader on an imaginary visit to the ruins of the dead city (which he himself had never seen, of course, and never would, but which he also did not need to see with his own eyes, so established were the reveries of Ani as a topos in the national literature of the nineteenth century). Why visit Ani, why enter this city of ashes, this Tomb of the nation, this "cemetery in which the bones of a past victory lie rotting" (l. 7)? "To weep, to embrace it, to remember, to reflect, to scream . . ." (ll. 1–3)?[22] Varuzhan speaks in the present tense. He is alone; no one accompanies him. The importance of this will soon become clear. I am, he says, the "last" bud, the "last" head reborn on the national Hydra (ll. 12–13). Art is what comes at the end—that is how the artist is habitually characterized in Varuzhan, and he expresses this on numerous occasions, as we will see. I want to "gently rock your death," he says, with the story of your past glory. Nothing remains of you but these stones, this dilapidation, this shame at having been taken apart by the wolves, one stone after another (l. 48). There follows a long rhetorical passage on the theme, "What remains of your past glory?" after which the poet begins an ascent up the city walls, which is also a movement toward a space of "liberty" (line 127). This ascent prefigures others that will come later in the same book, and then also in the poems in *Pagan Songs*. For the moment, he contemplates the city from these heights (within Ani, but already beyond it, above it), and he writes:

> Oh instinctive ascent,
> Oh drunken pursuit, be it
> Above a black tomb of bones,
> Oh sublime heights, you caress my sensitive soul,
> By making me, here on the ashes of my ancestors,
> Into a bud, still beautiful on the old trunk.
> Oh fascinating heights
> Where I hang from the purple thread of thought
> Between the azure and the darkness
> You give my heart the fleeting consolation
> That I will find below, beneath my feet,
> Reflected in Ani, the greatness of the heavens,
> That I will see on our tomb
> The planets pursuing their paths,
> That this darkness is the sublime face of the Idea
> That this collapse is the faltering of Eternity,

That the dust of Ani is the Milky Way, and
That the glow-worm is a beautiful star,
That this skull here is a moon and that I am God . . .
God? Ridiculous! This is nothing
But the caricature of God
Because our soul is the whore of nature
Because it produces only in the warmth of its womb,
Having nothing of its own, before this Nothing
Of a Fatherland, before this tohu-bohu,
As a first seed,
Not even a word of revolt that could create, or harmonize,
From the dust of Ani,
A Canaan new and free.   (*YLZ* 1:190, ll. 133–61)[23]

It is thus a question of this "Nothing of a Fatherland." And if I cannot hope for any
renaissance from this nothingness, then why go on living? Of course, the entire poem
is thus a sort of call or curse directed at the sons of this nation, which is not worthy of
living if it does not know how to revolt, if it cannot show itself to be worthy of its ancestors, if it cannot create a new Canaan on its own "ancestral lands." But that is only
one side of national aestheticism. The last lines of the passage just cited require some
commentary, which will perhaps show a completely different side. First, the ascent: it
allows one to discover that one is an heir. It also allows one to discover, in the historical ruins, a trace, a mark, a face—each time unexpected—of infinity, of the Idea, or
of eternity. The ascent offers thus a sort of dialectal inverse, like the darkness necessary
to light. It provides consolation for those ejected from history to think that ejection
has its necessary place (as a default, as a hidden face, as a revelator, as a historical
moment—these figures of spirit are well known and became widespread in the twentieth century) in the luminous system of historical meaning. But who will provide the
link between the ashes and the bud, between the tomb and the planets, between the
darkness and the Idea (terrible in its solar luminosity), between the collapse and Eternity? Who if not the one who has dared to confront the solitude of the ruins, who has
risen above the widow city so that this link can be established? I say all of this both in
seriousness and with irony, of course, and I have learned this irony from Varuzhan
himself, who turns the glow-worm into a star, and the skull at his feet into a moon.
But there is no Romantic art without irony.

We are quite far, it seems, from the nothingness of the fatherland and the default of
mourning, and the irony of the passage seems to accentuate its rhetorical aspect even
more. But throughout this passage Varuzhan has done nothing other than speak, in
a more and more detached and ironic way, of himself, this visitor to Ani, this climber
scaling the heights of the Idea; that is, he has done nothing but speak of himself as a
poet, and therefore, in reality, of art in the form of poetry. It is certainly not poetry

that will raise the dead, whose bones are dug up by the poet-traveler; poetry is not what will revive the heroes the fatherland needs. Poetry will not open or efface the tombs, it will not close the cemetery or transform it into a flourishing city. Nor will it create an artificial continuity in a space ruled by interruption and rupture. And yet, in a flash, it will tear open the space between the Tomb and the Idea. The fatherland has been annihilated, it is a sepulchral, tomblike universe, only because there is the Idea. But inversely, there is no Idea that is not above such a dark and terrifying universe of tombs, like the luminous realm of which the tombs are obscure remains, black holes, sources of dark emanation. Let us go a step further. Let us consider the natives, the survivors of this ancient disaster that does not speak its name. Here they are, many centuries later, full of fear, no shouts (*por't'kum*) in their throats, no revolt, hidden deep within the density of nature, unable to rise above it (toward the Idea, precisely), unable to demand their freedom, to become heroes, to return to their country (which, however, they have never left), unable to conquer the Promised Land, the new Canaan, the same (*nuyn*) country, their own country (*ink' iren sep'akan*), but one that would have become a fatherland, finally, for the first time, a fatherland they never had. And as long as they continue to be these fearful natives, there will be no fatherland, there will be only nothingness. These natives here are thus so many sepulchral stones, all of them mute, mute as the city is mute. And yet each of them, immured in his silence, is a fallen witness to past glory, and is like an inhabitant of chaos, of the tohubohu (*t'ohuboh* in Armenian, which Varuzhan shortens simply to *boh*).

Of course there is nothing new in any of this. What I mean is that the native in question here is the native of orientalism, this native whose presence was a riddle for national philology, which didn't know what to do with him or her except to send its travelers and *flâneurs* to visit them,[24] so that they could examine more closely these strange beings who had been promoted to their status as natives at the beginning of the nineteenth century, and so that they might discover, after all, what constituted them— these beings who were incapable of representing themselves or interpreting themselves, who could not write their own history. Is it at all surprising that aesthetic nationalism would rediscover the native, if we know that it was established through a violent affinity with the philological orientalism of the preceding century?

That is not what is surprising. Varuzhan obviously did not invent the figure of the native as a fallen witness, as a living ruin, as an inhabitant of chaos, or as a being who is responsible for the nothing of fatherland, and involved in it. He did not invent that; what he invented, or rather what he discovered, what he exposes, and what he assembles from the ground up for the very first time, is the *aesthetic logic* of the invention of the native. That is why I have been referring to an "aesthetic nationalism" that is articulated in this work and that will in fact be present throughout the work and thought of this entire generation, that of Varuzhan and his friends. Indeed, the exposition of the aesthetic logic that governs nationalism is certainly not a "deconstruction" of this nationalism. It is rather its *completion*, in a sense, and this completion is accompanied by the exposure of its most intimate inner mechanism—the aesthetic principle. Not for a moment does Varuzhan cast doubt on the nature of the fallen witness and the living ruin of the native, this obligatory figure in the philological orientalism of the nineteenth century. The Armenians had completely internalized this orientalism; the same is true of all the ancient peoples before them who had been *subjects* of the European and Eastern empires, beginning with the Greeks and the Serbs at the very beginning of the century, in a way that was much more rapid and concentrated in time. They had so internalized this orientalism that they turned themselves into natives and philologists, traveling into the past; then natives and explorers, traveling in the present; and finally natives and ethnologists, suspended between past and present. Natives and philologists, natives and travelers: these are the relations established in the first part of the century (from 1810 to 1820), as an immediate repercussion of European orientalism, among the Mkhitarist fathers in Venice. This is particularly true for two of their representatives who had established a living relation with the century (they are the first writers in modern Armenian): Minas Pzhshgean and Lucas Injijean—who, however, are far from being the best known among the extraordinary constellation of philologists, scholars, writers, poets, translators, and grammarians that the Congregation produced during the first half of the nineteenth century. Finally, natives and ethnographers: that is the relation announced by Khachatur Abovean around 1840, in the preface to his novel *Wounds of Armenia*, a relation that materialized three decades later with the immense wave of internal ethnography, or auto-ethnography, among both Eastern and Western Armenians, those living under the Russian Empire as well as those living under the Ottoman Empire. The entire project of national philology and national ethnography—that is, in fact, the project of the nation itself, the very idea of the nation—is thus put into place over the course of the century, triggered by the immediate internalization of orientalism, and therefore by the "autoscopic mimicry" that Stathis Gourgouris discusses in *Dream Nation*, his remarkable book on archaeology and Greek nationalism (Gourgouris borrows his terms and part of his approach from Homi Bhabha, the theorist of nationalisms in the age of diaspora).

With these brief remarks, which have been laid out and developed in more detail in the first part of this book,[25] I want to suggest how the construction of the figure of the native by orientalist discourse (which was and still is above all a discourse of philology) essentially determined the history of nationalisms, and how Edward Said's description of it in *Orientalism* (in 1978) was a decisive event for the understanding of this history (even though Said himself said almost nothing about it in this important work). This figure still had to be isolated, of course, and considered as the central moment in a general structure of interpretation that was at work throughout the nineteenth century.[26]

AESTHETICIZATION, ONCE AGAIN

Between the native and his archaeological past, there stands the philologist. Between the native and his mythological past, there stands the ethnologist. Or rather, both of these figures, the philologist and the ethnologist, weave together a signifying network that definitively turns the native into the tomb or the living ruin of meaning, the one to whom historical meaning, beneath its archaeological and mythological appearances, must be restored, as though in spite of him—whether he wants it or not, and whether he *knows* it or not. They too already establish the constitutive flash of light between the two extremes of the Ruin and Meaning, or the Tomb and the Idea. Yet they are quite incapable of saying what the law of this reciprocal constitution is. The native is the tomb of the idea and the ruin of meaning. He must therefore be restored to himself. He must be deciphered, the tomb must be brought back to the idea, and the ruin to its meaning. Did the native ever have a fatherland? What characterizes him, in the very moment when he is constituted, is his decline, his state of decay in relation to a superior civilization, circumscribed within a more or less distant past. He is not his own master. He is at once alienated and subjected. Taken together, alienation and subjection form the nothingness of the fatherland. We should recall what Hagop Oshagan wrote a few years later, in 1914, in the third issue of the journal *Mehyan*, in an article entitled "The Literature of All Armenians" (whose title echoes the name of the Armenian National Church): "Fragmented, aged, driven from its center, land, and religion, vagabond . . . without a name or body, a tottering multitude stands before us";[27] and on the same page: "To forge the integrity of our fragmented existence, we await our Dante." The "great workers," the "creators of the nation" will be its artists. Let us remember that in 1911 and 1913, in two important articles, one on the Armenian language, the other on the poet Siamanto, Varuzhan spoke of this same fragmentation within the language, which could be countered, he says, only by consistently working to give back language its "wholeness," or rather to make this wholeness emerge within it.[28] The debate of 1911 about language had been launched by the journal *Azatamart*, where it was framed in terms of the nature of the modern Armenian language. Many Armenian intellectuals had participated in this debate and had expressed some exceedingly nationalistic views. The "true" Armenian language was not the one that was being written at the time; it had to be a language inspired by the "central" dialects, from areas where Armenians were the majority population (the regions of Van, Erzerum, Harpoot, Bitlis . . .). This is the thesis of centrality. Varuzhan intervened in the debate by framing the problem in terms of aestheticization. Later he returned to the question in his essay on Siamanto. The following is an excerpt of particular interest to us here:

> The third criticism directed at our vernacular is that we have tended this language too much toward *grabar* [classical Armenian]. I think that such a notion is off the mark. Among the best Armenian writers in Turkey, you will not find a single one who has fallen into the trap of grabar. It is true that we have borrowed vocables and

roots from classical Armenian, but we have completely abandoned its grammar and its idiomatic forms, which are virtually incomprehensible today. The ancient language is a goldmine for a writer with taste who is able to draw from its semantic wealth; such a writer can select and polish what he finds, and he can be sure that his effort will be rewarded. I know that all of you, for as long as you exist, want the Armenian race to regain its long-lost force of will [korov], its combativeness, the proud and noble ways of life it had before, when Armenians made their language resound in the army and on the battlefield, or when they fashioned the arabesques of their language among the marble columns of their palaces or in the ceremonial halls of their princes [sepuh]. . . . If you want to restore to this race some of the character of its ancestors, why would you not also give its literature the powerful and expressive treasures that will best serve to reflect this character? That is the path on which our vernacular will progress. The first path is one that passes through the provincial dialects, in which one may find some lovely and useful flowers from the natural world [bnashkharh], untouched by artifice, with its naïve beauties that are close to our hearts. And it would be absurd to think that this whole and integral form of the language (to which the Armenian poet and writer can turn with much profit) will be imposed by grammarians, philologists, and a few strict minds besotted with systematicity—which would indeed be ridiculous. This is rather the task of the writer-aesthetes [geghaget-graget], and the success of the enterprise will depend on whatever talent and taste they are able to show. (YLZ 3:162–63)

In defending the archaizing tendency of Western Armenian, Varuzhan also promotes a certain recourse both to the classical language and to the "regional languages." But he does so only in terms of a takeover or a *sublation* of the old scholarly language and the popular forms of speech in literary language, referring to the latter as "the language that best reveals the treasures of the language in all their shining brilliance" (YZL 3:163). It is precisely this sublation that Varuzhan and his generation called an "aestheticization" of language, for the brilliance in question is that of an aestheticized language; it is the brilliance of art. This same will to aestheticization is found in a completely different domain in Komitas, who, during this same period, was systematically collecting popular songs in order to reconstruct them and work them into the sphere of art. The generation of *Mehyan* was perfectly aware of the similarity between these projects.

In my book on the history of the Armenian language and my essay on Charents in *Writers of Disaster: The National Revolution*, I have discussed the declarations made by Varuzhan and the generation of *Mehyan* in terms of a "buried misfortune" that struck the collective voice at its source.[29] I presented the same explanation once again at the beginning of this volume, in chapter 1, on the "variants and facets of literary erection." Art, aestheticized language, became imperative only because they were destined to take over for, to sublate, a voice that had become inaudible, drained completely dry.

At the same time, I believe that this imperative contains a chronic dissatisfaction concerning the literary modalities of their language that had never ceased haunting the Western Armenians. For Varuzhan and his friends at *Mehyan*, the literarization of the language was incomplete because it had not been an aestheticization! In his well-known articles of 1911 and 1913, Varuzhan ceaselessly repeats that very thing: one cannot write in the dialects, precisely because they are natural languages, and as such are incomprehensible, inaudible, stricken with the generalized exhaustion of the "natural" collective voice. One is nonetheless obliged to refer to them because they continue to be threatened by a violence at their source, to which in fact they have long since succumbed. The natural languages, much like the popular productions, are "sources" that must be brought to light by this aestheticization, which was demanded by the entire generation including Varuzhan and Oshagan, but also Komitas. The silence of the collective voice, the internal tearing apart of a communitarian body already shaken by disaster, here constituted the primary experience of a generation that produced the greatest Armenian writers of the century. We are therefore obliged to credit them, to follow what they say, and to heed the lessons of their incredible will to aestheticization, which becomes a desire to restore wholeness to a disintegrated communitarian body and to a collective voice stricken by an unnamed misfortune. The experience of the *Mehyan* generation thus allows us to discern the invisible event to which the phenomenon of literarization was a response. Hence Varuzhan's statement, already quoted above: "And it would be absurd to think that this whole and integral form of the language . . . will be imposed by grammarians, philologists, and a few strict minds besotted with systematicity. . . . This is rather the task of the writer-aesthetes." Much later, Hagop Oshagan would recall this phrase once again when, in his *Panorama of Western Armenian Literature*, he wrote: "We need philologists who are also philosophers and artists" (8:33).[30]

This experience to which Varuzhan and his friends respond with their will to aestheticization, this "buried misfortune," is thus given a name in Varuzhan's poetry. The experience, the misfortune, and the disaster: these are all designated by Varuzhan as the "nothingness" of the fatherland, the "tomb" of the Idea, and the "ruin" of meaning, which are the marks of the native. But then two questions arise: 1) If this originary decline and decay of the native can be qualified as experience, how can it be, at the same time, an assumption of the orientalism internalized by the subjected people? 2) The "aesthetic principle" functions as an imperative demanding the literarization of the language and the centrality of the artist in a process that restores integrity and wholeness to a disintegrated collectivity; it also requires the appropriation of popular productions, of treasures that were never seen, of the songs from which we are alienated, an appropriation always realized by means of art or understood in any case as a process of aestheticization, a reception into the light of art. In that case, how can the same "aesthetic principle" be used to account for the invention of the native?

In order to establish some common ground for these questions, let us recall a few points. Before the *Mehyan* generation, Komitas took on the task of recasting as art the popular songs he had collected and transcribed on his long wanderings through the provinces. For the members of the *Mehyan* group, and particularly for Hagop Oshagan, Komitas clearly offered something of a paradigm. His project obviously involved "aestheticizing" popular sources, rather than "popularizing" music. We recall that in 1914 Oshagan wrote, "A Priest of Labor has transformed our songs into music as marvelous as a revelation for us."[31] The "reappropriation" of what had become foreign (and of what in reality had been fundamentally foreign to us since always) can be accomplished in this way only through the "aesthetic" principle. Likewise, for the entire *Mehyan* generation, the aestheticized language is the one that takes over and sublates the "popular sources." It is precisely through this sublation that it creates the "nation." In doing so, it does not ignore the fundamental alienation from these sources referred to as popular. "We" have to reappropriate something that has become foreign, something that, paradoxically, is usually considered to be what is most "proper" to us, what is most our own. We have thus become "strangers to ourselves." This reappropriation requires an elaboration, a labor that is nothing other than the labor of art. The reappropriation of what has become foreign to "us" and that, in the end, constitutes this "we" as such, as a national "we," is possible only through the "aesthetic principle." In every case, this national "we" must be placed in quotation marks, for it depends in every way on the labor of art. And if "we" are a nation, the nation itself is clearly the product of an "aestheticization," the result of an aestheticizing process. That is the credo of the *Mehyan* generation. This position was precisely the one that would be proposed by Yeghishe Charents as a "third path" in his lecture of June 8, 1934 entitled "The Development of Our Literary Language." The phenomenon of aestheticization was understood by him as the completion of literary language, in both senses of the term. It completes the process begun by the literarization of the language; but it also means, quite simply, what happens at the very moment of this always-incomplete literarization. That is also why Charents spoke of an "aestheticized literary language," an expression that does not refer simply to "literature." What he had in mind was a "national form" as a transformative space in which the "popular sources," dialects, myths, languages, and natural productions, could be received, sublated, sublimated, and transmuted into something else—that is, into art.

It is in this sense that Varuzhan, twenty years before Charents, defended the archaic forms of Western Armenian, while also foreseeing a certain use of "regional languages," a use that could only take place as a transsubstantiation of popular idioms into literary language. For it is only literary language that is able to bring the "treasures of the language" to their fulfillment, their wholeness. In the same vein, the *Mehyan* Manifesto explicitly announced in 1914: "We want to create an aesthetics of the language." It was this sublimation and transsubstantiation of the popular idiom into a literary language—which thereby becomes a "national language" in an always renewed process—that Varuzhan and his friends at *Mehyan* called an "aesthetics" of language. Two decades later, Charents took up the same idea and used the same words to speak of it. The

shining brilliance that alone allows the hidden treasures of the languages and the popular productions to appear was interpreted by all of them as the brilliance of art. And
as I pointed out, this is the same will to aestheticize the popular sources that one finds
in Komitas.

We can now offer a provisional response to the two questions asked above (on the
experience of the disaster as the originary experience of the native, and on the aesthetic principle as a principle both for a transsubstantiation of supposedly abandoned
popular forms and for the philological *invention* of the very idea of "popular forms").
These are very difficult questions, for the entire status of aestheticization is at issue in
them. For Varuzhan and his contemporaries, what is involved in the literarization of the
vernacular language, the beginnings of philology, and the auto-ethnographic phenomenon cannot be understood in the terms used by these disciplines themselves
(ethnology, philology), nor in the terms of the historical phenomenon of literarization.
That is why, according to Varuzhan (as well as for Oshagan, let it be said in passing),
these terms must be opposed, or one must bring to completion the movements of
philology, literarization, and auto-ethnography. These disciplines contribute to the
advent of the "national form," and yet they are radically ignorant of its processes. That
is why we see in Varuzhan, and later in Oshagan, the establishment of a common front
against the philologists and, at the same time, a dependence on philology precisely because of this explicit opposition. The "integral" form of the language will be established
not by philologists and grammarians, who are incapable of such a task, but by artists
and writers. Clearly again, Varuzhan is not referring here to a merely linguistic project.
He articulates the necessity of completing the incomplete literarization of the language
as a reaction to a profound "disintegration," which corresponds to the annihilation of
the fatherland. He also speaks of the necessity for a reception of the buried "treasures,"
and a nationalization of "natural" productions, which correspond to their transferral
into the sphere of art, their transubstantiation and their sublimation, their elevation
to the Idea. National philology and auto-ethnography obviously did not correspond
to any of these conditions. They were ignorant of their own principle. They therefore
presented an obstacle to the "nationalization" of their objects, to the advent of the
whole and integral form; they had no idea of the collective disintegration, of the annihilation of the fatherland, to which they in fact contributed. It is thus indeed a question of disintegration and annihilation. These are the terms by which the aesthetic
principle is to be measured. But since the implementation of this principle aspires to
bring to completion, to fulfill, a program that was put into place with national philology and auto-ethnography—and therefore with the discovery or the invention of the
figure of the native, which was a central phenomenon in the establishment of philology in Europe—it must be admitted that the aesthetic principle also tells us something about how that establishment took place.[32] The native is in effect the monument
in ruins, the silent tomb of ancient culture, the fallen witness of past splendor. *Orientalist philology supposes and presupposes a disaster, always and fundamentally, in its very*

definition and realization. It obviously does not have the means to reflect on this sup-position. Nor does it have the capacity to integrate the assumed disaster in any way into its own language. Thus we see how the "writers of disaster," in the fulfillment of aesthetic nationalism, are quite strangely the only ones who revealed the hidden work-ings of orientalist philology. But they in turn can do this only by investing in the figure—both new and conventional—of the native.

That is why it is absurd, in the end, to ask whether there is an original experience of the native or whether the native is a pure invention. For the invention itself is *the in-vention of an experience of disaster,* which never appears to itself before the generation of aesthetic nationalism (except with Abovean, in a brief flash, in the initial moment of auto-ethnography). The experience and the invention are one. They coincide to the point of being one and the same thing, however paradoxical that may seem. But, one might object, an experience can't be invented! And yet, that is exactly what happened. The experience of disaster was invented by orientalism and philology. Invented, to be sure, but never reflected upon, never accounted for, never integrated. Hence the disin-tegration, the chaos, the tohu-bohu, the nothingness of the Fatherland.

Let us be very clear: Were the subjects of the Ottoman Empire not oppressed, ne-gated in their "identity," subjected to a tyrannical power, reduced to the status of cogs in a system of domination? Were they not "cut off" from their glorious past, like the thread of national destiny that Varuzhan spoke of, interwoven forever, perhaps, with the ruins of Ani—that is, doomed to decline without return? Were they not subjected, defeated, drained of their substance (that is, drained of their capacity to sculpt heroes in the marble of their native mountains and, simultaneously, drained of their capacity or their potential for mourning), were they not alienated from themselves? All of this is true, without a doubt. But all of this is true only today, for it is only today that we understand identity in terms of "culture," a culture that would belong to us as our "own," as what is "proper" to us, and from which we can therefore be alienated. It is only today that the history of the language and its continual vicissitudes are inscribed in and as the language itself and are decipherable as such. It is only today that one can be "cut off" from the past, since there is now, and from now on, a national subject who is the bearer of an experience, an assumption of continuity. By "today" I mean, roughly, from the end of the eighteenth century. That is what obliged the Congregation of the Mkhitarists, in the person of Mikaël Chamchean, to write a *History of the Armenians* in the 1780s, during that grand century, and during those same years when, elsewhere in Europe, with Herder among others, the idea arose of a culture proper to a nation, that is, quite simply, the modern notion of "the proper."[33] Finally, it is therefore only today that this subjection shows itself for what it is: a sacrificial exploitation of identity by the dominant people. So, once again: the invention of the native (objective genet-ive) and the experience of the native (subjective genetive) are one and the same. Philol-ogy (that is, all at once, the idea of a culture proper to the nation or the race,[34] the literarization of the texts from the tradition, the orientalization of the foreigner and of oneself) assumes a disaster, it *posits* the experience of a disaster in the very moment (the inaugural moment, the moment of its own inauguration) when it invents the native. There is no longer any mistaking this. But it is only today that this positing and assumption of the experience of disaster can be understood, repeated, and discussed. And this time, "today" is the moment when I am writing, as an heir to Daniel Varuzhan, to the *Mehyan* generation, and to the writers of disaster. It is here, then, for the first time, at the very heart of the matter, the heart of orientalism in its inaugural moment, that a critique of orientalism—which is to say also of philology and all its accompanying phenomena—can be fully carried out. What is the heart of the matter? It is the invention and the experience of the native as a witness and already as the *survivor* of a properly immemorial disaster, a disaster that would have preceded all memory.

But there is another objection that should be addressed. Whether this immemorial disaster is understood now as an experience posited and "assumed" by philology in the moment of its modern inauguration and its invention of the native, or as a "real" experience (although one that has been archived) of the survivors of a culture that was their own in ancient times, that was inscribed in their language, their history, their genes, their collective unconscious, or their memorial traces—in either case, the immemorial disaster belongs to an underlying structure that would seem to have little connection with contemporary events or even (perhaps) with the politico-sacrificial system of domination in which the subject people is enclosed. But Varuzhan did not need any underlying structure to know about subjection, alienation, and psychic and physical destruction. The continuous wave of the massacres in 1895, across the Armenian high plateau, and in 1896 in Constantinople, were fresh memories for all Armenians, in the provinces and in the capital. Varuzhan had lived through it as a child, in the Sebastea region as well as in Constantinople, where his father was imprisoned in 1896. And he would live through it again in April 1909, this time from a distance, with the massacres in Cilicia, the only region that had escaped from the massacres of 1895. He therefore did not need the experience of the disaster proper to the native in order to recount the butchery, the destruction, the desolation, the collective misery, the programmed disappearance of a national collectivity and, finally, the Catastrophe, which was emerging on the horizon or was already there. Moreover, his narrative poems from *The Heart of the Race* are largely a response to the desolation of an Armenian population that had been devastated and decimated by the will of the executioners in 1895. Why, in these conditions, would it be necessary to refer to an immemorial disaster and to the experience of the native, when it is a question of understanding the "nothingness of the fatherland"?

This is a serious and important question that cannot be avoided, but I can only partially address it in the present context. The objection implies that it is in reality the dominant people's will to destruction that determines the annihilation of which Varuzhan speaks. It implies that this will to destruction is determinant in the experience of the disaster for the native, for the survivor, or (as we would say in these circumstances) for the victim. But that is not the case, for several reasons. The first reason is that this disaster is at the very heart of the "national awakening" beginning in 1840, and no doubt before. The second is that the "annihilation" of which Varuzhan and his generation speak is one that, if we accept their categories, calls for and demands an "aestheticization," whereas the will to destruction and its effects are usually understood in terms of political oppression and resistance. The third reason is that this will to destruction does not appear as such until the end of the century, around the same time as the movement and the ideology of "national liberation." Far from being yet another manifestation of the imperial system of domination, the will to destruction marks the moment when this system is coming to an end and being dismantled. The problem is that the will to destruction, which was soon transformed entirely into a genocidal will, led to a Catastrophe that the Armenians have never been able to interpret except in political terms or, in the best accounts of the events, as the result of a "culture of violence" attributed to the perpetrator.[35] If we are to understand these events, we must begin to clear away this type of political or "cultural" interpretation of the will of the perpetrator, which is simply inadequate.

CATASTROPHIC MOURNING AND REPRESENTATION

After this necessary interlude on the theme of disaster and aestheticization, we must return for a moment to the city of Ani, and to these verses by Varuzhan that summoned us there:

> Because our soul is the whore of nature
> Because it produces only in the warmth of its womb,
> Having nothing of its own, before this Nothing
> Of a Fatherland, before this tohu-bohu,
> As a first seed,
> Not even a word of revolt that could create, or harmonize,
> From the dust of Ani,
> A Canaan new and free.

It should be clear that what has been described as "aestheticization" is also an appropriation, or an appropriative event, an *Ereignis* in Heidegger's language. Indeed, as I explained above, this aestheticization was a "reappropriation" of popular sources that had been used up, exhausted, and devastated, that had become inaudible or, in general, inaccessible. Aestheticization, as an event, is the advent of the proper, of what enables us to say "we"; it is what produces the "national." That is why in *Krake shrjanakë* (Circle of Fire), in his commentary on the lines just quoted, Krikor Beledian emphasizes the word *sephakan*, which can only be rendered as "proper," and he preserves the reading of the original text, with the phrase *nuyn ink' iren*, which as it stands does not make sense. Thus he writes: "What Varuzhan has in mind is an impropriety within identity itself, within sameness itself. In other words, the proper has somehow ceased to be proper, it has become other. Confronted with the nothingness of my own fatherland, I have no speech of my own, no proper speech."[36] And a little later: "For Varuzhan, the concept of fatherland . . . assumes, in general, a dimension of alterity, or we could say, a dimension of internal difference . . . The country is not the simple site of the proper. . . . Even within it, the proper is lacking to the proper."[37] What is at stake here is the entire logic of the invention of the native and of the assumption of the disaster. Let us approach it now from another angle, in terms of mourning.

Confronted with the nothingness of the fatherland, the native does not even have his own proper speech, a speech that would enable one to create a new Canaan, to give form to the national, to produce the national as form. The native cannot produce any form, since he belongs to nature, and everything he creates simply returns into nature's breast. Only art can create a form and produce the national. But the native remains a natural creature because he is unequal to the nothingness of the fatherland, to the chaos and the disaster that carry him along and define him. And how could he be equal to it, if it is true that the disaster is the ruin of meaning? Indeed, in order to articulate the ruin of meaning, there must be a meaning that is not in ruins. That is the general argument invoked here, covertly or explicitly, by Varuzhan. We do not possess as properly our own that which would enable us to say (to confront, to integrate, to formulate, to metabolize) the loss or the absence of the proper. We lack the proper by which to say the lack of the proper. There are many different ways to say this, in various equivalent formulations that would all have to borrow their language from the terms used by the poet. Let us attempt a few such formulations. How is it possible to mourn the fatherland, since one must have a fatherland in order to mourn, and since, in reality, the fatherland is but another name for the very capacity to mourn, for what was referred to above as the "ability to mourn"? What kind of mourning is possible for the loss of the fatherland (the ruination of meaning, the tomb of the idea), that is, for the loss of something that, in reality, is no doubt *the very capacity to integrate loss, the capacity not to be completely destroyed and disintegrated by it*? And today we would say, with somewhat different words—words that take up the whole terrible argument of Varuzhan's poem and that, in any case, invalidate all the right-thinking (and no doubt well-meaning) or moralistic discourses on the call to memory after the Catastrophe or (for that matter) after the Holocaust: How is it possible to preserve or to cultivate a memory of the Catastrophe when it is precisely a question of a catastrophe of memory? These are questions that try desperately, in an almost formalist way, to take into account the nature of the disaster at issue here. There is humanity only where there is mourning. But if mourning is lost, if the ability to mourn is lacking, then what are we to do? How can we mourn mourning? How can we respond to catastrophic mourning? We will encounter these same questions again later in similar terms, but this time not on the basis of the originary structure of the native and his immanent disaster, but on the basis of the present discovery of the sacred as lost and therefore of the very paradoxical relation between art and religion.

CHAPTER 5

The Other Scene of Representation

A few months after writing the poem on the ruins of Ani, when he received news of the terrifying massacres in Cilicia, Varuzhan wrote another poem about a visit to another ruined city. This time it was Adana, where the Armenian quarter had been completely destroyed in April 1909, in two successive waves that took place one week apart (April 1 to 4, then April 12 to 14). The poem is entitled "To the Ashes of Cilicia," and it was placed at the end of the first part of *The Heart of the Race*. This was the last poem that Varuzhan included in this collection. I would like to present a brief analysis of this poem, as an echo to the question of catastrophic mourning and in order to counterbalance what has already been said on the immemorial character of the disaster and on the invention of the native.[1] Indeed, the tone suddenly changes here. It is no longer a question of an imaginary visit to a city with a glorious past, a city that now exists only in ruins. It is a visit in the present, to a city which has just been devastated by a sudden, blind, atrocious violence. This time, Varuzhan does not make the visit alone. He is in the company of a "foreigner," a "stranger" to whom the entire poem is addressed. This is how it begins:

> Stranger, let us climb this little hill before us
> Beside which the weeping Sihon flows through the reeds,
> The Sihon, where tomorrow the sorrowing mothers
> Will wash the red chlamys. Stranger, hurry,
> For my feet are burning on these hot ashes
> And the hem of your long robe has begun
> To soak in the marsh. Stranger, hurry.[2]

And the poet proceeds to describe to the stranger, the foreigner, what he sees, or rather, what both of them see. The poem is punctuated by commands such as "See!" (two times), "Hurry!," "Remember!" and "Listen!" This last imperative enjoins the stranger to listen to the sounds of the celebration (in which Islam, for the first time, drinks a glass of wine in honor of the ashes) of the "executioner people" and to the deathly silence that rises from the other side of the city. The first "See!" points the stranger to the smoke, the flames that are still burning. The earth itself is burning: "See! the inflamed horizon surrounding us / Is a glowing crown, in its center we are standing, / Trembling like strange spirits in mourning" (*YLZ* 1:147).[3] Because the central image of the poem is ash, fire too is everywhere. Even the pilgrim's staff is half burnt, this staff that he points "in the direction of my words" (*khosk'is ughghut'eamb*), by which he means of course that he is indicating the scenes that he describes and privileges; but here the expression "my words" designates poetic speech, a speech that creates a meaning in a landscape now deprived of meaning and direction. In order to do this, this speech resonates from the heart of the fire's incandescence, its ravaging force. Indeed, this poem is obsessed with fire. The orchards are on the verge of being transformed to ashes (*mokhratsogh aygestan*), here as in the title of the novel by Gurgen Mahari, *Ayrvogh aygestanner* (Burning Orchards). It is the evening of a long day of orgiastic murder. The collapsed houses await the first night of mourning. The fields and the streets are littered with corpses. Seven men were crucified before a long wall of rock; from their naked corpses blood still drips, and from their hands and feet, and the setting sun sinks little by little into their horrified eyes. But just before he describes this scene of the crucified men—a scene that is central to the poem, but one that is (it must be said) quite grotesque—the poet-pilgrim exhorts his foreign companion: "Stranger, I beg you / Close your eyes, only listen to what my voice says" (*YLZ* 1:148). Once again, poetic speech alone is capable of saying the devastation, the speech that resonates from the heart of incandescence, from the heart of catastrophic mourning. Here, seeing is impossible. The incandescent speech reduced to ashes, the only speech sufficient to this mourning, does not describe or show. In a word (which might seem clear at first sight, but in fact requires an infinite elaboration), it does not *represent*. Catastrophic mourning cannot be a unified and coherent object of representation that could be placed before the eyes of the "stranger," so that he too could see what "really" happened.

THE TIME OF THE IMAGE AND THE TIME OF TESTIMONY

We have thus entered into a third aspect of our examination of the "aesthetic principle." The first aspect was the aesthetic logic governing the invention of the native. The second concerned aestheticization as an appropriation of self in the becoming-nation or the advent of the fatherland. The third aspect is the "representation" of the Catastrophe, or rather the complex relationship between testimony and representation. Before addressing this question more thoroughly, we should say that it has obsessed Armenians for almost a century, and it continues to do so today. The internal debate on the representation of the Catastrophe has resounded in very concrete ways throughout the twentieth century. It is worth recalling what Zabel Esayan wrote at the same time as Varuzhan's poem, after returning from Cilicia, in her book *Averaknerum mej* (Among the Ruins): "It is impossible to imagine the sum of the pain of each of the people that make up this crowd." Or: "I can try to recall details or partial images, but

I cannot calculate the sum of this infinite bloody history represented by each individual child."[4] I commented on these statements at some length in *Writers of Disaster: The National Revolution*. Here I will mention only one point: the insistence on the image. How can the heart of suffering, and the sum of many sufferings, be given an image? How can one imagine it? At any rate, with her testimony of 1909 (since *Among the Ruins* is indeed a book of testimony), Esayan rose to the task of erecting a monument of mourning to the victims of Cilicia. Her book is the only Armenian work of the twentieth century in which testimony succeeded in becoming literature or in turning literature to its own advantage, shaping it according to its own requirements, and even rendering problematic the very concept of literature in its confrontation with the Catastrophe. After 1915, Esayan was incapable of writing anything at all resembling a testimony on the Deportation or a monument of mourning. All the major authors of the century failed at the task. Hagop Oshagan stopped at the threshold of "Hell," which was to be the title of the third part of his novel *Mnatsortats* (The Remnants), the greatest novelistic work in the Armenian language of the entire century; he left this novel unfinished, for reasons that he was never quite able to explain. It was only in the second half of the century, after decades of mourning, that the great novels of Mahari (in Armenia) and Vorpouni (in the diaspora) appeared. But, indeed, these novels constituted a refusal to pay any tribute to the image. Let us say things somewhat differently now. Throughout the twentieth century, the Armenians never ceased recounting—to others and to themselves—their past sufferings, their years spent in the hell of the Deportation, and they did so both in Armenian and in the languages of the civilized world. The destiny of this testimonial literature, taken as a whole, was to provide an infinite number of items for the archive meant for "the stranger" or "the foreigner," items that are entirely illegible and that in fact have never been read by "the foreigner."[5] Must the question of representation, of the image, of the unimaginable and the "un-imageable" be distinguished, then, from the question of testimony? That is what would be necessary, but it is also precisely what is impossible, with an impossibility that is quasi-structural, since the most damaging effect of the Catastrophe is that it keeps its victims within the circle of the archive, or for that matter, within the circle of testimony transformed into proof. The recent film by Atom Egoyan, *Ararat*, addresses this problem by transporting it into the domain of cinema. This could only aggravate the dilemma, since film must of course entrust itself to the power of the image, even while problematizing it as Egoyan does through the *mise-en-abîme* of the events represented. So is *Ararat* a work of art or is it yet another testimony? To whom is the image addressed? The crux of the film is located, as we might expect, in the confrontation with the guardian of the law (the civilized law), who receives the speech addressed to the foreigner. This is exactly the same gesture as that of Varuzhan's staff, at the beginning of his poem on Cilicia, this half-burnt staff that is pointed toward the scene of the crime and the misfortune. By 1909, then, Varuzhan had already written and described the entirety of this delirious scene, in which the poet shows and points,

repeating the injunction "See!" while at the same time announcing from the very beginning that the reign of the image is closed, that no image can take account of the
Catastrophe. That is what Krikor Beledian writes in an extraordinary phrase found at
the center of his commentary on the poem "To the Ashes of Cilicia": "The time of the
image is past."[6] This does not mean that today we can no longer create images, that we
cannot make films, that we cannot recount, describe, or show, that we are not invited
always and again to *see*. On the contrary, that is all we ever do. Rather, the image is
past because the fire of destruction has burnt everything, and because today we live on
the ashes of what was. It is past because it still assumed an intact belief in the capacity
to frame, to imagine, to communicate, to represent. It is past, finally, because the image in art assumes a presence, and because art is supposed to present anew through its
own means. But the Catastrophe is anything but a presence that could be presented to
the gaze, or that could be inscribed into a sensible intuition. In reality, even Egoyan,
elaborating the endless proliferation of images, announces that the time of the image
is past.[7] The time of the image is also that of light, since light is necessary for the visibility of the image. But Varuzhan says: the source of the light is falling below the horizon and it is flowing away, it is sinking, it is disappearing in the eyes of the crucified.
No matter: Varuzhan needed this extravagant image of the seven crucified bodies in
order to say the end of the image. This fact ought to lead us to reflect. For Varuzhan
clearly understood that the end of the empire of sacrifice was also announced with the
fire and the ashes of Cilicia. With the image of a grotesque sacrifice, it is indeed the end
of sacrifice that is inscribed in bloody letters into his poem, onto the very surface of the
poem. By structuring it as an address to the foreigner who hears the description of this
scene, by asking him to close his eyes, by suggesting to him the infinity of the devastation, by evoking in an extreme image the end of the reign of the image—an end that
coincides with the devastation or the renewed "annihilation" of the fatherland—and
by writing that the reign of the image is dependent on the light and its source and that
its end coincides with a true solar twilight, or even a definitive eclipse,[8] an eclipse
that is definitive in the end only for the victim and the survivor—by doing all of this,
the poet-guide of the devastated city is exploring for the first time the obscure laws that
unite (or oppose) testimony, representation, and catastrophic mourning. The Catastrophe calls for testimony. The latter depends entirely on the former, it moves entirely within
it. But there is no testimony without an appeal to the foreigner, an appeal made in various
forms. Varuzhan's poem, of course, is not a testimony. It reveals the form of testimony,
by making itself into a dialogue with the foreigner. Besides, the testimony is doomed to
failure by its very nature. Captured by the archive, it will fail to testify in any case, if it
remains what it is. Perhaps what Egoyan had in mind with the *mise-en-abîme* of a
representation within a narrative was this very idea of law and dialogue, impelled by a
deep suspicion of testimony.[9]

However, there is another persistent doubt that remains: the relations between testimony and representation are not clearly established. In 1909, another writer, Souren

Bartevian, published a series of articles in Armenian on the atrocities of Cilicia; later he collected these articles in a book entitled *Kilikean Arhavirk'ë* (The Horror of Cilicia).[10] This work leaves the reader with a bitter aftertaste. Indeed, it is full of invectives addressed to Europe, the foreign observer, invectives designed to arouse Europe's conscience before the enormity of the events in Cilicia. However, we can be sure that no European, no foreign observer, ever read these lines written by Bartevian, for the simple reason (an empirical reason, to be sure) that they were written in Armenian. It is not the case that there were no articles written at the time in French or in English for the purpose of affecting and alerting public opinion in Europe.[11] But the articles by Bartevian were, in fact, not at all meant to affect this public opinion. They were addressed to an Armenian audience, and they express only the rage and powerlessness of the victim. This internal contradiction of testimony will become even more acute after 1915, after the Deportation and the systematic destruction of the entire Armenian collectivity of the Ottoman Empire. The appeal to the foreigner is inherent to this type of testimony, and yet it is without result; it is contradictory within itself. It is a matter, in effect, of showing the destruction. In order to show the destruction, how can one do otherwise than to *show oneself destroyed*? But, conversely, how can one show oneself destroyed? How can one appear destroyed in the eyes of the world? The Catastrophe deports the survivor to the limit of himself or herself, to the limit of what in other places one would name his or her identity. But "identity" is nothing other than the capacity to appear in one's own eyes as in the eyes of the world, and each through the other. That is why "to appear destroyed" is a pure impossibility. And yet, it is a necessity. In order to appear, one needs a frame, a stage, a theater. The Greek invention of the theater was already, and from the beginning, a direct confrontation with the underlying catastrophe that continually threatened to emerge. Hagop Oshagan no doubt knew this when in 1931, concerning the "narrative" of the Deportation or of Hell, he said: "There is in any case no question of a narrative, but rather of a tragedy, one that extends through the years, with the difference that instead of a stage we have an entire world, and instead of actors, we have to do with human flesh, in its greatest diversity and in its most spiritually differentiated value."[12] To appear, what is necessary (and here I am modifying the common formula concerning the identity of the subject) is a possible identification, a theater of identification, limits, and the establishment of a law (law and limit are the same word in Armenian: *sahman*). But possible identification is precisely what is destroyed in the Catastrophe. To appear destroyed, it might then seem that it would be necessary to use another scene, the scene of the Other, that of the foreigner. This has two consequences. The testimony that is proffered for itself can only suffocate in its own contradiction. But the testimony proffered for the Other, for the foreigner—whether European or not—is obliged to use the identificatory resources of the Other, the theater of the Other, and in that case (as Oshagan will say) it makes the Catastrophe its "theme." We are in a situation in which language is no longer capable of symbolizing violence or of working for the identification of the subject; either the power of symbolization and identification has disappeared, or we have to do with a form of violence that is henceforth beyond all possible integration and symbolization. To "appear destroyed," that is, to make the possible or actual destruction of appearing (of identification and symbolization) appear in the eyes of the world, an *other* scene would be necessary. The question of the witness thus becomes: Is it true (as we said a moment ago) that the Other scene is the scene of the Other? And is it still a scene? Is the intact power of the image, of the scenic presentation of the image, still necessary for it? Or is this Other scene not rather one in which the end of every scene must be played out, in which the end of every presentation must be presented? These questions, as formulated here, have the appearance of abstract or philosophical questions. And yet, they are questions that several generations of survivors have had to confront, questions with which some of them have struggled their entire lives. The narrative that is content to take the Catastrophe as a theme, the narrative that is content to parade a series of images, never takes into account the crepuscular end of the image, the loss of all possible symbolization when faced with the catastrophic event. In the Catastrophe, we are deported "from ourselves," dispossessed of our own law, of the "own" or the "proper" as a law; we are thrown toward the foreigner and toward his law, toward his world. That is why I said earlier that there is not, that there cannot be any proper memory of the Catastrophe. Only the foreigner can have a memory. Our memory is that of the foreigner. This disaster of the identificatory scene, whose effect is to deport us out of ourselves, to distend this "us" to the extreme, to give us over henceforth to a world without limits—this explains the strange structure of Varuzhan's poem, which is articulated as a multiple injunction addressed to the foreigner, in a language that is necessarily that of the foreigner (since the poem is a long address) but that is nonetheless read in Armenian, as if it were a *translation*. This can be understood in two senses. We could see it as an ignorance of the scene of the Other and yet another illusion concerning the address of the message, which is very common in the discourse of testimony. But we can also see it as an opening of the scene of the Other, or of another scene; we can read it as the necessity of another scene, a scene internal to the language in which this poem is written. This opening deports language outside of itself, it makes it other to itself within itself, according to a singular topology that would require a more detailed examination.

The literally mad logic of appearing-destroyed—which is always and in every case the logic of the witness-survivor—is one in which this witness-survivor (or the witness *as* survivor and the survivor *as* witness) constantly vacillates between the Other-scene and the scene-of-the-Other. Let us consider some examples. In his novel *Sovorakan or më* (A Day Like Any Other), published in Paris in 1974, Zareh Vorpouni recounts the first-person story of a family son in the diaspora, a son who goes mad by staring at the defeated and destroyed gaze of his father (in a photograph of him that has been preserved), and who believes that the father is trying, from beyond the grave, to destroy him and drive him mad, in order to make his own (the father's) destruction appear before the eyes of the world. For, in the end, the son must bear witness![13] The first English-language novel by Peter Najarian, *Voyages* (1971), clarifies the same structure of testimony, although Najarian of course had no idea of Vorpouni's novels, nor even of his existence.[14] In France, Janine Altounian attempted to explain in three important books that after the Catastrophe, there could be no restructuring of the psyche, and therefore, ultimately, no memory of the events, no self-identification and no reception of history, except in the scene-of-the-Other.[15] Finally, allow me to return for a moment to the film *Ararat* by Atom Egoyan, to explain how the structure of double representation (since the narrative of the events of 1915 appear in the film only as the subject of a pompous film-within-the-film whose filming is part of the story in *Ararat*) is for this filmmaker a way to call into question the duality and the dialectic (if it is one) between the two scenes, between the Other-scene and the scene-of-the-Other. It is always possible to narrate with images—and in the scene of the Other—the tragic events of the past; the cinema gives proof of this every day. But this will never tell us anything about the necessity of an *other* scene or about the catastrophic destruction of every identificatory scene. And yet, albeit necessary, this "other" scene is never given. In its absence, it only hollows out, or gives a negative, of the scene of the Other. The importance of this film thus lies in the fact that it seems to set into motion, in the terms I have just given, the entire problematic—now almost a century old—of post-catastrophic representation and testimony.[16] At the same time, it will be noticed that these complex questions of appearing-destroyed and the other-scene were not discussed in my essay on Charents (in *Writers of Disaster: The National Revolution*), even though Charents, in his thinking on the disaster as well as in his elaboration of the aesthetic principle, is always so close to Daniel Varuzhan. The reason for this is very simple: Charents never deals with the serious questions of the structure and function of testimony. But it obviously relates also to the fact that Charents felt assured of the ability to mourn that art confers on the fatherland (or the fatherland on art). What thus essentially distinguishes the poetic thought of Charents from that of Varuzhan, across a distance of fifteen years (Charents' poetic production occurred between 1912 and 1937, that of Varuzhan, between 1902 and 1915), is the presence in Varuzhan of a dimension of the aesthetic principle that is emerging only now. This dimension has to do, on the one hand, with representation and testimony, and, on the other, with appearing-destroyed and thus with the turbulences provoked by a failure of mourning that can no longer be overcome in any art or in any fatherland.

Beginning around 1995, this displacement of the limit between testimony and representation, and between testimony and literature—in their double confrontation with the Catastrophe—began to appear in the most remarkable way in Krikor Beledian's "novelistic" production. I place the word *novelistic* in quotation marks, of course, since in its traditional form the novel is no longer relevant when it becomes a matter of "representing" collective destruction and speaking from a position that we have been calling "appearing-destroyed." That is why Beledian's book on Daniel Varuzhan, published more than fifteen years ago, remains extremely important in this regard, even though it does not explicitly thematize the question of testimony. This book is in fact the first stage in a long trajectory of writing and philosophical reflection that now calls for rethinking and critical re-elaboration. But at the same time, this displacement and this interpenetretation between the traditional borders of "art" and "testimony"—and the resulting subversion of these borders—have been the subject of both literary and critical work carried out in other contexts, by novelists (Imre Kertész is one of the best examples in Europe), poets (Ruth Klüger, for example, who writes in English),[17] and the critical readers of their works, which attest at times to the refusal and to the radical questioning of testimony. These works have been addressed as a whole by Catherine Coquio in France, in a patient and extremely erudite examination presented in several essays, all of which are attentive to the details of this displacement and its various modalities. A specialist in comparative literature, Coquio attempts to provide a theoretical basis for what has remained, until recently, a poorly perceived phenomenon. It is not exaggerating to say that a new field of knowledge is emerging before our eyes. The following passage from her work, relating to the "transgression" of forms as an effect of testimony, will give an idea of what is at issue in this critical approach:

> The testimony on genocide is bound to carry out this transgression on every art form that it touches on, as we see in the major literary testimonies from the Shoah: the work of art, animated by this powerful core of iconoclasm constituted by the testimony to the inhuman, enters into critical combustion as soon as it begins to measure itself up to its object of thought by reflecting on its own formal means. It is thus by means of work carried out on its form that the extremity of genocide can be thought. By intermingling with literature in order to create a work, testimony thus poses three questions: what is man? what is a testimony? and what is a work? In its future repercussions, genocide challenges every human production in its forms, its reasons for being, and its very existence.[18]

It will be noted that the sentence "It is thus by means of work carried out on its form that the extremity of genocide can be thought" can be understood in several ways. It is of course a question of the form taken up by the work of art; but this can also be understood in terms of the form of "genocide." This point is essential. In this type of study, it is not only the "aesthetic" (or psychological, or social) *reactions* to genocidal violence that are in question, like deferred effects, observable beyond the event. What is characteristic of the catastrophic event is that it has no beyond, and that is precisely what the perpetrator wants. In the works and testimonies studied more specifically by Coquio (in the wake of the Shoah and the genocide in Rwanda), as well as those by Armenian writers of disaster, the "extremity of genocide"—that is, in reality, the true catastrophic event—can be "thought" only by way of works and testimonies in which this "extremity" is at stake within the very forms of language, since, to use the author's expression, the extremity of genocide is also the extremity of language. Art—the work—is one mode for exploring this extremity, which is at once the extremity of art and that of violence. That is why the word *genocide* here is totally inadequate, if it is true that "genocide" is the willed, programmed extermination by a historically assignable perpetrator. Testimony, when it crosses with literature to produce a work, not only interrogates the meaning of the words *literature* and *work*; it also allows one to investigate the historical assignation of an event whose true nature can only be "experienced" indirectly, by way of this crossing, this becoming-work or this refusal of the work, through all the convoluted paths in the encounter between testimony and representation. At present, Catherine Coquio is without any doubt the one who has taken this investigation and interrogation the furthest (particularly in terms of the *historical assignation* of the genocidal event), with the greatest tenacity and perseverance, by adopting an approach that is not only comparative (since all of the genocidal events of the century have their specific features and therefore need to be compared so that these features can emerge with clarity), but also attentive to the expression of the victim, that is, to the nature of testimony.[19] Any purely historico-political approach to the genocides of the past century, even if it is comparative (and such an approach is now common in the United States), will be incapable of saying anything of substance concerning "the extremity of genocide," because it never examines the testimony-work in its diverse aspects and multiple manifestations, for the survivors of the different genocidal events of the century. At most, such approaches today deal with testimonies in the guise of oral history. But, once again, this amounts to leaving aside the form of the testimony-work against "the extremity of genocide," the catastrophic event as such.

This long detour through the question of testimony and representation may, I admit, seem rather unusual and unexpected. Armenian readers are of course familiar with the poem that served as the point of departure for this development, but they usually limit themselves to reading it—if they read it—as a denunciation. Thus they use the poem in a way that runs counter to its own logic. We have just seen that, very early in the century and before the extermination without remainder in 1915–16, Varuzhan established the logical matrix of testimony, in which every later attempt at representing the Catastrophe would find its confirmation, up to that of Atom Egoyan. Denunciation is also a part of this logical matrix, of course. The victim always needs to denounce the barbarity of the perpetrator, and Varuzhan does not refrain from doing so. But he knows that this denunciation itself assumes an address to the foreigner, who is constructed, called forth, and instructed for the occasion. It is this construction and this instruction that he stages in the poem. Already, then, from the beginning, he stages testimony. And it is certainly a stage that is at issue here. "Among the Ruins of Ani," like "To the Ashes of Cilicia," establishes this height (the castle walls, the hillock) from which it becomes possible to have a wider view—over the city, over the event, over the disaster (immemorial or actual), over the ruins and the ashes, over the circle of fire. And we understand clearly that it is no longer a stage or a scene in which identi-fication is possible. Language now needs to make itself combustible, to receive the fire of destruction into itself, to make everything heard on the basis of this incandescence without return. Hence what we have called, following Beledian, "the end of the image," the age in which the image is past, which is also the age of the revolution of the image. For this scene of ruins and fire remains a scene only through the will of the poet, or by analogy. In reality, there is no longer any scene in which the action could be spoken and shown for the victim, in which the victim could thus identify himself, as a victim, as a being-subject, as a human being. Hence, as I have said, the constant temptation (and no doubt the ineluctable necessity) of the scene-of-the-Other.

ALREADY THE END OF RELIGION AND ART AS MOURNING

At the end of the poem, indeed, the poet-witness dismisses the foreigner. He asks him to return to Europe, to let the wind fill his sails and take his boat into the open sea, toward those countries more concerned with exploiting than with having compassion.

> When your horrified ship cuts through the waves and flees
> Pursued by tireless dolphins, who
> Came to our fertile inlets in search of corpses,
> When, still hiding your terrified eyes in your coat,
> You go back to your brothers in gold, do not forget
> To tell them how they cut Cilicia's throat
> To the treacherous music of the drums of freedom. (*YLZ* 1:150)

The "drums of freedom" are of course a reference to the festivals of reconciliation and the dreams of freedom provoked by the Young Turk revolution. As for the foreigner, in a way that is altogether conventional, he is placed among his brothers, worshipers of the golden calf, who will not come to the aid of the afflicted and the survivors, but who will rush to exploit the "miraculous metal" of their mountains. However we read this expression of resentment toward Europe, it is clearly a dismissal of the scene of the Other and therefore, ultimately, a refusal of testimony (or a provisional cessation of testimony, accompanied by a fundamental interrogation on the nature of testimony), even as the entire poem is constructed as a dialogue with the foreigner. In the last lines of this long poem, the poet, too, comes down from this stage:

> Foreigner, go now. You see that I too go down
> From these heights, and wrapped in my sad casaque
> I go to wander again in the city of the sacrificed.
> I must bury the dead, I must anoint the holocaust.
> The head of a wounded man moans on the altar stone . . .
> Next to the fountain, oh, a sister agonizes with no one there to watch over her . . .
> Tonight I must dig countless graves,

I must weave shrouds of light until morning comes
I must build mausoleums, I must erect monuments,
And into marble I must carve my songs as an epitaph.   (*YLZ* 1:51)[20]

We are no longer on a stage, in the scene of appearing-destroyed. For here, when the foreigner is dismissed, there is no longer any appearing that can hold together. There is no longer any appearing-destroyed in the eyes of the foreigner or, therefore, in my own eyes (since now my own eyes can only be foreign to me), even though this appearing has been the content of the entire poem. Indeed, now I must take care of mourning. I must dig the graves, carve the gravestones, erect the funerary monuments, inscribe the epitaphs, weave the shrouds of light. This is the poet speaking. He speaks of his art, of the work of mourning to be carried out in his language, which is no longer (or not yet) the language of the foreigner. Or perhaps it is, perhaps it is still the language of the foreigner, since the poet is still addressing him, one last time. Here language, having become foreign to itself, speaks its vocation to mourn. Perhaps one day a translation will be possible. Perhaps one day Varuzhan's poetry will be heard in French or in English, and catastrophic mourning will thus be heard throughout the world. The relation between art and testimony does not necessarily short-circuit representation. But it hollows it out, interrogates it, destroys it from the inside, brings it to the point of combustion. It brings a change of epoch, it declares and demands a revolution of the image.

In the introductory chapter of this book I discussed the journal *Mehyan* and the period surrounding its publication, and I introduced a certain number of the themes addressed here; there I stated already that in reality the relation between the poem and testimony was infinitely more complex than anything we could say by way of introduction. I pointed out that the testimony of the Catastrophe (whether that of the direct witness, the heir, the survivor, or the outside witness, the foreigner in the strict sense) can only be "foreign" in this sense. We now understood why, at least in part. A "successful" testimony can only be the testimony of the Catastrophe's *narrative*. Testimony must first have become speech, mourning, and art, so that the "foreigner" (and myself as foreign to myself) can hear it and make it heard, so that it will resonate in the world. And, in fact, it will have taken eight decades for the Armenians to understand this simple truth spoken in a poem by Daniel Varuzhan in 1909. At the end of the poem, the two themes are joined together. For testimony to be possible (for a foreign audience, a concerned *ear*, to be conceivable, for a *translation* to become effective), the Catastrophe must be (must have been) received into the space of mourning. Art is mourning, said Varuzhan (who capitalizes "Art"), and we repeat this with astonishment after him. Art is the space of catastrophic mourning (and this proposition will gradually become more familiar to us). For it is not only a question of burial, of singing for the dead, of laying them to rest in eternal peace, in the soul's rest, which are also the peace and rest of those who survive them. One must rejoin those who have been sacrificed without this sacrifice having anything religious about it. One must join with the holocaust. One must join and rejoin, this is an imperative—in a sacrifice that in fact does not join anyone together. And yet, it does—perhaps it joins the perpetrators together, among themselves, for a festival that is both savage and civilized, a festival in which the victim has no part (here I am referring to lines 94–109 of the poem, in which half the city has been transformed into a cemetery and the other half becomes a site of common and convivial rejoining and rejoicing). Once again, Varuzhan hesitates, as Oshagan will do regarding the same theme some twenty years later, in the third volume of his novel *The Remnants*.[21] Barbarous murder or civilized sacrifice? A crime devoid of meaning or a sacrifice full of meaning for those who carried it out? This is apparently the same uncertainty that is legible in the grotesque scene of the seven crucified. They were crucified, indeed, but for what religion? This is a very serious question. The poet would like to believe that it is an orgy of barbarism, on the hither side of the human, and a spilling of blood that will never be transformed into any meaning. He wants to believe, like all the victims of the sacrificial empire, that nothing was taken away from him but his life and his blood, or at least that not *everything* has been taken. He cannot admit that sacrificial murder, up to the very end, took away much more than life and blood, that it took away the power to transmute life and blood into meaning and symbol, into a religious joining together, into a festival, into rejoicing and song. For have we ever wondered what sacrificial murder extracted from the victim, in the very moment when it was carried out without any apparent sacrifice, without barbarity, in a purely symbolic and completely civilized manner? But, indeed, perhaps we are no longer in the sacrificial empire? Perhaps these bloody murders, at once sacrificial and grotesque (a parody of Christian sacrifice), mark the end of the symbolic blood of the victim? We would have arrived, then, at the end of sacrifice, which would also be the end of the empire of sacrifice, perhaps even the end of religion. For on this day everything changed in the history of the world, which is also the history of its religions. Earlier, in the scene of rejoicing that accompanies the silence of the corpses in the other half of the city, Varuzhan says: "Listen, Stranger . . . Islam for the first time today drinks wine in honor of ashes" (ll. 103–04). This clearly means that religion has come to an end, here too (though it is also an insult to Islam). And this is, after all, and in any case, a kind of freedom. To what end was this freedom established? Varuzhan had no way of knowing this. It was still much too soon for him to know it. If the empire of sacrifice came to an end with these grotesque and parodic sacrifices, it was no doubt because there was nothing left to sacrifice. But who can accept such a thing? Who can accept being collectively emptied of the totality of one's symbolic blood, the totality of one's ability to mourn? We must understand that the image presented a few lines before the descent toward the city and the announcement of the aesthetic work of mourning—this image of the foreigners obsessed entirely with the exploitation of the glorious metal to be extracted from "our mines heavy with their lode" (l. 128)—is a metaphorical displacement (this time in a psychoanalytic metaphorization, not a poetic one), the displacement of another exploitation, of another "extraction," that of the symbolic blood of the subject-people. It is not blood but milk that the Europeans are interested in extracting from our heavy, pregnant or impregnated mountains. With this milk they will construct "the idols of their ego . . ." (l. 129): yet another operation of postreligious erection (of statues, heroes, temples).

Marble is the prime element of the end of religion as it is figured here (as we will see again at various points below). In "Nemesis," poetic activity was metamorphosed by the cutting and the carving of marble. It raised a statue around which the people of freedom could assemble, could rejoin itself, could join itself to itself, could rejoice, against all the material, sacrificial, or symbolic exploitations, against the exploitation of blood, milk, and light. In the poem entitled "Luysë" (Light), written around the same time, art is also defined as that which sculpts the statue of the gods in the marble of light. "Light is the marble of the celestial mines / In which Art, in its immortal dream, / Sculpts the gods with their bodies of snow" (YLZ 2:90).[22] In "To the Ashes of Cilicia," it is marble that receives the poem as an epitaph, and light is the material from which the poetic (and therefore aesthetic) shroud of the dead is woven. In order to be real, and in order not to be expressed in the pure delirium of testimony in the scene of the Other, appearing-destroyed demands this absorption of death into the marble of light. But marble was already what the ancestors labored to remove from their fertile mountains, as they produced the wine from their vines (l. 87). Marble and wine? "Oh, the primordial milk of the nations that sing and sculpt" (l. 88). Here I use "primordial milk" for the Armenian word nakhasnund, which is the liquid that forms in the mother's breast before milk, properly speaking, before the substance that gives nourishment. This primordial milk is the element from which the singing and the statue are made; it is what the singing and the statue "are" before being, concretely, what they are, before receiving their form, before being born as art. Already for them, then, for these ancestors in the Cilicia of the royal age, there was Art. The "Race of Fire," alas, has shown itself to be more destructive than time, says the poem (l. 90), since it was able to destroy not only the products of Art, but the very activity of Art as a transformation and creative exploitation of the primordial milk, as the activity par excellence that brings the nation to itself, and makes it what it is.

Let us recall that in the poem "Native Mountains," written almost one year earlier, "marble" was also taken out by the ancestors who lived in these mountains of the fatherland (when we first read these lines in the former chapter, we did not know anything yet of its metaphoric significance). It was likewise "drawn" (in the sense of "milked") from those mountains by their active hands,[23] and we thus already see at work here the same strange image of exploiting the mountain and drawing out a primordial milk. Marble was already the matter in which "they erected their gods and their immaculate altars"; it was also the "milk" of which heroes are made. The "new generation" will find its salvation in these mountains, which will serve as a refuge and a fortress, and in the future, the "statues of the heroes" (YLZ 1:168, l. 72), made from the marble of these mountains, will be raised once again. It is important to understand that these heroes will only become heroes—that is, they will only be the heroes of the nation to come—through the artistic activity that raises their statues, and their stature, in patriotic marble. In the same impulse or in the same movement of inspiration, we might say, Varuzhan places the nationalist appeal to future generations alongside the central theme of becoming-nation through art.

Let us recall, too, that in the poem "Among the Ruins of Ani," in the middle of the rhetorical development on the theme "What remains?" (what remains of your ramparts, of your palaces, of your columns, your cathedrals and your temples?), Art was already presented as the supreme activity, the daughter of God and the bride of the Universe, but also as "the last epitaph and the last mortuary crown of dead peoples and fallen nations" (*YLZ* 1:89, ll. 93–94)—and all this in the same breath, as if the art of the millennial ancestors, the art of the sculptors of Ani, were already destined endlessly to accompany the disaster.

> What remains . . .
> From your thousand and one temples, where
> Statue by statue, ornament by ornament,
> A new art, an Armenian art,
> Art as God's daughter, as Nature's sister,
> Art as Universe's bride,
> As the final epitaph and garland
> Of deceased peoples and nations,
> Sculpted in the gilded outline of a dove
> Inside your holy steeples,
> Its head outstretched through
> Your hushed niches, capitals, and columns,
> Skyward, lovely, sublime,
> Broadly spread its wings . . .   (*YLZ* 1:88)

This was of course not entirely a slip on Varuzhan's part, even though this characterization is placed completely out of context here. We could say that this is the central difficulty of aesthetic nationalism, which first becomes visible in a passage dedicated to the glory of Ani's past, and to its present ruin. Aesthetic nationalism cannot do otherwise than to think simultaneously, under the same term—under the same art—both the past and the present, glory and ruin, appropriation and mourning.

If we return now to "The Ashes of Cilicia," we see that when Varuzhan thematizes art as the space of catastrophic mourning, he thinks in terms that are consistent with these same categories of aestheticization as appropriation and appropriative-event, that is, also, of aestheticization as nationalization. As indicated by the juxtaposition of the elegy to Ani, the city destroyed in the past, and the poem on Adana, the city destroyed in the present, Vaurzhan thinks within the same context both the immemorial disaster (assumed by the philological invention of the native, or as the object of an experience proper to the latter) and the historical Catastrophe. In the first case, art is the primordial element of national aestheticization (or aesthetic nationalism) and of the operation that unveils the nature of the native; in the second case, it is the space of mourning. But, in reality, it is no less the space of mourning in the first case. The previous chapter of this essay was called "The Disaster of the Native"; it is clear that this disaster does not come to the native from without. It is an integral part of his nature (or of his structure). It thus calls for mourning from the very beginning, as soon as the experience of the native disaster is invented. Nevertheless there is an unexpected conjunction here between aesthetic nationalism and art as a space of mourning, art as that which creates the Other scene on the basis of which a listening and a translation of appearing-destroyed will be possible. It is obvious by now that for me this conjunction is extremely troubling. It always has been. That is why more work is needed to understand how aesthetic nationalism and art as mourning could have been a part of a single system of thought for an entire generation, precisely the one that went through the Catastrophe, and the greatest generation of the century. Marble, primordial milk, luminous shrouds, the mausoleum, the funerary stelae, the tomb, the erection of statues and temples: so many ways of saying that art is catastrophic mourning, the space of presentation and production adequate to an appearing-destroyed that can one day be translated for the foreigner. But they are also so many ways of saying aestheticization as a nationalizing operation. This troubling conjunction consequently demands a work that ought to enable us to discern the common source (or the essential point of divergence) between national-aestheticism and the thought of catastrophic mourning.

One might guess that the conjunction just indicated derives from the fact that Daniel Varuzhan thinks art as the end of religion, or, we might say: *the sublation of religion into its end*. But, as we will see, he also thinks art in terms of a *history of mourning*. We must now explore these two sides of art. These themes were developed in strikingly similar terms in my *Writers of Disaster: The National Revolution*, in relation to the work of Yeghishe Charents, a poet who did not at all belong to the constellation of *Mehyan*. I will quote here the summary with which I concluded my introduction to *Yeghishe Charents: Poet of the Revolution*:

> The selections chosen for inclusion here are those which bear on poetic historiography, the confrontation between historical and poetic time, and therefore already, or once again, the Charentsian conception of the accomplishment of history in mourning, as the history of mourning. . . . It so happens that, for Charents, the birth of the fatherland and the emergence of the nation(al) are equivalent to the accomplishment of the post-Catastrophic work of mourning, which can only be carried out in art and through art. Thus an "aesthetic principle" is at work in Charents's thought no less than in that of the Western Armenian writers of his generation, who had for their part to confront the Catastrophe immediately, without intermediaries. Art presents itself in these writers as the sublated form of

religion in the function of mourning. [Charents's] "Requiem" accordingly proposes a meditation on the possibility of Komitas's return to the fatherland, and thus on the return of the fatherland to itself, as well as on the birth of the national. But the possibility of this return resides in the sublation of religion by art. That is why we find, at the heart of the poem, a section on the history of religion, which is in reality *a history of mourning*. Thanks to the Leninist revolution, Charents tells us, it is today possible, for the first time in history, to mourn the paternal Catastrophe, because art has managed to take the place of religion in the accomplishment of mourning.[24]

Similarly, but in a very different context, a history of mourning was sketched by Hölderlin in his poem "Mnemosyne," here too in relation to catastrophic mourning. It will be noticed that, in the account I just gave, the Charentsian idea of an accomplishment of history in mourning makes no distinction between the immemorial disaster and the historical Catastrophe, in a way that is conscious and deliberate. Charents' historical situation in the Soviet Union between 1922 and 1936 made such a foreshortened perspective possible. The arrival of the fatherland through art in the Leninist era came into play in the elaboration of a postcatastrophic mourning. That is also what allowed Charents to disregard entirely the paradoxes of testimony and representation. It is the fatherland's advent within the Soviet sphere (a cultural sphere that for Charents, we may recall, made a *Weltliteratur* possible at last), an advent that took place at the end of a history of mourning, which was also a history of religions— it was in this situation that appearing-destroyed would be able to become effective, without the madness and delirium of testimony. Varuzhan, in his thematization of the history of mourning between 1908 (the date of his first "pagan" poem) and 1913 (when his *Pagan Songs* appeared, and the time of the conference on Siamanto), obviously did not have as many resources available, to say the least. The entire question of the "end of religion" must therefore be taken up again according to his treatment of it. We can imagine that religions, like civilizations, are destined to die. But what is the relation between this theme of religion coming to an end and that of catastrophic mourning? This is a question that remains to be examined.

CHAPTER 6

Erection and Self-Sacrifice

Readers of Varuzhan's *Het'anos Yerger* (Pagan Songs), published in 1912, have always been intrigued by its structure. It contains two parts, two very distinct series of poems, the first of which is also called "Pagan Songs" (obviously giving its title to the entire collection); the second part is called "Flowers of Golgotha." The first part contains some of the most well known and most often reprinted of Varuzhan's poems.[1] But the second part forms a rather strange composite. I will therefore begin the discussion with a descriptive summary and an overview of the work's structure. Each of the book's two parts has a subtitle: "Glory to the Vine. Bacchus is Crowned with Flowers," and "Glory to the Vine. Christ Offers the Sacrifice." Bacchus had a place in the old Armenian pantheon, sometimes under his Latin name, but most often with his indigenous name, Vanatur. The Greek name that we might expect to see here, Dionysus, does not appear in Varuzhan's text; but it is clear that the two parts of *Pagan Songs* are placed under the patronage of the Greek god and the Christian god, these gods who offer themselves as nourishment to a coming community, in the form of a sacrifice or a dismemberment. In each case, it is thus the sacrificial process of a dismemberment for the sake of a "rememberment," of a death for the sake of a rebirth, of a bloody sacrifice for the sake of a renewed community, that is at issue. The "vine" (*sarp'inah* in Armenian) designates wine, of course, of which Bacchus is taken to be the god, but it is also wine as the symbol or transfiguration of the blood spilled in sacrifice. Is it then a question here of "religious" poetry? In a moment we will read the poem "Vanatur," placed at the beginning of the collection, just after the introductory poem. The latter, which opens the volume, is entitled "To the Statue of Beauty." In this introductory poem, we already encounter the theme of the poet's self-sacrifice:

> If we must give you a victim as an offering
> Let them cut me open on your altar
> So that your marble may drink the last drop of my blood.[2]

The word for marble here is very rare: *kuch*.[3] The poem thus takes up the entire sculptural metaphor in relation to poetry, as we have seen in "Nemesis" and elsewhere.

Here are the first lines of "To the Statue of Beauty": "I want your marble to be taken from the deepest womb of Olympus/And under my hammer I want it to take the shape/Of woman's fiery flesh, drunk with light and fever" (*YLZ* 2:7, ll. 1–3).[4] Here the word for marble is the one most commonly used, the Greek-derived word *marmarion*. From the very beginning of the poem, then, there are two metaphors for poetry: poetry as erection, and poetry as self-sacrifice. These metaphors are related through the desire to see marble absorb the blood of the poet. That is what Varuzhan said in his 1908 letter on Leconte de Lisle (cited at the beginning of chapter 4): "the poet's heart must let out a drop of blood, until he stands before his work like Jesus and consumes himself to the very end" (*YLZ* 3:364)—although this is not the "ultimate condition" of great poetry (364).[5] Varuzhan was of course familiar with French Romantic poetry, in which this is a prominent theme. But this insistence on poetry as gathering erection, as erection *and* sacrifice, suggests that the religious reference is central. We are given to understand that with the erection (of the temple, of the statue, or of the poem made of Olympian marble), and with the self-sacrifice (of the god, of the artist), the community comes to itself through a refoundation, a reactivation of its origin: it reappropriates itself to itself. And yet, poetry is not religion. Quite the contrary, we might say. But then, what kind of relation holds between them?

POETRY AS ERECTION

Vanatur is not exactly Bacchus, although they have a great many features in common. His mantle is steeped in the odor of the wine spilled during the New Year festivals, his eyes shine with sacred drunkenness; on his donkey, he visits all the arable lands from the spring to the fall; during the months of growth and production, he brings alive "the fields of the fatherland," and in his presence even the ruins are productive. He accepts the sacrifice of the ram for the sake of a renewed fertility. And the poet says to him in the present: "Drink the blood, eat the meat, O Vanatur/For in the fields of wheat shining in the sun/The scythes sing your glory" ("Vanatur," *YLZ* 2:10, ll. 71–74).[6] Is Vanatur then a kind of principle, before being a god? Is he the principle of fertility? It is he who dwells in "the heart of each fruit" (l. 84) and it is the saliva of his ox that fertilizes the fields (l. 86). He is the joyous god, a bon vivant, the god who drinks and dances. He is immortal. But he is the only immortal god, since

> All the great gods are now dead
> And only moss grows on their altars
> And only you have remained immortal
> As are the earth and the fire
> As is the salt of the oceans.   (*YLZ* 2:8, ll. 1–4)

We will encounter this theme of the immortality of the principle on several other occasions. But it appears here not only in the form of an abstraction or a subterranean force at work within the elements. And its name is not simply another word for life. For in this life, in effect, a community communes with itself. It seems, then, that the communion of community requires *a figure*. This figure is always essentially religious (later we will consider the significance of this essential necessity for the figure required by the communion of the community; at first sight, it is religious because it is formed and organized around ritual sacrifice and the narration in common that will be called mythical or mythological).[7] But poetry is not content to "sing" this immortal figure of the generative force and of joyous communion. Indeed, a new perspective is opened by the fact that this figure does not exist outside of poetry. The very last lines of the poem say precisely that: "For you are immortal after the death of the gods / Like the salt of the oceans / For in the depths of winter and its torments / Close to the happy hearth of the fatherland / Every guitar sings your song" (ll. 104–107). There is thus a common speech that is spoken and transmitted around the fires of the fatherland's hearths (*hayrenakan ochakhner*), and this can only be the speech of the bards and reciters, that of the myths and legends. We find clearly stated here at the end of the poem the old "function" of myth, which will concern us a great deal in what follows. It is the function of a common speech that gathers its listeners together as a productive and fertile community. That is the function of myth. Art and myth are merged here, in the happy orality of the self-productive (or self-producing) community.

Is this truly the old function of myth? There are grounds for believing that this function is not really so old, that it is even the invention of the moderns—who invented myth (the "myth" of myth), who invented its ancient and immemorial character, who invented the very idea of the community gathered together at the very moment when it was in fact breaking apart. There are even grounds for believing that this confusion between art and myth is the very matrix in which this function was invented. In this resolutely modern (mythopoetic) matrix, art and myth are reciprocally defined. We will say much more about this later. Let it suffice to recall once again what Hagop Oshagan would write a few years later (although here, in this statement of a mythic thinking that is being invented or rediscovered, what matters is the systematic character of the discourse, not the antecedence of the enunciation): "Some preeminent guises of universal fiction are becoming a necessity for us. " In this statement Oshagan used the French word *fiction* (since—let us recall this as well—at this point in March 1914, he had no Armenian word for this idea, although as an approximation he would use the word *keghtsik'*, whose usual meaning is "lie" or "deception"!), and of course "universal fiction" designates myth, a myth to be produced as fiction, but as a founding fiction, and as a fiction that gathers the community. Indeed, the task of the artist is precisely to produce such a fiction. Concerning the invention of myth, the myth of the function of myth, the "modernity" of myth, and the continuous exchange of values between fiction and foundation in the myth of myth, Jean-Luc Nancy has provided a number of decisive formulations.[8] In speaking of these questions here, after Nancy, I am thus pointing to an illustration provided by a group of writers whose thinking—insofar as it is poetico-religious, that is, insofar as it is *mything* or mythifying—coincides at every point with the general thinking of myth in the modern age, from Friedrich Schlegel to Nietzsche and beyond.

Let us briefly recall what Nancy says about "mything" humanity, by laying out several distinct points.

1. First of all, on the question of invention: "We know that although we did not invent the stories . . . we did on the other hand invent the function of the myths that recount these stories. Humanity represented on the stage of myth, humanity being born to itself in producing myth—a truly *mything* humanity becoming truly human in this *mythation*: this forms a scene just as fantastical as any primal scene" (*IC*, 45; Nancy's emphasis). The play on words, the infinitesimal approximation of *mythant* (mything) and *mutant* (mutating), is more than an ironic gesture. It suggests that according to the mytho-logic governing this scene, humanity (or community) comes to itself by way of an originary mutation, which is set into motion by the creation and/or the recitation of myth, but which is itself—as the origin of myth and of humanity—transmitted, recounted, and recited ever and again through the myth and its own power; this originary scene being that of a group gathered around a fire and listening to a singer, a storyteller, or a reciter—a scene that has been imagined countless times. Myth would thus recount the human community's birth to itself as human.

2. Next, concerning the necessary reinvention of myth, and therefore the necessity of a new mythology, an idea we find in Schlegel in 1800, but also, in fact, in all those obsessed with the idea of a repetition of the Greek experience: "And we also know that the idea of a '*new mythology*,' the idea of moving on to a new, poetico-religious foundation, is contemporaneous with the invention or the modern reinvention of mythology in the romantic epoch." And Nancy adds, referring to Nietzsche's inheritance of this Romantic invention: "—romanticism, or the will to (the) power of myth" (ibid., 45–46; parentheses surrounding "the" in published translation).[9] It is precisely to this poetic-religious foundation that Hagop Oshagan appealed, when he spoke of our need today (in 1914) for a "universal fiction," and thus for a mythology, which of course would be a new mythology, since the old one was no longer relevant, and since we were "torn, aging, driven from [our] center, land, and religion."[10] We can be certain that neither Varuzhan nor Oshagan knew Schlegel or the first generation of Romantics, or the entire reflection on myth in Germany, which culminates with Schelling's book on mythology.[11] But they had read Nietzsche. They reproduced the idea of a new mythology that pervaded Germany in the nineteenth century, for they were reproducing the invention of myth and the logic of a humanity that, in its origin and its essence, is a "mything" humanity. But in reality they were reinventing this entire logic for their own purposes, moved by the feeling of the disaster, which for them was obviously a disaster that had befallen mythic power, the founding power of myth. Here we can formulate somewhat differently what was said above concerning the birth and the

naturalness of the native: the native is *also* the one who is at once invested with and deprived of this founding power, the power of producing and recounting myths. That is why the "disaster" is in fact inscribed directly upon the native, onto his body, his absent speech, or onto the concept that defines him. It is through this mythological desire that the last generation of aesthetic nationalism reinterpreted and renewed the figure of the native, which in reality waited more than a century for this, hidden away in the hollows opened for it when it was brilliantly and instantaneously invented by the philology of European orientalism and by the national receptions of this philology (receptions which, as was pointed about above, are in fact constitutive of the "national," through the central phenomenon of autoscopic mimicry). But this mythological desire is also an artistic desire for myth. Oshagan expresses his deep wish for a universal fiction, that is, a new mythology, and with it the power of the lie; at the same time, he raises the artist to the rank of creator of the nation. Nietzsche evokes the mythic feeling of freely lying, and for him the "natural liar" is the artist. That is why we spoke earlier of the *aesthetic* logic of the invention of the native, a logic exposed for the first time, or reinvented, by Daniel Varuzhan. This logic is none other than that of philological ethnomythology, which developed in Europe during the nineteenth century and found an echo among the Armenians, according to a process and a temporality whose details remain to be elaborated.[12] Philology and ethnomythology could only be born within the aesthetic matrix in which the myth of myth is formulated.

Let us pause here to point out that philological ethnomythology is the most complete name that can be given to nineteenth-century European orientalism. This orientalism was able to gain dominance only by immediately becoming an auto-orientalism. In American universities, Edward Said's *Orientalism* is taught (and interpreted) in the context of postcolonial studies and a denunciation of all the evils perpetrated on colonized and orientalized peoples. Such a denunciation is necessary, but it must be recognized that there are also evils which colonized and orientalized peoples perpetrated on themselves. This orientalism was formed and developed in the mythopoetic crucible, and it is in this crucible that it first took the form of philology. It was also there that the nations and their nationalisms were constituted. This mythopoetic and quintessentially racist crucible is also what Said calls the "laboratory" of the philologist. The insistence on the "colonialist" nature of orientalism entirely occludes this conjunction between philology and the mythopoetic that characterizes orientalism as the major invention of the nineteenth century. Postcolonial studies would need to explain, on the one hand, the phenomenon of auto-orientalism in Greece and Serbia at the beginning of the nineteenth century (as well as among the Armenians in the second decade of the century, but with more of a focus on nationalist autoscopy, starting around 1840, or for auto-ethnography or ethnomythology, starting around 1870); on the other hand, it would need to place Said's *Orientalism* alongside another great book that is virtually unknown in the United States—*The Languages of Paradise* by Maurice

Olender[13]—in order to understand orientalism, and to arrive at a more Foucauldian reading of it as a discourse and not as an erroneous representation of the colonized by the colonizer. Only such a juxtaposition allows us to understand the extent to which orientalist philology is saturated by the myth of the mythopoetic, or how it was invented in the aesthetic crucible of this myth. It allows us to understand many different aspects of this orientalism: the historicity accorded to language (which Foucault places at the very heart of the philological invention); the simultaneous appearance of religion and literature (philology studies "religious" texts as "literary" texts, but in doing so it establishes our concepts of religion and literature for the next two centuries, which somewhat complicates the account Foucault gives of the beginning of literature, in the modern sense, as the other side of the philological invention, as a reaction to the "demotion" of language)[14]; and finally, the decisive invention of the native, in which all of these important features are at work. In sum, it would be necessary to reread *The Order of Things* in the light of these two books, written partially in its wake: Said's *Orientalism* and Olender's *The Languages of Paradise*.

The multiple nature (and the centrality) of the native, as a figure and as a concept, nevertheless does not fail to astonish. The native was first of all the bearer of an unconscious or degraded knowledge, the result of a disastrous and centuries-old forgetting, the mute preserver of a past that, of course, she or he did not think of as a past constituted as such.[15] The native was therefore a pure present that had to be restored to its historical dimension. She was a witness and a survivor, each through the other. First she was someone to be observed like a strange animal, she was philology's lackey, and the monumental remnant of history (in Armenian, *mnatsord* or *verapruk*, in sum, a vestige); then the native was someone to be interrogated in order to draw from him his unknowing knowledge and to give it back to him in the form of a narrative, in the form of art or as an ethnological account. But all this has now been reinscribed, sublated, in a new figuration of the native, the same native as before but this time cut off from the mythic power which, however, negatively defined him or her. It is in this reinvention of the native that the generation of aesthetic nationalism is entirely dependent on philological determinations, even as it never ceases to question them. Thus we have seen that Varuzhan spoke of his language as needing—in order to attain its wholeness and integrity—"writer-aesthetes" and not "grammarians and philologists"; similarly, Hagop Oshagan later demanded, in a Nietzschean mode, the arrival of philologists who are also philosophers and artists.

3. But this mythical world that was so desired, this myth of the community, can in any case only belong to the past. Not that it was something that existed long ago and has been effectively lost. On the contrary, it belongs to the very structure of myth that it has always already been lost. There is no myth that has not been lost, no mythic power that has not been extinguished from the beginning. Jean-Luc Nancy expresses it thus:

> In a sense, for us all that remains of myth is its fulfillment or its will. We no longer live in mythic life, nor in a time of mythic invention or speech. When we speak of

"myth" or of "mythology," we mean the negation of something at least as much as the affirmation of something. That is why our scene of myth, our discourse of myth, and all our mythological thinking make up a myth: to speak of myth has only ever been to speak of its absence. And the word "myth" itself designates the absence of what it names. (*IC*, 52)

The native was both invested with and deprived of the creative power of myth and of the mythological universe. He was thus cut off from himself in the same sense and to the same extent as myth itself. He was absent from himself because he had been deserted by the fullness of myth; hence his irremediable muteness. But, again, this absence to himself is equivalent to the absence of myth in relation to itself. Myth is cut off from itself, but also in a way by itself, in at least two senses. First, because the power of myth is never present, it does not belong to our present. It is always already lost, it always already belongs to the past. We do not exist "in" the mythical, in living mythical speech. We exist, therefore, in its death, and that is what is strange for us. We exist "in" its cut, its interruption. This second "in" still needs to be specified and thought through. But it is striking that these words "cut" and "interruption" are the very ones that Daniel Varuzhan uses simultaneously, attached to one another in his letter on the thread of past glory, a thread that has been cut, interrupted, a thread now entangled and entwined in the ruins of Ani. The city of Ani and its ruins may very well have been a historical and geographical reality, but it is no less the case that, in his nostalgia for "paganism," Varuzhan is speaking of myth, and from myth. Is it a myth that he wants to revive and make live again? There is every reason to believe so; he says it very clearly. But at the same time he also says the end of myth, and this is even his favorite theme, the one he places at the very center of his "poetic paganism." What he says of myth, then, is its mourning. I have said that for Varuzhan, art is mourning, it is the space of mourning. It has become even clearer now that art is the mourning of myth. But if this is true, then we are still moving within the mytho-logical circle, and have never ceased doing so. For art as the mourning of myth is entirely dependent on the modern dream of myth. This mythological circle is the very circle of the aesthetic principle.

4. Myth is cut off from itself in another sense as well. It is cut off, first, because when we speak of myth we are speaking of an absence, of a thing to which we are absent. But it is also cut off for another reason that appears to be very simple, a reason summarized in the phrase "myth is a myth." Thus Jean-Luc Nancy:

In order to say that myth is a myth . . . , it has been necessary to play on two quite distinct and opposite meanings of the word "myth." The phrase "myth is a myth" means in effect that myth, as inauguration or as foundation, is a myth, in other words, a fiction, a simple invention . . . This sentence contains, as well as two heterogeneous meanings for a single vocable, one mythic reality, one single idea of myth whose two meanings and whose infinitely ironic relation are engendered by a kind of internal disunion. This is the same myth that the tradition of myth

> conceived as foundation and fiction . . . Mythic thought . . . is nothing other than
> the thought of a founding fiction, or of a foundation by fiction. (ibid., 52–53)[16]

Myth (as foundation) is a myth, a simple invention. But myth (as invention) is foundational. This circularity, this complicity between foundation and fiction, makes it such that myth is interrupted by itself, from within itself. After a brief reference to Schelling's conception of mythology as "tautegory" (the fact that myth speaks only of itself), Nancy goes on to explain this circularity by saying that "myth signifies itself, and thereby converts its own fiction into foundation or into the inauguration of meaning itself" (53), which amounts to conferring on it the function of a "primary schematism" in the sense of the Kantian schematism, the operation of an imagination that originarily (that is, without empiricity) produces images.

This brief exposition on the meaning of the myth of myth thus brings us back to the same extreme point of ambiguity. If the disaster is the disaster of myth, there is every reason to believe that it is a mythical disaster. The question thus repeats itself without end: Is the mythical disaster not a real disaster? Were the ruins of Ani not real? Indeed, they were real. But they were also the very image of the mythic disaster (of the disaster of myth *as* mythic disaster) in Varuzhan's poetry. The problem begins, within this poetry itself, in the encounter with mourning; it begins when art takes on the function of mourning. In the ruins of Ani, the mourning in question is in turn a mythical mourning. And what about the ruins and ashes of Cilicia? Is it the same mythical mourning, the same art functioning as mourning, and therefore the same fiction that is repeated when the poet dismisses the foreigner whom he had called before the ashes of Adana, and when he goes down to the city to weave the shrouds of light and to erect mausoleums in memory of the dead? *This amounts to asking whether we can imagine the Catastrophe in a form other than that of the mythical disaster.* What mourning could be equal to it? We just saw that mourning (and art as mourning) is part of the very structure of myth and of mythological circularity. There is no myth, at bottom, without a mourning of myth. That is why myth is foundational. But it is also why the artist could be conceived as the one who erects the nation. For myth, as the mourning of myth, is already—or is still—art. It is *already* art since it is at the origin and principle; it sculpts the figure of the gods in light, says Varuzhan. It is *still* art since it is also at the end, it gathers myth into its endpoint, it gives life to the mythical figure of the god Vanatur in the cottages, around the fires of the fatherland's hearths, to the sound of all the guitars; it keeps him alive despite everything, even after the death of the gods, and much later, despite this death (or perhaps precisely because of it, thanks to it), it maintains him as what he has never ceased to be: the god of the autoproductive community. We will often have occasion to point out that there is mythological religion only because mythological religion has come to an end once and for all, has collapsed into itself and survives only in and as this collapse. "Theological" religion (Judaism or Christianity, as we will see) obviously plays a role in this collapse. There is thus an entire historical perspective concerning the different religions in Varuzhan, but always in relation to the prime importance and the "principiality" of art. This perspective is inscribed in a general history of mourning. But before returning to this central question, we must continue our descriptive summary by examining the other dimension of the "vine" (of wine and blood). After the dimension indicated by Bacchus, Dionysus, or Vanatur, we must look at the part dealing with Christ's offering of sacrifice.

POETRY AS SELF-SACRIFICE AND TRANSUBSTANTIATION

We find references in Varuzhan's correspondence, beginning in May 1908, to the new series of poems that he would write after his "patriotic" poems. Thus he writes to Chobanian: "If I find a patron, I want to conclude my patriotic poems by publishing a magnificent volume. I am already thinking of a new series of poems that will be entirely intimate and based on experience." And just after these lines: "For the pain of the fatherland, I have put pressure on my heart in order to bring new feelings and new passions to light. Now I aspire to dip my pen into my heart" (*YLZ* 3:371).[17] In the letter of October 4 that I have quoted several times already, he writes: "From now on I will only write of life. There is an immense flood in me that until now was held back by all the cadavers of the fatherland. I am about to change the strings on my lyre. Like the other worshippers who contribute to your journal, I too will approach the altar dedicated to *Anahit*, and there I will sacrifice my heart" (*YLZ* 3:387).[18] This very rhetorical formulation, presented here in a tone of joking seriousness, brings together the pagan vocabulary of sacrifice to the gods; the name of one of the most prominent goddesses in the Armenian pantheon—Anahid—and the title of the journal published by Chobaninan, *Anahit*; the announcement of a change in poetic tone; and the poet's desire henceforth to write a more personal and more intimate poetry, closer to himself. In November, Varuzhan writes to his friend Jizmejian: "After this book is published, I will move on to the 'Flowers of Golgotha' series, where I will analyze and sing nothing but life as it is [*chshgrit keank'ë*]" (*YLZ* 3:400).[19] But one of the most beautiful letters in this respect is that of April 2, 1909, in which he writes to Theotig (editor of an almanac that became a literary monument at the beginning of the century):

> I have begun to prepare a new volume, this time inspired entirely by lived experience; the poems will be somewhat more analytic, deeper and more psychological. The dough of my patriotic poems was ardently kneaded by my own fiery strength. They were addressed to the masses. The new volume I am preparing will explain the emotions of my soul, the composition of my heart, the tension of my nerves . . . Oh, how I would like to write the great book of Man. I am including with this letter the poem "Despondence" for your Almanac. . . . You will no doubt notice (or rather, I would like for you to notice) that in this poem I have not yet succeeded in describing all the violence of my emotions. It's only now that I am beginning to

know myself. The fatherland has greatly separated us from ourselves. We must gather together the relics of our hearts, shared out among three million people, and we must concentrate them in a single breast and feel its own proper Life, at least for a brief moment, for the love of art and for the love of the Song of Life. (*YLZ* 3:408)[20]

If these declarations seem to indicate that, after his patriotic period, Varuzhan was about to enter a more lyrical, intimate period, focused on his own "lived" experience and emotions, such an impression is soon dispelled. In the 1912 *Pagan Songs*, only three poems correspond more or less to this expectation: the poem mentioned in this letter, "Lk'um," or Despondence (written at a moment of extreme despair, it plays on the idea of suicide); a poem called "Menavor," or Lonely;[21] and finally the one entitled "Trtunjk'," or Laments (*YLZ* 2:145–47; 2:104–06; 2:91–98). The poet dedicated "Laments" to Yeghia Demirjibashian (1851–1908), the mad, "workless" poet-intellectual from Constantinople.[22] This poem had a special importance for Varuzhan; he published it in a small separate volume in 1911, in Sebastea. "Laments" is a sort of poetic autobiography; in it Varuzhan retraces the various phases of his inspiration. He describes the ordeals of his solitary years in Ghent (especially the painful experience of a love that was scorned and betrayed); he interprets the period of his patriotic or socialist poems as a repercussion of these ordeals, a period he now considers to be closed; and he ends on a note of complete despair, invoking Demirjibashian and his attempt to reach Nirvana by suicide in 1908. Here are some lines from the passage in which he interprets his socialist-inspired poetry:

> I had to devote myself to a cause. That was when I saw
> Wounds and sufferings more profound than my own.
> A People was being led to the slaughterhouse,
> A people who, hammer in hand, erected a century of marble over these years
> of clay.   (ll. 147–50)
>
> . . . .
>
> I felt a People beating in my breast
> A god had come to live in the chaos
> And deep into the empty crucible of egotistical loves
> Had thrown the immortal Idea, and it boiled with golden foam.
> There I was, then, in the sooty cottages where men
> Cursed the light of the coming day, which would soon freeze
> In their eyes, weakened by hunger and striving only for death.
> I was there where workers' arms dig the mines,
> Penetrate into the womb of gold, and abandoned to danger
> Open their own tombs, with as only shroud
> Their ragged shirts drenched in the sweat of exiles.

I was there where all the children fallen from Fate
Set fire in a rage to the domes of the great cities.   (ll. 154–67)

.   .   .   .

I sat astride the people, as on a horse running wild
And my eyes greedy for light were fixed on the Idea
I led it in a tempest over the thrones.   (ll. 176–78)

.   .   .   .

Rising under my whip, for three years it galloped
Through the ruins of tyrannical laws.
For three years it sank its feet into skulls
And it felt its flanks burn with boiling blood.   (ll. 181–84)

Is it possible to regard this as personal lyric poetry concerned with an "analysis" of the self and devoting all its attention to "lived experience"? In any case, we do not find any other poems in the collection that correspond to this idea of an intimate poetry or a return to the terrible moments of existence (except perhaps as an account of "man" in his totality), a poetry, finally, concerned with psychological realism, as formulated by the critics of the period marked by socialist realism in Armenia. What do we find instead? It is already clear in the passage cited: we find a compassion for—and the desire to participate in—the popular revolt against the tyranny of the thrones and of the capital; we find the "rhythmic beating of the self in millions of other hearts"(*YLZ* 2:96, l. 172). Referring to the first poem he wrote after his return home (Varuzhan left Europe at the end of August 1909), the poet wrote to Chobanian: "I am preparing to write in a way that is based entirely on real life, and to weave some new poems with irreproachable art, poems that will make up the 'Pagan Songs'" (*YLZ* 3:424), and he adds that he will send the poem entitled "Hrashk'i aghpiurë" (The Fountain of Miracles). This poem, then, will demonstrate the new style that will replace that of his patriotic poems. But what does this poem say? It was written just after an excursion to the fountain of Deghentan in Bardizag, a city not far from the capital, where many Armenians had settled. This miraculous fountain became a site visited by a great number of indigent, sick, and suffering men and women (the Armenian word is *akhtavarak*). Such is the miserable cohort that Varuzhan is describing here. There were women, particularly sterile women, who had exhausted themselves laboring in the tobacco fields, who had never become pregnant from a man's seed, who no longer possess the force necessary to give life. There were young boys born into the world of the factories or destroyed by premature labor. There were girls who had been abandoned. In sum, he sees there the dregs of society whom life had abandoned from within, but also the victims of social violence (*YLZ* 2:140–44). This is the great theme of decline, the destruction of human beings by an unjust and cruel society and by inhuman working conditions. Other poems in the "Flowers of Golgotha" series evoke European cities, factory workers, pauperization, old age,[23] lives ground down by machines and by industrial labor,[24] the prostitution that results from social inequality,[25] anarchist women and the fruitless sacrifice of their vitality.[26] These were among the many "socialist" or simply humanist themes that were so important to Varuzhan. Conversely, he also evokes a May Day celebration, a festival for the workers, in which he finds an occasion to recall their suffering and to awaken hope, to proclaim the imminence of the coming Hurricane (*amprop*) that will sweep away this old world, which devours the lives of those who work for it.[27] In this portrait gallery, among these teeming and at times apocalyptic images that would be at home in a Bosch painting, the anarchist woman just mentioned has a special place. Indeed, unlike the others, she is not a passive victim. To be sure, Varuzhan does see the anarchist (today we would say "the terrorist") as yet another "victim" of "the marble altar" (*marmarakert baginin vra*) (*YLZ* 2:152–53, ll. 3–4), but this resolutely sacrificial image (which does not really appear in any of his other poems on human distress and the socialist revolution) gives this figure a special status, since it presents her as the female alter ego of the poet—who is nevertheless extremely ambivalent about her. She does not have the gentleness of other women (l. 6). She spends her chaste nights studying the Prophets of the revolution (l. 9). Her beautiful hair has become the banner of Death (l. 16). In her vigorous body rages the fire that will consume the powerful thrones of this land (l. 20). She wants to strike down the laws and the heads that wear crowns (l. 23). Her heart drips poison into the hand offered to her by the poet (and he no doubt wants to be her ally, her life's companion). In the end, he offers her this "bomb" that "lit up the World one day" and that is perhaps poetry, or the poem we are reading (ll. 31–32). This is a recurrent image in Varuzhan, that of a world lit up for a moment (a day) in poetry, before disappearing in the general conflagration. Poetry *is* this fire that ravages the world, equivalent in that sense to the terrorism of the anarchists, the sacred terrorism that overturns thrones. We recall the final words of the fragment published from the letter to Theotig of April 2, 1909: "We must gather together the relics of our hearts, shared out among three million people, and we must concentrate them in a single breast and feel its own proper Life, at least for a brief moment, for the love of art and for the love of the Song of Life." The apotheosis of art is a final apotheosis, a fire illuminating the world for a brief moment with its truth. The song of life coincides in every way with this autosacrificial explosion. Now, just before this sentence, Varuzhan writes in an offhand way, without making much of it, and, it would seem, merely in order to explain the new genre of poetry: "The fatherland has greatly separated us from ourselves." Of course, this could mean that the patriotic poetry he had practiced up to then had prevented him from writing a more personal poetry. It could also mean that the fatherland's alienation from itself has also alienated us from ourselves. The fatherland's coming to itself as an aesthetic process, the appropriation of the self through art, will restore us to ourselves. And of course we should also read in this a thought of originary alienation: the fatherland is not what is most proper to us in an originary way. On the contrary, it is what most separates us from "ourselves." The gathering together of the self will occur (or will reveal its essence) in this ultimate moment of the illumination of the world in the fire of art. We are already familiar with these themes. But Varuzhan says something else here as well. He is beginning to understand that art as mourning and as erection, art as the figuration of the gods and heroes in the founding word, in sum, art as the self's entry into the fatherland, requires and includes another element, namely self-sacrifice. Thus, to the Greek figure of the re-membered Dionysus, he already (or still) opposes the Christian or Christic figure of the expiating god. He does not do this in order to return to Christianity—quite the contrary. At stake here are rather the essence and the function of art.

"Poetic paganism" would thus be concerned with the essence and function of art as a *mise-en-oeuvre*, a setting into the work, or simply as the revelation of a founding speech (*mise-en-oeuvre* and revelation always go together). But at the end of his book, Varuzhan adds a final poem in which he explains once again the meaning of his poetic approach; he summarizes and repeats everything we just said concerning the two dimensions of art (and the unity of these two dimensions): art as an appropriative erection, and art as self-sacrifice. This final poem is entitled "This Book . . ." (*YLZ* 2:157–58). The poet writes to his benefactor, dedicating the book to him and explaining to him what he will find in it: he will find the priestesses of Bacchus, he will find the gods who want Homer's heart as a holocaust, he will find the nights of Pompeii, the grenade ready to explode in the mouth of the volcano; but he will also find the present century, which bore on its side the Christic wound (l. 11; in Armenian: *Hisusi pes karever*), this century shaken by the pains of childbirth, as a new dawn is being born. He will find hearts that are darkening like bad-quality candles, struggles between man and steel, outright and unabashed murder destroying so many innocent lives. When he reads all this, he must remember that the poet's song has recounted "the pain of joy and the joys of pain" (l. 17). Bacchus and Jesus, Dionysus and Christ, the "paganism" of self-productive power and the "Christianity" of expiation in suffering are united in this single but divided project. And immediately afterward, we read these two lines:

> The heart is a chalice into which one pours wine
> That immediately becomes the sacred blood of the gods.   (*YLZ* 2:157, ll. 19–20)[28]

It is thus a question of transubstantiation. Is this a Christian image? Of course. But aside from the fact that this central idea of the eucharist is without doubt the most "pagan" aspect of Christianity, and aside from the fact that all thinking on self-sacrifice could be considered Christian in origin, we must not forget that here it is a question of poetry, of art in the form of poetry. The heart in question is the same heart that had to gather into itself the dispersed relics and bring the dispersion to an end for a brief moment (the time of the end of time). In "The Flowers of Golgotha," the poet sings all the pains of the world and of humanity in its suffering, precisely in order to gather them into this heart and into this chalice of art. It is therefore a question of art, and certainly not of religion. Art is what is in question here, exactly as it was (or rather will be) two years later, in 1914, this time without any explicit or at least apparent religious connotations, in Hagop Oshagan, who declares that we are strangers to the songs of the fatherland (to legends, myths, the entire popular production), fundamentally alienated from them, and therefore from ourselves—and who says that these songs (and the fatherland itself) will be restored to us only through the artistic work of a Komitas, through their transfer into the element of art, and thus, obviously, through a transubstantiation. The unnamed and anonymous song changed substance and was transformed into art. What was most "foreign" to us was becoming what was most "proper." Likewise, the entire aesthetic principle is at work when Varuzhan speaks of transubstantiation. The eucharistic time of art is the time in which dispersion reaches its final term.

But it is quite clear that transubstantiation is not a religious "metaphor" for the nature and function of art. In fact, it is not a metaphor at all, precisely because it is a question of a real change in substance. This can be understood in two ways that are closely related. It is a real change in substance, first because art is visibly an heir to religion as it reaches an end, and it therefore preserves some of religion's essential figures and operations. But also, and especially, because in the contrary sense art is in reality the very operation by which transubstantiation is defined and realized. It is through this artistic or aesthetic operation that the blood of the gods begins to circulate in their veins, that the gods become living gods for us (even if they become living gods only as gods of the past, gods that are already dead), and therefore that there is religion. We will have many opportunities to emphasize this point: the sacred (the sacred blood of the gods) is an aesthetic category. Here it is clear that the sacred is produced in the eucharistic time of art, by the transubstantiation of wine into blood—the blood of the gods—in this strange and mysterious crucible (this chalice) that Varuzhan calls "the heart." It is the self-sacrifice of the poet that makes this operation possible. The poet is the one who gathers all the sufferings of the world into one single heart. Which also means that, even in the age of the pagan religions, even in the time when the gods were not yet dead, transubstantiation as an artistic operation created gods that already belonged to the past. Religion itself was its own mourning, but (or therefore) its own mourning remained veiled and inapparent to it. In other words, by appropriating mourning, religion occulted catastrophic mourning. Later we will see what follows from this proposition.

LIGHT AND THE GOD OF RITUAL SACRIFICE

For the moment it is necessary to resume our descriptive summary: the two dimensions of the aesthetic principle (erection, self-sacrifice), taken together, are the subject of Varuzhan's entire book. The aesthetic principle is not only the one presiding over the "nationalization" of the nation, the advent of the fatherland, the appropriation of the "self," the reception of popular songs in the aesthetic space of the patriotic "we," the gathering of the self from out of dispersion, the transformation of the language into a language that has been aestheticized by the restitution or recomposition of its integrity. All of these elements make up the system in which Varuzhan thinks art, of course, and this system will be recorded a little later in the pages of the journal *Mehyan*. But there is more, which is not explicitly stated in *Mehyan*, except when its Manifesto proclaims that art, being "itself a species of religious zealotry, stands above religion." This something more is located in the complex relation between art and religion. We do not yet possess all the elements of this relation, since up to now we have largely set aside everything concerning the thinking of art as a *mourning* of religion, a thinking of art as mourning which is the subject of the first part of the *Pagan Songs*, itself called "Pagan Songs." But as we can see from what has been said so far, this relation is already extraordinarily complex. Art is apparently the result of a historical development (the end of religion), but it is also at the beginning of religion, and in two different ways. On one side, it designates the operation of self-sacrifice, and thus a transubstantiation that engenders the sacred blood of the gods, their *past* vitality, the sacred as *having been*. On the other side, it designates the operation by which the gods are erected, that is, sculpted in the marble taken from the celestial mines of light. This second determination of art, as an erection at the origin (or at the principle) of religion, intervenes—as I have mentioned—in the poem "Luysë" (Light; *YLZ* 2:88–90), which appears close to the beginning of "The Flowers of Golgotha," and therefore in the section devoted to art as a self-sacrificial operation. A brief commentary of this poem thus promises to provide us with some insight into this sublation of religion by art.[29]

The poem bears an epigraph attributed to the Rig Veda: "You shine for greatness and sacrifice," which could also be read as, "You burn brightly from grandeur and sacrifice."[30] We know that Daniel Varuzhan was a reader of the Rig Veda in the French translations available at the time.[31] This line is from one of the hymns to Agni, who shines his radiant light and who is the messenger of the gods. Here is hymn 12 of book 1, in which this radiant light and the role of messenger are described:

> We choose Agni the messenger, the herald, master of all wealth,
> Well skilled in this our sacrifice.
> With callings ever they invoke Agni, Agni, Lord of the House,
> Oblation-bearer, much beloved.
> Bring the Gods hither, Agni, born for him who strews the sacred grass:
> Thou art our herald, meet for praise.
> Wake up the willing Gods, since thou, Agni, performest embassage:
> Sit on the sacred grass with Gods.
> O Agni, radiant One, to whom the holy oil is poured, burn up
> Our enemies whom fiends protect.
> By Agni Agni is inflamed, Lord of the House, wise, young, who bears
> The gift: the ladle is his mouth.
> Praise Agni in the sacrifice, the Sage whose ways are ever true,

The God who driveth grief away.
God, Agni, be his strong defence who lord of sacrificial gifts,
Worshippeth thee the messenger.
Whoso with sacred gift would fain call Agni to the feast of Gods,
O Purifier, favour him.
Such, Agni, Purifier, bright, bring hither to our sacrifice,
To our oblation bring the Gods.
So lauded by our newest song of praise bring opulence to us,
And food, with heroes for our sons.
O Agni, by effulgent flame, by all invokings of the Gods,
Show pleasure in this laud of ours.[32]

Varuzhan's poem is made up of five stanzas, each ending with the words "And I go toward the source of the light." The various aspects and attributes of light are described (with certain features of an emanatist ontology), as when the poet speaks of feeling that surge up in him—"An exile's nameless, anguished yearning" (l. 29) from this source, this unknown and sun-filled region. The attribute that we are already familiar with is the one in which light is the original material of the gods erected by art and the womb from which a Dante or a Homer are born. But light is also that which "flowed one evening / From Jesus' side like a flood, / Flowed like forgiveness / Into the empty cups of desolation / Of men gathered round Sin's altar" (ll. 34–38). With the word *light*, Varuzhan thus names the unity of both sides of the aesthetic principle, erection and self-sacrifice. Moreover, it indeed designates the solar principle of all religions, which is not itself a religious principle, and which in any case does not belong to any established religion, whether that of the Greek gods, of Christianity, or of the gods of the Vedic tradition. Be it the wave of forgiveness that spreads from the sacrifice of the Christian god or the original marble of erection, light shines wherever there are hymns, myths, or active religious speech. Light is also another name for the god Agni, who "Creates even as it perishes / An Agni with eyes of fire" (ll. 43–44). The path followed by the poet as he travels again and again toward the "source" is therefore the one that leads him from religions to their origin and principle. Light is the bride of my Mind, God's daughter (l. 32),[33] the wine poured in the libations to the Universe (l. 33, translated as "the wine of the Universe's rejoicing" in appendix C, text 22), and the blood of nature (l. 39). This solar principle of religions penetrates all originary speech. However, it can be lost, or effaced, and this means exile. It inhabits the poetic word and the poets are responsible for dispensing it to men on this earth. Light is thus shared out to everyone, it is distributed, it creates a dividing-out and a partaking while itself remaining indivisible, like the sacramental host (*nshkhark'*). It is in fact what "descends / Every morning, on our altars, / To the bloody mystery of the birth of man" (ll. 61–63). The word translated here as "birth of man" is *mardeghut'iun*; thus the phrase "the bloody mystery of the birth of man" could also be rendered as "the mystery of Incarnation." But we must read here the articulation not of a religious thought, but rather of a resolutely antireligious thought. Indeed, as I read these lines, it is in fact a question of a religion of humanity. Through its participation in the solar principle, its preoccupation with human exile far from this principle, and its role as intermediary, poetic language is traversed and saturated by light. Art, as poetry, is thus realized in the sacrament (or the mystery, *khorhurd* in Armenian) of humanity. This is what was referred to above as "the eucharistic time of art." If we think in Christian terms, if we insist on attaching the function of art to its historical precedents, then this mystery is indeed that of the Incarnation. Historically, in fact, art was realized in the figures of Jesus or Agni. Today, the poetic word is finally capable of expressing the aesthetic (solar) principle that impelled this realization. The poetic word, in its return to the principle, becomes both the guardian and the lover of the aesthetic sun. Thus the word is drawn away and attracted toward the source of light. It leaves behind the earthly regions where religions still rule. The poet implores his contemporaries, his brothers "who make the sign of the cross" (l. 71) to let him pursue his path alone, not to hold him back, not to spread their evil shadow over him, like "a buzzard's wing" (l. 78). Four years after this poem to light, Varuzhan wrote another poem with a similar inspiration called "Pegasus," also included in *Pagan Songs*. This poem describes an identical journey toward the sun on the back of a winged horse. It is here that we find the formula of the poet as the one who dispenses the solar force: "What the sun gives me, my mind gives to Man" (*YLZ*, 2:63, l. 231).[34] But it is also here that he writes: "I sing / Drawn away by the sun / The freedom of Man and the servitude of God" (ll. 242–44)—which better clarifies the first capitalization of "Man."[35] Although the religions realize and incarnate the aesthetic principle within the limits of historical time, and although art as poetry must go back to the older hymns of the "mythological" religions in order to read and hear in them its own *mise-en-oeuvre* in the element of light, it is nevertheless the case that the religions kept man in captivity. The liberation of the solar principle of art also liberates man from this captivity, giving him back his primary mythopoetic capacity and enclosing God within his limits, which are those of the historical incarnation of this principle. Unless, that is, the God whose servitude Varuzhan announces here is the God of the theological religions, religions which in any case know nothing of man's mythopoetic power. In either case, this captive God represents a source of death, the converse of the solar source of art. Thus we see emerging here an immense aesthetico-religious system, whose elements we have not yet exhausted.

What we have just said concerning the relation established here by Varuzhan between art and religions nonetheless falls within a certain interpretation: Varuzhan's own, of course, but also ours, as readers separated from him by a century. Do we know any more than his contemporaries did about Agni or the Rig Veda? Nothing is less certain. However, I am convinced that the simple reading of this poem that was just presented would have been impossible without (for example) Heidegger's sustained reflection on the thinking of Being. In fact, before (and after) Krikor Beledian's commentary, written almost twenty years ago, no one else, to my knowledge, has attempted to grasp what was said here concerning religions (or, in reality, concerning the end of religion as such). What we need is a better understanding of the series of operations carried out by Varuzhan, or by our reading of him. I will present this examination in relation to three terms that are central to such an interpretation: being, recognition, and figuration.

1. First of all, it seems clear to me, after all, that Varuzhan's reading of the Rig Veda is at the origin of this poem dedicated to light and speaking from the midst of light. But the claim I made above, that light is also another name for the god Agni, is not exactly what Varuzhan says. Before translating this line with a clearer sense of what is at stake here, we must take a closer look. Indeed, Varuzhan writes explicitly, in the middle of the poem: "The light is the divine Agni" (l. 41). This "is" bears the weight of the entire problem confronting us in our attempt to think the relation between art (poetry) and religion after Varuzhan, or to think what we are calling "religion." In effect, if light is the divine Agni, it is also the god Vahagn; and it is the wine that, flowing from Jesus' side, flows in (and for) the libation of the Universe; and it is other gods as well; and finally, it is not without some sacrifice. Agni shines and radiates only through and for sacrifice. Varuzhan of course explains this relation between Agni and light very clearly, using the image of the Host that is divided among everyone while remaining indivisible. The light is thus entirely Agni, and yet it is divided up *within* Agni, it is divided up *between* Agni and other gods, and it is divided up and shared out *to* us *by way of* these gods. The "is" in the line from Varuzhan's poem is thus not the copula of a formal identity, but that of a speculative identity. Or, to use another vocabulary, light is being; and nothing can be said of being that it itself does not first say (or that it itself already *is* not) in different figures, in its coming into language for us. Moreover, Agni is a figure (even if we do not know whether the anonymous authors of the Rig Veda made a distinction between being and a figure). When we say "light is . . . Agni," on the one hand we have a figure, and on the other hand, we have something that is dispensed entirely in every figure, without being exhausted in any one. In every case, we must understand the identity between Agni and light in a strict and absolute sense. Varuzhan obviously assumes that this is what the authors of the hymns intended, insofar as they were religious authors. But this strict identity knows nothing about the withdrawal of light, which alone makes possible the fact that it "is" Agni. By "being" Agni, light is withdrawn, it is removed, it becomes shadow. This imperceptible withdrawal, this removal at the very moment of being given and of figuration, is what requires a journey toward the source of the light. If Agni "is" light, he is not its source. But the source is itself a function of the withdrawal of being (or, in yet another vocabulary, of being as withdrawal). That is also why in "Pegasus," which recounts a similar voyage toward the source of light, the poet can say that to the "children of clay" he gives the smiles of the stars and the fire of the roses, that he spreads over the Earth "the purple mantle of dawn," but that he could just as well spread his shadow

(*shuk'*) over it and darken it entirely (*YLZ* 2:63, ll. 231–38). Thus Being "is" only insofar as it is withdrawn from its giving/being given. It is obscured when it becomes light. It is a giving as much as it is a withdrawing. It is a shining radiance as much as it is a darkening. Varuzhan's interpretation of Agni thus calls for a reading similar to the Heideggerian interpretation of "Being" as a giving and withdrawal. Later, and conversely, we will ask how such an interpretation could already be found in embryo in the poetic thought of an author from the beginning of the twentieth century, a reader of the Rig Veda in the grips of the aesthetic principle.[36]

I want to open here a parenthesis on the philology of the Vedas. Presumably Varuzhan read the Rig Veda either in Paul Régnaud's 1900 translation into French of a portion of the work or in the Alexandre Langlois translation into French of 1872, but there is no way to know this with any certainty. In any case, if we consider all the philological interpretations of the "Vedic religion" that were developed in the second half of the nineteenth century, and which were therefore still current at the very beginning of the twentieth century (Bergaigne and Régnaud in France; Müller and his disciples in Britain; Hillebrandt and Oldenberg in Germany), we are struck by two things: on the one hand, the Rig Veda is generally seen as the "Bible" of the "Aryan race"; on the other hand, the "religion" of the Veda is interpreted by all these authors in terms of an evolutionist scheme, which obviously has a very limited value as a principle of explanation. These studies were carried out within the philological framework of comparative linguistics and therefore completely disregard the Veda's place within a performative ritualism and, therefore, within a sacrificial system.[37] Apparently, the evolutionist scheme was, for these nineteenth-century scholars, the only one to offer any sufficient guarantees of "scientificity." Hence Régnaud envisaged an evolution of the religious based on the need to maintain a domestic fire, and he imagined an evolution of hymnic language from concrete meaning (the lighting and maintenance of fire) to the metaphorical meaning of the expressions used, then to the mythological meaning in the personification of the metaphorical figures (these ideas are stated in the introduction to his translation of the Rig-Veda and in his book on the origins of religion, *Le Rig-Véda et les origines de la mythologie indo-européenne*). Despite all the variations in detail and all the debates between philologists, the same evolutionist scheme guides their interpretation of early religions. As we will see at the end of this study, Varuzhan was familiar with these evolutionist theories, and he offered them his own tribute on occasion. In these conditions, one can only be astonished by the radical change of perspective on the "origin" of religion and its relations with "art" as they appear in Varuzhan's poetry. It is not a matter here of spiritualism or Rosicrucianism, which have been common since the end of the eighteenth century. Rather, what provoked the change of perspective was indeed the aesthetic principle. It would be necessary to study the philological interpretations of the origin of religion from the beginning of the nineteenth century (particularly, and most essentially, in Schelling's *Philosophy of Mythology* and *Philosophy of Revelation*, both published posthumously, in

1854) and to ask whether they had an influence, whether explicit or hidden, on the conceptions of the philologists. We will return to these questions below, particularly the evolutionist interpretation of the origins of religion, from which, in reality, Varuzhan does not escape completely; or perhaps he does not escape it at all, and that is the entire question.

2. Poetry is recognition, in every sense. Historically, it is only now that light can be recognized (and recognize itself) in the fire of Agni, in the blood of Jesus, in the libations and rejoicing of the Universe, in the mythological religions and in the sacrifices to the gods. Only today can the word that is drawn away and traversed by its solar source say that man is free and God is captive. But poetry is also a path of recognition never assured of its end, a "rising up," an ascension that tears one apart, a journey on the back of a winged horse. Finally, poetry is a discourse of recognition in the sense of gratitude, an action of grace, a final address to the gods who go absent and to the gods who perdure in their principle, like Vahagn or Vanatur.

3. The mythopoetic capacity at the source of religion is a figurative capacity. It gives form, it figures, it gives birth to the gods, it makes them be in the process of self-sacrifice, as historical concentrations of light; it sculpts them in the marble of the celestial quarries in order to give substance to their beauty. This passage, this figuration, this coming into vision and into language, this insertion into the human realm, this presence in ritual and in mythology must also be thought if we want to highlight the relation between art and religion as it is expressed in Varuzhan's work. In other words, *light "figures itself"*; it is nothing before this transformation into religious figures, into Agni, into Christ or into the Greek gods; it is this transformation itself, the power of this transformation, of this coming into vision in a determinate form, of this "ontogony."[38] If it is true, on the one hand, that this principle of religion—being as light—is nothing religious, on the other hand, it is not anything that has *not* already been said, recognized (and self-recognized), or figured, in the divine figures of the great religions of humanity. It is this transformative capacity that is thought in Varuzhan in terms of erection and self-sacrifice. Varuzhan is of course often obliged to distinguish between the material of erection (this is the function of marble) and the activity that transmutes it into a statue, into God, into a hero, into a work. And of course he is also obliged to distinguish between the material of sacrifice and sacrifice itself. But, in the end, Agni "is" sacrifice, the Greek god "is" its own erection (and in neither case an incarnation of the solar principle or a determination of being, much less the result of a "deification of natural phenomena").[39] It happens that only poetry—again, poetry as a drawing away of being and toward being—could recognize this "is" and therefore recognize itself in divine figuration. It alone could recognize that Agni is the name, simultaneously, of the matter, the activity, and the result; that is, the name of the process that constantly and repeatedly gives to Agni the name Agni, an obviously sacrificial process in which the ritual offering to the gods of the nominating word is an essential operation. Of course, these three constitutive elements of the relation between art and religion can

be understood only in the framework of mythological religions, which are the product of the mythopoetic capacity of man.[40] We recall (from Varuzhan's letter of October 4, 1908) that such a capacity was refused to the religion of the Jews, and the prophet Isaiah was placed alongside Pindar as a poet and certainly not described as a prophet. Moreover, what we have said about the "eucharistic" time of art, about light in the form of the wine that flowed one evening from the side of Jesus, about self-sacrifice as one of the central operations of the aesthetic principle, about the grandiloquent Christic images used to express suffering, sacrifice, or the end of sacrifice—none of this should lead us to believe that Varuzhan had any sympathy for Christianity as an established religion. It is rather a question of aversion.

Varuzhan sometimes takes his aversion to Christianity to extremes. This is the case in a long and little-known poem of 1912, "O Century, O Century . . ." (*YLZ* 2:209–14), which is violently anti-Christian.[41] In this poem, Varuzhan salutes the new century. He salutes the peoples who break their chains, in the West as well as in the East; he salutes the Iranian democratic revolution; he salutes his contemporaries who are struggling for political freedom; he describes Armenia as the new Israel; he suddenly shows himself as completely optimistic regarding the fate of his compatriots in Ottoman Turkey; he recounts the fall of idols and of the powerful high priests, the end of the books of the law. And about the revolutionaries who overturn thrones and religions, he exclaims: "They pass by, they march, they are Gods, made immortal by the hand of man / So many Prometheuses, standing straight up, their heads reaching to the sun" (ll. 74–75). The socialist or anarchist revolution exploding on every side is interpreted here in a Promethean sense. "Up above, swiping their scythes at the feet of God / They cut down the fields sown with stars, the prairies of the moon. / And they sow celestial fire on our Earth" (ll. 76–77). Popular revolutions are beginning to gain momentum, against the king in Spain, against the Pope in Rome, against the colonizers and the slave-masters in Guadeloupe. "Socialist thought" finally opens the stony lips of the Sphinx, who can then address the masses, denouncing the Books of Lies, those bloody books imposed by the high priests, one after the other. And finally, it is profane wisdom, it is the godless thought (*imastut'iun* in Armenian) that gives the world a Law that neither Socrates nor Christ knew (ll. 88–99). The end of the poem is even more violent. The pseudo-doctrine is no longer able to connect the Evangel to the spirit of this world; the flocks prefer to move in the clarity of the Idea rather than to remain in the enclosure of an imposture. Sycophants reign in the Church, prostitution takes over the convents, perversions proliferate. Rome and Jerusalem are the new Sodom and Gomorrah (ll. 101–112). The Lamb of God is auctioned off. Still confident in their own authority, the religions, shaking a finger in warning, begin to threaten people. But the people no longer obey, they want no more of this class of profiteers and intermediaries, the priests. The spirit of Savonarola is reborn in this century. In the four corners of the world, the four Churches—so proud of their power—fall apart in their clashes with one another. This description, full of sound and fury, as we see, makes more explicit the "vengeance" referred to in "Nemesis." The descendents of Giordano Bruno, rebelling against all the illegitimate authorities, call for vengeance against their masters. They light a great fire, and into it they throw all the instruments of repression that Catholicism and Calvinism have produced to repress the mind, their bulls, their memoranda, their rings and their seals, with which they had attempted to silence truth and its light for twenty centuries (l. 132). Varuzhan also has some harsh words for the Armenian Patriarchs who have soiled their robes and brought shame upon the crosses they wear on their breast, by slipping into the harems of Sultan Abdül-Hamid disguised as eunuchs. They will all disappear, and humanity will finally become its own hero (it is strange that in Armenian, as well as in French or in Greek, the hero can be thought solely in the masculine form; only the figure of the anarchist woman could weaken this claim, but she thinks only of destruction). Glory to this century, which begins the morning of humanity. And it will be (it already is) a morning without religion. This anti-Christianity, much like French anticlericalism at the end of the nineteenth century, was of course inspired both by a revolt against the Fathers (the Mkhitarists) who had educated Varuzhan throughout his childhood and youth, and by a reaction against his immediate surroundings.[42] It is in any case another way—historical and somewhat naïve—to announce the end of religion.

CHAPTER 7

The Mourning of Religion I

THE IDEALIST MATRIX

At the origin of religion, then, there is art. Art produces the gods in the past through an operation of sacrificial transubstantiation or an erection in celestial marble.[1] It works in the element of light. It recognizes itself poetically in religious figures, these figures of gods burnt or sculpted, these figurations of self-sacrifice and of erection, who name and perhaps fix the movement by which being gives itself and withdraws itself. This poetic recognition, this solar force of attraction exerted on language, is already a sublation of religion at its end. It could not be otherwise: the recognition of light in the gods is, by the same token, the discovery of the gods as having been. We cannot say that this in itself is what brings religion to an end. It simply discovers religion always and again in the past. The matricial structure that thus governs the relation between art and religion was bound to give rise, as one can easily imagine, to every sort of interpretation and restoration. This structure was of course not invented by Daniel Varuzhan. Rather, it was invented by the early Romantics in Germany, around the end of the eighteenth century. And it was this structure that provoked the expectation of a *new* mythology. It was also what led Novalis to write his reactionary essays on Europe and Christianity.[2] Religion, Novalis argued, was no longer what it had been previously. It was necessary to reestablish a hierarchical society that also had to be a society based on Christian faith. It is this same historico-philosophical structure that would lead Schlegel, during the same period, and in a way that was much more complex, to shift from the religion of humanity and from the call to a new mythology toward the assumption and proclamation of Catholicism as the religion that had to be restored.[3] Now it is precisely because the theme—and the irresistible temptation—of restoration is one of the possible responses to this strange structure of recognition (in which light discovers or uncovers the gods in the past, at the very moment when it recognizes itself in them) that Varuzhan's interpreters have always read his "poetic paganism" as a desire to restore the pagan past. Such a reading can appear utterly absurd if we restrict ourselves to Varuzhan's poetic terms, but it is after all an integral part of the logic of historical meaning. Indeed, we have seen that in his first epistolary mention of paganism, Varuzhan speaks of "conversion" to poetic paganism. It is an impossible conversion, to be sure, but his use of the term nonetheless indicates a certain nostalgia for this past, which was opening under his feet through the action of the aesthetic principle. Similarly, it is possible to see the entire discourse on the grandeur of Ani, on the interrupted thread of a brilliant civilization that must be taken up again, as motivated by the desire for restoration. It certainly was motivated by that, among other things, and this is an important part of the system developed by national aestheticism. But this was obviously not the most essential element. I just said that the invaginated structure of the relation between art and religion, this idealist matrix through which art and religion are given to be thought and come to form a system, was not invented by Varuzhan. But neither did it reach him through the direct influence of German idealism and its major representatives, or through a knowledge, direct or indirect, of the early Romantics, which he certainly did not have. It reached him rather through the totally distorting prism of the nineteenth century—the century of philology—by way of an orientalism that several generations of scholars had constructed after the first works of comparative linguistics, an orientalism that had elaborated a philological memory of the Eastern religions. We cannot overestimate the decisive importance of this orientalism, which was crystallized and then diffused in the works of Max Müller in England and those of Ernest Renan in France, and whose counterpart was found in the evolutionist theories of anthropology during the same period. As a student of the social sciences in Belgium, Varuzhan had a thorough knowledge of this orientalism and this anthropology. He therefore had to reinvent the idealist matrix for his own purposes (and, moreover, in his own language), *in reaction* to this philological orientalism and this evolutionist anthropology, and therefore, despite his own best intentions, in a total dependence on both of them. He had to reinvent the circulation between being, recognition, and figuration, which necessarily led him to think of religion as a thing of the past and the gods themselves as past. It will be remarked that the Greek and pagan gods obviously do belong to the past. Granted, but what we find in Varuzhan is something else. It is no longer a consideration of humanity's religious past expressed in the terms used by philological orientalism or the history of religions as a discipline. It is rather a discovery in the present, in which the (poetic) power of discovery recognizes itself as light in the having-been. It is thus a discovery, in mourning, of the sacred, and therefore in reality a discovery of mourning, of the mourning of the sacred, a discovery that had taken place in Germany a century earlier, with Schlegel and Hölderlin (let us say), in a way that was at once astonishingly brilliant and fleeting (and in fact had no visible consequence, at least not until the re-elaboration of this category by Nietzsche in terms of the Dionysian, and then in Heidegger's reading of Hölderlin). I said "discovery, in mourning" (and I could have said "mournful discovery") because, as we know, in the very moment of its discovery, the sacred is lost; it is always discovered as lost. That is part of the very structure of the sacred as an aesthetic category, as a category following from the aesthetic principle. The sacred is *always already* lost. This is something of which philology is never sufficiently aware. We can go so far as to say that philology was invented (and that by the same token it "invented" religion) in order not to know this. It lives off this past, this loss that is consubstantial with religion. But these various ways of making this point only show the extent to which the invention of philology and that of the idealist or speculative matrix (which governs the relations between art and religion through mourning) are intimately connected and interwoven. Here again, it was Friedrich Schlegel who made the journey from one to the other, who spread the good news concerning these two aspects of the division between philology and philosophy. He wrote the first book in German that announced modern philology, *Die Sprache und die Weisheit der Indier* (1808); the same book also settles some scores with speculative idealism.[4]

We must now explicate this condition of being "always already lost" through a reading of Varuzhan's "pagan" poems, which present in broad daylight, as it were, this discovery in the present, this mournful discovery of the sacred. Before entering into this reading, it is important to specify one thing. It is true that Varuzhan's reception and thinking of the notion of loss came by way of the idealist matrix which he himself had recreated according to his own needs. In this matrix, mourning plays a fundamental, even a primordial role. Just as the native—the central invention of philological orientalism—carried his own disaster within himself, within his very definition, and thus called for a certain mourning, so did religion (thought from the perspective of its end) and the sacred (received as having been lost) call for a mourning which is the mourning of art or art as mourning. Poetic paganism is this art as mourning, a mourning of the sacred and of the gods in the very moment of the discovery of the sacred and of the gods. Here, discovery is loss. Poetic paganism is thus the art (and through art, the experience) of the mournful discovery that was just discussed. Certainly; but Varuzhan's project then repeated in its own way the entire German experience of thought and poetry, the entire German repetition of the Greek experience of the gods, although of course in circumstances that were very particular. But can we even refer to "circumstances" here? With the reinvention of the idealist matrix, he was confronting another experience, this time entirely implicit and, it seems, strictly unheard of: the experience of what we have called the *default of mourning*, the experience of catastrophic mourning, the disaster as a loss of mourning, as a loss of the very possibility of mourning. Certainly, no idealist matrix could hold its ground against the default of mourning, the mourning that defaults and defects from itself. And yet Varuzhan had no other means for thinking the default of mourning, for confronting this default, than (once again) art as mourning and therefore the all-powerful idealist matrix. This explains all the difficulties we encountered above in our various descriptions of the disaster, difficulties that we will no doubt find again in the description of religion reaching its end and sublated in its end, one last time, by art. But were there other means? Are there? Was it not in colliding with this question that Hölderlin lost his reason?

THE DOUBLE RETURN

We will begin with the long letter about return, dated November 11–17, 1908, sent by Varuzhan from Ghent to his friend Terenig Jizmejian (who had just returned home to Yerzinjan), and with the following passage in particular:

> How happy I would have been if you had traveled with my father. For a few days at least he could have believed I was there by his side and been gladdened by it. Send me your impressions, especially those having to do with Yerzinjan. I am not certain about next year, but in any case we will see each other the following year. I must absolutely visit all of Armenia. I want to kiss with my own lips every one of those sites where a martyr has fallen, or where a hero has tread. We are great only to the extent that we draw our feelings from the land. That is everything. To our ancestors. Which means: to the gods. Oh, Terenig, what a magnificent epic could be written about Tigran the Great. But this is not possible without first seeing Armenia. One must first have seen the great rocks that our ancestors used to make stones for their slings. One must first have seen those immense oak trees that they burned without uprooting them, in whose light they gathered to celebrate the great festivals of their heroic victories. One must have seen everything, everything that you have before you now. How fortunate you are, Terenig.[5]

For the sake of anecdote, it is worth adding that Terenig had been forced to return home, since the Mkhitarist fathers (who were financing his studies) had decided unilaterally to decrease his funds by half, which obliged him to abandon his studies. But Terenig did not remain in the country for long. After a journey around the Mediterranean that lasted a few months, he returned to Turin in 1909. What is important about this letter, however, is the central phrase, "To our ancestors. Which means: to the gods."[6] This phrase has echoed in our ears for decades. It is a double return, a double imperative to return. The past of the ancestors was thus the country of the gods. This equivalence established by Varuzhan will occupy us for some time. But this double return is indicated here as the condition for writing the great epic that Varuzhan already had in mind and that he would continue to think about until the end.[7] It was necessary to have "seen" the country in order to write the epic that Varuzhan planned to write. But it is this epic project that most clearly makes Varuzhan the heir (a dissident heir, of course, as is always the case for any true cultural heir) of the Mkhitarist fathers. For them, a national epic would have been the fulfillment of the nation par excellence, the work that would finally bring the nation into its own—which is how they saw (or interpreted) the distant examples of Virgil's *Aeneid* and Ronsard's *Franciade*. As I have explained elsewhere, three generations of the Mkhitarist fathers had worked on this project, first translating into (classical) Armenian the great "national" epics of Europe—even translating some of them several times, once every generation—and ending finally with the great erudite epic *Hayk Diutsazn* (Hayg the

Hero), composed by Father Arsen Bagratuni in 1858 in classical Armenian, at a time when the vernacular had been the language of Armenian literature for two decades, and when classical Armenian could no longer be considered capable of a linguistic restoration (if it ever had been).[8] The entire epic project of the Venetian Mkhitarists, which had been pursued with extravagant fervor throughout the first half of the nineteenth century—a nationalist project if there ever was one—was thereby rendered obsolete, and had been since the very beginning, for they had not foreseen the literarization of vernacular Armenian. Moreover, it almost goes without saying that none of the Mkhitarist fathers had ever set foot in "the country." The Armenian provinces, concentrated in the eastern villayets of the Ottoman Empire, were largely populated by "apostolic" Armenians, followers of the autocephalous church, and the Mkhitarists had no schools there. Their schools (aside from those in Venice and Vienna) were in Constantinople and in what was already called the *galouths*, the excentric or diasporic communities (Crimea, Bessarabia, Poland, Basra, Paris), although the word *diaspora* was not yet very common at the time. These are of course only external reasons. The more essential reason had to do with the nature of the native, that invention of philological orientalism, and in that regard the Mkhitarists were the purest representatives of orientalism for the sons of the nation! Even the auto-ethnographic program had not yet reached them. The native was for them what he was for Chateaubriand, Nerval, or Flaubert in their famous journeys to the Orient: the monument in ruins still visible after a secular collapse, not yet the bearer of an unconscious knowledge. For these successive generations of philologists and translators during the first half of the nineteenth century, the journey to the country and to the native—a journey which they nevertheless found necessary—had not yet taken place. The archeological descriptions of present reality could be elaborated on the basis of a knowledge of books and the impressions of a few travelers who had wandered into these distant lands that otherwise held little interest. It was only much later, after 1880, that the Armenians began to travel toward themselves, still as orientalist travelers, of course, but this time not as flâneurs but as ethnographers. The national project of the Mkhitarists at the beginning of the century was therefore in every way a philologist's project, even and especially when it was a matter of producing the "national" epic. However, the prestige of this nationalist project among Western Armenians (who were hardly capable of understanding a single line of *Hayg the Hero*, written as it was in a classical language that was certainly very beautiful, but also complex and often difficult) was such that Hagop Oshagan was compelled to write hundreds of polemical pages in his *Panorama of Western Armenian Literature* in order to deliver the final blow to this project by explaining precisely that it was entirely a philologist's project; in other words, a project that was not informed by what Oshagan then called "the literary concept," and what today we could call the aesthetic principle.[9] It was thus up to Varuzhan to take on the project anew in its entirety and to realize it according to the new demands of the age, that is, the demands of aesthetic nationalism.

To the ancestors, to the gods: this double return is the motto of poetic paganism. In the first term of the pair, we can read the necessity of responding creatively to the disaster that constitutes the native, tying the interrupted thread back together, and relating the present of the native to the past of the ancestors; it is the necessity of investigating the invention of the native yet further (of which, of course, Varuzhan knew nothing at all, in terms of an invention), of integrating the loss as an essential moment in the relation to the past or to the sacred. For, indeed, what can it mean "to return to the ancestors"? Is this a reactionary slogan? Is it a matter of returning individually and collectively to the past? Is it a matter of reviving their heritage? This first series of questions asks about the nature of the return. But there is also the question concerning the nature of the ancestors. Who were they? In the second decade of the nineteenth century, the Mkhitarist father Lucas Injijean was working on an archeology of the Armenian world, which was not published until 1835, in a posthumous edition of three volumes. This was no less a question of returning to the ancestors! It was an archeology without any digging or any terrain, a purely philological description and reinvention of the past on the basis of texts, and, in fact, on the basis of texts that were poorly dated and whose relation with this archeological past of the nation was itself poorly established. In Varuzhan's time, these uncertainties had been partly corrected, certainly, but this archeological past remained that of the kings of the Artashesian dynasty (second and first centuries B.C.), of which Tigran the Great is the most well-known representative;[10] or else that of the kings of the Arsacid dynasty (first to the fifth centuries A.D.). It is clear that Varuzhan wanted to traverse the texts and the memory of the nation, that he wanted to revive a capacity for heroism and a mythical stratum that were older than the philological reconstructions. He wanted poetry (and therefore, here, epic poetry) to inherit the "myth" of the ancestors, that is, both *their* proper capacity for heroization through mythic recitation and *our* capacity to mythify them. "To kiss with my own lips every one of those sites where a martyr has fallen, or where a hero has tread," wrote Varuzhan. The philological reconstruction of national memory was thus not sufficient. The reason for its insufficiency is not that it remained purely textual, that it did not know the real terrain. What it did not know was not the terrain, it was "the land." What was needed, then, was the fervor of the pilgrim, the one who *sacralizes sites* by his journey in the present. This sacralization of the sites of memory is the condition of art, but it is also, obviously, an effect of art. Condition and effect are not isolated from one another. Art "resacralizes" and "remythifies" the site. As we see, even with respect to the return to the ancestors as the condition for the epic, with respect to the native and the work of memory, Varuzhan's project can be formulated and specified only by discovering or affirming the mythical and "religious" function of art.[11] That is in fact the major difference between Varuzhan's epic project and the project of Khachatur Abovean, formulated some sixty years earlier. Abovean's formulation was made during the ethnographic moment of this long history of nationalism. He already saw the necessity of a "return." He spoke of the project of collecting legends and customs by returning to the native, in a reflexive gesture that definitively affirmed and confirmed the latter's centrality (and consequently, already that of the "land"). This gesture was an attempt to record the historical "accident" that had happened to the native, now forgetful of his past and possessing it only as a witness with no historical density, as a mute monument, and therefore in reality dispossessed of himself. What then is the difference between this project and Varuzhan's? It has to do with the resacralization of the site, as condition and as effect of the remembrance called *art*. Art is henceforth conceived as the epic remembrance of a power that is itself already essentially epic (that of the martyrs and the heroes), and not as the orientalist gathering together of a memory that must be restored to the native (to "the people") as his own, much less one that is merely used in a comparative examination which ignores both the mourning of the native and the mourning of the sacred, both the disaster of the native and the end of religion. At bottom, this is the difference between the Other-scene and the scene-of-the-Other discussed above in reference to the poem "To the Ashes of Cilicia." Here the Other-scene is that of the mournful discovery; the scene-of-the-Other is that of philology. It is an enormous difference, certainly, but one that from another angle may appear in reality quite small, since the "return to the ancestors" could also have been claimed by the two previous "moments" of nationalism: archeological nationalism and ethnographic nationalism. That is certainly the case, but it could not have been claimed by them, and in fact never was claimed by them, as resacralization. It is here, then (beyond the mournful discovery), that the aesthetic principle is concentrated. This resacralization of the site by and for art is expressed in the *equivalence* established by Varuzhan between the two ways of understanding the return: to the ancestors, to the gods. Art would set the sacred back into motion as the ancestors knew it and practiced it when they gathered around their sacrificial fires, around those great trees which they were able to burn standing, in celebration of their victories. As always, it is this image of the sacrificial festival that Varuzhan evokes in order to speak of the link between art and "the sacred." And as always, this link is presented in the two forms of erection and auto-sacrifice.

THE SACRED POET AND THE RED SOIL

Before offering a reading of some of the great poems addressed to the gods, I would like to open a short parenthesis on Hagop Oshagan's reading of Varuzhan's work. Oshagan first met Varuzhan in 1909, when the latter passed through Constantinople on his way back home. Later, in 1912, they became close friends when Varuzhan returned to the capital after three years in Sebastea and Tokat. Oshagan wrote a great deal on Varuzhan from the very beginning, first as a reader of his works, then as a stunned and inconsolable friend.[12] Here is how he described the impression Varuzhan

made on his contemporaries, based on his memory of the last evening they spent together (exactly one week before April 24, 1915), when friends had gathered at Rupen
Sevag's home with some other writers:

> I saw him for the last time at Rupen Sevag's home in Pera. The city was unrecog-
> nizable. In the company of several writers gathered around a table, he drank a
> glass of wine in honor of our literature. Then he read a few pages from his poem
> "The Red Soil." I will never forget the fire that filled his voice and his face at that
> moment, when the poem took shape before our astonished eyes. His body was a
> musical instrument. And we all felt that the inspired and the visionaries of past
> centuries [hin oreru] were not in any way different in nature from this man who
> was living his poem before us with such irresistible emotion. Even Sevag's wife, a
> German who had learned a few words of Armenian out of love for her husband,
> was drawn into the blanket of fire produced by his words, and she wept, no doubt
> without clearly understanding the sweet and terrible things, the infinite things that
> we Armenians who were there drew from it.[13]

In this passage, Oshagan speaks most vividly of the link between art and the sacred as
Varuzhan represented it in his very person. But, of course, his description preserves
the general atmosphere of this evening, which remained an indelible moment in his
memory, since Oshagan would never again see any of the friends gathered there that
evening for one last meeting. The link between art and the sacred was also represented
by Hagop Oshagan himself, as a novelist, a historian, and a critic. Much later, in 1931,
when he was living in Cyprus and working on his novel *The Remnants*, Oshagan
granted an interview to Benjamin Tashian, a journalist who had come from Cairo for
the occasion. The interview was later published in the monthly journal *Hayrenik* in
Boston, under the title "In the Shade of the Cedars." In this interview, in answer to a
question about his approach to critical work, Oshagan replied:

> You are speaking of a kind of writing that has nothing in common with what is
> commonly called criticism except its name. The act of writing is such a far-
> reaching and public phenomenon that we can only compare it to the ethos created
> by religions of the ancient centuries [hin dareru].[14]

As I pointed out years ago (in an essay entitled "Critique and the Experience of the
Sacred"),[15] Oshagan's response is strange, for the question that had been posed to him
had to do with the nature of literary criticism as he practiced or conceived of it. But he
answers with a statement concerning the link between "the act of writing" and the sacred ethos of the ancient religions. He responds as if the critic and the artist, taken together, were the last heirs to a very old *experience* of the sacred (or at least as if criticism
had to devote itself to the exploration of this experience in the *modern* reception of the
sacred). We can imagine that he shared this conception with Daniel Varuzhan or that

he had learned it from him. It is clear that none of this casts any doubt on what was said above about the sacred as a mournful discovery and the sacred itself as having-been. It is still in terms of "the ancient centuries" and "the inspired and the visionaries of past centuries" that Oshagan defines the sacred fire when he speaks of his lost friend. We may also imagine that the fire that "filled his voice and his face" as Varuzhan read "The Red Soil" is not unrelated to what the poet called "the circle of fire" (*hrap'oghp'ogh psak*)—if it is true, as I remarked above, that language needs to become combustible in order to receive or to render the Catastrophe, and if it is true that language needs to welcome the fire of destruction into itself, in order to make everything resound from out of this incandescence. That is Varuzhan's most central thought: the same scene (the same language, but on fire) as an Other-scene; the same Canaan as an other-country. It is, as we will see in a moment, the very thought of return and conversion. The return to the fathers, the return to the red earth, requires a word on fire, a word devoured by the blaze and destined for the ashes, and this word will in turn signify a return to the gods. We recall that it was already a question of red earth in the letter of October 4, 1908, written to a correspondent who had returned for a time to the country: "You are not far from the land of our fathers and already you must feel, in the depths of that red earth, the trembling of a joy covered with laurels" (*YLZ* 3:38). "The Red Soil" belonged to the earlier stage of *The Heart of the Race*, since it had been written in 1906. The piece of red earth on the poet's table was a "relic" inherited from the ancestors, a relic exiled in a foreign land. It was thus the last poem that Varuzhan ever read in public. Exile had come to an end. He was about to step with both feet into the Catastrophe.

THE GOD VAHAGN

Now we will begin a somewhat detailed commentary on Varuzhan's first "pagan" poem, "Vahagn" (*YLZ* 1:172–75). One of the most prominent gods in the restricted Armenian pantheon, Vahagn was the equivalent of the Iranian god Verethragna, the dragon-slayer, born in the morning reeds. We know that less than ten years later, Charents too would write a Vahagn poem; its inspiration and theme were different from Varuzhan's, but its underlying idea (the end of myth) was one that could easily have been taken on by the latter.[16] Here are excerpts from a previously unpublished translation of Varuzhan's poem by G. M. Goshgarian (for the entire poem in translation, see appendix C, text 20).

> O Vahagn, father of the gods,
> God of power, sun made man
> In the lineage of Tigran,
> Cleanse my soul, anoint these my lips
> With one ray—for behold, I kiss
> Your holy altar and, raising the dread hammer

With a mighty arm bent to your service,
Smash my bull's forehead, and dedicate
The freely gushing blood to your knees.   (ll. 25–33)

.   .   .   .

Accept, O Mighty One, these my gifts,
Which I pour out onto the flames
From a flawless, radiant urn.
Here is the wine. Open your nostrils and breathe in
Its sweet aroma, and be reconciled
With your apostate people
In the gay inebriety of a god.
Here is the holy oil. I pour it out before you
Pure, sweet, and abundant. . . .   (ll. 51–59)

.   .   .   .

O sublime one, are you satisfied? I have given you
All that I had in my cell and in my soul—
All that the enemy forgot to take
From deserted Ashtishat. the widowed city.[17]
Now, the last Vahuni of our race,
I kneel in holy fear before your altar,
And kiss the ground where something
Of your soul lets the pine-trees take root,
And, stretching my arms out toward you,
Sleeves rolled up, the bull's hot blood
Still dripping from my elbows,
O Vahagn, o god of my fathers,
I pray . . . I pray . . .

For the force, the faith in your arm,
With which, one day, you tore
The dragons' mouths to shreds and, like sun-seeds,
Scattered the Milky Way across the sky.
For the force that is the wings and the soul
Of the creation without end, the force
Beneath whose infinite kiss
The worlds bear flower and flame, and
The principle of immortality quickens in the atom
And the brain and the will; for the force
Beneath whose powerful finger

Seeds split open and the sap, singing,
Soars to the topmost branches of the oaks;
For the force that fills women's breasts,
Rocks our cradles, and carries us after death
As far as the stars, as far as
The creative cause of a second life, the force
That plants a Nation somewhere, like a pride of lions,
And pours the strength of your arm into its arm,
And, like the fire-condor, shelters under its wings of light,
In our mothers' wombs,
Heroes, geniuses;
I speak for that sacred Strength, whose wise
And overflowing source you are,
O Vahagn. Behold! My bloody arms
Stretched out towards you,
I pray . . . I pray . . .   (ll. 65–106)

Before engaging in a detailed reading of this poem, it will be useful to begin by briefly discussing the Armenian reception of mythology and the way in which the god Vahagn was conceived in Varuzhan's time. This will enable us to understand the densely layered historical and mythological allusions in the poem. The only written sources on the religion of the Armenians before christianization were the Armenian historians of late antiquity. We know that there is no Armenian historiographic "literature" until the fifth century A.D., when the Armenians had already been officially Christian for a century and a half. Everything we know about the "pagan" gods and their temples therefore comes to us from an entirely Christian-inspired literature, particularly *The History of the Armenians* by Agathangelos, the theologico-apologetic writing of Eznik, *Against the Sects*, and (no doubt much later) the *History of Armenia* by Moses of Khoren, who provides the only hymnic material concerning the god Vahagn. None of this means, of course, that the memory of Vahagn did not remain alive among Armenians for many centuries, despite the destruction of all the temples and the eradication of the pagan cults by Gregory the Illuminator, the official evangelist of the Armenians, and by King Tiridate around the beginning of the fourth century. Here is the narrative of one such act of destruction, as told by Agathangelos:

> When he arrived at the borders of Armenia, Gregory heard that here remained in
> the land of Taron the temple of Vahagn—a very wealthy temple, full of gold and
> silver, to which many offerings had been presented by the greatest kings. It was the
> eighth famous shrine and was devoted to the cult of Vahagn, called the Dragon-
> handler, a place of sacrifice for the kings of Greater Armenia, on the summit of
> the moutain Karke on the river Euphrates, which looks across to the great Taurus
> range; it was called Yashtishat from the frequent cultic sacrifices of the site. For at

that time there still stood three altars in it; the first was the temple of Vahagn; the second that of the Golden-mother, the Golden-born goddess, and the altar was called after her golden-built of the Golden-mother goddess; the third was the temple named for the goddess Astghik, called the spouse of Vahagn, who is in Greek Aphrodite. For this Gregory set out in order to destroy it also, since ignorant men still made profane sacrifices at these surviving altars.[18]

This quote is from R. W. Thomson's translation. "Temple of Vahagn" translates the Armenian *Vahevahean mehean*, where *Vahevahean* can be taken as an adjectival form or the proper name of the altar. The clan of priests in charge of the cult was the clan of the Vahuni.[19] The mention of the "eighth site of worship" is understood by the translator as "the eighth that Gregory destroyed."[20] "Dragon-handler" is the translation of *vishapak'agh*, dragon-slayer (or "reaper").[21] Traces of Vahagn remained in the memory and the language of the Armenians, for Vahagn, on the model of the Iranian Verethragna, slays dragons and scatters their remains in the sky. Or (according to a version reported by an author of the seventh century) he steals straw from the Lord of the sky and uses it to trace out the Milky Way (called in Armenian *Chanaparh Yartgoghi*, the Straw-Thief's Way) and, in that regard, he resembles Hercules. Finally, the very name of the sanctuary is already interpreted by the ancient author cited here, since it is given as "Yashtishat" and is understood as "the site where many sacrifices are offered" (*asht* being the Armeno-Iranian word for sacrifice). On the other hand, according to section 127 in Agathangelos, who cites an edict from King Tiridate before his conversion ("May there be greeting and prosperity with the help of the gods, abundant fertility from noble Aramazt, protection from Lady Anahit, valor from valiant Vahagn to you and all our land of Armenia"),[22] and according to Jean-Pierre Mahé's interpretation (who on this point takes up the ideas of Georges Dumézil), Vahagn incarnates "the warrior function in the triad Aramazd-Vahagn-Anahit" and can "carry out his bellicose activities in different domains (military, properly speaking, but also agricultural or atmospheric)."[23]

The other important source on Vahagn is Moses of Khoren, who repeats information from Agathangelos concerning the pagan temples and their destruction in the fourth century, but who also cites oral sources. Moses of Khoren's explicit quotation is the *only* written trace (aside from the brief mention of the straw thief in Shirakatsi in the seventh century) that we have of the mythologeme "Vahagn," and above all the only trace of a mythological poem or an ancient hymn in a form that can be considered as relatively original (that is, not embellished, condensed, abridged, or paraphrased by the author). The few lines thus transmitted by Moses, almost despite himself, are famous today among Armenians, literate or not, since they have been considered (and taught) since the nineteenth century as the oldest document of Armenian "literature" that has come down to us. They are found in a passage on the "descendents of Tigran," the Tigran of legend, the "son of Yervand," the supremely courageous, who, according to Moses, helped Cyrus take control of the empire of the Medes and the Persians (to be distinguished at least historically from the King Tigran of the first century B.C.). Vahagn is mentioned as one of the descendents of this Tigran. Here is the passage in its entirety:

> His sons were Bab, Tiran, and Vahagn; concerning the latter there is a song in the
>   legends of our country:
> "The sky was in labor, so was the earth,
> So was the sea with its deep blue water,
> The same labor, in the sea, took hold of the glowing red reed;
> From the stem of the reed arose the smoke,
> From the stem of the reed, a flame came forth,
> From the flame there leaped a young blond boy:
> He had hair of fire,
> He had a beard of flame,
> And his eyes were suns!"
> These praises were sung to the sound of the *p'andir'*, and I heard them with my
>   own ears; then one sang of his combats, his victories over the Dragons, and it
>   was said that he even became a god and that, after a statue was raised to him
>   in the land of the Iberians, he was honored with sacrifices.[24]

Faithful to his vocation as a rational historian (in his interpretation of myths) and as an euhemerist theologian (in terms of the origin of the gods), Moses reduces the gods to the stature of great men of the past and thus considers Vahagn as a princely hero around whom extravagant songs had been woven. But this leads him to keep silent on certain elements that he was obviously aware of, like the fact that the cult of Vahagn was prominent throughout Armenia and that the Vahunis' priesthood was devoted to a god (not an ancestor). In book II, section 8, he writes: "Among the children of Vahagn, King Vagharchak found some who spontaneously asked to be ministers of the temples. It was a great honor for them to be given this priesthood. He raised them to the rank of the first dynastic houses and called them Vahuni."[25] Moses's last mention of Vahagn concerns the importation of an eastern statue of Herakles (book 2, section 12):

> In Asia, Artashês found the gold and bronze statues of Artemis, Herakles and
> Apollo and had them brought to our country in order to erect them in Armavir.
> After receiving them, the chiefs of the priests, who were of the family of the
> Vahuni, raised those of Apollo and Artemis in Armavir. But when it came to the
> statue of Herakles, which had been made by Scyllas and by Dipenês of Crete, they
> saw it as a statue of Vahagn, their ancestor, and they erected it in Taraun, in their
> hereditary village of Ashtishat, after the death of Artashês.[26]

The rebirth of the god Vahagn in Varuzhan did not happen by chance. First of all, Varuzhan of course knew the passages just quoted, as well as the modern studies on the "pagan" religion of the Armenians. He was thus partly dependent on the philological tradition of the nineteenth century and on the interpretations that were current at the time. In particular, he knew the book by Father Ghevond Alishan, *The Armenians' Ancient Faith or Pagan Religion*, published in Venice in 1893, which contains two important passages on Vahagn: one on the solar origin of the gods, and another more historical and general passage on the cult of Vahagn.[27] However, he probably did not know the work of Manuk Abeghean on Armenian myths and popular mythemes, an extraordinary work that appeared in a journal in 1899, then as a book in 1900.[28] These two works attest in different ways to a renewed impulse to study the history of religions among Armenians and, in particular, to the favor enjoyed by "the ancient faith or pagan religion." With this in mind, it will be worthwhile to say a few words on the philological and comparative tradition. While the following remarks may touch on Varuzhan's work only indirectly, they will provide a clearer sense of the overall background.

The works of Alishan and Abeghean belong to two philological lineages that are very different in terms of their method. Abeghean had studied in Germany, where he wrote a thesis in the science of folklore rather than comparative mythology; but, in the work that interests us here, his method is entirely comparative. For that reason, although he is not addressing an audience made up exclusively of specialists, he nonetheless situates himself within an academic tradition that aspires to be strictly scientific. Finally, he is the culmination of a philological current that was quite prominent among the Eastern Armenians, a current that developed during a certain period in Russian universities and most of whose works were written in Russian. In terms of studies in comparative mythology, this current had emerged some fifty years earlier with Mkrtich Emin, an author of whom we already said that he had done pioneering work leading to the discovery of the epic and mythological character of a great many passages in Moses of Khoren, and was himself influenced, of course, by the German school that was already well established by 1850.[29] On the other side of the invisible border, Alishan was an heir to the national philological tradition of the Mkhitarists, a tradition he continued up to the end of the nineteenth century by completing the archeologically oriented projects that had been formulated at the century's beginning. This national tradition was also a nationalist tradition in its very essence. Alishan was an extremely popular author, known on both sides of the barrier that had divided Armenians into Eastern and Western (at that time, almost all of the Mkhitarist fathers in Venice were Western Armenians). His work on the ancient religion of Armenia is an erudite work, but not an academic one. In this book, written at the end of his life, Alishan presents the results of an entire life spent with manuscripts (most of which had not yet been published) on the theme of pagan religion, with the goal of providing a complete overview of religion as understood and practiced by pre-Christian Armenian antiquity. Finally, we must not forget that Alishan was a Catholic priest. He does not refrain from offering hasty judgments at times (though they may have been quite conventional) on the scandal that paganism represented to him. It so happened that Daniel Varuzhan, a faithful disciple and an heir to Alishan—one who pursued the literary and epic tradition of the Mkhitarists—became the greatest Armenian poet of the beginning of the twentieth century, something which would have been inconceivable for a disciple of Abeghean. These are considerable differences, but they are perhaps not the most significant in the context of concern to us here, and not simply because Alishan, too, when it comes to the details of his work (particularly in the sections on Vahagn) is obliged to work as a comparatist. Up to now our reading of Varuzhan has followed a precise thread, that of an interrogation on the *reception of philology within the national framework*, or rather an interrogation on the way in which this national framework was constituted essentially through the reception of philological orientalism and its different elements. The first issue was that of the native, which is at the very center of this constitution. But it turns out that the issue of religion is no less important. The incredible wager of comparatism in philology is one that puts at stake the ability, despite everything, to say something if not about religion, at least about mythology—and if not about the essence or origin of mythology, then at least about its function and structure—while still remaining, from the beginning (let us say, with August-Wilhelm Schlegel or, a little later, Max Müller) up to Dumézil, strictly within the Indo-European framework, in the form of a scientific archeology of the native. (This is what the ancestors of the natives and the natives themselves, in the earliest antiquity and in the Indo-European sphere, understood by religion; this is what they understand still today without understanding it, provided one knows how to make the texts speak together and make the beliefs of the native resound like the still-coherent remains of a system that is past, and perhaps surpassed!) It is not a question of casting doubt on the works of comparative mythology and the science of religions, particularly the most recent (in the lineage of Dumézil). That would be ridiculous. Here it will rather be a question, I believe, of highlighting in a general way the conditions and grounds for the discovery of the sacred in myth and ritual (a discovery that obfuscates its own mourning in the very moment when it institutes it historically), since these are the grounds that are taken up, interrogated, transformed, and brought back to their truth by the aesthetic principle (and if this is the case, the aesthetic principle, with its obsession with mourning, would be but a minute correction of philology, an auxiliary memory of the conditions of its birth). For Varuzhan, as I have said, the discovery of the sacred is the discovery of mourning, a strange mourning, a mourning that is consubstantial with the sacred. And in any case discovery and inference go together here. We have said that the sacred is a category inferred from the aesthetic principle, and that is a message that still has not reached the ears of philology. It is doubtful whether it ever will. But if it does, how can philology accommodate it?

In the last decade of the nineteenth century, we were very far from such a possibility. In *The Armenians' Ancient Faith or Pagan Religion*, Father Alishan offered a theory of paganism very similar to the one that Wilhelm Mannhardt had developed, based on the phenomena of light (sun worship, personification, divinization). It is within this framework that the examination of Vahagn as a divine figure occurs. Here is the passage in its entirety:

Whatever the etymology of the word [*Aregak*], it is likely that the Armenians, like other peoples, first honored and worshiped the sun in the heavens, in its apparent cycle, especially in its rising and setting; that they later represented it in the form of a disc, then in a human form; finally, like other peoples or following their example, they personified it and thus gave it a presence in sacred sites.—What form did they give it? If we are correct, it is the sun that the creators of our ancient legends describe in their song, "The Sky was in labor, and so was the Earth," and with the Sea they engender a glowing red Reed, from which smoke and fire arise, and from them a blond and glowing Boy, with small flaming eyes like suns, leaps and runs away. It is thus, I believe, that the worshipers and the poets of Armenia represented the legend and believed in it, or at least it is how they invented it; and, based on this, others came later and personified the fair-haired boy or wanted to see Vahagn in him, the grandson or the descendent of their beloved king and hero Tigran, the contemporary of Cyrus. Perhaps too the Indian priests from Taraun thus aligned their own faith and that of the Armenians, for these priests honored Agni, the supreme fire, like a god, as the vital principle of the elements and the seasons, whom they assimilated thus to the Sun. From there it was not difficult to assimilate Agni to Vahakn, which is also written Vahagn. As one of our ancient scholars says, "Some worshiped the Sun and called it Vahakn." And is it not the case that this Indian name, Agni, is a synonym of the Latin *Ignis* and the Greek *agnos*?[30]

A footnote here announces a later discussion of Vahagn as a hero. The passage in question is in chapter 9 and is entitled "The Gods: The Cult of Idols." In it Alishan explains first of all that in antiquity, as incredible as this may seem, beings other than the unique supreme being were called gods; that this is evidenced in their writings; and that they therefore believed in the existence of multiple gods and goddesses, "whether out of vice or out of habit."[31] Following the tradition of Moses of Khoren (whose work, we should recall, had been rediscovered in the eighteenth century and gradually came to be considered as the foundation of national identity, a sort of Holy Book immune to any textual criticism),[32] Vahagn is considered here as a historic figure, transformed into an idol or made into a god. Alishan then limits himself to repeating the information presented by the historians, which we have already indicated.

Manuk Abeghean's study is of a different caliber. It is written in an extremely polemical style. He wants to argue first of all that what was known about Vahagn is authentic mythical or mythological material, against the thesis that had been put forth recently by Grigor Khalateants claiming that this material sprang directly from Moses of Khoren's imagination.[33] He goes on to dismiss all existing interpretations, particularly two readings that were dominant at the time, according to which Vahagn was a solar god or a warrior god. He then discusses the comparative method, about which he writes the following (which is both a profession of faith and a good summary of the "neo-archeological" program, as laid out in chapter 3):

Nothing provides a better explanation of the physical origin of the myth of Vahagn than the method of comparison, in which—as is the case in the study of the mythology of other nations—the popular legends and myths of our nation will occupy a preponderant place. The modern period can be understood only through the study of the past. But even the study of the present unfolds the past before our eyes, since the present is the continuation of the past. It is thus that the present legends—many of which are the relics [*mnats'ord*] and the remains of ancient myths—can clarify these myths.[34]

By appealing to everything that the comparative sciences of his age had to offer,[35] but also to what he knew first hand of the Armenian legends and the popular expressions involving thunderstorms, Abeghean concludes that Vahagn is the god of thunderstorms—a god similar to Indra—who tears apart the clouds raised by his opponent, the dragon Vrtra, and brings down the sea contained in the heavens.[36] It is in this sense that he understands one of Indra's titles, *aptia*, meaning "born from the waters," which perfectly fits the Armenian mythic heroes, particularly the founding heroes in the epic of Sassoun, Sanassar, and Baldassar. As for the reed, it is through an analogous logic attributed to the creators of the myth that Abeghean, following Kuhn, explains its central presence in the mytheme of Vahagn's birth (the fire of heaven arises from the red reed of the glades the way that terrestrial fire comes from rubbing pieces of wood together). Thunderstorms would also be a fire in the sky. Other similarities with the Rig Veda help to explain the boy's blond hair, the redness of his beard, and his solar eyes. It is still necessary, says Abeghean, to explain, on the basis of popular beliefs and expressions, the relation between the dragon and thunderstorms, and then to articulate the passage from Indra *vrtrahan* (the dragon-slayer) to the Iranian Verethragna, which is the source of the Armenian Vahagn. As a whole, what we have is an exemplary study of comparative mythology as practiced by the German philologists of the time.

THE "CONVERSION" AND THE "LAST VAHUNI"

This long philological parenthesis will help illuminate the historical context for Varuzhan's sudden interest in the mythological figure of Vahagn, but it adds nothing fundamental to our understanding of his treatment of religion and the place of Vahagn in his "poetic paganism." Up to now we have done nothing else but browse the philological tradition centered around the "mythopoetic" and its Armenian fallout. Our present concern will be a reading of the poem "Vahagn."

> O god of my fathers,
> Behold! I approach your altar,
> Leading by the halter
> A bull from the valleys of Daron.

This is a scene of sacrifice, then, in which the poet-sacrificer addresses the god, calling him "god of my fathers," according to the formula of the double return (to the fathers, to the gods). It is not, of course, a ritual hymn like those of the Rig Veda, a text Varuzhan was studying at the time. Here, poetry mimics the hymn. Lines 5–25 describe the animal destined for sacrifice, whereas lines 26–65 deal with the sacrifice itself and already with the titles used to address the god. The first of these titles is *astvatsahayr*, "father of the gods," which echoes "god of the fathers" (l. 25) and institutes a divine paternity. This address demands further consideration, but it certainly is not one of the official titles for Vahagn that are found in the ancient texts referring to the pagan gods. Whatever his interpretation, Varuzhan has inherited an image of Vahagn as a solar god and a god of the morning who disperses the shadows and scatters the stars. We just saw that within the lineage of nineteenth-century comparative mythology, which insisted on finding the origins of the gods in meteorological phenomena (or in the impression these phenomena made on such naïve and primitive people . . .), Manuk Abeghean interpreted Vahagn as the god of the thunderstorm and the tempest, very close to the god Indra in the Vedas. But in the Varuzhanian titles, Vahagn is essentially the god of strength (*uzh*) or of power (*zorut'iun*), and here too it will be necessary to understand the meaning of this central attribute (if it is an attribute), which returns several times throughout the poem (ll. 51, 79, 102). It is at first a question of power in war. Meanwhile, Vahagn is the "sun made man" (*mardatsats Aregak*), a title in which we hear, on the one hand, a deliberate analogy with the Christian Incarnation, but also, and conversely, the expression of a circularity in the epic engenderment of the gods. Indeed, this incarnation is brought about in the "lineage of Tigran." This is a direct allusion to Vahagn's humanity, according to the Mkhitarist dogma, and therefore an echo of the Mkhitarist fathers' belief in the absolute orthodoxy of Moses of Khoren's book, which presents Vahagn as a hero, a descendent from the first Tigran, and thus as deriving his substance from him. But here, Vahagn is a solar god become man. We thus see how, from the beginning, Varuzhan establishes a new theology of Vahagn, using the elements available to him without critiquing them, but also thoroughly undermining the evolutionist rationalism of his master Alishan. But that is not all. I just said that Vahagn is also the expression of a circularity in the engenderment of the gods. He is in effect one of those "heroes" which the mythopoetic capacity of a people cannot do without. He is considered here by Varuzhan as the one who (or which) crystallizes the mythic narrative in relation to the gods, the one who (or which) gathers them together and, in the end, the one who (or which) engenders them. Only this mythical engenderment (which is also a genesis of myth) explains the attribute of "father of the gods" attached to Vahagn. We must not overlook the fact that Nietzsche attaches the same attribute of "father of the gods" to Apollo, another solar god, at the beginning of *The Birth of Tragedy* (section 3). "First of all we see the glorious Olympian figures of the gods, standing on the gables of this structure [of Apollinian culture]. Their deeds, pictured in brilliant reliefs, adorn its friezes. We must not be misled by the fact that Apollo stands side by side with the others as an individual deity, without any claim to priority of rank. For the same impulse that embodied itself in Apollo gave birth to this entire Olympian world, and in this sense Apollo is its father."[37] It must be said that there is a remarkable similarity here in the impulse behind Varuzhan's and Nietzsche's treatments of these "pagan" gods, which have a number of features in common, particularly their solar aspect.

As god of the fathers and father of the gods, and because he is an incarnation, Vahagn can have a human-divine "father" in the person of Tigran, the central heroic figure who merges with the mythifying or mything capacity of the "nation." This use of divine titles will be taken up again later in the second part of the poem. We must now follow the description of the sacrifice.

The sacrifice is carried out in the first person, as is the entire address to the god. The meaning of this is very clear: the hymn is part of the sacrifice. If the sacrifice is an offering, the poem and all the human gestures that accompany it are also part of the offering. It must be remarked, however, that this first person is that of the modern poet, who arrives at the end of history and repeats the gestures of his ancestors and fathers. He says that he is repeating them. Once again, then, he is miming. He mimes the hymn, but he also mimes the ritual of sacrifice. This miming is not an imitation. Let us say for the moment that it is a repetition. There could not be a modern sacrifice in and through the poem if there had not been an ancient sacrifice, the very memory of which has disappeared today. Is it yet another retrospective illusion, or has this structure always been the structure of sacrifice? Certainly, there are degrees of symbolicity in sacrifice, and it would also seem that one must establish a clear delimitation, a decisive discontinuity, between sacrifice as a religious act, in the Vedas or in the Christian eucharist, and the sacrifice by Varuzhan, who "merely" *says that he sacrifices.* But can we be sure that this delimitation is clear and definitive? In the symbolicity of sacrificial substitution, at whatever degree one wants to consider it (and if there are degrees), is not *saying* also *doing*? Here we are touching on the very center of our investigation into the end of religion and Varuzhan's poetic paganism as an experience (or already as a repetition) of the end. The question is the following: is religious experience (by way of this central moment of sacrifice, which is in reality a moment of generalized and ever-shifting substitution) not still and always an experience of the end of religion? In which case the "aesthetic principle," whose different figures and elaborations we have been following in Varuzhan, would simply be another name for the limitless substitutivity that governs the religious and that the religious in turn tries to govern, to stop, and to transform into a ritual fixity. To return to my first question: is it not the case that, in sacrifice, saying is doing? That is what Varuzhan says. The writing and the offering of the poem are in turn a sacrificial act, even if this is the last possible sacrificial act imaginable. Of course, this characteristic as the "last" act is essential. We will come back to this. But it is important to insist on the "reality" of the sacrificial act. I am aware that this term "reality" is strange, for it is a question here of thinking a repeated substitution without any assignable limit. But we must remain with the reality of poetic saying as a sacrificial act; otherwise we run the risk of completely misunderstanding what happens in the poem. We could also say that here sacrifice is a "metaphor" for the poetic act, provided that this metaphor is understood as being already internal to the sacrifice itself as a substitution.[38] Now, "saying as doing" is the formula for the performativity at work in the enunciation and in the function of the law.[39] In the poem that opens the Vedic hymns (which can be considered, at least symbolically, as the first identifiable document of religious humanity, that is, of humanity *tout court*), we read these words addressed to Agni: "You are the guardian of the Law." Through the sacrificial word, which is also performative speech, the god is thus confirmed in his function. That is exactly what happens in Varuzhan's "Vahagn." Is the latter then simply another poem, or is it rather the last hymn, and therefore the last sacrificial act, addressed to Vahagn?

The poet says that he sacrifices. For this he needs to describe in the first person an animal sacrifice, the immolation of a bull. He cuts the bull's throat, lights a fire, watches the flame rise up between the branches of the olive tree and the juniper, rising straight up to the heavens and "singing the transfiguration of the limpid soul of things." The word "transfiguration" translates the Armenian *verap'okhum*, which is the word used to designate two evangelical or postevangelical events: the transfiguration on Mount Moriah and the assumption of Mary. It is a movement upward or a change of nature. All the offerings to the fire are mentioned one by one, transported to the celestial palace (and palate) of the god. Then it is time for the wine and the "homa," whose purpose is to reconcile the god with his people who are now apostate or "converted" (*kronap'okh*). It is thus no longer a question of the ancestors here. Once again, the return—as in the first letter quoted at the beginning of this essay—is a conversion. The people turn toward their ancient god, whom they never should have left behind. They come back to themselves by remaining exactly where they were and turning around. We have already seen this movement in the first part of this essay (in the commentary on "In the Ruins of Ani"): it has the same structure as the movement that moves (or ought to move) the people destined to find a new Canaan in the very land they already inhabit. The promised land of the return is in fact not another land. Likewise here, it is through a movement toward oneself, a return to the proper, to the ancestrality of the proper, that the conversion is effected. Moreover, this conversion of the return takes place in a poem, one that is constructed according to the terms of poetic paganism, which are not (or not univocally) the terms of religion. But this also means that this people leaves behind Christianity. Consequently, Christianity is already interpreted as a disastrous interruption occurring between the sacred as actual (or presumed to be actual), that is, the sacred of the past, and the return to the sacred. This idea about Christianity as an interruption will be gradually specified as we proceed. The poem as a sacrificial act seals and countersigns this return. We must also note that wine and the homa are references to two sacrificial religions: that of Christ (but entirely dechristianized, brought back to its sacrificial core, disengaged from its historical byproducts) and that of the Vedas.

The second part of the poem (ll. 66–105) has a different tone. It no longer says "I, the poet, I sacrifice . . ." but "I, the poet, I pray, I implore . . ." and my prayer rises up to you. We are still in the register of "saying as doing." At the beginning we had the sacrificial performativity of the poem; here we have its performativity as an act of prayer, as a direct address to the god, as a hymn, and this no doubt amounts to the same. In both cases, we have a self-reflexive dimension that is undeniable, a folding-back of poetry onto itself, a "poetry of poetry," a "Dichtung der Dichtung."[40] The seam (so to speak) of this folding back can be located, I believe, in lines 66–71, decisive lines on which I will comment in a moment. First we must consider the last section on "strength" and "force." The first image here is that of Vahagn the dragon-slayer, his title of glory in Armenian mythology, as in the Iranian and Indo-European mythology of Verethragna, from which the former was adopted. According to Varuzhan, Vahagn's attribute is thus the strength with which he slays these dragons, and Varuzhan sees this "strength" itself as a religion. Certainly, you are a god, he says, but in you we worship strength and my prayer goes out to this strength. It is of course not a matter of brute strength or of a violence used to terrorize the weak. Here strength is that capacity to disperse the "sun-seeds" into the sky; it is the soul of Creation. Suddenly, then, we have a cosmological view of Vahagn as a vital principle giving birth to the things of nature, a principle that passes through the plants and the fire, infinitizes matter by breathing the breath of immortality into it, lives in the mind and the will (l. 88), rises in them like sap in a tree, breathes life into things, and makes milk rise into the mother's breast. (Each of these characteristics merits more attention than I can give them here.) It is this same strength that plants (*kë kangne*) a Nation like a pride of lions (l. 96). This is precisely the strength of erection (in Armenian, erection is *kangnum*). Strength is thus also another name for the aesthetic principle, this principle that presides over a people's becoming-nation, their communitarian gathering, and that brings the fatherland into being. Vahagn is the god of strength because he inhabits this movement of erection and because he provokes it. We understand, then, why he is the "father of the gods." The gods are fashioned and sculpted in light, they are engendered by the power of the aesthetic principle. If we have followed Varuzhan up to this point, we see that Vahagn (exactly like Nietzsche's Apollo) is not only a god among other gods, he is also the name of the principle that presides over engenderment in general, over erection. Vahagn is the religious name of the aesthetic principle, which is consequently a principle of figural self-engenderment. He thus plays exactly the same role as Agni in the Vedic hymns, since we have said of Agni that he was (according to an operation that may appear circular and therefore paradoxical) *the name of the process that produces names* and that produces the name Agni in particular. While he is a god, Agni is also the aesthetic name of the origin of the gods. Why "aesthetic"? Because at the origin of the gods there is art. At the origin of religion, there is an artistic "impulse." We thus understand how Varuzhan can write, "For the force, the faith [or religion] in your arm . . . I pray." It is of course not a matter of a religion of strength. Vahagn is the name of the power that engenders the Nation by *erecting it* as such. Here too we must venture a speculative reading, in order to hear behind these words the proposition "power is Vahagn" according to the model of "light is Agni" that we considered earlier. It is thus that Vahagn's "arm" (that is, his strength or power) can also merge into the "arm" of the nation, can foster heroes and geniuses in the belly of "our mothers," and can make Vahagn the "spiritual" (*imatsakan*) source of this formative force that is called "sacred." We already see in this first movement that Varuzhan is very far from the kind of historical reflection on Vahagn that we discussed before. He transforms all the elements available to him by reinterpreting them, fitting them into the pattern of the aesthetic principle or into the mould of the idealist matrix, which governs the relations between art and religion since the establishment of philological orientalism.

So far, there has been nothing unexpected in this paraphrase of the poem. Varuzhan's very first poem on paganism develops the entire system that we had already described above. But a certain doubt remains. This doubt concerns the line in which the poet-sacrificer says that he prays for strength, for the "religion" (or the "faith") of your arm. The use of the word *religion* (*kronk'*) in this phrase is quite strange, and Varuzhan is well aware of this. The word occurs at the precise center of the line and bears a mark of emphasis specific to Armenian. It is not very clear, in any case, whether this "force," this capacity of the gods for self-engenderment (which is also, among other things, the strength that erects the nation as such) is still essentially religious or whether it is beyond religion and the figures of religion. There is an ambiguity here, it seems, that we have no way of resolving. This is the moment of the turning and the returning of conversion. The god Vahagn is also the father of the gods; he is at the origin of their engenderment. Vahagn is thus both the name of the origin and the name of the figure. He is simultaneously a religious figure and the beyond (the origin) of all religious figures. He represents both a figure and the figuration of figures. In another vocabulary (which is in no way out of place in the present context), we could say that he is the name of fiction par excellence, that is, both the process of fictioning and the result of this process. The "return" to Vahagn is therefore a conversion to the origin insofar as it is located beyond all religious figures, and even if this origin lives only in them. It is true that this return is described with the religious term "conversion," but at the same time it invites us to leave religion behind. In art, the origin is unveiled. In art, religion shatters its structure and its limits; it undoes its fixity, it opens itself to that which engenders it, on the horizon of what makes it possible and makes it exist. By the same token, it obviously comes to an end. For there can be no religion of the principle. That is precisely what Varuzhan intends with the expression "poetic paganism," which is obviously not a religion among others, or the same ancient one revisited and revitalized. It is not a religion at all. As Walter Benjamin said of Kafka,[41] Varuzhan is not the founder of a religion. Nor is he attempting a renewal of the religious. Poetic paganism is the end of religion or religion as it reaches its end (and is thus sublated in its end as religion). Here is what Varuzhan says of this end:

> O sublime one, are you satisfied? I have given you
> All that I had in my cell and in my soul—
> All that the enemy forgot to take
> From deserted Ashtishat the widowed city.
> Now, the last Vahuni of our race,
> I kneel in holy fear before your altar,
> And kiss the ground where something
> Of your soul lets the pine-trees take root, . . .

Several times before, I said that the poet says that he sacrifices, and that we must take this "saying" seriously as a performative. He says what he does and he does what he says. However, he occupies a strange position as a performer of sacrifice. The mythical and sacrificial tradition was interrupted, the hymns to Vahagn no longer resounded. And even if sacrifice is a substitution that has no limit in symbolicity, we are nonetheless at the limit of this absence of limit. Of course, the sacred is at stake here through sacrifice, but it is at stake for the last time, through its own mourning. The poet is the last Vahuni, the last representative of the lineage of priests devoted to the cult of Vahagn. He is thus the poet of completion and termination. The French word would be *achèvement*. Thirty years later, Hagop Oshagan would present himself in the same way, and no less ambitiously, as the completion and termination of Western Armenian literature and culture, in every sense of the term, that is, also as the site of the inscription of the Catastrophe in its essence. With Varuzhan, the "last Vahuni," the poet of completion-termination is the one who puts an end to the religious tradition. He is the one who inscribes this end into his work. The poet of completion is the poet of disaster. But he is doubtless also the one who fulfills the religious tradition, who brings it into its own for the last time, who brings it into its own beyond its secular interruption. The poet belongs to the same tradition, he is one of them, one of these priests, although he is the last one of them.[42] At the same time, he does not at all belong to the tradition, since he intervenes at a point that is beyond its interruption, as a supplement, but also as a mournful memory, a memory in mourning. Thus it seems that the completion-termination of religion can occur only through the reception of religion into mourning, into art as mourning; and that only this late, this infinitely late reception says how things stand with religion. That is precisely what we have called the "idealist" matrix governing the relations between art and religion (a matrix in which erection and self-sacrifice intervened in order to articulate the origin of religion, what comes before religion, the space of light and being; with, moreover, an essential historical dimension in the phenomenon of the "completion" of the religious and the poetic assumption of "distress" and "dereliction," in sum, of exile; it is indeed a question of the completion of the religious in poetry and by poetry).

This "distress," "dereliction," and "exile," this "turning away" of the gods, recall very clearly what Hölderlin wrote during the period of his great elegies. In the next chapter (focusing on the historical determination of this distress), this comparison will become more explicit. In Varuzhan, as in Hölderlin, the "idealist matrix" comes undone and opens a space for a thinking that is still ungraspable and unformulated at the precise moment when the completion of the religious in and through poetry ceases being a loss of the sacred and becomes in reality a loss of mourning; in other words, at the precise moment when the history of mourning gives way to "history as mourning." But this "precise" moment is, in turn, hypothetical. Where exactly is it located? How can we apprehend it? That is the entire question. It is this precise moment, however, that marks (or should mark) the difference between art as mournful memory (of the religious) and poetry as the mourning of mourning.

But here Varuzhan says something more. He connects the completion-termination of religion again with sacrifice. He says something about sacrifice at the end of religion. In the deserted and desolate city, nothing remained after the enemy had passed through (I will return to the question of the identity of this enemy). Everything is destroyed. Ashtishat is a widow. The temples had been destroyed or burnt, the houses reduced to ruins. After Ani and Adana, this is the third city that was left entirely in ruins. After the storm, nothing remains. We can only imagine it as literally deserted, its culture wiped out, along with its wealth and its laws. Here Varuzhan is clearly describing the Catastrophe that has occurred. And yet, the poet-sacrificer has found something to offer in this devastated city, in this eye of the hurricane. He has found the most magnificent offering for the god of his fathers, a superb bull with all its adornments, which he sacrifices according to ritual observance, entoning the sacrificial hymn; and there is also the wine, the homa. What was it that the enemy—whoever he is—could have forgotten in Ashtishat? When everything has been destroyed, what remains to be sacrificed? What remains when the paternal law has been destroyed? Of what Remains could it be a question here?

It is impossible to say. And yet, our survival is at stake. The language is on fire, soon nothing will be left of it but ashes. The fatherland has been annihilated. The old question arises again, the old question of the other-scene, of the nature of the other-scene which cannot and must not be the scene of the Other. The foreigner, for his part, can wander toward his land. But for us even that is impossible. We have no other land. From now on, our land is the Catastrophe. Our fatherland is the Catastrophe. From now on, the fire of sacrifice is the fire that devours our language, in which this language devours itself and is consumed in itself. But is that what Varuzhan says? No, it is not. Could he have said this before the historical catastrophe came and wiped out the remains of the nation? Obviously not. On the contrary, what he says is that the fatherland will come (and will only come) in the mournful memory of an art meant for the "converted" people, for the people who have returned to religion in its principle, that is, to the principle of religion, to the "father of the gods," to the power of paternal engenderment, to the "strength" of Vahagn. Thus, still and despite every-thing, if religion was the patriotic ground of our ancestors, the element of the paternal law, the space of sacrifice and the intact capacity to mourn, and even if all this has been destroyed, there remains for us, still and despite everything, the ability to mourn, an ability or a capacity that has taken the name of Art. This is what Varuzhan explicitly says. And yet it must be admitted that this is a very strange logic. What was lost, we thought, was mourning, for which religion supplied a guarantee; and, with mourning, the foundation of the paternal law. When mourning is lost, which mourning is still possible for this loss? Which mourning for mourning? And yet, what still remains is mourning, says Varuzhan, what remains is still the ability to mourn. One can under-stand why we were unable to answer the question: "Of what Remains is it a question here?" When this ability is destroyed in the form of religion, it remains still in the form of art. In other words, the enemy has only succeeded in destroying religion. He (or should we say "it"?) was unable to destroy art, since art is itself the element in which religion is dissolved and completed. It is still necessary for us to reinvest the ability to mourn. What remains, in any case, is poetic language, which merges from now on with the holocaustic fire of sacrifice and with the offering to the gods. When every-thing has been devastated, language remains as a space in which catastrophic mourn-ing may be received and find a place. And we should be able to conclude thus: when everything has been devastated, what remains is devastation. However, faithful to the invention of mythological religion and to the structure of this invention (religion is lost, always already lost, it bears its mourning within itself, art is this capacity for mourning), Varuzhan concludes from this that what remains is mythopoetic mourn-ing, that is, in fact, the entire dimension of myth and religion, but received, absorbed, sublated and essentialized in poetry. Between the two formulations—a) what remains is the mythic and poetic capacity for mourning, what remains is language as a space, an object and a vehicle for sacrifice, what remains, in sum, is language on fire; and b) what remains is devastation without any possible mourning, for which a language is nonetheless necessary, the last language, a dead language, a language in ashes, a lan-guage of the end—, the difference is perhaps not so great. It is the difference between fire and ashes. Varuzhan constantly passes from one to the other of these formulations, as though crossing a transparent and invisible border. But this difference is sufficient to create the gulf that separates aesthetic nationalism from a possible historical think-ing of mourning, a thinking that is henceforth without mourning, without gods, without religion and without sacrifice, even if it is the last holocaustic sacrifice of the last Vahuni to the god Vahagn.

We must still ask who the "enemy" is in this poem. Who (or what), then, is the enemy that devastated Ashtishat, that put an end to the religion of the fathers, and to the fathers as religion?

CHAPTER 8

The Mourning of Religion II

THE ENEMY

In Varuzhan's hymn "Mer'ats astvatsnerun" (To the Dead Gods), we encounter the idea of a long and deadly interruption between the gods and us. Here is the beginning of the poem:

> Under the bloody-glorious cross
> Whose stretched arms flow in sadness
> On the whole world,
> I, vanquished, from the bitter heart of my art
> I mourn your death, O pagan gods.[1]

We soon discover that the poet is not speaking of the gods of the Armenian pantheon. Varuzhan enumerates at length, one after the other, the names of the dead gods, goddesses, and demigods of Olympus, and with them the heroes and creatures that populate Greek mythology: Zeus, Apollo, Hera, Hermes, Pan, Vanatur (which as we have seen was the Armenian name for Bacchus), Astrik (here the name of Aphrodite), Poseidon, and Eros, but also the satyrs, the naiads, and the sirens. It cannot be denied (though this is a point I will not insist on here) that in Varuzhan there is a desire to repeat the Greek experience of religion and poetry, a desire that one finds echoed in his wish to transform himself into Pindar.[2] The poem itself is thus a long lamentation on the death of the ancient gods. Their presence no longer animates nature, the lightning no longer has a master, the heavy rains no longer appear as the "golden seed" of Zeus, the deer now go to the lake without fearing the dogs of Anahit the huntress. The gods represented the glory of life, and life has been replaced by death. The obscurity of a "victorious cross" (l. 59) has spread "the glory of death" over the entire earth. These gods and satyrs were the figures of tradition, but now, the poet says, "I see Tradition in tears" (l. 29). They were the horizon of our world and the heart of our faith. Every day our ancestors offered "salt and nectar" to these divine figures, and with these offerings they "imprinted" their relation to their own fathers (l. 54). This verse is central because it clearly establishes the link between the living presence of the gods and the possibility of a fatherland.[3] The fatherland was possible then—that is, a faith transmitted from one generation to another, a sacrificial offering to the dead, a bond between the hearth (*akut'*) and the world. But today, look, "our forests and our seas/Our springs and our peaceful cottages/Are deserted and devastated" (ll. 66–68). The disappearance of the gods obviously coincides with the annihilation of the fatherland. The two go hand-in-hand for Varuzhan. In another poem, "Anahit," which develops the same theme of the disappearance of the gods through the particular figure of the goddess, Varuzhan expresses even more clearly the nature of the reciprocity (a lost reciprocity, of course) between the "hearth" and the "world," in terms of the sacrificial ritual:

> Your altar is buried in the grass. No longer
> Does fragrant incense burn there, no longer does the sacrificial animal fall under
>   the knife.
> Only a smell of amber rises from it,
> The smell of a red snake's dead skin.   (*YLZ* 2:44)

It is true that the cult of Anahit no longer exists, and that the goddess no longer lives on this land and in this country. Her bust is found in museums. But she will live for-ever "in heaven," in memory, like an abstract remnant, a reminiscence, a vital element (*tarr*), beyond even the cult, beyond sacrifice. Varuzhan offers an image of desolation, a loss of the fatherland, which is also a loss of the always ancient experience of "the sa-cred." At the same time, we see how these poems of "nostalgia" can seem lesser, some-how, than the long and properly religious poems, especially "Vahagn," which presents itself as a last sacrificial act.

In these poems, therefore, nostalgia and lamentation make themselves heard. These terms may be correct, but they do not tell us everything. In reality, these poems are songs of ritual mourning. At the beginning of "To the Dead Gods," the term that Varuzhan uses to say "I mourn your death" is *voghbal*, which in classical Armenian refers specifically to the role played by designated women in the funerary songs. The word *voghb* referred in general to the funeral songs and ritual lamentations for the dead. It is also the root from which the modern Armenian word for "tragedy" (*voghbergut'iun*) is derived (much like the word *Trauerspiel* in German). This song of mourning, this play of mourning, recalls the ancient glory of a world inhabited by the gods, and it addresses the present desolation, when the springs and the cottages are deserted and devastated. It mourns the loss of the sacred, as if a deadly storm had emptied these earthly sites of all divine presence (and therefore, no doubt, of all pres-ence, as if these sites needed a presence in order to become inhabitable, in order to occupy a place in the world). All of this was already apparent from our reading of "Vanatur" and "Vahagn." What is new in "To the Dead Gods" is that this devastating storm bears a name that is all too visible. It is Christianity and Christendom, with its mortiferous symbols, its bloody Cross, its crown of thorns, and the fanatic zeal of its saints. What is new is also that Art (which Varuzhan writes here with a capital) is explicitly designated, in its very essence, as a mourning for the gods, since here the voice of mourning arises from the very heart of art, from its most intimate moment. It is the artist who mourns and grieves, who remembers, who laments; it is he who initiates an immense work of mourning for the ancient gods, so many centuries after their disappearance—the artist, and not, say, the historians or the philologists. It is thus the artist who was "vanquished" by the Cross and by Christianity.

MIMICRY AND THE END

In the commentary on "Vahagn" above, I said more than once that the poet mimes. He mimes the hymns (the Vedic hymns or the hymns to Dionysus), he mimes Pindar, he mimes the sacrificial ritual within the poem. The poem itself becomes a sacrifice, offering to the gods the only thing remaining in the devastated city after the enemy has withdrawn (or, on the contrary, after the enemy has been installed forever): language on fire or in ashes, language as fire or ashes, language as remainder. This question of mimicry is one of the most profound questions raised by the notion of "poetic paganism." It is not unrelated to the place Nietzsche occupied at the time, and therefore also not unrelated to the element of Nietzschean inspiration in Varuzhan's thinking. There is no art without mimicry (without imitation or repetition). But neither is there any art without the catastrophe of whatever there is to imitate or to repeat. The fact that here this catastrophe bears the name of Christianity is something that must be more thoroughly understood. It is quite clear that in all of Varuzhan's "pagan" poems, these two propositions (concerning mimicry on the one hand, and catastrophe on the other) are at work. "Poetic paganism" is indeed a poetic repetition (or an imitation) of paganism, or of what is given as such. For Varuzhan, this necessity of a modern repetition of the Greeks comes directly from Nietzsche, at least from his book on the origin of tragedy, which was of course also a book on Wagner and the modern musical drama. Although it is thought univocally and (in the end) superficially as a decline (but one that begins at the very heart of tragedy, or a little later with Socrates), the idea of a properly Greek catastrophe is already found in Nietzsche, as a catastrophe that destroys the world of the gods from within.[4]

But in fact, beyond Nietzsche, the necessity for repetition comes to Varuzhan (without his being at all aware of it) from early German Romanticism and from Hölderlin, reader of the Greek poets and translator of Pindar and Sophocles. For Hölderlin, too, it was necessary to imitate or repeat the Greeks, for at least two reasons, which, however are opposed. First, it was necessary in order to "return" to them, to their gods, to their sense of the tragic, to their experience of the sacred, and necessary to do this by going against the grain of the catastrophe, by passing through it in the reverse direction, in a way by annulling it, all the while knowing that this "reverse direction" will have access only to the principle, the concept or the memory of the Greek experience. It was necessary to imitate their nature in our art, and, in sum, to practice a poetic paganism! But it was necessary to imitate or to repeat them for another reason, the inverse of the previous one, and a reason much more portentous. It was necessary to repeat, it seems, because their catastrophe is our own. It was therefore necessary to repeat their catastrophe so that we could appropriate our own, and first make it visible to ourselves. In the elegy "Bread and Wine," Hölderlin wrote: ". . . When the Father averted His face from mankind, / and all over the earth mourning, rightly, began."[5] Already, a century before Varuzhan, the powerful repercussions of the gods' disappearance were making themselves seen and heard:

> Happy land of the Greeks, you house of them all, of the Heavenly,
>
> .   .   .   .
>
> But the thrones, where are they? Where are the temples, the vessels,
> Where, to delight the gods, brim-full with nectar, the songs?
>
> .   .   .   .
>
> Where thrive those famed ones, the festival's garlands?
> Athens is withered, and Thebes; now do no weapons ring out
> In Olympia, nor now those chariots, all golden, in games there,
> And no longer are wreaths hung on Corinthian ships?
> Why are they silent too, the theaters, ancient and hallowed?
> Why not now does the dance celebrate, consecrate joy?
> Why no more does a god imprint on the brow of a mortal
> Struck, as by lightning, the mark, brand him, as once he would do?
>
> "Bread and Wine"[6]

Elsewhere Hölderlin refers to this disappearance of the gods as a "categorical turning away." The expression is precisely synonymous with the "catastrophe," a term that Hölderlin used as well for the same categorical turning away, having found traces of it inscribed within Greek tragedy itself. Philippe Lacoue-Labarthe has commented incisively on this structural moment of tragedy as Hölderlin understood it:

> When the Greeks, in the tragic moment of their "catastrophe," forgot themselves
> by forgetting the god—properly the moment of the caesura, of the gaping or
> interrupting articulation around which Sophoclean tragedy is organized, but
> which also perhaps (dis)articulates history itself—the divine probably withdrew
> definitively, definitively turned away, itself forgetful and unfaithful, but as such
> appropriating itself in its very distancing (it is of the god's essence to be
> distanced—*é-loigné*) and forcing man to turn himself back toward the earth.[7]

And yet, as Hölderlin writes, "we think of the Heavenly who once were / Here and who will return again at the proper time; / That is why in earnest too also the singers hymn the wine-god / And not vainly devised the ancient one's praises are sung."[8] Here, as with Varuzhan, mourning has a double meaning, and that is why it is so difficult to translate it. It is first of all the mourning of memory, as a "remembrance" of the

Immortals, and poetry is the fervent wait for the moment when they "will return again at the proper time." But when the Father turned his face from us, we were brought back to the earth. We no longer have the ability to mourn, and without this ability we can have no "remembrance." For the Father "is" this capacity for mourning. That is why this irremediable distancing brought such great distress. For mourning itself is now lost. And this time it is a question of catastrophic mourning, of which the poem "Mnemosyne" speaks. We are confronted with a fault or a default of mourning, a catastrophe of mourning. The last lines of "Mnemosyne" say: ". . . dem / Gleich fehlet die Trauer," which can be translated as ". . . likewise, mourning is in default," or ". . . at that very moment, mourning falters."[9]

Art in its essence is thus the mourning of the Immortals, as long as we continue to hear the double meaning of the word *mourning*, at once mournful memory and the catastrophic default of mourning itself (but the catastrophic default is always an imminent threat within mournful memory). In this way, we can better understand the absolute equivalence between the "return" to the fathers and the "return" to the gods in Varuzhan. There it is indeed a question of restoring the capacity for mourning, a restoration that art must accomplish or that it can at least claim as its proper task. But we also have to do with poetry's inscription of the paternal Catastrophe into language. For Varuzhan, and later for Yeghishe Charents, although in very different situations, the Catastrophe is a catastrophe of the Father, a forgetting of the "self" (of "oneself"), in a form analogous to the categorical turning away in Hölderlin. That is why it takes the form of an "end" of religion. Which does not mean that religions have now been surpassed and that we must move on to other things, to art or to skeptical indifference, for example. Quite the contrary. The end of religion, the disappearance of the Immortals and the turning away of the god open (or opened long ago) an infinite time of distress, which requires an "exploration" and a "reception" of the end (of disappearance, of the turning away). And, as Hölderlin asked, what are poets for in this time of infinite distress? A similar question impels Varuzhan when he writes that he (the poet) is the "last Vahuni," the last one to sacrifice to the god Vahagn, the solar god, Father of the gods, principle and origin of religion. Nothing remains to him but the "Remnant." The enemy has passed through and left pure devastation. Nothing remains except the necessity of completing the work of the enemy. This completion, which is the task of the poet, can take two forms: to receive the gods at their end (to sublate religion into art as mourning), or to receive the end of the gods (to inscribe "termination" into language for the very last time). There is hardly any distinction between these two gestures, as I said above. The poet, in any case, does not distinguish between them when, through the poem, he sacrifices what yesterday's enemy overlooked in the devastation of Ashtishat. He does not distinguish between them when he declares himself the "last Vahuni." He must receive the gods at their end or the end of the gods. He must receive one or the other, one and the other, in language and in mourning. He is the man of the remainder, when everything has come to a dreadful end. He is the servant of termination. He has nothing left to offer but the end. Nothing left but fire, language on fire. Unless nothing remains of language itelf but ashes. For the end of the god is also the end of mourning, the definitive annihilation of the fatherland, the disintegration of the community, a dispersion without return. What language is possible in dispersion, what language is there for saying disintegration, if it is true that every language assumes a community?[10] Varuzhan died in the torment of 1915. He did not have time to ask this question. Or perhaps it was already precisely this question that he was asking, before 1915.

THAT FOR WHICH ART MOURNS . . .

Art is in its essence a mourning for the Immortals. We can see that this is not a simple formulation. For if art is mourning, it contains within itself the determination of the "life" for which it mourns. It is the mourning for the mythical and the mythological world; it is the mourning for the fathers who "engraved," "marked," and "imprinted" their relation to their own fathers through the offering of salt and nectar; it is the mourning for the bond between the hearth and the world; it is the mourning for the fatherland (which, however, was already the expression of a capacity for mourning); it is the mourning for the bond with the gods and also for an exchange and a sharing with strangers. It is the mourning of the joy and cheerfulness of former times. It is the mourning for the Father. All of this, then, is part of the essence of art. But that is not all. For art also contains within itself the determination of the "death" of all these things, this death that coincides with the historical desertion and devastation of Ashtishat, the dispersion without return, the end of exchange and sharing, the categorical turning away of the god (the inscription without any possible mourning of his distancing). But, to return to the question at hand, this determination of death is Christianity. This principle of death, as Christianity, is thus also a part of the essence of art, of its historical emergence. In sum, no art without Christianity as its negative condition. This is indeed a provocative and paradoxical formulation. For, after all, the Greeks certainly had their own art. It is even said that they invented art. For them, was art not already a kind of mourning, in the form of tragedy, for example (but essentially)? Or rather, for them, was art not already the experience of a default of mourning, a catastrophic turning away? It is true that almost everything in these two questions has its source in Hölderlin. But if we must respond affirmatively to either one of them, then did they too—the Greeks— have the experience of the end of the mythical and mythological world through "Christianity" in order to accede to the essence of their own art? Did they need Christianity to have the experience of the Catastrophe, and in order to inscribe it in their tragedy?

This paradoxical formulation leads to some troubling reflections. It seems that in order to undergo the experience of the Catastrophe as an experience of thought, the Moderns always and absolutely needed to situate events within the framework of a historical narrative. Thus, it is said, there was a Greek experience of the sacred that was historically displaced by Christianity (or Socratic rationalism, or nihilism). The sacred *and* mourning were situated within a historical development, a historical perspective, and a historical temporality. The sacred *and* mourning could and should be the object of a history. It seems that the Moderns needed, in sum, a tradition. That is why the "tradition in tears" is named in Varuzhan's poem "To the Dead Gods." It is a tradition of the sacred, or tradition as sacred. At the end of this history of the sacred and of mourning, art remembers; art reveals the sacred world and its disappearance, while presenting itself as the sublation of one and the other. Art reveals in sublation. The two gestures, the two forms of completion, that we distinguished a moment ago (while also pointing out that they are hardly distinct: on the one hand the gesture of a completion of religion by art as mournful memory, with a preservation of the principle, that is, of the capacity for mourning, in conformity with the idealist matrix; on the other hand, the gesture of inscribing the Catastrophe into language as a remnant) always go together.

Since for the Moderns art reveals in sublation, it needs time. It needs a succession and a successivity (of events and quasi-events). That too is why, even though Varuzhan does not say who the enemy is that devastated Ashtishat, the logic of the argument clearly implies that it is Christianity (and even though it is the *present* devastation and distress that are in the background here, and these have little to do with Christianity). The Cross was a historical necessity, allowing art to accede to its essence, in mourning. It thus rendered any return to the death of the gods impossible. It monopolized mourning. Conversely, it called for a repetition, an imitation or a mimicry. A repetition of paganism, a mimicry of the practices of the sacred. Once again, no art without Christianity. But it is clear, this time, that the question raised here is the Moderns' question, it is our question.

The problem is that the sacred is a fiction of Modernity, and if the idea of "paganism" merges with the idea of the sacred, then this is no less true of paganism itself. We see that this double fiction is similar to the fiction of mythology (to the myth of myth), but without being exactly the same. In both cases, is it not the same presence of the gods and the same community founding itself around the mythopoetic recital and the substitutive sacrifice—that is, in the last analysis, around the offering of language? But in the myth of myth, we recall, fiction was supposed to be foundational *as such*, very explicitly; and this was essential.[11] The two senses of the word *myth* were linked by an "infinitely ironic relation," as Jean-Luc Nancy put it. Moreover, myth, like the sacred, designated "the absence of what it names." This absence is at the heart of "poetic paganism." But then it is no longer simply myth, it is also, indeed, the sacred, which the art of the Moderns articulates as mourning. Art is not only the space of mourning, nor is it only the mourning of myth. The art of the Moderns calls itself forth and invents itself as the mourning of the sacred. In doing so, it constructs itself in relation to a past (that of the Greeks, let us say) in which there was art, no doubt, but in which there was no mourning. In other words, paganism and the "sacred" are the (resolutely) modern fictions of a historical past in which they can appear to be exempt from mourning. Modernity needed this fiction for itself, of course. It needed an Ashtishat that was prior to the moment when she became a widow, deserted, destroyed, reduced to the state of a desolate city; it needed an Ashtishat *from before the disaster*, and even an Ashtishat from before any anticipation of the disaster, so that art can be named in its essence and so that the poet can proclaim himself the "last Vahuni"; so that the gods, finally, can be mourned "from the bitter heart of my art." This temporality, this historical necessity for a sacred without disaster and without mourning obviously required, in turn, a representation of the disaster in a historical form.

In the poem "To the Dead Gods," there are still two lines that we have not yet commented on:

Man has fallen under the giant heel
Of a deaf-mute Jewish god.

To my knowledge, this is the only occurrence of the word *Jewish* in the poetry of Daniel Varuzhan. But if man and the world are the victims of a Jewish god, deaf-mute or not, then Varuzhan's paganism, however it is qualified this time, is nothing other than the expression of a heretofore unsuspected Aryanism. Is this possible? This may well seem scandalous to the ears of a cultivated (Armenian) reader. But after all, this is the same Varuzhan who would later sign the Manifesto of *Mehyan*, in 1914, and who would thus endorse the lines that affirm quite explicitly, in a language that is not so far removed from his poetic language: "We believe that the Armenian Soul is Light, Power, and Life [*Luysn e, Uzhn e, Keank'n e*], embodied in the statuesque splendor of the *Aryan* race to which we belong."[12] There are certain statements that one might prefer not to cite, translate, comment on, or bring to public awareness. This is one of them, although it may be true that these lines did not come directly from Varuzhan's pen. But we cannot avoid citing and commenting on this statement, first of all because it appeared in *Mehyan* and was signed by three of the most important writers of the period, writers who defined our thinking on the Catastrophe for decades to come; and then also because it coincides with the poetic thought of Varuzhan, which itself functions as a perfectly ordered system, whose main features we have presented here. It is the system of aesthetic nationalism. Certainly, when Varuzhan wrote the lines cited above, on "the giant heel / Of a deaf-mute Jewish god," he did after all have a good century of European tradition behind him, an essentially philological tradition that had created the figures of the "Aryan" and the "Semite," had defined the distinctive features of each, had granted mythopoetic capacities to the Aryan, and had denied these capacities to the Semite. There is thus no originality in this overdetermined (because racial and racist) distribution of the mythopoetic. Varuzhan is simply repeating here the commonplaces of his age. He repeated them with the goal of defining the sacred in the time of its disappearance and the mournful memory of religion at its end. Nonetheless, we cannot help being struck by the fact that "light," "power," and "life," these Varuzhanian attributes of the sacred, these elements that intervene in the most extraordinary of his "pagan" poems ("Light," "Vahagn," and "Vanatur") are also the attributes ascribed to the Aryan race.

These simple remarks make it necessary to return to the historical explanations given in the first part of the present study and to recall the investigation that was conducted there beneath the surface, on the purely contextual aspects of Varuzhan's poetry—aspects that include, essentially (but implicitly), Aryan ethnomythology and ethnometaphysics, the philologist's laboratory dear to Edward Said (who takes the idea from Ernest Renan), the ethnographic project in its principle, and the unequal distribution of mythopoetic capacities among the "races." That investigation, as conducted there, had an introductory status and actually needs to be undertaken anew, this time on a larger scale, all the more insofar as we have not exhausted all the determinations of philology. We still have much to learn about aesthetic nationalism as the "philosophy" common to the generation that gathered around the journal *Mehyan*, and on the naïve (but in no way innocent) expression of ethnomythology in an author as important as Constant Zarian, the journal's owner and director, who was also the only one to direct an unsparing critique (one could even say an attack, and an extremely violent one in fact) against the work and the person of Daniel Varuzhan.

For now, let us conclude by recalling that we have in fact given very little space here to the question of context. It is from within Daniel Varuzhan's work (and even deliberately leaving aside his articles and public interventions) that we have studied the particular relations between art and religion as they are thought and practiced within his poetry. It has been a question of understanding how Varuzhan and his friends conceived of the catastrophic completion (of an age, of a culture, of a tradition, of a world) and how they situated themselves as writers in relation to this concept or this reality. Most generally, it was necessary to describe the aesthetic (or speculative) matrix that governed the reception of religion in its termination, the reception of the disappeared gods, and therefore the reception or the realization of the completion as such. This double reception (that of the gods as well as that of the *end* of the gods) defines art. It defines art in its relation to the sacred, a sacred that never appears without its own disappearance, since it is of the very nature of the sacred to be always already lost. We just saw that this aesthetic matrix is also a historicizing matrix; it locates the mourning of the sacred (and therefore mourning in general) within a history. It was through such an aesthetic matrix that Varuzhan thought the disaster that had happened (that had already happened, well before the Catastrophe) to his people. At the same time, I have tried to show that behind the aesthetic matrix a possibility (and, for us, a necessity) emerged, within Varuzhan's work itself, of thinking the disaster without aesthetics, of thinking mourning outside this essential relation with "the loss of the sacred" and "the end of religion." Varuzhan knew very well that the disaster is (also) the loss of mourning and not (only) the loss of the sacred. He knew this with a knowledge that was specifically poetic; he knew it as "the last Vahuni"; and he knew it when he offered the "remnant" to the god, when he sacrificed to Vahagn the language of devastation as that which "remains" after the devastation. He knew it when he defined art as mourning, as the "shroud of light." He knew it, finally, when he sent the foreigner home, so that he himself could go back down into the plain of the dead to erect mausoleums to the victims and to enter into the other-scene of representation, beyond the reign of images.

Is this to say that today we must destroy the aesthetic matrix (and with it even the extraordinary idea of language as *the fire of the last sacrifice*) in order to accede finally to the mourning of mourning, to language as remnant and ash, to the devastation "itself," to a possible other-scene? In a certain sense, yes. Is this matrix so powerful that we must constantly work "against" it in order to receive the Catastrophe into the language of thought? Here too, the answer is yes. But it is not entirely a question of power. Indeed, we must recall what was said above (at the end of the previous chapter) on the unexpected conjunction between aesthetic nationalism and art as the space of mourning (or art as that which creates an other-scene of language). Here too, the conjunction between the mourning of the sacred and the mourning of mourning is undeniable and troubling. As always, catastrophic mourning and the mourning of aesthetic appropriation appear together. The reader might object that a possible thinking of the Catastrophe has nothing to do, at bottom, with the end of religion and the loss of the sacred, as I have developed these notions in relation to Varuzhan in the last two chapters. But Varuzhan never thought one without the other. The reason for this is that he was completely dependent—as are we, still today, and profoundly so—on the philological invention that joined together, in a single movement, the sacred and the native (that is, at once, the mythological and the ethnological, the mournful memory of the religion of the ancestors and the various intellectual reactions—literary, linguistic, national, nationalist—to the constitutive disaster of the native, or, in another register, the sacrifices of Ashtishat and the ruins of Ani). For what, then, does art mourn? Is it the mourning of power, the mourning of myth, the mourning of the sacred (of a sacred without mourning), the mourning of religion and the dead gods? Or is it the mourning of the fatherland in the nothingness of the fatherland, the mourning of the "national" self? What we called in the beginning the aesthetic logic of the invention of the native finds its meaning only at the end, in the convergence of these two series. The central figure of philological orientalism was that of the native, the living ruin, the inhabitant of chaos, an integral part of the nothingness of the fatherland. But it happens that the native is also the fallen witness of the power of myth and the improbable *remnant* of the poetico-religious foundation. In the end, we see how the aesthetic matrix governing the relations between art and religion was fabricated in response to the intrinsic disaster of the native. It makes art function as the space of a speculative mourning. Conversely, of course, the disaster of the native was nothing other than the disaster of the mythopoetic capacity. In this perfect circularity, would there be nothing to learn about religion? No—precisely nothing other than what art says of it. On the other hand, concerning orientalist philology and the inauguration of ethnomythology that accompanies it, there is still certainly a great deal to learn. Throughout the nineteenth century, orientalist philology worked hand-in-hand with ethnology to imagine this "religion," this mythic power, this sacrality without mourning, this community founded in itself in sacrifice and recounting itself to itself in myth—and the native was the fallen bearer of all these things. Hand-in-hand with ethnology, philology thus invented mythology; it took up the myth of myth for its own purposes, and provided a powerful "scientific" impulse to this myth. This ethnomythology runs parallel to the philological invention of the native in the drive to constitute the "national."

ORIENTALISM AND RELIGION

The brief discussion on the end of religion that closed the previous paragraph, despite its idiosyncracies, recalls certain elements of a recent controversy among American academics on the theme of "religion and orientalism." An example of this controversy can be found in the book by William Hart on Edward Said and the religious effects of culture.[13] Hart uses a historical approach, attempting to take his author to task in relation to orientalism and its cultural assumptions. Hart claims that while Said denounces the orientalism inherent in European "culture," he in turn orientalizes religion; that is his prejudice and even his infantile disorder. In what sense can this claim be made? According to Hart, Said reads phenomena (especially religious phenomena) that existed prior to orientalism from a purely secular and secularist point of view, which Hart says is not only inadequate but is itself an effect of orientalism. It is therefore necessary to reconstruct a nonsecularized notion of religion, a notion that would not be subject to the orientalization that Said imposes on it. The task is thus to understand and to interpret European secularism by reconstructing religion as a discourse. Edward Said was working toward this central idea and according to Hart was "on the verge of an insight that eludes him nevertheless."[14] Instead of following this path, he took up the ontologizing views of Gibbon and even repeated, under the name "orientalism," what should have been explained in the context of religion as a discourse. This argument, rapidly summarized here, represents a rather strange treatment of the question. It could be said that Hart quite simply wants to save religion, to de-orientalize it (but without disorienting it); he wants religion to be more powerful than orientalism; and he wants religion to exceed orientalism on every side, however one understands it. It is clear, however, that there is a problem here that cannot be formulated in the terms already mentioned. One part of this problem is the connection between orientalism as Said conceives it and the religious avatar represented by the philological invention of the Semite (and the Aryan) in the nineteenth century. In terms of the critique summarized here, it is not difficult to understand the idea that secularism is an orientalism.[15] But this critique says nothing about the obligatory secularism of philology at the very moment when it was distinctively defining the Semitic religious sphere and the Greco-Aryan nature of mythopoetics. Nor does it say anything about the relation between secularism and racial thought. The "Semitism" of the nineteenth century is inscribed directly within a racial history of the religious, which is also a philological history.

The question, then, has to do with the obligatory (but "hypocritical") secularism of the philologist at the moment when, in a single movement, he invents the native and religion. I said earlier that the native is in reality a double figure. The first figure is the one that emerges when the native is approached philologically, as a pure transparence to itself, where the philologist is the one who would possess the truth of the native; the second figure appears when we approach the native "politically," based on the opposition between civilized law and customary law, as Mahmoud Mamdani does. The connection between the two is essential. William Jones, who is usually credited with the discovery of the Indo-European linguistic realm, is emblematic in this sense: like all his colleagues, he was a specialist in law before he was anything else. But we must not neglect orientalism's other success, which consisted in transforming everything into literature. This is true of Herder, for example (who in fact inaugurated this tendency), when he speaks of the "poetry" of the Hebrews. This is obligatory secularism. But it is also where we can locate the invention of literature. Thus we find ourselves one step upstream in the literature/criticism relation as defined by Schlegel. But this invention coincides entirely with that of religion. It is precisely at the moment when it transforms everything into literature that philology invents religion. Neither goes without the other. It is here that philology invents Judaism as a religion, with Herder, and Hinduism as a religion, with Jones and his English and British followers during the same period. This is what leads Schlegel to write his book on the Hindus in 1808, the same year as his conversion to Catholicism, and his book on the universal history of literature in 1812. Literature and religion always go together in this context, according to the secular obligation. However paradoxical it may seem, it is secularism that invents religion. That is why (to speak too hastily, no doubt) one can say that Schlegel had to convert to the religion par excellence, Catholicism, at the very moment when he was becoming the first theoretician of literature. He may criticize himself in 1808, ridiculing the "religion of art" of which he was the first thurifer in 1798, but the fact is that he is still the same man. We just saw that the two great Armenian philologists of the end of the nineteenth century, Alishan in Venice and Abeghean in Tblisi, both wrote books on religion (in 1893 and in 1895, respectively) completely independently from each other, the first based on written sources, the second based on oral sources.[16] Both were profoundly convinced that they were discovering the archives of the mythopoetic. They were obsessed (their age made them obsessed) with "religion" as a category, a category newly discovered by them. But because at the beginning of the century a secularizing decision had been made concerning religion, they were able, at the end of the century, to assume the religious division between everything belonging to the Semitic tradition (including Christianity) and everything belonging to the Aryan tradition (without the word being pronounced, but it was understood). The conclusion, then, is this: the religious discourse is in fact a racial discourse. But the religious discourse itself was only established in relation to the obligatory secularism of philology. And this obligatory secularism is that of literature and art. Religion is thus an aesthetic category. The fact that an aesthetic category can be a purely racist category—that is the scandal of the century.

THE TWO RELIGIONS

The last thing that remains to do now will be to read together two nonpoetic texts by Daniel Varuzhan on religion. Each of these two texts has a very distinct status. The first, called "The Hero," is an excerpt from a lecture that Varuzhan agreed to have published in the journal *Azatamart* in Constantinople in 1909.[17] The second, entitled "The Religions," was not written for publication. It was found in Varuzhan's papers and published in 1987, in the *Complete Works*. In it Varuzhan summarizes, apparently for himself, what he learned about the history of religions as it was taught in his time in Belgium, particularly the evolutionist theory developed by anthropologists (Herbert Spencer and John Lubbock are the only contemporary authors mentioned in these pages) and the reflections on the origin of religion by philologists and specialists in comparative mythology. First, here is the text of the "The Hero," almost in its entirety.

> Schopenhauer recognizes three types of superman: the Saint, the Genius, and the Hero. He becomes the most optimistic of optimists when he says that they experience the perfection and beauty of life, so that, thanks to this circumstance alone, it becomes possible to say that they experience the Universe. The Universe would of course have been created in vain were there no one to enjoy it, consciously or unconsciously. Let us limit our discussion to the Hero. He displays features so superhuman that the Ancients put him in the same class as the gods. The Ancients constructed their religion after the fact, rising from man to the hero and from the hero to God. The Greeks' gods are men, perfect in body and soul. . . .
>
> A great, harmonious being, in turn, is life's lawgiver: he is of the race of the gods. He is a hero either because he slew the dragon who was poisoning creation with the destruction and desolation he wrought or because he founded a historical golden age and a religion that not only brings the solar good news of life, but also illuminates the grave and its remote secrets. In the *man* endowed with this extraordinary force, men saw the germ of a god and, on his brow, a goddess's rose-scented kiss.
>
> In every condition in which the myths and legends show us heroes, these heroes possess something more than the prophets. Rather than merely feeling the gods' breath in their souls, they touched the body of an immortal with theirs: for the condition for being a hero is that the body become as divine as the soul. The prophet sees the future; the hero prepares it. One is a jurist; the other is a lawgiver. The former harvests God's word even before it is sown; the latter sows the still

unharvested word, and is extremely close to the inhabitants of this earth, in whose hand he often places his own; he takes from them the breast-plate, and the helmet, and the victor's crown, and the spear, and the sword and, following their lead, heads for the *Battles of Progress*. Heroes are the wheels on which progress advances from age to age. If evolution truly unfolds over the centuries without conscious intervention, it nevertheless always needs a hero to acquiesce to its verdict. The years are sown thanks to the peaceful labor of the human mind, but the centuries ripen thanks to the hero's blood. With their doctrines, the ideal of the best possible life, philosophers and sociologists mix the cement of progress; but it is the hero, the superman, who lays the foundations of the edifice of the ideal life to come; he piles marble on marble, puts the luminous columns in place, and runs the iron beams from wall to wall until the temple of civilization has been erected and the columns gleam and the altar is ready to accept the sacrificial victim of the Idea. He himself is that victim, the very hero who constructs the temple. His blood flows over the altar as the mark of the dominion of the ideal.

In this crude world, every superman is a sacrificial victim.

Without sacrifice, there can be no heroes.

First of all, let me say how utterly insufferable I find this kind of rhetoric. Nonetheless, it requires some commentary since, as I have said, it is congruent with Varuzhan's poetic thinking in general, if perhaps somewhat more brutal and naïve in its formulations. The speech from which these lines are taken was given by Varuzhan just after his return from Europe, at a time when he was already enjoying all the renown that his poems had brought him, at least from intellectuals. Who are the "heroes" that Varuzhan has in mind? Are they the dragon-slayers? Here it seems that Varuzhan is referring implicitly to "Vahagn." Or are they the founders of religion, those through whom the solar religion came to be, as Varuzhan very clearly suggests? This solar religion, for which the poet makes himself the messenger and the propagandist, is a religion of the will (the gods will, and their will is immediately transformed into action; they have the power to transform their representations into acts), and therefore also a religion of the will to power, of the will as power. This solar religion is of course opposed at every point to the religion of the prophets. The hero establishes a legislation of life, whereas the prophet merely applies an existing legislation (so we are told). The hero engenders the word that will give to men their earthly and spiritual nourishment, whereas the prophet only reaps (that is, he does not create). Even though the words *Aryan* and *Semite* do not appear in the article, it is quite clear that an Aryan religion, characterized as active, creative, and mythopoetic, is here being set against a Semitic religion of passivity. The hero erects the temple of civilization (of art, science, thought, religion), and he provides its material through his own sacrifice. Here we recognize the two elements—erection and self-sacrifice—whose articulation constitutes the essence of art for Varuzhan, the two elements that provide the basic structure for his book to come. These are, once again, the two elements of the aesthetic principle. But what is it that makes these pages so insufferable? Is it simply the fact that Varuzhan repeats in the most stupefying way the entire philological phraseology of the Aryan and the Semite, according to which the first is endowed with a boundless creative capacity, while the second only receives a purely moralistic religion? Throughout the nineteenth century, the philological discourse repeated these commonplaces with every possible inflection, racializing religion (or producing the religious as a mask for racial thinking)[18] and making art the creative (Aryan) faculty par excellence. It is partly this, of course, that is intolerable. But more than that, I think it is the preaching tone in which the good (solar) news of the "new mythology" is announced.[19] For that is indeed what is at stake here: Varuzhan, having recently returned to his country, is presenting the theory of the gods and the heroes forgotten by his contemporaries. There can be civilization only through the renewed myth, which is here given the name "progress." Everything that is carried out in a performative mode in Varuzhan's poetry—I sacrifice, I pray, I raise a language on fire as a sacrificial offering and as a sacred remainder, I go down the hillside to weave a shroud of light for the dead, I accomplish the mourning of the sacred through my art, which I thereby make live one last time, in a sort of final conflagration (without mentioning the more complex aspect of catastrophic mourning)—is transformed here into a rhetorical flourish on erection and self-sacrifice, into the pompous announcement (without the slightest irony) of a message of good news, all of which demand a hardy faith. I engender myself, I myself am my own hero and my own victim. Earlier I stressed that Varuzhan was obviously not the founder of a religion. This passage might well raise some doubts; we might well wonder whether Varuzhan did not vacillate for a brief moment, whether he did not confuse art and religion, in the brief space of a return and a pilgrimage to the "source." The discourse of faith, the retrospective illusion, the confusion of roles, the Aryan philosophy, the solar Evangel, the new mythology, the mimetism of oneself, the transformation (or the complete hijacking) of poetry as an instrument of politics and nationalism (this was in fact a speech given at a gathering organized by his friends at *Azatamart*)—which among all these things is the most disturbing in this short text? Hagop Oshagan would have chalked all this up to the use of a rhetoric that is necessary (or inevitable) in a time of crisis. One's uneasiness remains no less persistent, at this moment when poetics crosses paths with politics. Rhetoric does not pardon everything and does not explain everything.

Now for a few words on the text entitled "The Religions," found in Varuzhan's papers long after his death.[20] I must first confess something to the reader. The present essay on Varuzhan's poetry and "religion" has suddenly become possible (after years of shilly-shallying) only because I discovered this short text and first translated it into French for my own sake. I was dumbfounded by what I had found, without yet having a clear idea of the relationship between this text and the author's poetry. I will therefore finish with a rapid reading of "The Religions." This reading will allow me to briefly come back to Schelling and to link together the diverse historical elements that have appeared in the course of our inquiry: the Romantic invention of mythology, the philological revolution, the ethnographic nation.

What do we find in this text? Very simply, an evolutionist theory of religion that Varuzhan took from contemporary works. It is therefore quite uncertain whether we can see this text as anything other than a faithful reproduction of the theses circulating at the time, which Varuzhan heard in the university lecture hall. But here too it should be noted that Varuzhan faithfully repeats the opposition between the "mythological" religions and the "monotheistic" religions, which is only another version of the philological differentiation between Aryan and Semite as we find it in Ernest Renan or Max Müller. In these ideas on the origin of religion (which are developed in tandem with investigations in the science of language), we recognize also Varuzhan's choice of a unique origin of the divine, which informs both the polytheistic religions and monotheism. It is true that his summary of the "science of religions" of his time poses questions and develops arguments that were current in evolutionist anthropology, whose most popular representatives at the time were—other than E. B. Taylor—the two authors cited in the short essay by Varuzhan, Herbert Spencer and John Lubbock. The text might seem to be of limited interest since it is after all a piece of schoolwork. However, in a comprehensive study on the relations between art and religion, it is important to take it into account.

The name of Herbert Spencer has managed to survive the passage of time. Spencer is still known today as a contemporary and a critic of Auguste Comte, a founder of "sociology" and a supporter of evolutionism. His voluminous *Principles of Sociology* has been reprinted many times in various abridged editions. On the other hand, the name of John Lubbock (a banker and parliamentarian) has fallen into oblivion, despite the fact that during his lifetime he was the most well-known and active supporter of cultural evolutionism. His forays into the field of anthropology include *The Origins of Civilisation and the Primitive Condition of Man* (first published in London in 1870), but also *Prehistoric Times, as Illustrated by Ancient Remains, and the Manners and Customs of Modern Savages* (1875), and *Marriage, Totemism, and Religion* (1911).[21] Lubbock is cited by Daniel Varuzhan in reference to his discussion of tribes without religion and his mention of "the existence of a New Zealand tribe without any kind of religion at all," to which Varuzhan objects that the example "is by no means convincing grounds for denying the tendency of human nature to believe in a superhuman being." It is striking to find that Ignaz Goldziher, in his introduction to *Mythology among the Hebrews and its Historical Development* (1877),[22] reports exactly the same opinion and raises a somewhat different objection. Goldziher cites Lubbock's *Origins of Civilisation*. Here is the passage Goldziher quotes from Lubbock: "Even in Madagascar, according to a good authority, 'there is nothing corresponding to a Mythology, *or any fables of gods or goddesses*, amongst the Malagasy' "(emphasis in original).[23] It would be quite surprising if Varuzhan picked out exactly the same example (erroneously referring it to New Zealand) from Lubbock's entire work. My hypothesis is therefore that

Varuzhan had read Goldziher, and precisely in this edition in English (he did not read German)—unless, perhaps, he heard the reference to Lubbock at the university and the six pages found in his papers on "the religions" were simply an Armenian stenography of a course on religion given in French. Goldziher's conclusion with regard to Lubbock's remark, is the following: ". . . but this want of stories of gods and goddesses is very far from demonstrating the absence of myths of all and every sort."

Let us recall the point of departure of Goldziher's investigation: in *Mythology among the Hebrews* he argues that the mythopoetic power is not the exclusive attribute of the Indo-Europeans. All nations have had their mythological period. The Hebrews are no exception to this rule. Of course Goldziher wrote in reaction to the works of Max Müller and Ernest Renan, and he had followed the debate that took place between them around 1860 as to the origin of religion and (in veiled terms) the adequacy of a racialized thinking concerning this issue, and consequently of the philological distinction between Aryans and Semites.[24] This is the question confronted by Goldziher, the renowned Islamicist who began his intellectual career with his extraordinary book on the Hebrews, in which he attempts to show that the Hebrews too had originally developed a mythology. It is a fascinating project, precisely because it works against the very logic (the logic of orientalism, let us say) of the philological construction, and because it does so with the weapons provided by philology itself, and therefore in a total dependency not only on the methods applied in the science of comparative mythology, but also on the absolutely irreversible presuppositions maintained by philology concerning Aryan mythology and the Aryan as the producer of mythology. It is then to this debate that Daniel Varuzhan brings his own contribution, thirty or forty years after the fact. At the time when he wrote his great poems "The Light" and "Vahagn," Varuzhan thus wrote down a series of questions and responses, intended for himself, on the psychological origin of religion from the feeling of life (the feeling of the self), the artistic feeling (the feeling of nature), and the cosmic feeling, which is the proper element of religion, the latter thus having its foundation in every case in a "cosmogony." As for artistic activity strictly speaking, Varuzhan says that one finds its source "in the religions, because men fearfully rivet their attention on the superficial forms of nature."

I just mentioned the philological differentiation between the Semite and the Aryan in Renan and Müller. But in fact it was not necessarily a simple opposition. Maurice Olender has closely studied this tension between religious monotheism and mythological Aryanism in these two authors,[25] a tension existing within an intellectual climate that was, for both of them, entirely Christian. Thus Renan: "Originally Jewish to the core, Christianity over time rid itself of nearly everything it took from the race, so that those who see Christianity to be the Aryan religion par excellence are in many respects correct."[26] As for Max Müller, he provided philologists with the idea of a metaphorization of language and of a personification of vocables at the origin of the polytheistic religions and of that "disease of language" that is mythology.[27] According to him, these phenomena are characteristic precisely of the Indo-European languages and therefore, as an indirect consequence, of the Aryan race. But at the same time he postulates the existence of a primitive religion "in which each god, while he is being invoked, shares in all the attributes of the supreme being."[28] Nevertheless, for Renan, "the connection between Aryan characteristics, mythological talent, and scientific creativity" (to use Olender's formula[29]) is undeniable. It is undeniable even for Müller. It is true that for Müller the study of language in general is a way to highlight the divine in man, and in this respect the Aryans do not have any priority. But it is also true for him, as I have said, that a "mythological phraseology" is particular to the Aryan race. We therefore understand the theoretical difficulty of the undertaking that seeks to demonstrate the existence of a mythology among the Hebrews. It is explained by Olender in the following terms:

> Goldziher was thus in a position to appreciate the resistance to the notion that all peoples, including the Semites, have myths. This resistance, which he hoped to overcome, did not stem solely from theology. A certain transference had occurred. Old religious arguments for the supposed mythological incapacity of certain cultures had acquired new scientific legitimacy through the idea of "race." Race was at the root of the scholarly claim that not all peoples are capable of mythology. The attempt, then, to submit the entire Semitic sphere to a comparative treatment similar to the one constructed by the science of myths in the Aryan domain presumes the abandonment of the "prejudice" . . . affirming the existence of "unmythological races" [*unmythologische Rassen*].[30]

Such a project obviously went against the whole recent development of the philological tradition, particularly the theses of Müller, who saw the origin of myths in metaphorization and personification, and therefore in poetic power, even though the latter produces in the end a sickness of language (which is in reality a sickness of religion, since it perverts the original monotheistic Aryan intuition, itself an intuition of the origin). It also meant going against the theses of Renan, for whom "the Semites never had a mythology."[31] Moreover, Goldziher restored a historic dimension to religious and cultural phenomena and obliged his contemporaries to envisage a culture as a web of borrowings from a primitive source, borrowings that undergo phenomena of pressure and internal transformation, due to historical and political circumstances, without there being any particular primitive instinct involved, and without any sickly outgrowth.[32]

CONCLUSION

1. Between the evolutionist anthropology of the end of the nineteenth century (before Franz Boas) and the science of religion inaugurated by comparative linguistics and mythology, there is thus complete agreement; only their objects are different. This agreement is exemplified in the strange text which Varuzhan called "The Religions"; it consists in a firm belief that the following question can be given a coherent, historical

response: what is the origin of religion? At the very least, it consists in a firm belief that this question has a meaning even if it doesn't have an answer, that it is situated within the boundaries of human investigation—an investigation that is now thoroughly scientific. From this we can deduce a series of postulates that are foundational for philology: i) a science of the human spirit is possible; ii) it is a natural science (its object—language—is a natural object, even though it has a history); iii) this science studies the development of beliefs and thus deals with religion from the beginning; iv) it is also a historical science, whose archives are not necessarily given in the form of texts; v) philology and anthropology contribute, each in its own way, to the advance of this science of the spirit, whose vocation (or pretension) is to give to humanity a memory of itself. In both cases, then, the subject of the investigation is immediately transformed into a witness. The primitive tribes have preserved within themselves something of the primitive state of humanity. They are remnants, immobile monuments of early antiquity, vestiges; and they are this precisely to the same extent (but in the opposite sense) as the natives of ethnology or of comparative mythology, who are on the verge of disappearing, but who bear within themselves the remnants and vestiges of a much more ancient state of civilization. The ethnologist and the philologist therefore have the same position in relation to their presumed subject, who is transformed into a witness and a vestige of a past state of civilization, whatever the differences between the societies studied (a memory with an archive or without one, cultures that are oral or written, societies that are intact or already decadent). Hence, too, the contradiction that constantly inhabits the philosophies of the origin developed on anthropological or philological bases. The witness is but a vestige. He can be the vestige of humanity's childhood or of its golden age. Christianity (the perfected religion) is a final result, but the idea of God (necessarily conforming to the Christian idea) must be there from the beginning. However, what is common to the two currents that make up ethnophilology is that the original culture, gathered together or recreated by the philologist or the ethnologist, whether it is decadent or whole, is mythological in nature (and the "original" monotheism of the Hebrews then poses all sorts of problems). The "principle" of religion and of a national community can only be mythopoetic.

In terms of the Armenian context, Varuzhan becomes aware of this necessity by way of Max Müller and Ignaz Goldziher, either directly or through their epigones, propagators of the scientific Good News of ethnomythology. After all, the vocation of the poet is to restore the mythopoetic power or to make himself its mournful heir (the historical necessity of this vocation and therefore of "poetic paganism" thus becomes comprehensible). The poet will become the servant of Aryanism and will obey at every point the injunctions of orientalism: on the one hand, by taking up the flame of the national idea; on the other hand, by reflecting this same national idea in the colors of the mythic past and the mythopoetic present. It is true that Varuzhan (as the would-be incarnation of this historic poet) differs profoundly from his Mkhitarist teachers, who limited themselves to the bookish, erudite epic, simply continued the tradition of philological nationalism from the beginning of the nineteenth century, never once turned toward the native, and completely ignored the ethnographic determination of the very nationalism they strove for. In a word, the Mkhitarists did not register the ethnomythological revolution of the nineteenth century. It is clear that Alishan (author of the 1893 book *The Armenians' Ancient Faith or Pagan Religion*) had worked all his life to carry out this nationalist program of the 1810's (a program that was archeological, descriptive, and polyhistorical) and had taken into account the ethnomythological revolution (and consequently the "national" religion) only very late. In that sense, he was only obeying the philological laws of his century. In the end, he lent an attentive ear to what was being said about mythology and the ancient gods. Schelling had said that there can be no people without a mythology:

> Is it at all possible that a single people gave birth to a mythology as something that emanated from it, as it were? And, first of all, what is a *people*, and what makes it a *people*? Not the mere coexistence of a greater or lesser number of similar individuals in a given space, but rather their common consciousness. This community of consciousness finds only an indirect expression of itself in ordinary language. But where are we to find its ground if not in a common view of the world, and what other means does a people possess for preserving and affirming itself than in its mythology? It thus seems impossible that an already constituted people would receive a mythology afterward, either through the inventions of a single person or through a kind of collective, productive drive. This eventuality seems impossible also because we cannot conceive of a *people* without a mythology.[33]

We should also remark that in the next paragraph Schelling relates an ethnographic narrative (*Voyages dans l'Amérique méridionale* by Don Felix Azara) in order to show that certain small tribes of South America certainly did not have any religion ("no cults, no divinity, no laws, no chiefs, no obedience"), but that, precisely, these are not *peoples*! So it is that these unfortunate tribes with no religion or mythology migrated from South America to Madagascar, then, with Varuzhan, to New Zealand. But one immediately understands the stakes behind the argument.

In sum, mythology corresponds entirely with the being-people of a people. Max Müller took up this thesis, citing Schelling explicitly.[34] Goldziher also referred to it, citing both Müller and Schelling.[35] The fundamental intuition was that mythology and being-a-people are co-originary. Thus Schelling wrote: "If it is not the case that the mythology of a people is born from within this people, as its creation or its emanation, then we can only say that its mythology is born at the same time as it is, as its individual consciousness or its consciousness as a people, through which it becomes this particular people and not another, thus distinguishing itself from every other people no less than by its language."[36] And a little later: "The birth of mythology coincides with the birth of the people itself."[37] Of course, this coincidence between mythology and being-a-people took absolutely nothing away from the purely religious character of mythology in its origin; quite the contrary. It was indeed a question of the gods, and of gods who were indeed quite real. Thus religion became the new imperative of the century; although of course this was the imperative of mythological religion, not of theological religion.

Religion thus conceived is not a social phenomenon. It is the expression of a principle, precisely the mythopoetic principle. Alishan remained at the level of social expression, that of customs and beliefs. It became necessary, consequently, to take a further step and to make the principle itself the final term of a more far-reaching aim. At the same time, we must clearly state what is by now obvious: the principle of the religious is nothing religious. It thus becomes necessary to go back, to "return." We recall Varuzhan's double "return," pronounced as an imperative and an injunction addressed to himself: "To the fathers, that is, to the gods." We also recall what we said concerning the equivalence of these two returns. *The fatherland can only be mythical.* It is Varuzhan who says this. Or else: the fatherland will be mythical or it will not be. Is this the rigorous expression of an antinationalism? It is in any case the extreme limit of all nationalism. It is its most distant border, where nationalism is as much its own negation as its own institution and instantiation.

2. The only adequate modern aim for the mythopoetic principle of religion is that of art. This does not at all mean that the gods of mythology, whatever or whoever they were, were not real. Art may well be the domain of the imagination; it is not the domain of the merely imagined. This was explained above, following Schelling's explication of the essence of myth, in terms of Jean-Luc Nancy's reading of it. Mythology is an originary schematism, a pure giving of the image, by which a world is born for us (for them), with its gods, its nature, and its men. Of course, this can be understood (and set into a work through an autonomous activity called art) only at the end of a history of religion, at a moment when religion has exhausted all its resources. Here, the mythopoetic power is revealed quite simply as the power of the aesthetic principle, and that is why I have given it this name from the beginning. But in this state of completion, every sort of turning back is possible, particularly the one that imagines a new mythology, which this time would be a mythology of the artist, a new foundational fictioning, as foundational as the ancient myth that has reached its end. It is nevertheless the case that, in every sense in which this can be said and imagined, the principle of religion is an artistic principle. *Art is at the origin of religion.* That is the second central formulation of the generation of *Mehyan*, after the one which announces that the fatherland can be only mythical. It is art that brings about this supplementary step from religion to its mythopoetic principle. Hence the famous declarations in *Mehyan* that have been quoted several times here: "We want to found an aesthetics of language"; "Although art is a religious fanaticism, it is superior to religion"; "We want to erect a temple" (art as a pagan temple). Or from Varuzhan's pen: "If it were possible today, I would change religions and would joyfully embrace poetic paganism"; and from Hagop Oshagan's pen: "We need a universal fiction"; "The act of writing is such

a far-reaching and public phenomenon that we can only compare it to the ethos created by the religions of the ancient centuries . . . Besides, for superior spirits, art and religion are almost identical." Simultaneously, since the fatherland can be only mythical, it comes to be only through art. This singularly complicates our current representations concerning the fatherland, even if these representations are not radically challenged thereby. Art is the sublation of the mythical foundation, and it is the substitute for the sacrificial offering. This is the only way to understand why the national can come to be only during the age of art.

Thus, in a quite unexpected way, it is through its fulfillment in art that the prodigious philological invention (the invention of the historicity of language, of religion as coextensive with language in its origin, of mythology as the schematism of the pure image, and finally, of the native as a central figure and a historical vestige) discovers its own logic, which is the logic of the aesthetic principle. This fulfillment only confirms, up to a certain point, the incredible power of this invention. But art is also what takes responsibility for the *disaster* assumed by the philological invention—the disaster of the native, the loss of the sacred, and the constitutive absence of myth. What is happening, then, when a poet thinks of himself in the present as the last representative of the lineage of sacrificing priests, or when he proclaims that art, in its essence, is precisely a mourning for the sacred, for religion, for the gods of the fatherland? What is happening when a poet practices the performative offering of language as a last sacrifice? Is it the apotheosis of the philological (and therefore, in fact, theological) ethnomythology of Max Müller, for whom the science of language and the science of religion were one? Or is it only on the basis of such a poetic thought that we will be able to think mourning, to elaborate an idea of mourning that would finally be independent of philology? Is it only on this basis that we will finally be able to understand how things stand with the end of substitutive sacrifice, with language as a remnant, with the irremediable breakdown of the ability to mourn, with the disappearance of memory in mourning? And is it thus that one day, perhaps, catastrophic mourning will return to us from the future? To liberate mourning from philology—this is a task in which Varuzhan, perhaps, will have helped us despite himself.

—Part Two translated by Jeff Fort

Nietzsche in Armenian Literature at the Turn of the Twentieth Century

I

Throughout the present work, we have been discreetly pointing to the racialist thought of the group of writers around *Mehyan* and thus, in effect, to the fact that racialization and the aesthetic principle go hand-in-hand. In the final chapters of Part II, these pointers became more precise. In the nineteenth century, mythical-poetic power was clearly imaged as an Aryan capability, while, inversely, the category "Aryan" stood in close relation to what had been imaged in the form of the mythical and poetical. The polemic that Ignaz Goldziher carried on against Ernest Renan and Max Müller only confirms these categories' power, since the capacity to produce original myths and the identification of peoplehood with this capacity were by no means called into question by the man who would soon become one of the foremost representatives of Islamic studies. Everything that Constant Zarian and Hagop Oshagan say in unison and at great length in the pages of *Mehyan*, from the Manifesto to the March 1914 essays about the "return to the fatherland" and the appeal to create a new mythology, are in this vein. It is true that the appeal in question and the very idea of a "new mythology" already take us beyond philological categories and into the realm of what we have called, with increasing insistence in the course of this book, *ethnomythology*, that is, more or less, the pact between evolutionary ethnology and the science of comparative mythology, a pact that is one of the forms taken by mythopoetic faith and racialized thought—or, quite simply, the stock-in-trade of the philology of the day. This appeal and this idea are more than philological categories because they have, implicitly, a political dimension. We have referred repeatedly, in the preceding pages, to Oshagan's powerful declaration about the need for certain kinds of "universal fiction" or "universal lie," meaning, very precisely, a "new mythology" or, in a word, a modern mythology, an artistic mythology. With this declaration, Oshagan confirmed that he believed (at least in 1914, in the period when he was associated with Zarian) in myth's formative power. Myths are products of a "fictional" capacity. They have, by that very fact, the power to "form" the people or bring a people into existence by endowing it with form. When he uttered this sentence, Oshagan was perfectly well aware that he was formulating an appeal of a "political" nature, for, immediately afterwards, he says, in a passage I have not yet cited, "In prioritizing literature, the highest form of self-determination, we are not succumbing to a thankless illusion."[1] This very deliberate use of the term *self-determination* once again proves, were there any need, that the formative/fictional finality of literature (conceived here as creative of myth) was destined to compete with political action in the project of forming (that is, both educating and giving form to) a people, even if literature was in no sense whatsoever supposed to define a concrete politics. But that is not all. When he wrote this sentence, Oshagan was certainly unaware that the first Romantics had explicitly devised the same project for a "new mythology" a century earlier. And, above all, he could not have known that twenty years later, Nazi ideologues would conceive political action in the same terms, competing in their turn with politics, but without literature and with very different consequences indeed. On the other hand, Oshagan knew very well that the aesthetic will (the will for art) was a will to lie. It is in this sense that I have copiously cited his formula, pointing out its ambiguity and noting in passing that the source of this ambiguity is to be sought in the Nietzschean will for art, considered as a will for the lie.

To enjoy lying, Nietzsche said, is to enjoy "oneself as an artist," oneself as a "power" (*Macht*); it is to enjoy lying as that which is responsible for one's own power. Oshagan could not have been unaware of this. True, Nietzsche was engaged in a "deconstructive" enterprise *avant la lettre* when he made his statement. He was denouncing (and, at the same time, glorifying) "metaphysics, religion, morals, and science" as "different forms of lie" destined to overcome the reality of a world that was "unique, false, cruel, contradictory, seductive, and without meaning."[2] Nietzsche's earliest commentators seized on just one aspect of all this, the lie's formative power.

Nonetheless, even when it is understood that we are beyond philology here, and even when it is recalled how Nazism later utilized Nietzsche in putting its doctrinal apparatus in place, an appeal for a new mythology (common to both Oshagan and Zarian in 1914) and the belief in a mythological *religion* to come do not seem scandalous to the modern reader, even if she has been forewarned. After all, the aesthetic principle comprised the last moment in a history that was similar for all the ethnographic nations; and Zarian was not the only one to believe, in this period and thereafter, in gods who were yet to come and in whose coming he believed he had a part to play, that of prophet and herald. Much worse has been seen since. Where, then, is the worst *here*? Does it reside in these declarations in the Manifesto, which we have already glossed: "We believe that the Armenian soul is Light, Power, and Life, embodied in the statuesque splendor of the *Aryan* race to which we belong"? Or, again, in "On its columns, our Armenian, profoundly Aryan soul will discover lines sometimes unexpected and strange, and sometimes sublime"?[3] Following Maurice Olender, we interpreted these declarations as the echo of a general racialization of thought characteristic of nineteenth-century philology, a racial-

ization that the writers around *Mehyan* inherited and put to work when they proclaimed their aesthetic—that is, formative and fictional—profession of faith. (This is
not to say that the invention of myth that was the work of nineteenth-century philology in its entirety was not, for its part, political; on the contrary, it was political
through and through, because it had a direct stake in orientalism.)

It seems to me that the worst occurs when the open or hidden desire of the *founder of
a religion* (of the artist as a founder of religion, a manipulator of myths, of the artist with
collective pretensions) is combined with an openly avowed, unbridled *anti-Semitism*.
This combination/conjunction occurs, unfortunately, in the essays that Zarian published in *Mehyan*. It also finds expression (lest one imagine that the racism of the *Mehyan* period was just a youthful sin) in the overtly racist declarations of doctrine that the
same Zarian would later, in 1933, put in the mouths of certain of his fictional characters
who are in every sense representative of the thought of their author. Here, as I noted in
the introduction, racialist thought spills over into racist ideology, and this is absolutely
unbearable. It is the more unbearable because Zarian utilizes, from the outset, a phraseology with markedly Nietzschean overtones, which means that he bends Nietzsche to
the service of his own dubious ideology, interpreting him exactly the way all the racist
ideologues in Germany interpreted him between 1910 and 1930 (for example, Alfred
Baümler, a highly cultivated, prolific Nazi philosopher little known today).[4] All this
explains the cast of the present epilogue, in which I propose to read the texts to which
I have just referred a bit more attentively, especially those not yet touched on here, in
which Zarian's ridiculous (or, if one likes, revolting) anti-Semitism finds expression. But
I also propose to attend to what Nietzsche himself said about art.

In my first chapter, I spoke of the definition of art as a reaction to a basic alienation
and saw that it is art that brings the "national" into being. In sum, we defined the
Mehyan school's emergent "national-aestheticism," a term that I borrow from Philippe
Lacoue-Labarthe, who uses it in his analysis of National Socialism. National-aestheticism
is a kind of thought and politics that believes in the "fiction of a people as a work of art."[5]
Formally, this fiction should be distinguished from art and the work of art in the narrow
sense (literature, opera, theater). In reality, such a distinction is superfluous, and would
have made no sense to the *Mehyan* generation. This generation repeats what the period
thought about "great art" (about, thus, Greek art and, to a lesser extent—that is, in any
case, "to a mimetic extent"—Wagner's art): namely, that great art is the fiction of the
people. Through art and the activity of the artist, the people would be "saved" from disaster (from disintegration and a forcibly imposed silence). Heidegger says this in the
same terms in chapter 13 of his first course on Nietzsche, in connection with Wagner's
total work of art (and, of course, in a deconstructive tone): "The art work should be a
celebration of the national community: it should be religion itself."[6] This is, after all, one
possible formulation of the *aesthetic principle*. But it makes one uneasy to observe that,
when the *Mehyan* generation feels the need to run through the forms and variants of this

principle, it invariably does so in terms that have a Nietzschean ring. Does Nietzsche bear a share of the blame for this? Is that what Nietzsche thought about art? Was he himself already an adept of national-aestheticism?

2

We must, then, start by saying a word about the reception of Nietzsche, first in general, and then among the Armenians. As is well known, Nietzsche's work was astonishingly well received in Europe from the late nineteenth century on. At the very beginning, Nietzsche was interpreted as a "literary phenomenon," a sort of prophet, or, again, as Ernst Gundolf wrote in 1922, "the judge of our period." In a second phase, he was read essentially as a life philosopher in quest of new "values" immanent to life. In a third phase, he was assimilated to what was called existentialist philosophy, as, for example, in Karl Jaspers's two books of 1935 and 1936, *Vernunft und Existenz* and *Nietzsche: Einführung in das Verständnis seines Philosophierens*. In none of these three approaches characteristic of the first third of the century,[7] however, did the accent lie on that which is most characteristic of Nietzsche's thought throughout, namely, the place it assigns the artist. Here is one of his best known aphorisms on art gathered in the book that he was unable (or unwilling) to complete himself, *Der Wille zur Macht*: "Art as the single superior counterforce against all will to negation of life, art as . . . anti-Nihilist *par excellence*" [*WM*, no. 853].[8] Thus art is the "counter-movement" to nihilism, to what Nietzsche deemed the decadent forms of humanity (*WM*, no. 794). As for the artist, here is what Nietzsche says about him: "The phenomenon 'artist' is still the most *perspicuous* . . . from that position to scan the *basic instincts of power*, of nature, etc.! Also of religion and morals!" (*WM*, no. 797).[9] Art, as individually determined in the form of the artist, says more about religion, in particular, than religion itself does. At the very beginning of his career, Nietzsche wanted to found an aesthetic. His first book, *The Birth of Tragedy*, published in 1872, begins as follows: "We shall have gained much for the science of aesthetics when we have succeeded in perceiving . . . that art derives its continuous development from the duality of the Apolline and Dionysiac."[10] But this is also how Nietzsche understands his thought toward the end of his conscious life. In 1886, he declares, in the "Self-Criticism" he wrote for the reissuing of his book on tragedy: "So then, with this questionable book, my instinct, an affirmative instinct for life, turned *against* morality and invented a fundamentally opposite doctrine and valuation of life, purely artistic and *anti-Christian*."[11] This sentence provides a rather good summary of what Nietzsche wanted to accomplish between 1872 and 1886. It shows, in particular, that the Yes to life is of a "purely artistic" nature.

In the first third of the century, Nietzsche's readers largely ignored the "aesthetic" and "artistic" nature of his doctrine. Its aesthetic nature was likewise ignored in the first essays on Nietzsche to appear in the Armenian press, which reacted only to that doctrine's critique of morals as well as its anti-Christian dimension. In this, the Armenians remained faithful to the initial reception of Nietzsche in Europe. Moreover, the Armenian readers of Constantinople, students included, read Nietzsche only in French translation, and it would appear that they read, above all, translations of *The Genealogy of Morals* and *Beyond Good and Evil*. In a 1906 letter, Daniel Varuzhan wrote: "For my ideas, I prefer Byron and Nietzsche, but, for my art, I prefer Kuchag,"[12] thus opposing, in rather banal fashion, a national form (Kuchag was an "author" under whose name people had regrouped a corpus of popular poetry that was still a recent discovery early in the twentieth century) to a content that came from various currents of European thought, especially Nietzsche. It was only in 1909 that extracts from *Thus Spoke Zarathustra* saw the light in Constantinople's Armenian literary press. To the best of my knowledge, no further Western Armenian translation of Nietzsche appeared until the 1986 publication of my partial translation of *The Birth of Tragedy*.[13] For Eastern Armenians, contact with Nietzsche's work could be much more direct, because these writers studied at German universities, unlike their counterparts in Constantinople, for whom the culture of reference had always been French. That said, only one of Nietzsche's works was translated into Eastern Armenian before the war. Here too it was *Thus Spoke Zarathustra*, which appeared in Baku in 1914. The Russian Revolution and the Sovietization of Armenia called a halt to all attempts in this direction; the ban lasted for several decades.[14]

The Armenian writers of Constantinope had read Nietzsche in the years they spent in Europe. This is true, for example, of Indra,[15] and of Levon Shant. Indra is the author of a text issued in 1905 under the title *Nerashkharh* (Inner World), a major work that elaborates a complex poetic prose, with mystic accents, which does not, generally speaking, lead its reader to look for echoes of Nietzschean thought. Nevertheless, in 1986, when it became necessary for me to translate *The Birth of Tragedy*, it was to Indra that I most often turned in search of neologisms that could facilitate the task of rendering Nietzsche's German in Armenian. Let me give three examples: for the terms *Ureins* and *Einswerden*, which designate, in Nietzsche, originary unity and the act of becoming one with it, I borrowed words coined by Indra to express phenomena of the same order (*hanreut'iun, hanreanal, hamaynanal*). Similarly, neologisms invented by Indra (*khorhrtapatker, irapatker*) allowed me to translate what Nietzsche calls *Gleichnis*, the analogic image in which is inscribed the unrepresentable, that which belongs to the Dionysian world. Finally, it was yet another neologism of Indra's (*hmayap'okhut'iun*) which helped me translate what Nietzsche calls *Verzauberung*, the ecstatic transport of Dionysius' adepts. The fact that we can translate Nietzsche thanks to Indra does not, however, mean that Indra himself translated Nietzsche. Indra is not a writer who belongs to the Nietzschean sphere as read, in any case, through the lens of the aesthetic principle. We find in him none of the characteristic themes that would soon make their entry into Armenian literature: the turn back to Greece, "paganism," or historical criticism of Christianity. An absolutely original writer, Indra simply put in writing, in Armenian, a pantheistic experience he had to invent a language to express. Certain facets of Nietzschean theory helped him do so.

Levon Shant's relationship to Nietzsche was quite different.[16] The only great Armenian playwright of the twentieth century, Shant had received his higher education in Germany. He had read Nietzsche in German, given a great deal of thought to his work, and discussed him in his letters. His dramatic works are deeply marked by his familiarity with the German philosopher. Shant's first historical play, *The Ancient Gods* (1909), stages a kind of confrontation between paganism and Christianity; the "ancient gods" evoked in the title are the pagan gods, who seem to return to the Middle Ages in a period of Christian fervor by way of an unleashing of the human passions. This confrontation was plainly of Nietzschean inspiration. The most interesting feature of Shant's work is not, however, the idea of a "return" to the pagan gods. It is, rather, the fact that that work presents itself, from one end to the other, as the theater of the "will to power," a long meditation on the different types of power informed by a recurrent question: is the will to vanquish and overcome any and all propensity to the exercise of power itself a question of force and power? In the aporetic form in which I cast it, this question is typically Nietzschean.

Here, then, we have two instances of the reception of Nietzsche by writers who did not belong to the *Mehyan* circle. Let us adduce a third example, Edouard Frenghian. Frenghian was a politically committed Eastern Armenian who, in 1910, published a short book on Nietzsche, the only study of the philosopher in Armenian.[17] The book did not have much influence. Frenghian had studied philosophy in Germany with Alois Riehl (1844–1924) and refers several times to the book written by his professor, *Friedrich Nietzsche, der Künstler und Denker*, the first edition of which saw the light in 1897. According to Frenghian, "Nietzsche is the philosopher of life"; he defends "a biological point of view"; and "his conception of life is colored by Darwinist doctrine. The basic element in Nietzsche is the principle of 'the struggle for existence' and that of 'natural selection.' Life belongs to the strong, destined to triumph in this struggle for existence. At the same time, there exists a natural aristocracy." I take it for granted that these ridiculous affirmations require no comment. Frenghian also tells us that "Nietzsche raises the question of the genius, the individual genius. . . . The theory of the superman and that of the preparation of a superhuman race thus comes straight from his aristocratic radicalism, that is, from the principle of natural selection he inherited from Darwin."[18] Frenghian goes so far as to cite a remark of Elizabeth Förster-Nietzsche, Nietzsche's sister, about "creating, selecting a whole race of supermen"![19]

Frenghian also maintains that there exists a "Darwinism of the race." Constant Zarian, as we shall see, connects this "Darwinism of the race" or "aristocratic Darwinism" with the project of creating "new myths." The problem is that these two readings of Nietzsche are not entirely independent of one another. In particular, the Nazis' reception of the philosopher, even as it stood in the tradition of the vulgar reception and propagated that reception in the most shameful fashion, was also ideologically informed and guided by the "aesthetic principle," which means, here, the idea of the "formative (fictional) power of myth." When, in 1914, Oshagan wrote his sentence about the urgent need for a universal fiction, he went back to the idea of the artist as liar and creator of fictions, as elaborated by Nietzsche in fragment 853 of *The Will to Power*. He also—already—went back to the idea that art's formative or educational power came by way of the production of myth of a new kind. To be sure, he did not venture any further down this path. There is, nonetheless, an obvious consonance between his desire to produce a universal fiction to the end of collectively forming the nation, and what we have learned from other sources about the myth as power and *its implementation*:

> Myth is in no way "mythological." It is a "power," the power that is in the gathering together of the fundamental forces and orientations of an individual or a people. . . . Rosenberg interprets this power as that of the dream, as the projection of an image with which one identifies. . . . [Rosenberg is thinking] of the essence of the Germanic soul . . . in so far as it, like the Greek soul which was itself always Aryan, dreams the political . . . as *Formwillen*, the desire to form [*vouloir-former*] and the desire for form [*vouloir de la forme*] or *Gestaltung*: as *work*.[20]

These remarks by Lacoue-Labarthe encapsulate the central thrust of the 1930 book *Der Mythus des Zwanzigsten Jahrhunderts* (*The Myth of the Twentieth Century*) by Nazi ideologue Alfred Rosenberg.[21] Rosenberg, too, evokes the power of fictionalization, the "we" considered as a product of fiction, in other words, of an artistic-aesthetic activity. This is not very far from Oshagan's and Zarian's call for a new mythology, their "universal fiction," their artist's metaphysics, their dream of restoring a collective power that has obviously been lost, their "Aryan soul," and their desire-to-form (the race, the nation) as a work of art—in other words, all the themes of the "aesthetic principle" that we have examined at length. The point-for-point similarity between the terms is, at the very least, food for thought.

3

Constant Zarian was born in the Caucasus in 1885. After completing his secondary and higher education in France and Belgium, he moved to Constantinople in 1912. It was Zarian who decided to found the review *Mehyan*: he wanted to infect the Armenians with the spirit of the avant-garde movements of the day, especially Futurism. Theater was Zarian's grand passion at the time. We shall see later, when we analyze a few passages from essays he published in the review, that his project for the theater came straight from his reading of Nietzsche's *The Birth of Tragedy*. Zarian also wrote two novels. One of them, *Bancoopë yev mamut'i voskornerë* [The Pancoop and the Bones of the Mammoth], which was published in 1931–33 but never finished, is wholly autobiographical; it tells the story of the two years its author spent in Soviet Armenia between 1922 and 1924.[22] The other, published in 1943 under the title *Navë leran vray* [The Ship on the Mountain], is a novel well known to the broad reading public.[23] It relates, in the epic mode, the birth of a country. Zarian's major works, however, are the ones he calls his "travelogues"; here the author's peregrinations are transformed into a kind of grand cosmic voyage through countries and civilizations. The first of these narratives, *Ants'ordë yev ir chamban* [The Traveler and His Road], was published in serial form in the Boston monthly *Hayrenik* beginning in 1926.[24] Zarian had, from the very first, been an avid reader of Nietzsche. There are numerous, explicit references to Nietzsche's work in his texts, from his 1914 reflections on theater to the quite dogmatic expositions of his doctrine that we find in his novels, especially the 1933 *Bancoopë*. Indeed, throughout his work, Zarian falls back on Nietzschean categories to explain his vision of himself as a poet and prose writer. Here Nietzsche provides him with, all at once, a vision of the modern world, a vision of contemporary history, and a vocabulary in which to present both. Yet the situation is in fact still more complicated, since Zarian had also read Spengler in the 1920s. We find the first traces of this encounter in *The Traveler and His Road*. Putatively Nietzschean categories appear here at times in unadulterated form but, more often, in the form they take in Spengler's theory of cultures and civilizations.

Let us recall that Zarian always boasted that he had written the Manifesto published in *Mehyan* in his own hand, in French, giving it to his friends to translate. In a late interview, he says: "I went from Venice to Constantinople, where I began to write in Armenian. The best writers of my generation were in Constantinople. I founded *Mehyan* with Varuzhan, K. Parseghian, H. Kufejian, and Aharon. I was the one who wrote, in French, most of the Manifesto. Varuzhan finished it and translated it into Armenian. It was a marvelous period, a generation of artists, a splendid literary environment. Unfortunately, it came to a swift end."[25] In fact, Zarian and Varuzhan quickly fell out, as is indicated by the fact that Varuzhan left the group very early, in February 1914, and that his name does not appear in the review thereafter. Hagop Oshagan, in his monograph on Varuzhan, says that "his break with the group was not precipitated by antagonistic aesthetic positions, but by an unproductive sensitivity [on Varuzhan's part] and Zarian's rather bloated pretensions, which Kegham Parseghian and I tolerated for the simple reason that they made the review lively and innovative. We therefore accepted the posture of high priest that Zarian struck, however ridiculous it was."[26] This conflict is a chapter in literary history, but it also interests us because Zarian turned out texts in which he made open fun of Varuzhan. The first of them, entitled "Paganism?" appeared in the fourth issue of *Mehyan*. "Paganism?" takes the form of a dialogue between two characters whom Zarian calls the "Pagan" and the "Futurist." "The first time I saw the title of your review, *Mehyan*," Zarian has the Pagan, who is obviously Varuzhan, say, "I naturally assumed that you, too, would be on our side and would try to recreate the spirit of our ancestors' old religions." Thus Zarian pretends that Varuzhan was animated by a rather backward-looking, restorationist spirit, to which he opposes the idea of an art of the present and an art to come that deserves, in his view, to be called "Futurist." Indeed, he says so explicitly as early as February 1914, in an essay entitled "The Jesus of the Armenians." Those who foolishly tried to "go back to the 'old gods'" would, according to Zarian, come away from the attempt empty-handed, "for the old gods are in truth old, and dead. The very idea of a 'return' is a mark of intellectual laziness"(*Mehyan*, no. 2, 19). It so happens that Zarian admired Marinetti and wished to recreate in the Armenian world the collective movement spawned by his various manifestos. This did not, however, make Zarian a Futurist. The poetry he produced in later years never went beyond the Symbolist lyricism that he had inherited during his student years in Brussels; traces of it first make themselves felt in texts he wrote in French for Belgian literary reviews. In 1910, during his first stay in Constantinople, he had already published a manifesto, "The Crazy Wills," written in French and signed by both Zarian and his friend Hrand Nazarian. It is the only known manifestation of Futurism in his writings.[27] More characteristically, it is in the "Nietzschean style" that Zarian expresses his own version of the aesthetic principle and his metaphysics of the artist in his 1914 essays and articles.

Twelve years later, in the 1926 *The Traveler and his Road*, long after the death of Varuzhan, Zarian felt the need to revive his polemic against the Dionysian or paganism. I shall not go into the context. Zarian had to define poetry and the essence of the poet. "A poet," he writes, "is a man who dances on a tightrope. A tightrope artist."[28] But he is not satisfied with saying just that. He advances the idea that the poet is essentially a tightrope artist in opposition to Varuzhan, the representative of poetic paganism, who is brought on scene here in the form of a billy goat. "And while, up in the air, he is recalling the names of the saints and, holding angels by the arm, celebrating a mass for the universe in his own magnificent way, down below, someone else, wearing a wild animal skin and a mask with a goat's beard, terrifies, with the gestures of a creature from hell, the evil spirits, unbelievers, and all who jealously give others the evil eye."[29] Of course, the goat described in this manner is Dionysus. The passage is unbelievably invidious. Zarian needs this opposition in order to define himself. Astonishingly, his fierce, fanatic hostility to Varuzhan is cast in Nietzschean terms: he borrows the image and character traits of the tightrope artist from Nietzsche's *Zarathustra*. Tightrope artist vs. billy goat! In *Zarathustra*, the tightrope artist is the man who walks down the taut cord that leads to the "race of supermen."[30] He is the man who negotiates the dangerous "passage" (*ants'k'* in Armenian). Zarian describes his own destiny as a passage, a walk on the edge of the abyss. The Traveler (*ants'ord*), as emblematic figure, is this tightrope artist, this "passer."

Let us now turn back to the year 1914. Zarian published a series of essays in *Mehyan* under the general title "For Art." The titles of these essays are, in the order of their publication, "Creation, Madness, Heroism," "The Jesus of the Armenians," "The Theater," and "Paganism?" Zarian's constant preoccupation in these first years of his career was the theater. In his *Mehyan* essay on the theater, he announces a "unanimist" theater, whose model he finds in Greek tragedy. By "unanimist,"[31] a term he takes from Jules Romains, he means a totalizing theater, conceived as capable of bringing the whole people together, a synthesis of all the arts with universal aspirations. He says as much later, in 1922, in *Bardzravank*, a review that, like *Mehyan*, was published in Istanbul for a few months as, to some extent, the continuation of its predecessor. Zarian there describes the theater as "the synthesis of all the arts," adding that it is the "unanimist plot that takes place deep in the soul and exhibits the complexity of a total vision"; it presents itself as an "idealized mode of life, woven with the symbolic motifs of the possible and the real."[32] The Greeks' tragic theater, he goes on, is a model of such unanimist action, since, "derived from religion and life, it always maintained its religious character." Let us acknowledge that this need for a unanimist theater stemmed from the will to struggle against the real or imagined threat of fragmentation said to be characteristic of our age. Zarian thus repeats, in his own fashion, the theme of wholeness and fragmentation that we have already seen in Varuzhan and Oshagan, and that can also be seen in passages in Nietzsche on Wagner. What sets him apart from the others is the fact that, while he, too, wanted to see a renaissance of Greek theater, this renaissance coincided in some sort, for him, with the advent of a new religion. He conflates the two, as Stefan George and his disciples did in the same period, in their interpretation of both Nietzsche the man and his oeuvre.

Thus Zarian, in his 1914 essay on the theater, envisions the poet marching toward "the god," to whom will be proffered "a new song . . . before the new altar"; and he imagines the possibility that "one day new choruses may surround him." In producing a formulation and a project of this kind, Zarian plainly has Nietzschean descriptions of Menadic choruses, Dionysius' ecstatic devotees, and their hymns in mind. He also repeats a thesis popularized by Nietzsche, which has it that the theater was born of the odes to Dionysius. He even believes that Dionysius' altar stood in the center of the theater; for, he says, "the gods dwelt there." Thus, borrowing from Nietzsche the ideal of a modern revival or repetition of Greek tragedy, he wishes to restage this religious origin of the theater among his own people, in an uncertain future. Indeed, this is the task he sets himself: "If we attentively observe the present period of experimentation, we can happily confirm that the new Temple will be erected in a not-too-distant future and that new tragic plots will relight art's lofty flame in people's souls. Out of the lyric poetry that the Symbolist school brought to its zenith, there will inevitably emerge the quintessential *motif* of cosmic tragedy, *THE SONG THAT SPAWNS TRAGEDY*" (*Mehyan*, no. 4, 53; Zarian's emphasis).[33] Zarian is very plainly alluding to the Dionysian chorus and the Greek ode, which gave birth to "tragedy" and theater on a historical reading that was not Nietzsche's alone, but whose import Zarian had grasped thanks to Nietzsche. Zarian of course never realized this project of creating a "dithyrambic ode."[34] What is interesting, however, is his ambition to repeat and rediscover the origin: once again, art at the origin of religion!

How can art be the source of religion? This is possible because, in Varuzhan's formulation, the aesthetic principle presides over the erection of the gods; in Zarian's formulation, because the erected god is a *theatrical god*. The religious bond, the one that founds the human community and, at the origin, brings man into existence, is already a theatrical bond. This thesis is in accordance with the aesthetic principle, which each member of this "school" repeats in his own fashion. It is, nonetheless, a surprising thesis. It explains, in any event, Zarian's determination to create a theater of the origin, a theater before the theater. This generation of writers was obsessed by religious alienation, that is, by a form of alienation which it conceived of as a catastrophic dissolution of the original bond, which could obviously only have been religious. The Armenian word for *religion* is *kron*. Alishan, in his 1893 book *The Armenians' Ancient Faith or Pagan Religion*, suggests that the word is etymologically linked to *krel*, which means "carry," "support." The Latin word *religio* no doubt refers to an *original bond*. As for the Armenian word *kron*, it refers to an original "support."[35] Varuzhan conceived of this support as a stele. Zarian conceives of it as a stage! That is why the erected god is a "theatrical god." But who is this theatrical god? Is it Dionysius, as everything would seem to indicate? Dionysius, the masked god, the god of the theater?

Before answering, we must recall that this generation of writers uses Nietzsche for its own purposes, after all, in order to rethink the situation in which it finds itself: in order to rethink the original bond or support *by way of the dissolution of the bond or the collapse of the support.* This dissolution and collapse comprise its starting point, its primary experience; aestheticization is what they oppose to it. There was not enough art, according to these writers. One might imagine that their experience was not different from that of the Greeks, for whom Dionysius, the masked god, was also the *dismembered* god, that is to say, the divine figure who served as their representation of *disintegration*.

Who is this theatrical god? By a strange reversal, Zarian calls him "Jesus." In his essay on the theater, he describes the birth of the Church by establishing a parallel with the birth of Greek theater. It is in this essay that he writes: "There, surrounded by his choirs, Jesus was the leading performer, the most profound of the tragic masks"(*Mehyan*, no. 4, 50). Zarian here clearly identifies Jesus with Dionysius, his tragic mask, and his choruses. He carries this identification so far as to say: "[The Church] had recourse to virtually the same means employed by Greek tragedy" (ibid.). The birth of a religion—the Christian religion in this case—is here described in the same terms as the birth of the theater. We plainly have to do with a theatrical god, the leading, and the greatest, character in his own tragedy. What is more, this god bestrides a stage that he himself has erected. He finds himself on it from the outset. He is the one who created the scene at the same time as he created his role, in other words, himself. In his essay of February 1914 entitled "The Jesus of the Armenians," Zarian therefore writes: "Jesus is the supreme example of the genuine creator who is also a self-creator" (*Mehyan*, no. 2, 18).[36] At the same time, this purely theatrical god is, in Zarian's description of him, fitted out with all the attributes of the will to power: "To master oneself and gain control of all the virtues and mysteries that are a part of one's being is to become a universal force, a god"(ibid.). There is nothing surprising about this, because this theatrical god, this figure of all figures, is the artist par excellence, the prototype of the artist: "He can be understood only through aesthetic empathy, the penetration of the artist" (ibid., 19). The description of the theatrical god closes with a touch that makes this pure incarnation of the will to power the incarnation of art as well: "Jesus is Art." A prototype of the artist and an incarnation of art, he is the figure par excellence, the figure that will seal the fate of a people, his own, in its future life, intellectual as well as spiritual. This theatrical figure is the place of origin, the "support" and "bearer" of the origin. The bearer of the origin, the essence of religion, is by nature artistic and wholly theatrical. The idea that art is the founding principle of religion can hardly be pushed further than this, at least in the form in which it was revived by Nietzsche. The primordial figure is his own support, but he is also supposed to support the collectivity that makes him its god. Thus we find all the determinations of the aesthetic principle united in a very strange constellation. Zarian is obviously thinking in opposition to Varuzhan here, against the supposedly Dionysian Varuzhan, and he mobilizes against him, as a last recourse, purely Nietzschean resources. Of course, in this incarnation of art—in fact, of great art—there lurks a fantasy of self-creation. What is striking is the fact that this rigorous phantasmagoria of a self-created figure finds expression in the theatrical form of the god who erects himself upon a stage that he has himself erected, a god who imitates no one but himself so that everyone, *imitating him* (that is, imitating his imitation), can become what he is. Thus Zarian himself, in his own fashion, utters the "truth" of autoscopic mimicry (of *mimesis*).

In all of this, we hear the last echo of the philological invention of the previous century, mythology, taken so seriously by the writers of the *Mehyan* group that they had even come to dream aloud about mythopoetic power, that is to say, the need to restore, by means of art, the power that presided over the birth of myth and mythological religion. As far as this point is concerned, Varuzhan, notwithstanding the crucial assumption of mourning in his work and Zarian's hatred of him, does not substantially differ from Zarian. His writings show that he could even, at times, abandon all restraint, cease to be the poet of mourning, and become, quite simply, the ideologue of power, the power of myth, the power of art, and therefore, by an ineluctable necessity, of political power as well.[37] What perhaps characterizes Zarian and differentiates him from both Varuzhan and Oshagan is the fact that he moves entirely within the dimension of *power* and knows nothing at all about mourning (whether what is involved is the mourning "of philology" is of little importance here). It is this which drives him to the worst extreme, an extreme that I have so far been at pains to keep in the dark. Yet we are duty-bound to quote him, even if I do so with a certain reluctance. We are duty-bound to cite the essay of February 1914. We are duty-bound to evoke the racism that is on a continuum (or is it a break?) with the racialized thought that comes straight from nineteenth-century philology. Here is the passage in question:

> Jesus is a preeminent example of the genuine creator who is also a self-creator. He is the man of terrible battle, a battle he fought with himself. With a strange, magnificent effort, he annihilated, purged, put to death that which constituted the weakness of his blood, soul, and body: SEMITISM.

He was the first to grasp, with outstanding clairvoyance, the danger represented by the Semitic poison that was clotting his veins, exhausting his muscles, diminishing his mental capabilities, enveloping his heart, and filling his soul with apathy. The Aryan ideal was the first heavenly ray to enlighten his mind, opening up before him the emerald-spangled, bright-gold path that, as he knew full well, led to Golgotha.

To overcome oneself and master all the virtues and mysteries that one harbors within oneself is to become a universal force, is to become a god.

From the day he freed himself from the depravities of his race, this giant of a man became a fighter for an ideal.

The Semite never has an ideal. He has practical goals, but never has a dream. The Semite does not know infinity (Philo of Alexandria); he waits for a God, but does not seek him out.

The Semitic race is an inferior race. It is effeminate and materialistic (Otto Weininger).

The Semite does not soar. His is an uncreative race lacking genius, fearful of mystery and vision. The Semite knows how to imitate and repeat and grasps things easily, but never feels the music of the universe; he is a satirist with a lame soul.

Jesus is the anti-Jew. (*Mehyan*, no. 2, 18)

This is, manifestly, a profession of faith in Aryanism. But is it that and that alone? Do we have, here, a whole poetic, artistic, religious, and political project, the seduction of mythological religion, a whole program for a modern rehearsal of ancient tragedy in the process of being born, the will to return to the origin of religion in art, a revival of Nietzsche's formulas about power, affirmation, and the "artistic" nature of man, with "Semitism" acting simply as a foil and "the Aryan ideal" as an aspiration? We can see, at any rate, that Zarian's Jesus is not very far removed from the "Aryan Jesus" promoted by Stuart Chamberlain. Unsurprisingly, Chamberlain, the proto-Nazi who adored Wagner, hated Nietzsche from the bottom of his heart.[38] But mythopoetic power was obviously an Aryan "power," if it is true that its absolute contrary is the "impotence" of the Semite, his incapacity to create, inability to soar, wickedness, ignorance of the divine, inferiority, effeminacy, and materialism. Jesus is the proto-artist, the divine man who was able to discover within himself the power of the mythopoetic, the very power of art (that is the defining characteristic of art for this generation: the will-to-form as œuvre, nationalization as aestheticization). It is because Jesus is the proto-artist that he is "the anti-Jew" par excellence. Need we comment further? One more question: is there anything whatsoever that can be called Nietzschean in all this?

4

I have so far chosen to restrict myself to the year 1914 and texts published in *Mehyan*, in order to isolate the common core out of which the œuvres of the writers of this group developed. Now I need to add a section, the last, whose aim is briefly to indicate how the twisted evocation of Nietzsche, linked to the Aryanization of his thought, evolved in Zarian's later work.

In his unfinished novel of 1931–33, *The Pancoop and the Bones of the Mammoth*, Zarian revisits the first years of Soviet Armenian history, taking his personal experience as a guide (let us recall that he lived in Armenia between 1922 and 1924 as a guest professor of European literature). The novel is basically structured around two characters: an orphan who gradually rises through the ranks of the Communist Party, and Zarian himself, an Armenian intellectual come from nowhere, called "Iberian" in the novel. This Iberian expresses his views about the future of the Armenians and Armenia in Nietzschean accents. One long quotation will suffice to show how:

> In the present case, it means that we must revalue all our values, be anew [*vera-linel*], exist anew [*nora-goyanal*], put ourselves on new foundations [*verahastatvel*]. You're going to ask me how. Let me tell you right away. To begin with, to the myth of the divine-man, "'tormented on the cross and suffering with love,'" we must oppose the man-god, radiating light and strength, the pinnacle of worldly achievement. To an abstract, dualistic conception of the universe, we must oppose a naturalistic, free unity, self-contained and self-sufficient, the will to power [*tirapetakan kamk'ë*]. To the race of the "'servants and children of God,'" we must oppose that of the emancipated and the emancipators, who see in God the highest power that they themselves are capable of creating, to which they may submit, if they wish, or against which they may struggle, heads held high, manfully, without womanish emotion, without quailing, without prayer—because these god-makers participate in his divine nature and can embrace the universe with the same arms of fire, recognizing in it a musical expression of their own self. To feelings of dependence and need, these new men will oppose a feeling of capability and self-sufficiency. To the idea of equality, that of difference, distance, hierarchy [*kargapetut'iun*], nobility. To the idea of socialism, that of an individualism that has reached the highest level of spiritual development. To the demand for love, happiness, peace, and the need for consolation, they will oppose heroic disdain, the iron law of the immaculately pure will and absolute action. And, against providential conceptions of the world, they will pit their tragic conception of the world, for which man is by himself amid the chaos of nature and the elemental powers and becomes his own savior, bending his own heart and brain to his will. Ah, to reject, to refuse to accept that economistic, pancoopical creature, that partisan ant who is not the master of his fate, who has fallen from his throne into the dust and trots after history's and society's cart. To reject all that and assume all of one's responsibilities instead, barring the way to despair and weakness, reinforcing and arming the soul. Yesterday they were saying "'brother'" and "'Father,'" today they say "'citizen'" and "'comrade.'" Whose brother, whose comrade? The new man, the one we want, must have neither hope nor expectations. A self-

contained planet, the beginning and the end conflated inside him, a rock, a mountain-peak, endowed with his own strengths and weaknesses. Everyone manning his post in the battle and combat; everyone a peculiar value, a quality, a life sui generis, a pitiless solitude. A power that refuses to enter into communication with others or achieve self-understanding, refuses to become a " 'comrade' " or " 'brother,' " refuses to feel equal. And this not out of the arrogance typical of common creatures, but out of respect for other individuals. The powerful individual is the pioneer of absolute justice and unrelenting truth, and his relations to others can unfold only on clear grounds, where there is crookedness neither of mind nor of heart, nor cunning, nor pursuit of petty personal interests—but, rather, endless spiritual ascent, rank, cosmos, hierarchy, and gigantic, sunlike spiritual beings: a race of far-seeing Masters, self-fashioned creatures who do not take, but, rather, give the light and meaning of their strength. What we want, and want because we know it is possible, is the pre-Christian man who reached, with the priest-kings, the level of enduring existence. That world in which nature was not yet nature, nor spirit spirit, in which there were neither objects nor forms, but only forces. In which life was, in every one of its moments, a heroic necessity, replete with works, symbols, commands, magical and ritual gestures. (*Bancoopë*, 305–06)

Once again, the vocabulary is Nietzschean; but, once again, I am not certain that the "thought," the profound motivation behind this speech (which Iberian delivers to a sect made up of his followers) is equally Nietzschean. As I have already noted, however, the will to a formative power by way of the production of a new myth is an integral part of the "aesthetic principle"; it cannot even be called a perverted dimension of it. We want to make of our own nation "a race of masters"; we want to form "individuals" of a new type within a "hierarchized" society, individuals full of "heroism," of "magical and ceremonial gestures." Is this not, again, the expression of an "Aryanizing" project? For good measure, Zarian interprets the common, familiar theory of the ethnogenesis of the Armenians by way of a claim that the conquerors of the sixth century B.C. (Armens who had migrated from Greece and Thrace at the beginning of the first millennium before our era, on this theory) "constituted the noble warrior class and the royal family, because they were not only brave, godlike people, but also possessed the supreme religious wisdom and spiritual maturity that compels the peoples' respect and implicit obedience. The Armens rebuilt the ruined country; they put the Hattians to work and ruled over them. . . . To call the Armens back to life among us—that is our goal" (ibid., 306). This pseudohistorical fantasy backed up by a racist utopia is a period product. It is quite clear that it has nothing Nietzschean about it, the lexical similarities notwithstanding. Yet this is how Europe understood Nietzsche at the time, deeming Nietzschean even the rejection of "that economistic, pancoopical creature, that partisan ant who is not the master of his fate." Such, if Zarian is to be believed, are the typical features of the type of people created by the communist world. Of course, the paradox of a fantasy of this sort resides in the fact that the Armenians were a melange from their inception. They came into being in the form of a mixture between "god-like" Armens and the subjugated, unproductive "Hattian" tribes, a race of "slaves," needless to say. "Unhappily," the preponderance of the Hattians over the centuries ultimately led to the imposition of the name "Hay" on the country and its inhabitants. In other words, the "slave mentality" that triumphed elsewhere in the world triumphed here, too. Hence Zarian dreams of a world in which "[the Armenian] can rebuild his country in conformity with the idea of it that he has in his original soul, free of all mixture." Where is the essence of this pure soul free of all mixture to be found, if the fact is that the mixture was there from the start? The will to power is here a will to purification or, more precisely, self-purification. In this case, the "foreign," "impure" element of this soul "free of all mixture" is "within us"; it cannot be ascribed to some place outside. We know only too well where these dreams of metaphysical purification repeatedly led in the last century.

How will this self-purification come about? Naturally, by way of a "sacrifice"! In a long passage (*Bancoopë*, 299–306), Iberian explains to his dumbfounded listeners the essence of the pagan rite that consist of sacrificing animals, a rite that, among the Armenians, continues to exist alongside Christian beliefs. "The supreme life wisdom consists, not in separating spirit from matter, but, on the contrary, in locating spirit in matter and the world, where it's naturally at home." Thus it was through the sacrifice of animals that the Armenians expressed their "understanding of life," since "the animals . . . are not outside the Armenian people's individuality, but live with it, forming one and the same body and soul with it. . . . [The Armenian people's] supreme wish is that their hearts should beat in unison with theirs; they want to be united with the flow of their blood, the sensations of their flesh, their brains, lungs, and semen, in which they experience the limits of the law and a flight that soars endlessly upwards. That is why the powerful, terrible blow of the sacrificial knife is an expression of a boundless love eonian enough to encompass the universe, because, in the final analysis, the sacrificial victim is the one who offers the sacrifice"(ibid., 302). The whole of this passage purports to elaborate a non-Christian vision of the world, in which sacrifice would be the central expression of unity or unification with the world. Zarian, however, goes on to consider a second aspect of the matter, in direct relation with this "theory of sacrifice" of a metaphysical cast. The second aspect is altogether unexpected: "Armenian blood has flowed copiously on Armenian soil, the sacrifice[39] has been offered up time and again, and now the time has come when, at the price of a supreme effort and unremitting, exhausting labor, the miracle of radiance and color has to flower from that blood, forge the new race, and revive the new individual"(ibid.). To be sure, it is a question, this time, of the blood of "the one who offers the sacrifice" as the "sacrificial victim," but it is nevertheless clear that what is realized by means of this blood is self-purification; it is self-purification which will give rise to the new race. Self-purification is thus the result of a self-sacrifice. The logic of this passage may be difficult to follow, in part because of the usual paradox informing all thinking about sacrifice, but also because Zarian suddenly introduces a new theme, that of the blood the Armenians have shed on their own soil. All appearances are that this blood has to be understood as sacrificial blood (which is to say, as well, as the product of a metaphorical process), so that it can be assimilated to the logic of the "one who sacrifices as sacrificial victim." If Zarian is talking about the blood shed during the Catastrophe (and all indications are that he is, even if his intention is concealed or unconscious), may I confess, in my turn, that I find this type of reasoning, in a word, simply shameful? Even if it is true that every sacrifice is ultimately self-sacrifice (that proposition, too, should be treated with caution) and therefore self-purification, the Catastrophe (here, I am speaking in my own name) is precisely the unique human event with respect to which the discourse of sacrifice exhausts its resources and butts up against its limits. It must be added that the Catastrophe remains strangely absent from Zarian's œuvre.[40] It is true that, in *The Genealogy of Morals*, Nietzsche envisages self-sacrifice as self-purification when he writes that "the extent of an 'advance' is even measured according to the scale of the sacrifice required; the mass of humanity sacrificed to the flourishing of a single *stronger* species of men—now that *would be* progress,"[41] but he did so, for his part, in the middle of a passage on historiographical method, and, there again, the tone is plainly deconstructive.

What is perhaps more interesting (and this will be the last point we consider here) is the use to which Zarian puts the Nietzschean category of "nihilism." He does so in the framework of an attempt to produce a vision of the historical world (with features borrowed from Spengler's *Decline of the West*) within which it can seem possible that the future of his people will bring with it transcendence of the "economistic, Pan-Coopical creature," a resurgence of the religious, that is, of the powers of art, and, finally, an explanation for the misery of the present, the grip communism has on the country. At the same time, however, Zarian's effort has to be understood as a desperate attempt to open up a space in which the writer, the "traveler" through spiritual worlds, and the poet in exile (Zarian never ceased to regard himself as such) can find his place, reveal his "origin" and destiny, and justify his existence as artist. To account for "Bolshevism," the height of decadence and of the failure of the European tradition, in the form of a historical necessity—which is what Zarian does—is to display a typically nihilist attitude:

> The Bolsheviks are, unbeknown to themselves, the last representatives of Christian ideology. They represent the race of those rebellious slaves who destroyed the temples of Pythagoras in Greece, ridiculed the sublime knowledge of the sect of Orpheus, and put Christianity in its place. . . . They were unaware that, at the behest of an ineluctable destiny, they were clearing a path for the coming of the new man. To that extent, yes, the work carried out by the Bolsheviks was necessary.
>
> To attain the deepest depths of failure. (*Bancoopë*, 274)

The turning point will come later, after this two-thousand-year-long parenthesis, and as a consequence of it. The task of the individual—but perhaps one should rather say "of the poet"—is to be present at this turning-point, realize it in himself, and announce it to the world at large. The historical reflection on nihilism culminates in a reflection on the essence of poetry and art in general as exiled realities. The poet himself is in this sense an exile. This exile, which must henceforth be understood as a universal phenomenon, a parenthesis in the history of the world, is an ordeal in "nonbeing." Nevertheless, this ordeal of exile is itself necessary, since this ordeal alone can ensure that a renewal of "being" will become possible one day. This transcendence of nihilism is itself quite obviously bound up with the theme of sacrifice:

> At the outer limit, where nonexistence ends and birth has yet to begin, in the moment that lies between being and nonbeing, is a place of terror, of dread. . . . Fear and terror vanish from our minds to the extent that we are travelers born to cross borders and break through to new horizons. . . . In the life of peoples, just as in that of individuals, there are times [shrjan] when it is imperative to say " 'no' " to everything in the name of life. To alter, to overthrow [shrjel] the dominion of the grave. To chop off a part of our inner being as if it were a sacrificial lamb so as to save the rest, where the myth still lives. Sometimes history forces a people to migrate from one part of the planet to another, to follow the sun, to reduplicate its movement, to make a revolution [shrjel]. It seems to me that there are also moments when life's supreme requirements dictate that we accomplish that same migration within ourselves, following our inner sun in order to accomplish our own secret revolution [shrjan]. That moment has come for certain peoples, and they are now awaiting the true revolutionaries, those prepared to traverse, and capable of traversing, the region of fear, of passing from nonbeing to being.[42]
> (Bancoopë, 302–03)

The connections forged here between an extreme form of exile, an exile on the edge of the world amid a total forgetting of "being"; the need to cross the no-man's-land of nonbeing; and the firm resolution to endure the experience of forgetting as a poet rooted in the migratory, "solar" destiny of his people: this is, ultimately, what rescues Zarian to some extent, in my view, from his intolerable declarations and pompous prophecies. Yet, here too, the part to be saved at the price of a sacrificial act is the part in which "the myth still lives," that is, the Aryan (or artistic) part of ourselves!

In conclusion, it will have been understood that my aim, apart from denunciation of the kind of Aryanism characteristic of Zarian, was to grasp the moment in which the aesthetic principle yields to an unembellished racism. Where does this moment lie? Should we look for it in "aristocratic Darwinism"? Can we discern it in the fiction of the people as a work of art, which is the very definition of "national-aestheticism"? Is it present from the outset, in the announcement and expectation of a new mythology? Or even earlier, in the philological definition of religion as mythological? These questions are plainly appropriate in the case of the *Mehyan* group, Zarian's participation in which was anything but an aberration. But they are also appropriate to the whole of the European adventure, the one that led from the discovery of mythology to National Socialism. No attempt to determine Nietzsche's place in this European trajectory can sidestep them. What are we to make of the affirmation of art? Is it to be confined to playing a denunciatory, deconstructive role? Or should it be put back within the circuit of power, which is to be affirmed in its turn? The distinction between art as mourning and art as founding fiction is of no help here. The founding fiction and, with it, the whole system of the aesthetic principle are sustained by mourning. Even Varuzhan deferred, in this respect, to the pontification of the would-be founder of a religion. He did so despite the fact that he was the only member of his generation to try to come to terms (in his poetic work) with termination and disaster as such, that is, with the end of religion that is inscribed in the philological invention of religion. This is something Zarian never did and never dreamed of doing. But then we need to make another distinction, not, this time, between mourning and the founding fiction, but between mourning and itself: we need to trace a line of demarcation inside mourning itself. We have to learn to free catastrophic mourning, the mourning of mourning, from all the confusions to which it complacently lends itself. We have to learn to save mourning, in this way, from itself. Similarly, despite the immense efforts to salvage Nietzsche to which we have been witness for more than half a century now, I am convinced that the distinction we need cuts through his œuvre itself: the distinction that will allow us to interpret art, at one and the same time, as the affirmative power of denunciation (especially of the aesthetic principle itself) and as the negative power of the lie, open to every imaginable kind of manipulation.

—*Translated by G. M. Goshgarian*

Translations

Excerpts from Nineteenth-Century Works of Philology and Ethnography

As I announced earlier, I bring together here, in the first of these appendices, translations of extracts from books and prefaces that illustrate the archeological and ethnographic moments of the century-long history of the ethnographic nation, which began to take shape in Europe with the philological revolution of the early nineteenth century. The following selections are included:

1. Lucas Injijean, preface to his *Storagrut'iun hin Hayastaneayts': Ëst hin yev ëst mijin daru anvaneal zhamanakagrats* [Description of Ancient Armenia, After the Famous Chroniclers of Antiquity and the Middle Ages] (Venice, 1822).

2. Khachatur Abovean, preface to his *Verk' Hayastani* [Wounds of Armenia] (1841; published Tblisi, 1858).

3. Mkrtich Emin, the opening pages of his *Vebk' hnuyn Hayastani* [Epic Narratives of Ancient Armenia] (Moscow, 1850), which I take from *Mkrtich Emini yerkasirut'iunnerë Hayots lezvi, grakanut'ean yev patmut'ean masin (1840–1855 t't')* [Mkrtich Emin's Works on the Armenian Language and Armenian Literature and History (1840–1855)], a volume edited by Grigor Khalateants and published in Moscow in 1898.

4. Karekin Servantsdeants, an extract from his *Grots' u Brots'* [Written in a Rush] (Istanbul, 1874).

5. Karekin Servantsdeants, an extract from his *Manana* [Manna] (Istanbul, 1876).

6. Ghevond Alishan, the introduction and first chapter of his *Hin havatk' kam het'anosakan kronk' Hayots* [The Armenians' Ancient Faith or Pagan Religion] (Venice, 1893, 1895).

7. Manuk Abeghean, the opening pages of his *Der armenische Volksglaube* [Armenian Popular Beliefs] (Leipzig, 1899).[1]

8. Hagop Oshagan, an extract from his monograph on Servantsdeants found in volume 4 of Oshagan's *Hamapatker arevmtahay grakanut'ean* [Panorama of Western Armenian Literature] (Jerusalem, 1956).

The selections from Injijean and Emin have been translated from classical Armenian. The preface to *Wounds of Armenia* has been translated from the dialect of Kanaker, which Abovean used in both his preface and the novel itself (with, obviously, flashes of literary Eastern Armenian, then in its early stages). The passages taken from Servantsdeants and Alishan have been translated from literary Western Armenian (with archaic touches in both writers, especially in Alishan, who, even at the end of his life, had yet to make up his mind to write the way everyone else did and stubbornly continued to use a Western Armenian laced with classical Armenian, known as *grabar*). Finally, the extract from Abeghean's doctoral thesis has been translated from German.

The interest of all these selections lies in the fact that they afford us a glimpse of philology in its beginnings. National ethnography is announced in Abovean in the form of a project. It is realized from 1874 on, with Servantsdeants and the first publication of an extract from the popular epic *David of Sasun*. National philology appears for the first time with Injijean in 1822, in its archeological form. The discovery of myth and mythology is registered for the first time in the teaching of Mkrtich Emin at the Moscow Lazarian Academy, as well as in Emin's 1850 book. In each of these cases, philology has, since the period in question, accumulated works, modified the prevailing theses, altered its definitions, and deepened its study of the texts and analysis of the oral narratives. Our aim, in each of the areas considered (mythology, religion, archeology, oral narrative), is to show philology at work *in statu nascendi*. What I say here applies, in particular, to Mkrtich Emin, whose definitions of *vep*, *zruyts'*, and *ar'aspel* were taken up, re-examined, and profoundly reworked by Abeghean some fifty years later, in a way that is more closely attuned to modern sensibilities (which Abeghean acquired in Germany) as regards the mythic oral narrative and as regards Moses of Khoren's history as well, on which both Emin and Abeghean after him base their analyses.

All endnotes are mine, unless otherwise indicated.

I

LUCAS INJIJEAN
Preface to Description of Ancient Armenia

(Venice, 1822)

Motivated by a sublime passion, we have undertaken to examine the archeology [*hnagrut'iun*] of the world of the Armenians at greater length than that of other nations, as is the duty of a patriot, by culling information about our own geography from a large number of detailed works by ancient writers, classing it systematically according to province and locality, and rounding it out with a description [*storagrut'iun*] of each locality. For proper archeology not only describes the past [*hnakhosel*], but also identifies its auctorial sources.

We approached this task too lightly on our first attempt and encountered two major problems as a result. Initially, we decided to select, not everything that the ancient geographer had cited . . . but only that which seemed necessary for a modern geographer seeking to provide archeological place descriptions [*hnagrel*]. Thus contenting ourselves with what seemed essential, we often omitted to note what ancient authors said. Secondly, with the aim of simplifying our task, we began to mix descriptions [*sdoragrel*] of the old and the new. However, on due reflection, we understood that we would not be able successfully to complete the task of establishing the relationship between modern and ancient sites and then placing them side by side so as to facilitate comparison and correlation, and that it would be even more difficult to make a satisfying comparison of the divisions, regions, and borders of the old provinces with those of the new ones.

We therefore decided to take up this work again, but with new principles. This time, we unhesitatingly presented the archeological description of Armenia by itself. We made a fresh start and broadened our investigation somewhat, culling all the necessary information from works by ancient authors. This time, too, however, our study remained incomplete, because the citations we collected were too brief: we left out too many details that later seemed important and even indispensable to us. The human mind, for as long as it has not been confronted with diverse authors' views and has not learned to approach every text with caution, is inclined to follow common opinion in dealing with documents [*p'astivk'*] and to consider a single account sufficient, namely, the one it has to hand at any given time.

The need to make good this new insufficiency has led to new delays. To complete the descriptions of many sites, we have frequently had to turn back to ancient works, collate the various manuscript versions at our disposal, and clear up points that seemed questionable. Thus, for a single site, we have often gone laboriously from text to text for days on end, and have been obliged to correct and explain many toponyms found in Greek, Latin, and Syriac sources.

The resulting mental exhaustion and all these considerable problems have taught us once again, were there any need, the secret of the truth, which we have come to understand thanks to experience, application, and common sense. Which truth do we have in mind? First, philological endeavor is such that it has in fact only just begun when one considers it completed. Second, in all branches of knowledge, it must not be supposed that we can satisfy ourselves with a partial result before we have grasped the whole picture.

With that, we have explained the course of our research. We have tried to be candid so as not to be found wanting in the judgment of the philological tribunal, should that tribunal find errors and defects in our work that have escaped our attention. We may now, confidently commending our work to the archeologists' indulgence, move on to the description of Greater Armenia. We shall leave for another occasion the description of Ancient Armenia in the order and style that modern geography calls for. Again, we shall leave Lesser Armenia aside. Finally, we shall also put off the description of the six regions that were long ago overrun by our conquerors. We lack the strength to carry out all these tasks at present.

2

KHACHATUR ABOVEAN
Preface to Wounds of Armenia

(written 1841; published Tblisi, 1858)

King Croesus of Lydia was deserted in battle by his armies, loved ones, friends, and generals when Cyrus conquered the whole world, capturing Croesus' country as well. Croesus, who had grown up in palaces of priceless pearls and gems and considered himself the luckiest man on the face of the earth, was now at the mercy of a Persian foot soldier. He fled, his heart in his mouth, in hopes of saving his skin, at least, but the Persian caught up with him. The soldier's sword flashed over the king's head, everything went black before his eyes and, though he had not yet surrendered his head to the blade, he knew that death was upon him and, then and there, would carry off his soul. Just as he was resolving that his *own* saber should run through his heart so that he would not be slain by the foe—just as the soldier was raising his sword—the king's only son, seeing that his father was about to die, abruptly broke the twenty years' seal on his tongue; his tongue was loosened, and his heart, after a twenty years' silence, cried out for the first time. "Villain, who do you think you are killing? Hold back your sword! Do you not see that the man standing before you is Croesus, lord of the earth?"

The soldier's hands slackened and the king escaped with his head. His son, mute for twenty years, had saved his father.

The wretched prince of the blood had lived all these years, yet neither his parents' great love, nor their pity and their desire to hear his voice just once so that their hearts might be eased, nor glory and grandeur, nor honors and authority, nor treasures and wealth, nor the love of the world and its pleasures, nor the affection and agreeable conversation of countless loved ones and friends, nor the voice of the clouds, nor the sweet music of rivers and birds had, all those years, ever moved his heart to emit the slightest sound. Yet, when he was confronted with his father's, his beloved father's death, his heart cast off its fetters, his long-bound tongue broke its bonds, and his mouth, once sealed shut, uttered his pain. At death's door, his father, who had longed for this moment, heard his son's voice. The listener's heart burns even today at the thought that it was filial love which smashed nature's chains and reduced them to dust.

It has been not twenty, but thirty years and more, my dear father and my beloved nation, that my heart has been burning, has been consumed with emotion. Tears and grief have not quit my eyes day or night, plaints and laments have never quit my lips. O my countrymen and kin, if only I could tell you my thoughts and my heart's wish and then go to my grave in peace. Not a day but I saw my grave before me, not an hour but death's fiery sword danced over my head, not a minute but the grief in your heart seared and wasted my soul. I heard your sweet voice, I saw your dear face, I understood your noble thoughts and firm resolve, I enjoyed your tender love and friendship, I contemplated your lost glory and grandeur and our first, admirable princes' and kings' lives and deeds, the wonders and miracles once wrought in our Fatherland, our sacred country, and the peerless nature and bold exploits of our exquisite nation. Mount Ararat towered up before me day and night, pointing to the land of which I was a descendent and reminding me just what kind of land it was. The Garden of Eden was always in my thoughts and, whether I was dreaming or awake, it kept our country's renown and preeminence forever before my mind's eye. Hayk, Vardan, Tiridates, and the Illuminator told me even in my sleep that I was a son of theirs. Europe and Asia cried out to me without pause that I was a child of Hayk, a grandson of Noah, a son of Echmiadzin,[2] a dweller in Paradise. In the fields or at church, out of doors or at home, the very stones on which my nation's feet had tread, and still do, tugged at my heart, trying to pluck it from my breast. Very often, when an Armenian crossed my path, I wanted to take my last breath and give it to him—but, alas, my tongue was tied; though my eyes were open, my mouth was sealed shut; though my heart was full, my hand was empty; and words failed me. I didn't have the money I would have needed to show by my acts what I wanted. I lacked the kind of reputation that would lend weight to my words. And our books were in *grabar* and our modern language didn't count, so that I could not express my heart's wish in words. I was unable to command, and if I prayed or even begged, no one would understand my language. For I was afraid, too, that others would mock me, call me unrefined or ignorant, say I didn't know grammar or rhetoric or logic. I wanted them, too, to say: "Oh, he knows how to write such profound, convoluted prose that the Devil himself would be at a loss to make heads or tails of it." I, too, wanted them to point me out and admire me and praise my profound knowledge of Armenian. Some know only one language; I know quite a few. It would be hard to name a book that I haven't begun to translate and dropped halfway through. Poetry and prose—I've managed to churn out enough of both in *grabar* to make a very big book.

In those days, God also sent me several children I was supposed to educate. My heart wanted to break when I saw that they didn't understand any of the books by Armenians that I put in their hands, although whatever they read in the language of the Russians, Germans, or French delighted their innocent souls. I often wanted to tear out my hair because they loved those foreign languages better than ours. Yet there was a very natural reason for this. In those languages, they read about the exploits of famous people, what they said and what they did; they read about things that captivate the heart because they are things of the heart. Who hasn't delighted in reading such things? Who hasn't delighted in learning what love, friendship, patriotism, parents, children, death, and battle are? If there are such things in our language, I'll be hanged. But how else are you supposed to bring children to love your language? It's all very fine to sell peasants gemstones; but someone with no use for them won't trade you a hunk of black bread for your priceless jewels.

That's how it was. Had I not read in various books, when I was in Europe, that the Armenian nation must be heartless, since, despite all the storms that have broken over its head, not a single Armenian has come along to write about these things of the heart? What exists is about the Church, or God and his saints. But the books children tuck under their pillows are the pagan works of Homer, Horace, Virgil, and Sophocles, because all are about things of this world. It would be absurd to say that all Europeans are mindless unbelievers; that, putting aside the things of God, they have taken up frivolous things. Why do our children, putting our Narek aside, delight in those other books? I knew very well that our nation wasn't what the Europeans said it was. But what can you do? You can't turn the millstone if there's no grain in the mill.

I thought to myself that, when it comes to brave men, there have been thousands among us, and there are still many today. And when it comes to wise sayings, our old women know thousands of them. Hospitality, love and friendship, bravery and distinguished men—our peasants' hearts are full of such ideals. If it's parables, proverbs, or witticisms you're after, the humblest of ordinary men will tell you a thousand if he tells you one. What, then, did we have to do so that other nations would know what was in our hearts, and praise us, too, and love our language? I was in despair. I knew well that, in the lands of the Ottomans and the Persians, among all the distinguished, wise, talented people, all the good minstrels, singers, and balladeers at the gates of Khan and Shah and Sultan, many had been Armenians. It's enough to name Keshish Oghli and Kör Oghli to prove that what I say is no lie. Let someone go talk with Grigor Tarkhanov, observing his conversation, eloquent tongue, imposing stature and allure, and, of his talents, only the one for imitating the language and gestures of a hundred different individuals and nations, how they stand and how they sit—may I be struck blind if I ever saw his equal in the finest European theaters.[3] And when you consider that, if he ever saw the inside of a school, it was back in the day when, in our country, they played bingo with the alphabet[4] rather than learning to read, you'll understand what talent there is among the Armenians.

I wasted whole days of my life brooding over all this. I was very often tempted to stick my head in a noose. I had no idea when this evil would end. Believe it or not, as you like, but this tragedy weighed so heavy on my soul that I often went roaming like a madman over hill and dale, walking and thinking, and came back home with an overflowing heart. This and this alone was the reason that, one day at the beginning of summer vacation, I dismissed my students in the morning and, that afternoon, went wandering through the hills again. Not knowing where to turn, I set out for the German Colony to see a German friend. Distressed by the state I was in, the people there wouldn't let me go back to the city for three days. But, in the city, my dear students and my friends and relatives had long since been mourning my death. They thought I'd drowned in the Kura, where I used to go swimming every morning and evening, and the dear souls had gone looking for me, hoping they might learn something about what had befallen me. One morning, as I was sitting by the window, lost in thought again, they filed by. Hardly had I laid eyes on them than my heart leaped to my mouth. Who can express what it was like when we saw each other again that day? Anyone with a heart will understand. I may forget your love in the grave, my dear, beloved friends. Until then, for as long as there is blue sky above my head and breath in my body, you are saints in my eyes, and I'd happily lay down my life for yours.

Ah, but when has the sky ever remained cloudless, so that man's heart might, too? Hardly had my mental sun come back out than the clouds loomed up again, darker than ever, and thunder and lightning blazed a new path through my heart. I no longer could throw myself into the water. The fear of the Lord filled my mind, my innocent children's voices rang in my ears, and love and paternal piety flooded my soul. If I went to my eternal rest, who would look after my orphans?

But even as I was resolving to sit down and sing my nation's praises as best I could, and recount the brave deeds of our famous men, I again thought to myself: for whom will I be writing, since the nation doesn't understand my language? As well write in Russian, German, or even French as in *grabar*: ten people may understand me, but, for one hundred thousand more, what I write will be as meaningful as the wind whistling through a windmill. Since the nation neither speaks that language nor understands it, what's the use, even if my mouth should pour forth gold? Every man desires what is near and dear to his heart. What good is your honey-glazed rice if I don't like it?

Everyone I talked to tried to make me believe that our nation was averse to learning and saw no point in reading; but I could see that this nation of ours that "didn't like to read" passed Robinson Crusoe's story and the asinine tale of the City of Copper from hand to hand. And I knew that all distinguished nations had two languages, ancient and modern. The language of the cultivated is a fine thing, and even rocks ought to strain to understand it until they crack. Where have interpreters ever been given salaries, distinctions, and honors? Let the learned linguist go stand somewhere and shout out what's on his mind until he's blue in the face, and let his listeners figure out what he says. It would be such a shame to cause the cultivated unnecessary headaches.

Even a madman, I thought to myself, wouldn't do things this way. Mulling matters over, as usual, I would often, on my way through the city or going to visit friends, attentively observe the people. When they were chatting or having a good time, what did they like best? I often noticed that, at market or in the streets, they would stand watching and listening to a blind minstrel, fascinated, and give the man money, the water running out of their mouths. At feasts or weddings, who ever swallowed a single morsel without a musician? The lyrics were in Turkish, and many didn't understand a word, but the souls of those listening and watching went soaring to heaven and back. I thought about it and thought about it, and then, one day, I said to myself: go on, close your manuals of grammar, rhetoric, and logic, pack them away, and become a minstrel yourself. Whatever happens, happens. Your honor won't suffer and your gilding won't peel. You're going to get sick and die too one day, and no one will be there to say "have mercy on his soul."

On Mardi Gras, after turning my students loose, I started to churn over everything I could remember of what I'd seen or heard since I was a child. Eventually, my dear young friend Aghasi came to mind, and, along with him, another hundred brave young Armenians rose up and beckoned me to their sides. The others were well along in years, many of them still alive and kicking, thank God. Aghasi was poor and dead, Lord have mercy on his soul. I said to myself, no insincerity, now, and I chose him. My heart was in my throat. I saw that the number of those who still occasionally picked up Armenian books or spoke the Armenian language was steadily dwindling. A nation is preserved by its language and its faith. If we lose them, too, we shall fall upon evil days indeed. The Armenian language was running away from me like Croesus. Aghasi opened my lips, which had been sealed for thirty years.

Before I'd written a page, my dear childhood friend Mr. Aghafon Smbatian, an honest Armenian doctor, walked in. I tried to hide the page, but to no avail. God sent him to me at precisely that moment; Lord bless the man's soul. He insisted that I read out what I had written. Why hide things from friends? he asked. My heart fluttered as I read. I said to myself that, any minute now, he would, like others, shake his head, knit his brows, and mock my imbecility to himself, so as not to have to say things to my face. But I was unjust; I hadn't yet recognized the nobility of his soul. As I was finishing—the sword was descending, was about to cut into the bone—he said, "If you go on that way, it will turn out to be a wonderful piece of work." I wanted to jump up and kiss him on the mouth, the mouth that had uttered such kind words.

I am indebted to his sacred friendship for unsealing my mute lips. My soul was already on fire as he left. It was ten o'clock in the morning. I forgot all about food. I was so fired up that I wanted to kill the fly flying by. Armenia stood before me like an angel and gave me wings. Parents, home, childhood, things once heard or said, had all come alive in such a way that I forgot the world around me. All the nameless, stray, lost thoughts inside me blossomed and returned. Only now did I begin to see that *grabar* and the other languages I had learned had closed my mind and held it prisoner until then. All that I'd said or written down to that moment had been plagiarism or delusion. That was why sleep would overcome me or my hand would tire after I had scarcely written a page. Now I worked until five in the morning, and thought about neither food nor tea. My pipe was my meal and writing was my bread. I paid no mind to the entreaties, irritation, and anger of the other members of my household. Only after I had turned out thirty quarto pages did nature demand its due: I could no longer keep my eyes open. All night, it seemed to me that I was still sitting there writing. If only those thoughts had come to me by day!

Dear reader, do not be vexed because I have gone on at such length. I am telling you these things so that you will understand how seductive and powerful the love of one's nation can be. I wouldn't want what I went through in my house that morning to happen again, not even to my worst enemy. Hardly had I opened my eyes than the voice of my poor, immigrant German helpmeet met my ear. Clutching my only son to her breast, she was crying hard enough to make stones weep. Our servants and maids were standing petrified in one corner of the room, watching me and wailing. Whose heart would not have burst at that moment? I started up like a madman, looking at my child. Thank God, there was nothing the matter with him. I begged my wife to calm down, but she couldn't. I had no idea what had happened.

"You monster, you've practically killed me," I heard her say at last. "How could you do this to me?"

The servants, standing on the other side of the room, covered me with reproaches. Finally, I understood that I had been raving the whole night, and shouting, and sighing, and going on, and that I had responded to whatever the members of my household had asked me, not in German, but in Armenian, saying a thousand different, incoherent things before going back to my battle. Remaining in this state until nine in the morning, I had gone on doing what I pleased, while they, for their part, mourned, having abandoned all hope that I would recover. On that morning, and for the whole of the next week, the next month, I had only one desire, and still have only one: to go throw myself at the feet of a prince, beg him to give me a crust of bread, and then wander from village to village, day and night, in order to collect and write down the exploits of our nation.

Let people call me ignorant from now on. My tongue has been unloosed, o my extraordinary, beloved nation, so dear to my heart. Let the logician write for his guild; I, your lost, wayward son, shall write for you.

Whoever has a sword, let him first bring it down on my head or plunge it into my heart, for, if he does not, I shall cry out in terror, as long as I still have a tongue in my mouth and a heart in my breast: "Who is that you are raising your sword to strike? Do you not recognize the great Armenian nation?"

It is enough, it is enough, my noble nation, that you should love your son's deeds and rough tongue, that you should accept them the way a father accepts his child's stammering, which he would not trade for the world. When I grow up, we can talk a more sophisticated language. Aghasi is your little boy; you have many others who are older and more famous. Give me a heart and the courage to serve you, even at the risk of my life. See how I go and seek them out and line them up before you, so that you, too, will be astonished, and declare that a country that boasts such sons need not worry about a thing. I throw myself at your feet. Give me that sacred hand of yours, so that I may kiss it and that you may pardon me, and let us then go together to join our beloved Aghasi.

3

MKRTICH EMIN
From Epic Narratives of Ancient Armenia

(Moscow, 1850)

Preliminary examination

> I only say suppose this supposition.
> —*Don Juan*, c. 1, st. 85

Our people has no literary history. What Armenian and foreign authors have produced on this head to date is nothing but compilations of information on authors and their works, compilations that are, moreover, shot through with errors. To examine our ancient texts in accordance with the rules of scholarship [*makats'ut'ean*], identifying the characteristics and significance of each while discriminating between that which belongs, properly speaking, to the author and that which belongs to the period in which he lived—such a study is, regrettably, not to be found among us. Because such work has never been undertaken, many philological problems involving Armenian literature [*dprut'iun*] have yet to be resolved. Among them are those bearing on national epic [*azgayin yergs*], the existence of which among the Armenians has, for reasons unknown to me, been universally denied with a single voice. This is a pardonable misconception when it comes from a foreigner's lips, but it is unforgivable that we, too, should voluntarily blind ourselves to the Armenian heritage. For among the Armenians, as among all the world's other nations without exception, there have existed national epics, traces of which are hidden in Moses of Khoren's *History*. In the following study, I have endeavored to collect these traces, present them as a whole, and demonstrate their significance in the history of the Armenians. It is up to the reader to say whether I have succeeded.

We might well ask why philologists have felt no desire to investigate these traces when one of the essential sources is Moses, the Father of Armenian History. In my estimation, the one and only reason for this indifference is the way people understand certain words whose etymology our dictionaries do not correctly explain. That is why I consider it essential briefly to examine these words at the outset of my study in order to determine what they mean; only after that can we undertake to study the traces of our national historical epics preserved or mentioned in Moses's *History*. The words requiring elucidation, in my opinion, are *vep, vipasan, asem, zruyts'*, and *ar'aspel* or *araspelk'*.

The *New Dictionary*[5] defines the first of these words, *vep*, as follows: "Ancient narratives, real or imaginary; histories in prose or verse."[6] This definition is incorrect. The word *vep* is one of the oldest in the Armenian language. It meant, for our ancestors, what *epos* did for the Greeks: namely, a versified history or historical poem. Khorenatsi says that the history of the kings in the Books of the Kings was in verse, not prose. Moses's very terminology substantiates our claim: whenever he cites *zbans vipasanats* (the words of epic poets) in his *History*, he calls them *yerg* [song]. It follows that the Ancients' *vep* was simply a versified poetic history that sang the deeds of heroes and kings. This is what Europeans today usually call an "epic."[7]

From what has just been said, the meaning of the word *vipasan*, too, becomes clear without further ado. If a *vep* is a poetic history in verse, then a *vipasan* is a poet of the kind called an "epic poet" in the West.

The word *vipasan* is a compound that combines the word *vep* with the root of the word *asem* [I say], *as*. For our ancestors, *asem*, "I say," was synonymous with *yergem*, "I sing." Consequently, *asel veps* [to say an epic narrative] is the equivalent of *yergel veps*, *zpatmakan yerks* [to sing an epic narrative, a historical song]. Indeed, in contemporary colloquial Armenian, this older meaning of the word *asel* [to say] survives in the common expression *khagh asel*, which means "to sing a song."

Our ancestors called the opposite of the *vep* a *zruyts'*, meaning historical prose as opposed to verse narrative. In question here are old traditional narratives that, according to Moses of Khoren, were transmitted orally, handed down from century to century and, later, written down. Moses says that "today, we find countless *zruts'ats' mateank'* [books of *zrutys*] among them."[8] He means what Europeans call *Sage* in German and *saga* or *skazanie* in Russian.

As for *ar'aspel* or *ar'aspelk'*, the meaning of the term has changed in the modern period. Its older meaning was *vipasanut'iun*, that is, a story in which our ancestors transmitted truth allegorically.[9] Moses uses the word in this sense in many different passages to designate what Europeans call myth or fable. It was called *vera narratio* in antiquity.

Now that we have established the precise meaning of each of these words, let us embark on our investigation of what we are eager to submit to philologists' unbiased judgment as the first fruits of the Armenian literary tradition.

Among man's innate capacities is that of preserving the memorable acts of others in his memory and later transmitting them by way of a tradition. The exploits performed by a people's ancient patriarchs and leaders in defending it against enemy attack or resolving unforeseen crises would leave a certain impression on that people's imagination. In such cases, men did not content themselves with simply telling their fellow men about the events they had witnessed. Their inflamed imaginations breathed new life into their words, transforming them into harmonious songs. Thus we observe, at the beginning of nearly every nation's literary tradition [*dprut'iun*], a national epic containing that which is entertaining, memorable, and excites the passions. Among the many national epics known to us, we might cite those of a *historical* turn, such as the Greeks' Iliad, the Book of Kings (rechristened the *Shah Nameh* by the Persians), and countless others. We would naturally have liked to range our own epic songs [*yerg vipasanats'*], as we ourselves call them, alongside these epics. But we have not been so fortunate: our enemies' massacres and raids, as well as incessant wars, did not merely destroy our every nascent sublime thought, casting it into the flames, rivers, and winds; they did not so much as leave one stone upon another in Armenia. Yet, although the songs in question have disappeared without a trace, our erudite old historian [*hnakhos*] Moses of Khoren did not neglect them. He kept and offered us specimens of them in his *History*. These numerous songs are mentioned in the Father of Grammarians' work,[10] who used them to reconstruct the acts of Armenian patriarchs and the Haygazn kings, from the Armenians' forefather Hayk (2107 B.C.) to the last Haygazn, Vahe (328 B.C.), and then to reconstruct our history from Vahe down to the time of Khosrov, son of Vagharsh (Anno Domini 214), at which point the living fountain that nourished our ancestors' hearts and minds for so many centuries ran dry. Some of them were to be found among the oldest traditions in Vagharshak's day (147 B.C.), while others continued to live on the nation's lips until the turn of the sixth century, as Khorenatsi himself attests. These were not drab, graceless songs, as it has pleased certain foreign scholars to say.[11] Quite the contrary: they were impressive compositions, products of the very sublime thinking and flourishing imagination of the sons of Armenia. These songs, which Khorenatsi calls *Yergs vipasanats* or epic songs, once stood in for history [*zteghi patmut'ean unein*] with us, as they did with many of Asia's and Europe's oldest peoples. This is the view not only of modern philologists, but also of external philosophers,[12] among them Mar Abas and the "philosopher" Khorenatsi.[13] The latter, indeed, in the first book of his *History*, in which he recounts Aram's victories and gives an account of his reign, cites the words of the Assyrian archeologist [*hnakhos*], including the following remark, which merits attentive study: "But although they were not recorded in their original books [that is, the kings' or the temples'], yet, as Mar Abas Catina relates, they were collected by some lesser and obscure men from ballads and are found in the royal archives."[14] [Moses is here relating Aram's history and exploits.] It was indeed these humble, obscure individuals who, for centuries, sang heroes' brave deeds among all the world's nations, immortalizing them so that their nation could take pride in them later. It would appear that, albeit obscure, these men were not despised, inasmuch as what they said was collected in royal archives, furnishing the learned with the raw material with which to immortalize the memory of nations, princely families, and kings, such as Aram, in the case of our people. If we attentively consider the section of the Chaldean book cited by Khorenatsi that relates our ancestors' exploits, we will discern, precisely, the songs of the epic poets of an earlier day there.[15] The reader should not be put off by this claim. I do not advance it because I wish to make light of our nation's ancient history; nor do I wish to question the veracity of the Father of our History. God forbid! I would simply like to shed new, if still uncertain, light on the oldest stratum of our literature, which the authors of our Literary History, Armenian and foreign alike, have so far neglected.

4

KAREKIN SERVANTSDEANTS
From Written in a Rush

*(**Works** 1:83–86; Yerevan, 1978)*

§38

To satisfy philologists' curiosity, I hasten to make it known that, for several years, the right honorable bishop Yeremia Sarkisian of Van as well as the reverend fathers Ghevond Pirghalemian and Grigoris Aghvanian have been pursuing a worthwhile task: wherever they have gone, they have jotted down archeological descriptions [*storagrut'iun*] of antiquities, transcribed the colophons of old manuscripts and the inscriptions on stone crosses found in the ruins of monasteries, churches, and homes, and also written down popular tales as well as curses, legends [*ar'aspel*], and many dialectal words, in the intention, of course, of one day publishing all this material. Reverend Poghos Tomayan of Trebizond, a scholar doing similar work, has, for his part, been producing archeological descriptions of the Trebizond and Taron regions on the Holy Father's recommendation,[16] and has also turned out important commentaries on the ancient traditions and toponyms of those two regions. He has, further, made a description [*nkaragrut'iun*] of the customs and language of Taron's inhabitants.

§39

I, too, had long since adapted my pen and taste to the love of such subjects, publishing in Varag,[17] among other texts, "Prayers of the Old Women of Van" in *Artsvi Vaspurakani* [The Eagle of Vaspurakan]. In Mush, I published, in *Taronoy Artsvik* [The Eaglet of Taron], writings and a few songs in the language of Taron's inhabitants. But certain people repeatedly interfered with the eagle's flight and clipped the eaglet's wings, and both were eventually laid low by these foul deeds and treacherous acts. However, so as not to lose the thread of my thoughts, I shall say no more about that here. As for me, despite my intense wish to write, I frequently had to change my place of abode at short notice, traveling now to Van, now to Mush, now to Constantinople, now to Garin,[18] since I had to attend to official matters such as agriculture, economics, and . . . the administration of human beings . . . as a result of which I have lost both a considerable part of my studies and data and, above all, a good deal of time. I am nevertheless still in possession of things old and new that merit publication, and I promise gradually to bring them before the public.

§40

All that I have written so far was not first drafted and then revised; I simply jotted down whatever came to mind. I now append to this short book, as raw material, the narrative [*vep*][19] *David of Sasun* or *Mher's Gate*. It took me three years of hard work to collect it; I found no one who knew the whole narrative until June 1873, when the honorable schoolteacher Ohan introduced me to Grbo, the representative[20] of the village of Arnisd on the plain of Mush. Grbo said that the person from whom he had learned[21] had extensive knowledge of this story and that poems that were sung [*dzaynov k'erger*] occurred in many parts of it. He added that his former teacher had two young students who had learned the story quite perfectly, but that he himself had forgotten many passages because he had not recited it for a long time. I nevertheless retained him for three days, entreating him, showing him all the honors, and rewarding him, and, after resting up and preparing himself for the task, he recited it and I wrote it down in his words. Words used in the Baghesh[22] dialect occur in the Reciter's language. The reason is that, although the Reciter's village is in the Mush region, it lies close to Baghesh. Generally speaking, the language of Armenians from the villages of Khoyta and Chukhara is also of this type.

The subject of the story is the origins and the grounding of the principality of the Ardzrunis and the province of Sasun. We know from the Bible and our nation's history that King Sennacherib was about to sacrifice his sons Adrammelech and Sanasar/Sharezer to his idol when they killed their father and fled to Armenia, during the reign of our Skayordi.[23] Sanasar settled in Sasun and Adrammelech settled near Kaputkogh in the Lake Van region. Khorenatsi, Thomas Ardzruni,[24] and other historians all tell their story at length. There is no need to repeat the story of the successes they achieved and the honors bestowed on them by Armenia's rulers. Nor do we need to speak of their and their descendants' courage and the services they rendered.

In this oral narrative, we finds passages that correspond to the historical accounts. But there are also passages that fly in the face of chronology, toponymy, and probability. Events that occurred before Christ are related in Christian fashion; Adrammelech's and Sanasar's epoch is identified with that of St. Garapet monastery in Mush, and the Armenians are presented as worshipers of the cross. The country of Misir mentioned here is perhaps Musl or Mosul, which has a certain likelihood to it, because Mosul was not far from the limits of Sasun's sphere of influence. Baghdad, Khlat, and Kaputkogh are the real places of the same names. All other places are likewise accurate. As for Kaghzvan, it is near Kars; it is well known that this province was once ruled by the Georgians. . . .

The publication of this work will be of value to those who understand it; but I suppose that most readers will scorn it and that people will criticize not only the section I have transcribed, but the whole text, and me as well. That is of no concern to me. I will be heartened if only twenty people approve of this endeavor, and I shall carry on with it, encouraging others to follow me in striving to obtain and publish material of this sort.

5

KAREKIN SERVANTSDEANTS
From Manna

(Works 1:178–80)

I now hasten to say a little something about the epic narratives and legends of the fatherland [*hayreneats' veper yev zruyts'ner*].

We just saw that writing has a long history in our nation. But letters, cuneiform characters, and slates were used only for great, significant events and memorial inscriptions; they were a closed book for ordinary people, beyond their capacities. Did the same not hold in the Middle Ages, when it had become so much easier to produce manuscripts on paper? Were people not incapable of reading and writing then, too, until Gutenberg invented the printing press?

Although this was so, the mind and reasoning capacity of people could not remain idle and unfeeling. People talked about the things they saw or did or heard, composed accounts of these events, and produced oral narratives. They sang or murmured, either alone or in company, the love and sorrow they felt. Of course, the imagination added something to what had actually happened, and the listener added something in his turn when he communicated what he had heard to someone else. To the present day, narratives and legends are composed orally and in written form. We understand where the storyteller comes from thanks to the following sure sign: he composes his words using names, likenesses, and characteristics of the local customs of the inhabitants of his region and its climate, and also of the animals and places of his environment. . . . Narratives and legends, which the people call "tales" [*hek'iat*'], are composed to serve as moral guides; when they take the form of epics, it is to proclaim the bravery of the brave or provide an example for others. There is always an order to the composition of these tales: a journey to remote, unknown lands; marvelous, terrifying descriptions of places and people; events; adventures caused by the treachery of friends or brothers, and sometimes even of parents. . . . When heroes and heroines make their entry and an eloquent, well-turned tongue describes them, the heroic exploits of a Hercules diminish in people's eyes, like the Golden Fleece, the epic of Troy, Odysseus and his islands, the Garden of the Hesperides that so delights Homer, or Telemachus and Calypso. These are truly popular narratives.

Indeed, are the Albanian birth and youth, the passion and deeds of Semiramis as recounted by our great Khorenatsi not epic narratives and legends [*vep u zruyts'*]? . . . It is by way of myths of this kind that all ancient nations came into being and have maintained themselves as they were primordially.[25] Everyone knows that Alexander of Macedonia, the son of Philip, born in the days of Aristotle himself, was "descended of a dragon." The founders of Rome "grew up in the wild, living on goat's milk," and so on. The births of heroes, as well as their deaths or metamorphoses, are always miraculous events. Some are changed into constellations, others into storms; some live forever underwater or on islands, others in the depths of hell; some are changed into flowers, others into fish, and still others into savage beasts and wild asses, and so on. There are also heroes whose names—and mountains, regions, cities, forts, monuments, and bodies of water bearing their names—wordlessly recount their stories.

I admit that the legends collected here are not that old and sublime; but they can serve as examples to the philologists, so that, turning their attention to the people and all the legends and traditions it has on its lips, they strive to find older ones. Writers can make use of these legends to compose national literary epics [*azgayin grakan verper*]. The narratives of a good many foreign peoples have been translated into our language and, although the life and conditions of existence of those peoples are foreign to us, they are today better known to Armenian readers than our native [*hayrenakan*] life and the conditions depicted in our narratives.

6

GHEVOND ALISHAN
From The Armenians' Ancient Faith or Pagan Religion

(pp. 1–12; Venice, 1895)

Introduction

To know a nation's political and moral life (usually called History) well, it is absolutely necessary to know its religious conceptions and activity, too—simply put, its Faith. This holds especially for the nations that are mentioned in the oldest periods and have either disappeared in the course of time or still exist. No one is unaware that the Armenians are among the latter nations. They are known to have been present in the modern and medieval periods, and in ancient times and events as well.

With the exception of the Hebrews, the origins and early life of all or almost all nations are shrouded in darkness or the mists of time. We do not propose to dispel that darkness and those mists, to examine the Armenian nation's origins and development, but to study its religion, which is easier to know than its political life, as is true of other nations as well. In some cases, it can be said that a nation's political life is wholly unknown, whereas vestiges [*hishatakk'*] of its religion are still extant, and ancient sculptures and bas-reliefs, together with various artifacts, have come down to us. These reveal the essence of a people unknown or little known to history, telling us more about its religion than its acts and, sometimes, telling us about its religion alone.

There is nothing novel about studying the ancient religion of a nation that, as is the case with the Armenians, was a historical nation in ancient and modern times, and continues to be. Works about its religion have been written and published many times and by many, more or less learned, people. We felt no great need to refer to these works and little desire to do so, because they are generally depictions and accounts of confused, false, incoherent matters. Yet new light can emerge from darkness. The mind is never content to remain ignorant of what it is possible to know about what its ancestors and ancient forefathers knew. But, for us, the greater inducement to recall our ancestors' religion and bring it to others' attention again was the new knowledge that the learned are bringing to light in our day: newly discovered ancient monuments, cuneiform texts, inscriptions in stone, sculptures, all sorts of vessels and weapons recovered from tombs and ruins, mythological images on stone, clay, and metal supports, jewels big and small, tools, and so on and so forth.

The reader will perhaps think that we intend to discuss such things here, and that we wish to spread knowledge of our ancestors' faith with the help of these newly discovered things. But we do not; let us leave that to the more or less well-informed archeologists of our day, who are not only bringing new Armenian gods and religions to light (in particular, a certain Khaldi with a barbaric-sounding name),[26] but also new and old ancestors, old and hitherto unknown Armenians and, especially, non-Armenians: peoples and nations older than the Armenians who once lived in the land called Armenia. According to these archeologists, the ancestors of the Armenians of today arrived in Armenia or suddenly sprang up there not very long before the Christian era. Leaving it to them to cast more light on these very interesting nations and things, we propose to present in a different way, as succinctly as possible, their (and our) national tradition to philologists, both amateurs and specialists, without flying too far afield or delving too deeply into matters, since we have neither the wings nor the strength needed to meet the standards of these extraordinarily erudite people. We propose to do so by simply and plainly noting what both our own ancestors and foreigners have passed on to us about the Armenians' religion, in writing or in the form of material monuments, and also by indicating both what has been said and what remains to be said about the Armenians' national beliefs as well as their faith and customs, proper or perverse. To that end, we shall examine, first, the Armenians' general idea or understanding of religion and God and, second, their various articles of belief and their main objects of worship [*pashton*]— Nature or the Elements, Heavenly Bodies, Animals, Monsters, the Spirits of the Heroes, the Gods—as well as Magic, Witchcraft, Divination, the Meaning of Life after Death, Rites of Worship, and the Priesthood.

Chapter 1: Religion, Belief, and Worship

The deepest conceptions in man's heart or soul—that there exists a supreme being on whom he is dependent and that there is life after death—are common to virtually all nations and peoples, and also to all individuals. That supreme being is their "God." As for conceptions of this God and the actions that follow from them, as well as the relationship between earthly creatures and heaven or between the present and future life, they comprise "Religion," "Belief," and "Worship."[27] The last-named is an external sign by means of which man concretely testifies to his faith in the being or beings in whom he believes, whether the supreme God, idols, pagan gods,[28] spirits, or matter. Just as

Worship derives from Belief—for if one did not believe in something, one would give neither thought nor material things to it—so Belief derives from Religion. We ought to distinguish between these two concepts, which are usually considered identical and may be regarded as inseparable, but only in the sense in which a building and its foundations are. Religion is the foundation, Belief is the building. The pagans (a term we take to include the ancient Armenians) believed in many things or gods, just as Christians believe in various articles of faith (for example, those mentioned in the Creed), but neither pagans nor Christians would accept the things they do if it were not for an inner awareness or drive that has led them to adopt a belief in these things. Such is the supreme, deepest meaning of religion, which is stamped or impressed on human beings.

It is plain that, although, in a sense, all nations and individuals conceive of religion and God in virtually the same way, they use different styles and names to explain them, as they do with other things as well. These names or words can increase knowledge or pervert it. Philologists have not infrequently considered it worthwhile to examine the origins of these words and discern their meanings in each language. Leaving that detailed research to them, let us briefly observe about the words in our language that both ("Belief" and "Religion") are plural in form; although they are also used in the singular, their meaning is altered when they are. Let us also note in passing that the word "*Havatk'*" is similar in sound and meaning to a Latin word and its derivatives (*Fides, Fede, Foi*); here, the word is singular. Leaving these words, too, to the philologists, might we not, to establish the etymology of the word in our own language, bring it into relation with, or derive it from, the root *Hav*, which means "origin," "extremity," and "father's father"? But leaving this to the philologists as well, let us turn to Religion, after recalling in passing that "*Havatk'*" also signifies "pact," "a promise made to someone else," and "affirmation." The Romans, too, had a god of vows and treaties whose name, Fidius, meant "faith."

Kronk'. In Armenian, this noun announces its meaning, superbly and, perhaps, better than in other languages. Latin (with its derivatives) calls this *Religio*, which some, with reference to the usual meaning of the verb that is its homonym, derive etymologically from "to tie," "to bind," "to be bound"—that is, to bind man to God or Heaven and, especially, men to each other. For, among men, there is no bond stronger than religion. This is a lovely correlation. It is not, however, primary, but, rather, derives from a more primitive sense of the word. That is, if one supposes that there exists something in which to believe, it follows that one should be bound to it and to those who believe in it. Nothing about our noun *Kronk'*, however, indicates that it is derived from a more primitive signification; it appears to be independent or self-derived.

We have in our possession an old dictionary composed by an anonymous author (it also contains very old, rare words that have yet to appear in learned works), which gives the briefest and yet the most sensible etymology for the word *Kronk'*. "Kronk'— kir yev havanut'iun." That is the whole explanation. Anyone who knows a little literary Armenian[29] also knows that *kir* is the root of the word *krel* and that, like the word kronk', it is often employed in the plural; thus one writes and says *Kirk*'.[30] We all know what *kirk*' means, even if we have all learned to give slightly different senses to the word: *kirk*' is an intense, spontaneous inner feeling. But because this noun also signifies other psychological forces and feelings, the noun *kronk*' has been reserved for the feeling associated with belief. This means that belief is the rational man's primary and most powerful passion. It is the one, mentioned above, that leaves the deepest impression on us all: knowing one's origins, or one's dependence on, and obligations toward, a supreme being.

Appropriately, after "passion," the etymologist adds *Havanut'iun* [Accord], the immediate or inevitable consequence of such a passion of the soul being the accord among one's thoughts that constitutes, as we said earlier, *Havadk*' [Belief]. Thus this noun may be considered to derive from "accord" rather than "origin" (*hav*), or from both at once.

Truly, this word, with its meaning, is a very beautiful, philosophical, and even sacred find and correlation. It may be called the pride of the nation or language that possesses or has devised such a word or one with an equivalent meaning and, feeling its ultimate origin and supreme end in the depths of its being, has called it *Kronk*'— unlike those who consider that the beginning of everything, the gods included, comes from Chronos, infinite time. . . . But, when we say this, we think of the Greeks, that refined and most knowledgeable of peoples, and the Egyptians and Indians, their rivals in knowledge. And we wonder whether a national élan [*yer'ant*] gave this profound and superbly meaningful word to the Armenians, who were seemingly so far inferior to them in philosophy and were one of Asia's crude peoples, possessing neither an ancient literature nor the remains of temples [*mehenakan mnats'vats*]. Be that as it may; yet who would dare assert that, among the ancient peoples just mentioned, or others like them, the pure or patriarchal worship of God [*Astvatsapashtut'iun*] went back further than that of the Armenians? Our country's geographical position as well as both national and ancient history show, in our estimation, that the worship of God comprised the belief [*havadk*'] of the Armenians' ancestors, and that *Kronk*' was the name and the meaning given to the institution of this belief. In saying this, we are not stating any great novelty. For people with common sense take it for granted that the ancient nations' patriarchs or forefathers knew the true God. We count the Armenian nation among them, although we shall not enter into a debate about how old it is, for our concern here is with establishing, not how old the nation is, but how old its worship of God is, and with the fact that this worship constituted its first religion. Afterward, like other nations, it went astray and fell into error, degenerating into the historically known sects [*aghand*] that we shall be discussing here. It was therefore necessary that we begin by mentioning the worship of God or patriarchal [*nahapetakan*] religion, although we see no need to expatiate on it, since that worship is identical in all the old nations as long as they have not been perverted. When they go astray, however, they also go their different ways in the sphere of faith and worship; and, from that point on, we have to examine each nation separately.

7

MANUK ABEGHEAN
From Armenian Popular Beliefs

(pp. 1–5; Leipzig, 1899)

The Sources and General Characteristics of Armenian Popular Beliefs

Armenian ethnology began in Eastern Armenia with the emergence of modern Armenian literature, which is only a few decades old. Most writers concerned themselves with the life of the people in their works, depicting and faithfully recreating its mores, sagas, and religious or even superstitious practices. As a result, rather rich material for ethnological studies of Armenia is to be found in its fiction and poetry. Ethnology as such, however, began only in 1874. Bishop Servantsdeants blazed the path here, publishing, in the space of a few years, a rich collection of Western Armenian sagas, folk songs, fairy tales, riddles, and proverbs, as well as descriptions of mores and superstitious practices. Others have followed his example, so that the material now available suffices to provide the basis for a study (albeit one-sided) of Armenian popular beliefs.[31] One-sided, because those who have collected this material have unfortunately not proceeded in systematic fashion: the bulk of it has yet to be put in written form, and much of what has is still held in manuscript form by those who collected it, because books in general and, in particular, books containing such material sell too poorly.

I was unfortunately unable to make use of all published sources in writing the present overview of Armenian popular beliefs. The collections listed below have served as my main sources:[32]

AU = Allaverdian, J., *Ulnia kam Zeyt'un* [Ulnia or Zeitun], Constantinople, 1884.

EZ = *Azgagrakan handes* [Ethnographic Review], ed. E. Lalayan, vol. 1, Shushi, 1895; vol. 2, Tbilisi, 1897.

HB = Hovsepian, G., *P'shrank'ner zhoghovrdakan banahiusut'iunits* [Fragments of Popular Literature], Tbilisi, 1895.

LD = Lalayan, E., *Javakhk'i burmunk'* [Scents of Javakh], Tbilisi, 1892.

NM = Navasardian, T., *Hay zhoghovrdakan hek'iat'ner, zruyts'ner, yerger, aghot'k'ner, sovorut'iunner yev ayln* [Popular Tales, Narratives, Songs, Prayers, Customs, and So On], nos. 1–8 (part of my own collection has been published in nos. 6 and 7).

SV = Scherenz, *Vana saz* [Lyre of Van], Tbilisi, 1893.

SHH = Servantsdeants, G., *Hamov hotov* [The Way it Tastes and Smells], Constantinople, 1884.

SM = Servantsdeants, G. *Manana* [Manna], Constantinople, 1876.

SGB = Servantsdeants, G. *Grots' u Brots'* [Written in a Rush], Constantinople, 1874.

TT = Ter-Alexandrian, *T'iflisets'vots' mtavor keank'ë* [The Cultural Life of the Inhabitants of Tbilisi], Tbilisi, 1885.

I have also utilized the popular epic *Sasma Tsr'er* [The Heroes of Sasun], several variants of which have been collected by G. Hovsepian (Tbilisi, 1893), and another variant of which I have published under the title *David and Mher* (Shushi, 1889).

The value of the above-mentioned collections resides exclusively in the material that they contain; one can by no means say that they offer an understanding or, more exactly, a classification of the songs, prayers, etc., cited in them. That task is left entirely to the reader. The sole exceptions are the two volumes of the *Ethnographic Review*. Most of the material that I have taken from these sources I have also found myself in various regions of Armenia.

I am aware of no studies of, or work on, Armenian popular beliefs. Of the works on ancient Armenian beliefs, I have used the following as my source:

AHH = Alishan, G., *Hin Havatk' kam het'anosakan kronk' Hayots'* [The Armenians' Ancient Faith or Pagan Religion], Venice, 1895.

This book is a detailed compendium of material about the pagan belief of Armenia contained in ancient and medieval Armenian writings.

Other sources, not listed above, will be cited in the course of my exposé. Be it further noted that some material from my own unpublished collection is also utilized below, but not cited, to avoid repetition. I have collected most of my own material in my native village of Astapat. Some of this material, which is certainly not limited to just one village, may also be found in the sources cited above.

Of the ancient Armenian writings, I have had constantly to hand Eznik's[33] *Refutation of the Sects* (in the [1826] Venice edition), which also contains much material relevant to ancient Armenian popular beliefs. Eznik refutes in the first (pp. 68–110) and second (pp. 149–187) part of his text popular conceptions that are either purely Armenian or foreign, but already armenized. He hardly mentions Armenians but, in view of expressions such as "people say," "because some have asked whether," and the like, one can only conclude that Armenians are involved. Almost everything that Eznik refutes in the aforementioned passages with proofs from the Bible, in line with his general purpose (p. 111: "to refute foreigners with rational arguments, not the Bible, while refuting alleged natives who have not attained the truth [that is, Armenians who have preserved many pagan beliefs] with Holy Writ") may be found in present-day Armenian popular belief.

Popular Armenian beliefs are certainly Christian, in the first instance. But a people clings to its old traditions when it is deprived of writing and formal education (as most Armenians are) and lives in close proximity to nomadic peoples who do not possess writing. Consequently, many aspects of the ancient pagan faith, although they are, to be sure, dying out, have been preserved in the form of vestiges of the past in contemporary popular belief, especially among the lower classes of people, such as old peasant women. In addition to these two elements, Christian and pagan, we must mention the influence of Mohammedanism, due to the Arabs, Persians, and Turks under whose rule and as whose neighbors Armenians have lived for centuries. Thus we have the components of contemporary popular Armenian belief: Christianity, paganism, and Mohammedanism. However, if Mohammedan influence on Armenian mores and customs and even the Armenian language has been strong, Mohammedan influence on Armenian beliefs has been slight. Thus we are left with two main components: Christianity and paganism.

The pagan component, the subject of the present examination, represents a secondary mythology [*eine niedere Mythologie*] like that possessed by almost all the world's peoples. It comes to the fore in the belief in souls and the cult of the dead, in the veneration and mythical conceptions of physical phenomena and natural objects, in the belief in demons, and in magical practices.

The imaginary representations of Armenian popular faith, as well as most of its sagas and legends, are also found, of course, among other Indo-European and non-Indo-European peoples. Many of its notions, like those of every popular faith, may well constitute elementary ideas common to all humankind, and yet be authentically Armenian. However, most such aspects of Armenian popular faith are doubtless owing to borrowings or transfers. The neighboring peoples as well as those who have lived together with the Armenians in their historical homeland were always present in large numbers, and still are today. They have all certainly had some kind of influence on Armenian mores, customs, and popular beliefs. It is thus difficult to determine what has been borrowed from one or another foreign people in ancient or modern times.

The phrase "Armenian popular belief" must also be applied to everything that has attained general currency among the people, even if it is of foreign origin. What matters most here is to exclude those elements of popular belief that have not yet been domesticated and are perceived as foreign in the consciousness of the people themselves.

8

HAGOP OSHAGAN
From "Karekin Servantsdeants"

(Panorama of Western Armenian Literature 4:310–12;[34] written 1943,
published Jerusalem, 1956)

It is as if glory, anguish, and the torment of an irremediable loss were condensed behind this name, as well as the symbolic image of a generation on which it is impossible to pin a label. I hasten to add that for some twenty years, from 1870 until his death, Karekin Servantsdeants represented more in Western Armenian literature than all the supposedly big names. I am happy to be able to say that his reputation does not resemble the false, hollow, rigged glory of his teacher and countryman Khrimian.[35] While both made a name for themselves with a broad public, Servantsdeants's popularity and the respect paid him have a profound, remarkable beauty of a very special kind; for Venice as well as Vienna, Tblisi as well as Moscow were enthused by the man.[36] The affectionate admiration of these serious, authentic centers of national phi-lology [*hayrenagitut'ean*][37] goes to prove something, of course, and represents more than what Khrimian accomplished with his country priest's methods, exploiting his friendly relations with the booksellers to peddle his miserable prose. Thus the achieve-ment Servantsdeants has bequeathed us is of particular and profound interest to Ar-menology, a word it is hardly possible to toss about today as if it were a full-fledged concept. You are doubtless not unaware of the effort that notion cost. You are familiar with the crisis, experienced for two hundred years now, of our people's veritable glories and authentic customs, of the meaning of its history and its future existence. Venice, Vienna, Constantinople, Tbilisi, Vagharshabad, and Moscow are the big centers in which Armenology was cultivated and religiously pursued, with, of course, uneven results. Today we know more than we did in the day when an abbot from Sebastia laid the foundations, on an island, of that great enterprise, rediscovery of the Armenian fatherland.[38] What magnificent names come to mind as I dictate these lines! How hard those generations worked, revealing, as they pursued their moving mission, our people's virtues and the industrious creativity that distinguished all it did in the mate-rial as well as the spiritual and intellectual domains. Servantsdeants, one of those names, is a tragedy with a strange destiny. With regard to his qualifications for the work, that is, his aptitude and competence, he was the least favored of the group. He was an ordinary priest who had not so much as had a regular education, who knew no foreign languages, made do without the great, indispensable assistance of international philology, even without an office and a library, and may also have lacked the time re-quired to pursue an intellectual discipline. Yet he left us an œuvre that is, today, of in-estimable value. Some things are priceless; there is no haggling over their worth. Such is the most uncertain but also precious spiritual system of the Armenian fatherland—to put it differently, the Armenian soul's warp and woof, its inner expanses and the ulti-mate arrangement of its elements—that was saved [*p'rkvats*] by Servantsdeants. My remark takes on all its tragic density at the moment in which I dictate these lines (February 1943), when I let my mind's eye run over the picture presented by my father-land, entirely Turkified for the first time in its history as a result not only of the total elimination of its population from those regions but, in particular, of every vestige, big or small, of what once gave material form to its soul and culture. Servantsdeants collected everything that spilled from the lips of those who lived on that soil, all the images that had sprung from the land over the centuries, all the opulence of all the libraries that had for centuries been honored guests in monk's cells or in chapels or huts, in the guise of manuscripts, miniatures, paintings, books.[39] He felt, for the very last time (after him, we never had, from anyone's pen, a depiction of the experience of the Armenian fatherland or the feelings called forth by its soil; for more than twenty years, the censors outlawed descriptions of local conditions in the fatherland), the nameless, profound, indecipherable plastic manifestations [*patkerakerpum*][40] of that fatherland, salvaged for all time by his writings. His *Manna* is an irreplaceable exhibition of such pictures of the Armenian homeland's material forms. Not for nothing did people weep when they read his *The Way it Tastes and Smells*, a book that does indeed recreate the Armenian homeland's tastes and smells, which some magic alchemy seems to have carried off and imprisoned on paper forever. I remember *Bro' Toros*, which afforded me the occasion to read the loveliest handful of pages that I have ever read: I recognized, there, the most authentic of Armenians, with all his virtues and vices. And yet Servantsdeants's work hardly even approaches the concept of literature as I present it in the introduction to the present volume. This man, who rescued elements of such inestimable value for the ethnographic history of Armenian civilization, hardly considers the possibility (let alone the actual existence) of something called literature. Fate has decreed that, with his perfect indifference to art [*gegharvesd*] as well as his serene, contemptuous caution in the face of the base greed of Constantinople's booksellers, at the price of heroic sacrifices willingly made for the sake of realizing his project (Servantsdeants was a sought-after teacher, a well-loved bishop, an influential Armenian with a right to enjoy all the benefits and pleasures of life in Constantinople), and thanks to the vivid results that this eyewitness [*akanates*] and collector took straight from the land, Karekin Servantsdeants is more than just an Armenologist and ethnographer; he enters the field of Western Armenian literature, head held high, with a much richer and more authentic contribution to his name than those made by his big-wig fellow clergymen, from Nar-Bey through Turean and Kushagean to Ormanean.

I therefore associate with his name the whole phalanx of ecclesiastical authors of Western Armenian literature and the question of assessing them, independently of his other, awesome accomplishment: saving the Armenian fatherland, an enterprise that he conceived and carried out with the clarity of genius. Such was the gift that an itinerant parish priest's simple but iron will gave this people. Karekin Servantsdeants is loving kindness, beauty, and grace.

—Translated by G. M. Goshgarian

Essays in *Mehyan* and Other Writings of Constant Zarian

The review *Mehyan* appeared in Istanbul from January to July 1914. In all, nine issues containing a total of 112 pages saw the light before publication was suspended with the outbreak of war in Europe. The full title of the review was *Mehyan: Armenian Review of Literature and Art* (a French translation of the title appeared just under the Armenian title in every issue). Daniel Varuzhan, one of the five men who signed the Manifesto published in the first issue, soon left the group because of personal differences with the editor-in-chief of the review, Constant Zarian. There were no further defections. To the end, Kegham Parseghian and Hagop Kufejian (the future Hagop Oshagan) worked for *Mehyan* in their capacity as "editors." In the following pages, the reader will find translations of the Manifesto and of all of the texts written by Zarian except for the last, in the seventh and final issue, a text in which he makes a sort of gesture of defiance toward all who had shown hostility to the enterprise, or contempt for it. Zarian's articles and essays appeared under the general rubric "For Art," apart from the one included in the third issue, which was also the only issue organized around a single subject. This issue was given a title, "The Literature of All Armenians," and (on Oshagan's initiative) was devoted exclusively to that theme. We have accordingly inserted, in the middle of this appendix given over to Zarian, an English translation of Oshagan's piece for that issue.

We have made an effort not to edulcorate the Armenian texts, especially where they contain elements of overtly "racialist" thinking—for example, in the Manifesto, which proclaims the Armenians members of the "Aryan race." One of the reasons for publishing these translations is to show that the thinking based on the aesthetic principle came forward as what our philosophy professors called, in their day, "national-aestheticism," which could degenerate, simply, into racist ideology. In the present volume, we have tried to elucidate the conditions under which this degeneration came about. Thus we have tried, in a way, to save the aesthetic principle from its own ideological degeneration, while describing the historical system of which it was a part; or, rather, we have not quite tried to "save" it so much as to examine all its various facets, without ignoring the one dominated by racialist discourse (inherent in the aesthetic principle) or tainted by racist ideology (the aesthetic principle in its perverted form). It was Zarian who developed this ideology in *Mehyan*, in one text after another, culminating in the explicitly (and absurdly) anti-Semitic passages of his essay "The Jesus of the Armenians." Thus we have every reason to believe that the Manifesto's declarations about the Armenians' putative Aryan origins are also Zarian's work. But the fact remains that this Manifesto bears five signatures and that each and every one of its five signatories must be held responsible for his acts (even if these signatories rank among the greatest Armenian authors of the first half of the twentieth century).

All the articles and essays translated in this appendix appeared in Western Armenian. This is worth mentioning, because Zarian did not begin to write in Eastern Armenian (his native language, albeit not the one in which he was educated in his youth in Paris) until after he left Istanbul in late summer 1914 and took refuge in Italy. He lived in Italy, a few interruptions aside, throughout the war years, then returned to Istanbul in 1922 before settling in Armenia, where he remained until 1924. All the literary work Zarian turned out after 1914 is written in the Eastern dialect. Thus the texts he published in *Mehyan* stand out from all the rest. In fact, he wrote them in French; Kegham Parseghian translated them for the review as their author produced them (the sole exception was the Manifesto, translated by Varuzhan). Thus we have to do here with English translations of Armenian translations from French, the original versions of which have not come down to us; the translations of Zarian's essays made for the original French version of the present volume were translations into French of texts originally written in French, a fact that goes part of the way to explaining their rather hesitant and also rather bloated style. In making these French translations, we were guided by writings that Zarian published in French in the Belgian journals *Le Thyrse* and *La Société Nouvelle*, to which he contributed from 1909 to 1913. These texts had to wait half a century to find their place in a comprehensive reading of Zarian's work. They have not been included in the various volumes of his writings published in Yerevan in the past few years, volumes that bring together all his Armenian writings scattered in diasporan reviews and newspapers, while neglecting his publications in French, Italian, and Russian.

This group of closely related texts on art and the theater, all of which belong to the first stage of the writer's career, is here followed by two extracts from his greatest works. The first is from *Antsortë yev ir champan* [The Traveler and His Road], which was published in the Boston review *Hayrenik'* from October 1926 to February 1928; it was reprinted in 1975 by the Armenian Catholicosate in Antelias, Lebanon, in the Melidinetsi series, in a volume that bears the title *Yerker* [Works] and includes the great autobiographical texts that Zarian published between 1926 and 1930. The second extract comes from the novel *Bancoopë yev mamout'i voskornerë* [The Pancoop and the Bones of the Mammoth], which, beginning in 1931, also appeared in installments in *Hayrenik'* (a review that handsomely paid Zarian for his work). *The Pancoop* was reissued in a separate volume in 1987, again by the Armenian Catholicosate, in Antelias.[1]

I must here repeat what I said in the epilogue. My aim in the present volume has not been to give the reader a general idea of Zarian's œuvre, the most important part of which, in my view, consists of the works he wrote in the 1920s, all of them autobiographical, as well as those gathered under the title *Yerkirner yev Astvatsner* (Countries and Gods)—also published in *Hayrenik'*, from 1935 on, and only recently collected in two volumes by the Khachents publishing firm in Yerevan. My aim has simply been to "document" the racialist and racist aspect of the aesthetic principle, because there is no denying or ignoring it and because it represents the danger inherent in this kind of thinking. We witnessed the emergence of the same type of thought in Europe in the first half of the twentieth century, with intolerable consequences. It may be that I have not been fair to Zarian in proceeding in this fashion. I have, on various occasions, tried to explain why I have chosen to do so, and I am repeating myself here. Others may analyze other aspects of the writer's work; I have done so myself in several essays published in Armenian. For all these reasons, I have extracted from *The Pancoop* only the mind-boggling passage that the reader will find below; it takes the form of a monologue that one of the characters in the novel, Iberian, utters in the presence of interlocutors who are quite simply dumbfounded by what he has to say during their boat trip on Armenia's Lake Sevan. In *The Pancoop*, Iberian is, incontestably, the author's spokesman. (I firmly believe that Zarian named him Iberian because he was already planning the stay in Spain that he would make a little later in order to write the first part of *Countries and Gods*.) Although we have to do with a novel, the passage translated here has to be read as its author's racialist profession of faith: it has a generally Nietzschean cast, as Zarian undoubtedly intended. In fact, it is the most unabashedly racist passage in the whole of Armenian literature. It was written in 1934. This proves, at the very least, that Zarian's ideas were coherent and that he remained rather faithful to himself, both in what he said and how he said it. The texts he wrote in 1914 (the Manifesto and all the essays presented here) were not at all the products of accident.

All that said, I must add one more word. It bears on the translation of *ts'egh*, the Armenian word for "race." The word was commonly used early in the twentieth century to designate the nation. For example, Zabel Esayan uses it repeatedly in her 1911 book *Averknerun mej* (Among the Ruins° extended excerpt, translated into English by G. M. Goshgarian, may be found in my *Writers of Disaster: The National Revolution*). The common usage of the word, while obviously not fortuitous, is in no sense racist—far from it, in fact. It is not even racialist, except when one delves below the surface to study the reasons for which it came into use in nineteenth-century Europe and was then introduced into Armenian as an equivalent for "nation" meant to designate or connote the nation's "telluric" sources (I borrow the word *telluric* from Oshagan). That is why I originally decided to translate *ts'egh*, in the following selections, in two different ways, using the word *race* when the writer's intention is explicitly racialist, as in the *Mehyan* Manifesto and most of Zarian's other writings, and *nation* when what is involved is the common utilization of the term to designate the national collectivity (as in Oshagan's March 1914 essay).

But I have abandoned this idea. I shall leave it to the reader to make the necessary distinctions with the help of my commentaries. I would have had no need to provide all these explanations (indeed, I had no need to in Esayan's case) if we were not confronted, where the Armenian advocates of the aesthetic principle are concerned, with a kind of thinking that was at the roots of racialist discourse throughout Europe and, above all, in Germany. It should, finally, be pointed out that Zarian read German. He had probably read Spengler early in life, doubtless in the original. He spent a year in prison in Munich in 1906 for taking part in subversive activities intended to benefit Lenin's Bolsheviks. This did not moderate his taste for the race of the Masters or his contempt for "servile" races, however one interprets his apology for Masters past or to come.

9

"OUR MANIFESTO"

(Mehyan, no. 1, January 1914, 1–3)

Toward what veiled goal is the Armenian artist staggering, amid the turbulent scenes that an uncertain Fate has cruelly forged with the sweeping blows of affliction? What surrounding sphere will his errant eyes behold? Of what statue will his body assume the form? What sort of dance will his feet trace, weighed down with their leaden burden? And what magic will his tongue utter?

It was high time, we thought, that these vital questions vibrate deeply and intimately in the souls of all who feel within themselves the power to create, to build, to raise up. Wishing to see the facade of the Temple of Art shine at last on the race's breast, we cry, with a common will, burning with the fever of creative frenzies and cognizant of the powers still slumbering deep in this nation's soul:

Let us

1. worship and express the Armenian Soul;
2. pursue originality and individuality in matters of form;
3. cultivate the Armenian language with the help of revitalizing grafts;
4. keep pure literature at a far remove from politics and journalism.

We proclaim the necessity of *worshiping and expressing the Armenian Soul*, because the Armenian Soul exists, although it only rarely manifests itself. The verdict that has condemned it to silence must be revoked.

We say that, without the Armenian Soul, there can be no Armenian literature and no Armenian art. Every true artist merely gives voice to the soul of his race. The Armenian Soul has been forged out of a past filled with somber, majestic images, sadly illuminated by a black sun, and hardened in a life furrowed by roads to Golgotha. In our time, It seems to be a miracle whose mysteries must be revealed. The Armenian Soul is an element in the intellectual universe which, once It has been made manifest, will amaze all thinking mankind. To bring that Soul to light is every Armenian artist's basic duty.

We say that, although external factors—established customs, alien influences, deformations and perversions of feeling—have held sway over the Armenian Soul, they have failed to corrupt It. We discern It, the Armenian Soul, flashing bright from the strings of medieval lutes and Goghtn's lyres.[2] We discern its profound wisdom in our popular epics, gleaming nuggets of our race's genius. We sense that It lies coiled within each of us and that, animated by the breath of our ancestral heritage, It lives still. It will find its tongue the moment It is emancipated. Let us emancipate It, this Armenian Soul, from the shackles and the violence of foreign influences—struggling, if need be, even against ourselves.

We believe that the Armenian Soul is Light, Power, and Life, embodied in the statuesque splendor of the ARYAN race to which we belong.

We declare that we must pursue *originality and individuality of form* because—need we repeat this elementary truth?—it is incumbent on every artist to produce writings the manner and matter of which are original and individualized, because—need we add?—art is the very realization of the inner self, a mode of visionary creation that tolerates no predetermined influence. We say that our soul, which is to be the Armenian Soul Itself, will pass through all the forms dictated by the sensibilities and inner rhythms of each of us. We reject in advance all subjection to standing forms. We prefer all the means of expression and authentic, familiar forms that have served as vehicles for the Armenian Soul as manifested in our national art and literature down to the present day; yet we proclaim, we *demand* the freedom to employ all forms of expression, for we believe that, until there is originality and individuality of form, we shall have no innovation nor new creative riches.

We declare that it is necessary to *cultivate the Armenian language with the help of revitalizing grafts*, because we believe that, from the standpoint of the ideal of perfecting our language, the elements that Armenian employs at present must be considered inadequate. Not a single one of our provincial dialects can by itself satisfy our ideal of perfection—not even the "urban dialect," as the Armenian dialect of Constantinople is called.

We proclaim that the Armenian language must be purified of numerous foreign-sounding words; we are resolved to turn to the diverse sources of the language, classical Armenian and the language spoken on our native soil, and to adopt authentic Armenian words, expressions, and definitions. We propose to graft them onto our literary language without violating the laws that ensure its harmony. We want to found an aesthetics of the language, introducing new features, new hues, and new accents.

We declare that one must *keep pure literature at a far remove from politics and journalism*, because, in our day, politics and journalism are two of the dangers lying in wait for Armenian art. We are not opposed to the one or the other, journalism or politics, for as long as they remain in their proper roles. But we will rise up in protest whenever they try to come forward in the name of art or literature or to transform art and literature into weapons serving their own ends. *We demand the unconditional independence of art.*

Art is a kind of madness and, as such, stands above revolution or reaction. Itself a species of religious zealotry, it stands above every religion as well.

A race that wants to live has to create. There was a need to erect a temple. We want to help erect it. On its columns, our Armenian, profoundly Aryan soul will discover lines sometimes unexpected and strange, and sometimes sublime—perhaps unappealing, perhaps infuriating, but always sincere.

There was a need to create a temple: we want to create it. Whoso believes, let him enter, shedding at the door his prejudices about, and blindness to, the past and present, while bringing in with him his youth, enthusiasm, and, above all, creative power.

As he enters, this inscription will meet his gaze, carved in stone over the door: "Let us create."

Let us create, so as to live in what endures. Let us create there, in that enduring element, so as to add the new notes of our race to the world's great symphony.

Daniel Varuzhan	Constant Zarian
Hagop Kufejian	Kegham Parseghian
Aharon	

10

CONSTANT ZARIAN
"For Art: Creation, Madness, Heroism"

*(**Mehyan** no. 1, January 1914, 4–5)*

Creation, madness, and heroism: those are the three tragic faces of the making of Mystery.

If the period is historic, then let us plot angles, build the framework, and hail the insatiable surveyor who, at last, discerns the torches of new visions in the distance.

Rather than certainty, the enthusiastic pride of a new consciousness. As a foundation, the stubborn quest for a tragic ego.

In the desert?
    Yes, before the infinite.

What is tragic, for an artist, is the biting, merciless flagellation of the ponderous automatism of the life around him: a prison.

A prison with its monotonous movements, its uniform steps, its parasitic words, its dragging rhythms, its vain and savage, fawning and unvarying songs.

What is tragic is the pounding howl, the indecent game of life's stupid materialism.

Shamelessly, the grimacing belly usurps the place of the heart, laughing monstrously, cawing and cackling, wherever it discerns the faintest glimmer of intellect.

Thus it is that the veil the spider weaves spreads over every hue without distinction.

What is tragic is nature's weighty, thousand-ringed chains. The dreadfully massive, unsightly black prison devours us. We want to devour it in our turn, but with our blood, our griefs, our fevers, and all the strength in our straining bodies, whereas *it* devours *us* with icy indifference.

Nature does not know us.

And what is tragic is the human mind itself. Yet another prison. The enemy of dreams, an arithmetic cubed, pounded in by the brain. The $2 \times 2 = 4$, the logical lie, the uncertain certitude. Do you not see? The merchant weighs up every ware, the intellectual weighs up every idea.

They are decent folk.

The common man drags out his everyday existence and regularly does what others do. He regularly eats and drinks and regularly reads his paper every morning; he produces children and, the way dogs do, regularly dies.

Only the artist, the authentic creator, dares oppose his will *to be* against the tyranny of automatism. For he alone feels the prison's oppressive weight along the veins and longs to be free.

Against time and space, he pits *endurance*. Against automatism, he pits creation.

Free creativity is the key to all the mysteries of life.

With an effort at clairvoyance, it becomes possible to plunge one's eyes into one's soul, the eyes that strip the veils from the manifold play of the cosmic treasures and perceive the dreamy expression of all of life's tragic masks. In prison, they see the light and, bursting with their new-found awareness, set out on unhoped for, prophetic explorations.

The outset of a trying, tormenting spiritual drama.

Let us understand once and for all that life is the reflection of man's supreme ego.

Sometimes, during soundless nights, we hear the cry of suicides; sometimes, veiled, obscure appeals come creeping over our walls. Horrified, we understand . . . that they are triumphant voices.

For they say to the universe, "it's either you or us," and, striking their heads against stones, heroically work *miracles*.

Truly, only suicides and artists feel the need to triumph or be vanquished.

Artists love suicides, yet know that triumph means creation; that is, means weaving, from the tears and laughter of the dead, the *word*.

That calls for madness, and for heroism as well.

We know that when the animal went mad, man was born inside him.

We know that when madness kissed man on the forehead, he became religious.

Art is absolute madness.

In the thrilling leap toward the lands that dreams will create, admiring folly, soaring upward with open wings, is the indispensable condition for forging mystery. It is art's ground bass.

Madness means creative rebellion. If you are a rebel, cross everyday foolishness out with a black x and, if you aspire to the heavens, take wing and fly.

Who ever said that art is opposed to life? Quite the contrary: it is for life, but for *all* of life. Man, the wolf and the serpent, the plants and the trees, all the strange flora in the sea and all the precious stones shall once again magnificently flower and shall live amid sparkling, lightning-like laughter. We conceive the whole of life as a marvelous vision of our egos.

Who ever said that we are opposed to life?

But it is necessary to draw a magic circle around the ego to protect it. It is necessary to detach oneself from normality, from the merchant who sells everything and anything, from the blind and the short-sighted, from those who are never wrong and parasitic souls,

from the bourgeois, from the narrow heart and its petty calculations, from the sterile, somber, anti-aesthetic monster. One has to detach oneself.

There, in that circle, the creative spirit shall establish its kingdom, ringed by jutting towers confronting the unknown of the stars. There, the artist will suffer and, amid his suffering, will observe everything that appears. Demolishing the *real* and (journalistic) *fact*, he will redouble the essential rhythm, hear the secret music of existence, with its veiled voices, and the unrestrained pounding of its heart. Things, animals, and all the phenomena of our ego have disseminated their mysteries through the universe; one must learn to comprehend them and, advancing from discovery to discovery, to prophesy. Standing on life's headlands, one must proclaim the new image of the Universe amid struggle.

To look with eyes that have been ruined by habit, education, and all the things that take quantity as their measure is to perceive nothing.

One must possess the seer's blindness, inner sun, and creative madness.

Whoever can read the odes of his soul can also understand all the odes of the universe.

It requires heroism to do that.

Whoever dares to and knows how to see with his own eyes is a *hero*, for he is waging ruthless war on both himself and others.

God created heaven and earth because he *saw* them. The poet, sculpting new myths, sees them, and dares.

Revolting against nonexistence, God created; the poet revolts against the creator, against new nonexistence.

Art is rebellion against God.

Jehovah, Lord of lords, do you hear the magnificent *song* rising up over the columns? The nimble-footed choirs are dancing around the altar in order to raise up, out of the sacrificed corpses—dismembered, covered with gore—the new statues of new myths.

Do you hear, Jehovah?

II

CONSTANT ZARIAN
"For Art: The Jesus of the Armenians"

(**Mehyan**, *no. 2, February 1914, 17–20*)

I love Jesus of Nazareth and believe in him.

I love Plato as well, and Dante, and believe in them.

Against a background formed by the pure lines of Greek architectural forms, Plato appears, plainly visible, radiant, big with the pure light of the idea, his eyes fixed on life's great mystery. And although Dante forges complex apocalyptic visions with extravagant panoramas and crazily sculpted heavens in which he plants Hell and the Kingdom, his steps are assured and sublime and his person stands out as a totality before our eyes.

In our souls, Jesus is veiled in a pale indistinctness.

A Jacob Smith is right to show Jesus sitting at the table of a Flemish family. A Murillo or a Velazquez can depict his humiliated body and put glowing coals in his eyes, for Spaniards carry him in the inferno of their souls, souls always full of religious torment. And Italians paint his picture beneath a blue sky, on roads full of potholes, so that they can see him everywhere, always, as their mighty lord and brother.

But who has seen, who knows, the Jesus of the Armenians?

Our Jesus has remained terrifyingly *mute* and has never dwelt in the Armenian soul's inner depths, because no one has ever *seen* him.

In accursed nights, when the sky poured down maledictions like slaver, when Armenian cities were living in terror, when the doors of humble homes were blazoned with signs dripping with gore, we waited for him with great hope in order to lament the Feast of Crime—but he never came.

On Armenia's fields, Death and Crime have often danced their Düreresque saraband and veiled the verdure of our prayers with red shadows—but Jesus never passed that way.

The centuries of our suffering set heaven ablaze with our voices crying danger, and constructed the abominable temple of our skeletons. Jesus did not brighten that temple with a single lamp.

We howled out our misfortune, invoked Golgotha, and washed his imaginary feet with our blood. But we never once saw him.

Jesus is a foreigner for us.

The reason that Jesus has never dwelt in our souls and is distant from our conceptions, the reason that we have been unable to create an image of him, transform him into an icon and use it to produce art, is that his inner morality, spirit, and subconscious secret are remote for us.

While our national genius has received the commandments of Christianity's founder in a wonderful revelation, it has neither understood nor experienced his internal, personal struggle. The Armenian genius has not *recreated* it, has not felt the pain of bringing it into the world, has not relighted the moral pyre of the founder of a religion.

It is impossible straightforwardly to assimilate any idea, however new and beautiful that idea is, without the inner struggle and spiritual effort that impels us to create it afresh.

One and the same religion or doctrine, disseminated among different peoples, finds different forms and modes of expression. A race's virtues and moral riches fill a new religion with life, not the other way around.[3]

Christianity, which we accepted, as everyone knows, in tolerant, sympathetic fashion, has unfortunately remained impoverished. It is as if it lacked what is most essential, the heart; and Jesus remains something imposed on us by force.

Jesus is a preeminent example of the genuine creator who is also a self-creator. He is the man of terrible battle, a battle he fought with himself. With a strange, magnificent effort, he annihilated, purged, put to death that which constituted the weakness of his blood, soul, and body: SEMITISM.

He was the first to grasp, with outstanding clairvoyance, the danger represented by the Semitic poison that was clotting his veins, exhausting his muscles, diminishing his mental capabilities, enveloping his heart, and filling his soul with apathy. The Aryan ideal was the first heavenly ray to enlighten his mind, opening up before him the emerald-spangled, bright-gold path that, as he knew full well, led to Golgotha.

To overcome oneself and master all the virtues and mysteries that one harbors within oneself is to become a universal force, is to become a god.

From the day he was freed from the depravities of his race, this giant of a man became a fighter for an ideal.

The Semite never has an ideal. He has practical goals, but never has a dream. The Semite does not know infinity (Philo of Alexandria); he waits for a God, but does not seek him out.

The Semitic race is an inferior race. It is effeminate and materialistic (Otto Weininger).[4]

The Semite does not soar. His is an uncreative race lacking genius, fearful of mystery and vision. The Semite knows how to imitate and repeat and grasps things easily, but never feels the music of the universe; he is a satirist with a lame soul.

Jesus is the anti-Jew. He is the sublime inner metamorphosis, the diamond soul. He is a rock that burns forever, an ocean drunk with spirituality.

Jesus is the absolute and, simultaneously, the particular. He is movement itself, for he walks forever without tiring. To understand Jesus, one must suffer with him and espouse his profound struggle. One must contemplate him with a pure gaze and accept, not merely what he said, but what he went through so that he might say it.

Let us regretfully admit that there is no suffering in the Armenian Soul.

This people, which has experienced one hundred thousand Jesuses' one hundred thousand Golgothas, has never experienced an inner, moral Golgotha. Among us, the absence of religious quests and crises is striking. Also striking is the absence of consciousness of a mission and of Aryanism.

Where there is no profound spiritual life, no hard-fought battle of ideas, no inevitable hammering of accursed questions, there can be no art.

Art is the joy of mystic blood, and the joy of happy visions (Gaudium felicissimæ visionis).

The Sign will inevitably be born from amid wounds; otherwise, the void will swallow us up.

Snow and Blood are the very heart of creation, for the former is the sign of the immaculate, the latter, that of the wine of ecstasy. Jesus was a child and was snow, and he was ecstasy as well, for he vibrated like the petal of a sacrificially burned flower. That is why he must be ranked among the greatest artists.

Moralists, philosophers, and sociologists can readily understand Saint Paul, for example, but will never understand Jesus. Jesus can be understood only through aesthetic empathy, through the artist's penetration. The conception of him is poetic. He is color, music, line.

Jesus is art.

It is noteworthy that the peoples who love and see Jesus also *decorate* him. They make his wounds shine with precious stones and wrap his tortured body in parti-colored linen cloths embossed with gilded images. Jesus, despite the terrible torments he endured, appears to these peoples as joy—as, not a martyr, but a creator and artist.

The fate of the Armenian nation's intellectual and spiritual life is intimately bound up with the question of Jesus.[5]

Let us make an inventory of our values; at the same time, ignoring petty calcula-tions, let us make the heroic effort required to become aware of the emptiness that surrounds us and fills our souls.

For there is a servile, dead thing in the Armenian Soul, and it is incumbent on us to fight it.

Jesus, whom, for centuries, we seem to have accepted simply for form's sake, exists neither in our art nor in our literature nor in popular belief. As Armenian or as an im-age or as a living god, Jesus does not exist.

Consequently, if we are to lead a vital life, we must either recreate him by experi-encing his personal, inner struggle afresh, *so as to attain the Aryan ideal*, or we must struggle with him and overthrow him, so as to forge our new soul's new image.

Going back to the "old gods," as some ignorantly think we can, amounts to being left with nothing at all, for the old gods are in truth old, and dead. The very idea of a "return" is a mark of intellectual laziness.

To live in the spiritual poverty in which we are now living is to perpetrate a crime against ourselves and the mystery of the universe. A people that does not undergo spiritual renewal and create new values is doomed, if not to die, then to lead, at best, a corpse's shameful life.

I believe that the intellectual aristocracy about to be born has new Armenian blood in it, fiery and ecstatic.

I believe that it will encounter, very soon, on the path of its quest for a new art, the complicated but essential religious questions and, in the temple of its rebirth, accept a living god who will impel it to create.

May the Jesus I love forgive me. I should not like to see him in the pale, impover-ished form in which he is presented to us. I know that he would have preferred a sec-ond Golgotha to the colorless life he is leading in the Armenian Soul.

I sense that Jesus of Nazareth will prove me right.

12

CONSTANT ZARIAN
"The Heart of the Fatherland"

(*Mehyan*, no. 3, March 1914, 36–37)

We offer the Heart of the Fatherland a Wreath woven of the solitary, anguished flow-ers of our respect.

We offer it the hope and joy of the strange dance that it is our destiny to create—behold, here it is.

We offer the Heart of the Fatherland our ominous confessions, as do those who sometimes broke faith.

We offer it the sanguinary Love of the few who desire, create, and hammer out destiny on intimate terms with it.

O, that Heart. Many are those who, with flayed souls, sad, weeping, went roaming through its ruins to listen to its thundering, find its dispersed fragments, and behold, at least once, the ferment of its blood, a wine long since, very long since dead.

Let us remember:

Reverend Father Khrimian, a true Father, Abovean, the man of tough Ideals,

Servantsdeants, the intelligent Traveler,

Alishan, his Eyes fixed on the fatherland, and others, and others. . . .

Some pressed gory, bruised scraps of the Heart of the Fatherland to their breasts. They gave voice to the people's pain and the silent, wrenching ordeals of the fields and meadows, displaying the shades of exceptional, grief-stricken souls.

Some preserved fragments on which the kisses of affliction had left their mark, on which the bites of iron teeth had carved their traces; they roared out a red, savage art and, like a bell-tower in flames, excoriated the heavens.

But there were also those who, hopeless and spent, shouted out the horror of the desires consuming them, howled despairing leaps, and, enraged, went deaf so as not to hear, gouged out their eyes so as not to see.

"*A pair of eyes on the ground.*"

Yet also admirable are those who, slinging sacks over their shoulders, set out on rocky roads to find the scattered fragments of the Heart of the Fatherland.

It was they who recounted for us, in the plain language in which they heard them, the naive, ancient tales that the people continued to invent; they sang sad, melancholy songs of grief over the fatherland, the echo of who-can-say what Visions.

In mysterious, low, even fearful voices at first, then loudly and full of pride, they told and retold one another the new, miraculous tidings: the Heart of the Fatherland is not a corpse; it is not cold; it is still alive.

It is still alive!

Consciousness was born. They understood.

There where the heart had sown its blood, there, secretly, flowers have been born, mysterious and bashful, like new brides.

A people that tells tales and sings songs is a people that will live.

But, in order that the Great Heart might once again sing out with all its thunderous force, it is necessary to gather up its fragments and seek the new form of its existence and manifestation.

When, from an extensive fatherland's every corner—from its mountain-peaks, from the depths of its fields, from atop its boulders—the voices and songs of those who live by creating rise up, when they feel an imperative need to express, as destiny commands, their souls' secret and eyes' light, the Heart of the Fatherland shall, amazingly, vibrate with miraculous life.

No center anywhere.

Let us not look, with a poor man's eyes, at what others have done.

Let us not wait.

Visionary, unmediated creation.

And then—o, I know this past all doubting—then the choral song of the new *ashough*s shall rise joyous and clear, declaiming the new Mythology.[6]

For the Style will have been discovered.

Style is the race's image, its coat of arms, its crown, studded with gems charged with meaning.

There is no doubt that it already exists, but it is hidden in the depths of distant prospects, on people's features, in their skulls, in their eyes.

Quantity does not know of its existence and never shall.

Powerful personalities, the creators and geniuses who see everything, shall see style, too, and proclaim it.

The Heart of the Fatherland shall live by Art and in Art.

Scattered and divided, it shall become one in Art.

The Heart of the Fatherland, everyone's Heart.

And strange images and forms shall be born, loud colors, wondrous, astonishing melodies.

I tell you this.

13

HAGOP KUFEJIAN
"The Literature of All Armenians"

(Mehyan no. 3, March 1914, 38–40)

The time has come, we believe, to cast aside the colorless, pointless, old-fashioned explanations that have long enjoyed free passage through our literature and, for a time, strutted across the public squares.

Our literature is one. It comes from below, from remote regions. Beneath the diversity of dialects, the same blood flows, and has animated, among our race, the great talents whose light has flashed out over the clearings in the centuries.

Our literature comes from the multitude in the form of songs, statues, domes. It shapes the race's intellectual life (*vie d'esprit*)[7] and comprises the race's soul.

It is the heritage of all Armenians. It has the character of a center.

We reject the Constantinople Armenians' contemptuous chatter, which jeopardizes the unity of our literature.

The concept (*concept*) of a *literature of all Armenians* applies in equal measure to all the fragments of the Armenian race. It rejects inevitable constraints and the features that lend the dialects their pretensions; it is above the determination of ostensibly aesthetic linguistic phenomena.

It is too broad to be confined by the petty mutual antagonism between our literature's two branches. It is strong enough to live a life of its own with no need for the indispensable prop of *local color*.

The literature of all Armenians, like every phenomenon whose furnace resides in the heart of some vital organic activity, can be shaped only by the emanations that radiate from all living communities. It is, for that very reason, an expression of the race displaying, in many of its lineaments, unequaled fidelity to it.

While acknowledging the powerful influence of the primordial source constituted by the *mass of the race* and the external conditions framing it, and while giving the inescapable determinations of the *moment* (*moment*) and duration (*la durée*) their due, we believe that, over and above all this, strong individuals are particularly indispensable—great men who crystallize the soul of the race to perfection.

That is why we have to imagine *the literature of all Armenians* as unconstrained by servile fealty to various regional and ethnographic conditions.

In seeking the soul of the race in the souls of its great sons and daughters, we do not deny the importance of all the secondary factors or tangential influences that, stamping the individual with their stamp, help forge his psychology, bringing him forth in the form of a perfect, healthy animal.

We think or, more exactly, believe that, as with all great things, those most sensitive to the vibrations of the race will be its strong, great individuals. Snow and sun always kiss the mountains first.

But when is an individual great?

An individual is great when all of a race's scions can see their reflection in him as in a mirror while seeing their own traits just as they are, without distortion; when the host of shades rising from their graves kneel reverently before him; when, whatever the destiny of the different centuries and regions, the generations ebbing and flowing under the receding arches of time can recognize in Him the eternal, deathless reality that lives on, radiating like eternally burning musk from the urn containing his remains.

An individual is great when all the generations of a given race understand him. The individual focuses the countless rays scattered by the furnace of the race, in the full range of their hues, burning bright or half-extinguished.

There is nothing fortuitous in any of this, nothing that is due to the fluctuations of unrestricted caprice. Individual greatness obeys a mechanism so exact that it can be called scientific. The individual does not fall from the sky fully formed. He is the product of supreme effort.

He wages his first battle against the egalitarian tendency of societies. He knows by instinct how to despise the caresses and threats of which he is the object in order to subvert the mediocrity imposed by everyday life. Foam in his hair and light blazing in his eyes, he glides over the waves of mediocrity to freedom. He sculpts his detachment.

And, in his moments of weakness during this battle, he invokes all the great men of the past, calling on his race's hidden capabilities to bring the miracles he works to perfection.

It is obvious, then, that, before all else, the individual takes his race's most authentic cords in his hand. He is the truest type of the multitude among which he lives. He has condensed all the dreams of his race in the rainbow of his eyes, and his breath is anointed with the grace of all the ancient and modern melodies that, like lullabies, soothe his race's soul.

For the sake of greater clarity, let us add: great individuals are not of a metaphysical mold. Endowed with extraordinary powers of assimilation, they live through centuries of human history in their fledgling years. They very rapidly go through that which mediocrities would need exhausting centuries to digest. They embrace all the elements comprising the psychology of the race. . . .

The *literature of all Armenians* is an invitation to the sons and daughters of the race.

It is an invitation to go to those shores, those open spaces and heights where, after centuries of acclimatization, the race is discovering that it has become more daring, heartier in its pleasures, more fearful and fervent when it suffers.

It is an invitation to go to the land of our fathers, which, among enslaved races such as ours, should be the only divinity left standing.

We do not know how to hate. To this terrible vice, the greatest virtue we can oppose is the enthusiasm and the constancy of a dream, the existence of which is of decisive importance for our destiny.

"The races live within the circuit of a very limited number of conceptions and dreams," a contemporary thinker has said. Today, we have the impression that the oldest of the springs justifying our existence has been broken: the Armenian churches have ceased to be spiritual poles of attraction for our people.

Without a dream, life is impossible. A few important forms of universal fiction (*fiction universelle*) are becoming urgently necessary for us.

In prioritizing literature, the highest form of self-determination, we are not succumbing to a thankless illusion. We believe in literature.

We say to everyone, young and old:

We have our mission and our mystery, which come from the depths of the past, have been cherished by the past, and remain unrealized.

We have a possible kingdom before us. Our accomplishments in the intellectual realm are not signs of a negligible force.

We are not weak skeptics. We saw how the center of European thought repeatedly shifted over the past century. The great capitals always announce the gospel of possible wisdom to humanity. Remember Warsaw and do not forget Copenhagen.

The fate of doubting, nay-saying generations has been a sad one. Covered with a veil of suspicion, we will cease to live vigorously. Nay-saying leads to annihilation.

Be aware that the winds of equality are blowing unchecked on all sides. Resistance to such storms now will constitute the furnace of our capabilities. That movement is fateful and inevitable; let our reaction to it be just as tragic (*tragique*).

For, in this wrestling match, great individuals will once again enter the arena, nobly upright in the heroism of their desperate struggle.

Let us forge our great men. Let us forge them out of the elements of our fatherland that are the most refined and the toughest. Let us fill their souls with our mountains' rocky heights and iron strength, our flowers' blood, the foam of our silken streams, delicate as silk. Let us make incense for our great men's souls out of the ashes of our ruins. Let us pour the zeal of all our glories, real and fictive, into their hearts.

Waiting for us in our fields, like dreams still undreamed, are all the veiled, anonymous laments that pour from the lips of our peasants.

A Priest of Labor[8] has transformed our songs into music as marvelous as a revelation for us, for whom they had become something foreign. A handful of talented Armenians have succeeded in capturing the race's dreams and imagination in one or two legends with an art so novel that it has filled us with the optimistic belief that great creations await us.

How much remains to be done! Our future mythology is walking about on our native soil like a Milky Way suspended above our heads, afloat in a light-filled sheet's billows. In the recesses of who-knows-which monastery, our Faust is already sharing confidences with his devils.

We say to you: to forge the integrity of our fragmented existence, we await our Dante.

The Dantes did not come from India.

Our invitation is extended to all. It is addressed with equal urgency to Constantinople and the Motherland, the Caucasus and Persian Azerbaijan.

We will welcome the nationalist [*azgaynamol*] dream in all our writers, and learn to live with the dangerous illusion informing our young students' vain dreams, if only they—writers and students—are cognizant of the burden resting on their shoulders.

Fragmented, aged, driven from its center, land, and religion, vagabond, humiliated by its aimless wanderings, without a name or body, a tottering multitude stands before us.

Mighty laborers, race-builders, nation-creators, behold what we lack. It is our fervent belief that these capacities are still to be found in the race's secret treasure-house.

The Literature of all Armenians is our ark. Let us defend it firmly, fiercely, against the Philistines crawling in our midst.

14

CONSTANT ZARIAN
"For Art: The Theater (Synthesis)"

(*Mehyan, no. 4, April 1914, 49–53*)

In the period of crisis and soul-searching in which we now find ourselves, the question of the theater, too, becomes important, even essential. The future of the theater as well as the type and direction of the path opening up before it are matters that today preoccupy thinkers and philosophers of art in nearly all civilized countries.

In France, it has at last been understood that what has so far gone by the name of theater is no more than a vile, sordid commodity. In Russia, where serious, praiseworthy efforts have been undertaken to bring about changes in an intolerable situation that was an insult to noble, sensitive souls, it has at least proved possible to demolish what existed, even if nothing positive or solid has been said yet. Germany and England are giving serious consideration to this question and are attracting attention with a few audacious innovations. Belgium now feels the need to create a national theater and the government is even providing material assistance to this end. Ireland is expressing new ideas and producing new works. Finally, in almost every country in which intellectuals and civilization are to be found, people are giving serious thought to the theater.

What is the reason for this intellectually arduous quest? In a century in which airplanes, movie theaters, and other mechanical inventions are objects of general admiration, filling "progressives" with proud self-satisfaction, what motivates this interest, which has not been observed for centuries? It may be said that, since Roman times, people have never been seen to take so strong an interest in the theater.

We can find an easy explanation by taking a quick look at the past. We shall see that the crisis of the theater is, to a certain extent, the crisis of humanity itself.

When the Greeks first laid the foundations of tragedy, they immediately perceived its vital importance. The temple was about to be erected; knowledge was about to be proclaimed.

When it first emerged, tragedy was simply a fugitive from the Eleusian Mysteries that had slipped into the city. The Dionysian dithyrambic ode had its secrets, and its priests possessed lofty, esoteric knowledge that poets now revealed. Personified destiny hovered over the sacrificial altar and the chorus strode back and forth before it, preoccupied and full of tormenting doubt. The *thymel*—the altar—remained the theater's principal, indispensable ornament, for the gods dwelt there.

With roots in worship and religion, the Greek theater retained its religious character to the end: it was a ceremonial theater. When tragedy was subsequently brought to Rome, an unbelieving, plebeian, nature-worshiping environment, it was perverted and lost its greatness. All the efforts that Roman philosophers of art made to pump new blood into its veins and infuse new life into it were to no avail. The Latin race's mentality thwarted its development.

The theater degenerated into the *common play.*[9]

Christ endowed mankind with a new consciousness and enlightened men's minds with lofty knowledge. Struggling against a thousand obstacles, his ideas revolutionized the life of the spirit and blazed broad paths toward magnificent vistas.

Those initiated into the Mystery of Christianity built a secret Temple in the catacombs and grieved in harmonious dances around the martyrs' graves. And because tragic blood flowed in abundance and loud voices shouted prayers, the need for the altar of the Greeks' grew ever stronger. A little later, while the apostles disseminated the new cosmology by means of miracles and the word, the need to build the *House of God* made itself felt—the Church, the expression of the Sign. There, surrounded by his choirs, Jesus was the leading performer, the most profound of the tragic masks.

Developing until it had become the sole shrine of all knowledge, the Church multiplied its means of action and eventually felt the need—just as the Greek priests once had—to interpret, explain, and present the new doctrine's secrets in greater detail and, let us say, more tangible fashion. Hence it had recourse to virtually the same means employed by Greek tragedy. The Church became the theater of unanimist action.[10]

But because the ecclesiastical ceremony, under the influence of new interpreters, lost something of the simplicity of its forms and its means of expression, and because, on the other hand, the doctrine took on the character of an indubitable truth as it spread to broad sectors of the population, the need for a new ceremony began to be felt.

Mystery (*mystère, miracle*)[11] or, more exactly, ritual drama, became the new medium of tragic action in Christianity.

The ideas in the Old and New Testaments, historical memories and miracles, were represented in icons, plays, and *tableaux vivants,* with the result that Christian theater became a way of elucidating the worship service.

The community of the faithful—*sancta plebs Dei*—went to see these plays in order to admire marvelous miracles, the veracity of which it never doubted; and, because churches were too small to hold multitudes, Christian mystery had to go outside, to go public, to enter the polis and erect its stage in the streets. Before the performance, the actors, immersed in prayer, would kneel before the altar of the church in order to be spiritually united with Jesus; then, singing and accompanied by a priest, they made their way toward the public stage, in order to *live out* the tragedy of Jesus of Nazareth.

Unfortunately, what had to happen happened. The plebs, the commoners or, in a word, the street killed the pure Christian mystery: the street invaded the stage, that sacred preserve, bringing with it the trash of its vulgar mentality—idle chatter, gossip, politics, and other vile things. Christ's radiant tragedy was profaned and transformed into a . . . common play.

Later, Dante erected the mighty monument known as *The Divine Comedy*, and his genius became the tragic Christian vision's voice.

The theater, that is to say, the unanimist plot, died. The *thymel* (altar) was reduced to dust and, where no God was, prayers no longer rose up.

The common play, however, continued to develop.

Religious intuition and thought were divorced from the unanimist plot and retired to monastic cells, while the common play found new reasons to exist and evolve.

The first and foremost reason was *man*. Man, with his nature, passions, and budding powers dominated the stage, creating new forms and new movements before the eyes of the curious.

Shakespeare, turning to advantage all the possibilities opened up by the new trend, became the giant of this theatrical scene. Calderon accomplished nearly the same thing, while, in France, Corneille aspired to the greatest heights.

The materialistic, atheistic eighteenth century did not know the theater. Schiller, however, was to grasp its great importance, while Goethe was to concentrate, in *Faust*, all the concerns, torment, and questioning that filled his soul.

Faust stood alone.

With Ibsen, the family and society were put on stage. Ibsen's characters are torn painfully between these two institutions, a conflict that leads to the creation of what we may call interpsychological (*interpsychologique*) drama. The kind of character Ibsen shows us is strong and free, harkens to nothing but his own nature, is guided by his desires and caught up in an endless struggle.

Ibsen is a teacher.

In the late nineteenth century, Ibsen dominated the common play, creating an ennobled version of it that was unfortunately quite often at a far remove from art. His great merit resides, perhaps, in the fact that he gave expression to his own peculiar worldview and exhausted all the possibilities of his material.

Since then, social relations and the battle of the passions have provided writers with their basic material. Some pick a thesis and defend it on the stage. Others study man, basing themselves on scientific psychology, or try to find a satisfactory way of bringing contemporary society's conflicts and contradictions before the public.

The ruling class in contemporary society, in whose service official science and official culture stand, as does, consequently, the common drama as well, is conspicuous for its strange, parasitic intellectual laziness.

The theater—the common play—has become a place of amusement and superficial pleasures. Today's shallow, materialistic public, which lacks the intellectual capacity required for experimentation and creation, naturally proclaims its love of realism and naturalism and pays to see elaborate stage decor, so that everything will be tangible and readily visible, thus relieving it of the need to think or invent.

It is hard to imagine just how popular hams have become, now that they have gained the right to play roles in commercially successful works.

The common play has now reached the peak of its development and found itself a faithful, generous public. New, financially motivated "undertakings" are proposed, troops of writers spend their time realizing them, and new wares are brought to market, surrounded by a great deal of commercial advertising. These writers look for their material everywhere, in salons, hospitals, parliaments, or out on the street. Boudoirs, bordellos, and newspaper offices are becoming means to the end of producing new plays for the paying public's amusement. Seized by a feverish desire to "work something up," such writers suck in the dust of historical archives and lap up the latest "scientific" news. They shamelessly pillage each other's works and, if a few writers manage to devise a new expression or a new form for their profundities, others soon come along to capitalize on it, although they have had nothing at all to do with it.

> This giant factory produces everything:[12]
> The moralistic common play
> The pedagogical common play
> The doctrinaire common play
> The common play in the service of the fight against syphilis
> and common plays of many other kinds.
> Du théâtre vérolisé, as Baudelaire would have put it.

That's life, they say. That is indeed the life characteristic of the common play. The life characteristic of art and theater is something else.

If, in our time, there is no theater and the common play holds sway in its stead, the reason is that contemporary society brushes aside the rare artists and thinkers who independently seek their own way, and has neither religious, spiritual, nor universal concerns.

The Greek theater was a natural, inevitable further development of the ode, as Christian mystery was that of prayer.

Thus the tragic plot has its inception in lyricism (*lyrisme*).

The ode and the tragic plot unfold before Destiny, the Unknown, or Providence. People's presentiment of their Destiny fills their souls with a strange kind of suffering and spurs them on to action (*action*); for wherever there is conflict between bold actions and the secret powers, sacrifice becomes inevitable and blood flows on the altar.

The main motive for this action is to produce *knowledge* by means of worship, struggle, or self-sacrifice and to grasp the key to the mystery of the universe.

True theater is a means of comprehending *duration*. That is why it always stands in relation with God.[13]

Although contemporary society has no desire for such knowledge, a few isolated thinkers and poets are at least aware of the urgent need for it.

It was not long ago that people made obeisance to pantheistic, materialistic science, that loafers were capable of discussing and explaining everything with amazing ease, without straining their brains.

Determinism, *Darwinism*, *Monism*, and many other *isms* simplified everything, and, hand in hand with literary *realism* and *naturalism* (*isms*, again), filled people's souls with a terrible emptiness.

Now that science, with its relativistic laws, has been called into question, while philosophical inquiry has gone down a different road, the demand for true Theater is again making itself felt.

The Olympian gods are myths.

Philosophy is a vain intellectual game.

For some, the dominant religion is insufficient; for others, it has been deformed.

Science is little enough for the intellect, nothing at all for the soul.

What destiny, then, is rapping at our door? What kind of tragedy are we to create?

Two poets have made an honest attempt to create a contemporary Theater, and have succeeded in finding new paths. One is Maeterlinck, the other is Paul Claudel.[14]

Both have their roots in Symbolist lyric poetry, and the works of both are intimately bound up with Greek tragedy and Christian mystery.

In Maeterlinck's theater, Love and Death, under the dominion of destiny and providence, forge a strange, perspicaciously constructed plot. Imaginary characters who have taken from life its supreme reflection—or, rather, souls caught in the trammels of marvelous visions—turn about the Unknown and suffer from their desire to know. New wills well up from the depths of people's souls, new, veiled powers emerge from the heart of nature, and the plot is the result. Precisely when the living struggle against the dead, it is the dead who crown them, amid terrible laughter.

Maeterlinck plunges his eyes into the eyes of the Unknown.

Paul Claudel's theater is more idiosyncratic and more likely to generate controversy. His aim is to find a new form of expression for Christian doctrine and to bring the image of Jesus out from under all the veiled appearances of nature and humanity. His is an art of the parable, a missionary, doctrinaire, propagandistic art that opposes Platonic dialogue to Maeterlinck's interior dialogue (*dialogue intérieur*). But Claudel's art is sublime and pure, his visions are enthralling, and he shall have his place in the future development of the theater.

My aim in the present essay is not to make a detailed examination of all the new ideas and suggestions that have already appeared. I wish simply to glance at the difference between Theater and the Common Play.

If we attentively observe the present period of experimentation, we can happily confirm that the new Temple will be erected in a not-too-distant future and that new tragic plots will relight art's lofty flame in people's souls. Out of the lyric poetry that

the Symbolist school brought to its zenith, there will inevitably emerge the quintessential *motif* of cosmic tragedy, *THE SONG THAT SPAWNS TRAGEDY.*[15]

In a magic passage, Schopenhauer says "the epic or tragic poet shall discover that
he himself is destiny and shall be pitiless, like destiny."

Whether quantity and its servitors like it or not, understand it or fail to, the poet
shall stride toward his God, and shall display, on this wondrous journey, as the mirror
of his suffering and torment, the new song he has composed before the new altar.
Who knows?—one day new choruses may surround him, repeating his pure prayer.

What columns shall adorn this new theater? What forms shall the expressions of it
take? And with what past and what present shall we Armenians approach it?

Answering these questions means devising a new *ars poetica.*

One day I shall try to do that, if I feel the desire or the imperative need.

15

CONSTANT ZARIAN
"FOR ART: PAGANISM?"

(**Mehyan** *no. 5, May 1914, 65–67*)

Hethanosakan: Excuse me, my friend, I have an important remark to make.

Mehenakan:[16] Make two!

Hethanosakan: The first time I saw the title of your review, *Mehyan*, I naturally
assumed that you, too, would be on our side and would try to recreate the spirit of
our ancestors' old religions, which Christianity, unfortunately, distorted and then
wiped out. I couldn't help but think of Aramazd's, Astghig's, Nune's, and Vahagn's temples, which used to be found within the fortress of Ani, in Artashat and
Ashtishat, near Blacksmiths' Rock, on Mt. Paghat, and in many other places.
But—allow me to voice my disappointment—so far, I haven't noticed anything
pagan at all in the ideas you've expressed.

Mehenakan: Pagan? Now there's a word the meaning of which I don't
understand.

Hethanosakan: Look, paganism was a religion that preceded Christianity in
Armenia. All sorts of explicit testimonials confirm that fact.

Mehenakan: I know that much.

Hethanosakan: The pagans were the people who worshiped nature: fields, pastures, forests, mountains, rivers, and the sun, the primordial source of all life.

Mehenakan: I know that, too. But, tell me: what does that primitive religion of
our ancestors, which no doubt had its beautiful, appealing aspects, have to do with
modern life—and, in particular, with the kind of art we're after? After the pagan
period, mankind has gone through quite a few others, full of new trials, new
hopes, and different experiences and aspirations that naturally endowed us with

more refined sensibilities and deeper intellectual needs, affording us the chance to invent new ways of thinking and new approaches to things.

Hethanosakan: Yes, but the main features of life haven't changed.

Mehenakan: Which ones?

Hethanosakan: All the means of expressing people's instinctive inclinations. The love of power, strength, and virility, of the vastness of nature and its many beauties. The love of graceful, shapely human bodies, of wine and good food—in a word, of all the physical pleasures that a life of luxury offers. To live for the sake of living, praise wine and pleasure, plait wreaths of beautiful flowers and adorn Armenian brides with them: that's the purpose of life, that's what beauty is.

Mehenakan: What I love about you is the joyous leap of the young animal; if you had lived a few centuries ago, you would have been the young leader of the choirs of holy prostitutes devoted to Anahit's service. I like you: you're like a beautiful object among the beautiful objects in nature, like a horned deer that runs gracefully and has a simple mind; but our *Mehyan* hasn't been built in the Forest of the Poplars[17] and isn't dedicated to beautiful, glorious Anahit. We consecrated it to art.

Hethanosakan: Hasn't paganism produced art?

Mehenakan:[18] The Greeks produced very great art—but their paganism, you'll recall, wasn't objective. Their religion was a product of the creative imagination; even their idea of the gods came from their poetry. Greek art represented an admirable effort to escape the tyranny of nature and reconcile the soul with nature in a supreme, rhythmic equilibrium. The Greeks were the greatest symbolists in human history. Pythagoras reduced the radiant dream of the heavenly bodies to musical notes, while Plato was the first to describe the secrets of the heavens. To say nothing of the fact that they don't have anything to do with Armenian paganism, even if the Greeks did sell us wooden and silver idols.

Hethanosakan: And the Renaissance?

Mehenakan: I knew you were going to bring that up. The Renaissance was the product of many different circumstances, none of which exist in our case. To begin with, they had Greek and Roman art behind them, a huge storehouse of material with which to lay the foundations of a new art. What do we have? The songs of Goghtn? They come to a total of how many lines? And in what sense can they be considered novelties? We've stolen many of our gods from others and, as I said a moment ago and am ashamed to repeat, we had to turn to the Greeks to procure even our wooden idols. Secondly, our church wasn't narrow-minded, the way the medieval Catholic churches were: it didn't block the free expression of ideas and didn't stand in the way of natural intellectual development. Finally, who ever said that the Renaissance was fertile and progressive as far as art is concerned? In my opinion, the opposite is true: in blindly accepting the copies of classical works unearthed in digs, the Renaissance created a confused situation, diverting art from its natural path and spawning a tasteless, unbearable style known as the Baroque.

The consequences of that deviation can be felt even today. Renaissance artists copied the forms of the Greek masterworks, but didn't share the Greeks' spirit and worldview. If you look deeply into the reasons for the emergence of the Renaissance, you'll detect a certain relation—a distant relation, of course—with contemporary Futurists, for example.

Hethanosakan: That would never have occurred to me. That's a paradox.

Mehenakan: Call it whatever you like; the fact remains that both in that period as well as today, the motive for art was the object, the object for itself and in itself—*in sich*. In the Renaissance, people loved the visible—line, form, color— and, what is more, they observed it through the Greeks' eyes. What do the contemporary Futurists want, if not to express the object again? It's true that when we compare the two movements, our preference goes to the Futurists, because they imitate no one and, for better or worse, seek to express themselves with the help of new conceptions and forms.

Hethanosakan: Excuse me for asking: if the Renaissance was able to produce as many masterpieces as it did, why shouldn't we assume that we, too, will one day succeed in producing such works?

Mehenakan: Who's saying we won't? Art is freedom, and everyone is free to choose his own path; all he has to have is talent. However, as I see it, the object limits human consciousness, oppressing it and clipping its wings. Art is a means of freeing oneself from that objective realm, in order to dwell in the life of the universe as a whole. Objects, for us, are the thoughts of the universe: we regard them as grand symbols, breathe life into them, animate them and wash them in divine light. To love objects for their own sake is fetishism, whereas to discern symbols in them is to become a god. I think that the latter is art's proper path.

Hethanosakan: But you're forgetting that our people, after so much suffering, so many horrors and massacres, feel the need to live, to laugh, to have fun—in short, to enjoy life.

Mehenakan: Maybe. The only surprising thing is that just yesterday, they were still crying and bewailing the blood of their dead and the horrors of the massacres, whereas today, they raise their cups, invite people to dance, and construct the "temple" of sensual pleasure. I beg you not to assume that I mean to defend morality; do I need to repeat the elementary truth that art is beyond morality and immorality? A well-written work is always moral. What I wanted to say was that, if the people feel the need to laugh, that's no reason for the poet to take on the role of the one who makes them laugh. The people have their clowns and their servants, who exist in order to take advantage of them. The poet or the artist shouldn't sink to that level. He should always remember that only a few select individuals will understand him. The mob and those who serve it hate poets and exploit them. Every martyr has his mission; if not, he sheds his blood in vain. If the Armenian people's centuries-old martyrdom isn't capable of finding its mission in the life of the universe and forging the fabulous image of its suffering, if all these ordeals are transformed into dancing and laughter, then let us find the strength to say that we deserved our history. No, my friend, we Mehenekans are no pagans. We, too, love wine, women, and life; we, too, have many other natural needs, because we are mortal. But it's not from that that we want to create art. Our path is different.

16

CONSTANT ZARIAN
From The Traveler and His Road

(*Yerker, 132–38; Antelias, 1975*)

Literature

As I was about to leave Constantinople, Oshagan said, "I don't think they understand our literature there. In any event, go have a look . . . and write! We'll think about what to do."

The other day, pint-sized Charents, who had just come from Moscow, put his feet up on the table in Markar *agha*'s cafe. Turning to me, he said, in front of the Cheka spies, "You counter-revolutionaries. . . ."

I had no choice but to remind him, in very sharp terms, of his days as an official in the Dashnak government and as one of the volunteers with their "bandit morality." He became more sweet-tempered right away and began reciting my "Western City." I had long since forgotten that text of mine, as I had forgotten the "proletarian poems" that I had published in Russian in the Geneva monthly *Radouga*.

From 1906 to the present, what a complicated period we have gone through! What events have we witnessed! How arduous a slope of thought and experience have we scaled! And now, after negotiating so many roads, we stand before the same broken pitcher. The sole difference is that then our explorations were motivated by our selfless enthusiasm, thirst for novelty, spirit of self-sacrifice, and great dreams, whereas they are, today, the calculated expression of blind obedience and shrewd self-interest.

They are producing literature on state order and by Party decision and forcing people to produce poetry at gunpoint.

One or two authorized Party members aside, no one dares criticize for fear of being classed as a counter-revolutionary who "stands in the way of the cultural work of the peasantry and proletariat." In public, everyone sings hosannas of praise. In private, they mock and curse.

Every one of us, à la Arpiar Arpiarian, publishes exaggerated encomiums in the *Hayrenik* daily for Abdül Hamid's feast-day. The sole difference is that, here, every day is Abdül Hamid's feast-day.[19]

Yet literature and all other cultural questions are, now, for the Armenian people, matters of life-and-death importance.

In what sense are we part of the present?

How shall we present ourselves?

Of course, we have all come in order to play our part in the circus.

The circus is the plain of Ararat. The region at the foot of Mt. Ararat is complex, is a desert. Roads crisscross, travelers are disoriented. The shepherd sounds his flute to round up his flock but, once it has been rounded up, where is it supposed to go?

In Constantinople, we were trying to call the flock together. But we were in a conflagration after an earthquake. The flute was stained with blood and the crazed flock was scattered to the winds.

In the role of the hapless knight in the flaming forest, Siamanto was moving and tragic. Like a mother who has lost her children, he had clambered up onto the roof and was loudly weeping. Varuzhan, the last of the Mkhitarist poets, was, à la Delacroix, making the blood flow around the beautiful bodies of naked women and seeking the secret of the new life in a purely imaginary paganism. Others were collecting faded pictures in the ruins of devastated villages, fragments of reality's shattered mirror. All this was unfortunately lost beneath the cheap tintinnabulation of the language of Constantinople's Armenians. There were, of course, others: Medzarents's softly weeping soul, Indra's underwater bell, poor Zarifian's sighing, and other tears shed drop by drop; the Armenian people of the future will have to collect their diamond traces.[20]

In this bruised, contradictory century, Armenian life and its errant mind, scattered to the four corners of the earth, had thrown its doors wide open, and the winds blew as they liked. The Armenian spirit, despite its efforts, was unable to concentrate. The thinking Armenian lurched right and left, came up short before a thousand problems, reconciled himself with a thousand different realities. The Armenian mind had become a migrant.

In poetry, the people—the so-called educated public—demanded a national ideal. And Moses of Khoren's "I Weep Over You,"[21] in brand-new forms—or, rather, decked out in newly fashionable clothes—promenaded before the newspaper offices and reaped applause from Galata's[22] merchants. The political parties approached literature with their own calculations in mind. They had transformed poetry into posters and ads, and the poet into one of those sandwich-board men who, like beasts of burden, carry commercial announcements for stores through the streets of the big cities.

A few of the chosen writhed with pain amid inauthentic realities and two-bit ideas. Anarchy reigned. Barefoot, people hopped about on hot coals of emotion and inspiration. Coast-dwellers, they went fishing for the sigh of the waves and staggered about on shifting sands.

No one had understood that they were the true poets.

The dull-witted Armenian intellectuals demanded cheap, common wares. Anyone who could read and write wanted to understand everything. Poems were loose women; Armenian merchants would feel them up and, for a fee, enjoy them.

Yet it was then, in those days of our disgrace, that *Mehyan* preached heroism, pride, and solitude. *Mehyan* preached, as well, madness and freedom. Madness? Freedom? The Armenian bulls raged and the petty bourgeois guffawed.

Naturally, we ran a little too fast in our youthful enthusiasm. Many deformed our fundamental idea, didn't understand it and couldn't cast off old prejudices. Many others, men who had acquired rank and reputation, feared for their future.

It was symptomatic that, in *Mshak*, Mr. Surkhatian had already turned his bovine eyes on us and had strung out, in a long essay, all the manure in his mind.[23]

The Armenian poet needed to be heroically, proudly alone.

The migrant needed to return to his native soil.

This is no plea for the ivory tower. An ivory tower can be no one's native soil; and, in any case, there can be no mentioning us and ivory towers in the same breath. Solitude: the return to an genuine reality—not the superficial one that can be measured with a yardstick and weighed on a scale, nor the well-known "objective conditions" (environment, season, and weather), but the profound real, the one that connects us to the universe in its entirety.

There is no contraption more meretricious than a camera. This has been said time and time again. And there is no literature more meretricious than the one that goes by the name of *realism* or *naturalism*. This is not to say that life or the environment as a whole should be neglected. Simply, life has to pulse in time with our hearts, in step with the vital rhythm that fills everything with breath and elan.

We exclaimed "fatherland!" and "struggle, battle, progress!" But where was that fatherland? What were the struggle and the battle for? What constituted progress? Nobody knew.

In literature, they looked for the touching novel, the beautiful page, richness of language, the note of longing for the fatherland, and political squibs, while confusing poetry with literature.

A poet is a man who dances on a tightrope. A tightrope artist: a deeply devoted, religious, self-sacrificing man. A man who manipulates the attractive forces of invisible rhythms; whose every step is an instinctive effort; whose every leap is an act of courage; whose every muscular contraction is the result of an inner impulse. The believer's perilous walk along the edge of the abyss.

Under the impulsion of the wisdom of the centuries, the people have also understood the matter this way.

In a remote province, an Armenian mother, after waiting for many long years, gives birth to a son. Mothers are bound up with their children's future at an animal level. Profound life holds sway in their wombs and nourishes the future with the blood of the past, while the mystery grows amid a struggle between love and death. A mother has presentiments, goes on pilgrimages, makes vows, dedicates her child to an invisible flame.

And the tightrope artist of St. Garabed lives a strange, luminous life.

From an early age, the Chosen One readies himself for a great, important action. He can be picked out of a crowd of a thousand children. A modest, concentrated, luminous face. Healthy. In church, he kneels in the first pew, motionless, disciplined, serious, and devout. People regard him with respect, help him and support him. The holy spirit is in him, and inspiration as well.

Then, one day, he goes from saint to saint. He wanders through mountains and valleys, villages and towns, bound for the appointed sanctuary. Day after day, he worships, prays, finds inspiration and then, an amulet on his breast, strikes out for another sanctuary. On the way, he scales cliffs like a goat, walks along dangerous heights, leaps over broad streams, passes lightly over fragile planks. He is trying things out. He is trying himself out; he is trying out sainthood.

And then—a miracle: existence, the life around him, loses its sharp contours. The Chosen One is visited by new signs of another form of existence. He has set the laurel wreath of supreme madness on his head. He has been sacrificed.

His body becomes a pliant tool, an admirable means of spiritual expression. His muscles develop, he grows harmoniously taller, his head becomes a little smaller, his shoulders grow broader, his thighs grow harder and become as supple as rubber.

He attains this physical beauty by living an abstemious, virtuous, disciplined life.

He does not look at women, he does not marry, he eats frugally.

And there comes the appointed day: his spiritual riches are now piled high. All his channels of communication with the life of the universe are in place. His inspiration is abundant and deep. Rhythm has become body and body has become soul. A saint has assurance. The veils have been rent and his new perception of the world is perfectly clear.

The tightrope artist pulls his rope taut, summons the people and, after ordering up the music of drums and flutes, mounts.

He never once falls.

And while, up in the air, he is recalling the names of the saints and, holding angels by the arm, celebrating a mass for the universe in his own magnificent way, down below, someone else, wearing a wild animal skin and a mask with a goat's beard, terrifies, with the gestures of a creature from hell, the evil spirits, unbelievers, and all who jealously give others the evil eye.

Among our people, the poet has to don the skin of a wild animal.

But the poet is a tightrope artist.

To be alone is to go from saint to saint.

To seek the mystery of the equilibria that govern the universe. Not in vain imagination or in words, nor in the uncertain depths of a paper heaven of "dreams" held in place by a tack, but in little everyday realities: a piece of bread, a torn shoe, a dying monk, an electric light.

One has first to attain harmony, that is, the consciousness of unity.

The artist, the East teaches, must undergo purification rituals and then withdraw to a solitary place. There, he must recite "the seven-branched prayer," beginning with an invocation of Buddha's and Boddhisatva's armies and the rite of offering up real or imaginary flowers. He must realize in his mind the four immeasurable attitudes of loving kindness, compassion, empathetic joy, and ataraxy.

Then he must contemplate the void or the nonexistence of everything, because, "by the flame of the idea of nonexistence," it is said, "the five factors of self-consciousness are annihilated once and for all. . . ." Only then will godhead appear to him "like a reflection" or "as if in a dream," and "that luminous image will serve the artist as an example."

The poet is in this role of eternal prayer vis-à-vis life.

Alighieri[24] is an example; Blake is another.

Drunken, lice-ridden Verlaine and angel-faced Rimbaud, disgusted by the human race, are examples.

And here?

The Armenians of the Caucasus are still here.

17

CONSTANT ZARIAN
From The Pancoop and the Bones of the Mammoth

(299–306; Antelias, 1987)

"You say that the *matagh*, the sacrifice, that cruel monument left us by the pagan period, is the supreme expression of profound love? Yes, sacrifice is undoubtedly something natural. . . . It is, so to speak, the foundation of Christianity . . . on condition, however, that you yourself are what is sacrificed, on condition that you give, with your own hands and of your own free will, the most precious thing you have: wealth, happiness, or even life itself. But to take an innocent, helpless lamb, slit its throat and roast it, and then sit under a tree enjoying yourself in the belief that that makes God in his heaven happy—that, I'm sure you'll agree, Mr. Iberian, is at the very least anti-Christian."

"Grey, you speak very well, but if you don't shift a bit to the right, the boat's going to tip over and you'll have to pursue the discussion with the trout in the lake."

Grey, who had become rather warm under the collar, was filled with "holy rage" and was inwardly rejoicing over that fact that he had at last been able to nail Iberian to the wall with incontestable facts. He quietly moved to one side, threw his arms out in front of him to keep the boat on an even keel, and turned a guilty look on O'Connor.

"Yes, admit it, it's anti-Christian at the very least."

"We aren't understanding one another very well. . . . As often happens, we're using the same words to mean different things. I was saying"—O'Connor spoke softly, in a somewhat dreamy voice—"that the idea of the *matagh* is the logical consequence of that profound feeling of love that all the men of the classic age, in the case to hand, the Armenians, have for animals."

"That's paradoxical."

"So it might seem, if we were using the word 'love' in the generally accepted sense. It's only natural that everybody should love his cat, horse, parrot, or chickens. There even exist 'Blue Crosses' and societies for the protection of animals—those places that engage in the strange activity of catering to English old maids' and wizened American geezers' sensibilities, while soothing their consciences. You know, those poor, half-crazed, lonely, faded widows who, seeds clutched in their hands, sweet-talk chickens as they go trotting after them, or else the pot-bellied grocer who, in a moment of weakness, stops in front of the little birdy shut up in a cage and whistles a tender air. All that goes by the name of love. They even say that the longer man observes man, the more he loves animals, and so on. But that isn't the love I mean. . . . It's not that at all."

"I'm very curious to know what it is, then," Grey impatiently broke in, with the expression of a wrestler ready to ward off a blow.

"The true Armenian man, in whom, fortunately, the Dionysian and Zarathustran worldview or, rather, world-feeling is not yet dead, is bound to animals by a secret, savage love, an animal and, at the same time, divine love. He is a Zeus, capable of naturally changing himself into a bull. . . ."

"That's not Christianity, in any case."

"It's Christianity by its own standards, not by Christianity's. As a Protestant, you ought to be able to understand that."

"For me, your explanation of love is obscure. You say 'savage' and 'secret,' you say 'animal' and 'divine.' What do you mean?"

"Over the centuries, Christianity has tried to separate the human individual from nature and the animals. Hate the body, glorify the soul, whose homeland is elsewhere. Dualism, division. In my view, dualism isn't just a metaphysical error, it's a moral error, too. The supreme life wisdom consists, not in separating spirit from matter, but, on the contrary, in locating spirit in matter and the world, where it's naturally at home. The world is spirit's body and spirit finds full expression only when it succeeds in metamorphosing that body, in transforming the immobile into movement, work, and creation—not by division, by fleeing reality, dreaming up different worlds, and putting one's hopes in a supreme power, but by relying on one's own values, transforming spirit into reality and simultaneously carrying spirit to its highest possible expression. Now, if you try to understand this people a little, you'll see that they have adapted their psychological structures to the Nazarene's religious teaching, which was forcibly imposed on them in the past. They have transformed all the Christian symbols into natural ones. Jesus is the sun, light, fire. The external world is alive, it lives alongside them, is present. Whence this people's relations with other beings. Like mountains, lakes, and all the natural elements, so, too, the animals are not outside the Armenian people's individuality, but live with it, forming one and the same body and soul with it. This people's subconscious puts them, conceals them in the ox or the sheep, which they both are and are not, but in which they see their future and their happiness. Their supreme wish is that their hearts should beat in unison with the heart of the ox or the sheep; they want to be united with the flow of their blood, the sensations of their flesh, their brains, lungs, and semen, in which they experience the limits of the law and a flight that soars endlessly upwards. That is why the powerful, terrible blow of the sacrificial knife is an expression of love, boundless enough to encompass the whole universe, and eonian, because, in the final analysis, the *matagh* is the one who offers the *matagh*."

"For whose sake? If he doesn't believe in a supreme power, for whose sake?"

"For his own sake. For the sake of the will that wants to transform the earth by, first of all, transforming itself. Every creative effort leaves behind a trace of suffering and blood, but that blood, mingling with the earth, awakens its vital powers, and the suffering brings flowers shooting from them. Armenian blood has flowed copiously on Armenian soil, the sacrifice has been offered up time and again, and now the time has come when, with a supreme effort and unremitting, exhausting labor, the miracle of radiance and color must be made to spring from that blood, forge the new race, and revive the new individual."

Evening had already fallen.

For an instant, the whole scene was plunged into icy immobility. The lake took on a bluish cast, and, in the distance, the island seemed like a weird vision fallen by accident into that boundless waste.

"How transparent the evening is," said Elena, cradling her head in her hands.

"Yes, alabaster and glass. . . . One of those very old Venetian glasses, the color of pale gold and grape juice. Tap them, and they ring like crystal."

O'Connor quietly pulled up the oars and fixed his gaze on the sky.

"You have beautiful dreams," Grey said with a polite little laugh, after a long silence.

"It's friendly indulgence that makes you use the word 'dream.' Others don't hesitate to say 'delirium' about. . . ."

"It's amazing how fearful people are where intellectual effort is concerned," O'Connor broke in. "It's easier to raze a city or overthrow a state than to change people's ways of thinking or feeling."

"Fear. . . . People have a horror of transitional periods. At the outer limit, where nonexistence ends and birth has yet to begin, in the moment that lies between being and nonbeing, is a place of terror, of dread. Or, rather, dread is the eternal, inassignable mark of this transition. Fear and terror vanish from our minds to the extent that we are travelers born to cross borders and break through to new horizons. If the world didn't come to a stop where certain natural human capacities have their limits, soul and body would float in the heart of undefined space like a scrap of flag shredded by the winds. Only the courageous are capable of confronting that fear, crossing the wilderness of a transitional period with a firm step, vanquishing the devil, and approaching the gods as equals," said Iberian, smiling at Grey.

"How fortunate, after all," he continued, suddenly serious, "that people are so different. Yet how fortunate, too, that all are burning with the same fire, some with the flames of the serpent speaking from within the bush, others with the flames of the star-worshipers' zeal."

"The important thing is to burn, the important thing is to seek."

"In the life of peoples, just as in that of individuals, there are times [*shrjan*] when it is imperative to say 'no' to everything in the name of life. To alter, to overthrow [*shrjel*] the dominion of the grave. To chop off a part of our inner being as if it were a sacrificial lamb so as to save the rest, where the myth still lives. Sometimes history forces a people to migrate from one part of the planet to another, to follow the sun, to reduplicate its movement, to make a revolution [*shrjel*]. It seems to me that there are also moments when life's supreme requirements dictate that we accomplish that same migration within ourselves, following our inner sun in order to accomplish our own secret revolution [*shrjan*]. That moment has come for certain peoples, and they are now awaiting the true revolutionaries, those prepared to traverse, and capable of traversing, the region of fear, of passing from nonbeing to being. . . ."

"Which means?"

"In the present case, it means that we must revalue all our values, be anew [*veralinel*], exist anew [*nora-goyanal*], put ourselves on new foundations [*verahastatvel*]. You're going to ask me how. Let me tell you right away. To begin with, to the myth of the divine-man, 'tormented on the cross and suffering with love,' we must oppose the man-god, radiating light and strength, the pinnacle of worldly achievement. To an abstract, dualistic conception of the universe, we must oppose a naturalistic, free unity, self-contained and self-sufficient, the will to power [*tirapetakan kamk'ë*]. To the race of the 'servants and children of God,' we must oppose that of the emancipated and the emancipators, who see in God the highest power that they themselves are capable of creating, to which they may submit, if they wish, or against which they may struggle, heads held high, manfully, without womanish emotion, without quailing, without prayer because these god makers participate in his divine nature and can embrace the universe with the same arms of fire, recognizing in it a musical expression of their own self. To feelings of dependence and need, these new men will oppose a feeling of capability and self-sufficiency. To the idea of equality, that of difference, distance, hierarchy [*kargapetut'iun*], nobility. To the idea of socialism, that of an individualism that has reached the highest level of spiritual development. To the demand for love, happiness, peace, and the need for consolation, they will oppose heroic disdain, the iron law of the immaculately pure will, and absolute action. And, against providential conceptions of the world, they will pit their tragic conception of the world, for which man is by himself amid the chaos of nature and the elemental powers and becomes his own savior, bending his own heart and brain to his will. Ah, to reject, to refuse to accept that economistic, Pan-Coopical creature, that partisan ant who is not the master of his fate, who has fallen from his throne into the dust and trots after history's and society's cart. To reject all that and assume all of one's responsibilities instead, barring the way to despair and weakness, reinforcing and arming the soul. Yesterday they were saying 'brother' and 'Father,' today they say 'citizen' and 'comrade.' Whose brother, whose comrade? The new man, the one we want, must have neither hope nor expectations. A self-contained planet, the beginning and the end conflated inside him, a rock, a mountain-peak, endowed with his own strengths and weaknesses. Everyone manning his post in the battle and combat; everyone a peculiar value, a quality, a life sui generis, a pitiless solitude. A power that refuses to enter into communication with others or achieve self-understanding, refuses to become a 'comrade' or 'brother,' refuses to feel equal. And this not out of the arrogance typical of common creatures, but out of respect for other individuals. The powerful individual is the pioneer of absolute justice and unrelenting truth, and his relations to others can unfold only on clear grounds, where there is crookedness neither of mind nor of heart,[25] nor cunning, nor pursuit of petty personal interests—but, rather, endless spiritual ascent, rank, cosmos, hierarchy, and gigantic, sunlike spiritual beings: a race of far-seeing Masters, self-fashioned creatures who do not take, but, rather, give the light and meaning of their strength. What we want, and want because we know it is possible, is the pre-Christian man who reached, with the priest-kings, the level of enduring existence. That world in which nature was not yet nature, nor spirit spirit, in which there were neither objects nor forms, but only forces. In which life was, in every one of its moments, a heroic necessity, replete with works, symbols, commands, magical and ritual gestures."

Iberian fell silent for a moment. Never before had they seen him so calm and yet inwardly so agitated. His eyes glistened and he had become slightly pale.

No one objected to anything he had said.

"It's sheer madness," thought Grey. "There's no point in arguing with him."

"And this very place, the heart of this desert expanse, this profoundly mysterious eye in the opening between the mountains, Lake Sevan—what prodigious events has it not witnessed," Iberian continued, gazing into the distance. "Atop this plateau thrust between lakes and mountains, in this place of windstorms and snowstorms, gods have been born and gods have died. In this place, hostile worlds have stood face to face and fought. In this place, Surya, Tistria, Mithra, and Vaghuna, those Aryan sun gods, gigantic, stentorian, capable of moving mountains or casting bloody veils over the heavens—in this place, they waged battle against the lunar natures of Khaldi, Ardinis, and Sielaghdis.[26] Look at the boulders that loom up over the lakeshore: they resemble the petrified flanks of giant elephants. Vanguard armies ranged for battle. Frozen in the depths of the centuries, they have come to a halt and are listening for the sound of the battle trumpets that will call them back to life and order them to press their victorious attack. And the kings' race, the race of the Armens—look at the wasteland before you, there they are. . . ."

"Armens?" Elena asked.

"They were beautiful, well-built, daring people, mindful of god. Centuries earlier, with the invasion of the Thracian Phrygians, they had come to Asia from Europe. A few tens of thousands, superbly armed, that heroic race overthrew the Empire of the Khets and advanced as far as the mountains of the Caucasus. To establish their rule over that vast territory, they took with them people from the Hattian tribes, ten times their number. They themselves constituted the noble warrior class and the royal family, because they were not only brave, godlike people, but also possessed the supreme religious wisdom and spiritual maturity that compels the peoples' respect and implicit obedience. The Armens rebuilt the ruined country; they put the Hattians to work and ruled over them. Bear in mind that they were not barbarian destroyers or butchers, but, on the contrary, reconstructors and restorers who saved the land from ruin and created gods. Unfortunately, over the centuries and in the course of long struggles, the Hattian tribes slowly gained the upper hand. Eventually the country—which foreigners rightly continued to call Armenia—came to bear the name Hayastan, as the slaves wished, and the people took the name *hay*. It's not the name that matters, of course. The important thing for us at present is to admit the difference between two principles. There are Hays and there are Armens. Two opposing mentalities and two disparate spiritual worlds, which are sometimes joined in the same person, and clash, canceling each other out or undermining each other. Sometimes there is such a gleam in an ordinary Armenian peasant's eye, such vigor in his speech and bearing, that there can be no mistake about it: the man is an Armen. To call the Armens back to life among us—that is our goal. . . ."

"And to call the Armens of all countries back to life is ours," O'Connor exclaimed.

"Yes, the new race of powerful individuals, the spiritual man, the cosmic individual."

"Beautiful dreams, beautiful dreams," Grey muttered. "O'Connor, for the love of God, let's go back and see what's going on there, on the island."

"All right, all right."

The oars gaily churned up the water.

—*Translated by G. M. Goshgarian*

Daniel Varuzhan: Poems and Prose

The reader will find below a selection from the poetry of Daniel Varuzhan (1884–1915) in English translation. Three volumes of Varuzhan's verse were published in his lifetime: *Sarsur'ner* (Shivers; Venice, 1905), *Tseghin sirtë* (The Heart of the Race; Istanbul, 1909), and *Het'anos Yerger* (Pagan Songs; Istanbul, 1912). A fourth volume of poetry, *Hatsin Yergë* (The Song of Bread), saw the light in 1921, again in Istanbul; the manuscript had been confiscated in April 1915, when the poet was arrested, and was recovered by his widow in 1920. There exist several collections of Varuzhan's poetry in French translation (see the bibliography at the end of this volume). A choice of Varuzhan's poems in English translation can be found in the *Anthology of Armenian Poetry* (146–57), translated and edited by Diana Der Hovanessian and Marzbed Margossian; and "The Light," a translation by James Russell of the poem "Luysë," has been published in the winter 1994 issue of the *Ararat Quarterly* (New York). Unless otherwise specified, the translations offered here are the work of G. M. Goshgarian. Five of them (identified as such) are the work of Lena Takvorian or Nanor Kebranian.

In the selection presented below, the reader will find three poems drawn from the collection *The Heart of the Race*. These are, to begin with, poems about ruined cities such as Ani, Adana, or Ashtishat, marked by the powerful rhetoric of the image characteristic of Varuzhan. They are followed by four poems culled from the 1912 collection *Pagan Songs*: "Vanatur," "The Light," "To the Dead Gods," and "Anahit." Placed after this group of poems from *The Heart of the Race* and *Pagan Songs* are two prose texts by Varuzhan on which we have commented at length in Part II of the present volume: "The Hero," the text of a 1909 lecture that saw partial publication in the press of the day, and "The Religions," a text that was unknown until the eight-page handwritten manuscript was published in the 1987 *Complete Works*. The text's editors believe that it was composed sometime between 1905 and 1908, when Varuzhan was a student in Ghent; if so, it might represent notes he took under the immediate influence of his readings in the evolutionary theory of religion. However, this piece can just as plausibly be dated to the post-1909 period, if it is assumed that it represents the text of a lecture delivered in Armenian in Sivas, Tokat, or Istanbul. The manuscript bears no indication of the date of composition or the use to which Varuzhan may have put it. It should be pointed out that none of the poet's lecture notes from his days as a student in Ghent (that is, before 1909) or as a teacher in his native country (after 1909) have survived. The reason is doubtless that, in 1920, Varuzhan's family was unable to recover anything other than the manuscript of *The Song of Bread*.

I have added a few notes to the texts below in order to explain historical allusions that seemed particularly obscure. On one occasion, in a note to "To the Dead Gods," I took the liberty of criticizing an existing French translation by Luc-André Marcel and Garo Poladian.

18

DANIEL VARUZHAN
"Among the Ruins of Ani"

(From The Heart of the Race, *1909; YLZ 1:86–92)*

I.
Be it to weep, to kiss,
To evoke, to muse,
Be it to utter, onward, we enter.
Enter the vast city of a vast corpse,
Enter the Tomb of all Armenians . . .

Greetings, Ani, cemetery
Where rot the bones of a victorious Past.
Greetings, Ani, cradle,
Where beneath ruins, with black scorpion blood,
Our Future grows.
Greetings, Carcass, Mother, greetings.
Here I come, I, the final
Budding head of the Armenian Hydra,
I come to cradle your death with your life's glory—
To speak of your greatness,
Or the great promise of greatness, you became
A luminous steel breast where
Savage races, alien to suckling,
Came to shred their famished gums.

On the seam of Old Asia you were
For three centuries the heart, if Greece was the intellect,
Living heart, which cunning Byzantium,
That bastard of Rome, its eyes frozen in a stare,

Betrayed with a ravished appetite.
And it betrayed and it conquered—and alas,
When its flag stood erect on your idiot king
Hovhannes' grave,
And the kaftan was promised to Vest Sarkis,
It's with your keys in the Bosphorus prisons
That they locked solid chains around
Your young king's arms.[1]

II.
What a scourge. You were finally condemned
When Persian and Greek, your two rivaling rivals,
Lifted you as a shield between themselves,
Or like a hunted prey—having pierced its
Heart with its own claw—
Monomachus and Tughril
Peroz and wicked Alparslan passed you
From fang to fang, paw to paw.[2]
And shattering their jaws against each other,
They removed your foundations
In order to fashion your black headstone.
From that day on you as splendid construct
Where a thousand bolts of lightning struck at once
Collapsed marble by marble, plaster by plaster.
And, oh fury, oh shame,
Those who came to face and slash you wickedly
Were no eagles, merely wolves . . .

III.
Now in a wreck you rest,
And your fragments have lived for nine centuries,
The hand of time was not so cruel
To offer those tempests your remains.
But in your chest,
Sempat's bold stallion no longer neighs,
Nor hurls its blood-soaked hooves
Before Apshin's mare,[3]
And the golden rattles and bugles,
Which announced how the saber was cast with a cross,
Are silent over there, housing in their place
A thousand generations of owls.
Under the broad wing of that bat of silence,

The whore ripens with star-shed tears.
And there the ivy in its patriotic arms
Embraces your sullen earth,
Shattered flintstones and all.
And a blade of grass, scarcely budding
On the untread roads,
Hides a slithering snake from the roaming sun.

IV.
What remains, what?—from your stone barricades,
Which embraced you as they offered their chests
To the storming Asian tribes?
From your palaces, your fortresses, your pillars,
From your towers' daggers, where a swaying
Red Armenian flag
Wiped the sweat of eagles in flight;
From your capitals, your steeples,
Which once in the thundering clouds,
Mocking fate
Against the fist of time,
Became shields cast from fortune's mines;
From your barracks, temples, yes, from your
Thousand and one temples, where
Toward soaring faith
As arms tired, idled,
As ancient Aramian blood
Was curbed from its champion pagan thrust
And as Jesus was being born through tears
Lastivertsi and that sly Judas, Giragos,
From your thousand and one temples, I say, where
Statue by statue, ornament by ornament,
A new art, an Armenian art,
Art as God's daughter, as Nature's sister,
Art as Universe's bride,
As the final epitaph and garland
Of deceased peoples and nations,
Sculpted in the gilded outline of a dove
Inside your holy steeples,
Its head outstretched
Through your hushed niches, capitals, and columns,
Skyward, lovely, sublime,

Broadly spread its wings . . .
Now, alas, from them,
Those myriad beams, oh Ani,
Tell me, tell me, what remains? . . .

V.
It walls itself in silence. On
The spacious field, with the moon's sweet glow
The ruins glisten. From the distance
In the star-studded space
Can be heard only the whistle of voyaging winds.

Ani remains eternally silent . . .

I place my foot on a fallen stone,
Then on another, then another
And I rise toward the half-collapsed rampart.
The partition's clefts, wounds of time, become
My staircase, crumbling from my steps
Rubble tumbles,
And under my clawing fingers,
From the ivies, from the weeds
Sleepy lizards topple
And I climb—my soul
Overcome by deep intoxication
Pulls me toward the stars.
I wind, I climb.
My bare chest bleeds against the flintstones,
A shred of cloth remains
In the thieving talon of a thorn below.
But haughtily I, like a tiger approaching its prey
—If the freest heights are the spirit's prey—
In intense and feverish haste,
Shaking off the darkness and wreckage from my feet,
Over my ancestors' ten thousand parched skulls,
With a final gallant leap
On the ramparts I stand panting . . .

VI.
Oh you instinctive ascent,
Oh intoxicating scuffs even on
Black tombs of bone,
Oh sublime heights, which caress my tender soul,

Making me on my fathers' remains
A bud that still adorns an old branch.
Oh enchanting elevation,
Between blue and black you
Suspend me from a thought's azure cord.
You give my heart scant comfort,
So I'll find down under my foot
Inside Ani the sky's reflecting magnitude,
So I'll feel that on our grave
The planets still orbit,
That darkness is the sublime face of the Idea,
The ruins are Eternity's sin,
The wheel's dustcloud is a galaxy, or this wandering
Firefly a rare star.
This skull here is a moon, I God . . .
To be God, oh irony, this is
Merely to be a caricature of God,
For our soul is Nature's mistress,
And fertile only in its hot embrace,
Not having
Against this Nothingness, this abyss of Fatherland,
As its first seed,
A proper word to create, to harmonize, surging
From Ani's dust
A Canaan new and free.[4]

VII.
What, to have corpses inside one's eye
Which have in time become
Blood of your blood, sperm of your sperm,
And, oh, unable to revive,
To watch arms folded like so,
What, to see that today a snail navigates
Those immense buildings, on two spittle threads,
And in an altar's corner simply lives
The owl, black-clothed recluse,
To see that beneath the rubble,
Heroes' forearms silently decay,
Skulls, hearts, whose blood was
A venom to vipers, so spiteful it was.

To see that among crumbled barriers, a castle's
Crevices, dies
A ray of sunshine, an ancient Name, a mighty Nation,
And on fragments of vacant thrones,
The eagle spreads its dirt from a cloud . . .
What, meanwhile below, ahead,
Alongside this erasure
Souls dwindle and vanish,
Drowning in their very blood,
Or like the sheep and castrated bull
With dreadful patience, between each blow,
Say feebly, "Heave." Oh what, what,
Before all this,
In this dark undulation of corpses around me,
Of bones, sacraments, blood,
To stay erect, solitary, inept,
And from this chaos, not be able to extract
A renaissance, a radiant renaissance . . .

Oh derision, oh insult,
Then why live, why
Mutter like that a useless
Fatherland's name,
When the numb Living
Don't want to hear you, don't want to leap,
And from your war cry, horrified,
Their ears cowering in their chests,
They wish a thunderbolt upon your head,
Therefore why, why live?

VIII.
Below, there,
A giant snake head poking out of the pit,
Looks at me in the moonlight,—here, come—
You who in your eyes have green
Death's sweet relief—here, come—
My heel is yours, yours hot
These my veins—bite and sting—so I may in defeat
Tumble down, into Akhuryan's abyss,[5]
And on that black granite below
Smash my head, and on my pathetic

Fatherland's ashes here
My brain's pulp I may splatter . . .

(translated by Nanor Kebranian)

19

DANIEL VARUZHAN
"To the Ashes of Cilicia"

(From The Heart of the Race, 1909; YLZ 1:147–51)

Stranger, let's climb that mountain ahead,
Beside which flows weeping Sihon amid the
Canes, where tomorrow our anguished mothers
Will wash scarlet swathes—Stranger, hurry,
My bare feet sear on the hot ashes
And your long robe's brim's begun
To soak in the overflow—Stranger, hurry . . .
My semi-scorched staff points in the direction of my words,
Behold the city and villages and pastures and shores,
Where the Race of Fire tread with Attila's stallion.
The smoke rises there as does the blaze, which still creeps
Along the mountainside, billowing with the
Wind's breath, constricting and then again stretching
Like a tongue up and above the summit.
Even the soil smolders. See! the inflamed horizon
Is like a fiery wreath around us, in whose core,
Erect, we tremble and grieve like alien spirits.
Do you hear the sound of distant canes ablaze
Where forest nymphs turn to coal?
Such an incense-infused crackling of branches,
Such cindered orchards, such whoops of the turtle-dove.
The blaze passes, and the wind following behind,
Grasping the seared grass, blusters above the mountains.
What trembling nakedness among the moles' cottages,
Which like the porcupines emerge from the fields,
What razed huts built on the hillside,
Where the Armenian peasant used to appear with a morning prayer
To awaken the earth's Creator beneath his spade.
Stranger, you see how today those cottages
Wait lamenting quietly the first night of mourning among the ruins,
To moisten their ashes in the moonlight.

They demolished the roofs onto the tapers lit inside.
The doors, pliant, which even the breeze could push ajar,
Fell in pieces under the mob's bloody truncheons.
And now the toothless walls protrude like chins
From where they release hosts of souls into the sky.
Piles of ashes in the fields, and corpses along the road,
On that white road, from where the quick race of Aram,
Having loaded Western gods, Europe's crescive mind
Onto their mules, carried them to Asia.
Martyrs next to springs, martyrs in the furrows.
And there, up ahead, where the sun now sets,
Facing the steep cliff, they've crucified seven naked men,
The blood from their hair (Stranger, I beg you[6]
Shut your eyes and hear only my voice),
The blood from their nailed hands and feet
Runs over the dirt painting those pebbles.
As if the parting sun gently sinks in their enlarged eyes, still gaping in terror.
The executioners departed in the dark.
Peace, hosanna on the crimson heights . . .

Oh, my chin chatters so harshly; turn right,
And see the city, which seated in mourning among the fields
Still fumes at its heart like a furnace for human sacrifices.
The dawn of liberty had barely ignited its marbled front
When from under its solid foundations,
The Hamidian dragon shook itself from stem to shoulder.[7]
Those barbarians then awoke, spat at the sun,
Sprawling death's semen,
And one half of the city destroyed the other.
With the yataghan, the prox, the murderous fire,
Whatever genius remained was consumed by the ash heap.
Where are the temples now, inside whose scented steeples
The swallow had newly offered a spring prayer?
Where are the schools and palace for the future's lanterns?
Children's sacrificed hearts linger there as incense.
Where are the bright bathhouses, their pure marble
Where virgin girls sparkled in their bathing hours?
Where are the marvelous tombs and the ancient monuments
On which the Hetums engraved their victories . . . ?
Death and ashes—charred walls only
Protrude in the night summoning the owls.

Stranger, now rouse this country's past
In your memories and pity the century of another Race,
Consider that once it lived at the foot of the Taurus,
A diligent people that sang the deification of life.
Its caravan passed, and went always to flood
The good wheat of every hut where a fire flickered dolefully,
Its caravan passed, and Tarsus's jewels
Spilled like stars into the laps of queens.
And that road through the mountains from where the young Macedonian
Invaded the Ganges, and arose temples on this path
Where the beautiful Hellenic Mind was worshipped
Below the illuminated figure of Athena's sculpture,
That chaste trail of Rubenians' progeny of builders[8]
Saw the squeaking carriages move East to West
On which the relentless Armenian laborer had piled
Marble from opulent mountains and vineyards' copious wines—
Oh the primordial milk of the nations that sing and sculpt.
Now all that beauty of life has passed.
The Race of Fire, alas, was more ruinous
Than time, more disastrous than a plague,
It relishes basking like a contented dervish
On a stone from the rubble and gnawing on a stolen bone.
Listen, from the city's barricades, clamors approach,
The murderous Race celebrates its bloody victory.
Its victory in loosely slaughtering women, boys.
One part of the unfortunate city, on which the moon weeps,
Is now a grave. The other part is the scene of a feast.
The Muslim ignites his bonfires of delight,
Moaning skeletons burn on display,
All around, the mob with up-rolled sleeves rises to dance.
The blood-drenched Kurdish woman with hennaed hands
Beats a rhythm, and Islam, Stranger, see, for the first time
Today drinks wine in honor of the embers.
Half-scalded bodies groan in the distance.
But a wounded man appears in the dark,
Then crawling on his knees approaches the mob,
And mockingly, cackling, he spits
Into the festive bonfire.—

Pass the mournful winds
Over the corpses, and over the devastation,

And full with bloody semen, with moths of fire,
They travel to distant worlds to bloom a happy spring elsewhere.
Stranger, those winds there on the luminous sea
Hollowed your ship's swollen sails,
Leave this bitter country for your peaceful shores,
For the turtle-doves have died, and the peach-tree wilted.
When your infinitely fearful ship rips the waters and flees,
Always pursued by frolicking dolphins,
Who came to our fertile shore seeking corpses,
When still shielding your terrorized gaze in your overcoat,
You reach the laps of your golden brothers—don't forget
To tell them how Cilicia was slaughtered
To the treacherous rhythms of freedom's melody.
I know that those brothers with magnificent ships,
Will want to come . . . to our aid? . . . oh, no . . . for the dying remnants.
They'll want to come only to excavate our virgin, prosperous mountains,
And from our pregnant mines to miraculously drain metal.
Drain the metal and construct the idols of their selves . . .
Stranger, leave! I too now descend
From this height, and wrapped in my morose cape,
I leave to wander again among the city's victims.
I must bury the dead and anoint the holocaust.
A wounded man's head moans on the granite . . .
Near the spring, a sister, oh, perishes forlorn.
I must dig countless graves tonight,
And weave resplendent shrouds until dawn.
I must construct tombs, raise monuments,
And on the marble, my epitaph I must engrave.

(translated by Nanor Kebranian)

20

DANIEL VARUZHAN
"Vahagn"

(From The Heart of the Race, 1909; YLZ 1:172–75)

O god of my fathers,
Behold! I approach your altar,
Leading by the halter
A bull from the valleys of Daron.
Look! The sacrifice I bring you is fat.

In his milk-white breast
Is all the life of the soil.
His neck does not know what a crib is:
He has grazed freely in open pastures
And his teeth have been washed only
In the sacred spring at Heavenly Ash Groves.
When he pants, his powerful breath
Blasts the dirt and sand from the ground,
And all the smells of the fields' wet green
Come pouring from his black nostrils.
Look! the sacrifice I bring you is majestic and comely!
His spiraling horns set a blond crown
Of glory on his head,
And strength's black incense
Smolders in his savage eyes.
His shaggy tail slithers like an adder
Endlessly over his flanks,
Sweeping off hornets and horseflies
To keep his body spotless, to keep it holy.
O Vahagn, father of the gods,
God of power, sun made man
In the lineage of Tigran,
Cleanse my soul, anoint these my lips
With one ray—for behold, I kiss
Your holy altar and, raising the dread hammer
With a mighty arm bent to your service,
Smash my bull's forehead, and dedicate
The freely gushing blood to your knees.
. . . Behold! Already the sacred fire
Is smoking and crackling before you.
The flame curls its way through the olive branches
And, drunk with the juniper's melted gum,
Leaps straight up, singing the transfiguration
Of the limpid soul of things.
Here, take my sacrifice.—These are his bloody ribs.
This is his muzzle, these his shanks with their lard;
Here is the brain that regulated his instincts
And breathed rebellion into his horns.
Here is his warm, still-beating heart
And his gall, which I smear on his rump,
Hoping it will burn without a trace.

Take it—and the flame that, casting off its smoky crown,
Rises cleanly. It carries the bull upwards
One fragrant wreath at a time
To fill your heavenly palace with incense.
Accept, O Mighty One, these my gifts,
Which I pour out onto the flames
From a flawless, radiant urn.
Here is the wine. Open your nostrils and breathe in
Its sweet aroma, and be reconciled
With your apostate people
In the gay inebriety of a god.
Here is the holy oil. I pour it out before you
Pure, sweet, and abundant, just as
The tree poured it from its wounded breast
Into my splendid jars, rinsed seven times.
Accept it; regard it as you would the blood
Of an innocent baby,
Or the precious sweat of a woman with child.

O sublime one, are you satisfied? I have given you
All that I had in my cell and in my soul—
All that the enemy forgot to take
From deserted Ashtishat the widowed city.
Now, the last Vahuni of our race,
I kneel in holy fear before your altar,
And kiss the ground where something
Of your soul lets the pine trees take root,
And, stretching my arms out toward you,
Sleeves rolled up, the bull's hot blood
Still dripping from my elbows,
O Vahagn, o god of my fathers,
I pray . . . I pray . . .

For the force, the faith in your arm,
With which, one day, you tore
The dragons' mouths to shreds and, like sun-seeds,
Scattered the Milky Way across the sky.
For the force that is the wings and the soul
Of the creation without end, the force
Beneath whose infinite kiss
The worlds bear flower and flame, and
The principle of immortality quickens in the atom

And the brain and the will; for the force
Beneath whose powerful finger
Seeds split open and the sap, singing,
Soars to the topmost branches of the oaks;
For the force that fills women's breasts,
Rocks our cradles, and carries us after death
As far as the stars, as far as
The creative cause of a second life, the force
That plants a Nation somewhere, like a pride of lions,
And pours the strength of your arm into its arm,
And, like the fire-condor, shelters under its wings of light,
In our mothers' wombs,
Heroes, geniuses;
I speak for that sacred Strength, whose wise
And overflowing source you are,
O Vahagn. Behold! My bloody arms
Stretched out towards you,
I pray . . . I pray . . .

21

DANIEL VARUZHAN
"Vanatur"

(From **Pagan Songs**, *1912;* **YLZ**, *2:7–8)*

Seated on your plump ox, O Vanatur,
you travel from one side to the other of the patrimonial fields.
Dead are all the great gods, moss grows on their temples.
Only you have become immortal,
just like earth and fire, and like the
salt of the ocean.
From the purple robe on your shoulders still emanates
the scent of wine of the new year festivities.
Against the grain of so many centuries' destruction,
your eyes still express gaiety,
and your lively face is flushed
with the inebriate's red laughter.
And when seated on your plump ox
you visit the endlessness of the patrimonial fields,
the waves of life flow
from the furrows of the patrimonial fields.

Here comes spring and her vigorous awakening.
Be crowned with her irises, O Vanatur.
On your path, rays flow
like your replete veins.

And all the white stones
are forsaken in the dewy green.
From the rustic rooftops
rises the smoke, like peaceful incense.
Let me hang my necklace
with roses and with beads arrayed
around the neck of your ox,
your docile ox, that turned back,
periodically licks your naked godly feet.
Oh, its mighty bellow, that hence
from cavern to cavern
awakens the drowsy snakes and bears
and the peaceful life in the sun bursts out.
The stars seep honey from the sky
into the marble jars of the Naiads,
on the edge of sun-imbued fountains
pigeons take a bath
sprinkling pearls from their beaks.
Laugh, O Vanatur,
with your limpid pagan laughter,
for nature has arisen from its veils,
and mirth, fertile and infinite,
fills the air and passes, and like
a wild swan,
she sings your victory.

Here is summer and its flaxen lands.
Be crowned with the plenty, O Vanatur!
Under the hooves of your ox
the fields of tender wheat become plentiful and fertile.
Now take your golden bath in summer's seas.
Under the flower-laden bushes
the nests are filled with blessings
and the song of the skylark reaches us from the sun.
It is your fecund sweet breath that passes
athwart the green-flanked hills.
Sleeping on the roof

the villager opens his eyes, it is the Sun,
and closes them, it is the Moon.
The branches are heavy with the scent of spices,
even the ashen ruins are filled with
crops of nettle and mallow.
Under the willow, Vanatur, I sacrifice
the goat offered to you
the goat whose shiny and abundant hair
splits like a furrow on its backbone.
The goat who always gnawed away
at the sacred fence of your vineyard.
Drink blood and eat meat, O Vanatur,
with your ancient pagan merrymaking,
for in fields full of corn, sparkling
sickles sing to you.

Here is autumn and its fertile bleeding—
be crowned with the grape vine, O Vanatur.
Take your spear, entwined with
Vine leaves and blossoming fruits.
Let me adorn the horns of your ox
with bunches of grapes.
The fruit-bearing trees, like pregnant women,
heave under their weight.
All the trunks are sticky with sweet sap.
The kernel of each fruit
is hardened with your seed.
And the fertile land is blessed by
the spittle of your ox.
The granaries are filled with peace
and the jars with mirth . . .
let your ox eat corn among the heaps of unwinnowed grain
like stars. And you, O joyful God,
God corpulent, rosy-cheeked,
take your earthen pipes of Pan, drink the autumnal blood.
Near the fountain I will
attend upon you with wine
attend upon you with flames.
Laugh, O Vanatur,
O Vanatur, dance,
O Vanatur, dance,

For from the field where leaves are falling
appear the nymphs, all along the fences,
and girls whose laps are filled with pomegranates
advance toward your temple
for you are immortal after the death of idolatrous gods,
like the salt in the oceans,
like the tedious winter.
Next to the peaceful patrimonial hearth
every guitar sings your praise.

(translated by Lena Takvorian)

22

DANIEL VARUZHAN
"The Light"

(From **Pagan Songs**, 1912; YLZ 2:88–90)

You shine
For greatness and sacrifice.
Rig Veda

I go toward the source of the light.
The path is long, the path is paved
With flint and strewn with myrtle-thorns.
The path slants like a sunbeam. I go up it,
Putting my weight on my shaking knees;
From my knees, through which my brothers
Drove nails, the hot blood pulses.
My breast heaves, on my eyelashes is dust.
My heart is the empty pitcher.
And I go toward the source of the light.

The light is lovely. On high, it flows;
When it descends, it is just.
Once I saw a drop of its holy essence
In my mother's radiant soul, saw it
Shining from the verdant grave
Of an ancient hero in our village.
At midday I saw it
Stepping down my warm window-sill,
Like a big white butterfly;
Forgiving, clement, it poured

From the pavements and the foul road
Like steamy milk fresh from the udder.
In the evening it ribboned its way
From horizon to horizon like rivers of jacinth
Or formed dreamy pools
In the tranquil sky, where little islands
Of waterlilies burst into flame.
I saw it—and there arose in my soul
An exile's nameless, anguished yearning
For a remote, sun-filled province.
And now I go toward the source of the light.

The light is my Mind's bride and God's daughter.
It is the wine of the Universe's rejoicing
That flowed one evening
From Jesus' side like a flood,
Flowed like forgiveness
Into the empty cups of desolation
Of men gathered round Sin's altar, below.
The light is Nature's lifeblood,
Night's crown and the robe of day.
The light is the divine Agni,
Which, like a mother dying in childbirth,
Creates even as it perishes;
An Agni with eyes of fire,
Whose soul, spring after spring, pulses
In matter and men's minds;
The banks of the swelling Ganges
Still smoke with sacrifices to him.
And I go toward the source of the light.

The light is marble quarried in heaven,
Out of which Art, with its undying dream,
Carves gods with bodies of snow.
In its breast the brooding Dantes
And titanic Homers are born;
In its breast wisdom is a song
That poets, in the depths of night,
Drink from the stars,
And sing by day to Men.
It gives itself to all, is portioned

Out to all, and remains whole, like the host.
The light is the host that descends
Every morning, on our altars,
To the bloody mystery of the birth of man.[9]
And I go toward the source of the light.

How many thousands and thousands of years
Must I walk as I do now?
How often must I fall, mortally wounded,
On a path blazed with the stone-shattering
Hammers of my purpose?
I do not know—but, o my brothers,
You who make the sign of the cross,
Let me find my way alone,
Alone and so quietly that I can hear
My heartbeat, of tens of thousands of songs
The one that I love best.
Do not cast your shadow
Like a buzzard's wing on my sun-filled path,
On my path to the suns.
And do not call me
To your merry revels,
Where bawdiness plucks the strings.
In vain do you promise my heart
Virgins: my heart is the empty pitcher,
And I go toward the source of the light.

23

DANIEL VARUZHAN
"To the Dead Gods"

*(From **Pagan Songs**, 1912; YLZ 2:53–55)*

Under the blood-glorious Cross
whose outstretched arms spread gloom
over all the earth
I, vanquished, from the bitter core of my Art,[10]
I mourn your death, O pagan Gods.
Dead is the Mystery. And Nature bleeds
under the sharp edge of the laws' compass.
Only boredom remains, beautified with a wreath of thorns.

Man has fallen under the giant tread
of a deaf-mute Jewish god.[11]

Zeus, you are dead. You have died,
O Apollo, from whose four-horse-drawn chariot
was heard the neighing of the Sun.
Lightning, without a master, wanders amongst the stars
like a blind snake. Hera's chariot, held by reins of light,
is no longer pulled by peacocks.
Nor do they flow, as godly spermatozoa,
Zeus' golden showers, the Uranian blood.
Hermes' winged feet no longer revive
the orphan stars of the sky.
In the forest, Anahita,
I no longer hear the barking of your hounds,
running after your preferred game.
Buried away your quiver rots. The deer fearlessly
goes to the lake to drink its water.
Pan is not crowned with pine. Every birch tree
does not bloom enlivened by his vigorous breath.
Your cymbals are silent, good Satyrs.
I see only Tradition in tears,
seated on a tree trunk.
Nymphs, you have died.
The foaming rivers gnaw, in pain,
at their inconstant shores.
Naiads, from amidst the reeds,
you do not sing any more, when the moon appears.
The green seaweed is now your mantle.
In the moonstruck fountain I do not see
the spark of your eyes, unfortunate Narcissus.
The turtledoves, when in the pool they come to wet their beaks,
are startled by the toads.

O mighty Poseidon, the sea is emptied of you.
Your proud four horses do not spring up foaming
from the forest of corals.
Nor does your trident resound atop your holy dolphins' restless backs.
Dead is the Siren under the Sicilian rock,
the sailor passes it by without bewitchment.
The sea, O Gods, the sea is sad.
Where have you fled to, Teraphims,

far from my home's hearth? Which devoted saint
has pulverized you with her cross,
in you my fathers engraved their fathers,
by offering every day, salt and nectar.
You are no more, Eros. To whom will my enamored sister
offer the oblations of her vow?
And the keeper of the gate is no more.
Above my bed hangs only a victorious cross
where there is only the glory of death.
And now underneath that Cross,
whose outstretched arms spread gloom
over all the earth,
I lie vanquished, speaking from the bitter heart of my Art,
I mourn your death, O pagan Gods.
Look at all our forests and seas,
the fountains and cottages peaceful
are deserted and dispersed. Now, alas,
Man has fallen under the giant tread
of a deaf-mute Jewish god.

(translated by Lena Takvorian)

24

DANIEL VARUZHAN
"Anahit"

(From **Pagan Songs**, *1912; YLZ 2:44–45)*

Your altar is half overgrown by the grass. They burn
the sweet incense no longer,
the victim doesn't bleed there.
Only the amber scent of a cast-off skin
left by a red snake.
I sit there, a weary traveler. My horse grazes,
and Vahagn's mare, as if sensing the smell,
burns in a passionate orgasm.
But from the sun not even a god comes to us.
From the labyrinthine depths of the forest have disappeared
the wide-sleeved pagan priests. Vrooyr's lute
does not sing your breasts any more.
Around your altar reeds sob.
You don't tuck up your robe any more. No arrow-shot deer

colors your knees blood red.
In your museum your bust
lies weary, no longer crowned with spring.
But you live on, you will live eternally,
not on earth, but in heaven. Anahita.
Here the moon arises,
and you arise too, the crescent on your forehead.
I see you in the vicinity of the stars. From your breasts
light flows into the spring, whence the drinking
deer's moist chin
and its horns are anointed gold.
You look down—ladies of lechery
awaken to virtue, an amphora of wine falls off
the shoulders of the Bacchic nymph,
the virgin prays kneeling on her bed.
Your quiver on your shoulder, your wide bow strung,
you silently drive the chariot of the moon . . .
the spirits of the forest move,
frightened by the torch in your hand, the wolves howl.
The field dreams—and the rosebuds
under the sting of your arrows, one by one,
bloom like your mouth:
the liquid of life bubbles in the ancient vineyard.
Your breasts glide over us, you come and go—but people
do not worship you. They hardly accept a fragment.
The wind and the wave have destroyed
even your temple on the shore of Kerson.
Only at night, your abandoned hunting dog
sees your passage above, the crescent on your forehead,
and, seated at your altar,
it looks up at you and weeps, O Anahit.

(translated by Lena Takvorian)

25

DANIEL VARUZHAN
"The Religions"

(YLZ 3:83–95)

The critical study of religion may be said to have begun with Luther and, thanks to linguistics, peaked in the previous century. When, in the light of science, religious faith was cast into doubt, and doubt, as a spur to research, rooted fanaticism from people's hearts, the various faiths were subjected to scientific criticism; man, with his growing estrangement from religion, began to elucidate it. Religion does indeed merit study, from an historical, philosophical and, especially, psychological standpoint, because of the active influence it exerts on the individual and, in equal measure, society.

Three main emotions comprise the bases of man's physiological and mental life. The first, manifested at the unconscious level when life begins, is the vital sentiment (*sentiment vital*).[12] It emerges when the bodily functions begin to perform their roles, individually or collectively; the result is a feeling of pleasure or pain. Here man pays attention to himself or interprets these sensations of his without apprehending their causes or becoming directly conscious of them.

Here man is immersed in himself.

The second emotion is intellectual and aesthetic. Man dons twin wings, *the intellect* and *the imagination*, so that he can leave the nests of his heart and brain and mingle with objects from which he is separated in time or space. In this case, all sense phenomena—bodily pains and pleasures—become insensible, for consciousness is busy positively reflecting external images that have affected us at the mental level. These images or mental patterns cause us intellectual and aesthetic pleasure or pain and bear a relation to us only as pleasure or pain; their sources lie at other levels, which the mind cannot penetrate unless it forgets itself, to the extent that it can.

Here Man is immersed in a nature outside himself.

Another emotion, the third, is the *cosmic feeling* (*sentiment cosmique)*, where aesthetic emotion, or (taking the term in its most basic sense) the emotion of the *imagination*, awakens and inflames nature. Natural phenomena are not forever separated from man: by virtue of their power or the effects of fear, anguish, and admiration that they produce, they are of vital concern to him and simply elicit a new feeling of pain or pleasure in him. Man now feels that he is dependent on nature, that nature has the power to alter his destiny: a bond is consequently forged between man and nature. When men are civilized and cultivated, natural phenomena interest them, and that bond is constituted by *science*. In contrast, natural phenomena terrify the ignorant or the men of primitive times; in their case, that bond is constituted by *religion*.

That is why *cosmogony* is the basis for all religions.

It follows from what I have just said that poetry or art resides in the religions, because men apprehensively rivet their attention to nature's superficial forms. The germ of science (which men have deified, since they were unable to explain it) resides here, because the mind has almost fearfully observed natural phenomena and their metamorphoses. A partially developed *moral-philosophical* element resides here; it steadily developed in man's mind along with the germ of science and subsequently became the catapult that destroyed the irrational religions.

The most advanced ancient religions, such as Brahmanism, Confucius' teaching, and Judaism (or prophetism), have recognized a conscious, freely formative force standing above the Universe; they became *theological religions* or, at any rate, more theological religions than the others. Those that deified the natural elements or human vices and virtues, or even humanized them, assigning them genealogies as well as ways of life and modes of behavior, became *mythological religions*—for example, Egyptian, Greek, Roman, or Armenian paganism, and, to a certain extent, Mazdaism.

Finally, the religions that, rather than worshiping various natural phenomena *through the symbols* constituted by animals or statues of clay, ivory, or wood, worshiped them as true gods, became *fetishistic* or *idolatrous* religions; such was the religion of the Assyrians, of (intermittently) the Hebrews, Taoists, Lombards, Huns, and Celts, and of many savage peoples, the names of which there is no need to cite here.

We have yet to examine two main points. First, the question as to whether the peoples had a religion from their beginnings onwards, and whether all or only some of them had one; second, the question as to whether religion, when it first made its appearance among men, was *monotheistic* or *polytheistic*.

This problem (whether the first men had a religion or not) has not yet been fully elucidated; moreover, the means we need to elucidate it are lacking. Required is a study of the men of prehistoric times, of their way of life, customs, and beliefs. There is and can be no history or archive that would allow us to carry out such a study. All we have is the paleontological and archeological material in the museums, which is still incomplete and is not sufficient to allow us to draw a clear, definite conclusion in this matter.

We know very little—indeed, next to nothing—about the Stone Age. *Homo sapiens* (whose skeleton, discovered in a cave, has been preserved down to the present day) has been likened to a monkey on the basis of his anatomical structure, but many scholars have rejected this view because they find greater perfection in the formation of his skull. His weapon was a carved, almond-shaped [illegible word]. There exists no drawing or sculpture proving that he had the concept of an imaginary being or had conceived the idea of deifying the natural elements. It is possible, indeed, probable that this prehistoric man was quite incapable of utilizing any kind of marks at all to depict his instinctive worship or vague innate beliefs.

In the *Magdalenian or stone-carving* period, however, we do find signs of religious belief. Cro-Magnon man, who lived in this period, seems to have been more advanced than modern savages. He produced pictures engraved on ivory; his *deer-hunter* appears more beautiful to people with our tastes than the crooked torsos or elongated, deformed lineaments of the medieval or even Byzantine period. As far as religion is concerned, he has left graves. Food and weapons were placed in these graves alongside the dead to assure them a future life. Man's hope that he would have a life after death is sufficient proof that, while alive, he believed in the existence of a conscious power capable of determining his fate. We find the mark of religious belief in the sculptures, engraved signs, and more or less deformed statuettes that date from an era running from the Magdalenian and subsequent periods down to the historical period (the mythological periods included) and fill our museums today. The most important of these signs are the *Sun*, the *Cross*, and the *Lamb*[13]—first and foremost, the Sun. The root of all religions without distinction must be sought in that fecundating, life-giving globe of fire. That radiant heavenly body, full of glory and blessings, man's life-long companion, yet one that lives on eternally without him, so near and yet so far, could be and had to be the incarnation of a God in the sky, as, on earth, fire could only be that God's consubstantial descendant. From the first time that man saw fire come from two sticks rubbed together on Earth, the cross formed by those two sticks was sacred in his eyes. He worshiped it just as he did the sun, for he had discerned in those two crossed sticks a consubstantial fragment of the heavenly fire, and seen a descendant of his Sun, the Son of his God, descending upon it. (Later: how, in accordance with the law of evolution, the Cross is united with the Lamb. How this form of belief is more or less exactly developed in the Egyptian religions, with the idea, first, of Isis's son and then of Kristna and Prometheus, down to the union and condensation of these elements in Christianity and the formation of a new religion—all this would be matter for an extensive, valuable study, but it would be too long for me to undertake here and beyond my powers.)

As for the historical period, everyone knows with what beautiful forms of worship and what profound faith the nations, big and small, believed in their gods or God and served them. We observe the same phenomenon in savages, The fact that Lubbock can point to the existence of a New Zealand tribe without any kind of religion at all is by no means convincing grounds for denying the tendency of human nature to believe in a superhuman being. For I regard his savages, in view of their steady progress, not as natural human beings, but as absolute *degenerates*.

We must now consider a crucially important question. Were men originally *monotheistic* or *polytheistic*? Like all the partisans of the theory of evolution, Spencer proves the latter proposition, or, rather, tries to: men, he says, were originally *polytheistic*. Just as the theory of evolution accounts for man's physical and moral capacities, the various forms of human society, and all the different modes of production, so, too, does it account for *religion*. Enchanted by nature, man did not attribute only one Creator to it; rather, he attributed diverse creators to diverse natural phenomena. The number of his gods was subsequently augmented thanks to superstitious beliefs about spirits and shades and dream symbolism. Men did not, however, always keep all their gods. Every burst of intellectual development deposed a god from his throne, until the human spirit came to worship that which its mind was incapable of explaining—it might just as well be said that people have always worshiped their own ignorance.

Adversaries of the theory of evolution hold that, just as peoples advance from ignorance toward civilization, so it is not impossible (especially in view of the many instances of this) that they should lapse from civilization into barbarity. The anti-evolutionists accordingly believe that, as the result of a *regressive revolution*, men became polytheistic after having been *monotheistic*. In the beginning, by the grace of heaven, they worshiped a single Creator, but then, in the course of the centuries, for one reason or another, they lapsed into darkness, their minds clouded over and consequently began looking for a more concrete substance or tangible symbol, which they found in the *Sun*. Initially, they worshiped their Creator in the sun; thereafter, the Sun gradually took the Creator's place, and men began to sacrifice to Light, in the material sense, what they had previously sacrificed to their God.

Once they had struck down the wrong path, they no longer hesitated to deify the stars and the Moon as well, and then, gradually, all natural phenomena without exception.

Which of these two views should we adopt? In my opinion, both of them, partially, and neither in its entirety. With the exception of Judaism, all religions have been polytheistic, even if a number of other religions, although their origins are still shrouded in semi-obscurity, exhibit all the characteristic features of monotheism. When we take Buddha's or Zoroaster's teachings, we see that they preach monotheism—or, at any rate, that they have elevated *one Power* so high above the other, secondary powers, and presented it as so conscious and omnipotent, that the handful of other, insignificant Powers become nothing more than its attributes. This holds for Brahma and Ormazd.

However, neither Zoroaster's, Buddha's, nor Confucius's religion has been preserved in its virtually pure monotheistic form. Today we find that even religious books have been tampered with by alien hands and contain extraneous material. During the long march of the centuries, the peoples have surrounded their God with all sorts idols, spirits, and devils, the products of superstition. Nonetheless, everywhere and in every age, every people, from the Greeks and Romans to the most backward savages, have had their God the Father, or a God far superior to the others by his nature or function, with the result that nations and peoples have, sometimes vaguely and at other times with crystal clarity, sensed the impetuous force of a unique, superhuman Power controlling their destiny, a self-same Power that will remain eternally the same, even it is called by different names, Aramazd, Dios, Zeus, Thor, Nemesis, Baal, Brahma, Ahura Mazda, Jehova, or God.

26

DANIEL VARUZHAN
"The Hero"

(Azatamart, 1909; YLZ 3:116–17)

Schopenhauer recognizes three types of superman: the Saint, the Genius, and the Hero. He becomes the most optimistic of optimists when he says that they experience the perfection and beauty of life, so that, thanks to this circumstance alone, it becomes possible to say that they experience the Universe. The Universe would of course have been created in vain were there no one to enjoy it, consciously or unconsciously.

Let us limit our discussion to the Hero. He displays features so superhuman that the Ancients put him in the same class as the gods. The Ancients constructed their religion after the fact, rising from man to the hero and from the hero to God. The Greeks' gods are men, perfect in body and soul, whose arms converted into motion whatever violent action their minds conceived. Harmony of all physical and intellectual capacities is the basic condition for the greatness of a being.

A great, harmonious being, in turn, is life's lawgiver: he is of the race of the gods. He is a hero either because he slew the dragon who was poisoning creation with the destruction and desolation he wrought or because he founded a historical golden age and a religion that bathes not only life in sunlight, but also the grave and its remote secrets. In the *man* endowed with this extraordinary force, men saw the germ of a god and, on his brow, a goddess's rose-scented kiss.

In every condition in which the myths and legends show us heroes, these heroes possess something more than the prophets. Rather than merely feeling the gods' breath in their souls, they touched the body of an immortal with theirs: for the condition for being a hero is that the body become as divine as the soul. The prophet sees the future; the hero prepares it. One is a jurist; the other is a lawgiver. The former harvests God's word even before it is sown; the latter sows the still unharvested word, and is extremely close to the inhabitants of this earth, in whose hand he often places his own; he takes from them the breast-plate, and the helmet, and the victor's crown, and the spear, and the sword and, following their lead, heads for the *Battles of Progress*. Heroes are the wheels on which progress advances from age to age. If evolution truly unfolds over the centuries without conscious intervention, it nevertheless always needs a hero to acquiesce to its verdict. The years are sown thanks to the peaceful labor of the human mind, but the centuries ripen thanks to the hero's blood. With their doctrines, the ideal of the best possible life, philosophers and sociologists mix the cement of progress; but it is the hero, the superman, who lays the foundations of the edifice of the ideal life to come; he piles marble on marble, puts the luminous columns in place, and runs the iron beams from wall to wall until the temple of civilization has been erected and the columns gleam and the altar is ready to accept the sacrificial victim of the Idea. He himself is that victim, the very hero who constructs the temple. His blood flows over the altar as the mark of the dominion of the ideal.

In this crude world, every superman is a sacrificial victim.

Without sacrifice, there can be no heroes.

—Translated by G. M. Goshgarian, Nanor Kebranian, and Lena Takvorian

Introduction: Art, Religion, and Philology

1. "Das Grundgesetz aller Götterbildung ist das Gesetz der Schönheit." *Schellings Werke*, ed. Manfred Schröter (Munich: C. H. Beck, 1927), 3:417–18.

2. Ibid., 3:425: "Mythologie ist die notwendige Bedingung und der erste Stoff aller Kunst."

3. Friedrich Schlegel, *Dialogue on Poetry and Literary Aphorisms*, translated, introduced, and annotated by Ernst Behler and Roman Struc (University Park: Pennsylvania State University Press, 1968), 81.

4. Daniel Varuzhan, *Yerkeri Liakatar Zhoghovatsu* [Complete Works] (Yerevan: Academy of Sciences Publishing, 1987), 3:364. The reader will find the details of Varuzhan's biography below, at the beginning of Part II. The passage briefly quoted is reproduced at greater length there.

5. Later I shall try to explain this "two-sided orientalism" better. Let us note the following for the moment: one of the two sides is the orientalism that Edward Said brought to light (I say this with the proviso that we have to interpret the orientalist phenomenon that he describes as characteristic of philology even before it is linked to colonialism, Western hegemony, and the invention of the Other). The other side has been brought out, magisterially, by Maurice Olender in his *Les langues du paradis: Aryens et Sèmites, un couple providentiel* (Paris: Seuil, 1989) in connection with the racialist thought of nineteenth-century philology. See Chapter 6, n. 13.

1. Variants and Facets of the Literary Erection

1. In 1997, all seven issues of *Mehyan* were reprinted in a single-volume facsimile version by Kilikia Publishing House of Aleppo.

2. Hagop Kufejian changed his name to Hagop Oshagan in 1920, and with his new name (at first a pen name, then his name in "real life," after he fled Istanbul in 1922) he became the most powerful Armenian novelist of the twentieth century.

3. I contributed a preface to an anthology of Aharon's verse edited by Zoulal Kazandjian and entitled *Aharon Taturean, anzhamanak panasteghtsë* [Aharon Dadurean, the Poet

Out of Time] (Venice, 1997). A more elaborate version of this preface was published in *GAM*, no. 5 (2002). Another essay on Aharon, by Krikor Beledian, may be found in Beledian's *Tram* (Beirut: Atlas, 1980), 285–316, under the title "Aharon yev k'ertvats'in harts'ë" [Aharon and the Question of the Poem]. With this essay, Beledian inaugurated his criticism of the "metaphysical" determinations of poetry and, simultaneously, paid magnificent tribute to Aharon, the unloved son of Armenian literature.

4. Published in Paris in 1931, this volume of Parseghian's writings was the fourth in a series comprising the works of "Martyred Writers."

5. Hagop Sirouni began his poetic career in Varuzhan's orbit. In 1922, he moved to Rumania, where he lived until the end of his life, working as a philologist and, from 1924 to 1926, as the editor of the new series of the review *Navasard*. He was deported to Siberia in 1944, where he remained until 1955. Sirouni was extraordinarily prolific. He published a number of very useful works, notably a four-volume history of Armenian Constantinople, *Polis yev ir derë* (Antelias: Armenian Catholicosate, 1965–88), a book on the renowned Romanian historian Nicolae Iorga, and, beginning in 1965, an admirable study of Komitas in the pages of *Ejmiatsin* that merits publication in book form. Today Sirouni is better known than in the past thanks to *Ink'nakensagrakan not'er* [Autobiographical Notes] (Yerevan: Khachents, 2006); this publication at last makes available his account of the years 1915–18, which he spent slipping through police dragnets. Of all the writers I discuss here, Sirouni is the only one with whom I was briefly able to rub shoulders, when I myself was still a very young man.

6. This episode is now better known thanks to the autobiographical notes mentioned in the previous note. See *Ink'nakensagrakan not'er*, 147–74.

7. This essay appears translated in appendix B (text 15).

8. Original text in *Mehyan*, no. 1, p. 3. Hereafter, passages from articles in this journal, provided in translation in the text, will be followed by parenthetical citations of the *Mehyan* issue and page on which the original text is found.

9. Original text in Varuzhan, *Yerkeri Liakatar Zhoghovatsu* [Complete Works] (Yerevan: Academy of Sciences Publishing, 1987), 2:88–90. The entire poem appears in translation in appendix C (text 22), and a detailed analysis is provided in chapter 6. *Yerkeri Liakatar Zhoghovatsu* is hereafter abbreviated *YLZ*, and translated passages from it are followed by parenthetical citations providing volume number and pages on which the original text is found.

10. Oshagan's œuvre was subjected to a total boycott in Armenia for better than half a century. It proved impossible to publish any of his writings there before the appearance, in 1980, of a volume entitled *Yerker* (Works) that we owe principally to the efforts of Step'an Kurtikian. The result of this boycott, which was politically motivated but also due, it must be said, to cultural incompatibilities, is that even today, after so many years, Oshagan's work is all but unknown in Armenia. Moreover, for a long time, only the first five volumes of the *Panorama of Western Armenian Literature* were available in print (they were published in Jerusalem, by the Armenian Patriarcate, over a period of ten years, from 1945 to 1955). Volume 6 was issued by Hamazkayin in Beirut in 1968; volumes 7 to

10 were published in Antelias by the Armenian Catholicosate somewhat later, from 1979 to 1982. Thus it took no less than forty years to accomplish this Herculean labor. Hereafter, I shall consistently refer to this work as *Panorama*, and passages from it provided in translation will be followed by parenthetical citations providing volume number and page location of original text.

11. The only serious study of *Mehyan* to appear to date is Stepan Topjian, "A Sketch of the Aesthetics of Armenian Neo-Romanticism," in *Hay est'etik'akan mtk'i patmut'iunts'* [Studies on the History of Armenian Aesthetic Thought] (Yerevan: Academy Publishing House, 1974), 1:178–272. Krikor Beledian has published a superb book on Daniel Varuzhan, *Krake shrjanakë: Daniel Varuzhani shurj* [The Circle of Fire: On Daniel Varuzhan] (Beirut: Melidinetsi, 1988), in which the *Mehyan* group is of course considered as such. I shall return to this book often in what follows, discussing it in greater detail than I do here.

12. Chobanian might be called the "ferryman" of Armenian culture. Exiled very early in France, he lived in Paris to the end of his life, a few short interludes aside. He published the review *Anahit* in two different periods, 1898–1911 and 1929–49 (with an interruption between 1940 and 1946). Chobanian is well known as the author of the three-volume *Roseraie d'Arménie* (1918–29), about the Armenian poets of the Middle Ages; he also discovered the semipopular poems known as the *Antuni* as well as the poems attributed to Nahapet Kuchak. The *Antuni* comprise a genre of anonymous poems from the Agn region. Ringing variations on the basic theme of exile, they enjoyed an astonishing vogue from the fifteenth to the eighteenth centuries, and continued to be recited and sung in the Armenian world even thereafter. Chobanian's name will recur often in the second part of the present book, because he was one of Daniel Varuzhan's privileged interlocutors when Varuzhan was in Ghent. As for Vahan Tekeyan, a famous poet and publicist who belonged to the political faction opposed to the Armenian Revolutionary Federation, he was the author of *Hrashali harut'iunë* [Miraculous Resurrection], published in 1914.

13. Rupen Zartarian was a journalist who belonged to the Dashnak Party. He was born in the Kharpert region, like almost all the "local color" authors of the day. He published the Party's organ in Plovdiv (Bulgaria) before returning to Constantinople.

14. Siamanto was considered, at the time, to be Varuzhan's equal in the genre of "patriotic" poetry. It was Siamanto who introduced free verse and the epic spirit into poetry written in Armenian. The "Literary Lectures" (*Grakan asulisner*) are famous, especially the one on Siamanto. They were published in brochure form in 1914. Sirouni narrates the year 1913 in the review *Navasard* (see also *Sovetakan Grakanut'iun*, nos. 10 and 11, 1966). On Levon Shant, see the epilogue, n. 16.

15. On Indra (the pen name of Diran Chrakian), see epilogue, n. 18. As for Medzarents, I may perhaps refer the reader to the short biographical note in the *Dictionnaire des auteurs et des œuvres* (Paris: Robert Laffont, 1991).

16. Thus we find several essays in *Navasard*'s single issue that correspond to this movement of "return" (to the old country and the supposedly pagan past) and others on

the *Antuni* (p. 232) and the temples of the pre-Christian period (p. 148). It was in this review, as well, that Komitas's famous essay on "The Song of the Ox-Cart" in the Lori district was published (p. 312).

17. For a long time, we possessed no biographical study of Zarian, so that it was hard to say with any certainty when he actually lived in Constantinople. Today, after the publication of Vartan Matiossian's work on him, especially his recent book, *Kostan Zareani shurj* [On Constant Zarean] (Antelias: Catholicosate, 1998), we know that Zarian spent two distinct periods in the city: he was there briefly in 1910–11 and longer in 1912–14.

18. *Mayrineru shuk'in tak* (Beirut: Centenary Edition, 1983), 94. This is an interview that Oshagan gave to Benjamin Tashian, the editor of the literary supplement of the Cairo newspaper *Husaber*. The interview took place in summer 1931, in Cyprus, where Oshagan lived from 1926 to 1934. It initially saw partial publication in the Boston monthly *Hayrenik*. Extracts from this interview are available in French translation in my *Roman de la Catastrophe* (Geneva: MétisPresse, 2008).

19. I refer the reader interested in these matters to what I said about Esapan in *Writers of Disaster: The National Revolution* (Princeton, N.J. and London: Gomidas Institute, 2002).

20. See appendix C, text 20 for the entire poem in English.

21. In fact, the relationship between the poem and the act of bearing witness is more complicated than we can say in this opening chapter. I discuss all this in detail in chapter 5, in which I comment at greater length on the lines just quoted.

22. Oshagan, *Mayrineru shuk'in tak*, 95. Here are a few more of Oshagan's thoughts of 1931 about *Mehyan*: "The *Mehyan* movement was the fruit of psychological conditions. It found a broad echo among young people, who instinctively grasped its message. . . . A few of the survivors in the group have not abandoned the discontent they expressed in the Manifesto and have developed the perspectives they sketched there. Zarian, for example, has remained the fiery critic of old, and continues to excoriate the Philistines."

23. The word *hart'enk'* means "let us raze to the ground" or "let us wipe the slate clean." It served as a slogan for those who sought to negate received literary values. Oshagan had begun writing this series before *Mehyan* was founded. See my *Hakob Oshakani matenagitut'iun* [Bibliography of Hagop Oshagan's Writings] (Los Angeles: Open Letter Publishing, 1999).

24. I expand on this in my *Ages et usages de la langue arménienne* (Paris: Entente, 1988), which considers all the basic positions adopted by *Mehyan* in their conception and application—and thus also the phenomenon of literarization—from the standpoint of the history of the language. In the present context, I limit myself to the strict minimum about this question of language, that is, just as much as is required to understand the aesthetic principle.

25. There is even talk of "the statuesque splendor of the *Aryan* race."

26. The article by Zarian in which the idea of the "Aryan race" is most conspicuous is the one entitled "The Jesus of the Armenians," in the series "For Art," *Mehyan*, no. 2,

p. 17. We read there that the ultimate aim of art is to "attain the Aryan ideal." Jesus is said to have initiated this transcendence of "Semitism," a transcendence supposed to be both Aryan and artistic. Zarian's article is already clearly directed against Varuzhan's paganism, in the name of a renewal and transvaluation of values. The reader will find a translation of this article in appendix B (text 11). I shall comment on it in the epilogue, which is about Zarian and the Nietzschean influence on the *Mehyan* group.

27. Here is a rough translation of the whole passage: "A century and more ago, the Church was our living literature, our means of channeling things, and it was, as well, the vessel holding the secret of the magic transformation of the one into the other. Today literature is the substitute for this concept." "Living literature" obviously means popular tradition, whether that of myth, epic, or folklore. The phrase "channeling things" evokes the crystallization of a people in a "nation." Clearly, then, the question is: How are the popular sources and a national existence to be made to work in tandem? How is the metamorphosis of the one into the other to be achieved? The answer, aestheticization, is the answer comprised by the "aesthetic principle."

28. To convince oneself of this, it is enough to read an essay about *Mehyan* written by one of the best-known specialists in literature in the Republic of Armenia, Sergei Sarinyan: "K'nnadatut'iunë *Mehyan* yev *Navasard* hantesnerum" [Criticism in the Reviews *Mehyan* and *Navasard*], *Sovetakan grakanut'iun* (Yerevan), no. 9 (1973). This essay has been reprinted in the volume *Hay k'nnadatut'ean patmut'iun* [A History of Armenian Literary Criticism], edited by Sergei Sarinyan himself (Yerevan: Academy of Sciences Publishing House, 1998), 357–93.

29. These remarks are from Oshagan's "The Literature of All Armenians," published under the name Hagop Kufejian. The article is translated in appendix B (text 13).

30. The conversation that we are about to summarize runs from page 14 to page 25 of volume 9 of *Panorama* (a volume written in 1942). Rupen Sevag was a physician and poet who obtained his higher education in Lausanne, Switzerland and was, in his day, considered to be Varuzhan's equal. His legend has survived because he died in August 1915 at the same time as Varuzhan, under the same atrocious circumstances.

31. The double date reflects the thirteen days of difference between the Julian calendar, in use at that time in the Ottoman Empire, and the Gregorian calendar, introduced by the Catholic Church in 1582 and adopted by most European countries by the mid eighteenth century. In Turkey the Gregorian calendar was not adopted until 1927.

32. Oshagan's essay that deals with this last encounter was published in the daily *Arev* in Cairo in April 1924; his further mention of it in *Panorama*, in the context of his monograph on Varuzhan, may be found in vol. 6, p. 187.

33. Be it noted once again that I am using the word *nationalization* to designate the process of "becoming a nation" or "becoming national."

34. Hamasdegh (who was born in a village near Kharpert in 1895 and died in Los Angeles in 1966) is an author well known to the broad reading public. He immigrated early to the United States, where he made a name for himself with two collections of short stories revolving around his native village: *Giughë* [The Village], published in 1924,

and *Andzrev* [Rain], published in 1929. Ohan Garo (1890, Van–1933, Paris) is not as well known. His autobiographical writings have been collected in a single volume entitled *Khrchit'neren minchev Khorhrdaran* [From the Huts to Parliament]. See Krikor Beledian, *Du Même à l'autre: Cinquante ans de littérature arménienne en France* (Paris : CNRS Éditions, 2001), 206–08.

35. See Marc Nichanian, *Writers of Disaster: The National Revolution*, 67.

36. The Armenian equivalent of "provincial" is *gavar'akan*. Later in volume 9 of *Panorama*, Oshagan once again considers the relationship between *Mehyan* and this provincial literature, which the literary critic Ardashes Harutyunian (1873–1915) baptized, Oshagan says, "in a brilliant, harmonious phrase, 'the literature of tomorrow.'" This act of bestowing a name on an existing literature, represented by Tlgadintsi (1860–1915) or Zartarian, provided a definitive framework, according to Oshagan, for the efforts of a group of writers whose literary aspiration was to give form to the life of the nonurban "people." Oshagan regards both this literature and Harutyunian's theoretical project as the announcement and origin of the *Mehyan* movement as he conceives it. Tlgadintsi's students have published a volume containing the bulk of his published and previously unpublished work: *T'lkatints'in yev ir gortsë* [Tlgadintsi and His Work] (Boston: Association of Tlgadintsi's Students, 1927).

37. I have already commented (in the chapter on Charents in *Writers of Disaster: The National Revolution*) on the question of the "alienation" and "re-appropriation" that Oshagan speaks of here. It is because art is by its nature a re-appropriation of what was in fact originally foreign to us that it forges "the nation." Only aestheticized language and aestheticized song can be "national."

38. Oshagan inserts the French word *tellurique* in his text, here translated "telluric." His Armenian equivalent for it is *hoghayin*, which means "related to the earth/soil/land." The French term denotes a belief in force that comes from underneath the earth and is, so to speak, sacred, whereas the more pedestrian Armenian word tends to have an ideological resonance.

39. Zarian's "The Heart of the Fatherland" appeared in *Mehyan*, no. 3, pp. 36–37. The reader will find a translation of the essay in appendix B (text 12).

40. *Ashough* is the Armenian form of a common word in the Middle East (*aşık* in Turkish) for what we call in English *minstrels*, or in French, *troubadours*.

41. Manuk Abeghean's doctoral dissertation (the preface to which is included in appendix A; see text 7) was first published in Germany under the title *Der armenische Volksglaube* (Leipzig: W. Druglin, 1899). The reference to a "secondary mythology" may be found on p. 4 of the preface. The dissertation was later reprinted in volume 7 of Abeghean's *Yerker* [Collected Works] (Yerevan: Academy of Sciences Publishing,1975), 7:449–579, together with an Armenian translation (7:11–102). I shall come back to this thesis in chapter 2, in the context of a discussion of auto-ethnography, and again toward the end of chapter 3, when I discuss neo-archeology. I will take advantage of the present opportunity to note that Abeghean was a friend of Komitas. He taught alongside Komitas at the Gevorguian Seminary in Echmiadzin, Armenia and repeatedly carried

out "ethnographic" fieldwork with him at the turn of the century. This is an anecdotal, but unmistakable, point of intersection between the ethnographic and aestheticizing projects, and thus also a sign of the continuity between them. Abeghean recalls his friendship with Komitas in the essay "*Hishoghut'iunner Komitasi masin*" [Souvenirs about Komitas], also available in the *Collected Works* (6:431–39).

42. Ghevond Alishan, *Hin havatk' kam het'anosakan gronk' Hayots'* [The Armenians' Ancient Faith or Pagan Religion] (Venice: San Lazzaro, 1895). The preface to this work, as well as the first chapter, may be found in appendix A (text 6).

43. The first of Varuzhan's two essays, entitled "*Hay lezvi khntirë*" [The Question of the Armenian Language], is a response to an inquiry into the development of the Armenian language. This 1911 essay has been reprinted in *YLZ* (3:131–30). Those interested in the terms in which this inquiry was carried out may consult my *Ages et usages de la langue arménienne*, 354–58. Varuzhan's second essay is the text of his 1913 lecture on Siamanto. It is entitled "*Yarchaniani k'ert'oghut'iunë*" [Yarjanian's Poetry]; see *YLZ* 3:155–64 ("Siamanto" was the pen name of Adom Yarjanian). The expression "treasures of the language" comes from this essay, p. 163. In the wake of *Ages et usages*, I examined the stakes of these discussions in "Etats de la langue arménienne," in K. Témisian et al., *La Langue arménienne: Défis et enjeux* (Montreal: Cercle culturel arménien, 1995) and, thereafter, in *Writers of Disaster: The National Revolution*. Passages from Varuzhan's 1913 essay are cited in chapter 6 below.

44. See appendix B, text 13.

45. Theotig (1873–1928) was the editor of a yearbook called *Amenun Taretsuytsë* (Yearbook for All), published in Constantinople until 1922, then in Paris, which played the role of a literary review and an encyclopedia.

46. In Armenian, the word *people—zhoghovurd—*is derived from *zhoghvel* (to assemble) and is thus the designation par excellence for that which is "assembled."

47. Because of the need for this historical logic I decided to take up the whole question of Zarian's anti-Semitism toward the end of the present volume, after we have arrived at a better understanding of this invention of mythological religion and the determination (of Nietzschean origin, all indications would suggest) of art as the power of the lie and self-figuration.

48. " irents' yerangnerun bots'avar' kam shijanut amboghjut'eanë mej." See appendix B, text 13.

49. See appendix B, text 12.

2: Abovean and the Birth of the Native

1. One of these writers, the Mkhitarist Father Minas Pzhshgean, was not even deemed worthy of an obituary in *Bazmavep* (the literary-philological monthly published by the Congregation since 1843) during the year of his death. When his obituary finally did appear, it treated him as a secondary, nearly forgotten author. See *Bazmavep*, 15 May 1852, pp. 153–55.

2. At the time, I had no notion of the mourning of philology, of which Abovean is one of the grand figures. I therefore had no notion of the progressive self-invention of the ethnographic nation in the course of the nineteenth century. Above all, I had no notion of the original complicity between the self-invention of the nation and philological orientalism. The commentary that I offer here does no more than pave the way for the subsequent discussion of this complicity.

3. I am here relying on information supplied in a note by P. Hacobyan in his edition of Khachatur Abovean, *Verk' Hayastani* [Wounds of Armenia] (Yerevan: Academy of Sciences Publishing, 1981), 318. Patriarch Nerses's letter is held in Yerevan's Matenadaran [Mashtots Institute of Ancient Manuscripts], folder 167a, document 150.

4. The passage in question may be found in Khachatur Abovean, *Yerkeri Liakatar Zhoghovatsu* [Complete Works] (Yerevan: Academy of Sciences Publishing, 1948–61), 5 (1950): 382. Abovean's translation, or, rather, adaptation, is in classical Armenian. In English, it reads: "The soldiers pitilessly slew all those they encountered. One of them was getting ready to kill Croesus, when Croesus' son, who had been mute until then, cried out, in view of the bitter catastrophe [that was about to break over the head] of his dear father: 'Spare the king!' The soldier took the king prisoner and sent him to Cyrus." The word that I have here translated as "catastrophe" is indeed *aghet*.

5. An English translation of the preface may be found in appendix A (text 2). It should be added that Abovean's novel has a subtitle, *Voghb hayrenasiri më* [Lamentations of a Patriot], which is followed by the words "historical novel."

6. The original text appears in Abovean, *Verk' Hayastani*, ed. P. Hacobyan (1981), 46. Hereafter, translated passages from this work are followed by parenthetical citations providing the location of the original text in this edition.

7. There exists no satisfactory account of this seventeenth-century emigration, which took place in the wake of the wars between the Ottoman Empire and Persia. Raymond Kévorkian does, however, chart each of the waves of emigration leading to major Armenian settlements in various localities of the Ottoman Empire. See his *Les Arméniens de l'Empire ottoman à la veille du génocide* (Paris: Editions d'Art et d'Histoire, 1992).

8. See, on this subject, my essay "The Enlightenment and Historical Thought" in Richard Hovannisian and David Myers, eds., *Enlightenment and Diaspora: The Armenian and Jewish Cases* (Atlanta: Scholars Press, 1999). See also, on all the questions about the history and language of the modern period discussed here, chapters 7 and 8 of my *Ages et usages de la langue arménienne* (Paris: Entente, 1989).

9. In 1817, Father Pzhshgean translated *Robinson Crusoe* (the pedagogical eighteenth-century German version) from a French translation into modern Armenian.

10. In the passage following this one, Abovean relates an episode in which, overcome by his obsessions and overtaken by madness, he disappeared for several days, leading his pupils, who went looking for him, to the conclusion that he had drowned in the Kura. Later in the preface, we find another allusion to suicide: "Ah, but when has the sky ever remained cloudless, so that man's heart might, too? Hardly had my mental sun come back out than the clouds loomed up again, darker than ever, and thunder and lightning

blazed a new path through my heart. I could no longer throw myself into the water. The fear of the Lord filled my mind, my innocent children's voices rang in my ears, and love and paternal piety flooded my soul. If I went to my eternal rest, who would look after my orphans?" (*Verk' Hayastani*, 1981, 45).

11. Stepanos Nazareants (1812–1879), one of the first thinkers of modernity among the Armenians (and, with Mikael Nalbandian, the person who did the most to promote the literarization of the vernacular in Eastern Armenian), was an orientalist by profession. In a letter he wrote to Abovean (then in Tblisi) from Dorpat on 20 March 1837, he said that he was working on a translation of *Ideen für eine Geschichte der Menschheit* in his spare time and that he hoped to publish it soon, one section at a time. It is not known whether this translation ever saw the light. See Stepanos Nazaryan [Nazareants], *Namakani* [Correspondence], ed. Ruzan Nanumyan (Yerevan: Academy of Sciences Publishing, 1969); the original German version of the letter appears on pp. 48–49, and an Armenian translation is provided on p. 50.

12. I have translated this chapter of *La Communauté désœuvrée,* titled "*Le Mythe interrompu,*" into Armenian; see *GAM* (Los Angeles), no. 6 (2005). I discuss the idea of "interrupted myth" in chapter 6, in the course of a commentary on Varuzhan's poem "Vanatur."

13. This holds for my *Ages et usages de la langue arménienne,* and also for the interview I gave David Kazanjian, "Between Genocide and Catastrophe," in D. Kazanjian and D. Eng, eds., *Loss* (Berkeley and Los Angeles: University of California Press, 2003). "Literature does not save the father! It saves the 'disaster.' Do you understand the difference?" (145). The difference is easy to understand. But this difference makes no difference when it comes to the fact that philology has been the institution of mourning for the past two centuries.

14. This is, in fact, a (twofold) pun. *Grich* means pen, *brich* means pick. The title of the book could thus be taken to mean "with stabs of the pen and pick"; the suggestion hovering in the background would then be that the life of the peasantry has been transferred to the page. However, the familiar expression "*grots' brots'*" also designates an amateur writer with no special talent. The title thus also attests Servantsdeants's great, unfeigned modesty.

15. See Karekin Servantsdeants, *Yerker* [Works], 2 vols. (Yerevan: Academy of Sciences Publishing, Institute of Archeology and Ethnography, 1978–82), with a biographical preface in vol. 1 by A. Ghanalanyan. A brief study of the life and work of Servantsdeants by Jean-Pierre Mahé, cast in the form of a review of the first volume of the *Collected Works,* is available in French in *Revue des Études Arméniennes,* n.s. 14 (1980): 529–30. Hereafter, translated passages from Servantsdeants's *Yerker* are followed by parenthetical citations providing volume and page numbers of the original text.

16. The notion that oral culture represents a testamentary legacy established by national (and, of course, nationalistic) philology has been drawn straight from Stathis Gourgouris' *Dream Nation: Enlightenment, Colonization, and the Institution of Modern Greece* (Stanford: Stanford University Press, 1996), 148, a book that has had an enormous

influence on the present text, working something like a revolution in my life (which it could only do, of course, because I had been always waiting for this revolution, in precisely the terms that Gourgouris proposes for Greece and the establishment of Neo-Hellenism). We shall turn to *Dream Nation* again in the following chapter, where it is discussed at much greater length and plays an altogether decisive role. I shall, however, put off to the end of chapter 3 citing the passage on the testamentary legacy alluded to here. We will be in a better position to appreciate it by then, after having reviewed all the different aspects of philology as the institution of mourning and examined in greater detail philology's neo-archeological program, constitutive of the discourse of the nation.

17. "Holy Father" is a translation of "Surb Hayrik." Servantsdeants means, not the Catholicos, but Father Khrimian, who was given this name as well as that of "Khrimian Hayrik." Khrimian was elected Catholicos only toward the end of his life. He was a driving force behind the auto-ethnographic movement among the Western Armenians, as Servantsdeants very clearly notes here.

18. The reader will find a complete translation of these few pages from *Grots' u Brots'* (paragraphs 38–40) at the end of the present volume (appendix A, text 4).

19. This description of Servantsdeants's mission may be found in the biography of him by G. Sherents, one of his pupils who, like him, came from Van. See "Garegin Yep. Servantsdeants," *Azgagrakan Handes* [Ethnographic Journal] 9 (1902): 277. This journal was published by Edouard Lalayan in Tblisi.

20. Michel Foucault, *The Order of Things: An Archeology of the Human Sciences* (New York: Pantheon Books, 1994): "Language is no longer linked to civilizations by the level of learning to which they have attained . . . but by the minds of the peoples who have given rise to it, animate it, and are recognizable in it. . . . Language, in the whole architecture of its grammar, makes visible the fundamental will that keeps a whole people alive and gives it the power to speak a language belonging solely to itself. . . . In any language, the speaker, who never ceases to speak in a murmur that is not heard although it provides all the vividness of the language, is the people" (290). We agree: the philological revolution induces this change. But the change itself is what gives rise to the ethnographic nation. The reader will readily grant me that Foucault's discussion of the ethnographic nation here needs to be fleshed out a bit.

21. See appendix A, text 5.

22. There are, in fact, two letters from Khalateants to Servantsdeants, one dating from 1881, the other from 1883. Servantsdeants did not respond to Khalateants's demands but did publish his letters. I shall come back to Mkrtich Emin in the following chapter, in the context of an examination of "neo-archeology."

23. "Critical, archeological texts and oral discourses" is translated word for word from the Armenian: "grak'nnakan yev hnakhosakan grvatsk'nerë yev asats'vatsnerë." It follows that there is such a thing as an "archeological oral discourse."

24. The Armenian annex (Armfan) of the Academy of Sciences of the USSR was created in 1935. It became the "Armenian Academy of Sciences" in 1943.

25. Thereafter, 85 partial versions of the epic were collected, most of them in Western dialects, necessitating the publication of a fourth volume in 1979. These four volumes contained all the versions that had been collected until then. A fifth and final volume of variants appeared in Yerevan in 1999; Harutyun Simonyan was the driving force behind it. We should also mention the often-ignored work of Tigran Tchitouny, *Sasunakan*, published in Paris in 1942, a 1168-page-strong volume that presents Tchitouny's personal treatment of the epic, based on versions collected in the Van region.

26. Abeghean defends his work in a discussion the stenographic record of which was published in the last volume of his *Yerker* [Works] (Yerevan: Academy of Sciences Publishing, 1985), 8:637–48.

27. See Artin K. Shalian, ed. and trans., *David of Sassoun: The Armenian Folk Epic in Four Cycles*, original text with introduction and notes (Athens, Ohio: Ohio University Press, 1964). A review by Nina Garsoïan was published in *Speculum* 41, no. 1 (January 1966): 175–78.

28. It must, however, be added that there exists another homogenized variant of the epic, this time in Western Armenian; it was published in Beirut in 1947 by Hamazkayin Publishers under the same title, *Sasunts'i Davit'*. The text was established and edited by the writer Garo Sassouni, probably on the basis of versions included in the first collection issued in Yerevan in 1936. Sassouni did not have access to the official standard version, the one published in Armenia, while selecting and editing his text. So he says, at any rate, in the preface to his literary adaptation. It is plain that the desire to create a literary epic and transform the oral tradition to that end was shared by the two disparate fragments of the Armenian people.

29. Translated from Hagop Oshagan, *Mayrineru shuk'in tak* [In the Shade of the Cedars] (Beirut: Centenary Edition, 1983), 102.

30. Ernst Curtius later collected some of his essays on the French writers of his day in a volume called *Französischer Geist im neuen Europa: Gide, Rolland, Claudel, Suarès, Péguy, Valéry, Larbaud, Maritain, Brémond* (Bern: Francke Verlag, 1952).

31. These eleven volumes were reissued by Armand Colin in 1967. After a first, introductory volume, Brémond devotes three volumes to the period 1590–1620 (*L'invasion mystique*), and the following three volumes to the next thirty years (*La conquête mystique*). There follow several volumes on individual writers and particular topics, and then a description of the decline of the mystic sentiment.

32. Translated from Oshagan's *Hamapatker arevmtahay grakanut'ean* [Panorama of Western Armenian Literature] (Jerusalem: Armenian Patriarcate, 1956), 4:311–12. See appendix A, text 8. Hereafter, translated passages from this work, cited as *Panorama*, will be followed by parentheses providing volume and page locations of original text.

3. Orientalism and Neo-Archeology

1. For a history of the spreading interest in Sanskrit that stresses Hamilton's role, see, for example, Thomas Trautmann, *The Aryans and British India* (Berkeley and Los Angeles: University of California Press, 1997).

2. Schlegel's *On the Language and Wisdom of the Indians* is translated by E. J. Milling-ton and includes an introduction by Michael Franklin (London: Ganesha, 2001). Further texts by Schlegel have been translated by Millington and published in *The Aesthetic and Miscellaneous Works of Friedrich Von Schlegel* (London: Kessinger, 2006), which includes excerpts from Schlegel's work on India.

3. On Müller's career, see Nirad Chaudhuri, *Scholar Extraordinary: The Life of Professor the Rt. Hon. Friedrich Max Müller, P.C.* (New York: Oxford University Press, 1974), and, for a more compact account, Jon Stone's introduction to *The Essential Max Müller: On Language, Mythology, and Religion* (New York: Palgrave MacMillan, 2002).

4. On the great novelty (today a great commonplace) represented by Schlegel's treatment of the history of literatures as national literatures, and on his project, which is nothing other than the general project of philology, the best discussion, in my view, is Hans Eichner's preface to the second volume of the comprehensive edition of Schlegel's works, the 35-volume *Kritische Friedrich-Schlegel-Ausgabe*, edited by Ernst Behler, with Jean-Jacques Anstett and Hans Eichner (Münich: F. Schöningh, 1958–2002); see especially 2:xliv. Schlegel's whole conception of art and the critical approach to it is summed up in a sentence that dates from his first period: "Die Wissenschaft der Kunst ist ihre Geschichte" (*Kritische Ausgabe*, 2:290). There can be no theory of art apart from its history.

5. This way of formulating the philological project is Said's, his critique of orientalist philology notwithstanding. His model here, as everyone knows, is Auerbach. I expatiate on this somewhat in the following paragraph but, obviously, do not have room here for a full-scale demonstration of the triumph of *humanist* philology in Said. That will be the subject of a later work.

6. See the chapter entitled "On Orientalism" in James Clifford, *The Predicament of Culture: Twentieth-Century Ethnography, Literature, and Art* (Cambridge, Mass.: Harvard University Press, 1988), 255–56.

7. Stathis Gourgouris, *Dream Nation: Enlightenment, Colonization, and the Institution of Modern Greece* (Stanford: Stanford University Press, 1996), 122–54. Hereafter cited parenthetically in text, as *Dream Nation*.

8. From Wilhem von Humboldt, *Geschichte des Verfalls und Untergangs der griechischen Freistaaten* (1807), cited in Gourgouris, p. 123. See W. von Humboldt, *Humanist without Portfolio: An Anthology*, ed. and trans. Marianne Cowan (Detroit: Wayne State University Press, 1963), 87. The original essay may be found in Wilhem von Humboldt, *Schriften zum Altertumskunde und Ästhetik*, volume 3 of *Werke in Fünf Bänden* (3:73–124); the passage cited occurs on 3:87.

9. See, for example, Philippe Lacoue-Labarthe, *L'imitation des modernes: Typographies 2* (Paris: Galilée, 1986), which contains not only the author's decisive essays on Hölderlin ("La césure du spéculatif" and "Hölderlin et les Grecs"), but also on Nietzsche ("Histoire et mimésis" and "L'antagonisme"). In the first of these two essays on Nietzsche, we find the brilliant proposition, which bears on what Nietzsche said about the Greeks but is just as valid for the ethnographic nations (that is, as we shall see in a moment, for the

"internalization" of the orientalist gaze): "Imitation is not primarily that of the actor (subjective genitive), but is the imitation of that which the actor poses as something to be imitated by imitating it" (99; my translation). See Lacoue-Labarthe, "History and Mimesis," in *Looking after Nietzsche*, ed. Laurence Rickels (Albany: SUNY, 1989), 220.

10. Indeed, I am not even certain that the phenomenon of autoscopy was extended to the ethnographic nations "in a second phase." Western autoscopic imitation was designed to be imitated in its turn. That was its raison d'être and deepest significance. The first people to assimilate this phenomenon among the nations that would constitute themselves in reaction to the European movement, the Greeks and the Serbs, were exiles.

11. Jacques Derrida, "Onto-Theology of National-Humanism," *Oxford Literary Review* 14 (1992): 10, 13.

12. The full title of the book is *Voyage du jeune Anacharsis en Grèce vers le milieu du quatrième siècle avant l'ère vulgaire*. Jean-Jacques Barthélémy declares, in his short preface (I am following the 1799 edition): "I have written the description of a voyage rather than a story, because, in the description of a voyage, everything is in motion, and one may include details that the historian must ignore. These details, when they have to do with customs, are often only hinted at in ancient authors, and have often sparked disagreement among modern critics. I have discussed all of them before making use of any of them" (cxxxv). On the importance of this book for the Philhellenic malady that afflicted Europe in the early nineteenth century, see Gourgouris, *Dream Nation*, 129. See also Maurice Badolle, *L'Abbé Jean-Jacques Barthélémy (1716–1795) et l'hellénisme en France dans la seconde moitié du XVIIIème siècle* (Paris : PUF, 1926). The Armenian translation of *Le Voyage* is mentioned on p. 230. Of *Le Voyage* itself, Badolle says: "It is a veritable compendium of erudition and humanism in Europe from the Renaissance to 1780" (225).

13. The aspiration to comprehensiveness, which originates with Friedrich Schlegel in the 1810s, finds its culmination in the "humanist" self-perception of the great twentieth-century philologists. The names Ernst Curtius and Erich Auerbach spring immediately to mind, and have already been mentioned. I have also already pointed out that Said's ambition takes its place in this tradition, that of the accomplishment of humanism. It so happens that Hagop Oshagan's ambition, which found expression in the vast, comprehensive undertaking constituted by *Panorama of Western Armenian Literature*, was of the same order.

14. This is a point that I should have liked to examine more patiently, in order to point up the parallels and differences between Neo-Hellenism, Serbian "linguistic nationalism," and Armenian neo-archeology. I have to content myself with referring the reader to a few texts that seem to me fundamental. There is, to begin with, chapter 3 of Gourgouris's *Dream Nation*, a chapter devoted to Korais. There is also Claudia Hopf's published doctoral dissertation, *Sprachnationalismus in Serbien und Griechenland* (Wiesbaden: Harrassowitz, 1997), which examines linguistic planning using the examples of Korais and Karadžić. Gourgouris is a dedicated reader of Foucault and Said who strives to integrate Neo-Hellenism into their conceptual systems; Hopf bases her argument on the work of the theorists of nationalism in fashion in the Anglo-Saxon

world: Ernst Gellner, Benedict Anderson, and, finally, Joshua Fishman. (Fishman is an American sociologist who stands the usual political-cultural approach on its head: see his *Language and Nationalism: Two Integrative Essays* [Rowly, Mass.: Newbury House, 1972].) See also the collection edited by Reinhard Lauer, *Sprache, Literatur und Folklore bei Vuk Stefanović Karadžić* (Wiesbaden: Harrassowitz, 1988).

15. This preface may be found in vol. 11 of the "new, revised, and enlarged edition" of Byron's works, *The Works of Lord Byron* (New York: Octagon, 1966), pp. 44–45; the volume is also referred to as *Byron's Letters and Journals*, vol. 4. Lord Byron's reaction to Aucher's rejection of his preface, cited by George Eric Mackay, *Lord Byron at the Armenian Convent* (Venice: Office of the Poliglotta, 1876), 79, and later included in Byron's *Works*, is supposed to have run as follows: "What? You refuse to print this preface because it is severe on your masters and oppressors! Slaves and cowards! You ought to have hard masters; you are not worthy of the great nation from which you sprang." The reader will find a brief (and insipid) account of Byron's relations with the Mkhitarists in Christopher Walker, *Visions of Ararat: Writings on Armenia* (London: I. B. Tauris, 1997), a book that presents itself as a compendium of everything that Anglophone writers (especially travel writers) have had to say about Armenia. It is a panorama of orientalism as applied to the Armenians. The problem is that the whole of this book is itself of orientalist inspiration. It is as if nineteenth-century orientalism (and, what is more, the Armenians' orientalism vis-à-vis themselves) were not enough—as if one were under an obligation to give an account of orientalism from an orientalist point of view!

16. Armenophone readers will find more details in *Mkhit'arean Hobelean* [Mkhitarist Jubilee] (Venice: San Lazzaro, 1901) and in my *Geghagitakan azgaynakanut'iun* [Aesthetic Nationalism] (forthcoming, in Armenian), which will provide all the pertinent references.

17. Parsegh Sarkisian, *Yerkhariurhamea grakanakan gortsuneut'iun yev nshanavor gortsichner Venetiko Mkhit'arean miapanut'ean* [Two Hundred Years of Literary Activity and the Prominent Figures of Venice's Mkhitarist Congregation] (Venice, 1905), 49. Father Sarkisian's account is squarely in the Mkhitarist tradition, reflecting the legend about their activities in this field that the Mkhitarists themselves have fanned.

18. The Latin title is *Eusebii Pamphili Chronicorum Canonum, Libri Duo, Opus ex Haicano Codice A Doctore Iohanne Zohrabo, Collegii Armeniaci Venetiarum Alumno Diligenter Expressum et Castigum.* This title is followed by *Nunc Primum Coniunctis Latine Donatum.* It would appear that, in reality, Zohrabian first translated Eusebius' *Chronicle* into Italian, and that Mai then translated Zohrabian's Italian version into Latin. Certain details are available in Giancarlo Bolognesi, *Leopardi e l'armeno* (Milan: Vita e pensiero, 1998), 66–69. This book contains an instructive concluding chapter on the part that Ludovico Arborio di Breme (a colorful personality whom Stendhal also knew) played in awakening Byron's passing interest in Armenian.

19. The full title of Leopardi's book is *Annotazioni sopra la Cronica d'Eusebio pubblicata l'anno 1818, in Milano, dai dottori Angelo Mai e Giovanni Zohrab, scritte l'anno appresso dal conte Giacomo Leopardi a un amico suo.* The book, only 117 pages long, was published in Rome by Romanis in 1823.

20. Both publications are marvels of the art of printing. The Latin title of the second, in two volumes, is *Eusebii Pamphilii Caesariensis Episcopi Chronicon Bipartitum. Nunc Primum ex Armeniaco Textu in Latinum Conversum. . . .* The place and date of publication are given as Venice, 1818, although the book cannot have appeared before 1819. The Congregation was, however, furious that someone had gotten the start on it; and this was, after all, only a white lie. These magnificent books may be consulted in the UCLA Library's Rare Books department.

21. *Byron's Letters and Journals,* 4:42.

22. The word *flânerie* is in French in Gourgouris's text and evokes, of course, Walter Benjamin.

23. I maintain this formulation, although I am aware that it calls for a long explanation. The native is certainly a product of philological orientalism. But although he thus makes his entry with philology, the reason is that the object of philological seeing and knowing (*voir-savoir*) is historicized, in the sense of the "transcendental" historicity that characterizes the object of the human sciences and was put in place slowly or with stunning rapidity late in the eighteenth century; it must be detected between the lines in all the phenomena that we are describing here. Michel Foucault provides the best account of the establishment of this historicity, in chapters 7 and 8 of *The Order of Things.* One must, then, read these chapters in conjunction with Said's *Orientalism* in order fully to grasp the nature of the archeological subject-object known as the native. In the present context, I can only indicate this in passing and, for the time being, refer the reader to the articles on Foucault and "transcendental history" by Béatrice Han, for example: "Is Early Foucault an Historian? History, history and the Analytic of Finitude," *Philosophy and Social Criticism* 31, nos. 5–6 (2005).

24. Lucas Injijean, *Tesut'iun hamar'ot hin yev nor ashkharhagrut'ean* [An Overview of Ancient and Modern Geography] (Venice: San Lazzaro, 1791).

25. Very little has been written about these periodicals, in part because their very existence was obscured. The libraries of Armenia do not have complete collections of them and the relevant bibliographical works provide contradictory information about them (often confounding Injijean's three publications). See, nevertheless, Artashès Karinyan, *Aknarkner hay parberakan mamuli patmut'ean* [Sketches of the History of the Armenian Periodical Press] (Yerevan: Institute of Literature, 1960). This is an extremely valuable two-volume work, even if its author is an old Bolshevik. In the first volume, Karinyan traces the history of the Western (in Transylvania and Poland) and Eastern (basically, in India) communities. He opens the second volume with a long history of the educational and intellectual activities of the Mkhitarists before proceeding to review their periodical publications of the first half of the nineteenth century.

26. Minas Pzhshgean, *Yerazhshtut'iun: Vor e hamar'ot teghekut'iun yerazhshtakan skbants' yelevejut'eants yeghanakats' yev nshanakrats' khaghits'* [Music: A Brief Overview of the Musical Principles of Keys and Notes]. Long unpublished, but known to specialists, this book was published in Yerevan in 1997 by Aram Kerovpian.

344 NOTES TO PAGES 86–96

27. The last stipulation is important, because we have unpublished travel narratives dating from the late eighteenth century, including Father Chamchean's account of his journey to Basrah on the Persian Gulf. I thank Meroujan Karapetian for alerting me to the existence of these manuscript travelogues.

28. This is what Pzhshgean declares in the book's preface and repeats eleven years later in his 1830 book about his voyage to Poland. The Armenian formula is "vik'arakan ishkhanut'eamb yev Ar'ak'elakan pashtoniv" (as a vicar on an apostolic mission). I imagine that what was involved was an order to undertake a mission that originated in Rome, not just with the Mkhitarist Congregation, but I cannot say so with certainty.

29. See Pzhshgean, *Chanaparhordut'iun i Lehastan* [Voyage to Poland] (Venice: 1830), 89. This passage is about one of the rare Armenian-speaking communities in Poland. As is well known, the overwhelming majority of the Armenians in Poland were descendants of Armenians who had first immigrated to the Crimea, where they adopted the Tatars' language. The Armenian-speakers belonged to a later wave of emigrants, or had not come to Poland by way of the Crimea. Hereafter, translated passages from this work, referred to as *Voyage to Poland*, are followed by parenthetical citations providing location of original text.

30. See Nina G. Garsoïan, ed. and trans., *The Epic Histories Attributed to P'awstos Buzand (Buzandaran Patmut'iwnk')*, Harvard Armenian Texts and Studies 8 (Cambridge, Mass.: Harvard University Press, 1989).

31. See appendix A, text 1.

32. These works by Alishan are *Ayrarat bnashkharh Hayastaneayts'* (1881), about the plain of Ararat; *Sisvan* (1885), about Cilician Armenia; and *Sisakan* (1893), about the region of Siunik. There exists a French translation of the second, *Sissouan, ou l'Arméno-Cilicie: Description géographique et historique, avec cartes et illustrations*, trans. Georges Bayan (Venice: San Lazzaro, 1899), a work in a 539-page quarto volume. Also available in French is Alishan's *Schirac, canton d'Ararat, pays de la Grande Arménie: Description géographique, illustrée . . .* (Venice: San Lazzaro, 1881).

33. Foucault, *The Order of Things*, 293–94. The "history" which is thus revealed without intermediary is the history that language carries within itself. That is the cause of its historicity. The same holds for geographical space and will also hold, somewhat later, for the living and dead utterance of the native.

34. These formulations are, obviously, polemical. Benedict Anderson's *Imagined Communities: Reflections on the Origin and Spread of Nationalism* (London: Verso, 1983), a book about the formation of nations and nationalisms, made a very big splash in the United States on its release in 1983. Anderson's vaguely Marxist analyses of capitalism in the age of the printing press, like his analyses of the pilgrimages of colonial civil servants, were not exactly novelties. As for his analysis of the term *imagined*, it is quite simply impoverished. The book's success was owing to the fact that it played on an ambiguity surrounding the very notion of the "imagination," in the twofold prolongation of an Anglo-Saxon tradition: the one that criticizes nationalism as "imaginary," and a new tradition, that of "poststructuralism" (as it is called in the United States), for which

language is supposed to make every reality an "invention" and therefore something "imagined." Eric Hobsbawm, acting under cover of positivist historiography, has been another promoter of this astounding amalgam.

35. Edouard Lalayan (1864–1931) began the *Ethnographic Journal* in 1896 in Tblisi and published it regularly for a period of twenty years. In 1921 he became the first director of the newly created Ethnographic Museum in Yerevan.

36. The list of Injijean's models includes the following scholars: Johannes Gronovius (1611–1671) or his son Jacob Gronovius (1645–1716), cited by Injijean in his *Darapatum*, 7:197–98; Christoph Cellarius (1638–1707), the author of a *Geographica antiqua*, which went through several editions in the later eighteenth century in London; Jean Mersius (1613–1654); Samuel Bochart (1599–1667), the author of a famous *Geographica Sacra* (1646); and Adriaan Reelant (1676–1718), a specialist in Eastern languages who wrote on the origin of languages, notably a book called *De veteri lingua indica*. Injijean refers to him as well in his *Darapatum* (7:228–29), citing his *Antiquitates sacrae veterum Hebraeorum*. These, then, are the authors from whom Injijean drew his neo-archeological inspiration.

37. Joseph Pitton de Tournefort (1656–1707), *Relation d'un voyage du Levant, fait par ordre du Roy, contenant l'histoire ancienne et moderne de plusieurs isles de l'Archipel, de Constantinople, des Côtes de la Mer Noire, de l'Arménie, de la Géorgie, des frontières de Perse et d'Asie Mineure*, 2 vols. (Lyons, 1717). "Description des côtes méridionales de la Mer Noire depuis son embouchure jusqu'à Sinope" may be found at 2:164ff.

38. For a translation of Mkrtich Emin's preface to his 1850 book, see appendix A, text 3. The text by Manuk Abeghean that I refer to here is *Hay zhoghovrdakan ar'aspelnerë M. Khorenats'u Hayots' Patmut'ean mej* [Popular Armenian Myths in *History of the Armenians* by Moses of Khoren]. It was published in the review *Ararat* in 1899 and is available in Abeghean, *Collected Works* (Yerevan: Academy of Sciences Publishing House, 1985), 8:67–271.

39. The reference to Renan (which is crucial in this context) is to his 1878 essay "Des services rendus aux sciences historiques par la philologie," which Gourgouris cites in the 1904 edition: Ernest Renan, *Mélanges religieux et historiques* (Paris: Calmann-Lévy, 1904), 221–56. The last sentence in the passage quoted from Gourgouris is worth pausing over. The nation comes into being by endowing itself with an "Old Testament" by means of philology. This is the testamentary structure of neo-vetero-archeological culture.

40. I remind the reader that this passage is to be found on pp. 3–4 of the original German publication, Manuk Abeghean, *Der armenische Volksglaube* (Leipzig: W. Drugulin, 1899). See also Manuk Abeghean, *Yerker* (Yerevan: Academy of Sciences Publishing, 1975), 7:455–56; see *Yerker* 7:13 for a translation of the passage into Armenian by Dora Sakayan. The word she uses to render *Überbleibsel* in Armenian is *verapruk*, which means "vestige" in the sense of something that survives. An English translation of the opening pages of *Der armenische Volksglaube* is provided in appendix A, text 7.

41. Friedrich Hölderlin, *Sämtliche Werke* (Stuttgart: Cotta, 1953), 2:204. See Beissner's remarks in "Hölderlins letzte Hymnen," reprinted in Friedrich Beissner, *Hölderlin: Reden*

und Aufsätze (Weimar: Böhlau, 1961), about the task of deciphering Hölderlin's manuscripts. Mention must also be made of the radical attitude informing the "historical-critical" edition of Hölderlin and defended by its editor, D. E. Sattler, in his introductory volume to *Sämtliche Werke* (*Frankfurter Ausgabe*) (Frankfurt: Verlag Roter Stern, 1975), pp. 55–70. This edition provides typographical reproductions of the different layers of the manuscript of the poem and then proposes a reconstructed version corresponding, according to its general editor, to "the last intention" behind the nascent text.

42. For a justification of the choices informing my French translation of these lines, see my "Avons-nous vraiment perdu la langue à l'étranger?" in Alexis Nouss, ed., "Antoine Berman aujourd'hui / Antoine Berman for Our Time," a special issue of *TTR: Études sur le texte et ses transformations* 14, no. 2 (second semester 2001). *Deutungslos*, in particular, emphatically means "undeciphered" (it is a question of a lost language).

4. The Disaster of the Native

1. Translated from Daniel Varuzhan, *Yerkeri Liakatar Zhoghovatsu* [Complete Works] (Yerevan: National Academy of Sciences Publishing, 1987), 3:364. Unless otherwise indicated, translated passages of the poet's writings are based on this scholarly edition of Varuzhan's complete works. As in previous chapters, hereafter this edition will be designated as *YLZ*, and parenthetical citations will provide volume and pages on which original text is found. The first two volumes of the three-volume *YLZ* appeared in 1986, and it is the most recent edition of Varuzhan's complete work. It is also the only one based on the manuscripts, not only for the poetry, but also for the essays, articles, and unpublished prose works, which were not available when earlier attempts were made to collect the poet's work in a complete edition. Several Varuzhan specialists participated in this collaborative edition. We must first recognize the efforts of Gohar Aznavuryan, who throughout her life patiently and stubbornly collected Varuzhan's unpublished writings, but also those of A. Shraruryan, chronicler of the poet's life, and those of J. Mirzabekyan, who provided the notes for volumes 1 and 2. It must be said, however, that this edition is not without its problems. It received a scathing review by Abraham Alikian, in "Daniel Varuzhan Yerkeri Liakatar Zhoghovatsu" [The Complete Works of Daniel Varuzhan], *Hask Armenological Review*, new series, years 7 and 8, 1997. In particular, the name "Pindar," the natural association made by anyone familiar with Varuzhan, was read here as "Thindare" by the editors, which gives rise to the following rather surrealist note: "In ancient Greek mythology, Thindare was the son of the king of Sparta; he was driven out and ostracized by his own brother. He became king thanks to Hercules." This is obviously a misunderstanding, since here Varuzhan speaks of how much he envies the poets of ancient times, especially the Greek poets and the Old Testament prophets, whom he compares with the pre-Socratic Greeks. Varuzhan's "pagan" works must be read first of all as a repetition of the ancient Greeks, according to the German model from the end of the eighteenth or the beginning of the nineteenth century, especially that of Hölderlin.

Varuzhan came to know ancient Greek literature through his Mkhitarist teachers, a point that we will return to below.

2. I am referring to the text of a lecture that was first published in volume 3 of the *Complete Works* in 1987; see *YLZ* 3:83–89. The title of this text (which is in fact no more than a sketch, or a series of personal notes) is simply "The Religions." For a translation of this text, see appendix C, text 25, and see also a brief commentary in the last pages of the present essay (end of chapter 8).

3. These appreciative reactions can be found in the volume entitled *Namakani* [Correspondence], ed. Gohar Aznavuryan (Yerevan: Hayastan, 1965). This volume brings together many of the letters written either by or to Varuzhan that were available at the time. His correspondents' reactions to his first work can be found on pp. 221, 232, 238, 251, and 273. A list of critical articles responding to the publication of Varuzhan's first volume of poetry is given in *YLZ* 1:546. One of the most laudatory articles, written by Arshag Chobanian, appeared in *Anahit*, 1906, no. 6–7, 106–13, and was later printed in Chobanian's *Demk'er* [Portraits] (Paris: Massis, 1929), 105–16. In this article, the most prominent critic of the period praised the poem "On the Threshold of Eternity," saying that it contained "one of the most magnificent pages in all of Armenian poetry" (*Demk'er*, 111), which was certainly extraordinary praise for the first book of a twenty-year-old poet.

4. In the poem "Haverzhut'ean semin" [On the Threshold of Eternity], *YLZ* 1:45.

5. See the account by the actor Vahan Papazyan, in his book *Hetadardz Hayeatsk'* [Looking Back] (Yerevan, 1956), 1:53; or that of one of Varuzhan's disciples, Arakel Badrig, in his book *Daniel Varuzhanë im husherum* [Daniel Varuzhan as I Remember Him] (Yerevan: Hayastan, 1965), 26. For a list of articles on *The Heart of the Race*, see *YLZ* 1:554.

6. Badrig, *Daniel Varuzhanë*, 69. Cf. *YLZ* 1:553.

7. This expression comes from Hagop Oshagan, Varuzhan's unfailing friend and alter ego. It occurs in the last major text that Oshagan wrote on the poet, which appears in volume 6 of Oshagan's *Hamapatker arevmtahay grakanut'ean* [Panorama of Western Armenian Literature] (Beirut: Hamazkayin 1968); this work is referred to hereafter as *Panorama*. I will comment on these pages below.

8. The Young Turk revolution took place in July 1908. The proclamation of the constitution occurred on July 11/24, 1908. This constitution established a sort of constitutional monarchy. The sultan Abdül Hamid, however, was not completely divested of power. Only the following year, after making a bloody attempt to come back to power, in April 1909, was he definitively removed from the throne, exiled, and replaced by Mehmet V, who held the position of sultan until 1922, but without any real power.

9. Besides my monograph on Zabel Esayan in *Writers of Disaster: The National Revolution* (Princeton and London: Gomidas Institute, 2002), I refer the reader to a more recent essay of mine on her: "Zabel Esayan, Woman and Witness, or The Truth of the Mask," published in *New Perspectives on Turkey* (Istanbul: Bosphorus University), no. 42 (Spring 2010): 31–53.

10. See *Writers of Disaster: The National Revolution*, 198–200.

11. Cf. Chobanian, *Namakani*, 270–71, and *YLZ* 3:602. We can assume that Varuzhan was being cautious when he stated that the poem was written "before the Constitution," at least with regard to his Armenian readers, and perhaps in order to justify himself to Chobanian. Public declarations of "patriotism" were of course forbidden to Armenians and strictly censored by the dictatorship under Hamid. At the time of the Young Turks, however, censorship in the territory of the Ottoman Empire was relaxed at first, although this revealed nothing, in fact, concerning the real sentiments of the new leaders. Seven years later, these new leaders, who shared Varuzhan's socialist ideals, organized the complete extermination of the Armenians of the Empire.

12. Cf. *YLZ* 2:166–68.

13. This poem first appeared on August 9, 1908, in the journal *Razmig*, published by Rupen Zartarian in Plovdiv, Bulgaria. Varuzhan later included it in *The Heart of the Race*; cf. *YLZ* 1:198–203, and the corresponding notes, 1:570.

14. *Oliaba* appears to be the biblical name Olibamah (Genesis 36:14 and 36:18) or Oholibamah (Oxford Bible), which we also find in the form of Aholibamah (King James), thus modified by Varuzhan. I am unable to say why Varuzhan chose these biblical names for the Great Widow, the Mother of the Heroes and the Lady of the Ruins. Gayl Vahan (Vahan the Wolf) was the hero of the "Deeds of Taron," an epic narrative transformed into historiography following national events of the end of the sixth century and the beginning of the seventh. David Beg, one of the last local Armenian princes in the mountains of Siunik and of Karabagh, was the leader of local resistance (or of a protomovement of national liberation!) against the Turko-Persian rulers of the region in the eighteenth century. These are the obligatory episodes covered in any nationalist Armenian history, in versions that gradually took shape during the nineteenth century, finally leading to the modern "national liberation" movement after 1880. Was Varuzhan thus an heir to the Armenian nationalist discourse of the nineteenth century? Yes, he obviously was. But that is not really the essential question, since he is also the decisive interpreter of this nationalist discourse in aesthetic terms. That is what I would like to demonstrate here.

15. Mehmet Emin (1869–1932) was a Turkish poet who is known and appreciated in Turkey still today. When he learned of the arrest and exile of Varuzhan in 1915, he appears to have interceded in his favor, without result of course. But—since one does not exclude the other—he also appears to have written in favor of the policy of exterminating the Armenians initiated by the Young Turks. Cf. Badrig, *Daniel Varuzhanë*, 33; unfortunately, Badrig does not cite his sources.

16. The anecdote is related by Badrig, *Daniel Varuzhanë*, 37–38 (republished in *YLZ* 1:571).

17. On this unholy alliance between the Dashnaktsakan party—or the Armenian Revolutionary Federation—which spearheaded the national revolution, and the Young Turks, there is an abundant literature. For a good introduction, see Richard Hovannisian, *Armenia on the Road to Independence, 1918* (Berkeley and Los Angeles: University of California Press, 1967).

18. This is a good place for a few words concerning the existing commentaries on Daniel Varuzhan's work. The poet's friends and disciples all wrote down their memories. The most important testimony in this regard is that of Hagop Sirouni, who collected his writings into a book entitled simply *Daniel Varuzhan* (published in Bucharest in 1940). We also have the memoirs of one of his Venetian friends, Terenig Jizmejian, *Daniel Varuzhan, dprots'akan keank'ë, antip namaknerë, grakanut'iunë* [Daniel Varuzhan, His Life as a Student, His Unpublished Letters, His Literature] (Cairo: Houssaper, 1955). Two monographs on Varuzhan have appeared in Armenia, one by Hektor Rshtuni (1961), and another by Vazgen Gabrielyan (1978). These works conform quite faithfully to the norms of Soviet literatry criticism (in other words, they are completely useless). In the diaspora, after the writings of Sirouni and Jizmejian, there were monograph essays published in various histories of modern literature (those by Gurgen Mekhitarian, Hagop Oshagan, Minas Tölölyan, Mushegh Ishkhan), but quite astonishingly there was not a single book devoted entirely to Varuzhan, at least until the masterful work by Krikor Beledian, *Krake shrjanagë: Daniel Varuzhani shurj* [The Circle of Fire: On Daniel Varuzhan] (Antelias: Armenian Catholicosate, 1988), which is without doubt one of the most important books published in Armenian in the last quarter of the twentieth century. The present work makes frequent reference to this book, both for the information it provides and for its analyses, to which those presented here are, admittedly, extremely close, especially on the question of the "aesthetic principle," on the meaning of "paganism" for the poet, and on the relation between art and the fatherland. It is clear that Beledian is not one of those commentators who fall into the trap of "renaissance" and "nostalgia."

19. Cf. *YLZ* 1:110–11.

20. On the history of Ani and its place in the Armenian national imagination, as well as the archeological research that has been carried out there, see the excellent collection of essays edited by Raymond Kévorkian, *Ani: Capitale de l'Arménie en l'an mil* (Paris: Paris-Musées, 2001).

21. See appendix C, text 18.

22. These quotations (and all subsequent quotations from Varuzhan's poetry in this chapter) reflect my renderings of his work into French and can be considered my own translations, made with the help of Jeff Fort. Consequently they differ from the poetic translations by G. M. Goshgarian and others offered in appendix C. I did not try to reconcile slightly differing versions of the same lines and poems.

23. Here are the final six lines of this passage in Armenian, as printed in *YLZ*:

Զունենալով նոյն ինք իրենՑ սեփական
Հայրենիքի այս Ոչինչին, րոհիՑ դեմ՝
Իրը առաջին սերմնացու
Խոՙւֆ մՙոր սատեղծէ, ներդաշնակէ, պոռթկալով
Փոշիներէն Անիի
 Քանան մը նոՙր ու ագաՙո:

This is how these lines appear in the original edition. The manuscript (which I consulted in May 2006) does not allow any final emendation. "Of its own" can be related to the word of revolt and creation or to the fatherland. It is also possible to correct "nuyn inq" as though it was "nuynisk," and therefore relate it to the missing word (he has no word of his own when confronted to the lack of an "own"). In my translation I tried to keep all these possibilities as though they superimposed each other. In *Krake Shrjanakë*, K. Beledian comments on these lines, accepting the reading "nuyn ink' iren," while also admitting that it is a strange form that is never used, which he interprets as a doubling of the proper and an interrogation of the proper. But this does not give any more sense to the expression "nuyn inq iren." I will return to this point below.

24. I am here referring to Edward Said and to Stathis Gourgouris. See the latter's work *Dream Nation: Enlightenment, Colonization, and the Institution of Modern Greece* (Stanford: Stanford University Press, 1996), particularly the extraordinary fourth chapter, "The Punishment of Philhellenism," where we read the following: "The commodification of cultural observation becomes the central characteristic of the travel narrative, the conceptual matrix of the traveling experience itself. All travelers are *flâneurs*—'looking at all objects with a wild and vacant stare,' as Benjamin has put it . . , abandoned to the intoxication of an Other cultural landscape and writing of their adventures through personas possessed by an autoscopic presence. Indeed, the orientalist experience, of which Philhellenism is but a specific expression, is a most extravagant kind of *flânerie*" (137). The Walter Benjamin text referred to here is his posthumous book *Charles Baudelaire: The Lyric Poet in the Era of High Capitalism*, trans. Harry Zohn (London: New Left Books, 1973), 54.

25. It was while working on a book written in Armenian, *Geghagitakan Azgaynakanut'iun* [Aesthetic Nationalism], that I first came to understand the extent and the importance of this phenomenon of "autoscopic mimicry" theorized by Gourgouris in *Dream Nation*. It remained to provide a historical reconstruction of this process in the Armenian context, for which there is of course no phenomenon similar to European "Philhellenism." What was reconstructed (now in Part I of this book) was rather a "Neo-Armenism" (for which this unusual term had to be invented), parallel to Greek Neo-Hellenism, with its philological and ethnographic elements, and the importance given to the historiography of "pagan" origins. On the question of mimicry, aside from Gourgouris, see the article by Homi Bhabha, "Of Mimicry and Man: The Ambivalence of Colonial Discourse," in *Politics and Ideology: A Reader*, ed. James Donald and Stuart Hall (Milton Keynes: Open University Press), 198–205.

26. Recently, the concept and the figure of the native were described, from a different perspective, by Mahmoud Mamdani in *Citizen and Subject: Contemporary Africa and the Legacy of Late Colonialism* (Princeton: Princeton University Press, 1996). Here it is a question of the invention of the native in colonial discourse, as inflected by the distinction between civilized law and customary law, concomitant to the distinction between race and ethnicity. This description enables Mamdani to approach a genocidal event in his next book, *When Victims Become Killers: Colonialism, Nativism, and the Genocide in Rwanda* (Princeton: Princeton University Press, 2001). Such a description of the invention of the native through the examination of a "juridical" distinction cannot be undertaken here. It will be taken up elsewhere.

27. *Mehyan*, no. 3 (March 1914), 40. See also appendix B, text 13. (In 1914 Oshagan was writing under the name Kufejian. The name of the national Church is *Hayastaneayts' Yegeghets'i*, literally "Church of Armenias," in the plural.

28. The 1911 article, entitled "Hay lezvi khntirë" [The Question of the Armenian Language], may be found in *YLZ* 3:131–30. The 1913 essay, entitled "Yarchaniani k'ert'oghut'iunë" [Yarjanian's Poetry]— Siamanto was the pen name of the poet Adom Yarjanian—is in *YLZ* 3:155–64. See also chapter 1, n. 43.

29. *Ages et usages de la langue arménienne* (Paris: Entente, 1989), chapter 9, 358–69; *Writers of Disaster: The National Revolution*, 32–33.

30. This remarkable statement appears in the monograph on Indra (the poet Diran Chrakian) in volume 8 of *Panorama*. The phrase occurs as part of a discussion on the importance of the history of the language, understood both as a cultural achievement and as a testimony to this achievement. On Hagop Oshagan as a critic and literary historian, see my book *Le Roman de la Catastrophe* (Geneva: Métis Presse, 2008).

31. *Mehyan*, no. 3 (March 1914), 40. See also appendix B, text 13.

32. We will return to this central question below in chapters 7 and 8, in relation to religion, particularly in the final pages of chapter 8, where it will be a question of the major figures of nineteenth-century European philology, the founders of the "science of religion."

33. On the Armenian historiography that emerged at the time of the Enlightenment, but without any apparent relation to the latter, see my "Enlightenment and Historical Thought," in Richard Hovannisian and David Myers, eds., *Enlightenment and Diaspora: The Armenian and Jewish Cases* (Atlanta: Scholars Press, 1999). Regarding Nazareants and Herder, see note 11 in chapter 2.

34. The term *race* was commonly used by Varuzhan and his contemporaries. The "racialization" of culture and of tradition is a phenomenon inherent to the philology of the nineteenth century. We will return to this briefly at the end of chapter 5, where it will be a question of the invention of the providential couple Semite / Aryan and the respectful debates between Max Müller and Ernest Renan. Despite all the internal revisions within philology, it is clear that this racialization is constitutive of the discipline.

35. This is the interpretation offered by Vahakn Dadrian in his work *The History of the Armenian Genocide: Ethnic Conflict from the Balkans to Anatolia to the Caucasus* (Providence, R I · Berghahn Books, 1997).

36. Beledian, *Krake Shrjanakë*, 121–22. "Impropriety" here translates the neologism *ansephakanuthiun*, which means simply the "nonproper," the "absence of the proper," the "lack of the proper," but also the default of aesthetic heroization, according to a logic elaborated by the author and that I reproduce here with my own terms.

37. Beledian, *Krake Shrjanakë*, 123. Beledian is attempting here to construct a language with which to say the disaster at the heart of the proper or of the fatherland, the founding Catastrophe, as *Ereignis*, as the event of appropriation. It is clearly a question of thinking destruction (the destruction of the self) as a coming to be (of the self). Elsewhere (in his poetic work *Vayrer* [Sites]), Beledian creates an echo between *k'andel* (destroy) and *k'andakel* (sculpt, erect).

5. The Other Scene of Representation

1. The original text of this poem appears in Daniel Varuzhan, *Yerkeri Liakatar Zhoghovatsu* [Complete Works] (Yerevan: National Academy of Sciences Publishing, 1987), 1:147–51. As in previous chapters, translations are based on this edition, referred to hereafter as *YLZ*; parenthetical citations will provide volume and pages of original text. A translation of this poem has been included in appendix C (text 20). For an attentive, thorough, and decisive reading of this poem within a problematic quite similar to the one here (at least on this point), I refer once again to the work by Krikor Beledian, *Krake Shrjanakë: Daniel Varuzhani shurj* [The Circle of Fire: On Daniel Varuzhan] (Antelias: Armenian Catholicosate, 1988), 126–49 and 162–66. In fact, Beledian's book as a whole is constructed around a commentary on this poem. The importance of this commentary is such that it could not fail to inspire the present reading; it is to be hoped that the abbreviated summaries that are necessary here do not distort the author's analysis.

2. Here again I must alert the reader to the fact that the lines of Varuzhan's poetry presented in the main text reflect my own renderings of Varuzhan into French and can be considered my own translations, made with the help of Jeff Fort. Different translations, by G. M. Goshgarian and others, are offered in appendix C.

3. It is on the basis of these lines that Beledian called his book on Varuzhan *Krake Shrjanakë,* "The Circle of Fire."

4. Zabel Esayan, *Yerker* [Works], 2 vols. (Antelias: Armenian Catholicosate, 1987), 1:31; 45.

5. On this question of the proliferation of testimonies and their submersion in the archive, see my book *The Historiographic Perversion* (New York: Columbia University Press, 2009), in particular its chapter 4 ("Testimony: From Document to Monument") and its conclusion ("Shame and Testimony").

6. Beledian, *Krake Shrjanakë*, 136.

7. In this regard, see the fine study by Sylvie Rollet, "Hantises ou l'appareil, la mémoire et le politique," in *Le temps des appareils*, ed. Jean-Louis Déotte (Paris: La Dispute, 2004). In reality, in this article Rollet saves the very idea of the image; and more than that: she magnifies it. She argues that a new thinking of the image is necessary for understanding the intervention of the filmic image in historical memory, when history is the effacement of events and their disintegration. She refers to the concept of the "dialectal image" proposed by Walter Benjamin, which she presents as "the Benjaminian concept that is most promising for a philosophy of filmic time." The essential passage from Benjamin in question here is the following: "An image is that in which the Then and the Now come together, in a flash of lightning, into a constellation. In other words: an image is dialectics at a standstill." It may be found in *Benjamin: Philosophy, Aesthetics, History*, ed. Gary Smith, trans. Leigh Hafrey and Richard Sieburth (Chicago: University of Chicago Press, 1989), 50–51; also in *The Arcades Project*, trans. Howard Eiland and Kevin McLaughlin (Cambridge, Mass.: Harvard University Press, 1999), 476.

8. Beledian also cites line 57 of Varuzhan's poem in this sense: "Then the Barbarians spit toward the sun . . ."

9. On this question, see my paper "Representation and Historicity," presented in November 2003 at Columbia University, published in "Art and Testimony: Around Atom Egoyan's *Ararat*," special issue of *Armenian Review* 49, nos. 1–4 (2004–05).

10. On Bartevian, see Rubina Peroomian, *Literary Responses to Catastrophe: A Comparison of the Armenian and the Jewish Experiences* (Atlanta: Scholars Press, 1993), 117–50.

11. My *Writers of Disaster: The National Revolution* (Princeton and London: Gomidas Institute, 2002) includes a selective list of these articles, limited to the events in Cilicia in 1909, both by foreign witnesses and by Armenian witnesses and survivors. Articles published at the time in the French press, in the journal *Pro Armenia*, or in the English language press are not included there.

12. Hagop Oshagan, *Mayrineru shuk'in tak* [In the Shade of the Cedars] (Beirut: Centenary Edition, 1983), 16.

13. I developed and analyzed this scene in an article written in Armenian, "Zareh Vorbuni, Zhamanak yev Hayrut'iun" [Zareh Vorpouni, Time and Paternity], published in *Bazmavep*, 1996, 99–140. However, this analysis needs to be taken up within a general problematic of testimony as appearing-destroyed, of the role of the image and of representation in testimony (the latter part of the problematic is addressed here), of the Catastrophe as a disaster of the father—which was discussed in the first two essays of *Writers of Disaster: The National Revolution*, dealing with Charents and Mahari—and therefore of writing as a confrontation with the mourning of mourning.

14. Peter Najarian, *Voyages* (New York: Pantheon, 1971). *Voyages* is the first part of a trilogy, the second of which, *Wash Me on Home, Mama* (1978), is also presented in novel form, whereas the third part, *Daughters of Memory* (1986), breaks with narrative and begins to explore a very different literary space, that of impossible testimony and, therefore, impossible memory.

15. Janine Altounian, *Ouvrez-moi les chemins d'Arménie* (Paris: Dunod, 1994), *La survivance: Traduire le trauma collectif* (Paris: Dunod, 2000), and *L'intraduisible: Deuil, mémoire, transmission* (Paris: Dunod, 2005).

16. I say all of this with some reservations. My first impression of this film remains with me: the immense ambiguity of *Ararat* lingers as a kind of aftertaste, a sense that it still, and despite everything, wants to be *a testimony* addressed to the foreigner, concerning "our" suffering and "our" crucifixion, and that it does not even ask this foreigner to close his eyes, as Varuzhan did, but in reality plays with the fabrication of the represented image in order to show the atrocities, *after all and despite everything*, behind the screen of the second degree or of metarepresentation. It is a testimony on the scene-of-the-Other, supported by images (which is clear even without the filmmaker's declarations and actions after the film, all of which go in this direction). There is an immense ambiguity in the encounter with the foreigner, during which the young man smuggles in forbidden products by way of testimony. Forbidden products? Yes, these same atrocities or his own appearing-destroyed, once again, in the civilized space, atrocities and destruction that must be smuggled into the world of the law and of civilization. Grotesque atrocities, in any case. Thus the scene of the girls who are forced to dance before

they are burned to death, a scene taken directly from Siamanto and an obligatory commonplace for Armenians who have not read a single line of this poet obsessed by the atrocities of 1895 and 1909 (and who, like Varuzhan, was brutally assassinated in 1915 with his peers after being deported to Ayash), nor in fact a single line of real testimony in their lives (for it is evident that the epic narrative of the poet, like that of Varuzhan in fact, is *anything but a testimony*; it was no doubt taken by Siamanto from a first-hand testimony, then transformed by him into epic literature, destined to be received as such and to live on as a mythic scene in the memory of the Other, in one's own memory as a memory of the Other; and the filmmaker understood this perfectly, since it is thus that he "scenifies" Siamanto's narrative, shifting it into an image exposed on the scene-of-the-Other). Thus, too, the rape scene, in which the mother holds the hand of her little girl while she is raped, while the girl holds the hand of a stuffed bear. And thus, finally (but these are only three examples among others), in the scene in which the Armenian population of Van is deported at the end of the film, an utterly ridiculous scene, since the Armenian community of Van was precisely the only one in the entire Ottoman Empire not to be deported. Poetic license! I expressed another opinion in my presentation on the film (cited above, in note 9), in which I attempted to strike a balance between the two approaches: 1) one that sees Egoyan as a continuation or a fulfillment of the great debate of the twentieth century among Armenians concerning representation and testimony, on the interpenetration and the inevitable but controlled confusion between the necessity of an "other-scene" and the omnipotence of the "scene-of-the-Other"; and 2) one that reads this profound reflection on representation and historicity (as I have done in this note) as an illusory and learned *screen* for yet another testimony, another use of the scene-of-the-Other, resulting as always from the attempt to appear-destroyed.

17. On Kertész and Klüger, I refer the reader to an article by Aurélia Kalisky, "Refus de témoigner ou chronique d'une métamorphose: Du témoin à l'écrivain (Imre Kertész, Ruth Klüger)," in Catherine Coquio, ed., *L'histoire trouée: Négation et témoignage* (Nantes: L'Atalante, 2004), 419–48.

18. This passage is taken from a recent essay by Catherine Coquio, "Aux lendemains, là-bas et ici: L'écriture, la mémoire et le deuil," which appeared as the preface to a collection of essays entitled *Rwanda—2004:Témoignages et littérature*, edited by C. Coquio and Aurélia Kalisky, special issue of *Lendemains* 28, no. 112 (March 2004). These questions on the limits of literature, the insane paradoxes of testimony, as well as the relation between testimony and tragedy, have already been addressed by the same author in "Récits de rescapés: Y a-t-il une philosophie des témoignages?" in *Littérature et philosophie*, ed. A. Tomiche and Ph. Zard (Arras: Artois Presses Universitaires, 2002), and in many other articles, essays, and books (for a list of these, see the next note). In addition to Coquio, we should also mention Philippe Bouchereau, who in his essay "Le génocide est sans raison: Méditer la désespérance," in *L'intranquille*, 6–7 (2001), distinguishes between "figuration" (proper to the heir) and "testimony" (proper to the survivor). It is possible that in many cases this distinction is relevant. But it does not seem to

be so in the case of the Armenian figuration of the Catastrophe, where the distinction between figuration and testimony is not at all a question of generation (survivor or heir). Figuration and testimony have always cohabitated. The example of Daniel Varuzhan (for whom, as I will show in a moment, figuration becomes primary in the form of a matrix that emphasizes, from the beginning and in advance, the entire perverse, paradoxical, or demented logic—as one wishes—of testimony) is certainly proof of this.

19. See in particular the collection of essays Coquio has edited entitled *Parler des camps, penser les génocides* (Paris: Albin-Michel, 1999) and the introduction by her, "Du malentendu"; but also her new collection *L'histoire trouée: Négation et témoignage* (Nantes: L'Atalante, 2004), particularly Coquio's preface, "A propos d'un nihilisme contemporain: Négation, déni, témoignage"; as well as the following articles: "La littérature arménienne de la Catastrophe: Actualité critique," in C. Mouradian, Y. Ternon, and G. Bensoussan, eds., "Ici, ailleurs, autrement: Connaissance et reconnaissance du génocide arménien," special issue of the *Revue d'Histoire de la Shoah*, no. 177–78 (Spring 2003); and "L'émergence d'une littérature de non-écrivains: Le témoignage des catastrophes histo-riques," *Revue d'histoire littéraire de la France*, no. III (April–June 2003).

20. Here is the Armenian text of these extraordinary verses: "Օտարական՚ն, ա՚լ մեկնէ: Կ՚իջնեմ ես ալ աւասիկ / Այս բարձունքէն, ու փափքուած տատատոռկիս մէշ տրտում / Նորէն կ՚երթամ բախտախիլ քաղաքին մէշ զոհերուն: / Մեռելներն հարկ է թաղեմ, եւ ողջակեզն օձանեմ / Վիրաւորի մը գլուխն որձմարքին կը հեծեՙ . . . / Աղքիւրին քով քոյր մը, ո՚հ, կ՚ոգեկալի անտերունչ . . . / Պետք է փորեմ այս գիշեր գերեզմՙաննՙեր անհամար, / Եւ լուսեղէն պատան֙ներ հե֙նում մինչեւ առաւօտ, / Պետք է կերտեմ շիրիմ֙ներ, յուշարձան֙ներ կանգնեմ, / Եւ մարմարին վրայ տապանագիր քանդակեմ."

21. See my analysis (in Armenian) of the corresponding pages of volume 3 of *Mnatsor-tats* (The Remnants) in my essay "Yergin gerin" [Slave of the Song], *Hask Armenological Review*, 7–8 (1995–96). This analysis is taken up in my book *Le Roman de la Catastrophe* (Geneva: MétisPresse, 2008) in a slightly different form, but still in relation to the idea and the reality of sacrifice, with regard to the Turkish song as a "symbolic success" and to the transformation of "blood into meaning."

22. These lines were already quoted in the introductory chapter on *Mehyan*, and we will read them again later, in a commentary on the end of religion, the death of the gods, and the sublation of religion by art, all of which are themes proper to Varuzhan. It should be noted that erection, as the production of form, is an Apollinian activity. This Apollinian character is emphasized again by the fact that the erection of the gods is carried out by art "in its immortal dream."

23. *YLZ*, 1:167, ll. 36–40: "In your maternal belly the milk is the abundant mar-ble / That our ancestors drew out with their active hands / And with which they erected the gods and the immaculate altars . . ."

24. Marc Nichanian, "Introduction: Poetry and Revolution," in *Yeghishe Charents, Poet of the Revolution,* ed. Marc Nichanian with Vartan Matiossian (Costa Mesa, Calif.: Mazda Press, 2003).

6. Erection and Self-Sacrifice

1. A number of Varuzhan's pagan poems are included in appendix C at the end of this volume, in previously unpublished translations by different translators. For translations of other poems that appeared in *Pagan Songs*, see Diana Der Hovannessian and Marzbed Margossian, editors and translators, *Anthology of Armenian Poetry* (New York: Columbia University Press, 1978).

2. Translated from Daniel Varuzhan, *Yerkeri Liakatar Zhoghovatsu* [Complete Works] (Yerevan: National Academy of Sciences Publishing, 1987), 2:7 (ll. 12–14). *Yerkeri Liakatar Zhoghovatsu* is hereafter referred to as *YLZ*, and translated passages are followed by parenthetical citations providing volume and pages on which original text is found.

3. Varuzhan already used this word for marble in "Native Mountains": "The mausoleums of Ani were sculpted in your marble [*kuch*] / And the vases containing the ashes of the [Arsacides]." (*YLZ* 1:168) The poet is referring to Ani in Lower Armenia, where the funerary temple of the Arsacid kings was located.

4. This reference to Greece and this desire to repeat Greek art are not simply poetic conventions. We have already seen that Varuzhan dreamed of being the equal of Pindar.

5. See chapter 4, n. 1.

6. As in the previous chapters on Varuzhan, quotations from his poetry in this chapter reflect my own renderings of Varuzhan into French and can be considered my own translations. Different translations, by G. M. Goshgarian and others, are offered in appendix C.

7. Every attempt to separate ritual from sacrifice appears to be futile. It seems that there is no ritual without sacrifice and, conversely, no sacrifice without ritual. There is no period in which sacrificial violence was king, followed by another in which ritual establishes an ideal or idealized peace, an immutable order, far from the harsh realities of this world. See the very fine critical and polemical pages by Brian K. Smith in *Reflections on Resemblance, Ritual, and Religion* (Oxford: Oxford University Press, 1989), 44–46, where the discussion deals with the Vedic religion, based on the work of J. C. Heesterman, particularly his article "Other Folks' Fire," published in Frits Staal, ed., *Agni: The Vedic Ritual of the Fire Altar*, vol. 2 (Berkeley: Asian Humanities Press, 1983), and Heesterman's book *The Inner Conflict of the Tradition: Essays in Indian Ritual, Kingship, and Society* (Chicago: University of Chicago Press, 1985). The same critique was developed at greater length by Smith in the article "Ideals and Realities in Indian Religion," *Religious Studies Review* 14 (January 1988): 1–9.

8. Jean-Luc Nancy's decisive essay on myth and the modern myth of myth is included under the title "Myth Interrupted" in *The Inoperative Community*, ed. Peter Connor (Minneapolis: University of Minnesota Press, 1991); hereafter cited parenthetically in text as *IC*. I have translated this essay into Armenian; the translation appears in *GAM*, no. 6 (2005).

9. In this paragraph, Nancy cites a fragment from Nietzsche, who attributes to the Greeks a free creative power arising from a "mythic feeling of freely lying," a statement that was cited in Manfred Fuhrmann, ed., *Terror und Spiel: Probleme der Mythenrezeption* (Munich: W. Fink, 1971), 25. It is worth recalling what Nietzsche says in a fragment collected in *The Will to Power* (no. 853): "*We have need of lies* in order to conquer this

reality. . . . The task thus imposed is tremendous. To solve it, man must be a liar by nature, he must be above all an *artist*. And he *is* one: metaphysics, religion, morality, science—all of them only products of his will to art, to lie" (Nietzsche's emphasis). *The Will to Power*, trans. Walter Kaufmann and R. J. Hollingdale (New York: Vintage, 1968), 451. I will come back to this later, in the epilogue on Nietzsche and Constant Zarian.

10. *Mehyan*, no. 3 (March 1914), p. 40.

11. I am referring to F. W. J. Schelling's *Historical-critical Introduction to the Philology of Mythologie.* We know that Schelling paid homage to Schlegel (not without some hypocrisy) for having preceded him in a reflection on the essence of mythology.

12. I use the expression *ethnomythology* to indicate a) the "ethnologico-metaphysical" scene described by Jean-Luc Nancy in *The Inoperative Community*, and, at the same time, b) the conjunction between Indo-European studies of language and religion and the rise of ethnology in the nineteenth century.

13. Maurice Olender, *The Languages of Paradise: Race, Religion, and Philosophy in the Nineteenth Century*, trans. Arthur Goldhammer (Cambridge, Mass.: Harvard University Press, 1992). This book was recently reissued with a different subtitle (more faithful to the original): *The Languages of Paradise: Aryans and Semites, A Match Made in Heaven* (New York: The Other Press, 2002). The original French title is *Les langues du paradis: Aryens et Sémites, un couple providentiel* (Paris: Gallimard/Seuil, 1989), with a preface by Jean-Pierre Vernant. On the change of title in English between 1992 and 2002, see Gil Anidjar, *Semites: Race, Religion, Literature* (Stanford: Stanford University Press, 2008), 107. I will address some of the questions raised by Olender at the end of chapter 8 and in the epilogue on Nietzsche / Zarian.

14. I am again referring to the end of chapter 8 of Michel Foucault, *The Order of Things* (New York: Random House, 1970), 299–300, where Foucault describes the birth of literature in the modern (intransitive) sense of the term as a reaction to the philological stranglehold on language.

15. The gender of the native is entirely undecided and undecidable. In French, *le natif* is only defined by its grammatical gender, and therefore the use of *il*, the masculine pronoun, does not raise any particular problem. It is not the same in English, where the use of the pronoun has to be rethought each and every time anew.

16. Later, Nancy explains that it is a question of thinking community in terms of the interruption of myth, and thus of thinking it as resistance (as resisting communitarian immanence). "In the absence of community neither the work of community, nor the community as work, nor communism can fulfill itself; rather, the passion of and for community propagates itself, unworked, appealing, demanding to pass beyond every limit and every fulfillment enclosed in the form of an individual" (*IC*, 60). The interruption of myth (and with it, a thinking of interruption) is therefore also "the interruption of community, the interruption of the totality that would fulfill it" (61), that is, a resistance to the totalitarian. I would say that it is also a thinking of diaspora, a thinking that is much needed after the Catastrophe, whereas precisely such a thinking of diaspora is incapable of being constituted today. And if it cannot be constituted, it is because we

continue to try to imagine the Catastrophe in terms of the disaster of myth, which is a mythic disaster (unless we indulge in the now common practice of denying even that the genocidal event was a Catastrophe).

17. It must be admitted that the second part of the quotation corresponds to a text which, in Armenian, is quite obscure. It is difficult to understand in particular whether the poet is speaking of having put pressure on his heart in order to limit himself to patriotic feelings, or whether these new feelings and passions are rather the ones that were suppressed and oppressed. It is quite possible that this edition of the letters is faulty, but unfortunately I have no way to remedy the problem.

18. *Worshippers* here translates the Armenian word *k'urm*, which strictly speaking means a priest in the pagan era. Similarly, the word *altar* translates the Armenian *bagin*, which is used only for pagan sacrificial altars.

19. The expression *chshgrit keank'ë* (which I translate as "life as it is") alludes to a realist approach—in opposition no doubt to a more rhetorical approach—that Varuzhan practiced whenever he wrote patriotic poems addressed to the "masses." This long and important letter, from November 11–17, 1908, is essential for other reasons. Terenig Jizmejian had returned to his home country on the banks of the Euphrates, and after a very long detour that took him to Egypt, he had returned to Turin. In this context, it is the image of the *return* that emerges for Varuzhan. (I will quote these lines on the return in a moment.)

20. Curiously, this letter (in fact, the fragment of a letter) was not published in Theotig's *Amenun Tarets'uyts'ë* (Almanac for All), but in the daily *Zhamanak* (Times) of Constantinople in 1912.

21. "Lonely," which describes a deception or an emotional betrayal (related by Varuzhan in one of his letters to Jizmejian), dates from December 1908.

22. Yeghia Demirjibashian was one of the most visible Armenian intellectuals of the nineteenth century in Constantinople. He was a great reader (and propagandist) of orientalist literature and positivist philosophy as these were developed in France, and he integrated them into his multiform oeuvre (essays, poems, poetic prose, diaries) which was published almost entirely in literary journals. The image that remains of him is that of a tormented writer carried to extremes (both a mystic and a positivist) and relishing the shock of these extremes, dispersed like Kierkegaard in a multiplicity of pseudonyms, singing the praises of Indian Nirvana, and overcome with madness in the end. A relatively complete volume of his works was published in Armenia in 1986, edited by Stepan Topjian. But much work remains to be done if we are to have a more complete idea of his scattered writings. Krikor Beledian has written an innovative study on Demirjibashian which takes into account precisely the absence of the work, interpreted as a *désoeuvrement* in Maurice Blanchot's sense. See Krikor Beledian, *Mart* (Antelias: Catholicosate of Cilicia, 1997).

23. Cf. "Mamus aghot'k'ë" (My Grandmother's Prayer), *YLZ* 2:126–27.

24. In this series, we can cite "Banvoruhin" (The Worker), *YLZ* 2:102–03; "Spasum" (Waiting), 2:111–13 (a father crushed by work comes home and beats his wife in front of

their terrified children); "Ënketsikë" (The Bastard Son), 2:114–15 (a mother abandons her child); "Mer'nogh banvor" (The Dying Worker), 2:119–20; "Mek'enanerë" (The Machines), 2:123–25 (about men who have been destroyed by the all-powerful machine); "Dadar" (Workers' Break), 2:133–36 (the workers' degradation, but also the coming of the "Revolutionary Storm").

25. Cf. "Khap'vats kuyser" (Cheated Virgins), *YLZ* 2:121–22.

26. Cf. "Anishkhanuhin" (The Anarchist Woman), *YLZ* 2:152–53. This poem, which I will comment on in a moment, was published for the first time in a literary journal in 1912, before appearing at the end of the same year in *Pagan Songs*. These revolutionary poems (in the sense of the socialist revolution, we should say provisionally, and not in the sense of the national revolution!) were all written after Varuzhan's return to Turkey, and thus far from Europe.

27. Cf. "Mayis mek" (May Day), *YLZ* 2:137–39.

28. Here are these lines in Armenian: Սիրան ըսկիհ մ՚է ուր երբ լեցուին զինիներ / Աստուածնները սուրբ արինին կը փոխուին: In Armenian, the word for "transubstantiation" is usually (and logically) *goyap'okhut'iun* (*goy* is "being" or "substance"). The lines following the ones just quoted abandon this idea of transubstantiation for a moment and come back to the image of the poet riding his Pegasus, the poet who has undergone the self-sacrificial ordeal of suffering and can face the universe, the poet who is therefore entirely man, made up of both mud and light.

29. Cf. *YLZ* 2:88–90. A translation of "The Light" by G. M. Goshgarian is included in appendix C (text 22). Another translation, by James Russell, is available in the English-language *Ararat Quarterly* (Winter 1994) One of the original manuscripts of the poem is dated April 3, 1908 (*YLZ* 2:413) and was published for the first time in Chobanian's journal *Anahid* in 1909, before being included in *Pagan Songs*.

30. In Armenian: "Դուն կը փայլիս մեծութեան եւ զրհագործումին համար." This may be a reference to book 5, hymn 2, line 9: "Agni shines far and wide with lofty splendor, and by his greatness makes all things apparent." Ralph J. H. Griffith, trans., *The Hymns of the Rig Veda*, 2 vols., 2nd ed. (Benares: E. J. Lazarus, 1896–97).

31. However, we do not know whether Varuzhan read the Rig Veda in Langlois's translation into French from 1872, or in the translation into French of a portion of it by Régnaud, from 1900. These were the two translations that would have been available to him. Alexandre Langlois (1788–1854) had produced the first French translation of the Rig Veda in 1848. In 1872 an edition of his translation was published, corrected and augmented by Philippe-Edouard Foucaux (1811–1894). See Langlois, trans., *Rig-Véda; ou Livre des Hymnes*, 2nd ed., revised, corrected, and expanded with analytic index by Philippe-Edouard Foucaux (Paris: Maisonneuve et Cie, 1872). A facsimile reproduction of this second edition (minus the preface) was published by Maisonneuve in 1984 and reissued in 2009. The translation by Paul Régnaud (1838–1910) is a partial one, accompanied by a continuous commentary. See *Le Rig-Véda: Texte et traduction; Neuvième mandala, le culte védique du soma* (Maisonneuve, 1900).

32. I am again quoting the translation by Ralph J. H. Griffith (1896–97).

33. The capitalization is Varuzhan's. The Armenian word I am translating here as "Mind" is *Mitk'*. But if it were translated as "thought" (and this is very possible), we could reread the verse from "The Light" that presents light as "the Mind's bride" (now "the Thought's bride") and we could understand it in a Heideggerian sense, hearing in it the original affinity between being and thought.

34. Again the capitalization is Varuzhan's, and again instead of "mind" we could read "thought": ". . . my thought gives to Man. "

35. In *Krake shrjanakë: Daniel Varuzhani* [The Circle of Fire: On Daniel Varuzhan], Krikor Beledian offers a commentary on the lines "I sing / Drawn away by the sun"— which read in Armenian: "Կ՚երգեմ / Արեգդեմ" (in transcription, *"G'erkem / Aregdem"*)— in which he insists on the affinity between the poetic word-thought and the sun of being.

36. See above, note 31.

37. It is nevertheless the case that, at the beginning of the twentieth century, there was a certain conception of the continuity of the ceremonies devoted to Agni and of the ethnographic descriptions of these ceremonies (Willem Caland). For a modern treatment of the " "cult" of Agni, see the voluminous work (cited above) by Frits Staal, ed., *Agni*, vol. 2: *The Vedic Rituals of the Fire Altar*, edited with the assistance of Pamela MacFarland. What is fascinating in this work is precisely the impression of an astonishing continuity of ritual over three thousand years (but also of a gradual disappearance of the ritualist tradition) and therefore the importance of a knowledge of the rituals as observed today, in order to understand the Vedic "poetry" from three thousand years ago. It is a question here of the ritual performativity of the recited hymns, that is, quite obviously, their resolutely obsessional character. In the editor's brief preface to the second volume, after a reminder of the contrast between the Vedic nomads and the tradition of the Nambuduri tradition (the priestly families who knew and practiced the ritual of the ceremonies), we read: "The Vedic religion, however, has remained the same in at least one respect. Agni is the same fire reinforced by mantras and oblations whose names continue to be familiar from chants and recitations. Agni is not a deity like Siva, Vishnu, or Bhagavati, whose images are installed in temples. The Vedic religion of Agni and Soma is as nonanthropomorphic in the Nambuduri tradition as it was during the Vedic period" (*Agni* 2: xiii–xiv). And later, with specific reference to the Western concept of religion: "The concept of religion is a Western concept. . . . Scholars and laymen persist in searching for such religions in Asia. . . . What counts instead are ancestors and teachers—hence lineages, traditions, affiliations, cults, eligibility, initiation, and injunction—a concept with ritual rather than truth-functional overtones. These notions do not pertain to questions of truth, but to practical questions: What should the followers of a tradition *do*? This is precisely what makes such notions pertain to the domain of karman. Hence orthopraxy, not orthodoxy, is the operative concept in India. The Veda, for example, is not a sacred book: its power lies in mantra, and mantra is vidhi, that is, an injunction to karman" (ibid., xiv–xv). I have already cited one of the most interesting articles on these issues, that of J. C. Heesterman, "Other Folk's Fire" (in Staal, *Agni* 2: 76–94), which offers an agonistic

reading of the ritual. Staal, for his part, proposes purely structuralist readings of a ritual that is essentially "meaningless." See J. F. Staal, "The Meaninglessness of Ritual," in *Numen: International Review for the History of Religions* 26: 2–22.

38. In his commentary on the thinking of myth as developed by Schelling, Nancy writes of this originary schematism of the mythological imagination and of being's coming to itself through figuration, as it was desired and conceived by the Romantics: "The Romantic goal of a new mythology, one that would be fictioning, imaginary, playful, poetic, and performative, merely brings to light the thinking from which the myth of myth arises: it consists in the thought of a poetico-fictioning ontology, an ontology presented in the figure of an ontogony where being engenders itself *by figuring itself*, by giving itself the proper image of its own essence. . . . The myth of myth, its truth, is that fiction is in effect, in this ontogony, inaugural. In sum, fictioning is the subject of being. . . . The myth of myth is in no way an ontological fiction; it is nothing other than an ontology of fiction or representation" (*IC*, 54–55).

39. The entire philological school of thought, up to the middle of the twentieth century and beyond, said nothing other than this when it came to the essence or the birth of the gods. One example among many others is P. S. Deshmukh, *The Origin and Development of Religion in Vedic Literature* (Oxford: Oxford University Press, 1933), which is not without merit as a late synthesis of the discourse on Vedic "religion" among the philologists of the previous century. After a classification of the Vedic gods according to their natural origin, the author, repeating his teachers, writes the following: "The above description of the Gods of the Rigveda shows that they are, like the gods of the preceding periods, simple deifications of the natural phenomena, and on the whole the degree of anthropomorphism to which they have attained is incipient and their physical bases in most cases apparent. The powers and functions attributed to them are merely a poetical representation of the activities and manifestations of the physical phenomena for which they stand" (317). Religion as the metaphorization of nature—it's a rather simplistic explanation. To say this does not imply that the natural or meteorological characteristics of the "Indo-European" gods are negligible. The observation of these characteristics made possible the immense amount of work done in comparative mythology. Among the Armenians, Manuk Abeghean, who studied in Germany, produced a remarkable comparative work in 1899 on the Armenian pantheon, using the results of the German comparative school. But it is obvious that none of this has any pertinence for the *origin* of the gods and of religion. As Varuzhan writes: "Light is Nature's life-blood" ("The Light," l. 41).

40. For the moment I use the term *mythopoetic* without any further specification. However, in the last part of this essay (chapter 8), I will return to the ensemble of historical determinations that give Varuzhan's aesthetico-religious thought its particular coloration.

41. It seems that Varuzhan decided not to publish "O Century" in a book, since it could have been included in *Pagan Songs*, which did not appear until the end of 1912. It must be said that it is not among Varuzhan's best works . . .

42. In 1912, Varuzhan participated in the demonstrations, first in Sebastea, then in Tokat, against the Patriarch of Armenian Catholics, Paul-Peter X (Terzian), who refused to recognize the Ottoman constitution. We have a polemical article that he published on this affair in 1912. See *YLZ* 3:131–34, and the notes on 505–07.

7. *The Mourning of Religion I*

1. We must recall that "in the past" always means two things for Varuzhan which are not absolutely distinct for him: the gods were produced (in the past); they are produced as having been (and therefore as being no more).

2. For a straightforward account of Novalis's Catholicizing essays and his theocentric or theocratic politics, see the section entitled "Novalis et le génie du christianisme 1. *La Chrétienté ou l'Europe*," in Roger Ayrault, *La Genèse du romantisme allemand* (Paris: Aubier, 1969), 3:476–505. See also the ferocious satire of Novalis's essays in Schelling's "Heinz Widerpost's Epicurean Profession of Faith," a French translation of which is included in Jean-Luc Nancy and Philippe Lacoue-Labarthe, *L'Absolu littéraire* (Paris: Seuil, 1977), 248–59. The English version of the latter, *The Literary Absolute*, trans. Philip Barnard and Cheryl Lester (Albany: SUNY Press, 1988), has kept only the authors' commentaries.

3. For a history of the religious evolution of Friedrich Schlegel, one can consult the first major study in French on the subject, P. Anstett, *La pensée religieuse de Friedrich Schlegel* (Lyons: Annales de l'Université, 1940). The entire "reactionary" or "ultramontaine" (or simply Christian and Catholic) philosophy of Friedrich Schlegel, the theocratic philosophy that gradually begins to take shape around 1804, is based on the idea of a disaster of myth, a historical decline of the "original I" or the "Ur-I" (*das Urich*), in which the human community supposedly had a direct relation with itself.

4. This important work by Schlegel is available in translation as *On the Language and Wisdom of the Indians*, trans. E. J. Millington (London: Ganesha, 2001). Michel Foucault is the only one to have taken into account the important event of this book; in *The Order of Things* (New York: Vintage, 1994), 282–85, he locates it in the immediate prehistory of the modern philological episteme, in terms of the role it played in the establishment of comparative grammar as a discipline. But we are also familiar with the role *Die Sprache* played in the dialogue with Idealism, and in particular with Schelling, who wrote his essay "The Essence of Human Freedom" in *reaction* to the theses developed in the book by Schlegel. Finally, it should be noted that Max Müller mentions this foundational book (although without discussing it at length) in his *Lectures on the Science of Language* (1861): "'On the Language and Wisdom of Indians' . . . became the foundation of the science of language. . . . Schlegel was a man of genius; and when a new science is to be created, the imagination of the poet is wanted, even more than the accuracy of the scholar. It surely required somewhat of poetic vision to embrace with one glance the languages of India, Persia, Greece, Italy, and Germany, and to rivet them together by the simple name of Indo-Germanic. This was Schlegel's work." (I am citing the American edition of Müller's *Lectures* [New York: Scribner, Armstrong, 1875], 164–65.)

5. Translated from Daniel Varuzhan, *Yerkeri Liakatar Zhoghovatsu* [Complete Works] (Yerevan: National Academy of Sciences Publishing, 1987), 3:400. (*Yerkeri Liakatar Zhoghovatsu* is hereafter referred to as *YLZ*, and translated passages are followed by parenthetical citations providing volume and pages on which original text is found.) Yeriznjan (Yerzka in Armenian) was Terenig Jizmejian's native city. Jizmejian recounts the adventure of his return and his later journeys in the book that included his correspondence with Varuzhan: *Daniel Varuzhan, dprotsakan keank'ë, antip namakneë, grakanut'iunë* [DanielVaruzhan, His Life as A Student, His Unpublished Letters, His Literature] (Cairo: Houssaper, 1955). There is a certain sadness in seeing that it took several decades, almost forty years, for all the major witnesses of Varuzhan's life to publish their memories and the letters he had sent to them. During that time, Armenia was still inaccessible and the institutions that would have made it possible to gather and publish the correspondence of the authors who were killed in 1915 did not exist in the diaspora. But forty years is also the time of mourning.

6. In Armenian: "Depi mer paperë. Vor e depi astvatsnerë."

7. Several accounts of Changere (whence Armenian intellectuals were deported between April and—for the few who survived—September 1915) tell us that during these few months of a closely watched life spent at the gates of death, Varuzhan was hard at work on this epic.

8. I provide a detailed explanation of this in *Ages et usages de la langue arménienne* (Paris: Entente, 1989), chapter 7.

9. These polemical pages are found in vol. 1 of Hagop Oshagan, *Hamapatker arevmtahay grakanut'ean* [Panorama of Western Armenian Literature], published by the Armenian Patriarchate of Jerusalem in 1945. I said a few words about the *Panorama* in chapter 2. The 10-volume work is an immense war machine whose purpose was to traverse two centuries of philology in order to complete (or finish off) the invention of the native, and bring to its term the synthetic program of humanist philology.

10. This Tigran the Great is the one cited by Varuzhan, in his long letter on the "return," as the possible subject of an epic. He has to be distinguished from another Tigran, the one called Tigran "Yervandian" (i.e., of the dynasty of Yervand), mentioned by the historian Moses of Khoren as the ally of Cyrus against the Medes—a figure who had already been fully romanced, a subject of epic narratives in antiquity and venerated by the historian as the first true hero of the Armenians. But even this information must be corrected. In fact, the historian Moses of Khoren did not know of the Tigran the Great from the first century B.C. This means that the popular tradition from which he derived his knowledge, six or ten centuries after the events, had already long ago redistributed all the historical material of these events across other figures or other names, which then became the focus of the epic ancient narrative, particularly figures such as Tigran Yervandian and Artashês.

11. We should note that this new description of art as a "resacralization" need not make any reference to mourning, or in any case that it gives this impression. But I would argue that this is no more than an impression.

12. Here is a partial list of these articles by Oshagan: "Mer banasteghtsnerë—Daniel Varuzhan" [Our Poets—Daniel Varuzhan], *Hay grakanut'iun*, August and September 1913; an untitled article on *The Song of Bread* in *Bardzravank'* (Constantinople), no. 1, January 1922; an analysis of *The Song of Bread* in *Teghekagir Brak* [Newsletter] (Jerusalem), 1940–41; and a study in *Akos* (Beirut), 14–18 (1946–47). See also the pages on Varuzhan in volume 6 of *Panorama* (Beirut: Hamazkayin, 1968).

13. Hagop Oshagan, *Panorama* 6:187. "The Red Soil" is a poem published in *The Heart of the Race*; see *YLZ*, 1:110–11. Oshagan recounts this last gathering at great length at the beginning of volume 9 of his *Panorama* (Antelias: Armenian Catholicosate, 1979–1982) in the monograph on Sevag (mentioned in chapter 1 above), but there he does not explicitly mention Varuzhan's reading.

14. Hagop Oshagan, *Mayrineru shuk'in tak* [In the Shade of the Cedars] Beirut: Centenary Edition, 1983), 27–28.

15. M. Nichanian, "K'nnadatut'iunë yev *srbaznut'ean* p'ordzënkalumë" [Critique and the Experience of the Sacred], in *Kayk'* (Paris), 1993, no. 3.

16. Cf. Yeghishe Charents, *Yerkeri Zhoghovatsu* [Complete Works] (Yerevan: Academy of Sciences Publishing, 1962–68), 2:37.

17. In pagan times, Ashtishat was a temple complex in the province of Taron. The priests who officiated there were traditionally chosen from among the Vahuni family. After Christianity was established as the Armenian state religion in 301, the Vahunis led an armed rebellion against the king; it was crushed, and Ashtishat was razed.

18. Agathangelos, *History of the Armenians*, trans. R. W. Thompson (Albany: SUNY Press, 1976), section 809, 347–49.

19. On the Vahuni clan (or princely family), see Cyril Toumanoff, *Studies in Christian Caucasian History* (Washington, D.C.: Georgetown University Press, 1963), 215.

20. Cf. Agathangelos, *History*, 490, and the introduction, xl. In section 22, Agathangelos mentions "the seven altars of the temples" (*yot'n bagins mehenitsn*) where the king orders sacrifices to be made to the "statues of the gods" (*patkerats kr'ots ditsn*). R. Thomson explains this discrepancy in the text by the fact that there were seven sites of worship (Artashat, T'ordan, Ani, Erez, T'il, Bagayar'ich, and Ashtishat), but ten temples (Ashtishat contained three of them). On this subject, see the work that has remained authoritative for over a century: Alain Carrière, *Les huit sanctuaires de l'Arménie païenne* (Paris: E. Leroux, 1899).

21. On the "dragon," which has an important place in the myths of the Armenians, see Emile Benveniste, "L'origine du vichap arménien," *Revue des Études Arméniennes*, first series, vol. 7 (1927).

22. Agathangelos, *History*, 139.

23. Jean-Pierre Mahé, in Moïse de Khorène, *Histoire de l'Arménie*, trans. Annie Mahé and Jean-Pierre Mahé (Paris: Gallimard, 1993), 341. For the interpretation of Vahagn in terms of warfare, see Georges Dumézil, *Heur et malheur du guerrier: Aspects mythiques de la fonction guerrière chez les Indo-Européens* (Paris: PUF, 1969), to which we will return in a moment. Why "agricultural and atmospheric"? Mahé refers to the other great method

of interpretation, that of nineteenth-century German comparative mythology, on the basis of a representation and a personalization of natural phenomena. In sum, he reconciles Dumézil and the other great interpreter of the god's characteristics, Manuk Abeghean, of whom we will also speak later.

24. The translations from Moses of Khoren are mine. See also Moses Khorenats'i, *History of the Armenians*, trans. Robert W. Thomson (Cambridge, Mass.: Harvard University Press, 1978), 123.

25. See Moses of Khoren, *History*, 142.

26. See Moses of Khoren, *History*, 148.

27. Ghevond Alishan, *Hin havatk' kam het'anosakan kronk' Hayots* [The Armenians' Ancient Faith or Pagan Religion] (Venice: San Lazzaro, 1893), 96 and 314–24.

28. Manuk Abeghean, "Hay zhoghovrdakan ar'aspelnerë M. Khorenats'u Hayots' Patmut'ean mej" [Popular Armenian Myths in *History of the Armenians* by Moses of Khoren], published in 1899 in the journal *Ararat*, reprinted in Abeghean's *Yerker* [Works] (Yerevan: Academy of Sciences Publishing, 1985), 8:67–271.

29. Cf. Mkrtich Emin, *Vepk' hnuyn Hayastani* [Epic Narratives of Ancient Armenia] (Moscow, 1850). Emin returned to these investigations a number of times (in Russian), later situating himself entirely in the domain of comparative mythology. His 1873 article "Vahagn-Vishapak'agh armianskoy mifologii est' Indra-Vritrahan Rig-Vedy," which is reprinted in the collection of 1896, *Izledovanije i stat'i N.O. Emina po armenskoy mifologii, arxeologii, istorii i istorii literaturyi (1858–1884)* (Moscow: Lazarev Institute of Oriental Languages, 1896), is one of the important landmarks in the historical understanding of Vahagn in relation to the Indo-European pantheon. The article prompted a debate with Kerovbé Patkanean on the Armenian origin of the god and the etymology of the name. Dumézil mentions this debate in *Heur et malheur du guerrier* (119). In 1881, Emin went back to his older work on Moses of Khoren's reception of mythology, in a book written in Russian (*Moicei Khorentskii i drevni epoc Armianskii*), which was partially translated into Armenian under the title *Movses Khorenatsi yev Hin Haykakan Vep* [Moses of Khoren and the Ancient Armenian Epic], trans. Kh. Hovanniseants (Tblisi, 1887). Abeghean, to my knowledge, does not cite the 1873 article in his 1899 work on popular myths in Moses of Khoren.

30. Ghevond Alishan, *The Armenians' Ancient Faith*, 95–96. Alishan relies here on an etymology of Vahagn according to which *agn* (or *akn*) is the word for the source (of light), an etymology he found in Mkrtich Emin or that he reinvented for the sake of his argument. The reference to the "doctor" or "scholar" who assimilated Vahagn to the sun is not given, but the citation is from the *Tonakan Madean* (Book of Religious Celebrations). The comparison with Agni is also found in Emin. Later, in the chapter on the "Vishaps," Alishan explains that the language of "our ancestors" and the language of India were "sisters . . . if we can believe what the linguists tell us today" (186).

31. Alishan, *The Armenians' Ancient Faith*, 267.

32. On the beginnings of modern Armenian historiography and the place of Moses of Khoren, allow me to refer again to my article "Enlightenment and Historical Thought,"

in Richard Hovannisian and David Meyers, eds., *Enlightenment and Diaspora: The Armenian and Jewish Cases* (Atlanta: Scholars Press, 1999). This tendency to consider Khorenats'i's *History of the Armenians* as Sacred Scripture endures to this day. It was particularly pronounced with the Mkhitarists, among whom one can distinguish, without exaggeration, a veritable "religion of history" that takes on as much importance as any other religion.

33. Grigor Khalateants (1858–1912) had been Mkrtich Emin's student at the Lazarev Institute of Oriental Languages in Moscow, of which he served as the director later in his life (1897–1903). His work (in Russian) on Moses of Khoren and the Armenian ancient epic dates to 1896. He became famous in the small world of philologists for his discovery and publication of an ancient Armenian version of the *Book of Chronicles*.

34. Abeghean, *Yerker* 8:109–10.

35. His references are Max Müller, *Die Wissenschaft der Sprache* (Leipzig, 1893); F. L. W. Schwartz, *Indogermanischer Volksglaube* (Berlin, 1885); but especially Adalbert Kuhn, *Die Herabkunft des Feuers* (Berlin, 1859), and from the same F .L. W. Schwartz (something which is not obvious if we are content with the reference given by Abeghean), *Der Ursprung der Mythologie* (Berlin, 1860).

36. The references here are to Rig Veda, 2, 453, 10 and 2, 614, 3.

37. Friedrich Nietzsche, *The Birth of Tragedy*, trans. Walter Kaufmann (New York: Vintage, 1967), 41.

38. On the question of metaphor, its complexity and reversals, see Jacques Derrida's essay "White Mythology: Metaphor in the Text of Philosophy," in *Margins of Philosophy*, trans. Alan Bass (Chicago: University of Chicago Press, 1982), 207–71.

39. Jacques Derrida has of course written a number of essays on the question of performativity as well; I would refer the reader especially to one that I consider essential: "Before the Law," trans. Avital Ronell, in D. Attridge, ed., *Acts of Literature* (New York: Routledge, 1991).

40. This theme of folding back, of "the poetry of poetry," refers to Heidegger's commentary on Hölderlin, in his courses from the period between 1936 and 1942 and in his book *Erläuterungen zu Hölderlins Dichtung*, published in English as *Elucidations of Hölderlin's Poetry*, trans. Keith Hoeller (Amherst, N.Y.: Humanity Books, 2000). But it also comes from the Romantic reflection on poetry (especially that of Friedrich Schlegel). I cannot develop this comparison further here, but a number of remarks made in this essay already indicate that it is not gratuitous. Krikor Beledian insists on this self-reflexive theme in his first essay on Varuzhan; see *Tram* (Beurut: Atlas, 1980).

41. Walter Benjamin, "Franz Kafka on the Tenth Anniversary of His Death," in *Illuminations*, trans. Harry Zohn (New York: Schocken Books, 1969), 126. "Kafka was a writer of parables, but he did not found a religion." We might ask: why point this out? Why should we see Kafka as a possible founder of religion, which, after all, he was not? This was one of the subjects of debate between Gershom Scholem and Walter Benjamin in the summer of 1934. On the same page as the above citation, after comparing the village below the castle with a village in a "Talmudic legend" about the messiah,

Benjamin adds: "Exile—his exile—has gained control over him. The air of this village blows about Kafka, and that is why he was not tempted to found a religion. . . . The air in this village is not free of all the abortive and overripe elements that form such a putrid mixture. This is the air that Kafka had to breathe all his life. He was neither mantic nor a founder of religion. How was he able to survive in this air?" There is no religion possible for the exiles from the law, for the déclassés who live under the domination of the law while also being outside it once and for all, in the lowest depths of putrefaction. Fourteen years after Benjamin wrote his essay, Maurice Blanchot would echo the same ambiguous suspicion, the same depths and the same putrefaction, in his novel *The Most High*. Blanchot is of course very far from Varuzhan and his "poetic paganism." But the structure of the question remains the same: What religion can there be for the exiles from the law or from tradition? See also the following note.

42. "I am the last Vahuni." This formulation, which condenses all of Varuzhan's "paganism," is at once poetic and metapoetic. It is located at the precise point where poetry folds back on itself, where it becomes "the poetry of poetry." It is stated from within the poetic system, but it says the poetic singularity of the present as completion. This is exactly (I believe) the same structure proper to the completion that Walter Benjamin and Gershom Scholem put into play, each in his own way, in their extraordinary debate on Kafka in the summer of 1934, mentioned in the previous note.

8. *The Mourning of Religion II*

1. Translated from Daniel Varuzhan, *Yerkeri Liakatar Zhoghovatsu* [Complete Works] (Yerevan: National Academy of Sciences Publishing, 1987), 2:53. (As previously, this edition is referred to hereafter as *YLZ*, and parenthetical citations provide volume and pages on which the original text is found.) "To the Dead Gods" first appeared in Chobanian's journal *Anahid*, 1911, nos. 7–8, before being reprinted in *Pagan Songs* in 1912. A different English translation is included in appendix C (text 23). All translations appearing in the main text are mine and Jeff Fort's.

2. Varuzhan's statement to this effect, from one of his first letters on poetic paganism, was quoted at the beginning of chapter 4: "If it were possible today, I would change my religion and would joyfully embrace poetic paganism. Judaism is dull, though the prophets were able to beautify it somewhat. I am surrounded by ancient works. If only I could free myself from this mediocre condition and become a Pindar or an Isaiah" (*YLZ* 3:364).

3. The Armenian word translated here as "imprint" is *droshel*. This refers to the mark one leaves on a stone, the "type" engraved on it. In sum, with this engraving and this typography, our ancestors were able to become the sons of their fathers!

4. Even in Nietzsche, the catastrophe does not immediately bear the name "Christianity." In *The Birth of Tragedy*, the Greek decline begins from within. It was only later, in *Ecce Homo*, that Nietzsche wrote, referring to *The Birth of Tragedy*: "Profound, hostile silence about Christianity throughout the book. That is neither Apollinian nor Dionysian; it

negates all aesthetic values . . . it is *nihilistic* in the most profound sense, while in the Dionysian symbol the ultimate limit of *affirmation* is attained" (Nietzsche's emphasis). *Ecce Homo*, "The Birth of Tragedy," section 1, in *On the Genealogy of Morals and Ecce Homo*, trans. Walter J. Kaufmann and R. J. Hollingdale (New York: Vintage Books, 1989), 271.

5. *Hölderlin: Selected Verse*, trans. Michael Hamburger (Baltimore: Penguin, 1961), 112. In Friedrich Hölderlin, *Poems and Fragments,* trans. Michael Hamburger (Ann Arbor: University of Michigan Press, 1968), these lines are translated as follows: "When the Father had turned his face from the sight of us mortals / And all over the earth, rightly, they started to mourn" (251).

6. Hölderlin, *Poems and Fragments*, 245–49.

7. Philippe Lacoue-Labarthe, "Hölderlin and the Greeks," in *Typography: Mimesis, Philosophy, Politics*, ed. Christopher Fynsk (Cambridge, Mass.: Harvard University Press, 1989), 245.

8. *Hölderlin: Selected Verse*, 112; I added the line breaks, which are not included in the translation in that edition.

9. On catastrophic mourning and the history of mourning in Hölderlin's "Mnemosyne," see my two essays in French, "Avons-nous vraiment perdu la langue à l'étranger?" in the volume edited by Alexis Nouss under the title "Antoine Berman aujourd'hui / Antoine Berman for Our Time," special issue of *TTR: Etudes sur le texte et ses transformations* 14, no. 2 (2001); and "Témoigner et traduire: Du deuil catastrophic (De Hölderlin à Primo Levi),"*Revue Lignes*, no. 23–24 (November 2007).

10. Here too we can cite Hölderlin, "Bread and Wine": "Father Aether! they cried, and from tongue to tongue it flew on a thousandfold, not one endured life alone; shared out, such wealth delights and, bartered with strangers, it swells into exultation, asleep the word's power increases: Father!" (Hamburger translation, *Hölderlin: Selected Verse*, 108).

11. See the discussion of Jean-Luc Nancy's "Myth Interrupted" in chapter 6, in particular the discussion of the passage where he explains that "mythic thought . . . is nothing other than the thought of a founding fiction, or of a foundation by fiction" (*The Inoperative Community*, 56).

12. Cf. *Mehyan*, no. 1 (January 1914), 2. Here is the phrase in Armenian: "Kë havatank'. Hay hogin Luysn e, Uyzhn e, Keank'n e, marmnavorvats shk'eghuteanë mej ARIAKAN tseghin vorun kë patkanink'."

13. William Hart, *Edward Said and the Religious Effects of Culture* (Cambridge: Cambridge University Press, 2000). I am grateful to Gil Anidjar who, in connection with his work on race and religion, brought this book to my attention. See his article "The Semitic Hypothesis (Religion's Last Word)," now available as the first chapter of his *Semites: Race, Religion, Literature* (Stanford: Stanford University Press, 2008).

14. Hart, *Edward Said*, 83.

15. This is, in essence, Gil Anidjar's argument in "The Semitic Hypothesis" (the formulation "secularism is an orientalism" comes from him). This remarkable article begins with this formulation, and goes on to examine how the discourse on race, in the nineteenth century, masks itself behind the discourse on religion, in a hierarchized and

disciplinary hide-and-seek that Anidjar refers to as "co-concealment." The third part of the article provides a new summary of the invention of the category of the "Semite" by a philology whose intentions were not always the best.

16. These two authors were discussed in chapters 2 and 3 (as the heirs of the philological invention of the native and of what we have been calling ethnomythology or the power of myth) and in chapter 7 (this time in terms of their philological treatment of Vahagn and their divergent interpretations).

17. Cf. *YLZ* 3:116–18 and the editor's remarks, 3:502. "The Hero" was transcribed from a lecture that Varuzhan gave in September 1909 in Bardizag, at the time of an excursion with his friends and colleagues at *Azatamart*. On this occasion, Varuzhan read or recited his poem "Jardë" [The Massacre]. A full translation of "The Hero" is provided in appendix C (text 26).

18. Here I am again following a suggestion made by Gil Anidjar in "The Semitic Hypothesis," where he proposes a consideration of "race" and "religion" as "*contemporary*, indeed, coextensive and, moreover, co-concealing categories" (*Semites*, 28); and he adds in a note: "By co-concealing, I mean to follow upon what David Theo Goldberg calls 'the masks of race,' arguing that religion is one of those masks rather than a preexisting background to modern racism or simply one of the constitutive elements in what became racial or ethnic identity (see David Theo Goldberg, *Racist Culture: Philosophy and the Politics of Meaning* [Oxford: Basil Blackwell, 1993], esp. 61–89)" (*Semites*, 118 n. 52).

19. The verb *arp'avetel* was invented by Varuzhan, based on its two components *arp'i* (the sun) and *avetel* (to bring good news, hence *Avetaran*, the Evangel). Varuzhan announces (or has his heroic figure announce) a solar Evangel.

20. See *YLZ* 3:83–89 and notes, 3:494. See also the English translation in appendix C (text 25). We already mentioned this text in the second note of our essay on Varuzhan (chapter 4, n. 2). The manuscript is written in pencil, with no date and no signature, jotted down probably at the time when Varuzhan was still a student in Ghent. It is therefore something that Varuzhan wrote down for himself. The other possibility is that these pages were scribbled for a course at one of the institutions where he taught between 1909 and 1915, which would explain their lacunae. I consulted the text at the Museum of Art and Literature in Yerevan, in May 2006. The printed version has at least one incredible mistake, which I correct and point out in the translation (appendix C, n. 13). But this mistake is so crude that it awakens the reader's suspicion. We obviously need a new edition of Varuzhan's complete works.

21. Lubbock's *The Origins of Civilisation* is now available in the University of Chicago series Classics in Anthropology (Chicago: University of Chicago Press, 1978). His *Prehistoric Times* has also been reprinted (Freeport, N.Y.: Books for Libraries Press, 1971).

22. The book was first published in German: Ignaz Goldziher, *Der Mythos bei den Hebräern und seine geschichtliche Entwicklung: Untersuchungen zur Mythologie un Religionswissenschaft* (Leipzig, 1876). The 1877 English translation, *Mythology among the Hebrews and Its Historical Development*, trans. Russell Martineau (New York: Longmans,

Green), was reprinted in 1882, then in 1967 (New York: Cooper Square Publishers). The authors Goldziher refers to (Max Müller and Adalbert Kuhn) are the very ones Manuk Abeghean refers to in his work from 1899 on the popular myths of the Armenians.

23. Goldziher, *Mythology among the Hebrews*, xxii. Goldziher quotes the third edition of Lubbock's *Origins of Civilisation* (1873), p. 330, where Lubbock himself cites James Sibree, *Madagascar and Its People*, without further precision. The entire title and publication details of the Sibree book cited by Lubbock are as follows: *Madagascar and its People: Notes of a Four Years' Residence. With a Sketch of the History, Position, and Prospects of Mission Work amongst the Malagasy* (London: Religious Tract Society, 1870). The passage Lubbock quotes is to be found on p. 396.

24. This debate began with Renan's two book-length treatises, *Histoire générale et système comparé des langues sémitiques*, 2nd ed. (Paris: Imprimerie Impériale, 1858) and *Nouvelles considérations sur le caractère vénéral des peuples sémitiques, et en particulier sur leur tendance au monothéisme* (Paris: Imprimerie Impériale, 1859); these treatises were discussed at length by Müller in his essay "Semitic Monotheism" (1860), republished in vol. 1 of *Chips from a German Workshop* (New York: Scribner, 1869).

25. Maurice Olender, *The Languages of Paradise: Aryans and Semites, a Match Made in Heaven*, trans. Arthur Goldhammer (New York: Other Press, 2002), 51–81 for Renan, 82–92 for Müller.

26. Ernest Renan, *Oeuvres complètes* (Paris: Calman-Lévy, 1947–1961), 5:1142; cited by Olender, *Languages of Paradise*, 70.

27. The expression "disease of language" is often used by Müller to describe mythology; see for example *The Science of Language, Founded on Lectures Delivered at the Royal Institution in 1861 and 1863*, 2 vols. (New York: Charles Scribner's Sons, 1891). "Whenever any word, that was at first used metaphorically, is used without a clear conception of the steps that led from its original to its metaphorical meaning, there is danger of mythology; whenever those steps are forgotten and artificial steps put in their places, we have mythology, or, if I may say so, we have diseased language" (2:456). It assumes a divine revelation, which can be perverted through language (this is the linguistico-theological theory of roots), but nevertheless is a resilient intuition. Müller's theory is thus firmly positioned within the evolutionist debates on the originary form of "religion." Yes, so the argument goes, there was a primitive religion, but it was neither the monotheism of the Semites, nor the polytheism of the Aryans. This is more or less Varuzhan's position in this short text on religions.

28. Max Müller, *Lectures on the Origin and Growth of Religion as Illustrated by the Religions of India*, delivered in the Chapter House, Westminster Abbey, 1878 (London: Longmans, Green and Co, 1880), 280; cited by Olender, *Languages of Paradise*, 87. It is interesting to note that Edward Said almost completely disregards the intellectual figure of Müller, whereas he writes some very decisive pages on Renan.

29. Olender, *Languages of Paradise*, 168.

30. Olender, *Languages of Paradise*, 119. I have slightly modified Arthur Goldhammer's translation of Olender's original French text, *Les Langues du paradise: Aryens et Sémites, un couple providentiel* (Paris: Seuil, 1989).

31. Renan, *Oeuvres complètes* 8:148; Olender, *Languages of Paradise*, 129.

32. In particular, Goldziher's entire discussion in chapter 7 of his book ("Influence of the Awakening National Idea on the Transformation of the Hebrew Myth") is extremely interesting and requires a more thorough discussion, especially in terms of the transformation of mythic material into "religious" material, then into "history," and the use of the modern concept of a "national awakening." I cannot enter into this discussion here. I will address these issues elsewhere in relation to the "theology" of language specific to Müller.

33. F. W. J. Schelling, *Einleitung in die Philosophie der Mythologie*, in *Sämtliche Werke* (Stuttgart: Cotta, 1856–61), 11:62–63. My translation. See a different translation in F. W. J. Schelling, *Historical-critical Introduction to the Philosophy of Mythology*, trans. Mason Richey and Markus Zisselberger (Albany: State University of New York Press, 2007), 47–48.

34. See Max Müller, *Introduction to the Science of Religion* (London: Longmans, Green, 1873): "It was Schelling . . . who first asked the question, What makes an *ethnos*? . . . And the answer which he gave, though it sounded startling to me when, in 1845, I listened, at Berlin, to the lectures of the old philosopher, has been confirmed more and more by subsequent researches. . . . It is language and religion that make a people, but religion is even a more powerful agent than language" (145–47). Two pages later, Müller quotes Schelling's *Vorlesungen über die Philosophie der Mythologie*, 1:107, with his translation: "A people . . . exists only when it has determined itself with regard to its mythology. This mythology, therefore, cannot take its origin after a national separation has taken place, after a people has become a people" (149).

35. Goldziher, *Mythology among the Hebrews*, xxii–xxiii. After summarizing Schelling's argument, Goldziher adds: "However the question may stand with reference to savage tribes, modern science cannot possibly support the old thesis concerning the Semitic Hebrews and their incapacity of Mythology."

36. See Schelling, *Historical-critical Introduction*, 49. The German reads: "Kann die Mythologie eines Volkes nicht aus oder unter einem schon vorhandenen Volke entstehen, so muß sie mit ihm zugleich entstehen, als sein individuelles oder Volksbewußtseyn, vermöge dessen es eben dieses und kein anderes Volk wird, vermöge dessen eben es von jedem anderen Volke nicht weniger als durch seine Sprache geschieden ist" (*Einleitung*, in *Sämtliche Werke* 11·65)

37. Schelling, *Historical-critical Introduction*, 49. "Die Mythologie eines jeden Volkes konnte nur mit ihm selbst entstehen und geboren werden" (*Einleitung*, in *Sämtliche Werke* 11:65).

Epilogue: Nietzsche in Armenian Literature at the Turn of the Twentieth Century

1. Hagop Kufejian (Oshagan), "The Literature of All Armenians," *Mehyan*, no. 3, (March 1914), p. 39. Hereafter, quotations from articles in this journal, provided in translation in the text, will be followed by parenthetical citations of the *Mehyan* issue and page on which the original text is found.

2. All this is drawn from fragment 853 of *The Will to Power*. See note 8 below for the status of this fragment. Here is the original German of the passages that I am quoting: "Es gibt nur eine Welt, und diese is falsch, grausam, widersprüchlich, verführerisch, ohne Sinn . . . Die Metaphysik, die Moral, die Religion, die Wissenschaft—sie werden in diesem Buche nur als verschiedene Formen der Lüge in Betracht gezogen: mit ihrer Hilfe wird ans Leben geglaubt. . . . Die Aufgabe, so gestellt, ist ungeheur. Um sie zu lösen, muss der Mensch schon von Natur Lügner sein, er muss mehr als alles andere Künstler sein. Und er ist es auch: Metaphysik, Religion, Moral, Wissenschaft—alles nur Ausgeburten seines Willens zur Kunst, zur Lüge. . . . Und wann der Mensch sich freut, er ist immer der gleiche in seiner Freude: er freut sich als Künstler, er genießt sich als Macht, er genießt die Lüge als seine Macht." Friedrich Nietzsche, *Der Wille zur Macht; Versuch einer Umwertung aller Werte*, with an afterword by Alfred Bäumler (Berlin: Kröner, 1930), 575–76.

3. These sentences are extracted from the Manifesto published in the first issue of *Mehyan* (January 1914) and signed by Constant Zarian, Hagop Oshagan (Kufejian), Daniel Varuzhan, Kegham Parseghian, and Aharon (Dadurian). The five of them are therefore responsible for its content, although we know that much of it was written by Zarian himself; that, at least, is what Zarian said in an interview with Garo Poladian (1910–1968), published in the second volume of the latter's *Zruyts'ner* [Dialogues] (Cairo: Houssaper, 1961).

4. I recommend, for example, the afterword that Bäumler (1887–1968) wrote for the second edition of Karl Heckel's *Nietzsche, sein Leben und seine Lehre* (Leipzig: Philipp Reclam, 1922); his afterword to the 1930 Kröner edition of *The Will to Power*; and, finally, his 1926 book on Johann Jakob Bachofen, *Das mythische Weltalter: Bachofens Romantische Deutung des Altertums*, reissued in 1965 (Munich: Beck) with a postface ("Bachofen und die Religionsgeschichte"), in which Bäumler claims to have corrected the "errors of interpretation" to which he had been prone in his youth. This book allows us to understand how a Nazi ideologue could interpret, with a vast display of erudition, the "innocent" philological invention of the myth. Mazzino Montinari has examined Bäumler's interpretations in the last chapter of his *Nietzsche lesen* (Berlin: W. de Gruyter, 1980), an English translation of which, *Reading Nietzsche*, was released by the University of Illinois Press in 2003.

5. Philippe Lacoue-Labarthe, *La fiction du politique* (Paris: Christian Bourgois, 1990), 145; English version: *Heidegger, Art, and Politics: The Fiction of the Political*, trans. Chris Turner (Cambridge, Mass.: Basil Blackwell, 1997), 101. The term *national-esthétisme* occurs at the end of chapter 7, p. 112 in the French original. The equivalent should be found on p. 70 of the English translation, but the translator has unfortunately neglected to translate the parenthetical phrase in which it appears (national-*socialisme* comme national-*esthétisme*).

6. Heidegger, quoted in Lacoue-Labarthe, *Heidegger, Art, and Politics*, 68; *La fiction du politique*, 108. The sentence is borrowed from Martin Heidegger, *Nietzsche*, vol. 1, *The Will to Power as Art*, trans. David Farrell Krell (San Francisco: Harper and Row, 1991), 85–86. This volume contains the first course that Heidegger gave on Nietzsche, in 1936,

beginning with an interpretation of that part of *Der Wille zur Macht* that its editors entitled "The Will to Power as Art" (fragments 793–853). Of course, the use of the phrase *national community* is an interpretation. Heidegger's text reads as follows: "Aber über diese zahlen- und mengenmäßige Vereinigung hinaus soll das Kunstwerk eine Feier der Volksgemeinschaft sein: 'die' Religion." Martin Heidegger, *Nietzsche: Erster Band* (Pfullingen: Neske, 1961), 102.

7. To the second edition of his 1935 book *Nietzsches Philosophie der ewigen Wiederkunft des Gleichen* (whose ambition was to describe Nietzsche's philosophy as a "system in the form of aphorisms"), Karl Löwith added a useful appendix entitled "Zur Geschichte der Nietzsche-Deutung (1894–1954)." See Löwith, *Nietzsches Philosophie des ewigen Wiederkehr des Gleichen* (Stuttgart: Kohlhammer, 1956); in *Sämtliche Schriften* (Stuttgart: Metzler, 1987), 6:345–84. This appendix, the greater part of which was written in 1935, had, for political reasons, initially circulated only in private form (see pp. 363 and 542).

8. I am following the translation offered in Heidegger, *Nietzsche*, vol. 1: *The Will to Power as Art*, translated from the German by David Farrell Krell (San Francisco: HarperCollins, 1979; 1991 for the paperback edition), 73. Krell has made his own translations of all passages from Nietzsche's works in Heidegger's text, sometimes consulting the translation of *The Will to Power* by Walter Kaufmann and R. J. Hollingdale (New York: Random House, 1967) "for reference and comparison." Heidegger's quotations of Nietzsche are taken from the version of *Der Wille zur Macht*, with commentary by Otto Weiss, that appeared in volumes 15 and 16 of the second edition of *Nietzsches Werke: Grossoktav-Ausgabe* (Leipzig: Kröner, 1911). Here I use the reference system used in Heidegger, *Nietzsche*, where the abbreviation *WM* (for *Der Wille zur Macht*) is followed by the number of the fragment. The fragment numbered 853 had been slightly edited by Weiss for the 1911 *Grossoktav-Ausgabe* edition. In the *Kritische Gesamtausgabe*, initiated by Giorgio Colli and Mazzino Montinari (Berlin: Walter de Gruyter, 1967 ff.), to which I will refer using the abbreviation *KGW*, this fragment is found in two parts, *KGW* 8, 11 [415] and *KGW* 8, 17 [3]. Both parts stem from notebooks written in the spring of 1888, even if "the internal evidence for a date earlier than the preface [of *The Birth of Tragedy*] actually published in 1886 seems very strong," as Walter Kaufmann asserted in a note to his translation of the fragment on the basis of the classical edition (*The Will to Power*, trans. Walter Kaufmann [New York: Vintage, 1967], 451). The fact is that the first part of the fragment is the draft of a new preface to *The Birth of Tragedy*, which had been copied with some changes and completed a few months later. If this fragment is representative, it may be said that the editorial work done under the guidance of Nietzsche's sister for the composition of a book titled *Der Wille zur Macht* was not egregiously irresponsible. It may of course be doubted whether there was any need to compose and publish a work named *Der Wille zur Macht*, a project that Nietzsche himself had finally abandoned in late summer 1888. Nevertheless, it does not seem to me that this editorial construction is sufficient in itself to explain the incredible misinterpretation to which Nietzsche's work was constantly subjected for half a century. Karl Löwith voices the same doubts in a letter addressed to Jean Wahl (1936): "Car c'est un moment de la

pensée de Nietzsche lui-même qui explique qu'il ait pu . . . apparaître comme celui qui a préparé la voie aux fausses idéologies . . . La critique de l'abus que l'on a fait de Nietzsche doit être accompagnée par une critique de Nietzsche lui-même, comme origine profondément historique de l'influence qu'il a exercée." See Löwith, *Sämtliche Schriften* 6:453.

9. Krell's translation, in Heidegger, *Nietzsche*, vol. 1: *The Will to Power as Art*, 69 and 71; *KGW* 8, 2 [130], from fall 1885 to fall 1886.

10. Nietzsche, *The Birth of Tragedy*, trans. Shaun Whiteside, with an introduction by Michael Tanner (New York: Penguin Books, 1993), 14. This is the most recent translation of this work. In Walter Kaufmann's translations and critical accounts, the words *apollinisch* and *dionysisch* are rendered as "Apollonian" and "Dionysian," "following the precedent of Brinton, Morgan and the English version of *The Decline of the West*." Walter Kaufmann, *Nietzsche, Philosopher, Psychologist, Antichrist* (Princeton, N.J.: Princeton University Press, 1968), 128.

11. Nietzsche, *The Birth of Tragedy*, tr. Shaun Whiteside, 9. Emphasis in the original.

12. Daniel Varuzhan, *Yerkeri Liakatar Zhoghovatsu* [Complete Works] (Yerevan: Academy of Sciences Publishing, 1987), 3:274.

13. This translation was published in *GAM* (Montreal), no. 3–4 (1986).

14. Only recently were new translations into Eastern Armenian produced by Hakob Movses: *Baruts' yev ch'arits' andin*; *Ch'astvatsneri mt'nshaghë* [*Beyond Good and Evil and Twilight of the Idols*] (Yerevan: Apolon, 1992); *Ayspes khosets' Zradashtë* [*Thus Spoke Zarathustra*] (Yerevan: Van Aryan, 2002); and, finally, *Zvart' gitut'iunë* [*The Gay Science*] (Yerevan: Van Aryan, 2005), without critical apparatus but with prefaces that merit a thorough examination (I will conduct this examination elsewhere). I am reminded by Vardan Azatyan that a) Nietzsche's complete works were translated into Russian as early as 1909–1912, mainly by Simeon Frank; b) the Russian reception of Nietzsche was not free of religious and mystical undertones, particularly among Rudolph Steiner's followers; c) my assertion must be taken with a grain of salt if we consider the pre-Stalinist period (until 1928) and Lunacharsky's activity at that time; d) the 1909–1912 translation was not unknown to dissident Soviet intellectuals. In this vein, see also Bernice Glatzer Rosenthal, ed., *Nietzsche and Soviet Culture: Ally and Adversary* (Cambridge: Cambridge University Press, 1994), which is a disappointing contribution to the debate in question (a scathing review of the book by Richard Davies was published in the *Journal of European Studies* 5, no. 3, 1995). Finally, it was an Armenian philosopher, Karen Svasyan, who published the two-volume edition of Nietzsche's works in Russian in 1990.

15. Indra (Diran Chrakian) was born in 1875 in Constantinople. He was arrested and died while being deported in 1921 in a state of physical exhaustion and mental disarray. His masterpiece, *Nerashkharh* [Inner World], was published in 1905 (the standard edition of his works appeared in Yerevan in 1980.) *Nerashkharh* is one of the most powerful literary machines ever produced in Western Armenian. It is a prose work celebrated by its rare readers for, above all, its mystical tendencies and boundless linguistic creativity. Armenian admits the creation of neologisms, but Indra engaged, instead, in what would today be called Joycean wordplay, in which words are regarded as condensed entities the

aim of which is to reflect the absolute. This text has a philosophical cast: it spins out a continuous thread of reflections on language, madness, and art, all interpreted from a metaphysical standpoint. It is not, however, a theoretical treatise, but a poetic work that cannot be assigned to any immediately definable category; its linguistic weave is organized around places, situations, scenes, exotic objects, and memories. In several essays written after the book was published, Indra turned his attention to questions of pseudonymous identity, the relation between an author and his name, and that between writing and madness.

16. Levon Shant (who was born in 1869 in Constantinople and died in Beirut in 1951) was sent to Echmiadzin as a schoolboy and again as a college student; he became, as a result, one of the rare Armenian authors to take full part in the cultural life of both Eastern and Western Armenians, in Constantinople and Tblisi. Until 1921, Shant was also a committed participant in the political struggles waged by the Armenians. Thereafter, he lived in the diaspora, where he helped found Beirut's Palanjian Institute, one of the most important centers of Armenian education in the Middle East. He began his literary career as a novelist and began writing for the theater in 1900. His best-known plays are all historical dramas: *Hin astvatsnerë* [The Ancient Gods], 1911; *Kaysrë* [The Emperor], 1916; *Shght'ayvatsë* [The Man in Chains], 1921; *Inkats berdi ishkhanuhin* [The Princess of the Fallen Castle], 1923; *Oshin Payl* [Bailiff Oshin], 1927. Shant also translated Ibsen into Armenian. His complete works were published in Beirut in ten volumes between 1946 and 1949 by the Hamazkayin publishing house.

17. Edouard Frenghian, *Nietzsche* (Tbilisi, 1910).

18. Ibid., 39; 41; 41–42; 43.

19. Ibid., 84.

20. Lacoue-Labarthe, *La fiction du politique*, 135; *Heidegger, Art, and Politics*, 93–94. "Work" here translates the French *oeuvre*. See Lacoue-Labarthe's provocative formulation: "Le nazisme est un humanisme," *La fiction*, 138; *Heidegger*, 96.

21. Alfred Rosenberg, *The Myth of the Twentieth Century*, trans. James Whisker (Costa Mesa, Calif.: Noontide Press, 1982); published originally as *Der Mythus des Zwanzigsten Jahrhunderts* (Munich: Hoheneichen-Verlag, 1930). In chapter 9 of *Heidegger, Art, and Politics*, Philippe Lacoue-Labarthe makes use of the study that he wrote with Jean-Luc Nancy on this subject, *Le Mythe Nazi* (Paris: Éditions de l'Aube, 1991). Brian Holmes's English translation of the latter was published in *Critical Inquiry* 16 (Winter 1990).

22. *Bancoopë yev mamut'i voskornerë* was first serialized in the review *Hayrenik* from 1931 to 1933, and only later published in book form (Antelias: Catholicosate of Cilicia, 1987). This work is referred to hereafter as *Bancoopë*; passages that I translate from it will be followed by parenthetical citations providing the pages on which the original text is found.

23. Constant Zarian, *Navë leran vray* (Boston: Hayrenik Publishers, 1943). Twenty years after appearing in serialized form, the novel was published in Yerevan in heavily revised, bowdlerized form in order to bring it into line with Soviet censors' view of modern Armenian history, especially the period of independence between 1918 and 1920. Zarian

took part in this farce, which he was no doubt incapable of interrupting. After his immigration to Armenia in 1961, he had become the hostage of the regime. Boghos Snabian has published an incendiary book, *Avazakhrats navë* [The Ship Run Aground] (Beirut: Atlas, 1964), in which he exposes the thousands of modifications introduced into the letter and spirit of the novel. Zarian's novel (in the original version) has been translated into French by Pierre Ter-Sarkissian and published by Parenthèses in Marseilles (1986).

24. This work, too, was reissued in book form along with other travel narratives of Zarian's first period; the volume is entitled, simply, *Yerker* [Works] (Antelias: Melidinetsi, 1975) and contains other autobiographical narratives originally released in the review *Hayrenik*. Zarian published several more autobiographical texts in the same review, notably *Yerkirner yev astvadzner* [Countries and Gods] in 1935–38, *Hr'omeakan hushatetr* [Roman Notebook] in 1948, *Hollandakan hushatetrits'* [Selections from the Dutch Notebook] in 1949–50, and, finally, *Kghzin yev mi mard* [The Island and a Man] in 1955. *Countries and Gods* was recently issued in Armenia in two magnificent volumes (one on Spain, the other on the United States) edited by Yuri Khachatrian (Yerevan: Khachents, 1999 and 2003). I have published a number of essays in Armenian on Zarian, his autobiographical texts, and his theory of the theater: "Aghetin lr'ut'iunë Kostan Zareani ardzakin mej" [The Silence of the Catastrophe in Constant Zarian's Prose], *Bazmavep*, 1995, nos. 1–4, 343–74; "Kostan Zarean, Ankareli t'atronë" [Constant Zarian, the Impossible Theater], *Bazmavep*, 1996, nos. 1–4, 175–99; and "Kostan Zarean yev Oswald Spengler" [Constant Zarian and Oswald Spengler], *Kayk'* (Paris), 1989, no. 1.

25. Constant Zarian, interview with Garo Poladian, in Poladian, *Zruyts'ner* [Dialogues], vol. 2 (Cairo: Houssaper, 1961). See also Vartan Matiossian's essay on Zarian, "A Traveler and His Many Roads," in *Ararat Quarterly*, Spring 1994.

26. Oshagan, *Hamapatker arevmtahay grakanut'ean* [Panorama of Western Armenian Literature] (Beirut: Hamazkayin, 1968), 6:187.

27. See Vartan Matiossian,' "Bolisë yev Kostan Zarianë 'Mehean' en ar'aj" [Bolis and Constant Zarian before *Mehyan*], *Haratch Literary Supplement* (Paris), December 1988. It includes a French version of the Manifesto of "The Crazy Wills."

28. Zarian, *Yerker*, 137.

29. Ibid., 138.

30. The passages on the tightrope artist may be found in sections 3–6 of the preamble to *Zarathustra*. In section 4, Nietzsche writes: "Man is a rope, tied between the beast and overman—a rope over an abyss. A dangerous across, a dangerous on-the-way, a dangerous looking-back, a dangerous shuddering and stopping. . . . What is great in man is that he is a bridge and not an end: what can be loved in man is that he is an overture and a going under." *The Portable Nietzsche*, tr. Walter Kaufmann (New York: Penguin Books, 1984). Zarian, of course, keeps the passage and ignores the fall!

31. The Armenian equivalent is *hamatrop'*, a neologism forged *ad hoc* by Kegham Parseghian, who translated Zarian's French into Armenian in 1914. Zarian fell back on the word in his 1922 essays on the theater.

32. Zarian says all this in an open letter that was published in the February 1922 issue of *Bardzravank'*. The letter was written in (sharply negative) reaction to the production of a play by Hagop Oshagan, *Nor Psakë* [The New Marriage], the subject of which was a scandalous incident that had occurred in the Istanbul Armenian community. In Zarian's opinion, such "bourgeois" themes were unworthy of a writer of Oshagan's talent; Oshagan would have done better, he thought, to transpose the equivalent of his own Symbolist "visions" to the stage.

33. The Armenian word for "drama-creating" is *dramasteghts*.

34. Let us, however, note that unpublished texts of Zarian's have come down to us, one of which, *Tesilk'ë* [The Vision], is a theatrical work. See the essay on this subject by Arby Ovanessian in *Haratch Literary Supplement*, July 1995. This text by Zarian should long since have been published.

35. An interpretation of the word *kron* that has always existed among the Armenians ties this word for religion to the root *kir* and the verb *krel*, "to carry." This interpretation can be traced back to the fifth-century writer Eznik of Koghb and his theological treatise *Against the Sects*. The same interpretation recurs frequently in later centuries. (Alishan refers, in particular, to an anonymous sixteenth-century dictionary.)

36. The sentence reads, in Armenian: "*Hisus iskakan steghtsagortsi yev ink'nasteghtsi metsashuk' orinakn e.*" We know that Zarian wrote in French at the time and that his friends translated his texts into Armenian. The word *ink'nasteghts*, my translation of which, in the French version of the present book, is *auto-créé*, poses a real problem. In Armenian, the word is perfectly possible; it is not even a neologism. In French, on the other hand, *auto-créé* does not exist, and French is not as tolerant of neologisms. What French word did Zarian employ? This remains a mystery for me.

37. This assertion refers to (among others) a prose text, "The Hero," a lecture that Varuzhan agreed to have published in the journal *Azatamart* in Constantinople in 1909. See *Yerkeri Liakatar Zhoghovatsu* 3:116–18 and the editor's remarks, 3:502. I comment lengthily on this text in chapter 8.

38. Walter Kaufmann reminds us of this in the third edition of his *Nietzsche: Philosopher, Psychologist, Antichrist* (Princeton, N.J.: Princeton University Press, 1968), p. 41, referring the reader to Ernest Newmann, *The Life of Richard Wagner*, vol. 4 (New York, 1946). On Wagner's anti-Semitism, see Janine Altounian, "Haine antisémite et sublimation épique dans la langue de Wagner," *Les Temps Modernes*, no. 591 (June 1997). Wagner's fiercely anti-Semitic pamphlet, *Das Judentum in der Musik* (which was published under a pseudonym in 1850 and under Wagner's real name in 1869) is available in *Sämtliche Schriften und Dichtungen:Volksausgabe*, vol. 10 (Leipzig, 1871). A new German edition appeared in 1975, in a volume titled *Die Kunst und die Revolution* (Munich: Rogner and Bernhard) with commentary by Tibor Kneif.

39. In Armenian, *matagh*, a name designating the sacrificial victim—first and foremost, the animal offered up in sacrifice.

40. For a first attempt to understand the place of "sacrifice" as a concept in relation to Catastrophe in the Armenian case, see my "L'empire du sacrifice," *L'intranquille* (Paris),

1992, no. 1. A complete examination of this issue has been offered in my study on Hagop Oshagan's novel *The Remnants*; see my *Le Roman de la Catastrophe,* vol. 3 of *Entre l'art et le temoignange: Littératures arméniennes au XXe siècle* (Geneva: MétisPresses, 2008). With the Holocaust in mind, Philippe Lacoue-Labarthe wrote in *Heidegger, Art, and Politics*: "I argue that there is not the least 'sacrificial' aspect in the *operation* of Auschwitz. . . . Now, reconsidering the question, I wonder whether in fact, at a quite other level, which would force us at least to re-work the anthropological notion of sacrifice, one should not speak of sacrifice. This is, indeed, an admission that I am purely and simply at a loss—and I remain so" (52; in *La fiction du politique,* 80–81).).

41. Friedrich Nietzsche, *On the Genealogy of Morals,* trans. Douglas Smith (Oxford and New York: Oxford University Press, 1996), second essay, section 12, 59; emphasis in the original. The passage continues as follows: "I emphasize this central perspective of historical method all the more since it is fundamentally opposed to the prevailing instincts and tastes of the time, which would rather accommodate the absolute arbitrariness . . . of all that happens, than the theory of a *will to power* manifesting itself in all things and events."

42. In Armenian, the same word (*shrjan, shrjel*) is used three times in order to describe the "turning-point," the "nihilistic" period in the history of being that must be traversed, and the "revolution" of the sun. The tone of this passage, written in 1932, is strangely Heideggerian. The recurrent theme of the "sacrificial lamb" and, concomitantly, self-sacrifice should, however, make us think about the larger context in which this "turning-point" is here conceived. The passage also has biographical undertones: this was the period in which Zarian was getting ready to leave Europe for the United States.

Appendix A. Excerpts from Nineteenth-Century Works of Philology and Ethnography

1. *Der armenische Volksglaube* was Abeghean's doctoral thesis. It was published in book form in 1899 and later reprinted in volume 7 of Abeghean's *Complete Works* (Yerevan: Academy Publishing House, 1975), 449–75, together with an Armenian translation (11–102) by Dora Sakayan.

2. Echmiadzin, located in the city of Vagharshapat, is the seat of the Catholicos of All Armenians.

3. Information about the names Abovean cites here may be found in a book by the German orientalist poet and translator Friedrich Bodenstedt (1819–1892), *Tausend und ein Tag im Orient,* first published in 1849 and subsequently reprinted as the first four volumes of his 1865 *Gesammelte Schriften.* Bodenstedt has been largely forgotten today. We are indebted to him for the first German translations of many Russian and Persian works. He befriended Abovean in 1844, when the Armenian writer served as his guide during his stay in Yerevan and Echmiadzin (1:153), as Abovean regularly did for German visitors. It is Bodenstedt who, in his 1849 book (vol. 3, ch. 35), wrote the first biographical sketch of Abovean; it includes extracts from popular poems "in the vulgar tongue" sent

him by the Armenian, "along with a full commentary in German" (1:188). Abovean also sent him the poems of Keshish Oghli, an *ashugh* (bard) born in the first half of the eighteenth century, together with their German translations (3:15–19). As for Kör Oghli, he was an Armenian ashugh supposed to have lived, according to a more or less apocryphal literary tradition, in the seventeenth century. Tarkhanov, finally, was known to Bodenstedt in his capacity as a provincial government official.

4. "K'abov ein br'num, giullov ver k'ts'um." Translators generally skip over this sentence because they do not understand it. I have substituted bingo for the game Abovean refers to and added "rather than learning to read" to make the meaning explicit.

5. The reference is to *Nor Bargirk' Haykazean lezvi* [New Dictionary of the Armenian Language], published in two volumes by the Mkhitarist Congregation of Venice in 1836–37. The old edition of the same dictionary was prepared under the general editorship of Abbot Mkhitar; the first volume was released in 1749 (the year of Mkhitar's death), the second (which also contains a historical dictionary and a double lexicon, classical Armenian / modern Armenian) saw the light in 1770. The *New Dictionary* remains the authoritative reference work for classical Armenian even today.

6. *Nor Bargirk' Haykazean lezvi*, 2:819. [Emin's footnote.]

7. Emin here uses the French word for epic, *épopée*.

8. *History of the Armenians*, book I, ch. 3. [Emin's footnote.]

9. It is here that we can see how heavily Emin depends on his source, Moses, who wrote, be it recalled, one thousand or perhaps fifteen hundred years before he did. Emin's definition of the word *ar'aspel* reproduces Moses's definition word for word!

10. Here Moses of Khoren is called *K'ert'oghahayr* (the Father of Poets, or the Father of Grammarians and Interpreters), his official attribute in the Armenian tradition.

11. Eugène Boré, *L'Arménie*. [Emin's footnote.] Boré (1809–1878) was an orientalist who took orders in 1851 and, toward the end of his life, was named Superior General of the Congregation of the Mission. He served for fifteen years as a missionary in Istanbul. He is supposed to have been an assistant professor of Armenian at the Collège de France in 1833–34. In 1837 he published *Le Couvent de Saint-Lazare à Venise* (Paris: Société des Bons Livres), which offers a succinct history of the Mekhitarist Congregation, followed by information on the language, literature, and religious history of Armenia. *L'Arménie* was published as part of a collective work under the direction of Jean-Marie Chopin, *Russie* (Paris: F. Didot, 1838), in two volumes, which was part of the series L'Univers: Histoire et description de tous les peuples. (Eugène Boré's contribution on Armenia is to be found in the second volume of *Russie*.) Emin, writing in 1850, probably had this book in mind, and in particular pp. 99–100 in Boré's monograph.

12. The "external" historians and philosophers are those who are not in the tradition of "revealed" history, that is, the Old Testament.

13. As he is called by Lazarus of Parp. [Emin's footnote.]

14. Khorenatsi, *History of the Armenians*, book I, ch. 14. [Emin's footnote.] The English translation quoted here is Moses Khorenats'i, *History of the Armenians*, tr.

Robert W. Thomson (Cambridge, Mass.: Harvard University Press, 1978), 96. According to Khorenatsi, Mar Abas Catina was a chronicler who wrote an early Armenian history on the basis of chronicles preserved in the Royal Assyrian archives.

15. It is on this point that Abeghean, in 1900, subjects Emin's views to a thoroughgoing revision, by drawing a distinction between myth and epic narrative, and also between literary invention and the oral narrative tradition.

16. "Holy Father" is a translation of *Surb Hayrik*. Servantsdeants means Father Khrimian, who was given this name as well as that of Khrimian Hayrik.

17. Khrimian Hayrik's printing house was initially housed in the monastery of Varag, located in a mountainous area close to the city of Van; his newspaper *Artsvi Vaspurakani* was published there.

18. *Garin* is the Armenian name for Erzerum.

19. I hesitate, of course, over the choice of a translation for the word *vep*. The word cannot be translated as "romance" or "novel" (*roman*); Servantsdeants knew perfectly well what a novel/romance in the modern sense was. It cannot be translated as "epic," either. Why? Because Servantsdeants had at his disposal the word *diuts'aznergut'iun*, meaning "epic" in the ancient sense of the word (the one the Mkhitarists wished to revive). Yet he uses the provincial word, which was also the ancient word for the popular epic or chanted narrative of the *gusan*s. I prefer the translation "narrative," because it allows us to remain neutral. It should be noted, finally, that *gusan* itself is the ancient word for "bard." Oddly, there is no modern word to designate the popular teller/chanter of tales, neither in the literary language nor in dialect. It is as if the tradition of the bard had already fallen into disuse at the moment Servantsdeants was preserving it in writing.

20. The word Servantsdeants employs, *yeresp'okhan*, is a word of the literary language used to designate members of the Parliament. Grbo was obviously not a "representative" in that sense, but, no doubt, he was the only "man of letters" in the village and, consequently, was its spokesperson when it had dealings with the outside world.

21. This roundabout phrase, for lack of a better, is my translation of the word *varpet*, the "traditional teacher" who transmits the oral tradition to his "students."

22. *Baghesh* is the Armenian name for Bitlis.

23. For the Old Testament story, see 2 Kings 19:36–37. On Skayordi, see Moses of Khoren, *History of the Armenians*, book 1:23. The same story is told in the Assyrian annals of Essarhaddon (680–669 B.C.), known in the Bible as Asardon. The murder of Sennacherib is supposed to have occurred in 681 B.C. The episode in the Assyrian annals is available in English in D. D. Luckenbill, *Ancient Records of Assyria and Babylonia* (Chicago, 1926; rpt. London: Histories and Mysteries of Man, 1989), 2:225–36

24. Thomas was the first historian of the Ardzrunis.

25. I comment briefly on this sentence in ch. 3. Indeed, the present translation is already an interpretation, because Servantsdeants's sentence is grammatically ambiguous. It reads, in Armenian: "Ayspisi ar'aspelats' mejen tsagats en yev i nuyn mnats'ats amen hin azgats nakhnakanut'iunë."

26. "Barbaric-sounding" is my translation of the Armenian word *khaghtalur*. Alishan is here making a bad pun. The name "Khaldi," he says, is *khaghtalur*, which means "coarse, corrupted," but also (according to an uncertain etymology) "unrefined, like the language of the Chaldeans."

27. The Armenian chapter heading is "Kronk', havatk' yev pashton."

28. "Pagan gods" is my translation of the word *Dik'*, usually employed in the plural to designate the gods of mythology. The old word for mythology is *dits'abanut'iun*, "discourse about the gods," but this is also the old word for "epic," because Armenian made no distinction between epic and mythological narrative until the mid-nineteenth century. The only god in the popular epic *David of Sasun* is the Christian God; the epic is therefore not a work of mythology in the modern sense. The classical language, to be sure, had no need for a word to designate the popular epic, because it was quite simply unaware of its existence. As for the word *chastvats* (literally, "non-god" and thus "idol"), it is usually translated in what follows as "god," without a capital *G* or the modifier "pagan." *Dik'* has no negative connotations; that is certainly not true of *chastvats*.

29. Alishan means, of course, *grabar* or Classical Armenian, the Armenians' written language for an uninterrupted 1400 years, notwithstanding the intermezzo of "Middle Armenian" in Cilicia.

30. *Kirk'* means "passion." As in French and English, the word has come to signify a violent outburst of desire.

31. We have usually translated the German singular noun *Volksglaube* in this excerpt as "popular beliefs." In her translation of the German into Armenian, Sakayan sometimes uses the singular noun *havatk'*, which also means "religious faith," and at other times the plural noun *havatalik'*, which means "beliefs."

32. All the works Abeghean cites are in Armenian. He provides their titles in German translation. The titles are here given in Armenian, along with an approximate English translation.

33. Eznik of Koghb is a fifth-century author. [Abeghean's footnote.]

34. Translated here are the first three pages of the monograph on Servantsdeants included in *Panorama*. This monograph, which runs from page 310 to page 327 of volume 4, is one of the shortest in the entire work. It is also, without a doubt, the warmest.

35. The reference is to Mkrtich Khrimian. The most charismatic figure among the Western Armenians in the last quarter of the century, Khrimian dabbled in literature and was elected, late in life, Catholicos of All the Armenians. The monograph preceding the one on Servantsdeants in *Panorama*, vol. 4 is about him. Oshagan, who approaches Khrimian with a great deal of good will (he strains to find a trace of literary value in his work), does not, for that very reason, treat him very kindly.

36. Venice and Vienna designate the two subdivisions of the Mkhitarist Congregation. Tblisi stands for the Eastern Armenian intellectuals. Moscow means the Armenian philologists of the Lazarian Institute.

37. Oshagan has here invented a word that combines the idea of scientific philology (*gitut'iun*) with that of the fatherland (*hayrenik'*) or one's native (*hayreni*) soil. *Hayrenagitut'ean* thus means something like "fatherlandology" or "homelandology." We should perhaps translate it with a word that has become more familiar today, "Armenology."

38. The reference is to Mkhitar of Sebastia, who created the Mkhitarist Congregation that took up quarters in 1715 on the Island of St. Lazarus in the bay of Venice, and, on Oshagan's account of the matter, proceeded to lay the "foundations" of national philology.

39. Servantsdeants had been charged by the Patriarchate with organizing a census of the Armenians in the six vilayets in which a majority of Armenians lived, and also with conducting an inventory of their cultural riches (manuscripts, monuments, artifacts, and so on).

40. I am not entirely certain that *patkerakerpum* is the word Oshagan actually wrote. The "fatherland" must take graphic material form and be crystallized in concrete, pictorial manifestations, in the guise of architectural or intellectual constructs. But the word Oshagan wrote may have been *patkerakertum*, which, while similar in meaning, puts the accent on the creation of such forms, rather than on their physical manifestation or plastic nature.

Appendix B. Essays in Mehyan and Other Writings of Constant Zarian

1. Some effort has been made toward translating *Antsortë yev ir champan* and *Bancoopë yev mamout'i voskornerë* into English. There is a partial translation of the former by Ara Baliozian, published as *The Traveller and His Road* (New York: Ashod, 1981), and Baliozian has also made an early rendering of the latter into English, published under the title *Bancoop and the Bones of the Mammoth* (New York: Ashod, 1982). We are not using either of these translations here.

2. Goghtn, in northern Armenia, was the native region of the *gusans* and bards who, in antiquity and the High Middle Ages, kept narrative epics alive and sustained an Armenian popular cultural tradition, at least in the form in which they had been preserved and handed down by the historian Moses of Khoren.

3. That is why the Catholics' attempts, for example, to introduce the Latin race's red-cheeked Jesus among us strike us as ridiculous and pitiful. One need only cast a glance at the garb Armenian Catholic priests wear to see the contradiction between the Armenian beard or face and a Jesuit's headdress. This is the reason that, aesthetically, these clerics do not appeal to us. [Zarian's footnote.]

4. Both Philo and Weininger are of Jewish descent. I would write at length about the latter if Armenians were familiar with him. [Zarian's footnote.]

5. To be sure, our blockheads will find these ideas paradoxical and "incomprehensible." The present article has been written, not for them, but for the minority that thinks seriously about the future of Armenian Art. [Zarian's footnote.]

6. As noted where this line is quoted in ch. 1, *ashough* is the Armenian form of a common word in the Middle East (*aşık* in Turkish) for what we call in English *minstrels*, or in French, *troubadours*.

7. This and all other French words appearing in parentheses in the text were added by Kufejian, following the Armenian word.

8. This is an allusion to Komitas, a priest, musicologist, musician, and ethnographer. The very incarnation of the aesthetic principle, Komitas transformed "popular sources" into Art, thereby bringing the "national" into existence.

9. In Armenian, *hasarakats' khagh*. I have not been able to discover the word Zarian used in French (the writings on the theater that he published in French in Belgium are of no help here). I have therefore translated the Armenian term as literally as possible. What is meant is perhaps simply "bourgeois theater."

10. In Armenian, *hamatrop' gortsoghut'iun*. In 1922, in the review *Bardzravank'*, Zarian uses the term *hamatrop* again, accompanied, this time, by its French equivalent *unanime*. This is an obvious allusion to Jules Romains's "unanimism," although Romains's name is never mentioned.

11. This and all other French words in parentheses were added by Kufejian.

12. I have developed this theme at length in an open letter on the theater published in the Brussels review *La Société nouvelle* [in 1913]. [Zarian's footnote.]

13. For a more detailed examination of this question, see my essay in the review *Le Thyrse* [Brussels], 1913. [Zarian's footnote.]

14. Of course, I could name other contemporary dramatists, such as Vielé-Griffin, Paul Fort, Leonid Andreev, and so on, but they are still seeking their way and have not yet produced positive works. [Zarian's footnote.]

15. In Armenian, *tramasteghts yergë*, literally, "song-creative-of-drama." Zarian obviously has the Dionysian ode in mind.

16. *Hethanosakan* means a partisan of the "doctrine" of paganism. (The direct target of Zarian's polemic is Daniel Varuzhan.) *Mehenakan* means a member of the group around the review *Mehyan*. (Here Zarian means himself.) We have left these names in Armenian throughout.

17. The Forest of the Poplars (Soseats andar') was the Armenians' sacred forest in ancient times.

18. The published text contains an error here. In *Mehyan* no. 5, 66, Mehenakan's answer is printed as if it were part of Hetanosakan's question. We have inserted the word "Mehenakan" at the appropriate place. Only Zarian (for Mehenakan is Zarian) could describe Greek art as an art of the "symbol," and Greek artists as "symbolists," that is, people who are privy to the "knowledge" expressed in the symbol.

19. Among the Western Armenians, Arpiar Arpiarian was the most accomplished writer of the "Realist" generation. He was also a politically active member of the Hnchak party and an indefatigable publicist. He had to spend a good part of his life in exile, especially after 1896, during the Hamidian dictatorship. Zarian's remark is thus something of a blow beneath the belt. The newspaper he mentions here, *Hayrenik*, was the

Hayrenik published in Istanbul; the poem in praise of Abdül Hamid that Arpiarian had to write appeared in it in 1892.

20. Misak Medzarents (1896–1908) and Mattheos Zarifian (1894–1924) are two of the best-known Western Armenian lyric poets. Both died of tuberculosis in Istanbul in the flower of their youth.

21. The reference is to the "Lamentations" found at the end of Moses's *History of the Armenians.*

22. Galata is an Istanbul neighborhood that had a large Armenian population.

23. *Mshak* was an Armenian periodical published in Tblisi. Founded by Grigor Artsruni in 1872, it appeared regularly until 1921. Surkhatian was a literary critic who had his moment of glory in the Soviet period.

24. Both published versions of the text read "Alli," which makes no sense here. "Alighieri" is a conjecture.

25. The text reads *sti* (of the lie), here emended to *srti* (of the heart).

26. The first list comprises Indo-Aryan "sun gods." "Tistria" seems to be a misreading for Indra. Surya was the main solar god of the Hindu pantheon. "Vaghuna" should be read as Varuna, the Vedan god. In the second list, in contrast, we find the names of lunar gods associated with Assyrian-Urartian culture. "Sielaghdis" should be read as "Sielardis" or "Selardi" (as the name found in the cuneiform inscriptions of Urartu was read until recently, doubtless in relation with the Greek god Selenos). See Simon Hmayakyan, *Vani t'agavorut'ean petakan kronĕ* [The State Religion of the Kingdom of Van] (Yerevan: State University, 1990), and, in English, Raffaele Biscione, Simon Hmayakyan, and Neda Parmegiani, eds., *The North-Eastern Frontier: Urartians and Non-Urartians in the Sevan Lake Basin* (Rome: Istituto di studi sulle civiltà dell'Egeo e del Vicino Oriente, 2002).

Appendix C. Daniel Varuzhan: Poems and Prose

1. Here, in a few lines, Varuzhan summarizes the history of Ani's downfall as reported by contemporary historians. In 1022, the king Hovhannes-Smbat, or John-Sempat (r. 1020–1042) bequeathed the Kingdom of Ani to the Byzantine emperor, who was supposed to inherit it after John-Sempat's death. But after his death the kingdom resisted this transfer of power, and in 1042 the young Gagik II was crowned. Vest Sarguis, one of the dignitaries of the kingdom, was a kind of double agent; although he was the leader of Ani's pro-Byzantine faction, he also became the advisor of Gagik. The latter was summoned to Byzantium in 1045, locked in the jails of the emperor, and forced to resign. The keys to Ani had been sent to Byzantium by another member of the pro-Byzantine faction, Petros Getadardz, the Catholicos of the Armenians.

2. Varuzhan mentions here, side by side, kings and warlords from different epochs who defeated or devastated the kingdom of Armenia. They are successively the Byzantine emperor Constantine Monomachus (r. 1042–1055), responsible for Ani's downfall in 1045; Tughril Beg, commander-in-chief of the Seljuk Turks who invaded Armenia after conquering Persia in the second half of the eleventh century; and Alparslan, who became

sultan after Tughril. It is with Alparslan that the Seljuk invasion of Byzantine territories began. Ani was seized by the Seljuks in 1064. About the name "Peroz," I am less sure. Perhaps it designates the king of Persia (r. 459–484) at the time when Armenians revolted against Persian rule.

3. "Apshin" (Afshin) is the name a Seljuk beg who fought on Alparslan's side in the battle of Manazkert (1071).

4. These lines have been cited and commented on at length above, in chapter 4, with a different translation.

5. The Akhuryan is a river that flows by the outskirts of Ani. Today it constitutes the border between Turkey and Armenia.

6. The Yerevan edition of Varuzhan's *Complete Works* mistakenly closes the parenthesis here.

7. The Yerevan edition has here *vishapi* instead of *vishapn*. Varuzhan's interpretation of the events in Cilicia is that the massacres were tightly related to the Hamidian reaction of April 1909 against the newly established regime of the Young-Turks. It is true that they occurred exactly at the same time, and this was also Zabel Esayan's understanding of what happened then.

8. The Rubenians were the reigning family in the Armenian kingdom of Cilicia. The founder of the dynasty was Ruben (r. 1080–1095).

9. The Armenian word is *mardeghut'iun*, which could also be translated "Incarnation," the mystery of God's becoming-man. It depends on the way we understand this descending of the host onto our altars or tables (*seghan*), whether we situate ourselves in the existing religion or in the principle of religion, at its luminous "source." The reader will recall that in *Pegasus*, the pendant to "The Light" that was published in the same collection, the poet sings his "solar" ("sunlike" or "sun-driven") song, dedicated to the "freedom of Man" and the "enslavement" (or "servitude") of God.

10. The Armenian verse sounds as follows: *Yes partvats, Arvestis tar'n sërtên* . . . In their French translation, Luc-André Marcel and Garo Poladian translate it faultily: "Moi, que le cœur amer de mon art a usé" (I, worn out by the bitter core of my art), which would be possible in a pinch if there were no comma after *partvats*. This remark is important because Varuzhan's verse is the central formulation that allows him to say that at the very "core" of Art, there is mourning. Art, in its historical essence, is mourning for the dead gods. Art is the mourning of myth.

11. In Armenian: *Khul Astso më hrea*. *Khul* is the word for "deaf." But it is the question of a Jewish god, not a Hebrew one ("deaf-mute Hebrew god" is Marcel/Poladian's translation). Varuzhan racializes the Christian religion (which had not waited for him in order to racialize itself). This is a shade of meaning that needs to be considered seriously. Varuzhan thinks of religion and mythology (therefore also paganism and pagan gods) in terms of the immense opposition that he inherits from the nineteenth century's philology, between the Semite and the Aryan, between the one who has the mythopoetic gift and the one who is deprived of it.

12. This and all other French interpolations in the text are Varuzhan's.

13. The published version of the present text reads *gur'*. That this is not a mere misprint is indicated by the fact that the word *gur'* recurs in the text. A *gur'* is a basin or trough used to water animals; it is absolutely incomprehensible in the present context. Collation with the original manuscript in the poet's archives, which are housed in the Yerevan Museum of Art and Literature, reveals that *gur'* is a misreading. This speaks volumes about the shortcomings of the editors of Varuzhan's *Complete Works*. The manuscript, written in pencil in Varuzhan's hand, very clearly reads *gar'*, "lamb."

BIBLIOGRAPHY

Abeghean, Manuk. *Der armenische Volksglaube.* Leipzig: W. Drugulin, 1899. Reprinted
    in *Yerker* 7:449–75, with an Armenian translation by Dora Sakayan, 7:11–102.
———. "Hay zhoghovrdakan ar'aspelnerë M. Khorenats'u Hayots' Patmut'ean mej"
    ["Հայ ժողովրդական առասպելները Մ. Խորենացու Հայոց պատմութեան մէջ";
    Popular Armenian Myths in *History of the Armenians* by Moses of Khoren]. *Ararat*
    (journal), 1899. Reprinted in *Yerker* 8:67–271.
———. "Hishoghut'iunner Komitasi masin" ["Յիշողութիւններ Կոմիտասի մասին";
    Memories about Komitas]. *Yerker* 6:431–39.
———. *Yerker* [Collected Works]. 8 vols. Yerevan: Academy of Sciences Publishing,
    1966–85.
Abovean, Khachatur. *Verk' Hayastani* [Վէրք Հայաստանի; Wounds of Armenia]. Tblisi,
    Georgia, 1858. Reprinted in *Yerkeri Liakatar Zhoghovatsu* [Complete Works], vol. 3.
———. *Verk' Hayastani* [Վէրք Հայաստանի; Wounds of Armenia]. Edited by P.
    Hacobyan. Yerevan: Academy of Sciences Publishing, 1981.
———. *Yerkeri Liakatar Zhoghovatsu* [Երկերի լիակատար ժողովածու; Complete
    Works]. 10 vols. Yerevan: Academy of Sciences Publishing, 1948–61.
Agathangelos. *History of the Armenians.* Translated by Robert W. Thomson. Albany:
    State University of New York Press, 1974.
Alikian, Abraham. "Daniel Varoujani Yerkeri Liakatar Zhoghovatsun" ["Դանիէլ
    Վարուժանի Երկերի լիակատար ժողովածուն"; The Complete Works of Daniel
    Varuzhan]. *Hask Armenological Review* (Antelias, Lebanon: Catholicosate of
    Cilicia), new series, years 7 and 8 (1997).
Alishan, Ghevond. *Ayrarat bnashkharh Hayastaneayts'* [Այրարատ, բնաշխարհ
    Հայաստանեայց; The Plain of Ararat, Cradle of Armenia]. Venice: San Lazzaro,
    1881.
———. *Hin havatk' kam het'anosakan gronk' Hayots'* [Հին Հաւատք կամ Հեթանոսական
    կրօնք Հայոց; The Armenians' Ancient Faith or Pagan Religion]. Venice: San
    Lazzaro, 1893, 1895.
———. *Sisakan: Teghagrut'iun Siuneats' ashkharhi* [Սիսական Տեղագրութիւն Սիւնեաց
    Աշխարհի; Sissakan: Physiography of Siunik]. Venice: San Lazzaro, 1893.

—————. [Père Léonce M. Alishan]. *Schirac, canton d'Ararat, pays de la Grande Arménie: Description géographique, illustrée.* . . . Venice: San Lazzaro, 1881.

—————. *Sisvan: Hamagrut'iun haykakan Kilikioy yev Levon Metsagorts* [Սիսուան Համագրութիւն Հայկական Կիլիկիոյ եւ Լեւոն Մեծագործ; Sisvan: General Description of Armenian Cilicia and Levon the Thaumaturge]. Venice: San Lazzaro, 1885.

—————. [Père Léonce M. Alishan]. *Sissouan, ou l'Arméno-Cilicie: Description géographique et historique, avec cartes et illustrations.* Translated from the original Armenian by Georges Bayan. Venice: San Lazzaro, 1899.

Altounian, Janine. "Haine antisémite et sublimation épique dans la langue de Wagner." *Les Temps Modernes,* no. 591 (June 1997).

—————. *L'intraduisible: Deuil, mémoire, transmission.* Psychismes series. Paris: Dunod, 2005.

—————. *Ouvrez-moi seulement les chemins d'Arménie.* Confluents psychanalytiques series. Paris: Les Belles Lettres, 1990.

—————. *La survivance: Traduire le trauma collectif.* Inconscient et culture series. Paris: Dunod, 2000.

Anderson, Benedict. *Imagined Communities: Reflections on the Origin and Spread of Nationalism.* London: Verso, 1983.

Anidjar, Gil. "The Semitic Hypothesis (Religion's Last Word)." In *Semites: Race, Religion, Literature.* Cultural Memory in the Present series. Stanford: Stanford University Press, 2008.

Anstett, Jean-Jacques. *La pensée religieuse de Friedrich Schlegel.* Annales de l'Université de Lyon. Paris: Les Belles Lettres, 1941.

Attridge, Derek, ed., *Acts of Literature,* New York: Routledge, 1991.

Ayrault, Roger. *La Genèse du romantisme allemand.* 4 vols. Paris: Aubier, 1969.

Badolle, Maurice. *L'Abbé Jean-Jacques Barthélémy (1716–1795) et l'hellénisme en France dans la seconde moitié du XVIIIème siècle.* Paris: PUF, 1926.

Badrig, Arakel. *Daniel Varuzhanë im husherum* [Դանիէլ Վարուժանն իմ Հուշերում; Daniel Varuzhan as I Remember Him]. Yerevan: Hayastan, 1965.

Bardakjian, Kevork. *A Reference Guide to Modern Armenian Literature, 1500–1920.* Detroit: Wayne State University Press, 2000.

Barthélémy, Jean-Jacques. *Voyage du jeune Anacharsis en Grèce vers le milieu du quatrième siècle avant l'ère vulgaire.* 6 vols. Paris: Chez de Bure aîné, 1788.

—————. *Ughevoruti'un Krtseruyn Anakarseay Hellada,* trans. Edward Hurmuz, Venice: San Lazzaro, 6 vol., 1843–1846 (Armenian translation of *Le Voyage du jeune Anacharsis en Grèce,* Paris: Bure l'aîné, 1790).

Bäumler, Alfred. *Das Mythische Weltalter: Bachofens romantische Deutung des Altertums. Mit einem Nachwort: Bachofen und die Religionsgeschichte.* Munich: Beck, 1965.

Beissner, Friedrich. *Hölderlin: Reden und Aufsätze.* Weimar: Böhlau, 1961.

Beledian, Krikor. *Krake shrjanakë: Daniel Varuzhani shurj* [Կրակէ շրջանակը: Դանիէլ Վարուժանի շուրջ; The Circle of Fire: On Daniel Varuzhan]. Antelias, Lebanon: Armenian Catholicosate, 1987.

—————. *Tram* [Spամ; Drama]. Beirut: Atlas, 1980.

Benjamin, Walter. *The Arcades Project*. Translated by Howard Eiland and Kevin McLaughlin. Cambridge, Mass.: Harvard University Press, Belknap Press, 1999.

———. *Charles Baudelaire: The Lyric Poet in the Era of High Capitalism*. Translated by Harry Zohn. London: New Left Books, 1973.

———. *Illuminations*. Translated by Harry Zohn. New York: Schocken Books, 1969.

———. *Philosophy, Aesthetics, History*. Edited by Gary Smith and translated by Leigh Hafrey and Richard Sieburth. Chicago: University of Chicago Press, 1989.

Benveniste, Émile. "L'origine du vichap arménien." *Revue des Études Arméniennes*, first series, 7 (1927).

Biscione, Raffaele, Simon Hmayakyan, and Neda Parmegiani, eds., *The North-Eastern Frontier: Urartians and Non-Urartians in the Sevan Lake Basin*. Rome: Istituto di studi sulle civiltà dell'Egeo e del Vicino Oriente, 2002.

Blanchot, Maurice. *Le Très-Haut*. Paris: Gallimard, 1948. Published in English as *The Most High*, translated and with an introduction by Allan Stoekl (Lincoln: University of Nebraska Press, 1996).

Bodenstedt, Friedrich. *Gesammelte Schriften in 12 Bänden*, vols. 1–4: *Tausend und Ein Tag im Orient* (1849). Berlin: Verlag der Königlichen Geheimen Oberhofbuch-druckerei, 1865.

Bolognesi, Giancarlo. *Leopardi e l'armeno*. Pubblicazione della Università cattolica del Sacro Cuore: Scienze filologiche e letteraturea, 59. Milan: Vita e pensiero, 1998.

Boré, Eugène. *Le Couvent de Saint-Lazare à Venise*. Paris: Société des Bons Livres, 1837.

Bouchereau, Philippe. "Le génocide est sans raison: Méditer la désespérance." *L'intranquille* (Paris), 6–7 (2001).

Brémond, Henri. *Histoire littéraire du sentiment religieux en France*. 11 vols. 1916–33. Reprinted, Paris: Armand Colin, 1967–68.

Byron, Charles Gordon Lord. *The Works of Lord Byron*, vol. 11; *Byron's Letters and Journals*, vol. 4. New, revised, and enlarged edition. London: John Murray, 1904. Reprinted, New York: Octagon, 1966.

Carrière, Alain. *Les huit sanctuaires de l'Arménie païenne, d'après Agathange et Moïse de Khoren: Étude critique*. Paris: E. Leroux, 1899.

Chahinian, Krikor. *Oeuvres vives de la littérature arménienne*. Antelias, Lebanon: Armenian Catholicosate, 1988.

Charents, Yeghishe. *Yerkeri Zhoghovatsu* [Երկերի ժողովածու; Complete Works]. 6 vols. Yerevan: Academy of Sciences Publishing, 1962–68.

Chaudhuri, Nirad C. *Scholar Extraordinary: The Life of Professor the Rt. Hon. Friedrich Max Müller, P.C.* New York: Oxford University Press, 1974.

Chobanian, Arshag. *Demk'er* [Դիմքեր; Portraits]. Paris: Masis, 1929.

——— [Tchobanian, Archag], trans. *La roseraie d'Arménie*. 3 vols. Paris: E. Leroux, 1918–29.

Clifford, James. *The Predicament of Culture: Twentieth-Century Ethnography, Literature, and Art*. Cambridge, Mass.: Harvard University Press, 1988.

Coquio, Catherine. "Aux lendemains, là-bas et ici: L'écriture, la mémoire et le deuil." Preface to *Rwanda—2004: Témoignages et littératures*, edited by C. Coquio and

Aurélia Kalisky. *Lendemains: Études comparées sur la France* 28, no. 112 (March 2004). Tuebingen: Stauffenburg Verlag, 2004.

———. "L'émergence d'une littérature de non-écrivains: Le témoignage des catastrophes historiques." *Revue d'histoire littéraire de la France*, no. 111 (April–June 2003).

———, ed. *L'histoire trouée: Négation et témoignage.* Nantes: L'Atalante, 2004.

———. "La littérature arménienne de la Catastrophe: Actualité critique." In C. Mouradian, Y. Ternon, and G. Bensoussan, eds., "Ici, ailleurs, autrement: Connaissance et reconnaissance du génocide arménien." Special issue, *Revue d'histoire de la Shoah*, no. 177–78 (Spring 2003).

———, ed. *Parler des camps, penser les génocides.* Paris: Albin-Michel, 1999.

———. "Récits de rescapés: Y a-t-il une philosophie des témoignages?" In A. Tomiche and Ph. Zard, eds., *Littérature et philosophie.* Arras: Artois Presses Universités, 2002.

Curtius, Ernst. *Französischer Geist im neuen Europa: Gide, Rolland, Claudel, Suarès, Péguy, Proust, Valéry, Larbaud, Maritain, Brémond.* Berne: Francke Verlag, 1952.

Dadurian, Aharon. *Banasterghtsut'iunner* [Բանաստեղծություններ; Poems]. Edited by Zoulal Kazandjian, with a preface by Marc Nichanian. Venice: San Lazzaro, 1997.

Dadrian, Vahakn. *The History of the Armenian Genocide: Ethnic Conflict from the Balkans to Anatolia to the Caucasus.* Providence, R.I.: Berghahn Books, 1997.

Davies, Richard. Review of *Nietzsche and Soviet Culture: Ally and Adversary* (1994). *Journal of European Studies* 5, no. 3 (1995).

Der Hovanessian, Diana, and Marzbed Margossian, eds. and trs. *Anthology of Armenian Poetry.* New York: Columbia University Press, 1978.

Derrida, Jacques. *Margins of Philosophy*, trans. Alan Bass (Chicago: University of Chicago Press, 1982).

———. "Onto-theology of National-Humanism (Prolegomena to a Hypothesis)." *Oxford Literary Review* 14 (July 1992), 3–24.

Deshmukh, P. S. *The Origin and Development of Religion in Vedic Literature.* Oxford: Oxford University Press, 1933.

Dumézil, Georges. *Heur et malheur du guerrier: Aspects mythiques de la fonction guerrière chez les Indo-Européens.* Paris: PUF, 1969.

Dundes, Alan, ed. *International Folklorists: Classic Contributions by the Founders of Folklore.* Lanham, Md.: Rowman and Littlefield, 1999.

Emin, Mkrtich. *Mkrtich Emini yerkasirut'iunnerë Hayots lezvi, grakanut'ean yev patmutean masin (1840–1855 t't'.)* [Մկրտիչ Էմինի երկասիրությունները Հայոց լեզուի, գրականության եւ պատմության մասին (1840–1855); Mkrtich Emin's Works on the Armenian Language and Armenian Literature and History (1840–1855)]. Edited by Grigor Khalateants. Moscow, 1898.

———. *Movses Khorenatsi yev Hin Haykakan Vepë* [Մովսէս Խորենացի եւ Հին Հայկական վէպը; Moses of Khoren and the Ancient Armenian Epic]. Translated from Russian by Kh. Hovanniseants. Tblisi, Georgia, 1887.

———. "Vahagn-Vishapak'agh armianskoy mifologii est' Indra-Vritrahan Rig-Vedy." In *Izledovanije i stat'i N.O. Emina po armenskoy mifologii, arxeologii, istorii i istorii literaturyi (1858–1884)* [Studies and Articles of N. O. Emin on Armenian Mythology, Archaeology, History, and History of Literature, 1858–1884], edited by Grigor Khalateants. Moscow: Lazarev Institute of Oriental Languages, 1896.

———. *Vepk' hnuyn Hayastani* [Վեպք Հնոյն Հայաստանի; Epic Narratives of Ancient Armenia]. Moscow, 1850.

Eng, David, and David Kazanjian. *Loss: The Politics of Mourning*. Berkeley and Los Angeles: University of California Press, 2003.

Esayan, Zabel. *Averknerun mej* [Աւերակներու մէջ; Among the Ruins]. Beirut, 1985.

———. *Yerker* [Works]. 2 vols. Antelias, Lebanon: Armenian Catholicosate, 1987.

Eusebius of Caesarea. *Eusebii Pamphilii Caesariensis Episcopi Chronicon Bipartitum. Nunc Primum ex Armeniaco Textu in Latinum Conversum. . . .* Translated by Father Baptist Aucher. Venice: San Lazzaro, 1818.

———. *Eusebii Pamphili Chronicorum Canonum, Libri Duo, Opus ex Haicano Codice A Doctore Iohanne Zohrabo, Collegii Armeniaci Venetiarum Alumno Diligenter Expressum et Castigatum . . . Nunc Primum Coniunctis Latine Donatum.* Translated by Father Hovhannes Zohrabian and Angelo Mai. Milan: Regiis Typis, 1818.

Fishman, Joshua. *Language and Nationalism: Two Integrative Essays*. Rowley, Mass.: Newbury House, 1972.

Foucault, Michel. *The Order of Things: An Archeology of the Human Sciences*. New York: Vintage Books, 1994.

Frenghian, Edouard. *Nietzsche* [Նիցչէ]. Tblisi, Georgia, 1910.

Fuhrmann, Manfred , ed. *Terror und Spiel: Probleme der Mythenrezeption*. Munich: W. Fink, 1971.

Garsoïan, Nina G., ed. and trans. *The Epic Histories Attributed to P'awstos Buzand (Buzandaran Patmut'iwnk')*. Harvard Armenian Texts and Studies 8. Cambridge, Mass.: Harvard University Press, 1989.

Godel, Vahé. *La poésie arménienne du Ve siècle à nos jours*. Paris: Éditions de la Différence, 1990.

Goldberg, David Theo. *Racist Culture: Philosophy and the Politics of Meaning*. Oxford: Basil Blackwell, 1993.

Goldziher, Ignaz. *Der Mythos bei den Hebräern und seine geschichtliche Entwickelung: Untersuchungen zur Mythologie und Religionswissenschaft*. Leipzig, 1876. Published in English as *Mythology among the Hebrews and Its Historical Development*, translated by Russell Martineau (London: Longmans, Green, 1877; rpt. New York: Cooper Square Publishers, 1967).

Gourgouris, Stathis. *Dream Nation: Enlightenment, Colonization, and the Institution of Modern Greece*. Stanford: Stanford University Press, 1996.

Griffith, Ralph J. H., trans. *The Hymns of the Rig Veda*. 2 vols. 2nd ed. Benares: E. J. Lazarus, 1896–97.

Hacikyan, Agop, coordinating ed. *The Heritage of Armenian Literature*, vol. 3: *From the Eighteenth Century to Modern Times*. Translated and edited by Gabriel Basmajian, Edward Franchuk, and Nourhan Ouzounian. Detroit: Wayne State University Press, 2005.

Han, Béatrice. "Is Early Foucault an Historian? History, history and the Analytic of Finitude." *Philosophy and Social Criticism* (London) 31, nos. 5–6 (2005).

Hart, William. *Edward Said and the Religious Effects of Culture*. Cambridge: Cambridge University Press, 2000.

Heckel, Karl. *Nietzsche, sein Leben und seine Lehre*. 2nd ed., with an afterword by Alfred Baümler. Leipzig: Philipp Reclam, 1922.

Heesterman, J. C. *The Inner Conflict of Tradition: Essays in Indian Ritual, Kingship, and Society*. Chicago: University of Chicago Press, 1985.

———. "Other Folks' Fire." In Staal, *Agni: The Vedic Ritual of the Fire Altar*, vol. 2.

Heidegger, Martin. *Nietzsche*, vol. 1: *The Will to Power as Art*. Translated by David Farrell Krell. San Francisco: Harper and Row, 1979. Originally published as *Nietzsche: Erster Band* (Pfullingen: Neske, 1961).

———. *Elucidations of Hölderlin's Poetry*, trans. Keith Hoeller, Amherst, N.Y.: Humanity Books, 2000.

Hmayakyan, Simon. *Vani t'agavorut'ean petakan kronë* [Վանի թագավորության պետական կրոնը; The State Religion of the Kingdom of Van]. Yerevan: Academy of Sciences Publishing, 1990.

Hölderlin, Friedrich. *Sämtliche Werke*. Edited by Friedrich Beissner. Vol. 2. Stuttgart: Cotta, 1953.

———. *Poems and Fragments*, trans. Michael Hamburger, Ann Arbor: University of Michigan Press, 1968.

———. *Sämtliche Werke (Frankfurter Ausgabe)*. Edited by D. E. Sattler. Vol. 1. Frankfurt: Verlag Roter Stern, 1975.

———. *Selected Verse*, trans. Michael Hamburger, Baltimore: Penguin, 1961.

Hopf, Claudia. *Sprachnationalismus in Serbien und Griechenland*. Wiesbaden: Harrassowitz, 1997.

Hovannisian, Richard. *Armenia on the Road to Independence, 1918*, Berkeley and Los Angeles: University of California Press, 1967.

Hovannisian, Richard, and David Myers, eds. *Enlightenment and Diaspora: The Armenian and Jewish Cases*. Atlanta: Scholars Press, 1999.

Humboldt, Wilhelm von. *Werke in Fünf Bänden*, vol. 3: *Schriften zum Altertumskunde und Ästhetik*. Edited by Andreas Flitner and Klaus Giel. Stuttgart: Cotta, 1960.

Injijean, Lucas. *Darapatum* [Դարապատում; History of the Century]. 8 vols. Venice: San Lazzaro, 1824–28.

———. *Hnakhosut'iun ashkharhakragan Hayastaneayts' ashkharhi* [Հնախոսություն աշխարհագրական Հայաստանեայց աշխարհի; Geographical Archeology of the Armenian World]. 3 vols. Venice: San Lazzaro, 1835.

———. *Storagrut'iun hin Hayastaneayts': Ëst hin yev ëst mijin daru anvaneal zhamanakagrats* [Ստորագրություն հին Հայաստանեայց: Ըստ հին ու ըստ միջին դարու անուանեալ ժամանակագրաց; Description of Ancient Armenia, after the Famous Chroniclers of Antiquity and the Middle Ages]. Venice: San Lazzaro, 1822.

————. *Tesut'iun hamar'ot hin yev nor ashkharhagrut'ean* [Տեսութիւն Համառօտ Հին եւ Նոր աշխարհագրութեան; An Overview of Ancient and Modern Geography]. Venice: San Lazzaro, 1791.

Jizmejian, Terenig. *Daniel Varuzhan, dprots'akan keank'ë, antip namaknerë, grakanut'iunë* [Դանիէլ Վարուժան, Դպրոցական կեանքը, անտիպ նամակները, գրականութիւնը; Daniel Varuzhan, His Life as a Student, His Unpublished Letters, His Literature]. Cairo: Houssaper, 1955.

Kalisky, Aurélia. "Refus de témoigner ou chronique d'une métamorphose: Du témoin à l'écrivain (Imre Kertész, Ruth Klüger)." In Coquio, *L'histoire trouée*, 419–48.

Karinyan, Artachès. *Aknarkner hay parberakan mamuli patmut'ean* [Ակնարկներ Հայ պարբերական մամուլի պատմութJան; Sketches of the History of the Armenian Periodical Press]. 2 vols. Yerevan: Institute of Literature, 1960.

Kaufmann, Walter. *Nietzsche: Philosopher, Psychologist, Antichrist.* 3rd ed. Princeton, N.J.: Princeton University Press, 1968.

Kévorkian, Raymond. *Ani: Capitale de l'Arménie en l'an mil.* Paris: Paris-Musées, 2001.

————. *Les Arméniens de l'Empire ottoman à la veille du génocide.* Paris: Éditions d'Art et d'Histoire, 1992.

Kuhn, Adalbert. *Die Herabkunft des Feuers und des Göttertranks: Ein Beitrag zur vergleichenden Mythologie der Indogermanen.* Berlin: F. Dümmler, 1859. 3rd ed., 1886. Reprinted, Darmstadt: Wissenschaftliche Buchgesellschaft, 1986.

Lacoue-Labarthe, Philippe. *Heidegger, Art, and Politics: The Fiction of the Political.* Translated by Chris Turner. Cambridge, Mass.: Basil Blackwell, 1997. Originally published as *La fiction du politique* (Paris: Christian Bourgois, 1990).

Lacoue-Labarthe, Philippe, and Jean-Luc Nancy. "The Nazi Myth," in *Critical Inquiry* 16, n. 2 (Winter 1990).

————. "History and Mimesis." In *Looking after Nietzsche*, edited by Laurence Rickels. Albany: State University of New York Press, 1989.

————. *Typography: Mimesis, Philosophy, Politics.* Translated by Christopher Fynsk. Stanford: Stanford University Press, 1998. Originally published as *L'imitation des modernes: Typographies 2* (Paris: Éditions Galilée, 1986).

Lacoue-Labarthe, Philippe, and Jean-Luc Nancy. *L'Absolu littéraire: Théorie de la littérature du romantism allemand.* Paris: Seuil, 1977.

————. *The Literary Absolute: The Theory of Literature in German Romanticism.* Translated by Philip Barnard and Cheryl Lester. Albany: State University of New York Press, 1988.

Lang, Andrew. *Modern Mythology.* London: Longmans, Green, 1897. Reprinted, New York: AMS Press, 1968.

Langlois, Alexandre. trans. *Rig-Véda; ou, Livre des Hymnes.* Translated from Sanskrit. 2nd ed., revised, corrected, and expanded with analytic index by Philippe-Edouard Foucaux. Paris: Maisonneuve et Cie, 1872. Reprinted (facsimile of 2nd ed., with preface removed), Paris: Maisonneuve, 1984; 2009.

Langlois, Victor. *Collections des historiens anciens et modernes de l'Arménie.* Vol. 1. Paris: Firmin-Didot, 1867.

Lauer, Reinhard, ed. *Sprache, Literatur, Folklore bei Vuk Stefanovic Karadžić.* Proceedings of an international conference, Göttingen, 8–13 February, 1987. Wiesbaden: O. Harrassowitz, 1988.

Leopardi, Giacomo. *Annotazioni sopra la Cronica d'Eusebio pubblicata l'anno 1818, in Milano, dai dottori Angelo Mai e Giovanni Zohrab, scritte l'anno appresso dal conte Giacomo Leopardi a un amico suo.* Rome: de Romanis, 1823.

Löwith, Karl. *Nietzsches Philosophie des ewigen Wiederkunft des Gleichen.* Berlin: Die Runde, 1935. Revised and expanded, with appendix, "Zur Geschichte der Nietzsche-Deutung (1894–1954)," as *Nietzsches Philosophie des ewigen Wiederkehr des Gleichen.* Stuttgart: Kohlhammer, 1956. In *Sämtliche Schriften,* vol. 6: *Nietzsche,* edited by Klaus Stichweh and Marc B. de Launay. Stuttgart: Metzler, 1987.

Lubbock, John. *Marriage, Totemism, and Religion: An Answer to Critics.* London and New York: Longmans, Green, 1911.

———. *The Origin of Civilisation and the Primitive Condition of Man.* London: Longmans, Green, 1870. Reprinted in Classics in Anthropology series. Chicago: University of Chicago Press, 1978.

———. *Prehistoric Times, as Illustrated by Ancient Remains, and the Manners and Customs of Modern Savages.* New York, D. Appleton, 1875. 5th ed., 1908. Reprinted, Freeport, N.Y.: Books for Libraries Press, 1971.

Mackay, George Eric. *Lord Byron at the Armenian Convent.* Venice: Office of the Polyglotta, 1876.

Mahé, Jean-Pierre. Review of first volume of Servantsdeants's Complete Works. *Revue des Études Arméniennes,* new series 14 (1980): 529–30.

Mamdani, Mahmoud. *Citizen and Subject: Contemporary Africa and the Legacy of Late Colonialism.* Princeton, N.J.: Princeton University Press, 1996.

———. *When Victims Become Killers: Colonialism, Nativism, and the Genocide in Rwanda.* Princeton, N.J.: Princeton University Press, 2001.

Mannhardt, Wilhelm. *Wald- und Feldkulte.* Berlin: Gebrüder Borntraeger, 1875–77.

Matiossian, Vartan. "Bolisë yev Kostan Zarianë 'Mehean' en ar'aj" ["Պոլիսը եւ Կոստան Զարեանը 'Մեհեան' էն առաջ'"; Bolis and Constant Zarian before *Mehyan*]. *Haratch Literary Supplement* (Paris), December 1998.

———. *Kostan Zareani shurj* [Կոստան Զարեանի շուրջ; Around Constant Zarian]. Antelias, Lebanon: Armenian Catholicosate, 1998.

Mehyan, Revue arménienne de littérature et d'art. Constantinople, 1914. Reprinted in one volume, Aleppo, Syria: Kilikia, 1997.

Mkhit'arean Hobelean [Մխիթարեան Յոբելեան; Mekhitarist Jubileum]. Venice: San Lazzaro, 1901.

Montinari, Mazzino. *Nietzsche lesen.* Berlin: W. de Gruyter, 1980. Published in English as *Reading Nietzsche,* trans. by Greg Whitlock (Urbana: University of Illinois Press, 2003).

Moïse de Khorène. *Histoire de l'Arménie*. Translated by Annie Mahé and Jean-Pierre Mahé. Paris: Gallimard, 1993.

Moses Khorenats'i. *History of the Armenians*. Translated, with commentary on the literary sources, by Robert W. Thomson. Cambridge, Mass.: Harvard University Press, 1978.

Müller, F. Max. *Chips from a German Workshop*, vol. 1: *Essays on the Science of Religion.* New York: Scribner, 1869.

———. *The Essential Max Müller: On Language, Mythology, and Religion*. Edited and with an introduction by Jon R. Stone. New York: Palgrave MacMillan, 2002.

———. *Introduction to the Science of Religion: Four Lectures Delivered at the Royal Institute, with Two Essays on False Analogies, and the Philosophy of Mythologies.* London: Longmans, Green, 1873.

———. *Lectures on the Origin and Development of Religion as Illustrated by the Religions of India.* Delivered at the Chapter House, Westminster Abbey, in April, May, and June 1878. London: Longmans, Green, 1878.

———. *Lectures on the Science of Language.* 2 vols. New York: Scribner, Armstrong, 1875–78. Revised edition published as *The Science of Language, Founded on Lectures Delivered at the Royal Institution in 1861 and 1863.* 2 vols. New York: Charles Scribner's Sons, 1891. Revised ed. reprinted, New York: AMS, 1978.

———. *Die Wissenschaft der Sprache; Neue Bearbeitung der in den Jahren 1861 und 1863 am Königlichen Institut zu London gehalten Vorlesungen.* Translated from English by Dr. R. Fick and Dr. W. Wischmann. 2 vols. Leipzig: W. Engelmann, 1892.

Nancy, Jean-Luc. *The Inoperative Community.* Edited by Peter Connor. Translated by Peter Connor, Lisa Garbus, Michael Holland, and Simona Sawhney, with foreword by Christopher Fynsk. Minneapolis: University of Minnesota Press, 1991. Originally published as *La communauté désoeuvrée* (Paris: Bourgeois, 1986).

Newmann, Ernest. *The Life of Richard Wagner.* 4 vols. New York: Knopf, 1933–46.

Nichanian, Marc. *Ages et usages de la langue arménienne.* Paris: Entente, 1989.

———. "Aghetin lr'ut'iunë Kostan Zareani ardzakin mej" ["Աղէտին լռութիւնը Կոստան Զարեանի արձակին մէջ"; The Silence of Catastrophe in Constant Zarian's Prose]. *Basmavep* (Venice) 153, nos. 1–4 (1995). 343–74.

———. "Aharon Taturean, anzhamanak panasteghtsë" ["Ահարոն Տատուրեան, անժամանակ բանաստեղծը"; Aharon Dadourian, the Poet Out of Time]. *GAM* (Los Angeles: Abril Publishers), no. 5 (2002).

———. "Avons-nous vraiment perdu la langue à l'étranger?" In "Antoine Berman aujourd'hui / Antoine Berman for Our Time," edited by Alexis Nouss. Special issue, *TTR: Études sur le texte et ses transformations* (Montreal) 14, no. 2 (2001).

———. "L'empire du sacrifice." *L'intranquille* (Paris), 1992, no. 1.

———. "Enlightenment and Historical Thought." In Hovannisian and Myers, *Enlightenment and Diaspora.*

———. *Hakob Oshakani matenagitut'iun* [Յակոբ Օշականի մատենագիտութիւն; Bibliography of Hagop Oshagan]. Los Angeles: Open Letter Publishing, 1999.

———. *The Historiographic Perversion*. Translated and with an afterword by Gil Anidjar. New York: Columbia University Press, 2009. Originally published as *La perversion historiographique* (Paris: Léo Scheer, 2006).

———. "Introduction: Poetry and Revolution." In *Yeghishé Charents, Poet of the Revolution*, edited by Marc Nichanian with the collaboration of Vartan Matiossian. Costa Mesa, Calif.: Mazda Press, 2003.

———. "Kostan Zarean, Ankareli t'atronë" [Կոստան Զարեան. Անկարելի թատրոնը"; Constant Zarian: The Impossible Theater]. *Bazmavep* (Venice), 1996, nos. 1–4, 175–99.

———. "Kostan Zarean yev Oswald Spengler" [Կոստան Զարեան եւ Օսվալդ Շպենգլըր"; Constant Zarian and Oswald Spengler]. *Kayk'* (Paris), 1990, no. 1.

———, "Representation and Historicity." In "Art and Testimony: Around Atom Egoyan's *Ararat*," edited by Marc Nichanian. Special issue, *Armenian Review* 49, nos. 1–4 (2004–05).

———. *Le Roman de la Catastrophe*. Vol. 3 of *Entre l'art et le temoignange: Littératures arméniennes au XXe siècle*. Geneva: MétisPresses, 2008.

———. *Writers of Disaster: The National Revolution*. Princeton, N.J. and London: Gomidas Institute, 2002.

———. "Yergin gerin" [Երգին գերին"; Slave of the Song]. *Hask Armenological Review* (Antelias, Lebanon: Catholicosate of Cilicia,), 7–8 (1995–96).

Nietzsche, Friedrich. *Ayspes khosets' Zradashtë* [*Thus Spoke Zarathustra*]. Translated and with a preface by Hakob Movses. Yerevan: Van Aryan, 2002.

———. *Baruts' yev ch'arits' andin; Ch'astvatsneri mt'nshaghë* [*Beyond Good and Evil and Twilight of the Idols*]. Translated and with a preface by Hakob Movses. Yerevan: Apolon, 1992.

———. *The Birth of Tragedy*. Translated by Walter Kaufmann. New York: Vintage, 1967.

———. *The Birth of Tragedy*. Translated by Shaun Whiteside, with an introduction by Michael Tanner. New York: Penguin Books, 1993.

———. *Kritische Gesamtausgabe*. Edited by Giorgio Colli and Mazzino Montinari. Berlin: Walter de Gruyter, 1967–.

———. *On the Genealogy of Morals*. Translated by Douglas Smith. Oxford World's Classics. Oxford and New York: Oxford University Press, 1996.

———. *On the Genealogy of Morals and Ecce Homo*. Translated by Walter Kaufmann and R. J. Hollingdale. New York: Vintage Books, 1989.

———. *Der Wille zur Macht; Versuch einer Umwertung aller Werte*. With an afterword by Alfred Bäumler. Berlin: Kröner, 1930.

———. *The Will to Power*. Translated by Walter Kaufmann and R. J. Hollingdale. New York: Vintage, 1968.

———. *Zvart' gitut'iunë* [*The Gay Science*]. Translated and with a preface by Hakob Movses. Yerevan: Van Aryan, 2005.

Olender, Maurice. *The Languages of Paradise: Aryans and Semites, a Match Made in Heaven.* Translated by Arthur Goldhammer. Revised and augmented edition. New York: Open Press, 2002. Originally published as *Les Langues du paradis: Aryens et Sémites, un couple providentiel* (Paris: Seuil, 1989).

Oshagan, Hagop. "Daniel Varuzhan" ["Դանիէլ Վարուժան"]. *Agos* (Beirut), nos. 14–18 (1946–47).

———. *Hamapatker arevmtahay grakanut'ean* [Համապատկեր արեւմտահայ գրականութեան; Panorama of Western Armenian Literature]. Vols. 1–5, Jerusalem: Armenian Patriarcate, 1945–56. Vol. 6, Beirut: Hamazkayin, 1968. Vols. 7–10, Antelias, Lebanon: Armenian Catholicosate, 1979–82.

———. *Mayrineru shuk'in tak* [Մայրիներու շուքին տակ; In the Shade of the Cedars]. Beirut: Centenary Edition, 1983.

———."Mer banasteghtsnerë—Daniel Varoujan" ["Մեր բանաստեղծները_Դանիէլ Վարուժան"; Our Poets—Daniel.Varoujan]. In *Hay grakanut'iun* (Smyrna, Turkey), August and September 1913.

———. "Varuzhani 'Hats'in yergë'" ["Վարուժանի 'Հացին երգը'"; Varuzhan's "Song of Bread"]. In *Bardzravank'* (Constantinople), January 1922, no. 1.

———. *Yerker* [Երկեր; Works]. Edited and prefaced by Step'an Kurtikian. Yerevan, 1978.

Ovannessian, Arby. "Kostan Zareani 'Tesilk'ë'" ["Կոստան Զարեանի 'Տեսիլքը'"; Constant Zarian's "The Vision"]. *Haratch Literary Supplement* (Paris), July 1995.

Papazyan, Vahram. *Hetadardz Hayeatsk'* [Հետադարձ ակնարկ; Looking Back]. Vol. 1. Yerevan: Soviet Writer, 1956.

Parseghian, Kegham. *Amboghjakan gortsë* [Ամբողջական գործը; Complete Works]. Paris: Society of Friends of Martyred Writers, 1931.

Peroomian, Roubina. *Literary Responses to Catastrophe: A Comparison of the Armenian and the Jewish Experiences.* Atlanta: Scholars Press, 1993.

Pzhshgean, Minas. *Chanaparhordut'iun i Lehastan yev hayl koghmans bnakeals i Hayka-zants' sereloy i nakhneats' Ani k'aghak'in* [ՃանապարՀորդութիւն ի Լեհաստան; Voyage to Poland and Other Places Inhabited by Armenians from Ancient Ani]. Venice: San Lazzaro, 1830.

———. *Patmut'iun Pontosi* [Պատմութիւն; History of the Pontus]. Venice: San Lazzaro, 1819.

———. *Yerazhshytut'iun: Vor e hamar'ot teghekut'iun yerazhshtakan skzbants' yelevejut'eants yeghanakats' yev nshanakrats' khaghits'* [Երաժշտութիւն: Որ է Համառոտ տեղեկութիւն երաժշտական սկսբանց եղանակաց եւ նշանագրաց խաղից; Music: A Brief Overview of the Musical Principles of Keys and Notes]. Yerevan: Aram Kerovpian, 1997.

Poladian, Garo. *Zruytsner* [Զրոյցներ; Dialogues]. Vol. 2. Cairo: Houssaper, 1961.

Régnaud, Paul. *Le Rig-Véda et les origines de la mythologie indo-européenne.* Part 1. Paris: Leroux, 1892.

———, trans. *Le Rig-Véda: Texte et traduction; Neuvième mandala, le culte védique du soma.* Paris: Maisonneuve, 1900.

Renan, Ernest. *Histoire générale et système comparé des langues sémitiques*. 2nd ed. Paris: Imprimerie Impériale, 1858.

———. *Mélanges religieux et historiques*. Paris: Calmann-Lévy, 1904.

———. *Nouvelles considérations sur le caractère général des peuples sémitiques, et en particulier sur leur tendance au monothéisme*. Paris: Imprimerie Impériale, 1859.

———. *Oeuvres complètes*. 10 vols. Paris: Calmann-Lévy, 1947–61.

Rollet, Sylvie. "Hantises ou l'appareil, la mémoire et le politique." In *Le temps des appareils*, edited by Jean-Louis Déotte. Paris: La Dispute, 2004.

Rosenberg, Alfred. *The Myth of the Twentieth Century*, trans. James Whisker, Costa Mesa, Calif.: Noontide Press, 1982; published originally as *Der Mythus des Zwanzigsten Jahrhunderts*, Munich: Hoheneichen-Verlag, 1930.

Rosenthal, Bernice Glatzer, ed. *Nietzsche and Soviet Culture: Ally and Adversary*. Cambridge: Cambridge University Press, 1994.

Sarinyan, Serguei, ed. *Hay k'nnadatut'ean patmut'iun* [Հայ քննադատության պատմություն; History of Armenian Literary Criticism]. Yerevan: Academy of Sciences Publishing, 1998.

———. "K'nnadatut'iunë *Mehyan* yev *Navasard* hantesnerum" ["Քննադատությունը *Մեհյան* եւ *Նավասարդ* հանդեսներում"; Literary Critique in the Journals *Mehyan* and *Navasard*]. *Sovetakan grakanut'iun* (Yerevan), no. 9 (1973).

Sarkisian, Parsegh. *Yerkhariurhamea grakanakan gortsuneut'iun yev nshanavor gortsichner Venetikoy Mkhit'arean miapanut'ean* [Երկհարիւրամեայ գրականական գործունէութիւն եւ նշանաւոր գործիչներ Վենետիկոյ Մխիթարեան Միաբանութեան; Two Hundred Years of Literary Activity and the Prominent Figures of the Mkhitarist Congregation in Venice]. Venice: San Lazzaro, 1905.

Sassouni, Garo. *Sasunts'i Davit'* [Սասունցի Դաւիթ; David of Sasun]. Beirut: Hamazkayin, 1947.

Schelling, Friedrich Wilhelm Joseph. *Schellings Werke*. Edited by Manfred Schröter. Vol. 3. Munich: C. H. Beck'sche Verlagsbuchhandlung, 1927; rpt. 1958.

———. *Sämtliche Werke*. Edited by K. F. A. Schelling. 14 vols. Stuttgart: Cotta, 1856–61.

Schelling, Friedrich Wilhelm Joseph, *Historical-critical Introduction to the Philosophy of Mythology*, trans. Mason Richey and Markus Zisselberger, Albany: State University of New York Press, 2007.

Scheuermann, Karl. *Wilhelm Mannhardt, seine Bedeutung für die vergleichende Religionsforschung*. Giessen: Meyer, 1933.

Schlegel, Friedrich. *The Aesthetic and Miscellaneous Works of Friedrich Von Schlegel*. Edited and translated by E. J. Millington. London: Kessinger, 2006.

———. *Dialogue on Poetry and Literary Aphorisms*. Translated, introduced, and annotated by Ernst Behler and Roman Struc. University Park: Pennsylvania State University Press, 1968.

———. *Kritische Friedrich-Schlegel-Ausgabe.* Edited by Ernst Behler, with the collaboration of Jean-Jacques Anstett and Hans Eichner. 35 vols. Münich: F. Schöningh, 1958–2002.

———. *On the Language and Wisdom of the Indians.* Translated by E. J. Millington, with an introduction by Michael Franklin. London: Ganesha, 2001.

Schwartz, Friedrich Leberecht Wilhelm. *Indogermanischer Volksglaube: Ein Beitrag zur Religionschichte der Urzeit.* Berlin: O. Seehagen, 1885.

———. *Der Ursprung der Mythologie dargelegt an griechischer und deutscher Sage.* Berlin: W. Hertz, 1860.

Servantsdeants, Karekin. *Yerker* [Երկեր; Works]. 2 vols., with biography of Servantsdeants by A. Ghanalanyan in vol. 1. Yerevan: Academy of Sciences Publishing, Institute of Archeology and Ethnography, 1978–82.

Sherents, G. "Garegin Yep. Servandzteants'" ["Գարեգին Եպս. Սրուանձտեանց"; Bishop Karekin Servantsdeants]. *Azgagrakan Handes* [Ethnographic Journal] (Tblisi, Georgia), 9 (1902).

Sibree, James. *Madagascar and Its People: Notes of a Four Years' Residence. With a Sketch of the History, Position, and Prospects of Mission Work amongst the Malagasy.* London: Religious Tract Society, 1870.

Sirouni, Hagop. *Daniel Varuzhan.* [Դանիէլ Վարուժան]. Bucharest: Navasart, 1940.

———. *Ink'nakensagrakan not'er* [Ինքնակենսագրական նօթեր; Autobiographical Notes]. Yerevan: Khachents, 2006.

———. *Polis yev ir derë* [Պոլիս եւ իր դերը; Constantinople and Its Role]. 4 vols. Antelias, Lebanon: Armenian Catholicosate, 1965–88.

Smith, Brian K. "Ideals and Realities in Indian Religion." *Religious Studies Review* 14 (January 1988): 1–9.

———. *Reflections on Resemblance, Ritual, and Religion.* Oxford and New York: Oxford University Press, 1989.

Snabian, Boghos. *Avazakhrats navë* [Աւազախրած նաւը; The Ship Run Aground] Beirut: Atlas, 1964.

Staal, Frits, ed. *Agni: The Vedic Ritual of the Fire Altar.* Vol. 2. Edited with the assistance of Pamela MacFarlane. Berkeley: Asian Humanities Press, 1983.

———. "The Meaninglessness of Ritual." *Numen: International Review for the History of Religions* 26, no. 1 (1976). 2–22.

Tchitouny, Tigran. *Sasunakan* [Սասունական]. Paris: Araxe-Topalian, 1942.

Tchobanian, Archag. *See* Chobanian, Arshag.

Theotig. *Amenun Darets'uytsë* [Ամենուն տարեցյյցը; Yearbook for All]. 1907–15 and 1920–29. Istanbul: Der-Nercessian, 1907–15, 1920–22. Paris: Araxe-Topalian, 1923–29. Vols. 1907–25 reprinted, Aleppo, Syria: Kilikia, 2006–.

Topjian, Stepan. "A Sketch of the Aesthetics of Armenian Neo-Romanticism." In *Hay est'etik'akan mtk'i patmut'iunits'* [Հայ էսթետիքական մտքի պատմութիւն; Studies on the History of Armenian Aesthetic Thought], 1:178–272. Yerevan: Academy of Sciences Publishing, 1974.

Toumanoff, Cyril. *Studies in Christian Caucasian History*. Washington, D.C.: Georgetown University Press, 1963.

Tournefort, Joseph Pitton de. *Relation d'un voyage du Levant, fait par ordre du Roy,
contenant l'histoire ancienne et moderne de plusieurs isles de l'Archipel, de Constantinople, des Côtes de la Mer Noire, de l'Arménie, de la Géorgie, des frontières de Perse et
d'Asie Mineure*. 2 vols. Lyons, 1717.

Trautmann, Thomas. *The Aryans and British India*. Berkeley and Los Angeles: University
of California Press, 1997.

Varoujean [Varuzhan], Daniel. *Poèmes*. Translated by Luc-André Marcel and Garo
Poladian. Antelias, Lebanon: Armenian Catholicosate, no date [1969?].

Varoujan [Varuzhan], Daniel. *Chants païens et autres poèmes*. Translated by Vahé Godel.
Paris: La Différence, 1994.

Varuzhan, Daniel. *Namakani* [Նամականի; Correspondence]. Edited by Gohar Aznavuryan. Yerevan: Hayastan, 1965.

———. *Yerkeri Liakatar Zhoghovatsu* [Երկերի լիակատար ժողովածու; Complete
Works]. 3 vols. Yerevan: Academy of Sciences Publishing, 1987.

Wagner, Richard. "Das Judentum in der Musik" (1850, 1869). In *Die Kunst und die
Revolution*, edited and with commentary by Tibor Kneif. Munich: Rogner and
Bernhard, 1975.

———. *Sämtliche Schriften und Dichtungen: Volks-Ausgabe*. Vol. 10. Leipzig: Breitkopf
und Härtel, 1871.

Walker, Christopher. *Visions of Ararat: Writings on Armenia*. London: I. B. Tauris, 1997.

Zarian, Constant. *Ants'ordë yev ir chamban* [Անցորդը եւ իր ճամբան; The Traveler and
His Road]. Antelias, Lebanon: Armenian Catholicosate, 1980.

———. *Miats'eal Nahankner* [Միացեալ Նահանգներ; United States]. Edited by Youri
Khachatrian. Yerevan: Khachents, 2003.

———. *Navë ler'an vray* [Նաւը լեռան վրայ; The Boat on the Mountain]. Boston:
Hayrenik, 1943. Published in French as *Le bateau sur la montagne*, translated by
Pierre Ter-Sarkissian (Paris: Editions du Seuil, 1986).

———. *Bancoopë yev mamout'i voskornerë* [Բանկոոպը եւ մամութի ոսկորները; The
Pancoop and the Bones of the Mammoth]. Antelias, Lebanon: Armenian Catholicosate, 1987.

———. *Spania* [Սպանիա; Spain]. Edited by Yuri Khachatrian. Yerevan: Khachents,
1999.

———. *Yerker* [Երկեր; Works]. Publication of the Kevork Melidinetsi Literary Award.
Antelias, Lebanon: Armenian Catholicosate, 1975.

Zartarian, Roupen. *Clarté nocturne*. Translated from Armenian into French by Archag
Chobanian, Edouard Colangian, and Krikor Esayan, with a preface by Gaston
Bonet-Maury. Petite bibliothèque arménienne, vol. 5. Paris: E. Leroux, 1913.

INDEX